CHRISTIAN HERITAGE COLLEGE
2100 Greenfield Dr.
El Cajon, CA   92021

Evangelist of Race

Chamberlain in 1886

Evangelist of Race

The Germanic Vision
of Houston Stewart Chamberlain

Geoffrey G. Field

Columbia University Press

New York   1981

Geoffrey Field is Associate Professor of History at State University of New York, Purchase

Columbia University Press
New York   Guildford, Surrey

Library of Congress Cataloging in Publication Data

Field, Geoffrey G
   Evangelist of race.

   Bibliography: p.
   Includes index.
   1. Chamberlain, Houston Stewart, 1855–1927.
   2. National socialism—Biography.   3. Racism—
History,   I. Title.
DD231.C4F53   943.08′4′0924 [B]   80-21000
ISBN 0-231-04860-2

The author and publisher gratefully acknowledge the generous support given them by the National Endowment for the Humanities. Research leading to this book was funded by a Summer Stipend, and publication has been assisted by a further grant from the Endowment.

To my mother and father

Contents

Acknowledgments

In writing this book I have incurred a great many obligations. In particular I am indebted to the staff of the Richard Wagner Gedenkstätte who made my stays in Bayreuth pleasurable and gave me every encouragement and assistance in my research. Without the patient labors of Dr Wilhelm Einsle who catalogued the Chamberlain papers my work would have been immeasurably more difficult if possible at all. Dr. Joachim Bergfeld and Dr. Manfred Eger gave me the benefit of their extensive knowledge and practical advice on many occasions, while Fräulein Anna Schuster was generous with her time and expertise. Like so many others who have used the archives in Bayreuth, I was deeply saddened by news of her death.

My thanks go the William Bayard Cutting fund of Columbia University for a fellowship which enabled me to carry out the initial research for this study. Generous financial assistance in the form of summer grants from the American Philosophical Society and the National Endowment for the Humanities also allowed me to return to Bayreuth and to consult other libraries and records in Vienna, Munich, Strasbourg, Freiburg and Gloucester.

Fritz Stern supervised an earlier version of this study and offered valuable advice and criticisms. His friendly counsel and support, and the example of his own work, have greatly influenced my sense of the historian's task. My thanks go also to Istvan Deak, who provided suggestions, advice and encouragement at an early stage in my work. To Ismar Schorsch I am especially indebted: over the years I have benefited greatly from his knowledge of German and Jewish history and from his desire to see this book finished. It is a pleasure to record my intellectual and personal debt to these three friends.

Friends and colleagues have discussed aspects of my work. I should like in particular to thank Jim Briscoe, Eric Foner, Arno Mayer, Helene Moglen, Carl Resek, Jean Herskovits, Jim Shenton, and Seth Schein. Like many other scholars interested in German Jewry I have gained knowledge and pleasure from the seminars organized by Dr. Fred Grubel and the staff of the Leo Baeck Institute in New York. A special note of thanks also to Walther and Gerutha Knote for their hospitality and assistance and to Dieter and Joyce Hartung who have given me support and encouragement throughout my work. Joyce Hartung gave me great assistance in obtaining illustrations for the book. The photographs, except where otherwise noted, are reproduced with the kind permission of the Richard Wagner Gedenkstätte and Richard Müller of the Stadtarchiv, Bayreuth.

For their care and patience in typing the manuscript, I am grateful to Isabel Murray, Sydney Gura and Donna Symmonds. Also, I owe many thanks to Bernard Gronert and Leslie Bialler of Columbia Press for their scrupulous care in editing the manuscript, suggestions, and encouragement.

Greatest of all is my debt to Linda, my wife, who has endured the book in its different stages with good cheer and endless patience. Without her it would not have been written.

G. G. F.
November 1980

Introduction

This study examines a critical period of modern German history through the career and ideas of Houston Stewart Chamberlain. An Englishman by birth, he became a German by choice and left his mark on the development of popular racism and on the history of Bayreuth and Wagnerism. From the early 1890s until the 1920s he produced a steady stream of books and articles on religion, science, art, philosophy, and race that won him widespread fame and the friendship of Kaiser Wilhelm and Hitler. Both a critic and a boundless admirer of Germany, Chamberlain felt the pulse of his adopted land often with an uncanny accuracy; he voiced fears about the values and goals of German society, glorified the spiritual and cultural mission of Germans in the modern world, and suffered with other nationalist contemporaries the bitter disappointments of World War I and the destruction of the Wilhelminian Reich. His life and writings attest to the prominence of racialism and anti-Semitic thinking in German political culture before the fascist era and contribute to our understanding of the social and intellectual context of such prejudice.

Today Chamberlain is largely remembered as an intellectual precursor of Nazism. Alfred Rosenberg, the principal ideologue of National Socialism in its early days, hailed him as a pioneer and spiritual forerunner and viewed himself as Chamberlain's true successor. Konrad Heiden, Hitler's first biographer and a vocal opponent of the Fascist regime, por-

trayed this converted Englishman as "one of the most
astonishing talents in the history of the German mind" and
a man who "exerted a decisive influence on two generations
of German intellectuals."[1] In the years after 1933, Nazi
publicists—eager to demonstrate that the regime possessed
deep and authentic roots in the German intellectual tradition—made him the subject of numerous essays, speeches,
radio programs and books, while doctoral students took
aspects of his work for their dissertations. But it is misleading
to depict Chamberlain—as did so many of the early accounts
of his life—as a racist prophet on the periphery of society, toiling without due recognition of his talents and significance until
the National Socialist "revolution." His major books were
completed before the First World War and belong to the
cultural milieu of Wilhelminian rather than Weimar Germany;
his greatest success came as early as 1899 with the publication
of *Die Grundlagen des neunzehnten Jahrhunderts* [*The Foundations of the Nineteenth Century*].

Unlike Lagarde, Chamberlain was not an "outsider" who
lashed out against the values and institutions of the Imperial
Reich and harbored a deep pessimism about the future. His
"Hymn to Germanism," as the Kaiser called the *Foundations*,
though critical, nostalgic, and ambivalent toward many aspects
of modernity, was prompted not by a mood of cultural despair
but one of general optimism and faith in the further expansion
of German power and prestige in the world. It was not to the
anticapitalist agrarians or the depressed strata of the petty
bourgeoisie that Chamberlain addressed his message, but to
the nationalist middle classes; his tone captured their buoyant
spirit as well as their nagging fears of moral decline. Thus, it is
against the backdrop of Wilhelminian *Weltpolitik* that Chamberlain's views must first be examined. By 1914 he was already
59 years old and his basic outlook was already fixed: the latter
parts of this study reveal how his cultural and political vision
was further shaped by the combined impact of the war, the fall
of the Hohenzollern monarchy, and the discord of early
Weimar.

The organization of the book is largely chronological, al-

though on occasions I have departed from this to explain and
analyze more fully some aspect of Chamberlain's thought. His
life falls into three fairly distinct phases. The first runs from
his birth in 1855 into an upper class English family with strong
military and imperial traditions until the time he discovered
his vocation as a writer. Its central theme is his education,
meant in its broadest sense: the formation of his ideas about
society and aesthetics, the range of his interests and erudition,
and his gradual assumption of a cogent cultural and political
stance—shaped by the interplay of personal experience and
the larger shifts in society and attitudes that overwhelmed
Europe in the second half of the nineteenth century. The
Europe of 1850 was by 1890 transformed in the scale of industrial capitalism, and in the balance of power between the
individual states. Germany had become the dominant nation
of the Continent and Chamberlain, like many others, was captivated by the art, culture, science, and philosophy of this
emergent giant.

The second part of the book focusses on Chamberlain as a
writer and publicist. He was one of the most successful exemplars of a new literary type: the popular synthesizer who, in an
age of specialization, dispensed with academic caution and
strove to impose an order on the chaos of experience by drawing together all his knowledge in an easily grasped unified vision. He was one of several bold diagnosticians who rose to
prominence in the 1890s coinciding with a general spirit of self
questioning among Germans. It was in the cause of Wagnerism
that he served his literary apprenticeship; defending Cosima
Wagner's management of the festivals at Bayreuth, publicizing
the Master's aesthetic philosophy of redemption, and berating
its critics, Chamberlain honed his literary style into a fine
instrument of persuasion. Over the years he probably did more
to acquaint the reading public with Wagnerite ideas than any
other individual.

"I feel strongly out of place here" commented Mark Twain
on a visit to the Bayreuth festival of 1891.[2] Max Nordau
described the scenes of religious and aesthetic intoxication as a
yardstick of "the breadth and depth of the degeneration and
hysteria of our time."[3] Even Lord Redesdale, Chamberlain's

English translator, on a first visit in 1912, was bewildered by the intense devotional tone of this theatrical ritual. He was puzzled by these "minds that the great poet holds in the thraldom of his genius" and recalled how "with the silence of conviction they accept his preaching: the early Christians in the Catacombs could hardly have been more reverent."[4] Chamberlain, in contrast, found his spiritual home and personal mission in the "inner circle" of Wagnerites; in the "Temple of Music" his personal fears and loneliness were excised, his hopes were kindled, his views shaped, and he willingly let himself be carried into a mythical *völkisch* world, which was often more real for him than the one in which he lived. It is difficult to recapture the tone and mood of the Bayreuth *Kreis* that gathered around Wagner's widow determined to transform the small Franconian town into the focus of a cultural crusade. The writings and varied activities of Chamberlain mirror the growth of "the Bayreuth Idea," revealing the spirit and ideals that inspired the cult, the way it adjusted to developments in German society and politics, and its impact upon German national consciousness. In recent years historians have begun to show greater interest in the Wahnfried circle around Cosima, but no account has placed Wagnerism in the cultural and political matrix of Wilhelminian *Weltpolitik*, the defeat of 1918, and the politics of the radical right during Weimar. In shaping the destiny of Bayreuth, Chamberlain's central role is undeniable.

It was Chamberlain who constructed an ideological bridge between Wagnerism and the broader tradition of nationalist and racist thought; his work stands at the confluence of Bayreuth and the Germanic ideology. In breaking out of the narrow confines of the cult he became nationally—even internationally—famous as a popular philosopher and cultural critic. Beginning with *The Foundations of the Nineteenth Century*, a panoramic racial history described by one English reviewer as an "Iliad of conflict between German and Semite," he elaborated an integral *Weltanschauung* that was thoroughly Wagnerian and also supplied a cultural justification for doctrines of Pan-German imperialism. With Chamberlain popular racism reached a new stage: more than any other writer he synthesized the various strands of German racism around 1900, endowing his books with a scientific and scholarly aura, disassociating himself from vulgar prejudice, and offering an apparently balanced and informed judgment. His public success provides an example of the ways in which racism and anti-Semitism, under the guise of a search for truth, penetrated social circles that found more popular ethnocentrism too crude and radical. It also reminds us that race thinking is a central theme not an aberration or minor byroad in the intellectual history of Europe from the French Revolution to the Nazi Reich.

Above all Chamberlain's writings attest the pervasiveness of anti-Semitism in Germany both before and after World War I. Until recently it was widely believed that animosity toward Jews abated with the economically prosperous years after 1896 and the simultaneous slow decline of the anti-Semitic parties in the Reichstag. But a growing body of evidence now casts doubt upon this assumption and indicates that prejudice against Jews remained deeply ingrained in social and political life and assumed a variety of new forms outside parliamentary politics. Indeed, it was during the 1890s that Jews began to organize nationally in defense of their civic rights, protesting the arbitrary actions of the bureaucracy and the continued discrimination they suffered in the army and civil service, as well as taking issue publicly both with legislation that threatened Jewish interests and the steady stream of anti-Semitic literature. Admittedly, German Jews had made startling gains since the beginning of the nineteenth century, but the problem of successfully assimilating while preserving a Jewish identity remained at issue. *Causes célèbres* like the Xanten ritual murder trial in 1892, social slights and rebuffs, and the prevalence of "respectable" or scholarly anti-Semitism among the elites of German society continued to give cause for alarm. Chamberlain's large readership was merely one of many signs that hatred of Jews was far from being an unfortunate remnant of a past age, an outmoded superstition that time and experience would eradicate.

Recently historians have unearthed a mass of new evidence about the Wilhelminian Reich and have pointed to the

years 1890–1914 as a crucial period in the evolution of German
politics and of the nation's sense of its role in Europe and the
world. Tariff debates, imperial rivalries, the construction of a
battle fleet, the rapid growth of Social Democracy and
increased political pressures from newly mobilized strata of the
petty bourgeoisie all placed a heavy strain on the political
system and fostered the development of new techniques and
styles of politics, and new pressure groups which played a
potent role in opinion-making. These years saw rapid changes
in the German right, hastened by pressure from such groups as
the Pan-Germans and the Naval League; sharp differences of
interest and goals continued to divide the right and helped to
fragment organizations, but this did not prevent a marked
degree of ideological consensus of a negative sort from developing. Anti-Socialism, anti-liberalism, and mounting dissatisfaction with the existing parliamentary structure were coupled
with sweeping assertions about the mission of German culture
and a broad *völkisch* ideology that contained a varying but
ever-present quotient of anti-Semitism. Although he was not a
political activist in the usual sense, Chamberlain's thought
must be placed in this larger context: his cultural vision
embraces the complicated structure of nationalist feeling at
the turn of the century and discloses something of the gradual
process whereby large numbers of educated Germans became
accustomed to racialist rhetoric and forms of argument and
desensitized to the plight of Jewish fellow citizens.

The third and final section of the book deals with Chamberlain's life after he had gained the acclaim of Kaiser Wilhelm and had won widespread attention as a prophet of Germanism. It opens with a portrait of Chamberlain the private
man, beset with domestic troubles, but then focusses primarily
upon his public image even as Chamberlain came to regard
himself largely in terms of his public significance. After moving to Bayreuth in 1908 he grew steadily more apprehensive
about the direction of German politics and the materialist
values which seemed everywhere triumphant. Though his
private life was now happy and peaceful, he experienced deep
disquiet at the deterioration of Anglo-German relations, appalled by the approaching prospect of having to choose

between his birthplace and his adopted land. With the outbreak of war in 1914, Germany's total defeat four years later,
and the establishment of a republic, Chamberlain saw all his
hopes for a German-dominated Europe destroyed. His final
years (hard in some ways to describe because he was more an
observer than an active participant in the right's campaign
against the hated *"Judenrepublik"*) dramatize the bewilder-
ment and despair felt by so many conservative minded
Germans at the collapse of the *Kaiserreich*. His ultimate destination in the ranks of the National Socialists is well known,
but here, for the first time, the details of his political journey
are retraced, suggesting something of the common ideological
and psychological terrain of the pre-war right and post-war fascism. In these years the politicization of art at Bayreuth rose to
new heights, foreshadowing the complete identification of the
Festspiele with the Nazi state. How far this alliance of
Wagnerism and fascism can be ascribed to ideological agreement has, of course, been a subject of heated debate ever since.

Biography is today an astonishingly popular genre; studies
of Hitler and other figures of Germany's recent past abound on
the shelves of bookstores and public libraries. But this vogue
among general readers has been parallelled by declining
interest among academic historians and researchers. Apart
from attempts at collective biography or prosopography,
biography is not—as Fritz Stern has recently reminded
us—usually considered the most apt medium for treating the
kinds of problems concerning historical structures that currently dominate scholarly investigations.[5] Even successful
practitioners of the craft like Martin Duberman have raised
serious doubts about the possibility of ever recapturing a past
personality, of comprehending and unraveling the tangle of
human motives and emotions.[6] These are worries that plague
anyone who tries to reconstruct a life. As Stefan Zweig wrote:
"Intuition knows more of a man than all the documents in the
world." A biographical portrait is pieced together out of large
numbers of separate fragments. Nothing should be invented,
but it is of necessity a process of imaginative reconstitution, of

overcoming lacunae of evidence that inevitably exist—and this makes us uneasy. But, for all its hazards, a strong case can be made for biography on the grounds that it helps us grasp the very complexity of the past, the web of associations that link an individual to his times, and the manifold sources from which social, political, and cultural attitudes are formed. And while it carries the obvious peril of narrowing the historian's focus and inflating the historical role of the individual, it can also provide an antidote to the temptation to reduce people to ideological types and to distort the nuances, mental outlook, and moods of the past under the weight of concepts and structural abstractions. This seems to me especially true when attempting to grasp the character, depth, and resilience of racial prejudice which has too often been treated as a political device of negative social integration or analyzed purely as an epiphenomenon of class relationships.

Psychobiography, in contrast to more conventional forms, has attracted greater scholarly interest of late, especially among those writing about National Socialism; this is not surprising since the enormities of Nazi terror seem to defy all rational explanation and to exhaust the conventional categories of historical analysis. In a review of recent research, Peter Loewenberg has assessed the now-extensive psychohistorical literature on German political figures, the German family and social structure, national identity and racism.[7] The list is long and impressive, ranging from Erik Erikson's pioneering studies in the 1950s to the recent psychobiographies of Hitler by G. L. Waite and Rudolph Binion. In considering the life and milieu of Chamberlain I have learned a great deal from this literature, particularly from several of the earlier contributions—by N. W. Ackermann, M. Jahoda, M. Wangh, and H. V. Dicks—on the role of projection, displacement, and identification in the psychodynamics of racism.[8]

But mine is not at all a psychobiography; not only do I lack the professional competence to undertake such an analysis, but also the task itself is, as Robert Coles has suggested, fraught with theoretical problems and difficulties over evidence.[9] Even in a case such as Chamberlain's, where at first the documentation appears surprisingly voluminous and varied, there are serious gaps. Psychoanalysis stresses the significance of origins and repetitious patterns of behavior, placing an emphasis on infancy and childhood, but most of Chamberlain's letters as a schoolboy and reports about him as a child have not survived. Other lacunae include information about his always fragile health: the extent to which his ailments were psychosomatic can only be guessed at, and there is virtually no hope of finding out more than we know now. Further, his relationship with his first wife, Anna Horst, as well as a range of other significant aspects of his private life and emotional states, are largely veiled from the historian as he tries to probe the many-layered personality behind surviving records. Frequently, biographers concerned to incorporate psychological theory into their work have become preoccupied with diagnosis, with accounting (often in highly speculative fashion working backwards from later evidence) for the genesis of specific patterns of thought and feeling. As for the theoretical difficulties, they largely concern the relationship between psychodynamics and social development; much of what has been written centers upon intrapsychic conflict, interpreting individual behavior in terms of neurotic and regressive drives and defenses, and runs the risk of treating subjects almost in isolation from their historical milieu, as self-contained little monads. The most glaring examples of this are undoubtedly in the past but even those like Fred Weinstein and G. M. Platt who are sympathetic to the enterprise see theoretical pitfalls ahead and refer to "the coming crisis in psychohistory."[10]

My goal has been, then, to analyze Chamberlain's dominant character traits, the formative personal and social influences upon his intellectual development, and through his writings and letters to convey something of the atmosphere of both Wilhelminian and Weimar Germany: to describe his style of mind rather than trace his psychic history. For this the sources are rich indeed. He was an extraordinarily prolific letter writer and kept a variety of diaries and journals, recording even his dreams on many occasions. A careful, methodical man when it came to organizing his papers, and one with a well-developed sense of his own importance, Chamberlain threw away little despite a peripatetic life. His second wife, Eva, the youngest daughter of Richard Wagner, was also anxious to preserve everything (or almost everything) and regarded even scraps of paper, insignificant notes hastily made in his "elephantine" scrawl, as sacrosanct. Chamberlain is also more accessible to the historian than most other race thinkers because of the sheer range and number of his published writings. He wrote plays, a scientific treatise, large studies of Wagner, Kant, and Goethe, popular works on religion, and literally hundreds of essays on race, literature, philosophy, politics, and, of course, Bayreuth. Because of the number and scope of his writings—augmented by the ample unpublished materials—it has been possible to give a very full description of his mental world: to show how he brought his opinions about history, religion, philosophy, science, art, and politics into a more or less coherent unity, principally by placing everything in racial categories. Few attempts have been made to analyze the aspirations and fears, the intellectual justifications and political allegiances, in short the private and public existence, of leading race theorists and popularizers, possibly because the subject occupies a position somewhere between intellectual and political history. Gobineau is the one exception who has prompted a number of detailed studies, the most recent in English being a fine account by Michael Biddiss.[11] Arguably the most influential race publicist in Central Europe around the turn of the century, Chamberlain, perhaps more than any other comparable figure, lends himself to this kind of cultural biography.

Reading Chamberlain's letters and books I found that a composite picture of the man and his times soon emerged. More troublesome was the task of gauging his influence upon contemporaries. The success or failure of a publicist is registered by his impact on readers, and the most successful—Chamberlain included—are not original thinkers: they draw heavily on the views of others or put into a sharper and more polemical focus ideas that already possess a wider resonance in society. In consequence, it is frequently impossible to separate one writer's impact from that of contemporaries expressing similar views. And while I have tried to avoid making larger claims than the evidence warrants, it is important to show Chamberlain's ideology as more than symptomatic of broader attitudinal shifts in society, even if his influence must, in the end, be unquantifiable. His work both offers insight into a larger racist and nationalist pathology and was instrumental in promoting it. To illustrate this I have analyzed as wide a selection as possible of contemporary comments, together with newspaper articles and reviews of his most successful book, *The Foundations*. Such sources are admittedly fragmentary and sometimes tenuous: interpreting newspaper reviews, for example, involves assumptions about the relationship between reviewers and the readership of a journal. But, used in sufficient numbers, a generally accurate, if impressionistic, picture emerges of the reception accorded to his book and supplies a basis for generalizations about the mental climate of the time.

The central theme of this study is anti-Semitism and its role in the political culture of modern Germany. Few subjects have attracted as much attention from historians over the last three decades and my indebtedness to earlier scholars—among them Fritz Stern, George Mosse, Uriel Tal, Eva Reichmann, and Ismar Schorsch will be readily apparent. The relationship of Germans and Jews, as many writers have recognized, contains in microcosm the major strands of German history from the late eighteenth century until the Third Reich. It is a subject, in Stern's words, that "touches the raw nerves of German society," one that casts a searchlight on the complex responses of Germans to the forces of social, political, and cultural change.[12] "In no other European society," Ismar Schorsch asserts, "were Jewish-Christian relations shaped by such a comprehensive structure of ideological anti-Semitism."[13] Thus, although an Englishman by birth, Chamberlain's life intersects some of the principal themes of German history: among them the impact of industrial capitalism upon a tradition-bound state, the character of German liberalism and nationalism, German perceptions of the state and the place of politics in national life, and the process of secularization.

There are, of course, many aspects of German-Jewish history, and of the development of German anti-Semitism, which fall outside the chronological scope of this book. Chamberlain knew little of Germany before the 1880s and died before Hitler became Chancellor. The long and widely debated process of Jewish emancipation, ending with the granting of full legal equality under the new German federal constitution of 1871, has recently been the focus of intensive research. As Reinhard Rürup and others have shown, the politicization of anti-Semitism was already well advanced by 1850 and, two decades later, "formed part of the foundation stock, as it were, of the new *Reich*."[14] Chamberlain, then, was one of the inheritors of these earlier forms of prejudice; he in part continued and in part renewed the anti-Semitic tradition, joining recently developed doctrines of eugenics, craniometry, and anthroposociology to the older themes of romantic *völkisch* thought, and strengthening still older Christian superstition with secular arguments. His ideas should not be equated with the racial elitism of Himmler or Heydrich, though the former read and admired his work. Chamberlain was a man of earlier and more settled times. Jean Réal reported a conversation with Eva Wagner-Chamberlain in December 1938, a month after the *Reichskristallnacht* set off a country-wide pogrom. Eva, who was an ardent Nazi, nevertheless commented: "My husband would not have liked this!"[15] She was probably right: it is essential to keep in mind the distinction between vicious rhetoric and brutal action, between those who theorized about and those who commanded the lives of others. Chamberlain never explicitly advocated violence toward Jews, let alone their extermination; but the germs of violence were undeniably present in his rhetoric before 1914, and in the reception of his writings we find ominous signs of that attitude which later made so many Germans, who were not necessarily anti-Semitic, insensitive to the sufferings of Jews. It has become almost the fashion for historians of Germany to warn against the temptation to look forward to 1933, claiming that the "search for parallels and prototypes" distorts the history of the *Kaiser-reich* and possibly Weimar as well. And yet most of the literature on German anti-Semitism, either explicitly or tacitly, involves an attempt to situate the Nazi era more coherently in the wider framework of German and European history. I have tried to resist falling into the teleological trap but inevitably the career of Chamberlain does lead us on toward the horrifying reality of the Nuremberg Laws and Auschwitz. And if this book offers some enlightenment as to the cultural and political origins of that tragedy it will have served its purpose.

Part I

The Making of a Wagnerite

I must confess I doubt whether humanity ever produced a greater, perhaps as great a genius as Richard Wagner

—Chamberlain (1883)

This opera Tristan and Isolde *last night broke the hearts of all witnesses who were of the faith and I know of some, and have heard of many, who could not sleep after it, but cried the night away. I feel strongly out of place here. Sometimes I feel like the one sane person in the community of the mad, sometimes I feel like the one blind man where all others see; the one groping savage in the college of the learned; and always during service I feel like a heretic in heaven.*

—Mark Twain at Bayreuth (1891)

Chapter One

An Englishman Uprooted

A LITTLE MORE than 50 miles northeast of Nuremberg lies the town of Bayreuth, roughly in the geographical center of the *Kaiserreich* and yet still within the confines of Bavaria. In the eighteenth century it had enjoyed a brief period of distinction as the residence of the Margraves of Brandenburg and Bayreuth and as the home of the poet Jean Paul. By the close of the nineteenth century it was famous as the center of a growing cult associated with the life and works of the composer Richard Wagner. Wagner had visited the town in 1871 and, after negotiations with local dignitaries, gained permission to build there his ideal National Theater. It took considerably longer and cost more than he expected, but in 1876 the first music festival was staged, inaugurating a tradition which continued after his death and still survives, though greatly modified, in the present day.

A commercial center for the surrounding agricultural region, with little industry apart from a few textile factories, Bayreuth was and still is a quiet town, bypassed by the transforming forces of industrialism. At its heart lies the ornamental eighteenth century *Hofgarten* and the palace of the Margraves, the seat of their administration; close by, bordering on another section of the park, is Villa Wahnfried, the somber stone mansion Wagner had built for himself, which became synonymous with the orthodox Wagnerism publicized by his widow, Cosima, and her circle of devoted helpers. Just a few yards away, across the street, stands another house, of more recent construction, with nothing distinctive about it except perhaps for the small observatory on the roof. It was here on January 9, 1927, that Houston Stewart Chamberlain died after a long illness. Letters and telegrams poured in from all quarters to his widow, Eva: from politicians, academics, students, writers and royalty. Albert Schweitzer, long an admirer, wrote: "What he has done for the advancement of knowledge will exist as a noble contribution for the good of the *Volk*"; "I will never forget," he added, "that I was permitted to see him in his suffering, a spirit who triumphed over suffering."[1] At his graveside none of his English relatives were present, only fellow Wagnerites and Germans: among them a Hohenzollern prince representing the exiled Kaiser Wilhelm and Adolf Hitler, now beginning to emerge as a political figure. In Wahnfried, Cosima, perhaps the greatest single influence on his life, sat uninformed of the death but clearly aware of it; ninety years old and very fragile, she waited patiently for her own end and never asked after Chamberlain again.

That Chamberlain should die in Bayreuth was fitting, for the town was a symbol of everything that he revered; more than a shrine to Wagner and his philosophy, it was the focus of a campaign to change Germany, to re-create a German nation free of the evils of liberal capitalist society. Chamberlain's life and work were haunted by this vision of an alternate Reich: conservative, idealistic, antimaterialistic and antimodern in its hankering after the simplicity and community of a mythic past. His belief in the ennoblement of man through art, his deep sense of estrangement from the standards and ideals of bourgeois society, his anti-Semitism and contempt for western rationalism all place him within the romantic, *völkisch* tradition of German thought; Chamberlain's achievement was to become one of the leading prophets and moralists of Germanism. Yet unlike the others he was a foreigner, a German by choice and assimilation, not birth. To grasp how this happened we must first turn to the very different surroundings of his early life.

Although as he grew older Chamberlain's acquaintance with his family was to be very limited, confined mostly to letters and short visits, it would be a mistake to conclude that his

background was of little significance in shaping his later
career. Throughout his life he retained vivid memories of
childhood and showed a strong interest in his own ancestry.
Characteristically he began his autobiographical reflections
with an account of his forebears, not out of conventional piety,
but because no matter how far he drifted from the attitudes
and priorities of his English relatives, he never ceased to be
proud of his heritage or to measure himself against it in one
way or another.[2]

There were indeed remarkable personalities on both sides.
The Chamberlain family was said to have originated with the
earls of Westmorland and through them was connected to
Plantagenet blood. The more immediate founder, however,
was Henry Orlando Chamberlain, born in September 1773 in
London, the illegitimate son of the Earl of Westmorland. An
adventurous and spirited youth, he ran away from home as a
boy, went to sea, and spent several years wandering about
Europe; part of the time he was employed by the Portuguese
government. Later he entered the British consular service and
lived in Rio de Janeiro as Consul-General for South America,
enjoying considerable power at the Brazilian court in a
particularly turbulent period. For his services he was rewarded
with a baronetcy in 1828, but died in the following year at the
age of 56. He had been married twice and the title descended
to the sons of the first wife. From the second marriage came
five sons, of whom Houston's father, William Charles Chamberlain, was the oldest. All five brothers entered the military
and each had a distinguished career. Houston's father joined
the navy, going to sea as a cadet at the age of 12 and after a
lifetime in the service attained the rank of Admiral. The other
brothers went into the Indian Army: one became a General,
another a Lieutenant-General, and a third a Colonel. Most
decorated of all was Houston's favorite uncle and boyhood
hero, Sir Neville Chamberlain, who won fame for his bravery
in the Afghan and Sikh Wars and in the Mutiny. He was
eventually promoted to Field Marshal by Queen Victoria and
made a Knight Commander of the Bath.[3]

On the maternal side, Chamberlain's genealogy was Scottish. His mother came from a landed family near Edinburgh,

although her father, Captain Basil Hall, had served in the
navy and achieved some fame for several long voyages of exploration. The Hall family had more of a scholarly heritage
than the Chamberlains, although Henry Orlando had been a
keen astronomer and botanist. Captain Basil Hall's writings
about his passage to the Lutschu Islands, south of Japan, and
his travels on the European Continent were still popular in the
1860s, and Chamberlain's great grandfather, Sir James Hall
had earned distinction as a geologist, explorer and onetime
President of the Royal Society at Edinburgh. Educated for a
time in a French military academy at Brienne, Sir James also
became acquainted with the young Napoleon Bonaparte; in
deed, Hall—the French Emperor later recalled—was the first
Briton he ever encountered.[4]

Such was the family: wealthy, aristocratic, a mixture of
scholars, explorers, and soldiers of the Empire. Uncles and
cousins possessed landed estates in England and Scotland;
some relatives had married into the highest social circles,
others established reputations in business, banking, and public
administration. They were widely travelled, living for periods
in Brazil, the West Indies, Portugal, France, Malta, and India
as well as on the European Continent. And yet, in spite of
these experiences, they remained—at least to Chamberlain's
mind—very British in their prejudices, manners and loyalties,
exuding all the patriotic and chauvinistic fervor associated
with the upper classes in the Palmerstonian era.

Chamberlain was born at Southsea on the southern coast
of England on September 9, 1855. At that time Britain and
France were at war with Russia and his father, Admiral Chamberlain, was commanding a ship off the Crimea; his mother
who had recently been in Malta visiting her sister, had
returned to England for her confinement. Houston was the last
of her four children: the oldest, a girl, had died in infancy and
there were two small brothers, Basil and Henry ("Harry") aged
five and three years respectively.[5] His birthday was a date of
double rejoicing, for on that day the fortress at Sevastopol fell
into British hands, marking a turning point in the war. England
was entering a quarter century of unprecedented material prosperity; Britain was the world's workshop, the world's carrier,

ship-builder, and banker. Progress and wealth seemed, as though by some new law of nature, to have been showered on this one nation, and success bred a mood of comfortable complacency among the ruling classes and Chamberlain's family among them; their mood was buoyant, optimistic, frequently arrogant and nationalist. Theirs, in the words of W. L. Burn, was an "age of equipoise," less anxious, less divided and less introspective than the generations that followed.[6] There was, admittedly, no shortage of criticism about its moneyed, materialist ethos, no dearth of anger at the crassness and vulgarity of its Podsnaps and Veneerings, but the mid-Victorian era was predominantly confident and secure, assuaging its doubts by a certain conservative caution and self-protective belief in established institutions.

Consonant with this sense of stability were the long-range plans the Chamberlains made for the sons of the family. It was never doubted that all three would enjoy the same privileges and live up to their duties as subjects of the realm and responsible members of the upper class as their family had done before them. Their paths in life were confidently mapped out by the older generation; their education was to be tailored to their ultimate destination in the armed services or colonial administration. In the event, Harry alone served in the navy as a second lieutenant before being invalided home and discharged; he then went into business. Basil and Houston, who had more in common with each other than either had with Harry, never followed in their father's footsteps; but their scholarly bent reflected nonetheless the influence of family tradition—in this case the Hall family. After the Sorbonne and Oxford, Basil (whose passion for Japanese culture and the Far East was clearly ignited by the example of his grandfather and namesake) made his home in Japan where he became Professor of Literature at Tokyo University. Similarly, Houston's early enthusiasm for science—botany in particular—derived in no small measure from an awareness of the career of Sir James Hall; even his youthful attraction to Germany seemed to him in later years curiously anticipated by his mother, who had been educated by a German governess before that became a fashionable convention and who, when

Houston was six months old, had written: "I have decided to speak only German with this little one from the beginning; it would be such a shame if the child missed the sole opportunity of becoming really familiar with this difficult tongue." [7]

Within a year of Chamberlain's birth his life took a dramatically different course from that envisioned by his parents and relatives. Already sick and weakened by her pregnancy, his mother died before the end of 1856. The problem immediately arose of what to do with the children: their father was constantly away at sea and they were far too young for boarding schools. Of their two grandmothers, Mrs. Basil Hall, who resided in England, travelled too frequently and was too involved in society to be able to provide them with a suitable home. So the task fell to their paternal grandmother, Lady Anne Chamberlain, a formidable woman who as wife to Sir Henry Orlando had spent years in Portugal, Spain, and South America and since his death had lived on the Continent, most recently in Versailles. [8] Her unmarried daughter, Harriet Mary Chamberlain, was her constant companion and now took over the responsibility of the three young children.

Chamberlain lived on the Avenue de St. Cloud in Versailles for the next ten years. The upbringing of the three brothers was strict, religious, and on the whole happy. Their Aunt Harriet supervised their education in the first few years, assisted by tutors; then, Basil and Harry were enrolled in local schools and attended the nearby Lycée Impériale. Basil alone completed his studies in France while Harry was entered at an early age in a military training school in England. Houston's earliest years were spent largely in the company of his aunt. Such glimpses as we have of him suggest a solitary, sensitive, and imaginative child who did not mix well with others of his own age; later, he recollected that his favorite pastime was to retreat into an empty room, wall himself off in a corner with chairs, and play alone, cut off and isolated from the household around him. His sickly constitution and paleness, which won him the nickname "Poor Little One" or "P.L.O." from his brothers, was a constant source of family anxiety, but when old enough he too attended the lower classes at the Lycée, although he was taken away in the afternoons and sent out for

long, refreshing walks. In these years Houston saw almost
nothing of his father, who was either in England or on active
service at sea: "You wouldn't know your own father," Lady
Chamberlain once told him sadly, "if you met him on the
street." [9] But, though absent, Admiral Chamberlain took his
obligations seriously and worried a good deal about the fate of
his sons; it troubled him that Houston spoke French with
greater facility than his own tongue and that his contact with
England was so tenuous. In the autumn of 1866, following the
pattern of other English parents whose children lived abroad or
in the empire, he enrolled his son in a small private academy
in Portsmouth to make the boy sure of his own roots.

The small school he entered, which claimed to train
gentlemen for careers in the military and colonial services, was
the worst conceivable experience for Chamberlain at this juncture and one that he never forgot. There were many such
schools in England (one thinks immediately of Dr. Blimber's
establishment in *Dombey and Son*) of varying quality but
often with poor living conditions, harsh discipline, and low
academic standards; and though the Taunton Commission in
1868 publicized some of the worst abuses in them, they had
been and remained for some time completely free of state interference. There can be little doubt about the horror which
this shy, sensitive boy experienced at his sudden exposure to
English school life. Pampered by his indulgent aunt and
grandmother in Versailles, he was now cast into a sports-
oriented, rough, and intolerant society where his timidity and
"foreignness" and even the Gladstonian liberal politics he had
imbibed from Aunt Harriet, made him a frequent target of
ridicule and bullying by classmates. He was certainly not the
only youth exiled from his family—the school undoubtedly had
its share of sons of Anglo-Indian administrators and military
families—but he could never conquer his homesickness for
France or overcome his terror at the coarseness of the other
pupils. Even in later years the memory was still vivid: "I have
never again," he wrote, "felt and could not again experience
such pain. It was the absolute, inconsolable, helpless misery of
an abandoned soul, suddenly torn away from love, comfort,
gentleness, and friendship and thrown into a Hell of mob rule

[*Faustrechts*]." [10] He pleaded to be taken away; in June 1867 the request was granted, but after a brief vacation in France he was again dispatched to England, this time to the more prestigious Cheltenham College, which specialized in turning out future officers for the army.

Cheltenham, one of the newer boarding schools founded at the beginning of Victoria's reign, combined the ideals and outlook of Arnold's Rugby with a stronger emphasis upon mathematics, modern languages, and science than was true of many of the older foundations. Expanding numbers of such schools, claiming to produce the self-reliant, cultivated Christian gentleman, reflected not only the increasing weight given to matters of class and status in education but also a general trend toward higher educational attainments and qualifying examinations among recruits for the army, civil service, and clergy. For Chamberlain, Cheltenham provided a very different atmosphere from the school he had just left. The teaching staff, many of whom were Anglican clerics, were better qualified; scholarship among the students was more highly valued; and, being much larger, it enabled less gregarious boys to withdraw into their own shells without interference. Here Chamberlain was able to forge a program for survival: he was diligent in his studies, wrote his own plays and stories, and pursued hobbies, especially his life-long interest in astronomy. "The starlight," he later recalled, "exerted an indescribable influence on me. The stars seemed closer to me, more gentle, more worthy of trust, and more sympathetic—for that is the only word which reflects my feelings—than any of the people around me in school life. For the stars I experienced true *friendship*." [11]

Religion was an essential part of daily existence at Cheltenham. Since the 1820s the town had been a center of Evangelicalism and the college was directly under the influence of that party in the Church. Previously Chamberlain's church-going had been mostly confined to Calvinist services which he attended with his aunt at Versailles, but he readily accepted Evangelicalism with its moral fervor, strict discipline, and emphasis upon contrition, work, and prayer as the way to salvation. As a solitary, largely friendless youth who hated the regimentation of school life, he channelled his anxiety into religious observances; his Christianity was curiously intertwined with a realization that as a son he was subject to a father he barely knew, and as a schoolboy he was subordinate to the college authorities. Years later while living in Dresden, he recalled:

> I remember the period of ardent and absolute faith in the religion I had been taught. How unspeakable was the joy of recollecting when I woke in the morning, that Christ was there, near my bed, and that he loved me. How delightful the evening prayers in the college chapel, the prostration before God in the half-darkness, broken only by some few, flickering gas-flames, and whilst the monotonous chant of the responses rose up on alternate sides. Perhaps I was not very orthodox, even then,—for I rarely listened to the service; my child's mind was filled by the actual presence of God, and I used to continue repeating between my lips: "Oh Jesus, I love thee, I love thee, I *love* thee!" And then I would pray to Him to love me; and when I had the conviction that He did, then I was more happy than words can say, and at night my friends the stars glittered more brightly than ever. But gloom always soon came over this image; the remembrance of the daily miseries of school-life, of the ever-fretting dependence of a child on the will of others. [12]

Neither at school nor later did he subscribe to church orthodoxy of any kind. In later life he found simple Calvinist services most sympathetic, but his faith was always undogmatic and ill-defined, centered around the personality of Christ rather than church doctrine. As far as is known, no crisis of belief or loss of faith troubled him even temporarily; Christianity remained central to his outlook and, unlike many contemporaries, he experienced no real tension between religion and his growing fascination for science.

Chamberlain disliked Cheltenham but began to accept his fate, especially after the death of his grandmother, Lady Chamberlain, in December 1867. Her house in Versailles was sold and he was forced to spend his school vacations with relatives in England. Among them—now as later—he felt completely out of place, and they soon dubbed the rather priggish and withdrawn youth "the distinguished foreigner." His sickly and nervous disposition cut him off from most of his contemporaries; he was not good at organized games and was frequently excused for health reasons. Finally, a serious breakdown brought his Cheltenham career to an abrupt close in the fall of 1869. Oblivious to the signs of psychological strain, the doctors who attended him diagnosed a respiratory condition and prescribed an immediate change of air. Houston was once again placed under the care of his Aunt Harriet and sent first to English seaside resorts and then to the Continent. Though the doctors had envisioned only a short rest and recuperation, Chamberlain's English education was in fact over. He never again lived in England and returned there only for brief and infrequent visits. It would have astonished him to discover, as Sir Maurice Bowra relates in his memoirs, that some fifty years later he was reckoned by at least one Cheltenham master as a distinguished old boy of the school.[13]

In his boyhood Chamberlain lacked any firm sense of nationality, and it troubled him greatly. Living in Versailles with his aunt and grandmother, he felt himself neither English nor French. The language he wrote and spoke most of his first thirty years was French, but he was always regarded there by friends and acquaintances as a foreigner. Indeed, his early environment cultivated this feeling of separateness. His family were friends of the André, Pressensé, and Neuflize families, wealthy Protestant bankers who were extremely conscious of their Calvinist faith and their distinctiveness as a religious minority.[14] At home on the Avenue de St. Cloud, English was always spoken, except when addressing servants. Houston, of course, spoke French with his childhood acquaintances in the park at Versailles. Lady Chamberlain's French friends (mostly army officers and government officials, apart from the Protestant bankers) came to the house, but more memorable to the impressionable child were the visits of relatives, businessmen, and diplomats from England. Their bearing and conversation left no doubts as to national superiority, and French attitudes were a constant source of ridicule. Aunt Harriet was the sole member of the family to immerse herself in French culture and to respect French ways, but even for her British superiority was unquestionable. "Already when quite young," Chamberlain wrote, "I had imbibed this superciliousness, and had learned to mock 'French frogs' to despise 'French liars,' and to ridicule 'French vanity.' If the teacher in a history lesson spoke of a French victory or the glorious conclusion of a peace for France, the conquest would be represented at the family table as a let-down or a fluke, and the world imperium of Britain would be counterposed to the French success."

He was taught the blessings of English rule and believed the fate of India and Ireland was enviable; unquestionably, the political traditions of England outshone all others. "What child," he asked, "would have been able to withstand the influence of such ideas. And the result of this influence was that even as a child I felt foreign in the France I loved." And yet, on the few occasions he visited his maternal grandmother, Mrs. Basil Hall, in England, Chamberlain felt even more alien and out of place. On one occasion after being run-over by a tradesman's cart, kicked by an irate ass, and tormented by other children as the "French fop" [*französische Laffe*] Houston could not wait to return to France. "Already in my fifth year," he claimed, "I felt completely foreign and uncomfortable in the island kingdom and shrieked with joy when, after a short sojourn, I felt the soil of the Continent beneath my feet again." [15]

This sense of isolation, of having no home or roots, dominated the first twenty years of Chamberlain's existence, or at least so it seemed to him in later life. Departure from Versailles and school in England never had for Harry the same catastrophic consequences as for Houston, while Basil settled down easily to life at the Lycée and the Sorbonne and then Oxford. After his departure from England in 1870, Chamberlain spent the next nine years travelling in Europe; of his birthplace he had only bad memories. This knot of national estrangement and personal anxiety remained entangled in his character, and his sense of homelessness reasserted itself later in an impassioned search for roots in Germany. His hostility to England was also mixed with strong elements of guilt and self-doubt, a sense of failure which at times accentuated his bitterness and at others compelled in him a respect for the strength, values, and traditions of his native land. His travel-

ling companion and surrogate parent during these nine years
was Aunt Harriet. Little information about her survives: she
was intelligent, well read, selfless, and intensely devoted to her
brothers and their families. After travelling with and caring for
her mother, she never married but took on the task of raising
first Houston and his brothers, then a niece who had been or-
phaned. After 1878 she mostly lived in England looking upon
Houston as a son, providing him with money when he needed
it, and corresponding with him every few days until her death
in September 1899.

After leaving England in June 1870, Chamberlain and his
aunt first visited Bad Ems. Conflict between France and
the German states was imminent, and Chamberlain always
claimed to have witnessed personally the celebrated encounter
between the Prussian monarch and the French ambassador,
Benedetti, in the public gardens of the spa which provided the
final push toward war. Still in Germany when the conflict
began, the youth spent hours at the railway stations at Ems
and Heidelberg watching the troops embark for the front. The
electric atmosphere, the early news of victories, and the sound
of the guns around Strasbourg were exhilarating to Chamberlain and he was overwhelmed with admiration for the
military prowess of Prussia.[16] This was his first experience of
Germany: years later, in 1915, he described it, with suitable
embellishments, for the German wartime public, in part to be-
moan the loss of national vitality and to exhort a spiritual
rebirth of the German *Volk*:

> From the beginning, before his [i.e. Chamberlain's] eyes was not
> a philistine Germany, not a Germany of travelling salesmen
> and company directors, still less a nation of unrealistic
> dreamers and professors, and least of all a Germany of chatter-
> ing parliamentarians and weak-kneed ministers. Rather, it was
> a *heroic Germany*, establishing itself with the insuperable
> power of right and its knightly cadres commanded by immortal
> heroes.[17]

No letters or comments written by Chamberlain or his
Aunt Harriet in these months survived; only his wartime reminiscences exist, written after he had lived for three decades

in Central Europe. Considering their years at Versailles and their love of French culture, it would be surprising if Chamberlain or his aunt were as militantly pro-German as he later suggested. Possibly, the boy had no deeper understanding of what the war meant and perhaps he was oblivious to all but the excitement of uniforms, parades, and the reports of battles; but his aunt and other relatives, like Sir Neville Chamberlain, were undoubtedly troubled by the major redrawing of the European frontiers and the shift in the Continental balance of power that the conflict brought about.

As the war entered its final stages with the German armies occupying large areas of northeastern France and laying siege to Paris, Aunt Harriet returned to the difficult problem of Houston's education. No further plans had been made after he left Cheltenham, as it was assumed that he would soon recover sufficiently to resume his studies in England. But several relapses in his health lengthened the period of recuperation and necessitated some alternative solution. A private tutor was obviously most suited to Houston's circumstances and, while staying at Montreux with Sir Neville Chamberlain, Aunt Harriet hired the services of a young German theology student, Otto Kuntze, who had travelled south after two serious hemorrhages. The son of a pastor from the north Prussian town of Stralsund, Kuntze was a learned and remarkable teacher who put order and discipline into Chamberlain's studies for the first time, and—as an ardent nationalist—helped fire his pupil's enthusiasm for the cultural and scientific heritage of Germany. And while Kuntze was Chamberlain's tutor for only a brief period, his significance in the youth's imaginative *Wendung zum Deutschtum* can scarcely be exaggerated; they remained lifelong friends and correspondents (though most of Kuntze's letters have been lost) and the tutor read critically and advised Chamberlain on all his later books.[18]

Initially Kuntze was hired to give instruction in the German language, but this experiment proved such a success that by May 1871 he took on the task of full-time tutor. Chamberlain's health continued to give rise to alarm: in May 1871 he contracted scarlet fever and some weeks later, while convalescing at Lucerne, was found to have pleurisy, which brought

both Houston's father and Sir Neville to his bedside for fear of
his death.[19] It was not until 1872 that his condition began
gradually to improve, and during the next years he lived an
itinerant existence, spending the winters in Italy or the south
of France and returning north to the higher altitudes of Switzerland for the summer months. Despite a slow start, the boy
began to derive great benefit from the teaching of Kuntze. In
addition to mathematics, religion and the German language,
Chamberlain read widely, chiefly poetry, plays, French
classics, and history. He read Montaigne, Pascal, Rousseau,
Voltaire, Balzac, and Flaubert; he studied Schiller and avidly
consumed historical classics like Prescott's *Conquest of Mexico*
and Motley's *Rise of the Dutch Republic*. But, most of all,
Kuntze kindled Chamberlain's enthusiasm for botany—a
healthier pursuit than his previous passion for astronomy and
one which allowed him to spend hours tramping in the open air
across the Swiss countryside. At the hands of his tutor, this became more than a pleasant hobby: Chamberlain's notebooks
from the period reveal a systematic reading of botanical
scholarship and show that he soon possessed a fairly extensive
knowledge of the flora of the Swiss mountains.

In May 1873, however, his association with Kuntze came
to a sudden end when Admiral Chamberlain recalled Aunt
Harriet and Houston to England. Having abandoned all plans
for a military career for his son, the father remained anxious
about his future and intent on settling him in a suitable vocation. His latest solution was for Houston to attend an agricultural college as preparation for farming in Canada or
another part of the empire. Houston, who had no taste for
these plans at all, remained in Britain for almost seven
months, spending much of the time on the Scottish estates of
his uncle, Arbuthnot Guthrie, a wealthy financier and lan-
downer; but it soon became evident that his health could not
withstand the rigors of the British climate, let alone the more
exacting regime of Canada.

Chamberlain returned to the Continent, but by now
Kuntze—who in the interim had completed his theology
degree—was pastor to the German evangelical community at
San Remo. During the summer of 1874, however—a period

which Chamberlain always regarded as the high-point of his education—they continued their earlier studies. "Now that I was free of other preoccupations," he wrote, "I was incomparably more industrious—besides, with greater travel, I had learnt to value better what significance your teaching had for my whole life. In these months I worked enormously hard, and you responded to my zeal with a devotion which still today arouses the deepest gratitude in my heart. Latin, German, philosophy, and mathematics were the main diet. Also, we read together many other things such as Huxley's 'Lay Sermons.'"[20] At the end of the summer Kuntze returned to his congregation and soon after left for Germany where he became a *Gymnasium* teacher. Chamberlain continued as before, travelling with his aunt, and for the next three years received no formal instruction. The main question troubling him was whether he could pursue his scientific interests at a university without endangering his fragile health; and if he could, whether his father would accept that choice of a career and allow him to stay outside England.

By 1875 Chamberlain's ties to England had worn very thin; he was convinced that his health could not withstand the northern climate and, in any case, felt more at home on the Continent. From Kuntze he had learned of the excellence of German scientific scholarship and, as his health recovered in the following years, he grew more confident that he could take the strain of a university career. Periodically, Admiral Chamberlain offered more advice about a possible vocation, at one point suggesting that his son should enter the ministry and become a naval chaplain, but he was less insistent than before and accepted Houston's negative responses quietly. Aware of Houston's dedication to botany, he even raised the possibility of a scientific career. Elated, his son confessed: "This has long been my silent desire, never mentioned to you nor to anyone else because I thought it was against your wishes."[21] Inquiries were made about several German universities but some of the doctors consulted about a choice insisted that the northern winters would ruin his health. Hence it was decided to wait for a while and to continue the therapy of the Swiss mountain air. But from 1875, at least, Chamberlain had a goal: to take a degree in science leading perhaps to a career of research or teaching.

His growing fascination with everything German was reflected in his correspondence. In June 1875, for example, still apprehensive about the recent efforts of his father to enroll him in an agricultural college, Houston confessed to Aunt Harriet: "My three greatest wishes in life are: first, to be allowed to remain in Europe and not to emigrate to the colonies, second, to stay far away from England, and third, to settle in Germany." Descriptions of England were enough to make him despondent: "Your letter containing the description of all your London social life, and the breakfasts and dinners with the high nobility, has put me in a depressed state because of the realization that I could at any time be compelled to return to that world which I hate so." He added: "The arrival [in Cannes] of dear old Dr. Meyer and his wife from Rostock first lightened the burden of my sorrow. With these good people I feel what I have experienced among so many Germans: that they understand me and I them—a feeling which I have never had with an Englishman."[22] In the following year he asserted: "The fact may be regrettable but it remains a fact; I have become so completely un-English that the mere thought of England and the English makes me unhappy." Repelled by the coldness and formality of his birthplace he began to seek refuge in an idealized homeland which he called Germany. "I would give my left arm to have been born a German," he once told Kuntze.[23] In fact, he knew little of Bismarck's Reich; his picture of Germany was derived from science, literature, philosophy, and music. This attraction was also clearly entwined with his feelings of rebellion against a father whose authority he continued to fear. Also, before long, additional emotional ties greatly reinforced Chamberlain's feelings.

During the winters at Cannes Chamberlain mixed mostly

with the substantial German colony there, and in the fall of 1874, at a charity bazaar organized by the German residents, he first met Anna Horst. The daughter of a state prosecutor in Breslau, she was in her thirtieth year and earned a living by private tutoring. Chamberlain left no record of their first encounter, but Anna recalled it vividly: "I was struck," she wrote, "by the shyness of this very slim young man in a huge grey hat, whose beautiful eyes were hidden (unnecessarily it seemed to me) by spectacles." They were alike in many ways: both were nervous, shy, and lonely, and both longed for more intimate companionship; they also shared enthusiasms for poetry and music as well as for botanical expeditions into neighboring countryside.[24]

With the exception of Aunt Harriet and Kuntze, Chamberlain had never before experienced a close relationship with anyone. Seeing a great deal of each other in Cannes and then in the spring and summer of 1875 at Montreux, where Anna had a job tutoring, Houston soon became completely infatuated—much to his aunt's disquiet. Already in 1875 he was contemplating marriage, although he recognized the obstacles were formidable: he was 20 years old and had not yet embarked on a career; his income was inadequate to support a wife, and his family were certain to object to so youthful a marriage to a Prussian girl ten years his senior with neither social position nor wealth to her credit. Anna was also troubled by the age difference between them, but allowed her reservations to be swept aside by Houston's insistence.

Expectations of a hostile response in England proved correct and for the next three years they saw each other at Cannes in the winters and corresponded during the spring and summer seasons.[25] Meantime, Chamberlain tried unsuccessfully to publish the poems and plays he was engaged in writing, and pressed on with his botanical and scientific studies. Recurrent bad health, especially a severe case of jaundice in the summer of 1877, reawakened family suspicions about the incurable delicacy of his constitution and made university study a receding goal. So his frustrations increased. He was forced to postpone marriage till he was older or at least until the strength of his affections had been tested by time; moreover, his eagerness for a career in science was checked by his family's conviction that taking a degree course might irreparably damage his health.

Amid these disappointments, his attraction to Germany and German culture grew still stronger: it seemed connected in his mind with all his desires for independence, his scientific and marital aspirations. "England," on the other hand, became almost synonymous with his father's well meaning but arbitrary interference, and with all that restrained his hopes. His earliest declaration of spiritual allegiance to Germany dates in fact from this time: after writing several descriptive letters to Anna while on a tour through Spain in 1876, he tried to set on paper his feelings for her birthplace. The result was an astonishing outpouring of German idealism which anticipated in a remarkable way his later admonitions to Germans and eulogies to the Reich:

Seville, Tuesday 23rd May 1876

I cannot tell you how much my reverence, my passionate love for Germany and my faith in her, increases. The more I learn of other nations, the more I mix with people of all classes—educated and uneducated—from all the countries of Europe, the more I love Germany and the Germans. My belief that the whole future of Europe—i.e. the civilization of the world—rests in the hands of Germany, has now grown to a firm conviction. The German's existence is quite different from that of other men—in him self-awareness and the feeling of his own worth have reached their high-point. He is both artist and practical organizer, thinker and activist, a man of peace *par excellence* and the best soldier, a sceptic and the only man who is really capable of belief. But, as always, the greater the natural gifts, the greater the responsibilities which go with them. Germany's role is a tremendously difficult one and if she is to fulfill it, the whole nation must recognize the task and strive together as one for its accomplishment. Not only does Germany have so much to perform and develop, but in the meantime, she must preserve herself against the animosity and misjudgments of all Europe. If one is not caught up in all this, but can observe the course of things from afar, the question often arises: "Will Germany be able to fulfill her alloted task? Will she accomplish it?" And though one may love Germany with all one's heart

without seeing any overhanging clouds still one must reply: No!
—if the fundamentally corroded moral relations are not
improved (and they will not stay as they are; if they do not
improve, then they will deteriorate) No!—if the whole nation
does not understand that purity is the greatest strength of a
people. And so, while the future of Europe depends on
Germany, Germany herself can only have a future if the roots
of the present condition are attacked and if morality is raised
aloft as the principal weapon against the rest of the world. If
Germany does not understand this, then she too must fall—fall
prey to the barbarians, without having fulfilled her role. . . .
(Ah God! What kind of a German am I to write in this way!
Don't be angry with me, for certainly I am no German).

6:45 in the evening. Ah you beloved German nation! Will
you never discover your exalted role and see that your ordained
path is not to be that of the other nations? [26]

These passionate lines on the moral duty of Germans are
curiously reminiscent of Wagner and Lagarde, and yet at this
time Chamberlain knew little of Wagner and nothing of Lagarde. He had read the Grimms and some of the German
romantics, and had imbibed the staunch Prussian viewpoints
of Kuntze. But neither the immediate circumstances surrounding the letter nor the exact origins of his thoughts is evident.
Since the letter is one of the very few to have survived from
this period of his life and since similar sentiments do not recur
in his writings until more than seven years later, it must
remain something of a mystery. Certainly, it is significant that
his thoughts were addressed to Anna Horst, and clearly his
feelings for her and his love for Germany had become closely
intertwined, especially in view of the rather snobbish disparagement his relatives felt for Anna both as a foreigner and
as a working woman of decidedly middle class family. [27]

In 1878, after years of overwork as the naval commander at
Devonport, Admiral Chamberlain died. Houston felt little
grief; although he recognized his father as a limited but well-
meaning man, they were almost complete strangers. The
father's death did, however, mean financial and personal independence for the son, and Chamberlain now began to chart his
own course. His four-year relationship with Anna was his immediate concern. Despite continuing family dissatisfaction

they were married on April 9, 1878. "Aunty's" mood especially worried Chamberlain but his brother Basil assured him it was only the transient reaction of an over-possessive woman to the loss of her youngest. "I *do* know," wrote Basil a few days before the wedding, "the terribly jealous temper that has caused her and others so much unhappiness through life. I had the same experience of it with regard to the very dear friendship that binds me to Aunt Fan. . . . Perhaps you may not know that there was the same sort of thing in my father's case when he first married. She was, I believe, almost frantic with jealousy but it all past [*sic*] over." [28] After the marriage Aunt Harriet accompanied the newlyweds on the first stage of their honeymoon along the shores of Lake Geneva. She then left them to meet her niece, Mary, a sickly girl whose father had recently died in Abyssinia and who now received the attentions which had earlier been lavished upon Houston. [29]

After a brief vacation in Switzerland, Anna and Houston travelled north to Breslau, where her family lived. No evidence survives about the Horst family. There are some flimsy indications that her father was a Jew who had converted to the Christian faith; if true, this could possibly have had some bearing on the later development of Chamberlain's racial views, but nothing resembling hard evidence is available. [30]

Another aspect of Chamberlain's life about which he was eager to act was his education. His first plan was to reside in Florence, where the climate would be beneficial to his health, and where he could study botany at the university under the guidance of Professor Parlatore. Having improved their Italian, Houston and Anna travelled south to Italy by way of Munich, arriving in November 1878. The architectural and artistic splendor of the city overwhelmed Chamberlain, and though he at first applied himself diligently to mastering Italian and extending his knowledge of plant physiology, he was soon completely distracted by his surroundings. Recalling the experience later, he wrote:

> I had intentionally not prepared myself at all for Florence as an artistic center: my plan was to learn the language and then to dedicate myself to the study of botany; nothing should divert me from it. It turned out completely otherwise. Never shall I

forget the hour when, one evening, I was strolling aimlessly through the town, and came for the first time unexpectedly, across the Piazza della Signoria. The sight of such beauty was so overpowering that a kind of dizziness overcame me and I had to withdraw into a door-way, lean against something and gradually recover. I returned home stunned. This was a different order of ecstasy to that which I experienced in the stars and later in flowers. These works of beauty fashioned by man, took my breath away and destroyed my equilibrium. Nurtured in a completely unartistic environment, I had not the slightest foretaste of such things. They produced a complete revolution within me.[31]

He hastened to purchase art books, eagerly devoured large numbers of histories, and studied carefully the works of Burckhardt. His days began with violoncello lessons and continued with tours of the Uffizi and other galleries. Scientific research was momentarily forgotten: "I was no longer aware that a man named Parlatore even existed, let alone that I had come to Florence on his account." Only in May 1879 did Chamberlain's mood of elation and artistic enchantment give way to one of self-doubt and worry. He began to reprimand himself for his carefree existence, fearing that he was becoming a mere "dabbler," disengaged from society and given over to his own amusements:

Suddenly a kind of vision of my future existence rose before my eyes. I saw myself—like so many of my English countrymen, whom I had observed from a distance—vegetating without any goals in life; in part connoisseurs of art, in part amateur musicians, perhaps occasionally dabbling in botany and geology—a dilettante in the bad sense of the word, namely a dilettante in life, a man without responsibilities, and without any self-imposed obligations. Confronted with this picture I shuddered with horror.[32]

Chastened by these thoughts, and convinced that his talents lay in science rather than the fine arts, Chamberlain felt a compelling need to escape the distractions of Italy. He made a sudden decision to move to Geneva, which offered the advantages of a prestigious university as well as reasonable proximity to the Mediterranean. When he arrived the univer-

sity semester was already in progress, but he settled in quickly
and easily surmounted the first hurdle of matriculation exams,
and was formally admitted to the faculty of Natural Science in
the fall of 1879. During the next two years he worked hard, taking a wide range of courses in physics, chemistry, botany,
anatomy, anthropology, and zoology. Then, in the fall of 1881,
instead of taking his exams for an undergraduate degree in parts
spread over two or three years, he did them all at once, learning
shortly afterward that he had placed first in the university.
After the many trials and setbacks of his youth this achievement was especially gratifying, as it crowned with success the
first stage of his chosen career, helped to buttress his self-confidence, and enabled him to justify his way of life to his relatives
in England. Eager to make up for lost time, he proceeded at
once to the doctorate, which his professor of chemistry, Carl
Graebe, had intimated could be completed in a little over a
year, leaving him free for postdoctoral research or a regular
teaching appointment.[33]

His thesis was to have been on some aspect of plant
chemistry. "If I am not mistaken," wrote Chamberlain later,
"it was concerned with the vegetable fats of a certain botanical
group."[34] But a renewed bout of sickness soon forced him to
discontinue laboratory work for a time, and further reading
and reflection focussed his attention on a problem of a very
different kind from the biochemistry envisioned by Graebe.
The new interest concerned the motion of sap in plants, a
tricky subject for research and one which involved the philosophical debate between mechanism and vitalism. In 1882 when
he started on the subject, Chamberlain had little real grasp of
what it entailed. He was hopeful that the research could be undertaken without complicated apparatus and planned to establish a laboratory at home, which would allow him to work as
his health permitted, without necessitating long hours at the
university.[35]

He began diligently but without adequate supervision
found himself sinking deeper and deeper into a bog of endless
and mystifying detail; each question, each set of results
opened massive new avenues for research and the prospect of
obtaining the doctorate in 1883 rapidly faded. It was not until

the spring of 1884 that he felt "firmly in the saddle," and even this proved too optimistic. The first task was to select suitable plants for long periods of experimentation and then to design an accurate manometer for measuring sap movements. Previous research had failed, in part, because of insufficient readings, and so Chamberlain molded his daily existence to the requirements of his work. "I imposed a regimen on myself so that, even in the evenings and nights, not more than four hours at most would be allowed to pass between two successive readings of the various plants under observation. If, for example, I had left my laboratory at eleven in the evening, I set the alarm for 3 A.M. and early at 7 A.M. I was again at work. If, on the following night, I permitted myself to retire at 9 P.M., so I got up again at 1 in the morning and again at 5." [36]

Such was his mode of life as a doctoral candidate. Discussion of the direction of Chamberlain's research, may be postponed until a later chapter, for he was not to finish the thesis until 1896. The more immediate consequence of the exacting work schedule he set himself was that it further undermined his health and contributed to a complete nervous breakdown which he was to suffer in 1884—although, as will become clear, it was far from being the only cause of his collapse. [37]

Life in Geneva was not all work. There were trips into the mountains and journeys further afield to Germany. In September 1882 Chamberlain and Anna left their small apartment in town and moved into a large rambling villa at Vert Pré with splendid views of Mont Salève to the south. The bucolic existence suited them both and was enlivened by a constant stream of house guests. He spent a great deal of time reading widely—Buckle, Spencer, Kant, Schopenhauer—and took piano lessons from Ruthardt, a friend of Nietzsche and one of the few welcome visitors at the retreat in Sils Maria. Though many of Chamberlain's friends were later critical of Anna, and Hermann Keyserling for one snobbishly referred to her as a "second-rate governess type," their marriage in these early years seemed to be working well. Chamberlain appeared happy and at ease; he contentedly assured his Aunt Harriet: "My first impression at each letter from London, always is—thank heavens I'm not there!—so please don't think it necessary to tone down your glowing descriptions, in order not to 'mir das Herz schwer machen.'"[38]

Though Ruthardt regaled Chamberlain with stories about Nietzsche, it was not the solitary prophet of Zarathustra who increasingly absorbed his intellect, but rather Nietzsche's cultural antagonist, Richard Wagner. He had become a patron of the Bayreuth *Festspiele* as early as 1878, although he did not attend the performances until four years later. Like many young students and aesthetes, Chamberlain was enthralled by the prospect of an "artwork of the future" and clutched eagerly at the chance to participate in publicizing Bayreuth and raising contributions. Wagnerite friends like the French writers Edouard Dujardin and Theodor de Wyzewa, and the highly talented but as yet untried stage designer Adolphe Appia, soon became regular visitors at Vert Pré. And before long, the volatile, dilettantish side of Chamberlain's nature, which he had suppressed after fleeing Florence, began to reassert itself in a desire to devote more and more of his time and energy to the cause of Wagner. Yet he still wanted to complete his thesis and obtain a university appointment of some kind. The result, in 1882 and 1883, was a deepening tension between his interests in science and his fascination for Wagnerism; and it was this indecision and general restlessness which seems to have prompted him to a surprising but—in terms of his future life—very significant course of action.

At the beginning of 1883 Chamberlain suddenly left his laboratory in Vert Pré, went to Paris, and began to concentrate on his financial affairs. We know almost nothing of his reasons: he had shown no interest in business before and carefully omitted all reference to this episode in later life—in his invectives against contemporary Mammonism he conveniently forgot that he too had once sullied his hands. There is no sign that he and Anna faced any sudden or unaccustomed pecuniary problems; they lived on investments and were able to travel, pay for Houston's education, keep up an expensive villa with at least one full-time servant, and make donations to favorite causes like Bayreuth. Possibly the financial instability of the early 1880s had reduced the returns on Chamberlain's stocks and he was afraid of eating away his capital reserves. He had spent two years on his dissertation and had made little headway; the prospects of finishing quickly and earning money by teaching were remote. But his decision may also have been influenced by the very frustration of his botanical research, and perhaps his behavior may to some extent be interpreted as the attempts of a 28-year-old man who had never worked to prove to himself and to others that he could succeed in the business world. In addition, the Wagnerite circles in which he hoped to move were, generally speaking, wealthy, and possibly he felt he would need more money for travel and other expenses which might result from his activities for the cause. Finally, it may also have been that his growing acquaintance with wealthy Parisian Wagnerites persuaded him that he could, without much difficulty, gain a quick success on the *Bourse.*

Whatever his reasons, Chamberlain began to gamble in the Paris money market and at first could boast some gains.[39] By the end of October 1883, he had entered into a small partnership with a Frenchman named Cerceau. They engaged in small-scale brokerage and hoped later to expand into the discounting area. Cerceau was "the *Bourse* man," and looked after the half dozen clerks they employed, while Houston described himself as "the calculator, the plan-maker, the organiser."[40] In fact, Chamberlain's main task was to make the right contacts in France and Switzerland and to attract new clients, which he hoped to do through his family's friends and business associates, and also through his fellow Wagnerites, for in 1883 he had managed to get himself delegated as the official Paris representative of the Wagner Association.

The timing of Chamberlain's entry into business was singularly inauspicious, for the European money market was everywhere unstable. In Germany the early 1880s were years of uncertainty, while in France the collapse of the Union Génerale in 1882, after a bitter rivalry with the Rothschild Bank, resulted in a panic on the *Bourse* and a flood of bank-ruptcies. Between 1882 and 1887, France faced mounting budget deficits, industry stagnated, and prices and wages de-clined. Anti-Semitism became more vocal among those de-pendent on the financial market, although Chamberlain's cor-respondence reveals little of this. The kind of business in which he engaged was extremely risky, and by February 1884 his affairs were in a state of crisis. Interestingly enough, however, he traced his difficulties to immediate internal prob-lems within the firm, rather than laying the blame on either the general state of the market or the alleged manipulations of "Jewish finance."

In the absence of other evidence, we must rely entirely upon Chamberlain's view of the firm's failure. Some of his relatives were critical of his own role, but Chamberlain placed all the blame on his partner Cerceau. Houston had spent long periods away from Paris, returning to Anna in Geneva or searching out new clients or attending various Wagnerite func-tions. When he returned after one of these trips in February 1884, he found the business on the verge of collapse. Without prior discussion, Cerceau had speculated, incurring heavy losses; then, to retrieve the capital he had lost, he ignored the wishes of the firm's customers, failing to execute their orders on time or selling without their instructions in the hope of repurchasing the stock later when the market prices dropped. As Chamberlain admitted to Aunt Harriet: "To make a long story very, very, *very* short: my position is a most critical one." He denied any knowledge of his partner's dealings and set to work to assess the extent of the disaster. The company had not only accumulated losses from its own capital reserves but also owed large debts to its investors. He wrote despairingly: "I see two possibilities: borrow money on which to make a fresh start or pay each man his due and then see how I can earn my liveli-hood as a crossing-sweeper or something else. As for the first solution to my present difficulties, I can hardly take it into consideration, for I am far too practical to borrow from the

Jews; it is impossible for an honest man to pay their percentage and gain his own livelihood." In any case, he reflected, most of the customers he had cultivated in Germany and Switzerland would desert the firm.[41]

Behind these letters to Aunt Harriet was a tacit request for help. He concluded that after everything had been worked out, he and his partner would owe some £1500, "which I cannot possibly hope to raise for some months." He was also insistent that he could succeed and recover his losses if given another chance: "If . . . it would be *possible* for me to begin again, I should do so full of hope and confidence, for the more I see and know the market, the more sure I am of success—and I have a certain number of customers who I know would remain true to me and facilitate a fresh start."[42] Far from impairing his reputation on the exchange, he argued rather unconvincingly, his recent misfortune had in some ways raised confidence in him.

On April 7, 1884, the partnership with Cerceau was formally dissolved. With Aunt Harriet's assistance, including the transfer of £2000 in securities, Chamberlain made a new start. He worked hard in the following weeks, allowing himself only one relaxation: his activities for the Wagner Association. "I think," he wrote, "it is my passion for Wagner which enables me to stand everything; as soon as the door of my office is closed behind me, I know it's no good fretting, so I eat a good dinner and stroll on the Boulevard, thinking of the *Kunstwerke der Zunkunft*, or I go to see one of my Wagnerian friends, or I write to one of my numerous Wagnerian correspondents."[43] His relatives in England continued to be disturbed, for they obviously believed Houston completely unsuited for business and doubted that he was persistent enough or sufficiently hardheaded to succeed. Aunt Harriet had from the first been critical of his decision to devote so much time to making money, and other family members harbored doubts as to his innocence in the Cerceau affair. One uncle, Arbuthnot Guthrie, a very successful businessman and a director of the Bank of England, felt the market was far too unstable and refused to assist Chamberlain in gaining new clients. Irate, Chamberlain complained to Aunt Harriet: "Uncle Buth

[Arbuthnot] refused point blank to do the only thing I asked him for and which he better than anyone else *could* have done, which was to help me with my business connections." He added defiantly "Last month I earned very nearly £200 in commissions, so you see that my aptitudes are appreciated by some people." [44]

Yet, for all his air of confidence, Chamberlain's second venture also began to go badly, and the constant strain of recent months took its toll. During the summer of 1884 he was plagued with migraine headaches, and in September decided to quit Paris for a while. He told Aunt Harriet: "But now I am *really* going to Vert Pré. I must, I should certainly break down in my best season if I did not try and have a little absolute rest, at least absolute quiet." By the end of September he fell ill, exhausted and overstrained from his recent trials: "In the state in which I am [I am] often very capable and wide awake, but also often at the lowest ebb, so that any trifle can make the balance tip to a serious crisis." He complained of "contraction of the heart and chief blood vessels" and feared increasing deafness. Dictating his correspondence to Anna, he wrote: "You must not be alarmed, dearest Aunty, but it is right you should know that I can now neither *read* nor *write at all!* That is to say, I *can* of course read a few lines but immediately it is as if a hundred daggers were being plunged into my head, and I have to lie down with closed eyes till I recover." Frequent fainting fits, nightmares, and other nervous disorders added to his plight. [45]

With Houston sick, it became Anna's task to tie up his affairs in Paris. Her account of the situation is certainly colored by her loyalty to Houston; the chief problem, she argued, was that of recovering sums owed to her husband by Cerceau and others. A small sum was forthcoming from the sale of furniture and effects from their Paris apartment, but the £2000 in securities loaned to Chamberlain by Aunt Harriet had been disbursed in payments of the partnership's debts. In the eyes of his wife Chamberlain had sacrificed all to ensure that his customers would not lose; his own debtors meantime had defaulted and "there [was] no hope of seeing this money ever!" Aunt Harriet suggested that a lawyer be hired to unravel the whole affair but Anna rejected the idea firmly on the grounds that Houston would be too distressed. [46]

On the Paris exchange Chamberlain had attempted to prove his ability to succeed in business as he had recently done in the academic world. The resultant loss of financial security was a bitter blow. Not only did he feel a deep sense of humiliation and personal failure, but also the financial dependence which had characterized his life till his father's death in 1878 was now restored. His doctorate was only half completed; he had no private income and no way of earning a living. Failure meant he was again attached to the pecuniary strings of his family in England and it was they who supported him in the following years.

While Anna was in Paris, Chamberlain tried to recuperate at Cannes. She soon joined him and they spent a quiet winter, resting and consulting medical specialists who, after puzzling over the case for some time, finally concluded he was suffering from "the innate, excessive delicacy of the nerves and the great irritability of the *nervous membrane* in general and of that surrounding the nervous system generally." For the moment they prescribed fresh air and leisure, and cautioned Chamberlain that he must abandon in the forseeable future all scientific research which required long hours of experimentation and broken nights. [47]

Chamberlain's breakdown brought the Genevan period of his life to a close. He no longer wished to remain in Switzerland now that he was unable to finish his doctorate and could not anyway afford the upkeep of a house like that at Vert Pré. Aunt Harriet suggested that Italy might be good for his health, but Chamberlain and Anna preferred Germany, both because living there was relatively inexpensive and more especially because of the availability of good theater and music. Although none of Chamberlain's letters from Geneva had repeated the encomiums of the Seville letter quoted above, he had visited Germany often in the previous five years and found the country increasingly appealing. "I have been to Germany repeatedly these last years," he informed Aunt Harriet, "and I must say that I felt there more completely happy, more at home, more in my *own* element, than anywhere else." In addition, in Germany he could hope to continue his activity for Bayreuth and Wagnerism. "Thus," he wrote, although I cannot hope ever to be again able to do the smallest thing *materially* for the cause I love above all others, I can be really useful"[48] After some discussion with friends, he chose to settle in Dresden, a flourishing center of the Wagner movement.

Thus ended Chamberlain's first thirty years. He had entered the world with considerable advantages of wealth and social position, but the course of his early life was heavily determined by his delicate health. Outwardly he looked strong enough, and pictures of him in 1885 reveal a tall, well-built man; but—whether from physical or psychological causes or both—he was weaker than he appeared. One breakdown at fifteen years destroyed his father's hopes that the boy would have an English upbringing followed by a socially acceptable career in the military or some arm of government administration. The second, and more serious, collapse he suffered in 1884 prevented the realization of his hopes to become a scientist. In between, there was a happier period: his association with Kuntze, the early years of his marriage to Anna Horst, and university at Geneva. Not only did the second breakdown nullify his recent academic success, but his financial losses also took away much of the independence and security he had enjoyed since 1878 and made him reliant on the charity of others. He looked forward to substantial inheritances later, but in 1884 as a sick man, with little property and unable to make his own way, his plight resembled the conditions of his youth. The difference was that he was now thirty and had a wife to support.

Already in his broad and unconventional education we see developing those qualities of mind—the originality of the autodidact and the encyclopedic knowledge of the dilettante—that

Chamberlain in 1878

later characterized Chamberlain's writings. But in his own recollections be believed that the strongest legacy of his peripatetic youth was a sense of having no nationality, of being in a way the product of three cultures—England, France, and Germany. Had he stayed at Cheltenham, its traditions and rigid training would either have forced his personality into some socially acceptable mold or otherwise created a nonconformist; conformist or rebel the result would assuredly have been a familiar English type. As it happened, Chamberlain grew up feeling equally "foreign" in England, France, and Germany; he lived on the margin of all three cultures. In some cases, sociologists have suggested, this may exacerbate psychological uncertainties and self-division; it may culminate in a vehement *Selbsthass* which gnaws at the self or is projected outward into hatred for others.[49] But such feelings of "marginality" can also, under certain circumstances, lead to an open-mindedness and receptivity to a wide range of ideas and influences. This was true of Chamberlain's restless, dilettantish spirit in his years at Geneva. He was an English-style liberal in politics, as well as an admirer of German cultural nationalism; a Wagner enthusiast who also liked Berlioz and even Mendelssohn; a student of Kant and Schopenhauer who tried to keep up with the latest works of Flaubert and the Symbolists. Later, in the different atmosphere of the German Reich and with his closer tries to the world of Bayreuth, he began slowly to change; his interests became more exclusive, began to flow in channels dictated by the twin influences of Wagnerism and Bismarckian Germany. As a result, his "marginality" led him, in this new context, to become more assimilationist, more fiercely Germanophile and eager to stress the importance of "rootedness." The passionate Germanism of the Seville letter is absent from the letters he wrote at Geneva; in Dresden that style was rediscovered. Even his appearance changed, indicating a kind of compulsion to find a new self in Dresden; before they left for Germany Chamberlain went off to town and had his long beard removed and his shoulder-length hair cut short.[50]

Finally, Chamberlain had discovered the music of Wagner and in the next years it was by his activity for Wagnerism that

Chamberlain at Vert Pre, 1885

From Anna Chamberlain, *Meine Erinnerungen an H. S. Chamberlain*, Munich: Beck, 1923.

he surmounted his sickness and depression in Dresden and regained a sense of purpose. When he went to Dresden, Chamberlain had only just begun to explore the true meaning of the "Bayreuth Idea." Four years later, when he left, he was emerging as a prominent and valued exponent of the cause.

Chapter Two

The Education of a Wagnerite

IN AUGUST 1870, during a boat trip on Lake Lucerne, Chamberlain heard the name Richard Wagner for the first time. The composer was then living at Triebschen, a spacious villa overlooking the lake where he had been exiled four years before from the court of King Ludwig of Bavaria. Repeated meddling in politics had infuriated the royal ministers, while his adulterous relationship with Cosima Bülow had aroused the disgust and homosexual jealously of the King. Exile had given Wagner perhaps the happiest years of his life: free from the distractions of Munich, looked after by Cosima, and surrounded by a growing brood of children (including his son Siegfried, who was born in 1869), he was enormously energetic and creative. There were periodic visits from admiring friends like Nietzsche, then a young philology professor at Basel, and ample time to plan for a festival theater. Around the estate was a high wall which cut the house off from the noise and gaze of boat excursions and coaches, packed with inquisitive sight-seers. On one of these boats sat the 15-year-old Chamberlain, intrigued by the heated conversation which animated his fellow travellers at the sound of Wagner's name.[1]

In later life Chamberlain asserted that his early upbringing had restrained his strong musical inclinations. His family and early teachers had little interest in music and, as a boy, Houston had little opportunity to hear any orchestras. Though he asked his father to allow extracurricular musical studies at Cheltenham, the request was refused: the general consensus of

the Chamberlains was that, though a necessary accomplishment for young girls who had to ensnare then amuse a husband, musical attainments were quite irrelevant to a young
man destined for the military. But, after leaving England, his
love for music began to grow. Convalescing near Lago Mag-
giore in 1872, he listened as a fellow guest at the hotel played
selections from Beethoven and was deeply moved. "In these
hours," Chamberlain wrote, "a new world opened to me, a
world of whose existence I had till then not the remotest suspicion. . . . All pain—and as a sick youth reputedly destined for
an early grave, I had experienced much of it—was transformed
into ecstasy . . . the world had acquired a new significance."
Soon he was himself taking piano and cello lessons during the
months he spent at Cannes each year.[2]

Ironically, Chamberlain first learned of the music dramas
and Bayreuth from two Jews whom he met at Interlaken during the summer and autumn of 1875. The first, a Parisian
schoolteacher named Lowenthal, was an accomplished pianist;
he introduced Chamberlain to the work of Schubert, Weber,
and Chopin, as well as Wagner. Unfortunately, Chamberlain
recalled, "he knew only a little of Wagner, for one got to hear
little of him in the Paris of that time. But some pieces he
played wonderfully—such as the overtures to [Fliegende]
Holländer and Tannhäuser and the beginning of Lohengrin."
Attempting in 1917 to reconcile his friendship for this baptized
French Jew and his racial outlook, Chamberlain wrote: "Obviously Lowenthal stemmed from the Sephardim; rarely have I
encountered the Oriental type so beautifully and nobly educated; but he suffered because of it, for the poor man was inconsolable over his Jewish heritage and all my words could not
appease his feelings; certainly, this grief played a part in his
early death."[3] Lowenthal, it seems, was the first of several
Jews in Chamberlain's life who showed him the deep psychological sufferings, the corrosive self-doubt, and self-abnegation which resulted from their being the victims of anti-Semitism. His response was that of pity, rather than rejection of
racial ideas and stereotypes.

More important as a source of information about Bayreuth
was a second Jew, named Blumenfeld, who came from Vienna,

where the ideas of the Wagnerian *Gesamtkunstwerk* had made an especially great impact upon the musical and literary avant-garde. The Vienna Academic Wagner Society, founded in 1873, was the largest and wealthiest Wagner club; not only did it collect funds for the *Festspiele* and encourage perform-ances of the dramas, but it sought as well to propagate Wagner's social and religious philosophy among the in-habitants of the Austrian capital. Among university students and in groups such as the "Pernerstorfer circle," where young writers and artists confronted the social and spiritual crises of the Hapsburg monarchy, Wagner was a hero and Bayreuth the symbol of cultural regeneration.[4] Blumenfeld's enthusiasm was typical of his generation, and he urged Chamberlain to attend the first *Festspiele*, which was planned for 1876. But Houston could not afford the tickets and travelling expenses, and his father refused to finance such entertainment and was unmoved by the claim that a new age was dawning in music. Sadly, Houston wrote to Aunt Harriet: "If only I had enough money at my disposal, August 12 would certainly find me in Bay-reuth. It will be a tremendous experience and those who attend this performance will have witnessed a turning-point in the history of art."[5] Such was his enthusiasm before he had at-tended a single performance of any Wagnerian drama. He followed reports of the festival in the *Kölnische Zeitung* and other newspapers and studied the poem of the *Ring*, which Blumenfeld had urged him to buy. Not surprisingly, when in 1878 he finally saw *Tannhäuser* in a provincial German city, it was a great disappointment: the average provincial theaters were of poor quality when it came to performances of Wagner, and his expectations were enormous. Inadequate productions of Wagner's dramas were to distort their public reception for some years, and it was not until much later that Chamberlain achieved a full appreciation of the earlier works.[6]

Chamberlain's first real exposure to Wagner's art came in November 1878. Shortly after their marriage, he and Anna travelled to see her relatives in Breslau and then, on their way south to Florence, passed through Bavaria where they at-tended the Munich première of the *Ring*. The experience overwhelmed Chamberlain: "Wagner's work," he told Aunt

Harriet in a particularly effusive letter, "has fulfilled my expectations in every respect and in some has far exceeded
them." "What struck me most" he wrote "was the miraculous
simplicity and the crystal clear quality [of the work]—which I
find lacking in French and Italian operas with their numerous
singers and unconnected accompaniment." It was *Rheingold*
especially which captivated him: "the marvellous orchestra
charmed the ear and invited whoever was capable to gaze
deeper and to take pleasure in tracing the ethical and philosophical ideas of the tone-poet; truly an ocean in which man
may blissfully immerse himself to gain learning." "As for
Wagner's ideal of a new theater," he added, "just one evening
was sufficient to convert me and destroy any last reservations
of mine." [7]

He at once joined the Bayreuth Patrons Society [*Allgemeine Bayreuther Patronatsverein*] which had been set up in
1872 to raise money for the festivals and to coordinate the
activities of local Wagner clubs in Germany and elsewhere.
Since his father's death earlier in the year, Chamberlain had
become financially independent and was able to give small
donations to the cause. He still knew very little of Wagner's
work or of the social and political attitudes associated with the
elusive "Bayreuth Idea," but his enthusiasm for the cause at
once assumed the high seriousness of the most fervent devotees. For him, as for so many contemporaries, the Wagner
movement heralded cultural rebirth: he was deeply attracted
by its anticapitalist longings and its critique of the spiritual
emptiness and fragmented nature of modern society. Bayreuth
was a precarious venture undertaken in the expansive era that
followed German Unification; it might even be viewed as an
artistic analogue of the risky business promotions of those
years. It embodied both the ebullient, hopeful mood of the new
Reich and also the deeper anxieties and sense of cultural
unease that swept across Germany, particularly after the economic crash of 1873. [8] Wagner saw his creation as a national institution, a center of the struggle for German race and culture,
but Chamberlain's initial enthusiasm was diffuse and had little
to do with nationalist or political feeling. It was the aesthetic
utopianism of Bayreuth that fascinated him, its stress on the in-

ward condition of the individual and on self-realization through art.

As a patron of the *Festspiele*, Chamberlain received the *Bayreuther Blätter*, a journal founded in 1877 to provide a forum for Wagner's ideas and to publish news and correspondence from the growing number of Wagner societies. The first number appeared in January 1878, edited by a Prussian aristocrat, Baron Hans von Wolzogen, who had settled in Bayreuth so as to devote full time to the project. A man of fanatical and idealist temperament Wolzogen, whom Chamberlain once dubbed "the Pope of Wagnerism," edited the *Blätter* until his death in 1938: under his guidance it became the focal point of the Wagner cult, the mediator between Wahnfried and the public, and the official vehicle for espousing Wagner's aesthetic, social, and political views and for interpreting the music dramas themselves. Wolzogen's work and longevity, like that of Wagner's widow, Cosima, gave continuity and stability to the "Bayreuth Idea." No greater contrast could be imagined to Nietzsche, whom Wagner had first eyed for the task. Wolzogen was hardworking, reserved, and deeply religious; and while his confused ideas and mystical utterances sometimes aroused irreverent amusement among other members of the inner circle of Wagnerites, nobody doubted the enormous significance of his dogged and persistent labors for the cause.[9] Even in 1885 Cosima, who expected self-sacrifice in others as almost a matter of course, could still marvel at his extraordinary dedication. To the conductor Hermann Levi she wrote with unaccustomed frankness: "Wolzogen can certainly not vie with Nietzsche as a stylist at present, but I most decidedly hope that he will train himself to be a writer; I agree with you that he is not a born one. Wolzogen has one of the most curious natures I have ever come across, a life so completely absorbed in an idea would seem incredible had one not seen it."[10]

In later years Chamberlain too came to appreciate Wolzogen's personal qualities, but their first dealings with one another, in 1879, were marked by disagreement. Chamberlain was not yet ready for the doctrinaire style of the *Blätter*, and he found himself annoyed by its "outspoken tendency . . . to

oblige the members of the new Patrons Society to support a
specific philosophical, religious, or political confession of
belief." Often thinking about the efforts of devotees like
Heinrich Porges to endow Wagner's work with such a fixed religious and philosophical content, Chamberlain decided to
reply with an essay of his own. It was his first attempt to expound his ideas on art, and his strictures of official Wagnerism
often sound like criticisms later directed against his own views
as a publicist for Bayreuth. His youthful attack, like the opposition he later encountered himself, derived from social and
political principles as well as aesthetic ones, for it was with
some surprise that he realized that many of his own ideas
about politics and social organization were contrary to those
sanctified by the *Blätter*. Although his ideas on Wagner and
Bayreuth underwent a marked transformation in the next
decade, in 1879 he firmly asserted:

> It is a completely false and most reprehensible procedure to ex-
> tract a specific philosophical teaching from art-work. In con-
> sidering an artist's creations we need not enter into his personal
> views.
>   His works breathe a higher spirit, and there is scarcely a
> more unfortunate and harmful notion to the cause the [Wagner]
> Verein represents than the idea of "exposing the philosophical
> views of the Master by means of his works." Outside pure en-
> joyment of beauty the effect of an art-work is and can only be
> an aesthetic and—indirectly—an ethical one. . . . Art affects us
> directly, and its advantage morally is that it, to some extent,
> elevates man above himself and purifies his spirit without his
> having to retrace the many stages of ratiocination. For an in-
> telligent man the consequence will naturally be that he is in-
> duced to think a lot. But Art—a product of genius which
> reflects general and absolute Beauty and Truth—can never act
> as the vehicle for a particular and specific teaching.[11]

His essay measured the opinions of the *Blätter* against the
ideas of Kant, whose *Critique of Judgment* he studied in detail
during this time. Chamberlain's argument rested upon a
separation of logical concepts and aesthetic ideas. The former
were abstracted from empirical experience and could not be

used to communicate inner feeling, whereas the function of art and aesthetic ideas was to reveal inner experience. Judgments of taste and beauty were individual, not universal, and were totally different from logical judgments. For Chamberlain, art was free from the external world and the restraints of conceptual thinking; it obeyed its own laws and formed a free and independent world of its own. Though it might stimulate individual imagination, encourage liberality of mind and receptivity to ethical ideas, it could not itself supply the content of those ideas. Thus by attaching a framework of philosophical and social ideas to Wagner's art, the *Blätter* had transgressed the distinction between aesthetics and logical thinking and thereby devalued art. "We need" he wrote to Wolzogen "neither philosophical, nor moral, nor political systems. The real duty [of the *Blätter*] is to spread and extend *understanding* for true, pure Art—as it ought to arise from its temporary demise, greater and holier than before." [12]

He was especially incensed by the identification of Wagner's art with Christian concepts of regeneration, and asserted: "It would not be difficult to prove that whoever holds opposing views could just as easily believe they were represented in the *Nibelungenring*. Many who do not subscribe to the Christian dogma—but whose moral worth and search for truth is not less sincere than that of church-goers—may have felt their convictions strengthened by hearing the *Nibelungen* drama." Such ideas clashed sharply with the aesthetic religion that Bayreuth was attempting to build and they reveal the broad gulf which separated the young Chamberlain from his later viewpoint. Only a year later, in his essay "Religion and Art," Wagner set forth more clearly than ever before the nature of his aesthetic religion and its "Christian" teachings, insisting that "all real drive and effective power for realization of the great Regeneration can spring only from the deep soil of a true religion." Equally heretical was Chamberlain's dismissal of the ties between Wagner's art and Schopenhauer's philosophy, which Wolzogen and Wahnfried were carefully extending and elaborating; not only did he reject Schopenhauer as an inferior thinker to Kant, but roughly admonished: "those men who in the journal lament so loudly the wickedness and indifferent materialism of the present day, should open their eyes and ask themselves what it is that has poisoned German youth, if not that pessimistic doctrine which they disseminate so enthusiastically."[13]

Wolzogen, not surprisingly, did not publish Chamberlain's essay, although he did answer the charges with a veiled reference in the next issue of the *Blätter*. In an article which exuded all the chauvinism for which the journal became famous, Wolzogen maintained: "Only the German in his deepest necessity can feel and conceive that which should lie nearest to the heart of we Germans who share in the strivings of Bayreuth." He added: "A communication from Italy from a cultivated English admirer of Wagner's art has recently confirmed once more, in a remarkable manner, the view expressed above as to the role of foreigners in our strivings."[14]

Wolzogen's rebuke was a profound shock to Chamberlain, who had viewed Wagnerism as a cosmopolitan aesthetic movement in which all were welcome; now it seemed he was being informed that although his financial support might be helpful, his birthplace prevented him from ever appreciating fully Wagner's art and the mission of Bayreuth. "I felt," he wrote, "as if I had been thrust out of a place which was for me like a sanctuary." His immediate response was to stop reading the *Blätter* for three years. In this time, while Chamberlain was completing his degree at Geneva, the Wagner cult was taking a more definite shape. Troubled by growing debts and conscious of his declining health, the composer labored to finish his musical testament, *Parsifal*, and, as he did so, poured out his frustrations in a series of polemical essays about racial regeneration, aesthetic religion, antivivisectionism, and the parasitical social role of Jews. Published in the *Blätter*, these essays were to set the tone of orthodox Wagnerism in the years to come; for the moment, however, they had no impact upon Chamberlain.[15]

Then, in 1882, Chamberlain and Anna visited Bayreuth for the first time. They saw *Parsifal* six times and were overwhelmed by the experience. "Hitherto," Chamberlain later wrote, "my life had been so artistically barren, but now I had reached the font of the purest Art. Schiller speaks of an 'aesthetic culture which should combine the dignity and bliss of humanity': I have discovered the place of this culture." Now—in contrast to 1879—he was entranced by the pseudo-religiosity of Bayreuth, and fascinated by the mystical brotherhood of the Grail. Amid the camaraderie of the festival visitors and the intoxicating effect of the performances, he found himself happy as never before. To Aunt Harriet, he confessed: "I fear you will think us very Wagner-mad when we come back. My position in regard to Wagnerism, my appreciation of the fundamental idea of the music drama have greatly changed in the course of the last week." He added: "Even Wolzogen, whom I used to laugh at, states the simple truth when he says: 'with these divine harmonies, the heavenly spirit of love at once seizes the stirred hearts of the listeners, who are lifted upwards toward the divine source of the pronouncement' etc. etc. Yes 'borne upwards' that is the term; you feel as if you were being carried up to the heavens on angels' wings." His visit ended with a brief glimpse of Wagner, dining with performers in a local tavern. He returned to Geneva a convert; in the secular shrine of the festival theater Chamberlain had discovered his spiritual home.[16]

The following year Chamberlain returned to Bayreuth, where the atmosphere of triumph had given way to one of uncertainty and gloom. The Master had died at Venice in February, leaving the festival without a leader. There is no evidence that Wagner ever considered that his widow would step into his place, and not for years would the young Siegfried be able to take over his birthright. Wahnfried remained quiet, dark, and shuttered in mourning—in contrast to the celebrations of the previous year. Cosima shut herself off from all but her closest friends and took little part in the organization of the festival. In the absence of one dominating personality, factional squabbles soon arose between figures like Hermann Levi, the conductor, and Julius Kniese, a fanatical anti-Semite and director of the festival choir; they had always been mistrustful and jealous of each other, but now their bitter quarrels threatened to disrupt the whole performance. But if Bayreuth seemed adrift from its moorings, it was only momentarily so: Wolzogen, Heinrich von Stein, and other leading Wagnerites responded to the crisis with a more intensive personality cult of the deceased Master and an even greater insistence on theoretical orthodoxy than Wagner himself had required. Since the early years of his career a Wagner party had clustered around the composer, but after his death an elite group, an "inner circle" of Bayreuth supporters, assumed the task of interpreting his artwork and disseminating his cultural, political, and philosophical ideals. The *Wagner-Lexikon*, published in 1883, laid down the doctrines of what Wolzogen called "the orthodox party"; in the following years emphasis upon doctrinal purity, and selfless devotion to the cause was the counterside to fears about the prospect of preserving the *Festspiele* and continuing the Master's life work. [17]

Chamberlain was eager to involve himself in the Bayreuth cause. At the festival in 1882 he had made the acquaintance of a number of prominent Wagnerites, and in 1883 he assiduously attended the meetings of the Patrons Association. "What occupies my thoughts most at the present moment," he told Aunt Harriet, "is the question of the future. What is to be done to insure in the first place the continuation, in the second the progress of this art." He now reckoned himself "among the small cohort of *real* Wagnerians" and sought to obtain the post of Paris representative to the Richard Wagner Association. "At any rate," he confided to his aunt, "I now know enough influential people to be sure of being in some way active in the cause of the progress of modern music." [18] Having recently set up his brokerage partnership with Cerceau in Paris, he anticipated spending a large part of the year there, which would allow ample time to devote to activities for Bayreuth.

The task of the Paris representative was a delicate one, for public reaction to Wagner's works was often infused with revanchist and Germanophobe sentiments, and even the avowed defenders of Bayreuth were often divided and at odds with each other. Chamberlain was successful in his bid for the job, a striking illustration of the confidence he was able to inspire, even in his youth, among older and more experienced men. After all, he was largely a stranger to the world of Parisian Wagnerites, and it had been only a year since he had first attended a festival and met the major personalities associated with Bayreuth. But he had a perfect command of French and German, and could, it seems, get along with both the younger literary Wagnerites and the old guard of Lascoux, Nuetter, and Lamoureux. An admirer of French and German culture, Chamberlain was eager to overstep national boundaries and foster common efforts on behalf of "the artwork of the future." It promised to be an uphill struggle. To many Frenchmen, Wagner was the hated composer of the chauvinistic *Kaisermarsch*, a *reichsdeutsche* artist who had seen in the smoking ruins of Paris the retribution for his own personal sufferings and reverses in that city. But Chamberlain, reacting against both German and French "ultrapatriotism," saw Wagner as undeservedly abused and felt that "his character like his genius was universal." During 1883 and 1884 he was active in gathering new subscribers and supporters for Bayreuth, corresponding with members of the Association, and trying to found a journal which would reach a broader audience and begin the task of opening the eyes of Frenchmen to the subtleties and full breadth of Wagner's dramas and ideas.[19]

These time-consuming activities may well have contributed to the failure of his business, for, as we have seen, he apparently neglected to check or supervise the transactions made by his partner until affairs had reached a crisis. Soon after, exhausted by his efforts to save the brokerage firm and distraught at his failure, he was forced to leave Paris, and it became unclear whether he should continue his role in the Wagner Association. Until spring 1885 he remained nominally the Paris representative, but prolonged absence led him to resign, although he continued to keep up a busy correspondence with Parisian friends and was even able to play a role in *La Revue Wagnérienne* which they founded. Then, gradually during his years in Dresden his interests were to shift

away from the concerns of French Wagnerism to the dissemination of the cult in Germany itself.

Chamberlain and Anna arrived in Dresden in November 1885.
They lived for the next four years in a small apartment on
Reichenbachstrasse, enjoying a quiet, leisured existence and
travelling each year to Berlin and Bayreuth, and sometimes
further afield to Schleswig and even Norway. These were years
of great significance for Chamberlain's psychological and intellectual development, forming a transitional period during
which he had no fixed goals in life—a prelude and preparation
for his later careers of Wagner publicist and cultural prophet.
    Convinced by his doctors that his health could not with-
stand a scientific career, his future seemed empty and unclear.
Recovery from his breakdown was the first task, and Chamberlain adopted a careful daily regime which would speed his
recuperation. After frequent consultations with doctors in
Berlin, and nursed attentively by Anna, he soon grew stronger
and became more active, especially in the business of the local
Wagner club. All his financial needs were met by relatives in
England, although Chamberlain sometimes complained that
his style of life was misunderstood by some, at any rate, of his
family. "I am positively incapable of work," he wrote in 1886
to Aunt Harriet," and yet my sufferings are such, and of such a
nature, that nobody considers me a sick man, a patient, an in-
valid. Nobody sympathizes with a man who 'goes to the
theater'! who is told to travel and amuse himself as medicine; I
have never for one moment doubted that most 'people' look
upon me simply as an unmitigated humbug."[20] The absence of
medical evidence and lack of any but the most fragmentary accounts prevents us from saying more about the nature of his
sickness; but what is important is that he was sufficiently well
to read extensively and to take an active role in the affairs of
Bayreuth. He had more free time than most contemporaries to

devote to self-education and to Wagner.[21] Gradually, over the next four years he began to write and by 1889 had taken the first steps toward his literary career.

Anna was his constant companion in these years, but she is scarcely mentioned in the following pages. For, though they read and travelled together, she cannot be said to have influenced greatly the development of Chamberlain's ideas. She helped him in his work, attended to his wants, and took up his interests. Her life revolved entirely around his, and her autobiographical reflections contain no hint as to her opinions and thoughts—only those of her husband. It was Cosima Wagner, Countess Coudenhove, Baroness von Schleinitz, the members of the Wahnfried circle, and other Wagnerites whom he met at performances that influenced Chamberlain. They recommended books to him, discussed their interpretations of Kant and Schopenhauer, and told him their political views. Anna's letters have not survived and Chamberlain's comments about her are perfunctory and usually concern her health or domestic details. It would seem that in Dresden, as later in Vienna, he kept her out of certain areas of his life: and as he drew closer to the leading circles of Wagnerism, so he entered a social world in which Anna never really participated.

Dresden had, of course, old and deep associations with Richard Wagner. It was here, as royal *Kapellmeister* that he first staged *Rienzi, Fliegende Holländer*, and *Tannhäuser*, and completed *Lohengrin*. Dresden had also been the scene of his revolutionary involvement in 1849 and of his first schemes for a national theater. When Chamberlain arrived the town had a small but flourishing Wagner society, some of whose members, like the sculptor Ernst Kietz, had been close friends and supporters of the composer. During his visits to the *Festspiele*, Chamberlain came into contact with a wide circle of friends and, encouraged by some of them, he began to try his hand as a publicist. At first, in spite of his geographical separation from Paris, he saw himself as a mediator between Bayreuth and the French public. Even as late as 1889 he was contemplating a French translation of Wagner's prose writings and sought a publisher in Paris.[22] But, for the most part, by 1887 the first "French phase" of his activities was over; from then

on, as he became numbered among the trusted friends of
Wahnfried, he turned his attention away from France toward
Germany. This coincided with significant changes in his views
on art, society, and politics, and reflected the general tendency
of Bayreuth to identify itself more and more with German nationalism of the *völkisch* kind.

Chamberlain's place in the development of French
Wagnerism is closely connected with the journal *Revue
Wagnérienne*. At the *Festspiele* in 1883 he met Edouard
Dujardin, a young French writer who had studied music under
Debussy and Dukas and was eager to publicize Wagner's
dramas in France. They became friends and saw each other
again in Munich in the following year, where the *Ring* was being performed. Together with another acquaintance, Theodor
de Wyzewa, they discussed the possibility of founding a French
journal modelled after the *Bayreuther Blätter*. Wagner's music
and writings were little known in France and since the fiasco of
Napoleon III's *Tannhäuser* in March 1861 (the lavish performance had been disrupted by members of the Jockey Club,
largely for political purposes) only fragments of the dramas
had been performed. Even these were often the scene of
disorders, sometimes mounted by extreme nationalist groups
and at others by those intolerant on aesthetic grounds of the
"music of the future." [23] "The management of the Société des
Nouveaux Concerts," so explained the program for *Tristan
und Isolde* in 1885, "is desirous of avoiding any disturbance
. . . and urgently and respectfully begs that the audience will
abstain from giving any mark of their approval or disapproval
before the end of the act." [24] Since the 1860s a small coterie of
intellectuals—among them Baudelaire, Auguste de Gasperini,
Théophile Gautier, Catulle Mendès, and Gérard de
Nerval—had rallied to Wagner's defense. But even these
champions were often surprisingly ignorant of the dramas and
their underlying aesthetic. They were seldom able to attend
performances abroad, and were in most cases unequipped lin-
guistically to study the librettos and prose writings in depth.
"In 1884," Dujardin explained, Wagnerism "was a new world

which had to be discovered" by the French intellectuals. The new *Revue Wagnérienne* would, it was hoped, remedy this ignorance.[25] As the Paris representative of the Wagner Association, Chamberlain gave the venture an air of authenticity, and through his connections he was soon able to interest several wealthy patrons, including the prominent Parisian Wagnerite Judge Lascoux, the Belgian industrialist Alfred Bovet, and an old friend of Chamberlain's, the Genevan millionaire Agénor Boissier.

The editors of the projected *Revue* began soliciting support from Parisian writers and Wagnerites. Dujardin arranged a banquet attended by Lamoureux, Victor Wilder, Léon Leroy, and many other leading figures, while Wyzewa made the rounds of the Paris cafés. Stephane Mallarmé had recently returned to Paris from the provinces and gathered a group of disciples around him. Dujardin and Wyzewa soon became regular visitors to his Tuesday evening soirées at 89 rue de Rome, proselytizing and searching for further recruits for their journal. Their visions were grandiose. Dujardin declared his intention of preparing new improved translations of Wagner's works and of breaking down the barriers of existing language. Heavily influenced by his friend, Chamberlain tried to explain to Aunt Harriet: "A language must live, must be capable of adapting itself to the wants of a new generation. . . . and those who stand as we do, at the early dawn of a new epoch, of a reaction of idealism against materialism, of poetry against science—call it what you will—those men must all forge the language in which their ideas can be expressed."[26]

Wyzewa, meantime, claimed that the *Revue* would bring order to modern aesthetics and give some cohesion to the varying tendencies prevailing in current literature: to this end he proposed a series of articles that would relate Wagner's work to contemporary literary movements, and analyze the moral purpose of art. Chamberlain shared the lofty aims of his two co-founders and was, in addition, anxious that the *Revue* create a large and unified bloc of French support for Bayreuth; but—after their initial discussions—he could offer relatively little assistance both because of his business difficulties, which demanded most of his time and energy, and the subsequent

collapse of his health. Nonetheless he aided Dujardin with
preparations for the first issue and kept in close correspondence with his Paris associates. Gradually, as his health
improved he began writing notes on Wagnerism in Germany,
reviewed performances in Central Europe, and eventually
contributed longer articles on several of the music dramas. But
more important, perhaps, than his essays, was his role as mediator between the avant-garde of literary Wagnerism and the
more traditional and conservative Wagnerites who financed
the *Revue*, for sharp differences soon arose.

Wagner's significance for the artistic avant-garde in
France was vague and confused. Poets like Philippe Villiers de
l'Isle-Adam, Valéry, Laforgue, and Mallarmé believed they
had discovered in Wagner a kindred worshipper of the religion
of Art who shared their particular aesthetic views and whose
works provided a wealth of myths and symbols to evoke inner
experience and illuminate their revolt against bourgeois philistinism and the sterility of modern society. Through Wagnerism
the Symbolists tried to extract from the German Idealists, and
especially from Schopenhauer, a philosophical and aesthetic
basis for their movement. Wagner, they asserted, had translated these abstract philosophical ideas into forms of beauty
and emotion. The "Artwork of the Future" had a mighty appeal and even the level-headed succumbed readily to its spell.
"Writers," wrote Romain Rolland, "not only discussed musical
subjects but judged painting, literature, and philosophy from a
Wagnerian point of view. . . . The whole universe was seen and
judged in the light of Bayreuth."[27] Another contemporary
warned years later: "The men of today can absolutely never
grasp what Wagner . . . was for us, the vast expanse of light
which his magic opened to us, the ground swell [*lame de fond*]
he aroused in our souls, the dreadful disgust he imposed on us
for everything that was not his."[28] *Revue Wagnérienne* rapidly
became the Bible of the avant-garde, the focus of literary
Wagnerism and Symbolism; its appearance in February 1885
marked the dawning of a new era, just as the burial of Victor
Hugo two months later more ostentatiously epitomized the
passing of the old. A list of contributors to the 36 issues which
appeared in the next three years attests to the significance of

the journal, but it was precisely these strong literary associations which made the *Revue* a subject of bitter controversy. It is arguable, indeed, that far from unifying French Wagnerism, as Chamberlain hoped, the journal hastened its division into opposing factions.[29]

While Wolzogen's *Bayreuther Blätter* excluded all but the orthodox Wagnerian view, Dujardin proved unable to impose a rigid editorial direction on his publication and it soon encompassed many divergent opinions. Though in its first months the *Revue* included lengthy discussions and analysis of Wagner's ideas, musicologists and conservative Parisian Wagnerites became increasingly restive at the use of Wagner's name to justify all manner of literary experimentation. Even in early issues, essays such as Mallarmé's *"Richard Wagner, Reverie d'un poète français"* failed to mention a single music drama or passage from the composer's prose writings; then, in January 1886, eight sonnets to Wagner appeared whose perfervid, decadent style was scandalous to more traditional minds. Not surprisingly, by September Agénor Boissier and other financial backers were fast losing their patience and made it clear "that, if they were willing to support *Revue Wagnérienne*, it was because it published studies of Wagner and not Symbolist poems."[30]

The feud developed rapidly. Dujardin and Wyzewa levelled vehement criticism at Lamoureux and Wagner's French translator, Victor Wilder, for obscuring the true meaning of the dramas. Chamberlain supported Dujardin throughout these disputes, and collaborated on a translation of *Rheingold*, together with some introductory notes, parts of which were published in the *Revue*. Their opposition, of course, regarded the translation as too "decadent." After months of dissension, Bovet and Boissier, encouraged by Lamoureux, withdrew their financial support and the journal closed down at the end of 1887. A last farewell issue was printed later, in July 1888 (to which Chamberlain contributed) and then most of the *Revue's* supporters shifted their allegiance to Dujardin's new venture, the *Revue Indépendante* whose editorial policy called explicitly for toleration.[31]

In spite of its brief life, *Revue Wagnérienne* was ex-

tremely important in cultivating Wagnerism in France. Its
influence left a deep imprint on the poets and artists of the *fin
de siècle*, although Jacques Barzun exaggerates when he suggests that "it left Paris almost more Wagnerian than the home
of the Master."[32] The articles of Dujardin and Wyzewa were
among the first careful and informed analyses of Wagner's
works in France, and while Chamberlain at first provided only
summaries of Wagner news from Germany, he soon after—at
Dujardin's prompting—contributed longer studies of *Lohengrin*, *Tristan*, and *Götterdämmerung*. Detailed and meticulous, his essays revealed a considerable knowledge of Wagner's
art works and prose writings, as well as the growing corpus of
secondary literature. The main emphasis of these writings was
psychological: like the Symbolists, he found in Wagner's
balance of tone and word (in fact he coined the word *Wortton-
drama*) a perfect means of communication between the subjective, unconscious realm and the objective world. Wagner was a
poet who had turned to music as the only means of recapturing
inner psychological experience. But Chamberlain remained
unmoved by the philosophical mysteries elaborated by
Wyzewa and by Wolzogen's vision of Wagner as an intuitive
Schopenhauerean. In words reminiscent of his first irascible
essay of 1879, he berated those "who pretend to discover in
Wagner's dramas religion, political systems, and philosophies." He added: "If Tristan and Isolde are interpreters of
Schopenhauer's theory, one can see they have it backwards; it
is simpler and truer to avow they have nothing to do with it."
As for Wagner's final work, the man who later became an
apostle of Aryan Christianity wrote: "There is no more Christianity in *Parsifal* than there is paganism in the *Ring* and
Tristan."[33] Thus, while concurring in many details with Bayreuth's interpretation of Wagner, Chamberlain—at least when
he wrote for Frenchmen—did not echo the distinctly Christian
and national political chords that were being struck by
German Wagnerites. Parisian Wagnerism was aesthetic rather
than Christian or political, and the *Revue's* significance, in
Dujardin's words, lay in providing "the connecting link
between Wagner and Mallarmé, between Schopenhauer and
Symbolism . . . it helped the Symbolists of 1886 to take note of
the deep musical necessity which imposed itself on them."[34]

If Chamberlain's first "phase" of Wagner activities ended with the demise of the *Revue*, the second began almost at once with the publication of his first essays in the German language and his movement closer to the Wahnfried circle.

Since 1883 the Bayreuth cult had been establishing itself, presided over by Cosima who had emerged from mourning to provide forceful leadership. She was assisted by a remarkable group of young men—mostly in their twenties or early thirties—who worshipped Wagner's memory. These faithful lieutenants—Wolzogen, Glasenapp, Schemann, Stein, and Thode especially—sought to expound for the German public their interpretation of what Wagner's art and vision meant, and to discredit all variant opinions. Wolzogen, in particular, was interested in the expansion of Wagner societies which, he hoped, would act as oases of Germanic values amid "the desert of modern materialism."[35] To coordinate the activities of the more than 100 branches of the *Wagner-Verein* and to supervise the literary campaign, an "inner circle" or elite of Bayreuth supporters grew up whose members were highly conscious of their special place in the cult. Needless to say the heavy emotional and religious atmosphere of the Wahnfried circle was very different from that surrounding *Revue Wagnérienne*.

The essays Chamberlain wrote for the *Revue* had attracted some notice in Bayreuth, but it was only in 1888, with the publication of his first German article, that his potential as a publicist was recognized. The essay was a detailed analysis of the relationship of music and poetry in *Tristan und Isolde*, which illustrated the orthodox view that all Wagner's dramas embodied the same basic artistic conception and the same reciprocal relationships of the various arts within the *Gesamtkunstwerk*. Elated by its success, Chamberlain jubilantly reported to Aunt Harriet:

> My German article on the language in Wagner's Tristan and Isolde has created quite a sensation among the people who study these matters. . . . The greatest philological authority on these questions, Baron von Wolzogen, who has himself studied Tristan specially and written on it, assures me that it is a revelation to him. Madame Cosima Wagner herself—the severest authority—says it is "remarkable" and it was Hofkapellmeister Levi, the celebrated Bayreuth leader, who I have for

long been on bad terms with, who was so *"begeistert"* that he
insisted upon her reading it.[36]

This was his first step toward Wahnfried; the second came
with the publication of a brief newspaper article dealing with
the relationship between Wagner and Cosima's father, Franz
Liszt. It was prompted by an attack on Wagner, delivered in a
lecture to the Dresden Music Society, by Moritz Wirth, an
anti-Semitic publicist and right-wing social reformer, who had
once been close to Wahnfried but had moved into opposition.
With a delicate combination of fact and eulogy Chamberlain
asserted that Wagner had always been frank in acknowledging
his debts to Liszt. The implication was that Cosima and
Wahnfried had been similarly generous: a reply to the
considerable criticism aroused by her cold and almost indifferent response to the death of her father at the Bayreuth festival of 1886.[37]

The timing of Chamberlain's essays was opportune, for
the high priestess of the cult was looking for new talent. In
1887, the death of Heinrich von Stein, a brilliant young
philosopher who had taken the post of tutor to Wagner's son,
Siegfried, deprived Bayreuth of its most able protagonist and
thinker. At the same time, another of the young Wahnfried
supporters, Ludwig Schemann, who later became one of the
chief race publicists in Central Europe, began to drift apart
from Cosima's circle, uncomfortable in so confining an intellectual environment.[38] Stein's death and Schemann's
gradual defection dealt a hard blow to Wagnerism, and Cosima
was overjoyed at the emergence of Chamberlain as a vigorous
champion of the cause. They met in June 1888 in the Dresden
home of the Kietz family. The encounter was a great success
and the beginning of a long and devoted friendship; it also
marked, as Wolzogen quickly noted in a congratulatory letter,
Chamberlain's formal induction into the "inner circle" of
Wagnerites.[39]

Chamberlain was overcome with admiration for this tall,
gaunt woman with her regal airs and penetrating gaze, who
over the years was to have an enormous influence upon his personal life and intellectual development.[40] It is difficult to re-

capture the exaggerated awe with which she was regarded by the votaries of the Bayreuth cult. On the face of things she seemed to contradict in many ways the dominant bourgeois ideals and conventions, although under her guidance Wagnerism became associated with a national cult that was strongly bourgeois. Born the illegitimate daughter of Franz Liszt and a French noblewoman, Countess Marie d'Agoult, Cosima was raised as a strict Catholic and converted to Protestantism only in 1872. After marrying her father's favorite pupil, Hans von Bülow, she left him for Wagner by whom she had three children. The scandal of their relationship echoed throughout Germany and continued later to be an awkward subject for many Wagnerites. Only recently, with the long delayed publication of her voluminous diaries, has it become clear just how traumatic and guilt-provoking her leaving Bülow was—anguish, bad dreams, and pangs of conscience about her children constantly recur in her daily entries.

Cosima's devotion to Wagner was total, all consuming; while he lived she accepted his conviction that "woman has nothing to do with the outside world," although her influence on his last works, and especially upon the racial and religious turn of his thought in those final years, was probably great. Much about her is mysterious and will undoubtedly remain so. The origin of her anti-Semitism is, for example, obscure: as Bülow's wife she had mixed freely with Ferdinand Lassalle, Karl Varnhagen von Ense, whose Jewish wife, Rahel, had presided over one of the most brilliant literary salons, and various prominent Jews in Berlin, but by 1862 she was outspoken in her prejudice. Some authors have asserted that Cosima's bigotry arose in part from nagging anxieties about her own pedigree and her family connection to the Frankfurt banking family of Bethmann; but, like so much else about her, this is mere speculation. To Chamberlain and his contemporaries, this dedicated recluse, accessible only to her trusted advisors, was an exceptional woman, conspicuous for the power she exerted in the German musical world and consumed by the task of advancing Wagner's work. Strong-willed, intelligent though intellectually somewhat narrow, she was unquestionably the driving force behind the Wagner cult.

"Cosima," wrote the equally tough-minded Elizabeth Förster-Nietzsche, "has for me always been the personification of will and a longing for power in the noblest sense of the word."[41]

Wagnerites saw her in several ways. At times she was a woman, frail and lonely, who needed guidance to perform the duties which had been bequeathed to her. "It is impossible," wrote the Austrian Wagnerite, Friedrich von Hausegger, in a rather critical letter to Wolzogen "that a woman, no matter how gifted . . . or energetic, or willing to make sacrifices (all that is present)—could embrace the broad horizons of a man like Wagner. . . . I wish I were wrong. But many . . . many . . . think like me."[42] Her enemies and critics, beginning with Nietzsche, invariably used her sex as a means of explaining alleged distortions in the interpretation and staging of Wagner's art. "Seldom," admitted Chamberlain soon after their first meeting, "has a woman had to play so crucial a role in the development of the human mind and spirit [Geist]"; but, he added reassuringly, "you know it and are up to it." When further criticism of Cosima's authority over the festival was raised in 1891, he wrote to a Wagnerite friend in Dresden:

> It is certain that any artistic undertaking can only find life in *one* person—for this reason I don't believe that the group will of a number of gifted people can compensate for one excellent individual. We are so fortunate (in spite of all the narrow-minded and spiteful attacks) to possess an exceptionally gifted leader of the *Festspiele* who knows, moreover, the intentions of the Bayreuth Master like no second person on earth and who took an outstanding part in the festivals of 76 and 82. That the present leader is a woman should also be seen as a downright blessing: first because she clings, with a piety that only the most self-sacrificing love can inspire, to the intentions of her immortalized husband. . . . and secondly because those most highly gifted men who properly constitute the "general staff" of Bayreuth—Kniese, Mottl, Levi, Humperdinck etc. and also the singers—are *happy* to subordinate themselves to Frau Wagner. So, let's thank God and hope that He will also watch over the great cause of the highest art in the future.[43]

Her supporters generally overcame attacks on Cosima's abilities as a woman by elevating her to the position of a divine

Cosima Wagner, c. 1877

priestess through whom breathed the will and spirit of the composer himself. In their cult of Wagner's widow the Wahnfried circle broke all bounds; witness, for example, the tone of adulation in Chamberlain's words in 1896:

> Among us closer associates it is regarded as a pious rule that we should not in public speak the name of the person who from now on placed not half but her entire strength in the service of the festival. The reasons for this attitude are embedded in the heart, in the soul, and permit no discussion. [44]

Unsympathetic toward the "new woman," both in reality and in fiction; too healthy, as she once expressed it, for Ibsen, Cosima left her signature on every aspect of the Bayreuth cult—by claiming that she alone understood fully the will and the aims of Wagner.

After his very first meeting with her Chamberlain confessed to Wolzogen: "I never suspected she would from the first meeting be for me what nobody else could be. Respect and admiration for her I had already—but now I have what is infinitely more—the deepest love. That she possesses such strength and such youthful freshness of spirit has filled me with hope for our cause." "Her presence," he once told Aunt Harriet, "makes one always feel as if one had been suddenly transported to some other planet"; she "electrified" those who approached her. [45] Though rather more restrained in her tone, Cosima was also pleased with her new recruit and wrote to her good friend and confidante, Baroness Wolkenstein: "I am now in close contact with Chamberlain for whom I have come to feel a great friendship because of his outstanding learning and dignified character." [46]

Impressed by his abilities she soon began delegating tasks to him, including the delicate mission of collecting the correspondence between Wagner and his friend the Dresden violinist Theodor Uhlig. As she planned to publish an expurgated version of the letters, Cosima was anxious that all the evidence be safely under her control. "That I entrust you and nobody else with this commission," she told Chamberlain, "will perhaps say everything to you." He responded eagerly to such requests and was soon visited by her once more in Dresden;

invitations to stay at Wahnfried and also to attend festival rehearsals soon followed. Their mutual sympathy and admiration ripened into warm friendship, as shown in the frequent letters between them, in which they exchanged ideas, gossip, and personal confessions; long before Chamberlain moved permanently to Bayreuth in 1908, Cosima had come to regard him as almost a son.[47]

Growing contact with the "inner circle" at Bayreuth exerted a great influence upon Chamberlain's view of the role of Wagnerism as well as his social and political outlook. From surviving sources it is difficult to trace exactly the transformation of his ideas, but his meeting with Cosima seems to mark an important transition. Until 1886 Chamberlain had espoused a basically Kantian position whereby art was considered a free and separate world beyond conceptual thought and having no specific philosophical or religious content. By 1889 he was moving closer to Wagnerian ideas of man's redemption through art and began to view art as anchored in the *Volk* and religion. Reading Schleiermacher, Novalis, Friedrich Schlegel, and E. T. A. Hoffmann, Chamberlain began to break with the Kantian emphasis on a Newtonian moral law as the goal of human development and to stress the cultivation of distinctive national personalities as the true aim of ethical endeavor. He drew upon Romantic ideas about collective folk personalities, which found expression in *völkisch* or populistic art. Art became the incarnation of national genius and also the inspiration for an alternative aesthetic social ideal quite different from existing reality. In a continual dialogue with his German Wagnerite friends and in his correspondence with Cosima, Chamberlain gradually moved away from the cosmopolitan, aesthetic stance he had shared with Dujardin.

While he continued to admire Mallarmé and the Symbolists he nonetheless felt them too fastidious of life, too narcissistic; he was deeply moved by that apotheosis of the *fin de siècle*, Huysman's *À'rebours*, but rejected its hero's wish "to hide himself away, far from the world, in some retreat, where he might deaden the sound of the loud rumbling of inflexible life as one covers the street with straw for sick people."

The solution for the malady of the age was not aesthetic

withdrawal and the elevation of the Beautiful rather than Being to the rank of Absolute.[48] Not denial of life but regeneration and the ennoblement of man through imaginative truth: this was the message of Bayreuth. "I cannot avoid the conviction that German art is ordained for a special and especially exalted mission in the history of mankind." "Never," Chamberlain insisted, "have the truly great among Germany's poets in words and tones wished to content themselves with *l'art pour les artistes.*" Unlike the self-absorbed French avant-garde, German artists, rooted in the soil of the *Volk*, sought "to awaken the artistic element in man to conscious life, to arouse and develop it, impelled by the conviction that they thereby brought to fruition something important as a national work and significant for the culture of all mankind."[49]

It was especially in Schiller's *Letters on the Aesthetic Education of Man* that Chamberlain discovered an intellectual bridge between Kant and the socially regenerative mission of art espoused by Bayreuth. A favorite with Bayreuth "initiates," the work replaced the rigorous Kantian emphasis on duty with a doctrine of aesthetic humanism, contrasting the unity and harmony of ancient Greek society with the division of the modern age. In Schiller Chamberlain found a penetrating analysis of cultural evolution, which coincided with his own growing critique of industrial and commercial society, and a poignant analysis of the plight of modern man who, in Schiller's words, "grew to be only a fragment . . . and instead of imprinting humanity upon his nature . . . becomes merely an imprint of his occupation, of his science." Schiller's concept of Art as the unifying agency that could overcome the self-divisions, conflicts, and fragmentation in man's mental and social world had become—with varying shades of interpretation—a central tenet of the Romantics. For Chamberlain, Wagner's art fulfilled Schiller's ideal. By reconciling man's sensuous inclinations and moral will, it could produce the *schöne Seele*, harmonious, morally sensitive, and unalienated. Bayreuth offered a vision of man redeemed, restored through the twin integrating myths of Art and Volk. Writing somewhat later, Chamberlain expressed succinctly the conviction he had arrived at during his Dresden years:

Every German who is concerned about the cause, should bind together Schiller's *Briefe über die ästhetische Erziehung des Menschen* and Wagner's *Religion und Kunst*. He should continually immerse himself in these works and model himself upon their spirit and teaching. My deepest conviction at least, is that not German politicians but these two poets have pointed the way to the German *Volk*. They have shown the path the Volk must tread if it is to fulfil its mission, if it is to bring to fruition its particular "spirit of pure humanity," "the infinitely important plan which Nature wills for her redemption" (as Wagner expressed it). Yes, I go so far as to find Schiller and Wagner indispensable for a full, comprehensive understanding of the German regeneration doctrine. [50]

How Chamberlain and Bayreuth interpreted "German regeneration" will be shown in a later chapter; for the moment it is sufficient to point out that his Wagnerism and his other views became "Germanized" during the four years he spent in Dresden. "For the decisive movement of my life," he later wrote, "was towards *Deutschtum*. I attached myself to the German system—if I may be permitted an astronomical image—and at its center stood Richard Wagner." [51]

The evolution of his ideas mirrored the development of a more strident national cult in Bayreuth in the 1880s. And yet *Festspiele* performances always—until the Nazi years—drew an international crowd and Cosima was known, and sometimes criticized for, her willingness to engage foreign artists for major roles. Thomas Mann once described the "Germanness" of Wagner's music as "deep, powerful, unquestionable" but added with his usual acuity: it "has many traits which *foreigners in particular* find German." [52] This was true of many non-German Wagnerites—Bayreuth embodied their vision of the admirable qualities of German *Kultur*. Yet the reconciliation of the chauvinist and international sides of Bayreuth was not always so simple and Wolzogen at times found himself confusedly referring to "a musical association of national and supra-national character." At times Bayreuth could shelter behind cultural imperialism, and the German mission to be the ennoblers of mankind; at others, Cosima and her circle made good use of the racial ideas of Count Gobineau, tacitly viewing true Wagnerites

as a kind of European elite of superior moral and racial characteristics. Certainly, Chamberlain was forced to ponder the relationship between French and English Wagnerism and what he
increasingly felt to be a basically German artwork—but his conclusions were vague and ill-formed in this transitional stage of
his development. His ideas grew clearer as he developed his own
racial theories in the next decade.

As a student in Geneva, Chamberlain followed closely the
politics of Britain, France, and Switzerland. He read *The
Times* and French newspapers regularly, occasionally attended
debates in the Swiss parliament, and frequently discussed
politics with friends and family. With regard to England he
approached issues from a firmly Gladstonian perspective and
showed a marked antipathy to the philosophy and policies of
Conservatism. Perhaps the best way to illustrate his outlook is
to examine briefly his opinions on two of the chief issues facing
the new Liberal government in 1880–1881: Ireland and South
Africa. In both cases his correspondence records a continuing
clash between his convictions and those of his family, who deplored what they regarded as Gladstone's vacillation and weakness.

The combination of agricultural depression, bad harvests,
and neglect by the previous Conservative government had
created a mounting crisis on the land in Ireland. In April 1881
Gladstone introduced a new Land Bill designed to fix "fair"
rents, grant tenants greater security of tenure, and alleviate
some of the distress caused by the massive increase in evic-
tions by landlords. In effect the bill proposed to recognize legis-
latively a difference in property rights between England and
Ireland; it immediately prompted strong opposition from the
Conservatives, as well as deep disquiet among the Whig
aristocrats of the Liberal Party who feared that the precedent
might well be applied elsewhere. Chamberlain studied the
land question carefully: he read Royal Commission reports,

absorbed available newspaper and magazine articles, and kept informed of the debate in the Commons. Sympathetic toward the plight of the Irish peasantry, he soon found himself at odds with his relatives, including Sir Neville Chamberlain, who deplored the bill as a violation of sacred property rights and an unpardonable breach of trust. Houston, however, insisted that the Liberal proposal was both practical and just. Not only had landlord intransigeance wrecked earlier, more moderate legislation but even the claims of Anglo-Irish absentees to ownership was questionable:

> the tenants are the *real, original proprietors*. The holdings have remained for centuries in the same families and all that they are worth is due to the toil and sweat of these occupants whereas the landlords are successors of real spoliators who stepped in and forced the original proprietors to pay what may be called a tax on their property. As I understand it, Gladstone cannot be said "to confiscate the landlords' rights" (as Uncle Neville puts it); on the contrary he admits their proprietorship and draws a veil over all the iniquities of the past. What he does is to admit and enforce *tenants rights* . . . and if this does imimpose sacrifices upon the present landlords, it is only just to put the unrighteous gain of centuries in the other scale of the balance. [53]

To the idea of increased compensation for landowners, he answered angrily: "Compensation for those blood-sucking Jews who have trebled their fortunes by unjust means; one might talk of compensation to the people who have been cheated for so many years." [54]

When his English relatives wrote furiously of the methods of parliamentary obstruction practiced by Irish MPs at Westminster as a means of resisting coercion measures, Chamberlain insisted that these tactics had matured only after long provocation. "The policy of Parnell and Co.," he wrote to Aunt Harriet, "I quite agree to be unjustifiable but I well remember that not many years ago, when an Irish member got up, the House used systematically to ignore him and either members began conversing or walked out; at least they have forced Parliament to listen to them." [55]

More disturbing to him were the reckless and irresponsible

filibustering tactics of a small Conservative "ginger group" led by Lord Randolph Churchill whose noisy interruptions of House business during the time-wasting Bradlaugh imbroglio reflected the extent to which Disraeli's legacy had debased and coarsened English political life. On the Conservative benches he had respect only for Sir Stafford Northcote—in many ways the real target of Churchill.

As a good Gladstonian, Chamberlain's real *bête noire* was Disraeli, the man whom he blamed in large measure for the injection of selfish class interest and jingoism into British public life in the next decades. He backed Gladstone's efforts to liquidate Conservative foreign policy by disengaging from "forward" positions in South Africa and Afghanistan, where Disraeli's efforts to stabilize volatile political situations had led to growing involvement, expense, and finally failure. After annexing the Transvaal in 1878, for example, Britain faced a growing revolt among the Boer farmers. Once again opposed to the pro-imperial views of his family, Chamberlain wholeheartedly endorsed the Liberal decision to restore Boer independence and praised Gladstone's moderation even after the massacre of an English detachment of troops at Majuba Hill. "If we had not men like Gladstone," he argued, "one might well doubt of the existence of 'English love of justice and truth.'" He looked forward to intermarriage and closer ties between the Boers and British settlers in Cape Colony, and predicted that eventually this would lay the foundation "to one of those vigorous nationalities such as have always sprung up from the intermixture of races."[56]

Both Chamberlain's sympathy with the Irish peasantry and his hatred for aggressive British imperialism anticipated his later attitudes. Twenty years later he largely blamed the decay of English politics and the heightened competition between imperial nations on misguided Conservative policies, although by then he explained the trend more elaborately in terms of racial degeneration and the dominance of moneyed interests. Chamberlain never subjected Prussian Junkers to the same scrutiny as the Anglo-Irish landlords, nor did he examine German *Weltpolitik* with the same critical eye as British expansionism in southern Africa.

Outside England as well Chamberlain favored liberal politics. He admired, for example, the liberal republicans in France and particularly Gambetta whose death he characterized as "a disaster for the whole nation, perhaps all of Europe."[57] Also, for a time, after the assassination of Czar Alexander II, he even seemed somewhat sympathetic to the Russian anarchists living in Switzerland—again causing some consternation among his relatives. Sending a pamphlet by Dragomanov, the Ukrainian anarchist, to London, he added the comment: "You will see how little ferocious the man is, who is credited with being the head of the revolutionary party." In another letter he urged Aunt Harriet to "Tell Uncle N[eville] that in sending him *Revolté*, I didn't think or suppose anything about his political opinions—but merely wanted to give him an opportunity of forming a judgment at first hand on those held by the best sort of present socialists—for the *Revolté*, unlike *Revolution Sociale*, the *Ni Dieu ni Maître*, and many others is a paper which counts Elisée Reclus and other savants among its editors."[58]

He had met Reclus in Geneva and had a great respect for the famous geographer and friend of Kropotkin who ten years before had taken part in the Commune. It is difficult to judge how deep Chamberlain's understanding of such thinkers went or to what extent he accepted socialist and anarchist theories. More than likely he was chiefly drawn, like so many contemporaries, to the anarchist critique of bourgeois values and conventions; this was compatible, at any rate, with his growing enthusiasm for Wagner. Even in later years, however, he still admired the works of Proudhon—"one of the most acute minds of the century"—and identified with his attacks on Mammonism and condemnation of Jews and financiers. "I find many points of contact," he wrote in 1895, "between the Wagner-Schiller mode of thought and the anarchism of Proudhon."[59]

It was as an inhabitant of Dresden that Chamberlain first experienced life in the German Reich. He had visited the country before and was educated in the German cultural tradition, but now he confronted the everyday reality of Bismarckian Germany. This period of four years was, in fact, his only sustained contact with the Reich until 1908, when he settled in Bayreuth, although most of his writing in the intervening two decades was directed toward German readers. First impressions are important and Chamberlain's vision of Germany was that of a Wagnerite; his outlook on contemporary social and political issues was influenced deeply by the attitudes prevalent at Bayreuth as well as the situation in Dresden and Saxony. The result was a dramatic shift in his opinions away from the liberalism of his Genevan period.

The German Empire in which Chamberlain lived was a society in the throes of rapid social and economic change. Alongside the old Germany of princes, nobles, and peasants was emerging a new one of industrialists, financiers, corporation managers, trade unionists, and proletarians. The Wars of Unification had forged the most formidable concentration of military and economic power on the Continent, but the new nation was deeply divided and faced staggering tasks of social and psychological adjustment. Regional rivalries continued, and confessional and class tensions were accentuated in the first decade of the Empire; Prussian hegemony interfered with efforts to create national unity, and the attempt to fasten a traditional authoritarian political order to a dynamic industrializing society promised continuing friction and conflict. Instead of a period of tranquil domestic development, the first years of the Reich were a frenzy of speculation and overexpansion—the so-called *Gründerjahre* when the old order seemed to retreat suddenly before a culture that was ostentatious, brash, and obsessed by money. To conservative critics and those who identified with a pre-industrial order, the heroic era of battlefield victories had created a secular and selfish nation whose commercial success signified a collapse of values and spiritual impoverishment. Then, in 1873, revelations of company frauds and a weakening of public confidence precipitated a wave of selling; the stock market plunged, wiping out share values overnight, and the country experienced a sharp depression. The repercussions of the slump are well known. In politics Bismarck shifted the balance of forces dramatically, abandoning his partnership with the National Liberals and forming a conservative alliance of agrarian and industrial interests around the principles of economic protection and opposition to socialism. Culturally the crash prompted a wave of self-questioning and a vehement critique of contemporary society and capitalist values. The Germany that Chamberlain got to know in the mid 1880s—conservative, troubled, and divided as well as aggressively nationalist and posturing—had been forged in this climate of crisis. [60]

Generally speaking, Chamberlain became within the space of two or three years a firm opponent of liberalism. Like many other Wagnerites he was preoccupied by what he saw as a complete divorce between the German state and German culture; the nation he insisted had yet to find a distinctive political form. Rejecting the existing political establishment and its party structure, he called for a "spiritualizing" of public life and embraced a vague idealism that vented itself in exaggerated praise for the monarchy and authoritarian bureaucracy. While he admired Bismarck, Chamberlain concurred with Wagner's opinion that the Chancellor had allowed himself to become too entangled in electoral and factional politics.* "I honor and love Germany as the birth-place and home of much of what is best and greatest and most beautiful," he told Aunt Harriet, "but I don't believe the present . . . political system is an adequate expression of German thought and feeling." [61] Summing up his standpoint in 1889, he referred to himself as "a thorough conservative—but not in the party sense of the word." [62]

The most important change in Chamberlain's opinions during these Dresden years was his growing anti-Semitism. Hitherto anti-Jewish slurs and jokes had been interjected in

---

* One aspect of Bismarck's policy that troubled Chamberlain deeply was the Chancellor's manipulation of Anglophobia. "You must not believe," he informed Uncle Neville in 1889 after a particularly strident official campaign, "that the present attitude of the Germans toward England is anything new. The government has been preparing this for years through the medium of the press." "The violence and general tone of such a paper as the *Dresdener Nachrichten* towards England—always, not only now—a well bred Englishman can scarcely picture himself. And this paper is read daily by the 150,000 inhabitants of this town." The same animosity, he added, could be heard in the schools where children were "brought up . . . to mistrust and dislike, and in a measure to *despise* England." HSC to Sir Neville Chamberlain, Jan. 13, 1889 (CN).

his letters in a sporadic and unsystematic way; he might deplore Jewish finance or refer to Anglo-Irish landlords as "blood sucking Jews," but his prejudice was vague and not very coherent. Now, influenced both by the intolerant atmosphere of Bayreuth and the mood in Germany as a whole, he began to weave anti-Semitism consciously into his whole political and cultural outlook. Chamberlain's repudiation of liberal norms and institutions was couched in the language of race: the Jew became the symbol for all that he loathed and the central conceptual principle of his new cultural stance. In this, as in much else, his personal evolution mirrored a wider trend among many Germans in the aftermath of the economic crash of 1873.

Much has been written about the significance that the *Gründerzeit* and the onset of depression had for German anti-Semitism.[63] Only a few comments are needed here, as reminders of the broader context in which Wagnerism took shape and the opinions of Chamberlain were formed.

In the Reich Constitution of 1871, German Jews were finally given full equality after almost a century of continuous and fierce debate; the legal barriers which had been gradually lifted since the Napoleonic Wars were swept away entirely in the general climate of economic prosperity and rising expectations created by the boom of the 1860s. As R. Rürup has demonstrated, Jewish emancipation had by that time become linked to the wider development of a bourgeois-liberal society; it was one element in the larger program of liberal economic, political, and social reforms.[64] This protracted emancipation process also coincided with and facilitated a rapid transformation in the social position of German Jews who since the end of the eighteenth century had been progressively assimilated and integrated into German culture and society by the accelerated pace of modernization. Recent studies of educational attainments, urbanization, occupational concentration, and tax rolls illustrate clearly their dramatic rise in three generations from an underprivileged situation within a traditional society to a highly successful and largely middle class element within the emergent capitalist one. Their prominence in finance, commerce, textiles, and the professions as well as their increased representation in civic associations and in various areas of intellectual life, was out of all proportion to their numbers within the population (500,000 or 1.25% in 1871) and symbolized the *embourgeoisement* of the Jewish community as a whole.[65]

And yet, though Jewish economic integration and cultural assimilation were far advanced and Christian resistance to civic equality had subsided, the "Jewish question" had far from disappeared; and it was reopened within a few years in a flood of denunciations against alleged Jewish domination of German society. Part of the explanation for this reversal lies in the emancipation process itself. Owing to the political fragmentation of Central Europe there was never a single, circumscribed debate over Jewish rights, but rather a series of concurrent disputes occurring against a background of uneven, piecemeal change. For almost a century the issue was discussed by the press and parliaments of the separate states, which in many cases had the effect not of dismantling traditional prejudices among Christians but of hardening negative stereotypes and further enriching the common store of anti-Jewish arguments. Emancipation was always strongly contested and many Germans either remained opposed or accepted it only grudgingly in 1871. Even the liberals and the enlightened civil servants who championed full equality often defended their views not on the grounds of abstract rights of man or equal justice, but as a practical solution: only the elimination of legal disabilities, it was asserted, would allow the assimilation and reformation of Jewry. In short, to improve the Jew it was first necessary to abandon the special laws that defined and shaped his present existence. Opinions varied about the speed and scope of such legal changes, but the common denominator was that they ought to be linked to Jewish "civic betterment." Underlying emancipation was always a strong presumption that Jews would lose their separate group identity, and become no more than a denominational category; in fact, insofar as religion was never purely a private affair in Germany, it was often assumed that a solution to the "Jewish question" could only be achieved by eventual conversion. Finally, the slow and fragmentary nature of the emancipation process both helped to reinforce the habit of regarding Jews as lesser and inferior citizens and to couple the controversy over Jewish rights firmly with the general debates over industrialization, liberal politics and economics, and the changing character of German society.[66]

Had the new Reich enjoyed a period of continued prosperity, it is possible—although many historians raise serious doubts—that legal equality would have opened the door to social acceptance and gradually eroded the restraints that still blocked Jewish advancement in many spheres. As it happened, the sharp economic downswing, as we have seen, created widespread disillusionment and uneasiness. The crash and ensuing depression was interpreted as more than an economic crisis: it stimulated a collective appraisal of the spirit and goals of the new nation and fostered a repressive and vindictive mood. It was in this atmosphere of anti-liberalism and deep ambivalence toward modernity that anti-Semitism emerged as a significant political force. All the accumulated resentments built up during the emancipation debate now suddenly broke to the surface in an outcry against the Jew as symbolic of all that was judged corrosive and debased in German life. In these outbursts Jews were no longer represented as unqualified for equality because of their cultural or economic backwardness; rather, they were attacked as an excessively powerful minority who had gained control of society and subverted its traditional values. The slogan "emancipation *from* the Jews" became a common battlecry of conservative critics, those who felt penalized and uprooted by the functions of capitalism, and those searching for a scapegoat to explain the bewildering course of events.[67]

The formative significance of these years in the shaping of modern German anti-Semitism is widely acknowledged. In vehemence and specious detail the exposés of Jewish swindling and political corruption crafted by Otto Glagau, Franz Perrot, Rudolf Meyer, and Wilhelm Marr—to name only the most important—constituted a new era in anti-Semitic journalism. Their analysis shifted back and forth from denunciations of individual Jews such as Bleichroeder and Strousberg (of Jewish descent) to a more generalized indictment of Jewry as an antithetical racial principle responsible for the corruption of German life. Their writings mark the first stage in the process by which anti-Semitism was detached from particular Jews and became an integral part of an anti-liberal, anti-modern, and nationalist cultural stance. Their polemics also represent a new departure by virtue of the size of their readership and their appearance in eminently respectable press forums such as the formerly Liberal *Gartenlaube* and the Conservative *Kreuzzeitung*. Even more important, however, in endowing anti-Semitism with a certain social and intellectual respectability was the association with the cause of such university scholars as Paul de Lagarde and Heinrich von Treitschke, while the widely publicized speeches of court chaplain Adolf Stoecker, who sought to build a political coalition in Berlin on an anti-Jewish basis, also helped to create the impression that these new attacks were distinct from earlier and cruder forms of *Judenhass*.[68]

In addition to this vigorous campaign against Jews, in print, one other development of these years deserves mention: the establishment of small, independent anti-Semitic parties which aimed to nullify Jewish emancipation and reestablish special restrictive laws. There were many of these groups, small in membership, underfinanced and deeply divided by personal rivalries among their leaders.* They were never capable of unifying into a national organization, but all subscribed, broadly speaking, to the demands of the Anti-Semitic Petition, circulated in 1880, which called for prohibition of further Jewish immigration, a census of Jews already in the country, and their exclusion from positions of governmental authority, teaching, and the judiciary. Characterized by its originator, Bernhard Förster, as a national plebiscite, the petition eventually obtained 225,000 signatures. For the most part the small anti-Semitic parties made a poor electoral showing. While they built a fairly durable political base in both Hessenland and Saxony, and in 1881 mounted a forceful but unsuccessful campaign to challenge left liberal strength in Berlin, their progress was on balance fitful and the results poor until

---

* Among the most important were the *Christlich-Soziale Arbeiterpartei* (Adolf Stoecker); *Mitteldeutscher Bauernverein* (Otto Boeckel); the *Deutscher Volksverein* (Liebermann von Sonnenberg and Paul Förster); the *Soziale Reichspartei* (Ernst Henrici); *Deutsche Reformpartei* (Alexander Pinkert). For the most detailed analysis of them see: Richard S. Levy, *The Downfall of the Anti-Semitic Political Parties in Imperial Germany* (New Haven: Yale University Press, 1975). Still useful is Kurt Wawrzinek, *Die Entstehung des deutschen Anti-Semitismus 1873—1890* (Berlin, 1927).

1893.[69] These party activists moved in a different social world
from men like Treitschke and Lagarde: the German bourgeoisie, even when sympathetic to their general outlook, abhorred their extremist rhetoric and populist character. But they
were highly significant in developing new techniques of mass
politics and demagogic propaganda and their local successes
showed the potential of racist and anti-modernist ideology for
mobilizing diverse *Mittelstand* groups.

It was, then, amid the turmoil of the decade after the
Gründerkrach, that the Bayreuth cult took shape. Wagner's vision of national regeneration, his racist polemics in the *Bayreuther Blätter*, even the racial odyssey *Parsifal*, should be
recognized as products of this time as well as being the outgrowth of his earlier Judeophobic writing and his growing despair over the failure of Germans to come to the aid of the
debt-ridden festival. In these Wagnerite circles Chamberlain
first became acquainted with the range and intensity of
German anti-Semitism. It is also very possible that the
particular circumstances of Dresden and Saxony played a role
in the sudden intensification of Chamberlain's racism from the
mid 1880s, for the state proved a very receptive ground for
anti-Semitic organizers even though Jews made up only a
minuscule portion (0.27%) of the population. Rapid industrialization caused widespread suffering among craftsmen
and small businessmen and their mounting protest and demand for protective legislation frequently assumed anti-
Semitic form. In addition, the Saxon government was particularly hostile to Jews, excluding them from civil service appointments, publishing its releases in blatantly anti-Semitic newspapers, and eventually prohibiting kosher slaughtering as a
means of curbing the influx of orthodox *Ostjuden*. Not only did
anti-Jewish feeling attain a high degree of respectability in the
state, it also made political headway among the Saxon Conservatives and in the formation of small *Mittelstand* parties.
Dresden, for example, was the birthplace of Alexander Pinkert's
Deutsche Reformpartei, and in 1882 was host to the first
international anti-Semitic conference, with delegates from
Germany, Austria, and Hungary. Anti-Semitic *Reformvereine*
sprang up in many Saxon towns in the 1880s, the most important being that in Leipzig whose leader, Theodor Fritsch, es-

tablished the newspaper *Anti-Semitische Correspondenz* in 1885 and rapidly became one of the most active anti-Jewish campaigners in the Imperial Reich. And though in general it is difficult to evaluate the effectiveness of such agitation, in Saxony some confirmation can be found in the results of the *Reichstag* elections of 1893 (the *annus mirabilis* of the independent anti-Semitic parties); the Saxon anti-Semites obtained 6 seats and 116,000 votes out of 16 seats and 263,000 votes achieved by such groups nationally.[70]

There is no evidence to suggest that Chamberlain either supported or was particularly influenced by the activities of men like Pinkert and Fritsch. Indeed, it is very likely that he was offended by their brand of *radau-Antisemitismus* and rabble rousing, and found their political panaceas exceedingly simplistic when compared to the exalted Wagnerian goal of human regeneration. Such judgments certainly appear with some frequency in his letters during 1890, while in one instance in 1889 he reported ironically to Cosima that attendance at an anti-Semitic meeting left him "full of pity and love for all Jews."[71] Wolzogen and other supporters of Bayreuth voiced similar sentiments, although Ludwig Schemann made contact with several of the anti-Semitic political leaders, including Fritsch. But, in spite of the rather snobbish disdain in Wolzogen's letters, he did advertise such journals as Pinkert's *Deutsche Reform*, Oswald Zimmermann's Dresden daily, the *Deutsche Wacht*, Otto Glagau's *Der Kulturkämpfer* and several others of like orientation as suitable reading for Wagnerites. Moreover, Zimmermann and Bernhard Förster were invited to write for the *Blätter* and Adolf Stoecker remained a friend of at least some Bayreuthians for many years. None of the leading anti-Semitic agitators appears to have been a member of the Dresden branch of the Wagner Association, however, but that is not surprising given its upper middle class composition and intellectual (rather than activist) bias.[72]

Yet, if the relationship between Chamberlain's development and these political anti-Semitic groups remains obscure, it is clear that his four years in Dresden greatly intensified his opposition to Jews, and saw his adoption of a form of cultural criticism which ascribed all social ills to their malicious influence. Writing to Cosima from Berlin, which he saw as a fas-

cinating but terrible example of a town overrun by Jews, he
wrote:

> In front, behind and beside me—Jews! One of them who
> perhaps smells in me a business competitor, is constantly look-
> ing over my page. He must find the handwriting very unbusi-
> nesslike; perhaps he is astonished to see that in this house [the
> Central Hotel] someone should be writing from left to right. [73]

Another example of his feelings is the letter he dispatched
to Aunt Harriet after the death of Kaiser Frederick III in 1888.
Chamberlain astonished his relatives by admitting his pleasure
at the death of the Anglophile liberal ruler. In Germany, he
insisted, "the *Jews only* have regretted the late emperor—along
with some weak-minded liberal enthusiasts." Claiming that
Frederick's reign would merely have augmented the already
excessive power of the Jews, he explained:

> For Germany it would have been no blessing to begin dabbling
> in liberalism; liberalism (so called) is adapted neither to the
> genius of the nation, nor to its momentary position between
> dangerous neighbours. And not only was Emperor Frederick in-
> clined to that disastrous line of politics, but he was quite spe-
> cially a Jewish liberal, and has been well nicknamed: "Der
> Juden Kaiser." And in that he was diametrically opposed to
> what every intelligent and upright German feels—for the
> Germans are everyday awakening more and more to the fact
> that—in spite of their splendid position as an empire—they are
> menaced by a complete moral, intellectual, and material ruin if
> a strong reaction does not set in in time against the supremacy
> of the Jews, who feed upon them and suck out—at every grade
> of society—their very life blood. [74]*

---

* This is the same uncompromising tone to be found in Wagner's last essays; similar
outbursts can also be discovered in the manifestoes and proclamations of master artisans and anti-Semitic politicians. The Wagnerite mood had much in common with
the popular version of antimodernism, forged in the last two decades of the century.
They were alike in their monarchism and patriotism, their attacks on classical
liberalism and religiosity; similar, too, was their lack of clear social or political objectives. Wagner's *Meistersinger*, with its celebration of Hans Sachs, the cobbler, and the
culture fostered by the medieval guilds, was a particularly popular expression of this
advocacy of artisanal values. This vaguely delineated Golden Age was the positive
myth that linked Wagner's aesthetic reformism with *Mittelstand* ideology of the 1890s;
the negative myth was anti-Semitism.

It would be a mistake to exaggerate the extent to which Chamberlain was either concerned with politics or conceived of society's problems being soluble through political means. For in Dresden he was still primarily interested in art, and his hopes for cultural regeneration centered upon the aesthetic reform movement rather than the Reichstag or Bismarck's government. Sick and disheartened when he arrived in Dresden, with no immediate goals and aspirations, it can be seen how important Wagnerism was in his life during the next four years—it was a kind of aesthetic psychotherapy that provided him with a sense of participation in a significant cause, and allowed him to escape the depressing uncertainties of his health and to forget the interruption of his scientific research. At first he had embraced the pure aesthetic movement and, under the influence of Dujardin, immersed himself in the latest Symbolist literature from France. He studied the works of Huysmans, Jean Moréas, Baudelaire and Mallarmé, Gautier and Verlaine; and he became close friends with the poet Jules Laforgue, who resided in Berlin and was to die suddenly in 1887.[75] It was a literary education that few of the Wahnfried circle had, and Chamberlain always remained more sympathetic to the "moderns" than the other principal personalities around Cosima. Wagner's art, at this stage, seemed to Chamberlain to restore wholeness to divided modern man—psychologically it integrated passion and intellect just as artistically it united tone and word. A little later, as he moved closer to the Bayreuth circle itself, he saw in Wagner's art a means of welding together a new kind of national community, and he began to reject the decadent doctrines of art for art's sake. The social and religious mission of art now began to preoccupy him. At the very same time that Nietzsche warned that "one pays heavily for being one of Wagner's disciples," Chamberlain succumbed increasingly to that "Cagliostro of modernity."

When he was not occupying himself with the affairs of Bayreuth and the Wagner society, Chamberlain spent his time reading widely. He studied Wagner's dramas and prose writings and then delved into the legends and sagas on which they were based; he read the German and English Romantics, and was inspired by Schleiermacher's writings to make a thorough study of the Greeks; he found a life-long companion in Carlyle, whose *Lebensphilosophie* was to find echoes in his writing later on. Then, under the influence of Cosima's letters and conversations, he made a careful study of Schopenhauer's philosophy, though he could never fully accept the intellectual juggling act which purported to reconcile Schopenhauer's theories on art and the underlying principle of *Gesamtkunstwerk*. Out of his contact with Schopenhauer, however, came deep interests in Oriental religion and literature, for which he began learning Sanskrit. He was captivated by the East as a mysterious and compelling alternative to contemporary western materialism; gradually, these interests in eastern religions were joined to racial theories about Indo-Aryan culture and then once again to the all-encompassing art of Wagner, who had himself referred to the *Ring* as "certainly the most characteristic work of the Aryan race." Finally, alongside all these other pursuits Chamberlain began a long study of Kant, Goethe and Plato, reading a little each day, thinking and contemplating about what he had read.[76]

It was a full and busy existence. He became conscious of time in a new way and started to list meticulously in diaries all the reading he did, including newspapers and journals. And in this extensive reading schedule as much as in his changing views themselves one can perhaps detect acceptance of another German passion: the cult of *Bildung*, of which many historians have written. Chamberlain's course of study was designed to turn himself into the embodiment of the cultivated man, the well-formed and integrated personality; it was also a part of his general search for values, for a "new humanism" that would resist the corroding materialism and "steam intellect" of the present. But, in the practical realm, this veneration of *Kultur* and appeal to Idealism—so popular among the German bourgeoisie—meant a repudiation of politics and a separation of the realm of ideals and morals from the realm of power. Thus the counterside to *Bildung* was acquiescence to authority, to Bismarck and the *Obrigkeitsstaat*, and later, a justification of imperial ambitions on the grounds of cultural superiority.

Thus it was that Chamberlain could call himself a conservative "but not in the party sense of the word." For him Wagnerism and Idealism came before politics—and, to a large degree, shaped them. After expressing his satisfaction at the death of the liberal Kaiser Frederick III, he welcomed the accession of Wilhelm II—"the most intelligent, the most interesting face of the whole Hohenzollern family since the great Frederick." It was Wilhelm's genius that he was able to "unite in a really rare manner strength of character and practical insight into affairs with a really high idealism and appreciation of art" in contrast to his parents, "the apostles of 'industrial art' and similar beastliness." In politics his succession meant that Bismarck's hand "once more holds fast the reigns of government." [77]

In art, Chamberlain hoped, it meant the era of Bayreuth. "We Wagnerians," he wrote (and Cosima was similarly jubilant in these months), "are happy to see on the throne of the mightiest empire a man who is a member of the *Allgemeine Wagner-Verein* and who in '86 at Bayreuth said to my young friends, ex-minister Puttkammer's sons: 'When I am Emperor it will be my business to see that this only home of German dramatic art does not perish.'" [78] Wilhelm did encourage military officers and members of his entourage to join the Wagner Association, and from time to time made high-sounding declarations of allegiance to Bayreuth. But eventually in this respect—as in so many others— Wilhelm was to be a disappointment, confining himself to a few festival visits and maintaining an air of official reserve. Yet, in 1888 Chamberlain envisioned royal support for the task of cultural regeneration: Wagnerism would help nurture a new unified German *Kulturstaat* and Judaism of the spirit would be expunged for good. This loosely related collection of ideas, emotions, and fantasies was both profoundly "unpolitical" and deeply illiberal. In such unguarded statements we see that the Genevan science graduate had been transformed into the Bayreuth publicist.

Chapter Three

First Years in Vienna (1889–1892)

BY THE SPRING of 1889 Chamberlain had largely recovered from his breakdown, and as his health and stamina returned he began to think again of resuming a career in science. He put aside plans for a French translation of Wagner's prose works which he had been toying with, and devoted his time to a study of Darwin, Huxley, and the scientific writings of Goethe. In 1881, when searching for a dissertation topic, he had been profoundly impressed by the botanical studies of Julius Wiesner; now, once again it was Wiesner's work which revived his enthusiasm for plant physiology. By the summer months he and Anna had decided to leave Dresden and settle in Vienna, which had an agreeable climate and many cultural attractions, and was also the home of Wiesner. Chamberlain's goal was to complete his doctorate within a year, and he began salvaging the results of his Genevan research. After a short holiday visiting the Paris exhibition with Dujardin and Wyzewa, they travelled to Vienna.

It was cold and raining when they arrived in September, and the town seemed very foreign; but before long Chamberlain was welcomed into the circle of Viennese Wagnerites, whose leading figures he knew from the *Festspiele*. "The amiability, the pleasant sociability and real *Zuvorkommen* of the Viennese are quite unique," he told Aunt Harriet. "I had new proof of it yesterday when I was received with never-ending applause as the *berühmte* Herr 'Tschembelay'! by the one hundred and fifty most active members of the Akademischer

Wagner Verein." To Dujardin he praised the amiability of the inhabitants, admired "the pretty women of easy morals," and, after describing the picturesque setting of the town and its excellent university, concluded "I feel very comfortable in this medley of peoples and centuries." The one thing he found "frankly disagreeable," he admitted, was the "enormous quantity of Jews" but at least they kept to their own districts.[1]

After searching for a month, Chamberlain found a large, quiet apartment at 1 Blumelgasse, in the Mariahilf quarter to the southwest of the town center, on a high floor overlooking the Esterhazy park. This flat was to be his home for the next two decades. He enrolled in the university at once and began attending lectures in the new neo-Renaissance building on the Ringstrasse, not far from the parliament. He quickly became acquainted with Wiesner, who later recorded his first impressions of this rather intense English student:

> Regularly, after my lectures a smaller circle of listeners gathered around me, who wished to have a more detailed exposition of the subject of the lecture. Chamberlain soon appeared in this circle and I was immediately struck by the direct and felicitous manner he had of delivering his questions and remarks, testifying to his cultivation and knowledge. Often enough the conversation rapidly departed from the theme of the lecture and turned to other questions of philosophy and religion. These conversations were certainly among the most enjoyable and most stimulating which I have had in my life.[2]

For the first ten months after their arrival Chamberlain was hard at work trying to write a first draft of the thesis for submission to Wiesner. At first, in Geneva, he had devised a complicated series of experiments to document the movement of sap in plants; subsequently, in Dresden and Vienna, his interest turned more to the philosophical implications of the subject—in particular to the scientific debate between the proponents of vitalism and those who argued that there could be no understanding of the complex processes occurring in plants and animals until they were reduced to the principles of theoretical mechanics. Initially, under the influence of the extreme materialist Karl Vogt, Chamberlain's interest had been in the mechanics of sap movement; now, after several years of reading Kant, Schopenhauer, and old Indian texts, along with recent scientific papers, he approached his subject from a broader, more philosophical and vitalist standpoint. With Wiesner's encouragement he began a serious study of the limits and nature of scientific explanation which led to the conviction that contemporary research in its stress upon mechanical and materialist reasoning, its blind faith in "pure empiricism," and its crusading zeal for the doctrines of evolution, was hopelessly confused and philosophically impoverished. "All the facts," he asserted, "which are advanced in support of the evolution doctrine allow themselves to signify something else; it only requires the right builder to arrive, who knows how to erect a new building with the same material."[3] The immediate task, he insisted, was to admit that while causal and mechanical concepts enhanced our knowledge of physics and chemistry, they seriously impeded our grasp of biology and botany. What was needed was a new attention to scientific method, particularly in the life sciences. With this goal in mind, Chamberlain returned to eighteenth-century French writers like Bichat, Cuvier, Buffon, Lamarck, and Geoffroy Saint-Hilaire, as well as to such Germans as Karl Ernst von Baer, Caspar Friedrich Wolff, and most importantly, the hitherto neglected scientific writings of Goethe.

As a result, Chamberlain's dissertation altered shape; his meticulous experimentation, instead of showing exactly how the sap moved in plants, became part of a larger negative proof of the existence of a life force (*élan vital*). Only by postulating a life force, he argued, could sap movements be understood; and this meant drastically revising the methods of science and recognizing the validity of a subjective, imaginative, almost artistic, insight into living things—akin to Goethe's "graphic vision" of nature (*Naturanschauung*). Although he was to achieve a widespread reputation as a Wagner publicist and popular race theorist, Chamberlain always regarded himself as a natural scientist as well. In later years he repeatedly returned to questions about the status and validity of scientific knowledge and, in his major works, greatly elaborated his critique of positivism and scientific materialism, striving always to integrate his ideas about science, religion, philosophy and art into a coherent and unified system. Discussion of his views is best deferred until later: suffice it to say that the thesis on the sap, of no special consequence by itself, anticipated all his later scientific speculation and that its vitalist underpinnings were closely linked to the crystallization of his doctrine of race.[4]

By July 1890 Chamberlain managed to present Wiesner with a description of his experiments and the tentative conclusions he drew from them. On July 18 he jubilantly dashed off a card to Aunt Harriet announcing: "After studying my memoranda more carefully, [Wiesner] seems to consider my work really remarkable. He confirms my opinion that it is really *new*, that the results are unexpected and of great interest. . . . An early publication in some form or other [is] desirable. He strongly recommends my only publishing . . . the fully worked out and quite new part; the rest would form material enough for one or two more essays."[5] In fact, these publication plans were premature: *Récherches sur la sève ascendante*, as the book was titled, did not appear until 1897—after another substantial revision. The reasons for the delay are difficult to unravel and although Chamberlain declared later that a recurrence of ill health and nervous disorders prevented once more the continuation of his scientific pursuits, his own letters and activities would seem to belie this conclusion. A more convincing explanation appears to be that his restless and dilettantish spirit felt too constrained by the specialization and professionalism botany required; other interests, particularly his time-consuming activities in the service of Wagnerism and growing journalistic ambitions had temporarily supplanted his scientific research. In the following years, his original goal of earning a doctorate receded: even when *Récherches* . . . was completed he decided against presenting it for a degree, since university requirements at Geneva mandated a broad oral exam that Chamberlain had no desire to prepare for.

In the summer of 1890, however, after submitting the fruits of his research to Wiesner, Chamberlain gave himself up to "an orgy of mountain climbing," spending his time on the limestone bastions of the Rexalpe and the Schneeberg, or trekking with his friend Adolphe Appia to the Kahlenberg Heights and the Wienerwald. Then, at the end of August, the possibility of a more exciting journey arose. The Austrian government, as part of a wider campaign to publicize its administration of the protectorates of Bosnia and Herzegovina, and to encourage investment in and promote a wider understanding of the area, decided to sponsor a tour. Through acquaintances, possibly some of his Wagnerite friends, Chamberlain managed to secure an invitation, and set off with Anna early in September. "I am assured," he informed Dujardin on the eve of their departure, "that this almost unknown corner of Europe is is more in the middle ages and more oriental than Constantinople, Asia Minor or Egypt; in a few years this will no doubt disappear, but for the moment it is true."[6]

Although only about three weeks in duration, the journey was sufficient to kindle Chamberlain's enthusiasm, and he decided at once to arrange for a second and more extensive visit. Throughout the winter months he and Anna took intensive lessons in Serbo-Croatian and studied the history and geography of the region. The Austrian imperial finance minister, Benjamin von Kállay, who was in charge of Bosnian affairs, offered to meet the expenses of the second trip, provided Chamberlain agreed to publish some articles after his return; but the offer was declined. After several postponements, they finally left in May, travelling by horseback to the most remote parts of Bosnia. A keen photographer, Chamberlain took a large number of pictures, some of which were later published and others placed in an exhibition. The whole experience had a profound influence on him: here he met Catholic, Greek orthodox, and Moslem inhabitants—the latter, expecially, who formed the aristocracy of the region, impressed him greatly.[7]

Years later, in 1917, in conversation with the Indologist Leopold von Schroeder, he recalled that Bosnia first made him really aware of the significance of race. Rudolf Kassner, the Austrian mystic who was for a time an admirer of Chamberlain, was shocked by his "*Schwarmerei*" for the Serbs of Bosnia, "those genuine, still almost pure Slavs," as they were described in the *Foundations*. From the "tallness of the men and the prevalence of fair hair," Chamberlain was convinced they were close racial cousins of the Germans; they manifested none of the deterioration he associated with other Slavic types.[8]

On his return to Vienna at the end of September 1891, Chamberlain began writing articles about Bosnia and its customs. Already in the previous year, acting on the advice of Dujardin, he had written three brief essays of a political nature for the Paris *Figaro:* one on the coming significance of Canada, another on Kaiser Wilhelm II, and a third on modernization in Austria. Hastily done and inadequately researched, they were immediately refused by Francis Magnard, the editor. Flushed with enthusiasm after his first trip to Bosnia, he again tried his hand at political journalism, and sent off accounts of his travels to the *Standard, Morning Post,* and *Murray's Magazine* in England and wrote a feuilleton for the prestigious *Neue Freie Presse* of Vienna. All these essays were refused.

Chamberlain tried to explain his activities to Agénor Boissier, a wealthy Genevan friend who adopted an avuncular role toward him, "It is precisely," he told Boissier, who was perturbed by his excursions into the "mire" of journalism, "my family who have pushed me energetically to work at this trade." "One does not have to be an anti-Semite in the odious sense of the word," he added, "but it is at least true that all journalism is Jewish filth."[9] In the face of his family's insistence he claimed to have little alternative but to carry out their wishes. Actually, Chamberlain's family letters would seem to indicate that it was his will not theirs which was behind his efforts, although there are signs that some of his relatives were critical of his leisured life and his failure to settle down in a profession or career.[10]

His earlier failures did not dissuade him from writing more essays after the second Bosnian tour. These were more successful: Boissier helped get one published in a prestigious Swiss review and three others were accepted by journals.[11] His intention was to arouse public support for Austrian policy in Bosnia since the occupation of the region in 1879, and more especially to praise the judicious administration of his friend Benjamin von Kállay. "As a bulwark against Russian or Serbian and, in general, against all Pan-Slavic covetousness,"

he wrote, the area was vital to Hapsburg interests. Even England should recognize its supreme importance: "The Russian,"
he told his aunt, "is our deadly enemy, and the enemy of all
western civilization . . . our policy in regard to eastern Europe
must be dictated by the clear knowledge of this fact." As a
"moral outpost" against the Czars, Bosnia "could, from one
day to the next, become one of the pivots on which all European politics will revolve"—words which proved only too
true a little over two decades later.[12]

Chamberlain's view of Bosnia was markedly pro-govern-
ment. Though uninteresting as analytical accounts of Austrian
policy, these articles are significant in showing his growing
regard for autocratic rule: Bosnia he argued was a working
example of Wagner's illiberal ideal: "Absolute monarch—free
people." Benjamin von Kállay was Plato's benevolent tyrant
come to life, achieving more in ten years than representative
institutions could have accomplished in half a century. "I
really believe," Chamberlain wrote to his Serbo-Croatian language teacher, "that the Bosnians are at this moment the most
fortunate *Volk* of the whole earth; they are still 'natural' men
enough to feel free and healthy, and yet are already endowed
with the best sign of civilization . . . no parliamentary regime!
May God protect them from this for many years."[13] Admiration for enlightened dictatorship in Bosnia coincided, as we
shall see, with his growing hostility to representative institutions in Austria and Germany; gradually he was moving
toward a belief in a vague corporatist system of government
where an absolute monarch and trained bureaucracy ruled,
advised by corporations of the separate elements of the nation:

> The general credence is that Austrian bureaucracy is a
> somewhat rotten and irretrievably sluggish machinery. Be this
> as it may, the short history of the occupation of Bosnia suffices
> to show what an amount of talent and go-ahead administrators
> this empire disposes of, if only neutral ground can be found
> where party passions and national rivalries do not eat up the
> best of every man.[14]

Bosnia also raised other issues to which Chamberlain was
sensitive as a Wagnerite: for example, the destruction of traditional patterns of life by modernization. The Bosnian was

Chamberlain's idea of 'natural man,' in contrast to the urbane, overcivilized bourgeois of industrial Vienna. Regretfully reflecting that Austrian domination would mean "westernization," he wrote:

> He [the peasant] builds his house, he makes his shoes, and plough, etc.; the woman weaves and dyes the stuffs and cooks the food. When we have civilized these good people, when we have taken from them their beautiful costumes to be preserved in museums as objects of curiosity, when we have ruined their national industries that are so perfect and so primitive, when contact with us has destroyed the simplicity of their manner—then Bosnia will no longer be interesting to us.[15]

A few years later, again thinking of the Bosnian, he wrote:

> The spirit of a natural man, who does everything and must create everything for himself in life, is decidedly more universal and more harmoniously developed than the spirit of an industrial worker whose whole life is occupied with the manufacture of a single object . . . and that only with the aid of a complicated machine, whose functioning is quite foreign to him. A similar degeneration is taking place among peasants: an American farmer in the Far West is today only a kind of subordinate engine driver. Also among us in Europe it becomes every day more impossible for a peasant to exist for agriculture must be carried on in 'large units'—the peasant consequently becomes increasingly like an industrial worker. His understanding dries up; there is no longer an interaction between his spirit and surrounding Nature.[16]

Chamberlain's pride in the technological and scientific prowess of the "German" nation was always mixed with despair at the consequences of migration to the cities, the commercialization of agriculture and the breakdown of peasant life.* Bosnia rein-

---

* In one of his plays, written in the 1890s, Chamberlain depicted the tragic lot of the peasant—subject to the hazards of weather and rapacious landlords, and with traditional values at odds with the urban, commercial ethos of the rest of society. A second play, set in Vienna, dealt with the themes of love, marriage, duty, and money: it portrays, among other things, the venality and superficiality of bourgeois life in the Austrian capital. Taken together they illustrate Chamberlain's critique of urban values and nostalgia for "natural man." See "Der Weinbauer" and "Antonie" in *Drei Bühnendichtungen* (Munich, Bruckmann: 1902). The first was unsuccessfully performed in Zurich in 1896, the second appears to have been staged by the Prague Stadttheater in 1906.

forced his *völkisch* nostalgia and bolstered the antidemocratic and racist outlook he had adopted in Dresden. Later, even he was a little embarrassed by the excessive sentimentality of these early articles and tried to persuade a somewhat skeptical Cosima that one of them was an intentional satire of "Jewish feuilleton style." But the lingering significance of these journeys is indicated by repeated references in later years.[17]

For more than a year Chamberlain's concerns had fluctuated between Bosnia, journalism, photography, and a growing range of activities associated with the Wagner Society of Vienna. Convinced that he was not cut out for a scientific career, his quick, eclectic mind shifted easily from one thing to another. A lively correspondence with Cosima attests to the breadth of his reading—Scott, Milton, Schopenhauer, Kleist, and a staggering array of other names fill the pages of their letters. A hasty note to Edouard Dujardin was equally typical of his catholic tastes: "Things go better with me. I am over my head in plant physiology, the philosophy of Anaxagoras, English language philology, the music of Gluck and the projects about the dramas in which I hope to collaborate with you." He lectured to the Photographic Society at the University; he allotted a portion of each day to Kant, Goethe or Schopenhauer; and he remained abreast of the latest cultural trends in France—the popular novelist Pierre Loti, the satirist Eugéne Labiche and the cabaret singer Aristide Bruant (whom he had seen at the famous Le Chat Noir while visiting Montmartre in 1889) were just three of his favorites.[18]

He also busied himself with plans for books but at first had little success: when he tried to put pen to paper his ideas seemed feeble, flat and insignificant, at which he would hurl the results into a waste basket and dash out into the streets or a nearby coffeehouse. There was a feverish intensity even to Chamberlain's dilettantism; by the autumn of 1891 he had abandoned all hope of a scientific career; now he began to devote all his energies to Wagnerism, and it was service to Bayreuth that provided the necessary catalyst for his development as a writer.

It was as a favorite of Wahnfried that Chamberlain was

welcomed by the prominent Wagnerites of Vienna. Through Wagnerism he met music critics like Arthur Seidl and Gustav Schonäich, composers such as Anton Bruckner and Engelbert Humperdinck, and a range of literary and academic friends, among them the versatile philosopher and *littérateur*, Baron Christian von Ehrenfels. But, while Chamberlain's life mostly revolved around the Wagner societies, his closest and oldest friend during these first years at the Blumelgasse was the remarkable young stage designer Adolphe Appia whom he had known in Geneva. Their friendship deserves notice, not merely because of Appia's posthumous fame as one of the founders of modern stagecraft, but also because it reveals another, clearly defined side of Chamberlain's character; it shows him a solicitous and cultivated mentor to a younger disciple, for Appia was the first of several younger people whom he befriended. [19]

Their first encounter cannot be dated exactly: it was probably sometime in 1884 when Appia, a young music student at Leipzig University, returned to his home in Geneva for a vacation. Sharing deep interests in music and natural history (both had, for example, been at Bayreuth in 1882) their relationship quickly ripened into a deep friendship, and Appia was a constant visitor at Vert Pré. Seven years younger than Chamberlain, he was nervous and inhibited—the product of a strict Calvinist upbringing at the hands of a domineering father, a doctor, who disapproved of a musical career and wanted his son to study medicine. Walther Vollbach, Appia's most recent biographer, finds it odd "that two men so dissimilar in their outlook on most human and cultural affairs" should have been on such close terms. but this judgment derives from a series of misunderstandings. Chamberlain's views were not fixed from youth—he did not enter the world a full-blown fascist; his illiberal and anti-Semitic tendencies, far from being a personal aberration, were in conformity with the attitudes of large groups of contemporaries; anyway, the notion that no villain can enthrall or befriend the right-minded is a questionable assumption at best. The fact is that Appia was happier and, in the early days at least, more creative in the company of Chamberlain than when he was with anybody else.

They were indeed very different: Chamberlain, for all his underlying nervousness and sensitivity, presented to the outside world an air of confidence and aristocratic sociability; his engaging manners, brilliant conversational style, and polished affability were in striking contrast to the awkward, inarticulate Appia, plagued by a speech impediment. Whereas Chamberlain was an accomplished linguist—fluent in French, German, and English and capable of getting along in Italian, Spanish, Dutch, Norwegian, and Serbo-Croatian—Appia found it impossible to master foreign tongues. While Chamberlain's erudition was broad in the sciences and arts, the younger man was relatively unschooled and had large gaps in his knowledge.

Not surprisingly, Chamberlain became the dominant personality in the relationship—a mixture of an older brother and teacher. Appia was intellectually and emotionally very dependent on him, and yet Chamberlain never doubted the genius of his younger companion. Later, after their friendship had cooled, Appia still referred to him as "the ideal intermediary [who] gave to me with one hand, while he was willing to receive with the other." He added: "Lucky the young man who finds such a friend on his way." [20]

When the Chamberlains moved to Dresden in 1886, Appia followed them and stayed for three years. Frequent conversations with Houston and Anna—of whom he was very fond—helped clarify and sharpen his early insights, and gradually his musical interests gave way to a fascination for the problems and techniques of stagecraft. Chamberlain's growing intimacy with the Bayreuth circle and local Wagnerites was also invaluable in obtaining permission for Appia to observe backstage the technical equipment not only of Dresden's Royal Opera House—the scene of Wagner's first performances of his dramas—but also the theaters at Bayreuth and Munich. Gradually, with Chamberlain's strong encouragement, Appia began to formulate an entirely new vision of stagecraft that would complete Wagner's synthesis of the arts. In 1882 and again in 1888 Bayreuth had disappointed him because of inadequate staging: "The most effective means of expression—light—without which there can be no depth is ignored. The drama which is all shadow and light, violent contrasts and infinite shades of meaning, is projected against a monotonous background." [21]

Well aware of the exceptional nature of Appia's talents, Chamberlain advised him on matters of prose style and expression, offered suggestions about his general reading, and explained difficult sources on the principles of electricity and magnetism, as well as helping with the interpretation of Wagner. From him, Appia gained in his own words "a pregnant and documented image of Wagner's personality, transfigured through the enthusiasm and adoration of a thoroughly informed artistic disciple." [22]

As early as 1888 Chamberlain began mentioning his friend in letters to Cosima, hinting at Appia's ideas about the unity of music and light in the drama. That October he also passed on to Wahnfried some of his friend's thoughts about costumes and was pleased by Cosima's initial murmurs of approval. "What he says," she acknowledged, "is ingenious and correctly grasped," and she invited more details. [23] Chamberlain's secret hope that Cosima would allow Appia some role in the *Festspiele* came to nothing. The more she saw of these new proposals, the less she liked them, for her chief aim was strict traditionalism, to preserve Wagner's style of production by a constant ritual of repetition. Though conceding that more could be done with electric light than in the old gaslit days, Wahnfried remained obdurate in its refusal of Appia's spatial arrangements, his simplified costumes, and his use of shadow and movement.

Chamberlain was quietly persistent: when he visited Bayreuth in 1892 and 1893 he carried with him Appia's designs for the *Ring*; a little later, he counseled his friend to send another portfolio of sketches, along with a recently published pamphlet, "La mise en scène du drame Wagnérien." Other Wagnerites, including Wolzogen and Prince Hohenlohe-Langenburg, a close friend of Cosima, were also approached for their views, while in his biographical study of Wagner, published in 1895, Chamberlain footnoted some of Appia's ideas, predicting "that the next great advance in the drama will be . . . in the art of the eye, and not in music." [24] All the gentle coaxing and obvious hints met with firm rejection: "Appia does not seem to know," argued Cosima rather sharply, "that the *Ring* was produced here in 1876, and therefore there is nothing more to be discovered in the field of scenery and production. Consequently, all that is right in his writing is superfluous since it is in accordance with the directions in the score, and all the rest is wrong to the point of childishness."*

"All your concepts," Chamberlain consoled Appia with a confusing piece of generational arithmetic, "are about 75 years ahead of their right time and the mother of the kind of people who will blaze with excitement at contact with your ideas, is still only a little girl who goes to school." [25] The words were prophetic. For as long as Cosima lived Appia had no hope of participating at Bayreuth; indeed, it is a testament to her enormous influence that he was unable to translate his vision of the Wagnerian drama into practice on any stage for over a quarter of a century. Only after 1951 were his suggestions incorporated into the "new Bayreuth" style of Wagner's grandsons. Chamberlain, alone of the Wahnfried circle, appreciated the revolution Appia pioneered, extending Wagner's union of music and drama by integrating all visual aspects of the staged presentation with the musical forms.

After Chamberlain moved to Vienna, Appia often visited him for weeks and even months at a time and met prominent Wagnerites like Felix Weingartner, Arthur Seidl, and Siegmund von Hausegger. He felt less comfortable amid this broader circle of Chamberlain's acquaintances and decided to return to Switzerland where between 1895 and 1897 (while Chamberlain worked on the *Foundations*), in seclusion at

---

* Another great figure in modern stage design received a similarly frosty reception. Gordon Craig describes lunching with Cosima in Dresden in 1905: "I always think it was rather wonderful that I met Frau Cosima Wagner that once, and had the honor of sitting at her right hand. I don't know who else was there—two or three people. I didn't realize much about that great lady in those days: all I realized was whether I felt well or not. And I felt very well that day, so I naturally talked a lot, and talked about the theater a lot. . . . I cannot remember much what we talked about at table, but I got quite excited talking about Wagner's music, and I said to Frau Cosima that I could not see the stage trappings at Bayreuth or anywhere else were anything like the visions his music conjured up. And I think I remember her saying: "And what pictures do *you* see, Mr Craig?" And I described something like the wild pampas of South America, the rushing of the wind, perhaps a prairie fire, and so on.

When I looked at Frau Wagner I could hardly see her face, because she had turned the same color as the table cloth, into which she seemed to be vanishing. I came to a stop, thank goodness, in time—something shot me out into reality. By then everybody was getting up from the table, and before long I said goodbye to everybody, and to Frau Wagner, kissing her beautiful hand—'Gnadige Frau . . . .'" E. G. Craig, *Index to the Story of My Days. Some Memoirs of Edward Gordon Craig 1872-1907* (New York, 1957), p. 271-72.

Bière, he wrote his most important book, *La musique et la mise en scène*. Its progress is chronicled in voluminous and somewhat disjointed letters dashed off to his friend. The scores of chatty and impulsive letters from Appia elicited somewhat less frequent but warm responses from Chamberlain. Among other things, Chamberlain advised that the book be published in German—the language that dominated musical studies—and, when Appia hesitated, he agreed to supervise the translation. He also persuaded his Munich publisher, Bruckmann, to accept the manuscript and found time in 1898 to read and correct the first draft meticulously despite the heavy burdens of his own work. When it appeared in the following year, Appia's *Die Musik und die Inszenierung*, one of the outstanding texts of modern stagecraft, bore a dedication to Chamberlain "who alone knows the life which I enclose in these pages." [26]

In later years, as Chamberlain became increasingly immersed in his personal mission as a publicist and cultural prophet, the two men saw less of each other and slowly drifted apart. Appia, in middle age, was no longer so emotionally dependent as he had once been; also, in Emil Jacques Dalcroze, the founder of eurhythmics, he discovered a new collaborator with whom he worked on several fine productions, culminating in Gluck's *Orpheus and Eurydice* in 1913. When in 1905 Chamberlain's marriage began to collapse and Anna grew sick and more of a burden than he wished to shoulder, he displaced some of his feelings of guilt in anger at Appia whom he accused of meddling and disloyalty. Yet, apart from several years silence after Chamberlain's divorce, their correspondence continued intermittently until 1924—by that time both had moved far apart in their political and artistic attitudes, although each clearly cherished the memories of a long friendship, once so intense and supportive.

In championing Appia at Bayreuth Chamberlain was mildly rebellious, but in all his other associations with Wahnfried he remained firmly orthodox and unreceptive to any criticism of Cosima. When he came to Vienna a Wagner fever was sweeping the town: among the students of the *Leseverein der deutschen Studenten* and the budding *literati* gathered in the coffeehouses, and in the salons of the aristocracy and the wealthy bourgeoisie, Wagner's music and the amalgam of aesthetic and social philosphy that went with it was enjoying a remarkable vogue. The sensuality and startling psychological insights of the dramas, their mixture of pessimism and spiritual redemption, their alluring fragrance of sacrificial *Liebestod*, and even their difficulty (to master them required handbooks and a struggle) were all part of the composer's appeal. "I remember having been dominated by the Wagnerian idea," Romain Rolland once admitted, "when the Wagnerian art was still half obscure to me." The same was true of a good many Viennese enthusiasts; as Hermann Bahr commented, exaggerating only a little, many of the younger generation were ardent Wagnerites even before they had heard a single note of the music. [27]

After Bayreuth, Vienna was the second center of the Wagner cult. [28] Not only did the town have the *Hofopera* (under the direction of Hans Richter and later Gustav Mahler), where fine productions of the dramas were regularly staged, but it also boasted the largest and wealthiest Wagner society, the Vienna *Akademischer Wagner-Verein*. With over 900 members, including prominent socialites, musicians, academics, and composers, it sponsored frequent meetings and concerts and collected sizable sums of money for Bayreuth, thereby obtaining some measure of influence over the actions of Cosima and the Wahnfried circle.

As was to be expected in a city so deeply torn by national and political tensions, the most serious differences among Viennese Wagnerites erupted over whether the *Verein* should associate itself with the radical Pan-Germanism of the student societies and Georg von Schoenerer. The majority of the Wagner Society were strongly opposed to any move that would intrude the factionalism of German nationalist politics into their cultural activities; many found the demagoguery and crude anti-Semitism of the Pan-Germans repulsive; others looked to art as a kind of personal religion—an escape from the futility of political and civic action, not an enticement to collective involvement. A vocal minority, however, insisted that Wagner's whole crusade for culture necessitated a firm en-

dorsement of the Pan-German ideology and its vigorous opposition to Jews and Slavs. The leader of the *Verein*, Alois
Höfler—a teacher and later university professor—strove to
avoid a rift, arguing that its sole concern should be art. But
compromise proved impossible and in December 1889 the
dissident group split off to form their own *Neuer Wagner-
Verein.*[29]

During his first year in Vienna Chamberlain regularly attended meetings and concerts but, largely occupied with his
university studies for Wiesner, took little part in *Verein*
"politics." At first he was unsympathetic to the political
Wagnerites and deplored their dragging art through the swamp
of everyday politics, but gradually his views altered, especially
when the older society became more vocal in its criticism of
Cosima. Her controversial staging of *Tannhäuser* at the 1891
festival and her efforts to gain greater control over the
Festspiele funds, collected by the various local branches of the
Wagner Society, provoked considerable dissatisfaction. Discontent increased further when she imperiously announced her
decision to found a music school at Bayreuth and tried to gain
control over the allotment of free festival seats (subsidized by
the general fund) from the local societies.*

Chamberlain had no doubts about Cosima's judgment or
authority, and he grew angry at those who questioned her actions. At first he tried to support Wahnfried on the inside: his
letters to Cosima are full of *Verein* gossip and occasionally included caricatures of her opponents and parodies of their conversations. But he became steadily more hostile to Viktor
Boller, a lawyer and leading organizer of the Vienna society,
and by early 1892 explained to Hans von Wolzogen and

---

* Chamberlain's hope was that a substantial part of the Wagner Society funds would
be used to purchase free seats for worthy Germans without financial means to attend
the festival, thereby fulfilling the original wishes of the Master. He especially wanted
to subsidize German schoolteachers who could have the largest possible impact on the
younger generation. "If we want to preserve the sublime and sacred thoughts, strivings
and art of our Master as more than something fashionable in the soul of the *Volk*,
there is only one way: send hundreds and thousands of good German teachers to Bayreuth." He lobbied for this idea as a way to celebrate the proposed revival of the *Ring*,
but when Cosima made clear her preference for a music school Chamberlain
abandoned his plans and acted as her spokesman. HSC to Hans von Wolzogen Dec. 2,
1891; HSC to C. F. Glasenapp April 25, 1892 (CN).

Friedrich Glasenapp that he felt obliged to leave "this society of puffed up and impotent philistines" with their "completely negative immoderate, violent and destructive criticism of Bayreuth" and "their disgraceful treatment of Frau Wagner." [30]

As the author of several articles on Wagner and a known confidant of Wahnfried, Chamberlain was asked in October 1891 to lecture at the *Neuer Verein*. His report to Cosima was wholly enthusiastic. *"For the very first time,"* he wrote, "I was in a Wagner society where one could sense an eagerness, where something serious happened and where . . . the whole discussion concerned itself exclusively with the things which justify the very existence of a Wagner society." Though numerically small, it contained people "who approach our cause with a holy seriousness"—in contrast to the lax and negligent meetings of the *Akademischer Verein*, where newer composers and celebrated Jews like Gustav Mahler were regarded almost as highly as the Master himself. Subsequent evenings strengthened his first favorable impressions and, after a short delay arising from political tensions within its ranks, Chamberlain was formally admitted to the *Neuer Verein*. "If only," he remarked to Glasenapp, "we can succeed in restricting the all too passionate nationalism and the all too aggressive anti-Semitism within suitable limits so that the name of the Master shines over all and in everything—then something useful will come of it." [31]

Over the next years he became the leading figure of the society and exercised a strong influence over its program and evolution. Hard at work by that time on two books and numerous essays publicizing Bayreuth, he was in demand as a lecturer and began to try out his ideas on a variety of audiences, journeying, for example, to Graz to address the society dominated by Friedrich von Hausegger and Friedrich Hofmann, two fanatical anti-Semites and nationalists who had completely disrupted the sedate *Musikverein fur Steiermark* some years before with their political activism. Outside the Wagner clubs he lectured to German audiences at the *Deutscher Jugendbund*, the student fraternity *Germania*, and the philosophical faculty of Vienna University. Fifty years later one listener still recalled how this tall, blond man sent "a powerful wave of excitement flooding through the hall" and Chamberlain himself was surprised by his effectiveness as speaker and his ability to master his nervousness.[32]

In this way Chamberlain's activities for the *Neuer Verein* brought him into *deutschnational* circles in Austria and introduced him to such Pan-German leaders as K. H. Wolf, the founder of the *Ostdeutsche Rundschau*, for whom he was soon writing articles. So completely is Chamberlain identified with the German Reich that it is easy to forget he wrote most of his major books and essays in Vienna. Spiritually he may have been more at home in Bayreuth and Germany, but he always acknowledged that the intellectual and political ferment of the Austrian capital (which Hitler would later call "the hardest though most thorough school of my life") gave powerful stimulus to his creativity. Viennese echoes reverberate through all his writing; he sat at home most of the day and his life was outwardly uneventful, but noises of the struggles outside floated up into his study on the Blumelgasse and shaped his ideas permanently. His passionate defense of everything German and exaggerated fears of political Catholicism, his obsession with social disintegration and focus on the instinctual rather than rational origins of human behavior all bore traces of his Viennese milieu.

Chamberlain had settled in the Hapsburg Empire at a time of rapid political change as new social groups, hitherto excluded from power—the peasantry, workers, artisans and Slavic peoples—successfully challenged the twenty year ascendancy of Austrian liberalism.[33] The sufferings of craftsmen and workers created by sharp economic fluctuations, tensions arising from large-scale immigration of Jews and Slavs from the east, and the resentments of nationalist Germans who witnessed the dwindling of their former monopoly of power in the empire converged to produce a general crisis which dissolved the old political order. In Vienna, a storm center of national and social conflict, the three movements that were to dominate the political future—Pan-Germanism, Social Democracy, and Christian Socialism—were already in existence by 1889, and within a decade had shattered the parliamentary power of liberalism. Chamberlain had moved to the Austrian capital in time to witness its transition to mass politics. His diaries and letters point to a deepening concern with public issues. When liberals downplayed German nationalism as a disruptive force in a multinational society, Chamberlain viewed them as traitors. He sympathized with the discontents of artisans and small traders and their opposition to laissez-faire liberalism, but deplored the swift success of Karl Lueger's Christian Socialism among these strata. To him it signified a dangerous revival of the Catholic church's authority, disguised by a new demagogic and populist style. Similarly disturbing was Victor Adler's creation of a united movement out of the scattered elements of Austrian socialism. When Adler (himself an ardent Wagnerite) organized the first symbolic May Day parade in 1890, Chamberlain anticipated violence. To Aunt Harriet he reported: "People here seem to be rather frightened of the first of May. The late troubles, which you will have read of in the papers, cause real alarm. I suppose the rabble won't care to come up to a fifth floor flat, but I am having my revolvers cleaned so as to be able to furnish them with some digestive pills if they did." [34]

Mixing almost exclusively with German Austrians, he shared their outlook, particularly their rancor against the demands of the radical Young Czechs for legal and cultural equality. Thus, in April 1897, when Count Badeni's speech ordinances placed Czech on an equal footing with German as a language of official use in Bohemia, his letters echoed the explosion of anger among the German population. Jubilantly he reported the demonstrations of students and respectable bourgeoisie in Vienna, Graz, and Salzburg, and applauded the patriotic feats of those like Dr. Karl Lecher, the Bohemian German leader, whose filibusters obstructed the business of parliament. "Everything that is German," he complained, "is systematically persecuted in this country, the object almost avowedly declared, being to obliterate the German element entirely." [35] Though at first alarmed by the abrasive, inflammatory style of Georg von Schoenerer, Chamberlain soon came to value the Pan-Germans as the only group totally committed to the defense of German interests and culture in the empire.

In some respects, of course, Vienna merely reinforced tendencies already pronounced in Chamberlain's thought. Since leaving Geneva, as we have seen, he had rebelled against his Gladstonian liberal heritage. In place of bourgeois rationality, he affirmed instinct; in place of the liberal concept of progress, he asserted that the modern era was retrograde. Like many contemporaries he looked to art as a source of value and a means of restoring spiritual harmony to individuals atomized by social and economic evolution. Wagnerism symbolized this mood: in it aesthetic theory and cultural criticism were joined, offering a vague but deeply felt alternative to liberal ideals. One result was Chamberlain's growing attachment to a vison of *Volksgemeinschaft*, a perfectly integrated community foreshadowed in a remote, mythical past. Another consequence—intensified by the bitter class and ethnic conflicts of Vienna—was an increasing preoccupation with race and anti-Semitism, which became the cohesive and unifying element of Chamberlain's ideological repudiation of liberalism.

But, if Chamberlain's fascination with race had already been awakened in Dresden, the web of historical and racial theory that he began to spin around his cultural stance was entirely new, and there is no trace of it in his comments before the early 1890s. Several scholars have emphasized Chamberlain's debts as a race thinker to Gobineau, whose celebrated *Essai* he began to study around 1893 at Cosima's suggestion. It is true that he learned much from Gobineau and several other French authors, including Edouard Drumont, Edouard Schuré, Hippolyte Taine, and Emile Faguet. But Chamberlain did not contemplate these writers—nor other German and English ones—in isolation: he read with a critical eye, comparing and measuring their insights continually against his daily experience of the "racial" conflicts of Austria. Moreover, since he identified more closely with Hohenzollern Prussia than the polyglot Hapsburg realm which seemed to him to be slipping down the slope toward imminent disaster, Chamberlain repeatedly drew parallels between the fate of Germans in the two states. Karl Kraus once called Vienna "the laboratory of the apocalypse;" for Chamberlain it was the scene of an ongoing racial experiment, an absorbing but destructive arena of physiological struggle, whose lessons its northern neighbors would do well to learn.

The details of Chamberlain's race theories are fully analyzed in a later chapter. His depiction of the emergence of modern European civilization was rich in resonances from contemporary Austria. Like Gobineau and most other racists, Chamberlain was fascinated by the demise of ancient Rome; its collapse under the assaults of the courageous Teutons formed a central element of his historical analysis. Centuries of miscegenation had sapped Rome's power, creating a mongrelized chaos of races incapable of true culture and unfit to carry forward the twin legacy of Graeco-Roman civilization and Christianity. While the northern Teutonic peoples struggled successfully against Roman decadence, constructing the vigorous nation states that had dominated subsequent history, the chaos retained the upper hand in southern Europe and the Hapsburg domains. For Chamberlain, the dynastic authority of the Hapsburgs was the historical successor to Rome, and he echoed Treitschke's belief that "Austrian Germanism" was "unspeakably corrupted by Semitism."[36] Witness, for example, the description of the anarchy of late Rome given in the *Foundations:*

> The annihilation of that monstrosity, a State without a nation, of that empty form, of that soulless congeries of humanity, that union of mongrels bound together only by a community of taxes and superstitions, not by a common origin and a common heartbeat, of that crime which we have summed up in the definition "Chaos of Peoples"— that does not mean the falling darkness of night but the salvation of a great inheritance from unworthy hands, the dawn of a new day. Yet even to this hour we have not succeeded in purging our blood of all the poisons of that chaos. In wide domains the chaos ended by retaining the upper hand. Wherever the Teuton has not a sufficient majority physically to dominate the rest of the inhabitants by assimilation, as for instance, in the south, there the chaotic element asserted itself more and more.[37]

The allusions to Austria in the passage are clear. In its language and images, in the piling of one descriptive phrase upon another at the outset of the statement, this passage seems modelled upon Pan-German polemics from the 1890s. At other times he referred more explicity to contemporary Vienna, as in the following casual aside:

> What the French call *un charme troublant*—superficial cleverness combined with a peculiar sort of beauty—is often characteristic of the half-caste; one can observe this daily at the present in cities like Vienna where people of all nations meet; but the peculiar unsteadiness, the small power of resistance, the want of character, in short the degeneracy of these people is equally marked. [38]

The most striking contrast, in Chamberlain's view, was Prussia—a state bound together by ties of blood, where the government and institutions fostered "organic evolution." At Königgrätz in 1866, he argued: "the invincible strength of a noble race triumphed over racelessness and the moral power of a true nation conquered an agglomeration of territory . . . patched together by mere dynastic interest and lacking all unity." Bismarck's Prussia demonstrated "in what simple ways it is possible not merely to theorize about race . . . but to breed and preserve it." [39] Even Chamberlain's exaggerated Prussophilia echoed the tones of Pan-German speeches and broadsheets.

But Vienna not only encouraged Chamberlain to ponder more systematically the qualities and mission of the Germanic race, it also shaped and accentuated his conviction that the Jew was its historical antithesis. To be sure, his antipathy for Jews was already well developed before he arrived in the city, but he had never before lived in a place with such a large and conspicuous Jewish population. The figures—119,000 in 1890 or 8.7% of the total population—tell only part of the story, for Vienna's Jews were if anything more conspicuous than they were numerous. Their rise had been spectacular and their prominence in finance, newspapers, politics, the arts, and the professions was immediately evident—and appalling—to Chamberlain. Anti-Semitism pervaded Viennese life and politics in the 1890s: one has only to read Schnitzler's *Professor Bernhardi* or his novel *Der Weg ins Freie* (*The Road into the Open*, 1907) to enter the morass of contemporary prejudice and the complicated responses of Jews. In an autobiographical jotting, Schnitzler reflected:

> It was not possible, especially not for a Jew in public life, to ignore the fact that he was a Jew; nobody else was going to do so, not the Gentiles and even less the Jews. You had the choice of being counted as insensitive, obtrusive and fresh; or of being oversensitive, shy and suffering from feelings of persecution. And even if you managed somehow to conduct yourself so that nothing showed, it was impossible to remain completely untouched; say, for instance, a person may not remain unconcerned whose skin has been anaesthetized but has to watch, with his eyes open, how it is scratched with an unclean knife, even cut until the blood flows.[40]

For Chamberlain the Jew was woven into the very texture of his image of Vienna. His earliest letters from the Blumelgasse record a growing obsession with their numbers and alleged power. When he heaped abuse upon Baring and Jewish financiers in a letter to Aunt Harriet, he could not resist a parting shot against "English sentimentalizing about the poor, persecuted Jews and speechifying about religious intolerance, just as if religion had anything to do with the matter." When in 1894 he visited a spa to cure his skin disorders and rheumatism, he complained: "Unfortunately, like everything else . . . it is fallen into the hands of Jews which includes two consequences: every individual is bled to the utmost and systematically, and there is neither order nor cleanliness."[41] In the following year, when contemplating a move to Munich—for financial reasons mainly—he ranted:

> However, we shall have to move soon anyway, for our house having been sold to a Jew . . . it will soon be impossible for decent people to live in it . . . Already the house being almost quite full of Jews, we have to live in a state of continual warfare with the vermin which is [sic] a constant and invariable follower of this chosen people even in the most well-to-do classes.[42]

Further quotations are unnecessary. Sometimes he

focused on "Jewishness" in the abstract—a synonym for "liberalism" and all the aspects of modernity he loathed—and sometimes his invective was more pointed, aimed at *Ostjuden* immigrants or the Jewish press or financiers. At times he even held out Jewry as an example of a people who grasped instinctively the sacred principle of race and the importance of safeguarding its purity. Over the space of five years in Vienna, Chamberlain's prejudice became more vicious in tone and he began to formulate a racist world view whose driving force was the dialectic of German and Jew. His racial hostility became ever more systematic and intellectualized.[43] Finally, more even than in Dresden, he learned in Vienna the political effectiveness of anti-Semitism in mobilizing the anger and frustration of Germans. This was clear from the demagogic campaigns of Lueger and Schoenerer; it was also borne out by his own limited experiences as a lecturer before audiences of students and Wagnerites.

Chamberlain's early years in Vienna mark the end of the first stage of his life: one of false starts in his efforts to find a suitable career, a peripatetic education, and a growing identification with the cultural mission of Bayreuth. It was also a period of preparation, even if unconsciously, for his vocation as a publicist. To those who met him in his late thirties, Chamberlain seemed cosmopolitan, charming, cultivated, and generous to friends like Appia. His erudition was impressive: from years of reading in Dresden and Vienna he had acquired an encyclopedic, if ill-assimilated, knowledge of many subjects and both in Bayreuth and among friends in Vienna he inspired hopes of great achievements to come. His family in England, on the other hand, regarded him with some puzzlement and found his enthusiasm for Bayreuth a mystery. On a lengthy visit to England in October 1893, he found his relatives inquisitive but almost impossible to talk to. Expressing his mingled amusement and frustration to Cosima, he wrote: "The kinds of hair-raising questions that are put to me, you could not conceive; it is impossible. Nobody doubts that you have chosen Bayreuth because it is a 'center of traffic;' a standing question is 'How much money do they make out of it'" Even Sir Neville Chamberlain, whom he had admired since childhood, referred to *Tannhäuser* as "the opera where there are a lot of girls at the beginning."[44]

Despite several failed attempts at journalism and playwriting—his thespian talents were rather meager although three of his plays were later published—Chamberlain was nonetheless convinced by 1892 that his future was a literary one.[45] Later he recalled in characteristically dramatic terms the moment that realization swept over him:

> In this my thirty-seventh year the writing demon [*Schreib-daemon*] seized my soul and gained power over me, so that I have never again been able to relinquish the pen. . . . On the morning of the nineteenth January 1892—I can still picture it as if it were yesterday—I was seized, as if from outside myself, by a spirit of resolution. The first command of this spirit was a mechanical one. I had never in my life written while standing up; now I picked up a small table and placed it upright on a small cupboard, which I then moved to a suitable place. Having built, in this way, an improvised standing-desk, I hastened to lock both doors so that nothing would disturb me at the magical work. I then approached this newly constructed desk, firmly resolved to write down everything that was going through my head—without questioning whether it was old or new, deep or shallow, well-expressed or trivial. Soon, the unexpected occurred: from the less good thoughts arose better ones, and from these better still. Before long—out of the writing and occasioned by it—brain-waves and ideas streamed forth on all sides, such as I had never before experienced. My vocation was revealed to me; or, more correctly, it had overpowered and taken possession of me.[46]

Dujardin had for some time urged him to write a book about Wagner for French readers. He began work on it and wrote several sections in the form of lectures. At first he was content to see himself as a mediator or interpreter of Wagnerism for those unable to understand the dramas in their original language. But soon he decided to switch to German, for the audience that he wanted most to impress was in Central Europe. Progress was very rapid: he wrote easily and had a complete command of his subject. A young Wagnerite friend,

Rudolf Louis—a Jew as it happened—whom Chamberlain described to Wolzogen as "perhaps the most specifically philosophical brain I have ever met," helped with stylistic revisions and the book appeared in July 1892.[47] *Das Drama Richard Wagners*, as it was called, was Chamberlain's first book. It was a fine, lucid analysis of the development of Wagner's dramatic ideas, and although it sold few copies it gave Chamberlain confidence to press on with other projects. Even before it appeared he was hard at work on other literary schemes and scarcely relaxed his taxing schedule over the next two decades. Reflecting often on how much time he had lost in finding his true vocation and fearing that his delicate health portended a short life, he acted like a man in a desperate hurry—eager to realize his own ambitions and to fulfill the high expectations of Wahnfried.

Part II

The Writer and His Public

As soon as I hold pen in hand I feel alive again and happy

—Chamberlain (1899)

The three pillars on which the structure of my spirit rests are: Science, Art, Religion

—Chamberlain (1919)

Englishmen may well be proud of a fellow countryman who is recognized in Germany as one of the most brilliant writers and profound thinkers of the day

—Lord Redesdale (January 1914)

Chapter Four

The Bayreuth Publicist

ALTHOUGH PROUD OF the Reich, its military might and technological progress, many Germans felt deep disquiet about the future and believed that their nation was suffering from moral decline. While similar self-criticism and cultural pessimism can be found elsewhere, in Germany (the "belated nation" in Hellmuth Plessner's words) attacks on modern "philistinism" and on the failure of the nation to generate shared values and goals were particularly widespread.[1] As early as 1878, Paul de Lagarde's *Deutsche Schriften* sounded the main themes of this critique. His bitter polemic against liberalism and secularization, his contempt for the bourgeois *ethos* of Bismarck's empire and call for a spiritual rebirth of the *Volk* had a growing appeal for educated Germans, especially in the 1890s. Later writers and intellectuals echoed Lagarde's strictures, while a myriad of cultural reform organizations were founded, pledged to protect Germans from the corrosive impact of modernity. Some advocated reforms of pedagogy and education, others saw a revival of religion as the only solution for a corrupt and individualistic age; many groups stressed the virtues of the small town against the city environment or articulated some form of agrarian romanticism; and still others venerated art as a means of revitalizing the nation.

The Wagner cult was one of these numerous movements for reform. Its faith in the redemptive power of art found echoes in several other organizations (the Arts and Crafts

Movement, for example, whose journal, *Der Kunstwart*, was edited by Ferdinand Avenarius), so did the social and political ideals expounded by Wagner in his rather turgid prose writings. But Bayreuth was a unique cultural experiment. It claimed that the Reich could be transformed from the stage outward through the artistic genius and philosophical doctrines of one man: the dramas were sacred works and Wagner an artist redeemer through whom coursed the true spirit of the *Volk*. No other movement for cultural reform carried self-inflation to such heights,* no other movement won so many ardent supporters or had a comparable impact on the myths and symbols of German nationalism.

From 1892 when the *Schreibdaemon* took possession of him, until 1896 when he began work on the *Foundations*, Chamberlain devoted his efforts to Bayreuth and the mission of cultural reform. His Wagnerian literary apprenticeship coincided with the dawning of a new era, as Bayreuth moved toward a wider popularization of its message.[2] The period of constructing the Wahnfried dogma was largely over; the shaky times following Wagner's death had been endured and the *Kreis* kept intact. In the 1890s the time was ripe for expansion; for intensifying the literary campaign and reaching out to embrace other *völkisch* groups professing related ideologies; for transforming the *Festspielhaus* from a great composer's mausoleum into a place of pilgrimage for all Germans who cherished the national mystique. In this process, it was Chamberlain who came to the fore: a stream of books, articles, and lectures flowed from his pen, reaching a far wider audience than Wolzogen's rather abstruse *Bayreuther Blätter* or Glasenapp's pedantic and specialized studies. Chamberlain, more

---

* Nietzsche returned continually to this theme, depicting Wagner as one who had transformed a desire for power into artistic creativity: "When the ruling idea of his [Wagner's] life—the idea that an incomparable amount of influence . . . could be exercised through the theater—seized hold of him, it threw his whole being into the most violent ferment. . . . this idea appeared at first . . . as an expression of his obscure personal will which longed insatiably for power and fame. Influence, incomparable influence—how? over whom?—that was from now on the question and quest that ceaselessly occupied his head and heart. He wanted to conquer and rule as no artist had done before, and if possible to attain with a single blow that tyrannical omnipotence for which his instincts obscurely craved." For Nietzsche Wagner was Napoleon as artist. Quoted from *Richard Wagner in Bayreuth* (1876) by R. J. Hollingdale, *Nietzsche, The Man and His Philosophy* (Baton Rouge, 1965) p. 129.

than anyone, fashioned the popular vision of Bayreuth and constructed the ideological bridge between Wagnerism and the mainstream of the Germanic ideology. His broad knowledge, easy, colorful style, and propagandist talents were remarkable.

To promote the festivals and publicize the Bayreuth Idea, Wahnfried supporters launched a multifaceted campaign to dominate contemporary writing on Wagner, collect prestigious and potentially helpful patrons, expand existing Wagnerite clubs, and safeguard Cosima's authority over the whole cult.

Convinced that while alive Wagner had been the victim of an insidious press campaign which "did all that fanaticism and malice could do to ruin Bayreuth," his supporters paid special attention to journalism. Chamberlain was among the most prolific, writing for a wide range of German, French, Dutch, and English periodicals as well as specialized musical reviews and mass circulation newspapers. His articles were carefully tailored to his readers—whether of such popular journals as Harden's *Zukunft*, the *Revue des Deux Mondes*, or Philadelphia's *Ladies Home Journal*, or the more explicitly political subscribers of the Pan-German *Ostdeutsche Rundschau* or the nationalist *Deutsche Zeitung*. The need for conscious restraint in his writing was sometimes wearisome. In 1896, after an especially active year, he conceded to Glasenapp that none of his more popular essays were completely frank expressions of his ideas "but rather a diplomatic or—better said—a tactical attempt through eloquence and conscious bias to pave the way to a better understanding and reception for the art and teachings of our Master." As for the publications themselves, he continued, "the *Börsencourier* and *Zukunft* are outspokenly Jewish papers; the *Redende Kunst* is gutter press [*Revolverblatt*], the Berlin *Deutsche Zeitung* is anti-Semitic of a Duehring stamp which says in its program that Wagner's art casts "a shadow" over Germany etc.—Nowhere can *I* find true expression." "Each of us," he concluded, "has his cross to carry; mine is perpetual self-renunciation, the suppression of what the inmost recesses of the heart feels."[3] The same kind of dissembling was to be found in his public lectures, where he carefully modulated his anti-Semitism to suit different audiences.

Propagating Wagnerism not only meant publication, it also involved gathering recruits and patrons for the cause. Wahnfried carefully cultivated relations with the nobility and ruling families of Germany. Among those in some way associated with Wagnerism were the Grand Dukes of Mecklenburg-Schwerin and Anhalt; the Grand Duchesses of Baden and Oldenburg; and prominent public figures like Price Philipp Eulenburg, Prince Ernst Hohenlohe-Langenburg; Prince William of Hesse-Darmstadt and Prince Max von Baden. The Wagner society of Berlin boasted the names of many of the capital's leading families, and though very few were close to the Wahnfried circle, their interest and concern for Bayreuth was of great significance to Cosima.

Wealthy industrialists were also courted for financial contributions, and here Chamberlain was able to use his influence with the Swiss millionaire Agénor Boissier, and later with his friend and patron August Ludowici, to obtain generous donations. Equally important were the efforts of Bayreuth to attract a widening circle of helpers from the ranks of German scholars, journalists, publishers, and intellectuals. The earliest generation of Bayreuth enthusiasts, especially the young Nietzsche and Heinrich von Stein, had been heavily criticized by academic colleagues for their *Wagner-Schwärmerei*; but despite such opposition Bayreuth remained eager for university recruits, who would lend to Wagnerism their academic prestige. By 1900 a considerable number of Wagner publicists held regular teaching posts—among them Wolfgang Golther, Max Koch, Leopold von Schroeder, Richard Sternfeld, and Henry Thode—while a great many other teachers and professors were regular participants in the meetings of the Wagner societies. When Chamberlain met someone who impressed him, he invariably tried to interest him in Bayreuth. Thus, he urged Wolzogen in 1893 to capture his young friend Rudolf Louis, a talented philosopher and aesthetician, for the "Zauberkreis"; he did the same later in the case of Hermann Keyserling. And when Wolfgang Golther obtained a professorship of philology at Rostock, Chamberlain viewed it a success for Wagnerism:

Yes that is the victory of Bayreuth—or rather the foundation of
the future victory of Bayreuth—that such men as you are becoming the recognized teachers of our *Volk* . . . We need now
men of the first rank in all areas, men whose scholarly abilities
can be denied by nobody. . . . pugnacious, subtle men: one position after another must be won.[4]

It was assumed that these apostles of Wagner would
champion the cause in their professional activities. For many
intellectuals, of course, Wagnerism was merely a passing fad,
something they threw off in time; others proved impervious to
Wahnfried's blandishments—even where their ideas paralleled
those of Wagnerism in many respects, as was the case with Lagarde. Despite the efforts of both the theologian Franz
Overbeck and Ludwig Schemann to attach this prophet of
Deutschtum to Wahnfried, he proved deaf to all invitations to
Bayreuth and requests for essays for the *Blätter*. But, if he
evaded them in life, Bayreuthians appropriated Lagarde's
spirit after death: he enjoyed a seat of special honor in the
Wagnerite pantheon.[5]

The main activities of the Wagner cult in the towns of
Central Europe revolved around the various branches of the
Wagner association. By 1891 there were more than a hundred
local groups with over 8,000 regular members, and their numbers expanded considerably during the next decade. In 1909, a
Richard Wagner-Verband deutscher Frauen was founded to
raise scholarship money for the festivals, though not until after
World War I was a specifically Wagnerian youth Bund established.[6] In between festivals these local societies sponsored
lectures and discussion evenings, encouraged local performances of the music dramas, and tried to relate Wagnerism as a
movement to the political, cultural, and social concerns of the
day. It was here that the main publicists of the cult, like
Chamberlain, came into direct contact with the wider public
who were inquisitive, enthusiastic, or mildly supportive of the
mission of Bayreuth.

In composition, influence within the cult, and even in
their aims there were marked differences and local variations
among these clubs. At one extreme there was the *Vienna*

Akademischer Wagner-Verein, a large body of over 900 members, by no means all of whom were convinced of the social and cultural prognoses that formed part of the Bayreuth Idea and were articulated regularly in the *Blätter*; at the other extreme was the small coterie of intellectuals who rallied to the club which Chamberlain and Dujardin founded in Paris (actuálly in 1884 this branch still had only 21 fully paid up members, 7 of whom were from Chamberlain's family!). The Berlin Wagner society was dominated by the rich and aristocratic families of the capital; the much smaller branches in provincial German towns had an entirely different class and occupational composition.[7] Some societies, like the *Neuer Verein* in Vienna, were highly political; others, like the *Akademischer Verein* in the same city, tried to preserve an unpolitical stance. Most members of the clubs, however, were staunch German nationalists, and many were openly anti-Semitic. Furthermore, a great many Wagnerites were active in a wide variety of other organizations, such as the *Alldeutscher Veband*, the *Bodenreform* movement, various veterans groups, religious societies, and political parties. Hence the branches of the Wagner Association formed meeting points for many elements of the *völkisch* movement, and as such helped foster a sense of their close ideological and sentimental ties.[8]

Given these differences among the various Wagner societies, one might ask whether it is justifiable to speak of Wagnerism as a distinct ideology or cultural outlook. The frequent letters of Prince Hohenlohe-Langenburg to Cosima Wagner, for example, reveal a conservative and racist mind very different in tone and style from Ludwig Schemann or the *völkisch* Pan-Germans in Vienna with whom Chamberlain spent so much time. Georg Meurer, who wrote for the extreme racist journal *Hammer*, bore little trace of intellectual similarity to that versatile student of Brentano, Baron Christian von Ehrenfels, who befriended Chamberlain. And yet all were, at least for a time, firm Wagnerians.[9] Even within the more select ranks of Bayreuth publicists there were differing shades of religious, racial, and political views. Thus, it is with some caution that we speak of a Bayreuth outlook, indicating the areas of accord and the points of disagreement within the Wahnfried circle.

Through Chamberlain's writings, however, the main contours of "The Bayreuth Idea" are discernible. Until 1896 he was the willing instrument of Cosima's wishes, conferring with her over his essays and books, and championing her authority over the cult. He placed before the Central European public what the *Manchester Guardian* once called "the official and authorized pronouncement of the inmost circle of Wagner's friends and relatives."[10] As his views developed, differences were to arise which cooled somewhat his relations to Wahnfried, but eventually it was Bayreuth that largely conformed to Chamberlain's viewpoint rather than the other way round. Meantime, before 1896 he showed himself the "perfect Wagnerite," explaining Wagner's music and ideas, defending the actions of Wahnfried, and entering the lists against all critics of the cult: his activities provide an excellent picture of a Bayreuth publicist.

No visitor to the Bayreuth *Festspiele* could escape the deeply religious atmosphere encouraged by Cosima and her closest supporters. The *völkisch* professor W. H. Riehl accurately perceived the way the exaltation of culture led, in some degree, to the substitution of art for religion and the deification of Wagner. "The inmost, hard core of Wagner's party," he wrote, "is more than a party, it is simultaneously a congregation which believes in its Messiah and listens to his revelations with the devotedness of believers. The veneration for his person and work grows to a cult, his books are seen as a confessional writings, the outward symbols of the new, aesthetic faith."[11] Believing themselves the vanguard of a cultural and spiritual crusade, the Wahnfried circle exhibited in their writings and correspondences a degree of self-

Haus Wahnfried 1876

Bayreuth Festspielhaus, 1900

righteousness, dogmatism, and emotionalism difficult for the historian to recapture. Letters between members of the inner "charmed circle" [*Zauberkreis*], as Chamberlain once called it, overflowed with dedication, camaraderie, and a distinct note of paranoia about the rest of society. Wagner and his widow were regarded as semi-divine, while the leaders of the cult fantasied themselves as Grail knights, guardians of the sacred cup; their prose was laden with the words "duty" and "selflessness"; their actions and interrelationships at moments evinced an unhealthy quality of masochism and self-abasement. Chamberlain once confessed to Siegfried Wagner: "If it benefited Bayreuth, I would without hesitation let myself be roasted over a slow fire." [12]

The core of the Bayreuth gospel was an intense personality cult of Wagner. The Master of Bayreuth had helped initiate this mythopoeia himself in his carefully written autobiography, *Mein Leben*. Though it remained unpublished until 1911 (by which time, of course, many of his enemies were dead and unable to question its contents) Wagner's "confession" provided well-drawn guidelines for his widow and her close supporters. In the decades after the Master's death, the Wahnfried circle exercised a vigilant watch over relevant new publications and collected and edited his letters—deleting, obfuscating, and distorting those episodes of his career which failed to conform with the vision of an ideal artist-redeemer they wished to create. Wagner emerged as a secularized saint, misunderstood and maligned by contemporaries. He was the incarnation of "selflessness" and "purely human" values, "a brave and noble knight" fearlessly striving for mankind's ennoblement. He was the aesthetic genius of whom Schiller dreamed; the culmination of German musical and poetic traditions; a tone poet whose intuitive *Anschauung* seized upon the deep religious and moral strivings of the *Volk* and gave them mythic and symbolic expression in his dramas.

The writings of Chamberlain are excellent exemplars of Bayreuth hagiography, especially his handsomely illustrated *Richard Wagner*, which was published by Bruckmann in 1895. When he first received Bruckmann's request for such a book, Chamberlain had dutifully sought Cosima's advice on whether he should accept. In fact, it had been Cosima who had secretly arranged the whole thing and her choice of Chamberlain, rather than Henry Thode or one of the other literary Wagnerites, was a special mark of esteem.[13] Cosima was eager that a colorful, well-written account of Wagner's life and the "Bayreuth Idea" should appear; Glasenapp's monumental life was far too long and factual to obtain any popular readership, and now the expanding cult needed a new synthesis. Wolzogen, Glasenapp, and Heinrich von Stein were Chamberlain's main sources, and his goal, as he explained to Aunt Harriet, was to grasp intuitively the "individuality" of Wagner, to strip away the accidental and outer layers of detail and depict the "inward and spiritual man."[14] In consequence, Chamberlain treated the details of Wagner's life only briefly and sometimes very elusively; more attention was given to the composer's position within the broad tradition of Teutonic art, although here too Chamberlain's approach resulted in a very static and nonevolutionary interpretation—an ahistorical view of Wagner characteristic of the Bayreuth circle.

Chamberlain nevertheless took great care over the brief biographical sketch in the book—and not merely out of deference to Wahnfried. A part of the cult's "idealization" of Wagner was to protect his memory from the taint of criticism. For Bayreuth art was a moral force, elevating and ennobling the audience—it could scarcely issue from anything but a faultless, unblemished personal life. If the good life did not always produce great art, at least great art had to be inspired by a noble personality.

The defender's task was not easy, for Wagner had been a man of large appetites and little restraint. He had lived the romantic artist's life; he had spurned conventions, acting out the dreams and repressed desires of the bourgeois in a genteel, inhibited, and eminently civilized age. Others obeyed the rules, or pretended to do so; but Wagner had lived high on unpaid debts, mixed with royalty, taken part in a revolution, and lived openly with another man's wife—all the while he was creating some of the greatest music of the century. His ego-worship was inordinate and notorious; his victims were many. Yet, while contemporaries found his behavior shameless and outrageous, they could not help being fascinated by it, nor could they resist the subconscious appeal of his art.

Neither Chamberlain nor Wahnfried, of course, acknowledged any of this. Wagner's life had to be interpreted and explained in the light of his old age, when conservatism, morality, and religion were the watchwords of Bayreuth. There were a number of delicate aspects of Wagner's career which a biographer had to address. One was the question of paternity, a problem which had troubled the composer and which was raised by a number of his critics. Was Wagner's father the police actuary Friedrich Wagner or his actor friend Ludwig Geyer? In his first postscript to *The Wagner Case*, Nietzsche had claimed that his father was Geyer, a fact Wagner had concealed, because it was very likely that Geyer was a Jew. Chamberlain preferred to avoid the issue and merely alluded that Geyer "was in every respect worthy of the warm friendship Friedrich Wagner had felt for him." In a letter to his English translator he was more straightforward, asserting that Wagner's mother had been "a delightful, modest, pure woman, bred up in a pious family"—not for a moment, he added, could he believe "she could have behaved like a mere strumpet."[15]

More complicated were the Master's own marital entanglements, and here Chamberlain needed all his skill to thread the difficult path of Bayreuth orthodoxy. Wagner's abandonment of his first wife, Minna, his adulterous relationship with Mathilde Wesendonck, and his fathering of children with Cosima Bülow before she was separated from her husband, let alone divorced, was all public knowledge. Chamberlain's strategy was simple: he praised Minna as a limited but well-meaning woman, ignored Mathilde almost completely (to her intense annoyance), and implied—by careful juxtaposition of sentences rather than by direct statement—that Wagner had turned to Cosima only after the death of his first wife in 1866. Cosima's role in the estrangement of Wagner and King Ludwig was omitted, and no mention was made of Hans von Bülow. A vague reference to narrow bourgeois moralism was included, followed quickly by the assertion that Cosima had by her actions obeyed a "higher duty," a "holy duty," and the commandment of "a higher power."[16]

There were other irksome criticisms hurled at Wagner: his large debts and penchant for luxury were frequently spoken of, so too was his alleged exploitation of the emotions of his young, unbalanced patron, King Ludwig. Nor had the volume of accusations decreased to any extent since Wagner's death. Chamberlain's explanation—and that of Bayreuth—for this continuous scandal-mongering was that a press conspiracy existed whose goal was to destroy Bayreuth and defame Wagner. The Bayreuth circle was convinced that, at every step of Wagner's career, Jews had tried to block his path. The composer Meyerbeer for example, was alleged to have done his best to see that Wagner's works were not performed. This claim, made by Glasenapp and reiterated by Chamberlain and other supporters of the cult, prompted considerable controversy in musical journals.[17] More damaging than the individual malice of Meyerbeer, was, in Chamberlain's words, "the poisonous daily bilge dished out by the Jewish press" which Germans uncritically consumed. "I can think of no greater spiritual poison, which enhances more the progressive 'materializing' ['Judaizing'] of German families, than the majority of today's popular newspapers." Wagner's famous enemy, Eduard Hanslick, the critic for the *Neue Freie Presse* of Vienna, was viewed as the commanding general of a press campaign which continually injured Bayreuth "by alternately pouring ridicule upon it, then smothering it in silence."[18]

If the scandals of Wagner's private life could be attributed to the fabrications of a hostile press, his public actions and his politics were not so easily explained. Wagner had participated actively in the Dresden revolution of May 1849 and as a result spent almost fifteen years in exile. Whereas modern Wagner scholars have distinguished at least two distinct periods of his life—a liberal one coinciding with the era of democratic nationalism in Europe in the 1840s, and a later reactionary period—the Bayreuth "orthodoxy" insisted that he had been consistent throughout. Those, like Hugo Dinger, who denied this were rapidly expelled from the cult. The political and social vision of Bayreuth was that of Wagner's final years, and the idea that he had once been a republican, hand in hand with Bakunin and the revolutionaries, was intolerable. Echo-

ing Wagner's tone of injured innocence in *Mein Leben*, Bayreuth publicists rejected all evidence of his complicity: he was
a revolutionary of the spirit, not a political insurgent.[19]

It was in the interpretation of Wagner's politics that
Chamberlain, active in the highly politicized Wagnerite circles
of Vienna, went far beyond earlier writers like Glasenapp. His
writings were timely because they coincided with the wider
popularization of the cult and efforts to relate its mission to
other *völkisch* groups. Indeed, when Chamberlain first lectured
on the subject before the Wagner society of Graz, the local
police feared demonstrations and demanded that they be able
to check the contents of the speech in advance.[20] The main
task Chamberlain set himself was to disassociate Wagner from
the taint of republicanism, communism, and political demagoguery without condemning outright the popular nationalist
movement of 1848. Though Wagner was a fervent German nationalist who had advocated unification of the German states
long before that became a political reality, Chamberlain
claimed he had never been in the vanguard of the revolution.
His actions had been those of an artist visionary, an unpolitical man, rather than a political agitator like his friend,
August Roeckel.

Wagner, wrote Chamberlain, was stirred by an awareness
of the materialism and mammonism of the age; he saw "that
society was standing on the verge of a mighty crisis, and that
effective and thoroughgoing aid must be sought, not in politics
but in regeneration." There were two pieces of evidence for
Wagner's complicity in the revolution: a speech he addressed
to the *Vaterlandsverein* of Dresden in June 1848 and police
claims that he had mounted the barricades in the insurrection
of May 1849. Chamberlain dismissed the flimsy evidence of active intervention in the May uprising and turned to the *Vaterlandsverein* speech, in which Wagner had urged the Saxon
king to be "the first and truest of all republicans" and called
for sweeping social reforms. Chamberlain completely rein-
terpreted the speech, insisting that Wagner had valiantly
remained outside party politics, and had sought to galvanize
king and people behind the moral and religious goal of cultural
rebirth. The only way forward, in Wagner eyes, had not been

via constitutionalism and parliamentary majorities, but by an alliance of "absolute monarchy" and "free Volk"—for, Chamberlain argued, only when monarchy was absolute and unchecked in its power by democratic assemblies could a people enjoy true "inner freedom." Democracy, for Wagner, was a "foreign un-German" idea, impeding spiritual transfiguration. At Chamberlain's hands Wagner's proposals, including his call for the acquisition of overseas colonies and a measure of popular participation in politics and social reforms, were refashioned into a *völkisch* German creed with close affinities to the Pan-German nationalism of the Second Reich. "This one man," he concluded, "has done more to spread the German language, German feeling and thought, throughout the whole world than all the statesmen, generals, and politicians of the century put together."[21]

Cosima was delighted with Chamberlain's rescue of the early Wagner's political reputation, especially since in 1892, the year before the Graz lecture, two books had appeared which presented a very different interpretation of the Dresden uprising. One of these was by Hugo Dinger, whom Chamberlain attacked in his lectures for claiming that Wagner had been a communist revolutionary associated with Bakunin. The other author was Ferdinand Praeger, a piano teacher who met the Master in London in 1855 and subsequently became a friend and correspondent. Before he died in 1891, Praeger had written a book of recollections about Wagner, entitled *Wagner as I Knew Him*, which Lord Dysart, a leading figure of the London Wagner Society, had published in English and German in the following year.[22]

The Praeger affair, in which Chamberlain was the foremost champion of Cosima and the chief spokesman for Wahnfried, shows the fanatical zeal with which the Bayreuthians defended their orthodoxy. Praeger's book dealt mostly with the early career of the composer, contravening all the most sensitive aspects of the Bayreuth "gospel." To the delight of Hanslick and other critics of Wagner, the work deplored Wagner's sybaritism and his vehement anti-Semitism, claimed that he had deliberately concealed the degree of his political involvement in 1849 and, most unforgivable of all, implied that the

Master had badly mistreated his first wife, Minna. Such a book, which soon gained widespread publicity, was guaranteed a vituperative response from Bayreuth.

The campaign against Praeger began during the *Festspiele* of 1892, led by Chamberlain and William Ashton Ellis, an Englishman who later translated all Wagner's prose works. Ellis, the editor of *Meister*, the journal of the London Wagner Society, was already at odds with Lord Dysart. On comparing the English and German versions of Praeger's book, Chamberlain and Ellis found several discrepancies between the two. Also, many points in the book seemed suspicious: some of Wagner's letters quoted by Praeger did not resemble the Master's style of writing, while in several cases the chronology appeared fallacious. Finally, given the fact that Wagner and Praeger were never really close friends, it seemed questionable that he could have been privy to some of the information now published.

All these objections to the book were woven together by Chamberlain into a devastating critique for the *Bayreuther Blätter*. This was sufficient to discredit it among most Wagnerites, but Wahnfried was still troubled by its success with the general reading public.[23] For this reason Chamberlain decided to follow up his critique toward the end of 1893, when he made one of his rare visits to England. Using well-placed family connections he managed to gain entry to Lord Dysart's private archive, where the original Praeger letters were housed. Ashton Ellis had been refused permission in the previous year, but Chamberlain took advantage of Dysart's absence abroad to prevail upon his employees. Implying that he wanted the letters for his own private information, not for any specific purpose of publication, Chamberlain scrutinized and transcribed 20 out of the 34 letters cited in the Praeger book; the rest were missing. Returning to Vienna he wrote another blistering attack for the *Blätter* reproducing the original letters and exposing Praeger's distortions.[24]

Chamberlain's first article, which he had proudly sent to Cosima as a Christmas present, had aroused widespread attention. "Bismarck's paper, the *Hamburger Nachrichten*," he told Aunt Harriet, "had a long 'feuilleton' on it last week (five

columns) in which the critic says 'Ch's Kritik ist an sich eine
geradezu klassische Leistung' "[25] The second essay produced an
immediate response from the publishers of the German edition, who announced publicly their thanks to Chamberlain for
having revealed the defects of the book, and at once withdrew
it from publication.[26] Chamberlain was overjoyed at his success. In England, however, the book had not been withdrawn
and Ashton Ellis set about chronicling every error and misrepresentation in its pages, causing Dysart further discomfort,
and occupying column after column in the *Musical Standard*
for months on end. Dysart resigned from the London society
which gradually dissolved under the strain of these internal divisions. The debate grew increasingly bitter, as Praeger's
widow claimed that Bayreuth was out to destroy her husband's
memory because he had favored Minna over Cosima; Dysart,
who had suffered considerable monetary loss as well as public
embarrassment, began to fight back, threatening suit against
Chamberlain, and then issuing warnings of a different kind.
He announced he would publicly disclose the whole affair, and
the manner in which Chamberlain had obtained his evidence,
and also spoke of publishing certain other letters "recently discovered, also possibly letters of what I understand are of a very
offensive nature, which I think certain persons whose names I
do not care at present to mention, will not care to see the
light." He was almost certainly referring to correspondence
concerning Wagner's first marriage, which Cosima would not
want to be placed before the public.[27]

By this time the affair was becoming a burden for Chamberlain and Bayreuth. Praeger had been discredited and
further prolongation of the dispute could only sully the name
of Wagner. Dysart continued to insist that Chamberlain had
made inaccurate copies of the letters and that "every single
word in the book from beginning to end is absolutely true."
Bayreuth answered by reproducing Chamberlain's two articles
in book form with a separate introduction by Wolzogen. It was
a victory for Wahnfried, but Praeger's assertions contained too
much truth to be easily forgotten. Even as late as 1908 Chamberlain still found it necessary to publish a second edition of
his critique, with the explanation that "There are still people

who repeat Hanslick's old lie that Praeger's book was bought up by me, and talk of Praeger as an impartial and trustworthy witness."[28]

It is unclear why Praeger should have written so flawed a book. It did contain serious errors of fact and chronology, some of them, admittedly, arising out of problems of translation. Ernest Newman was puzzled by the whole affair and wondered whether "the author of it is not to be regarded as a diseased rather than a criminal type." Yet this distorted account of an unbalanced man who wanted to write himself into history was in many respects closer to the truth than the Wahnfried mythology—and this is what made it so dangerous. The explanation eventually adopted by Chamberlain and the Bayreuth circle for Praeger's actions was characteristic of their conspiratorial outlook: Praeger was a Jew, trying to get revenge for Wagner's outspoken anti-Semitism. Though Wolzogen preferred to play down the "Jewish" aspects of the affair at the beginning, anti-Semitism had become the central issue by 1894. Chamberlain warned of Praeger's book: "It does not stand alone, but is a symptom; the disposition of mind from which this symptom springs is everywhere around us, waiting only for a favorable opportunity to besmirch the honor of the German Master in the future as it has done in the past."[29]

The Praeger controversy indicates the lengths to which Bayreuth zealots were prepared to go in their defense of Wahnfried's Wagner, a national hero untainted by personal vice or political perfidy. Especially interesting is the alacrity with which Wagnerite journalists joined the fray on Chamberlain's side. Theodor Antropp was active at the Pan-German *Ostdeutsche Rundschau*, so was the fanatical Dresden Wagnerite August Püringer; Oskar Bie supported Chamberlain in the *Allgemeine Musikzeitung*; the radical anti-Semitic *Deutsche Wacht* and the *Deutsche Zeitung* publicized the dispute, while Chamberlain's friend, Theodor de Wyzewa, backed Wahnfried in the *Revue des Deux Mondes*.[30] They did not rest until the book was removed from print. In addition, the affair made Cosima more aware than ever of the enormous talents of Chamberlain as a publicist. By 1895 he had become the foremost popularizer of the cult.

Another task of Bayreuth publicists was to demonstrate the importance of the *Festspiele* for German national culture and also to interpret the dramas in accord with Wagnerian "orthodoxy." The problems facing Cosima in 1883 were enormous: the festival was deep in debt and few music lovers were prepared to make the long and relatively expensive pilgrimage to this remote Franconian town. Even those who considered themselves Wagnerites, Chamberlain once reflected sadly, occasionally voiced the opinion that the whole festival should be moved to Munich or some other accessible large urban center. In addition to Bayreuth's geographical inconvenience, there was the rivalry of well-funded state operatic companies (like the one in Munich under the leadership of Ernst von Possart) which were capable of excellent performances. By skillful negotiations with the Bavarian government Wahnfried was able to keep exclusive control of *Parsifal*, but the other dramas were frequently staged before large and enthusiastic audiences. Finally, it was argued by many critics that the *Festspielhaus* had been established for the *Ring* and *Parsifal*, and that Wagner's earlier works were quite different and were designed for all opera houses, not merely Bayreuth.[31]

If Bayreuth were to survive, it had to counter each of these objections. Thus, it was emphasized in all Wahnfried-inspired literature that the *Festspielhaus* was a "sacred place," a shrine of Germanism. Its performances were not merely "model" productions which could be imitated elsewhere; they were intrinsically different, offering "a living symbol of German idealism," "an ideal world within the real one." Remote from densely populated and industrial areas, the festival transported the audience into a world which was the negation of modern materialist and cosmopolitan civilization. In large cities art acted as a mere diversion from worldly cares; in Bayreuth it aimed to be an inspiration for life. Those attending were drawn into the drama as in a religious celebration, "a communal rite to remove the votary from the pressures of space and time, from the pain and corruption of modern life."[32] "These works," wrote Chamberlain, "are a moral power in our century; in them a hidden power 'of German being' comes forth from the light; they lead us away from the frivolity of the modern theater and with holy fervor transport us into the depths of our own being."[33]

Völkisch art required not only a rustic, *völkisch* setting but also a popular German audience. With this in mind Wagner had hoped to support his national theater by patronage and public subscription, allowing free places to be awarded to the deserving, and freeing the festival from ordinary social and commercial conditions of theatrical enterprise. The attempt to raise sufficient subscriptions failed, but the ideal remained important to Wahnfried. Chamberlain was especially active in trying to raise money for "free place" scholarships—although no Wagnerite could fail to perceive the growing embourgeoisement of the festival, which by 1900 was a social occasion, dominated by the famous and wealthy. Through the symbolism of the drama, it was argued, the *Mythos*, or eternal Germanic truth, was carried to the people. As Chamberlain's close friend Leopold von Schroeder wrote in a book which gave Wahnfried great pleasure: "For the first time since the dispersion of the Aryan peoples, they can, once more, congregate at a predetermined place . . . to witness their primeval mysteries." "Bayreuth," he added, "has become through Wagner the ideal center of the Aryan peoples and Germany and the Germans have thereby been assured immeasurable pre-eminence as the appointed guardians of this consecrated place where the wonder of the Grail is revealed."[34] Schroeder's prose was more torrid than most, but all Bayreuth publicists shrouded the cultic rites in an air of mystery. The "Bayreuth Idea," Chamberlain insisted, defied verbal description or logical analysis; to be understood it had to be absorbed, ingested, at first hand.

But what of the claim that only Wagner's last dramas were suited to the Bayreuth stage? Clearly, if the festival were to succeed it had to include in its repertoire all the Master's works—not just the *Ring* and *Parsifal*. Thus, a major part of Chamberlain's activity as a publicist was devoted to showing that all Wagner's dramas and writings were perfectly compatible parts of a single unified vision of art and life—that his artistic development from the earliest work, *Die Feen*, until the last, *Parsifal*, was a series of closely linked stages in the evolution of the Word-Tone-Drama, "a new, more perfect form of drama, fully answering to the requirements of the Germans."[35] Both Chamberlain's first book, *Das Drama Richard Wagners* (1892), and his larger biographical study three years later were of major importance in presenting concisely and eloquently the Wahnfried contention that all the dramas belonged to Bayreuth, and that only there could they be seen and heard as originally intended.

It was not easy to fit all Wagner's artworks and writings into one consistent theory. The Master had toyed with several philosophical and aesthetic theories, and though his goal was always cultural regeneration, his hope of realizing it shifted from politics to art, and finally to religion. At one moment he professed himself a follower of Feuerbach, and at another a firm adherent of Schopenhauer. Such earlier writings as *The Artwork of the Future* (1849) and *Opera and Drama* (1851) called for a reunification of the separate art forms into a new equal synthesis—the re-creation on a higher plane of the Greek tragedy, where dramatization of myth had taken the form of a communal religious celebration of life. Each art, he reasoned, could only reach its fulfillment in union with the others. Not long after, under the powerful influence of Schopenhauer's aesthetics, Wagner underwent a change of heart, tacitly accepting music as the supreme art which alone could explore the depths out of which emotions arose, communicating otherwise inexpressible feelings, and merging the individual soul with the underlying force of the universe. But though he changed his ideas about the relationship of the arts, Wagner never admitted it; he never repudiated his earlier theories. Uneasy about his own contradictions, he tried in later essays like *Beethoven* (1870) and *The Destiny of the Opera* (1871) to make his theories compatible, but succeeded only in further muddying the waters for his subsequent interpreters.[36]

If Wagner believed in the unity of his artistic theory and practice, Bayreuthians could scarcely contradict him. The dilemma was simple: either Wagner had not clearly understood the theories of those like Schopenhauer whom he professed to follow, or his dramas derived from more than one aesthetic conception—in which case it was arguable that not all of them were intended for or suited to Bayreuth. In the face of these difficulties, Chamberlain's explanations were understandably confused and vague. He relied largely on the early essay *Opera and Drama*, and viewed Wagner as a Word-Tone-Poet who had created an organic relationship between words and music, combining the advances made by Shakespeare in poetic drama with those made by Beethoven in musical expression to forge a new synthesis. Wagner's own inconsistencies, not surprisingly, reappeared in Chamberlain's exegesis. He shifted ground constantly, at times arguing that music was the only art form which could evoke the timeless, spaceless realm of religion or arouse the most profound feelings of the *Volk*, and on other occasions flatly insisting that no one art was preeminent. The same kind of prevarication prevailed in Chamberlain's discussion of Wagner's debts to philosophers. Thus, in *Richard Wagner* he both acknowledged that the Master had built upon the rock of Schopenhauer's philosophy and declared that Schopenhauerian pessimism was completely incompatible with the Wagnerian doctrine of aesthetic redemption! But, if his arguments were tortuous, Chamberlain's conclusion was firm: all Wagner's works grew out of the same aesthetic vision, and represented the culmination of "Germanic" poetry and music.[37]

It was not enough for Chamberlain and other Wahnfried supporters to contend that the festivals were intrinsically different from all other operatic performances, they had also to support their claim in extensive reviews of the performances themselves. In this respect, too, Chamberlain was active, providing newspapers and journals with descriptions and analyses of the *Festspiele*. Cosima's task had been a difficult one: in 1883, as Chamberlain recalled, every performance was like a requiem, and it was not until 1886 that the festival again came under a single strong hand. Beginning in 1886, Cosima sought to demonstrate that Bayreuth was a necessity for all Wagner's works and began expanding the repertoire, starting with imitations of Wagner's Munich productions of *Die Meistersinger* and *Tristan und Isolde*. Her first major challenge came in 1891, with the decision to stage *Tannhäuser*, a costly and difficult drama which the Master had never staged satisfactorily himself and which had been produced by every major opera company in Germany. As Wagner's best-known work it was the supreme test for Bayreuth's contention that the festivals were essential for all the dramas. Cosima admitted to George Davidsohn, the sympathetic editor of the *Berliner Börsen-kurier*: "I knew we had set ourselves the Bayreuth task *par excellence*." [38]

Cosima's *Tannhäuser* was a great success, although it also aroused considerble criticism. Chamberlain was in the forefront of her public defenders, declaring in later years that this festival was a turning point separating the real Bayreuthians from the general mass of Wagner enthusiasts. "This year," he wrote in the *Bayreuther Blätter*, "Bayreuth has brought us a drama which we have hitherto not had. . . . this drama has revealed to many of us what Bayreuth is, what Bayreuth aims for, and what Bayreuth can achieve." In a published letter to a French music critic, Paul Flat, who had doubted that Wagner would have attempted to dramatize *Tannhäuser* in this way, Chamberlain explained that only lack of money had prevented the Master from executing such a plan in 1880. Now, for the first time since 1845, it had been properly performed. "The fate of Bayreuth," Chamberlain assured Flat, "lies in the hand of one person, and this hand carries out what the Master had wished." Equally lavish was Chamberlain's praise when, three years later, Cosima consolidated her achievement with a new version of *Lohengrin*. In an early essay in *Revue Wagnérienne* Chamberlain had dismissed this particular work as that "of a moment of feebleness, of discouragement, of doubt." Now it had been transformed by the Bayreuth style into a masterpiece. [39]

By 1896 the Bayreuth tradition was established. Chamberlain had played a major role in the expansion of the cult, and was closer to Wahnfried than perhaps any of the other leading Wagnerites with the exception of Wolzogen. In the weeks of the festival he was in his element, attending banquets for the artists, receptions at Wahnfried, strategy meetings with delegates from the Wagner societies, and enjoying reunions with friends and acquaintances from all over Europe. Romain Rolland, who attended the *Festspiele* that year, recalled: "I got myself introduced to H. S. Chamberlain. Very tall, blond, lean, still young, about 35 years in appearance, moustache and blond beard. . . . the air of a professor at the Ecole de Chartes, not yet tired and very enthusiastic about his work." [40] (It was actually the last year Chamberlain would devote exclusively to his work as a Bayreuth publicist, for he soon became too burdened by the *Foundations* and other books to give as much time and energy to the cause.)

It was not surprising that Cosima asked him to write the official history of the first two decades of Bayreuth. Chamberlain was honored by the request, but felt a little disturbed (he admitted to Wolzogen) when she dispatched quite a detailed "skeleton sketch" outlining exactly what was required in the essay. The finished essay completely satisfied the High Priestess, capturing precisely the mood she desired: it carefully recalled the years of hardship and heroic struggle; the empty rows of seats in 1884; the selfless devotion of the few, and the growing triumph under Cosima's leadership. Ending with a clarion call to the faithful to redouble their efforts, Chamberlain prophesied a broader task ahead, that of inspiring the whole German nation with the ideals of Bayreuth. [41]

Apart from his history of the festivals, Chamberlain also crowned his efforts in 1896 wth a spate of reviews and articles on Cosima's new version of the *Ring* cycle, staged for the first time in twenty years. These reviews were typical examples of Bayreuth propaganda. The major theme was the success of the "Bayreuth style" inaugurated by Cosima. In 1892 one of Wagner's chief ambitions had been realized with the establishment, under the direction of Julius Kniese, of a Bayreuth music school which would train artists specifically for Wagnerian roles. Chamberlain had been very active in trying to raise money for the school, and he saw the *Ring* festival as a vindication of all these efforts. In the first, third, and fifth cycles of the *Ring* the roles of Siegfried and Brünnhilde were played by internationally famous operatic stars, Wilhelm Grüning and Lilli Lehmann. In other performances, Alois Burgstaller, a graduate of the Bayreuth school, and Ellen Gulbranson, another unknown prodigy of Cosima's, undertook the parts. For Chamberlain the result was "an incontestable victory of the Bayreuth school" and "one of the most important stages on the path towards discovering a new German style for the new German drama." He was especially bitter in his criticism of Lilli Lehmann, both because she was a Jew and because Cosima had developed an intense dislike for the singer. "The cooperation of this operatic prima donna," wrote Chamberlain, "was the one painfully disturbing thing in an otherwise unforgettably harmonious overall impression. . . . the one really dark shadow."[42] Lehmann, who had been one of Wagner's original Rhine maidens, commented angrily: "Many roads lead to Rome, but to the Bayreuth of today only one, that of slavish subjection." "The *Ring*," she added, "was here quite dislocated in the very place that was its home."[43] With its carefully prearranged gestures and movements in strict subservience to dramatic form, Cosima's new style eliminated all spontaneity and improvisation by individual artists: it reproduced on stage the same kind of subordination and subservience to the Bayreuth dogma as existed in other aspects of the cult.

In his presentation of Wagner's ideas and his analysis of how they should be carried out, Chamberlain was the loyal disciple of Cosima. But in one area, that of lighting and scenic design, he opposed her conservatism and tried to convince her to adopt the radical new theories of Adolphe Appia. The more Cosima became acquainted with Appia's proposals, however, the less she liked them. Though conceding that thanks to electric power more could be done with lighting than in Wagner's day, she flatly objected to Appia's spatial arrangements, his simplified costumes, and his use of shadow and movement.[44] Bowing to Cosima's preferences in public at least, Chamberlain was content to use conventional illustrations and sketches in his *Richard Wagner*; in his journalism too he remained the complete disciple: "the exact knowledge which [Cosima] has of every part of the tone poem, of every note, of every particular in the costumes and of every gesture and movement in the acting, is simply incomprehensible. She watches over everything herself."

"That Frau Wagner came to believe that she had a kind of divine mission," the conductor Felix Weingartner reflected many years later, "was less tragic than that nobody had the

courage to point out to this woman . . . that even a highly
gifted person undertaking a new and unaccustomed task
makes pardonable, comprehensible, and natural mistakes."[45]

While Chamberlain looked back happily over the first
twenty years of the festival, Weingartner surveyed them
critically. In a spirited attack in 1896 he ridiculed the dogmatism of Wahnfried, the servility of Cosima's supporters, and
the fanaticism directed to all who could not accept the Wagnerian "commandments."[46] But to say that a man like Chamberlain was subservient to Cosima, while true, gives only a
part of the picture. For, as their correspondence shows, his was
a loyalty and a willing subordination of self, rooted in deep
friendship and reverence. He embraced the views of Wahnfried
so completely that they became—for a time at least—his own,
and he was extremely indignant when critics claimed that his
books were nothing more than summaries of Cosima's ideas. For
Chamberlain the theatrical ritual of Bayreuth was a key to
understanding the world in which he lived and a national religion which could transform it. "What constitutes the cultural
significance of Bayreuth," he reflected in 1919, "is the fact that
here a 'pinnacle of humanity' [*Gipfel der Menschheit*] lived
among us and created and gave immortal form to his thoughts;
in this way the teaching, which otherwise exists everywhere as
mere theory, becomes an experienced doctrine; for in the
Festspiele . . . an example is raised up corporeally before our
eyes."[47] The teaching was that of *völkisch* nationalism and
Germanic Christianity. It is to an analysis of the "Bayreuth
Idea," to use an expression coined by Nietzsche and then appropriated by Chamberlain, that we now turn.

At the heart of the Bayreuth world-view lay the concept of
spiritual regeneration. In an important article in the *Bayreuther Blätter* in 1895, and also in his biography of Wagner,

Chamberlain carefully explained the meaning of this central doctrine. It consisted of three main assumptions: first, that the original state of man was free and harmonious, without any contradiction between the needs of the individual and those of the community as a whole; second, that humanity had been deflected somehow from its natural course of development, leading to the degenerate state of contemporary society; and finally, that only by returning to its "purely-human," pristine state could mankind rediscover its true path. "Regeneration," Chamberlain was careful to point out, was an inner, spiritual process of rebirth, quite different in meaning from the political terms "revolution" and "reformation." Revolution, as preached by the socialists, merely substituted one political order for another without altering the basic condition of humanity; "reformation" was its conservative counterpart: "gradual, progressive change and betterment of a social and artistic order considered eternally valid." In contrast, Wagnerian "regeneration" sprang from the deep, rich soil of a "true religion" and implied a transformation of the very nature of man, not mere legislative and political transfers of power.[48]

It had been this kind of inner, spiritual change which Wagner had championed in Dresden in 1848–49, although his efforts had been misconstrued. As the culminating figure in a long tradition of German art, Wagner recognized that only the artist could give voice and form to the moral and religious mission of the *Volksgeist*. Aesthetic redemption was the solution to the divisiveness and alienation of the modern world, for art expressed the underlying reality of things; it penetrated the outer crust of appearances, revealing the "realm of freedom," the Kantian *Ding an sich*. Artists like Wagner and Schiller, through their creative, intuitive insight, could alone deflate the arrogance and dogmatism of scientific and religious thought; they alone could achieve a total, integrated vision of the cosmos, which enabled them to perceive subjectively truths about society, politics, and religion, inaccessible to logical, rational thought. "In my deepest conviction," wrote Chamberlain in 1893, "it is not politicians, but these two poets [Wagner and Schiller] who have indicated to the German *Volk*, the way it must travel, if it wants to fulfill its mission."[49]

Fifteen years later he remarked to his friend and admirer, Kaiser Wilhelm: "As Homer created Greece, so Wagner's art would be suited to be the ideal life-nerve of a reborn Germany—if it can only be saved from the crushing embrace of the Jews and the Court opera Intendants and its message vigorously disseminated." [50]

While accepting that art could redeem society, most Bayreuth supporters, including Chamberlain, did not confront the many intricate questions such a conviction involved. What strikes the observer most, perhaps, about the Bayreuth style of thought is its lack of clarity, its willingness to settle for hazy, emotive rhetoric, and its refusal to confront the reality of mass politics and society. Wagner's cultural critique and his vague, mystical alternative to modern society were adopted with uncritical servility, and neither Chamberlain nor the other members of the *Kreis* did much more than echo and elaborate upon the Master's texts. Tricky problems such as the relationship between artistic genius and the *Volk*, the connection between racial biology and aesthetic redemption, or the extent to which foreigners could comprehend Wagner and participate in the movement were left largely unresolved. But, vague though it was, the Bayreuth Idea offered Chamberlain an ideal fantasy world from which he could launch his criticism of existing society. Though he remained intellectually independent on some issues, in the early 1890s, at least, his cultural outlook was dominated by Wagnerism.

The "Bayreuth Idea" rested on two major myths, one positive, the other negative. In answer to the question "What is German?" Wagner and Bayreuth enthusiasts conjured up an idealized vision. The German possessed a loyal and deeply religious character, he had inner depth [*Innerlichkeit*], was close to nature, and had a fundamental sense of the identity and shifting interdependence of life in all its diverse forms. He was strong yet compassionate, individually free but not the slave of his own desires; he was naturally conservative and felt strong ties to the *Volk*, its language and traditions. For Wagner the German was the noblest specimen of humanity, whose mission was to ennoble the rest of mankind. But the German character also had its weaknesses—though they often stemmed from an excess of virtues rather than anything else. Bayreuthians saw in the bold, naive figure of Siegfried their image of the character defects of the race: the German was too often prey to the deceit and lies of his enemies, who took advantage of his guilelessness and childlike innocence. In short, Siegfried and Parsifal were the paragons of Germanic virtues according to Bayreuth, its *Wunschbild* of the superior race.[51]

But even the most myopic of Wagnerites could perceive that the *Kaiserreich* was not a nation of Siegfrieds. Indeed, as industrialization altered the face of the country and intensified political and class tensions, so Germany manifested all the traits which Bayreuth doctrine deprecated as flagrantly *undeutsch*. The contemporary German showed every sign of being as mediocre, utilitarian, egotistic, greedy, and hedonistic as the rest of men. As industrial capitalism undermined traditional beliefs and ways of life, so the individual became separated and estranged from the rest of society. "Like a wheel that spins faster and faster," wrote Chamberlain, "the increasing rush of life drives us continually further apart from each other, continually further from the 'firm ground of nature'; soon it must fling us out into empty nothingness."[52] German and Christian heritage was being sacrificed at the altar of Mammon, while a never ending succession of secular and materialist doctrines filled the vacuum left by the decay of true religion. "If we do not soon pay attention," wrote Chamberlain to a friend in 1896, explaining the task of the Wagner societies "to Schiller's thought regarding the transformation from the state of Need [*Notsstaat*] into the Aesthetic State, then our condition will degenerate into a boundless chaos of empty talk and arms foundries [*Kanonengiesserei*]. If we do not soon heed Wagner's warning—that mankind must awaken to a consciousness of its 'pristine holy worth'—the Babylonian tower of senseless doctrines will collapse on us and suffocate the moral core of our being for ever."[53]

Echoing the anti-capitalist rhetoric of Lagarde, Constantin Frantz, Carlyle, and other critics of modernity, Chamberlain inveighed against the philistinism and materialism of his age, epitomized by Alberich, the ugly dwarf who renounced love and beauty in his obsession for gold. His lectures and essays on behalf of Bayreuth were anti-liberal, despised the shallowness of rationalist philosophy, feared the rise of priestly and scientific dogmatism, and cursed the moral frailty of contemporaries. They were negative rather than positive and offered little by way of alternatives—Wagner's spirit, Bayreuth, and the music dramas were society's panacea. Satisfied with vague assertions and nostalgic longings, the supporters of Bayreuth concentrated most of their energies toward explaining the divergence between the Germans as they were and the "authentic," natural Germans they should have been. Wagner had offered several answers during his lifetime: in his early writings he concentrated upon the evil effects of money, the power of greed, and the emasculating effects of luxury. Later he placed the blame increasingly upon foreign influences and racial debilitation. Decline resulted from the transference of French egalitarian values and English commercial attitudes to the unsuitable soil of Germany. More significant still was the actual physical deterioration of German blood because of interbreeding with inferior racial types. Exploitative business, liberalism, Marxist socialism—in fact all the un-German characteristics of the modern age—were ascribed to alien, especially Jewish, corruption. The positive myth of German character thus required the negative counterpart of conspiratorial and national enemies. In the years after Wagner's death, the role of race in the cult became steadily more important and Bayreuth soon emerged as one of the chief ideological centers of German anti-Semitism.

Bayreuth supporters had varying racial views, and no effort was made by Cosima or Wolzogen to impose strict uniformity. Wagner's own writings on the subject fell into two groups: the essay he published in the *Neue Zeitschrift für Musik* in September 1850 and such tracts as *"Erkenne dich Selbst"* and *"Heldenthum und Christentum"* which he wrote for the *Bayreuther Blätter* at the end of his life. There were several differences of tone and argument between the two. The first essay, entitled *"Judenthum in der Musik,"* won widespread attention; it represented the Jew as the perverter of the nation's values and synonymous with materialism and commercialism. Most of the essay, however, was devoted to the influence of this alien element upon art and the theater. The prominence of Jews like Meyerbeer and Mendelssohn, argued Wagner, prevented the theater from acting as a powerful agency for social reform. These newly assimilated Jewish composers were alienated from the life of the nation and lacked the deep cultural roots which allowed the German artist to express the tensions and strivings of the nation. Their compositions, seductive to the ear, were mere entertainment, celebrations of the bourgeois and materialist spirit. "Alien and apathetic," argued Wagner, "stands the educated Jew in the midst of a society he does not understand, with whose tastes and aspirations he does not sympathize, whose history and evolution have always been indifferent to him." But though he might call the Jew "the evil conscience of our modern civilization," Wagner's views were vague and unscientific—with none of the pseudo-scholarly trappings race theory was to acquire in the following decades.[54]

Wagner's last essays, published in the *Bayreuther Blätter*, were strongly influenced by the French aristocrat Count Gobineau, whom he had first met in Rome in 1876, and had invited to Wahnfried in 1881. Gobineau's chief work, *Essai sur l'inégalité des races humaines* contained a far more detailed and closely argued explanation for cultural decadence than anything Wagner had written. Indeed, this synthesis of anthropology, theology, linguistics, and history was unquestionably the most impressive and ideologically coherent racial analysis produced in the pre-Darwinian era. Written after the revolutions of 1848–49, the *Essai* was a post-mortem of the old aristocratic order in Europe, characterized by reverence for hierarchy, social status, and family lineage. "The racial question," Gobineau asserted, "overshadows all other problems of history . . . it holds the key to them all." Although careful to reconcile his views with the biblical account of creation, he argued that climatic and environmental forces had worked to create three distinct human types—white, yellow, and black— with different physical and mental aptitudes. Superior in beauty, intellect, and creative vigor, the white race (and especially its illustrious Aryan branch) was the bearer of culture and civilization, responsible for the triumphs of the past. But the process of civilization inevitably involved miscegenation with inferior breeds, leading to the slow debilitation of the noble race over centuries. For Gobineau, history revealed the tragic "fall" of man from a presumed racial purity into a degenerate condition of racial corruption and mongrelization. Pockets of Aryan blood remained, especially among the nobility, but decline was inevitable and irreversible.

Contemporary society, argued Gobineau, offered abundant proof of his conclusions. Revolutionary convulsions, false egalitarian and democratic ideals, the selfish materialism of the bourgeoisie, and the phlegmatic response of the nobility to these challenges were inescapable symptoms of depravity. France was exhausted, Britain was being slowly corrupted by liberalism, while, as Michael Biddiss has shown, Gobineau was by no means sympathetic toward Prussia. If anything, in his last years he viewed the process of decay as accelerating: in a cold, objectivist, and ironical tone he depicted a global crisis and a vision of racial doom.[55]

"My husband," wrote Cosima to Gobineau in May 1881, "is quite at your service, always reading the Races when he is not at work with the staging." Gobineau replied warmly: "I assure you that there is no Bayreuthian more faithful than I."[56]

No less than seven articles about or by the French aristocrat appeared in the *Blätter* in 1882 and many more were to follow. Wagner discovered in the *Essai* a much more grandiose analysis of racial decay than he had formulated, and his admiration led him to appropriate a number of ideas and a more biological phraseology in his last polemical essays. Yet, while deeply moved by Gobineau's aristocratic pessimism, Wagner could not accept the conclusion that racial degneration was irreversible. Rather, he incorporated the *Essai's* critical analysis of modern society into a much more optimistic doctrine of regeneration. Art and the Christian religion, he maintained, offered the possibility of an antidote "provided to cleanse the blood of the human race from all impurities."[57]

There were other differences as well: Gobineau never placed the same importance upon the Jews as an anti-race, nor was he as sanguine about the redemptive mission of the German Reich and the Protestant religion as Wagner and Bayreuth. His *Essai* bolstered the vague Aryanism associated with the Wagner cult, but gradually as Aryan and German became almost synonymous for Wahnfried, a new racial synthesis was necessary and one which took account of post-Darwinian science. This was the task Chamberlain was later to set for himself in his *Foundations*.

After Wagner's death the influence of this transmuted Gobinism remained strong and even those, like Chamberlain, who criticized the *Essai* as unscientific sympathized with the fears of imminent decline which it voiced. Ludwig Schemann was the leading exponent of Gobineau's ideas both in the Bayreuth circle and in the Reich. Encouraged by Cosima he began a lifetime task of translating and publicizing the *Essai*, and founded in 1894 the small but influential *Gobineau Vereinigung* to promote the cult. Its membership was drawn principally from the German upper classes, but both German and foreign supporters of Bayreuth were active in the society.[58] This Germanized brand of Gobinism involved considerable misinterpretation of the original, and was vague and sketchy on many important questions, but it had great significance for the spread of racial ideas in the Second Reich. It was largely through the influence of Bayreuth that Gobineau entered the mainstream of German racism, helping to bestow upon deep anti-Jewish prejudices a mantle of intellectual respectability.

Many reviewers of Chamberlain's *Foundations* were exasperated by the vagueness and apparent inconsistency of so many of his statements on race. In part, at least, his imprecision can be traced to the Wagnerite environment in which his racial ideas were formed. The writings and correspondences of Bayreuth enthusiasts abound with racist comments, but very little attempt was made to define the race concept or to limit consciously the ways in which words like "Jewish," "German," "Semitic," or "Aryan" were used. At times "race" is employed to denote a biological group with definite physical, moral, and spiritual characteristics, transmitted "through the blood." On other occasions "race" is used to refer to certain ideas, values, behavior and styles of thought, not necessarily connected to any specific biological structure. Hence the word "Jew" might imply a member of a cultural, historical, or religious group; a distinct biological type; or, sometimes, a Gentile who had assimilated "Jewish" attitudes and ideas.

This same linguistic imprecision veiled Bayreuth's deep uncertainty about several crucial issues. First, if Wagner's art was "rooted" in the Germanic race, what should the role of foreigners be in the cultural mission of Bayreuth? Second, if the Jewish question was the main problem facing modern man, could it be solved by religious conversion or cultural assimilation, or was a Jew unable to overcome his born nature? Wagner's early writings suggest both that his music dramas were accessible to all and that the answer for Jews was to become good Germans. Later, however, he came to associate his art more exclusively with German national revival and adopted a more specifically biological phraseology when discussing race. There was an increasing adherence to racial determinism among members of the Wahnfried *Kreis* after the Master's death, but little attempt was made to think through the philosophical and social implications of this. Thus, Chamberlain eagerly befriended foreigners who wished to help Bayreuth—after all he was himself an Englishman—but he voiced doubts to Wolzogen in 1897 that non-Germans could appreciate the dramas: "man," he wrote, "can only understand what he is." [59] Similarly, in his *Richard Wagner* he sympathized with Wagner's early view that Jews could throw off their "Jewishness," but in other essays around the same time he borrowed the uncompromising rhetoric of the Master's final essays, calling the Jews the "plastic daemon of mankind" and the deadliest foe of regeneration, which had to be subdued.

Once, when questioned about his anti-Semitism, Chamberlain replied: "I have remarkably many Jews or half-Jews for friends, to whom I am very close." [60] The same could have been said about the Bayreuth cult as a whole. A number of Jews played important roles in the development of Wagnerism: the writer Heinrich Porges and the pianist Karl Tausig; the neurotic young Russian, Joseph Rubinstein, who committed suicide a year after the Master's death; Angelo Neumann the concert impresario and George Davidsohn, editor of the *Berliner Börsencourier*—to name only the most prominent.

Two Jews, Max Koch and Richard Sternfeld, were among the academicians who became active Bayreuth publicists, while even Chamberlain's publisher and friend Hugo Bruckmann was considered a Jew at Wahnfried. Cosima called him "an agreeable, cultivated Semite" and Chamberlain admitted that while probably one by race, in manner at least Bruckmann was not an "unadulterated Jew." [61] There was a consistent streak of pragmatism from Wagner's lifetime onwards—what advanced the cause ("*der Sache*") was acceptable. If this meant writing for Harden's *Zukunft* and Kraus's *Fackel*, as Chamberlain did, or employing Jewish singers and conductors, so be it. Once, when questioned about the numbers of foreigners attending the festival, Chamberlain merely responded curtly that if enough Germans came the problem would not exist. Although it is difficult to generalize it would appear that Chamberlain, and other members of the "inner circle," grew increasingly doubtful that a Jew, no matter how congenial, could ever fully change character. As a result Jewish Wagnerites could enjoy the genuine friendship and affection of Cosima and her lieutenants, but they could never escape condescension and the reminders of their "inferiority" that went with it. The Jew who acquiesced to such treatment was condemned to one long penitence for the tragic flaw of his birth, regardless of his talents and personal qualities.

Perhaps the best example of the way in which this anti-Semitism pervaded personal relations between Jews and Gentiles associated with the cult, is the career of Hermann Levi, a brilliant conductor, who was born the son of a rabbi at Giessen. One of the few contemporaries to master the new and difficult scores, *Hofkapellmeister* Levi was forced upon Wagner by King Ludwig of Bavaria to conduct the Bayreuth première of *Parsifal*. Outraged that his *Bühnenweihfestspiel*, designed to consecrate the temple of music, should be handed over to the ministrations of a Jew, Wagner tried without success to dissuade the King. Levi conducted the première and all subsequent *Parsifals* down to 1894; indeed, in the period immediately after the Master's death, his knowledge of the dramas made him almost indispensable.

Wahnfried demanded much from all devotees; from Levi, a nervous man, deeply conscious of his birth and easily wounded, it exacted more than from most. In return for his loyalty and deference, he was subjected to all kinds of slights and condescension. Theodor Adorno once wrote that, with respect to Levi: "Sadistic impulses to humiliate, sentimental conciliatoriness and above all a will to bind the mistreated person emotionally to himself, all flowed together in the casuistry of Wagner's conduct." [62] After 1883 the same unpleasant amalgam of revulsion, pity, and respect characterized Cosima's dealings with him. The young composer and conductor Felix Weingartner recalled an evening spent with Levi at Wahnfried:

> I noticed that his attitude to both Frau Wagner and her children was uniformly submissive. He seemed to be continually bowing, both actually and metaphorically and this affected me painfully because I had known Levi only as a great artist and unbiased thinker and also because it was soon apparent that the members of the Wagner family were faintly contemptuous of him, an attitude which they only imperfectly concealed behind the mask of friendship. On our way home that evening I asked him how a man of his standing could allow himself to be treated like that. He looked at me sadly and stammered hoarsely: 'It is easy for you in that house, Aryan that you are!' [63]

A long suffering victim of Wagner, Levi could not overcome his addiction to the composer. Anxious and self-abnegating, he was the target of the obsessive anti-Semitism of the Bayreuth circle; in turn he adopted many of their nationalist and racist views.

When Levi died in May 1900 his Wagnerite obituary, which demanded a delicate balance of praise infused with tactful disparagement, was entrusted to Chamberlain. Cosima had already given her judgment just before Levi's death when she told him that though a Jew could become a Christian, he could never become a Teuton; she had added that she valued the Christian above the Teuton but as she later admitted to Chamberlain: "I fear I did not speak the truth." [64] Cham-

berlain's essay struck the same note: Levi was a tragic illustration of what Wagner had described in *Judenthum in der
Musik*, a confirmation of the inability of man to escape his
race. Levi's enormous services to the *Festspiele*, his genuine commitment to the German cultural tradition, merely
heightened the overall tragedy of an existence dedicated to the
impossible task of "assimilating German culture as his own
real possession."

"It was Levi's religion," wrote Chamberlain, "to direct his
glance upwards to German culture. Goethe, Mozart, Richard
Wagner: they were the saints to whom he prayed. But he did
not restrict himself to the greatest figures. The living atmosphere of German culture was a daily necessity for him,
from Gottfried Keller to Wilhelm Hertz; he spent his whole
time in the company of richly gifted creative Germans. What
he lacked was the innocent impartiality, whose gaze fixes itself
effortlessly upon the truth." Levi's life, Chamberlain argued,
was a homily on the irreducible significance of race: if there
were an answer to the Jewish question it was that of Levi, as
encouraged by Wagner's words: "In order to be men in common with us, cease to be Jews!" Levi had tried, but had never
quite managed it. Chamberlain himself, Cosima, and even
Levi's widow were all well satisfied with the finished
obituary.[65]

If the Bayreuth circle did not have a well formulated view
of how the *"Judenfrage"* could be solved and what the fate of
German Jews should be, they at least agreed that a legislative
or political solution could not be successful. There were many,
like the Förster brothers, who advocated restriction of immigration and the exclusion of Jews from specific areas of economic and social life. But, whereas the new anti-Semitic
parties growing up in the 1880s placed their hopes in such protective legislation, the attention of Bayreuth was upon a more
sweeping process of cultural regeneration. In consequence,
Wahnfried tended to keep political anti-Semites at arm's
length. Some of the leading anti-Semites were entertained by
Wolzogen, and the Wahnfried circle took considerable interest
in the writings of Wahrmund, Glagau, Stoecker and Schoe-

nerer, but the *Blätter* avoided too close an identification with such popular and demagogic political organizations.[66] Moreover, while some Wagnerites in Vienna and elsewhere were very much involved in *völkisch* politics, many of Bayreuth's supporters were shocked by anti-Semitic rabble rousing and were hostile to the pronounced anti-Christian motifs in much of their propaganda. Thus, Prince Hohenlohe-Langenburg wrote to Cosima to express his deep regret that the antics of Ahlwardt and similar hysterical agitators were injuring the whole anti-Semitic movement.[67] Wolzogen was also worried that the anti-Christian orientation of journals like Theodor Fritsch's *Antisemitische Correspondenz* decreased all hopes of galvanizing support for a religious-based regeneration of the *Volk*.[68] With this in mind Wolzogen urged Chamberlain in 1893 to be careful to maintain a proper distance from the anti-Semitism of the streets in the lecture he was preparing on Wagner's *Regenerationslehre*. Indeed, he urged Chamberlain to stress that the duty of Germans was to desire "not exactly the physical expulsion of the Jew from our midst, but rather . . . his elimination morally from within us!" Jewish power could only end if Germans transformed themselves; certainly measures would have to be taken to "push back the material predominance of this shameful minority," but, he added, "it would be bad if the result of so penetrating a lecture . . . were nothing other than a brutal, joyous *Juden raus!*"[69]

Chamberlain echoed these words when he advised a Viennese friend, Karl Haller, who was about to start a new journal, that anti-Semitism was too negative a program: "I confess," he added, "that a German idiot or a Teutonic ass is much less congenial to me than a serious and productive artist of Jewish heritage. . . . I need only refer to Lueger and Mahler."[70] "Whose fault is it," he asked at a lecture to the *Jugendbund* in Vienna, "if the Jewish press possesses such an enormous influence?" Such papers would not be influential if Germans did not read them.[71]

For a time, however, one political movement did arouse the enthusiasm of Wahnfried: this was the conservative Christian reformism and anti-Semitism of the Berlin court preacher

Adolf Stoecker. Wolzogen, long attracted to Stoecker's Christian Social party, which placed racism firmly within the context of religious revival, showed some signs he was trying to steer the *Blätter* toward open endorsement. This was in 1892-93, when Stoecker's prestige among conservative and anti-Semitic Germans was at its highest. Cosima was interested in the idea, probably hoping that Stoecker's influence among traditional conservatives might be used for Bayreuth's benefit; but, after dining with Stoecker in Berlin, her enthusiasm declined. She found him rather naive on race questions and rejected his emphasis upon conversion as a solution to the Jewish problem. Chamberlain also opposed the use of the *Blätter* for partisan purposes, and insisted that Christian Socialism was fundamentally different in ideology from Bayreuth. After the failure of all her efforts to protect the Bayreuth monopoly over *Parsifal* by a vote of the Reichstag, Cosima became increasingly dispirited about politics and parties. Writing to Countess Wolkenstein in 1907 she deplored "the cancer of the German being which is now ruining Germany: that is parliamentarism." Her correspondences, like those of Chamberlain and other members of the "inner *Kreis*," contain a deep contempt for "a regime which has enslaved itself to the Reichstag." Cultural regeneration could not be legislated; politics was the symptom not the root of the question. It was remarkable, Chamberlain reflected, how little even so great a politician as Bismarck "was in touch with the higher aspirations of the nation, and how he reaped but could not sow." [72]

For some Bayreuthians racial ideas were supplemented by the firm conviction that meat-eating and vivisectionism were also either causes of degeneration or at least symptoms of it. Wagner, who took quite literally Feuerbach's assertion that "Man is what he eats," had long been a firm supporter of vegetarianism and toward the end of the 1870s publicly declared his opposition to vivisection. Beginning with Schopenhauer's concept of a single world will and adding an asssortment of ideas derived from race theory, Darwin's *Descent of Man*, and the Bible, he became convinced that the killing and eating of animals was sheer cannibalism. Primeval man, he alleged, had recognized the unity of all that lived, and the carnivorous habit was a later sign of human corruption, related in some mysterious way to the predatory heritage of the Jews. Meat-eating, Wagner believed, actually deteriorated the blood and he enjoined his supporters to heed his reinterpretation of Christ's message at the Last Supper: thou shalt not eat meat![73] Exactly how many Bayreuthians became herbivorous as a result of this injunction cannot be determined, but their correspondences often referred to this issue and the related one of vivisection. Certainly, vegetarianism enjoyed a brief period of popularity among the young Wagnerites of Vienna (Gustav Mahler, for example, told a friend in 1880 that he felt transformed by the experience and expected "a regeneration of the human race from it").[74] George Bernard Shaw, who proved a more reliable prophet, was less convinced that such abstention would triumph and commented caustically:

> Vegetarianism, the higher Buddhism, Christianity divested of its allegorical trappings (I suspect this is a heterodox variety), belief in the Fall of Man brought about by some cataclysm which starved him into eating flesh, negation of the Will-to-Live and consequent Redemption through compassion excited by suffering (this is the Wagner-Schopenhauer article of faith); all these are but a sample of what Wagnerism involves nowadays. The average enthusiast accepts them all unhesitatingly—bar vegetarianism. Buddhism he can stand; he is not particular as to what variety of Christianity he owns to; Schopenhauer is his favorite philosopher; but to get through *Parsifal* without a beefsteak between the second and third acts he will not.[75]

In theory, at least, Chamberlain was opposed to meat eating. He was also a confirmed anti-vivisectionist: as a student in Geneva he had defended one of his zoology professors in a local newspaper, but subsequently revised his views and never again countenanced the experimental use of animals. This conviction was doubtless strengthened by his experiences in Dresden where Ernst von Weber and Alfred Lill von Lilienbach, both very active campaigners against vivisection, were prominent in Wagnerite circles. But even Chamberlain had to admit that much of the evidence Wagner produced to support his ideas was a little far-fetched, and argued in *Richard Wagner* that false reasoning had been used to justify a valid but essentially intuitive insight. Wagner had grasped instinctively that the basis for a revived religion had to be a sense of the unity and harmony of all living beings; *Parsifal* was a poetic and dramatic representation of this. Cosima agreed with Chamberlain: "Only when we recognize animals as living beings like us can we speak of true religion, namely the bond between ourselves and the whole of Nature." [76]

The "Bayreuth Idea," as formulated in Chamberlain's writings and in the *Blätter*, presented to contemporaries a critique of bourgeois society and the values of liberal parliamentarism, together with premonitions of racial decline and cultural suicide. It diagnosed the crisis of the age as spiritual and racial and sought the renovation of German society not in politics but through the uniquely German genius for art. This firm conviction that, in a fast-changing and chaotic age, art could fulfill the supreme task of social cohesion, of inculcating values and teaching *völkisch* pride, arose in the period of *Sturm und Drang*, in its repudiation of eighteenth-century rationalism and empiricism, and combined with awakening nationalism in the age of the romantics. Wagner in many ways was the consummation of German Romanticism, a man who contrived to build a German philosophy, politics, racial and social vision, and even a religion—all out of art. For the essence of the noblest art, Wagner believed in his last years, was religion; its task was to revitalize the Christian faith, now ossified under the weight of ecclesiastical dogma and false doctrine, by allowing men to experience repeatedly in the present the truths Christ had embodied. This apotheosis of art attained its fullest expression in *Parsifal*, which became the focal work of the cult, performed almost like a religious rite at every festival except one down to the Second World War. [77]

A massive racial theodicy, laden with blood imagery and confused Christian symbolism, *Parsifal* wove together Wagner's racial and religious ideas in what Carl Schorske once called "some of the sweetest yet most penetratingly sickish music ever written." [78] The plight of Amfortas and the community of the Grail Knights on the heights of Montsalvat was that of Aryan man, debilitated by intermixture with inferior breeds. Fusing Aryan myth and Christian legend, Wagner re-created the odyssey of Parsifal, now depicted as the chaste champion of Aryan superiority who alone could retrieve the sacred spear that had penetrated Christ's flesh, and preserve the Grail, the talisman of the race. By overcoming the insidious temptings of Kundry, he revealed the power of will and renunciation; his victory, like the original sacrifice of Christ, exemplified "the redemptive will's supreme endeavour to save mankind at death throes in its noblest races." [79]

In *Parsifal* and in his final prose writings Wagner proclaimed the urgent need for a Germanized Christianity, divested of the old orthodoxies and the constraining organization of the churches. His efforts to fuse the secular mystique of the *Volk* and Christian revelation were not original but coincided with a broader movement that was attempting to enliven Protestantism with the fire of nationalist passion. Beginning with such publicists as Lagarde and the Viennese Orientalist Adolf Wahrmund (a contributor to the early issues of the *Bayreuther Blätter*), and continuing to the 1930s, this Germanic religion–or mystical nationalism with a Christian veneer— was to make serious inroads into German Protestant opinion. The key to the new faith lay in severing Christianity's ties to Judaism and integrating it with the doctine of race. Denunciations of Roman Catholicism as semitized and inferior, criticism of the Protestant churches as too shackled to Catholic dogma, the conviction that Germans had a special capacity for grasping the teachings of Jesus, and the vision of an Aryan Christ were all elements of this ideological mélange. Following Wagner's death, Bayreuth became one of the leading centers of this Germanic faith. "We consider," wrote Chamberlain, "Lagarde's unabashed exposure of the inferiority of the Semitic religious instincts and their pernicious effects on Christianity as an achievement that deserves our admiration and gratitude." [80]

But beyond these vague appeals for a purified national faith, Bayreuth publicists remained quite divided over specific religious doctrines. Wolzogen and Cosima were both ardent Protestants who hoped to strengthen the links between Wag-

nerism and reformist movements within the Church, whereas
Chamberlain favored a highly personal, nonconfessional religion of Christ divested of all sacraments and doctrine; other enthusiasts of the cult inclined toward Indian religion, various
mystical beliefs, and even theosophy. Wolzogen cultivated ties
with liberal Protestant and social Christian elements within the
Church and, while he tried to exclude from the *Blätter* extreme
anti-Christian statements which might give offense and
alienate church opinion, he wanted it to act as a forum for religious discussion. Thus, in a long and passionately argued open
letter to Chamberlain in 1895, Wolzogen urged him to abandon
his nonconfessional position and work for reform within the
existing church structure. After deploring the weak state of organized religion and intoning the usual racial and political dia-
tribes against modern society, Wolzogen launched into a long
eulogy of Stoecker, complete with quotations from his speeches
and sermons; Stoecker was seen as a Wagnerian pastor who
recognized the bonds between *Kunst* and *Kirche* and who
managed to wage the crusade against *Judenthum*, without un-
dermining the power of Protestantism or slipping into the kind
of anti-Christian sentiments which marred so much anti-
Semitic propaganda.[81]

Although Chamberlain rejected it, Wolzogen's appeal
illustrates both the centrality of religion in the Bayreuth Idea
and the confusions and problems inherent in Germanic Christianity. The main difficulty was that in embracing the race
theory of the Darwinian era, German Christians found it difficult to avoid a thoroughgoing biological determinism which
substituted race for God. This dilemma, of which both
Wolzogen and Chamberlain were fully cognizant, often resulted in a strangely schizophrenic outlook on religion and
race. While professing a Christian ethic of love and tolerance,
writers poured out their anger and hatred; while using such
concepts as sin, redemption, and revelation, they radically altered the original content and substituted a range of anthropological and political meanings. In some cases Germanic Christianity led to desertion of the church in favor of some form of
occultism or neopaganism, but the Bayreuth circle never
doubted the compatability of racism and Christianity. Thus,

they rejected the militantly anti-Christian tone that surfaced in the writings of anti-Semites like Eugen Duehring and Friedrich Lange, but in their own essays left the relationship between race and religious experience vague and mysterious.[82]

Differences over religious doctrine and on the emphasis to be put on race continued between leaders of the Bayreuth cult. But more important were the many beliefs and ideas they shared. Wolzogen and Leopold von Schroeder might consider themselves more orthodox Lutherans than Chamberlain but they were fervent admirers of his books and praised his race theories almost without qualification. After 1900 Chamberlain emerged as by far the most influential Wagnerite exponent of Germanic Christianity. His broad learning and literary skills attracted a wide readership both among churchgoers and extreme *völkisch* Christians like Wilhelm Schwaner, Max Bewer, and Wilhelm Stapel.[83] For Chamberlain and the Bayreuth circle Wagner's art was fundamentally religious: the dramas represented allegorically the inner kernal of Christianity and thereby pointed the way toward religious rebirth.

With its vehement attack on the general embourgeoisement of German society, Wagnerism was particularly appealing to the German bourgeoisie, well schooled in the conventions of self-criticism. Wagner's art was rich, sensuous, overripe—"heavily upholstered," as Thomas Mann called it; it smacked of the bourgeois. And it was greeted with such impassioned feeling for and against precisely because it expressed deep human and social ambivalences.

Thomas Mann once suggested that a book be written about Wagner the psychologist, the bohemian destroyer of conventions who nonetheless reeked of "the atmosphere of the bourgeois," and who teased, thrilled, and overwhelmed his audiences.[84] Many contemporary writers described, often exaggeratedly, the impact of the music dramas. One thinks of

Musil's depiction of Walther, the idle and frustrated young man in *The Man Without Qualities*, whose piano playing turned "with or without his will" into improvisations of Wagner's music: "and in the splashings of this dissolutely swelling substance, which he denied himself in his days of pride, his fingers waded and wallowed, gurgling through the flood of sound. . . . His spinal cord was paralyzed by the narcotic influence of this music, and his lot grew lighter." [85]

Much of Wagner's immense power, as many later commentators and some contemporaries recognized, was in releasing emotional forces otherwise pent up and repressed. In Robert Gutman's words: "The composer offered the faithful an easy spiritual experience on an intensely physical level. Wagnerians could dream of purity and renunciation as they embraced the flesh." [86] The music was at once sensational, erotic, religious, and mysterious. By conjuring up archetypal psychosexual situations on stage (the second act of *Tristan*, for example, or the exploration of incest in *Parsifal*), the composer probed a range of anxieties and impermissible fantasies, using the technique of motif-building to hone music into a fine instrument of psychological allusion.

Wagner invited extreme responses. For some his "magic" was a kind of aesthetic psychotherapy, a cathartic release of tensions; others denounced it as downright unhealthy and liable to unhinge the sensitive. Max Nordau's bestseller *Degeneration* (1893), depicted Wagner as the supreme decadent: "the last mushroom on the dunghill of romanticism;" he marveled at husbands and fathers "who allow their womankind to go to these representations of "lupanar" incidents." [87] The Wagner hysteria, as it was sometimes called, had roots deep in the terrain of bourgeois sexuality and repression; in this sense the composer, with his profound grasp of the significance of myth and dreams as mirrors of the unconscious, anticipated the psychic insights of Freud.

The use of art to explore emotions otherwise subject to strict constraints was one aspect of Wagnerism, but the other, the institutional, aspect sought to channel and direct the emotional energy released into social and cultural regeneration. Like other cultural reform movements that proliferated in the

1890s, Bayreuth was overwhelmingly a cult of the middle and upper classes. The most active supporters included titled nobility like Wolzogen, Stein, and Countess Wolkenstein; those with aristocratic relatives like Chamberlain and Cosima herself; sons of industrialists and bankers such as Schemann and Thode; and a large number of professors, teachers, journalists, lawyers, and bureaucrats who formed the bulk of the literary publicists of Wagnerism. Festival performances tended to be largely upper middle class in composition (seat prices and travel being expensive), with more than a smattering of nobility and even royalty, but the membership of the local Wagner clubs included a broader cross section of the bourgeoisie and overlapped with other cultural and nationalist organizations.

But while the festivals were a preserve of the wealthy and privileged, through the ever-growing popularity of the dramas themselves and the intensive efforts of publicists like Chamberlain, Wagnerism invaded the language, symbolism, and mythology of German nationalism. Speeches, newspapers, books, even grocery advertisements were redolent with Wagnerian references, while Kaiser Wilhelm II even had his motor horn tuned to the Donner motif in *Rheingold*. Nazi trivialization of Wagner was perhaps more consciously undertaken and extreme than anything that had gone before, but it followed many precedents. It was not only the Nazi Fuehrer who allowed himself to be depicted in the shining white armor of Lohengrin; there is also the portrait of Wilhelm, standing with his Lohengrin helmet before a swan—the Knight of the Grail of German imperialism.

The growth of the Bayreuth cult coincided with a widespread decline in the power of liberal and progressive ideas among German *Bürgertum*. In a time of rapid social and political change, of heightened international rivalry and imperial expansion, the grip of nationalism on the imaginations of Germans grew stronger. In the political sphere, powerful new pressure groups (the Pan-Germans, the Naval League, and the *Kriegervereine*) mobilized popular support for national goals. Less aggressively and on a much smaller scale, Bayreuth and other cultural movements helped to reinforce national myths and values in the artistic realm, transmuting social fears, estrangement from the conventional political process, and visions of an embattled *Reich* into a vague dream of national destiny. By 1914 Wagnerites were active in many patriotic organizations—the Pan-German League, the *Deutscher Sprachverein*, and the *Heimatkunst* movement, to name but a few. Bayreuth's vague "nonpolitical" solutions, its romantic and illiberal antimodernism suited the German mood; it offered little in the way of concrete answers to Germany's problems but expressed the collective uneasiness, longings, and discontents of the Wilhelminian era. Even its counterfeit populism was a sign of the times: at every turn Wagnerites invoked the name of the *Volk* to justify their cultural stance, but their "people" was a romantic myth, a relic of Wagner's democratic past with little basis in reality.[88]

It was in the society of Wagnerites then that Chamberlain first developed his views on culture, politics, and race. His activities in the Wagner clubs and as a publicist dominated his first seven years in Vienna. But Chamberlain was not merely a passive recipient of Wagnerian orthodoxy; he soon found his own voice and by 1896 had acquired the necessary confidence for larger and more ambitious literary projects. In the next years he turned his mind increasingly to historical and philosophical subjects; in some of them Wagner received only a brief mention. But in a larger sense they were all thoroughly Wagnerian in spirit and together constitute the most sustained attempt to enlarge and refine the Bayreuth Idea in the light of the late Wilhelminian era.

Chapter Five

The Foundations of the Nineteenth Century

ON FEBRUARY 6, 1896, Chamberlain received a letter from his Munich publisher, Hugo Bruckmann, who had for some time cherished an idea for a large book—intended for publication in 1900—which would cast a farewell glance over the magnificent cultural achievements of the nineteenth century, a kind of literary homage to European *Bildung* as the new century dawned. With this in mind he approached several writers and scholars for their suggestions, but found the results surprisingly disappointing. Some of those consulted had in mind an encyclopedic work requiring the collaboration of numerous authors; others seemed totally incapable of viewing the century from any but the standpoint of their own specialization. Despairing of these academics, Bruckmann had turned to Chamberlain for any thoughts he might have on the projected book.[1]

The request reached Chamberlain at an opportune moment. He was restless and eager to broaden the scope of his writing, which for five years had been concentrated almost entirely upon publicizing Bayreuth. A letter he wrote to his Swiss friend, Agénor Boissier, at Christmas 1895, revealed his mental exhaustion with Wagnerism. Although he contemplated a final volume to complete his Wagner trilogy (a speculative summation attempting to relate Wagner to nineteenth-century German culture) he was clearly not im-

mediately ready for such a task and preferred to toy with the
idea of writing a Kant encyclopedia, a brief history of
German art, or of revising his dissertation for publication.
Boissier sympathized with his longing for fresh tasks and replied encouragingly:

> I understand perfectly your desire, your *need*, to escape for a
> certain time from the *obsession* of which you tell me. Wagner
> is a "devouring fire" and he does not with impunity take
> possession of those who, like you, plunge themselves for so
> many years in the world that he reveals to us. Also, your idea of
> stopping, of changing the orientation and subject of your work
> for, I don't know, one or two years, appears very good and right.[2]

Other domestic problems also disturbed the relative calm of
his daily life: his disinheritance by his Aunt Catherine* made
him anxious about his long-term financial security, while tensions arose from what seems to have been a growing estrangement from his wife. Their marriage had degenerated into little
more than a convenient routine and Chamberlain was beginning to feel that Anna—ten years his senior, frequently sick,
and a little dull compared to some of his new Viennese
friends—was becoming a millstone around his neck. Bruckmann's letter appeared as a welcome relief from these preoccupations and he clutched at it with all the tenacity of a drowning
man.

Chamberlain had been revising his doctoral thesis, but a
bout of influenza had, for the moment, hindered further
progress. As a result he had ample time to ponder Bruckmann's idea and quickly became absorbed in its possibilities.
"I found no rest," he told Cosima Wagner, "until everything
was worked out." In six days he had drawn up a complete outline and submitted it to the publisher, who enthusiastically offered a contract. Later, Chamberlain announced he had been
extremely reluctant to undertake the work, and consented only

---

* Aunt Catherine, a spinster who lived in Versailles and a good friend of the Countess de
Charnace (the stepsister of Cosima Wagner) left her property to Houston's brother
"Harry" in 1895. The reasons are unclear, although Houston hinted that it had some-
thing to do with his activities for Bayreuth. HSC to A. Boissier Dec. 28, 1895; HSC to
A. Ludowici May 11, 1906 (CN). For further details of Chamberlain's finances see
chap. 8.

after Bruckmann's repeated efforts at persuasion. But this was a literary flourish, inserted into his autobiography to reinforce the desired impression that fate had guided his life's work, and that he, like the prophets of old, was merely a pliable instrument in God's hands. If he hesitated at all, it was at the prospect of devoting an estimated three years to the venture. He would only undertake the book, he told Cosima, if convinced that it would be first-rate: either "a small masterpiece or nothing at all."[3]

Cosima strongly encouraged him, for she believed the book would be a Wagnerian *Kulturgeschichte*, and Chamberlain's first outlines of the project held out the prospect of a complete history of humanity, shaped and evaluated in accordance with the ideals of Bayreuth. Thirty centuries of human development would culminate gloriously with Richard Wagner, "the towering genius of the century." German history, religion, science, art, and philosophy would be Wagnerized and the Bayreuth ideal linked indissolubly to the national, racial mission. If, with the death of Heinrich von Stein and the defection of Nietzsche, Wahnfried had lost its most promising philosophers, in Chamberlain at least it might still find its cultural historian. Wagner himself had always attempted to cast his theories in a historical framework, and a scholarly vindication of these insights was long overdue.

The initial plan proposed to Bruckmann called for a three-part work.[4] The first was intended as a preparatory study, reviewing the cultural development of Europe from the ancient world to 1800. Three chapters, each covering six centuries, would depict the main themes of human history from Christ to the nineteenth century, events being evaluated and selected for discussion according to the yardstick of their contribution to the modern world.

The second part of the book was more complicated. Divided into nine chapters and 37 sections, it was intended to analyze the cultural attainments of the nineteenth century itself—its politics, social forces, technical and scientific advances, philosophy, and art. This huge survey would range over subjects as diverse as the philosophical "errors" of the English empiricists, the insidious power of the modern press, the consequences of uncritical *Darwinismus*, the expansion of new forms of wealth, the effects of Jewish emancipation, and would culminate in the religious art of Wagner.

Finally, the third part of Chamberlain's original sketch envisioned a reevaluation of the nineteenth century as an integral part of the total historical process. "Then, at last," he wrote, "the century would stand out before our eyes clearly shaped and defined—not in the form of a chronicle or encyclopedia, but as a living 'corporeal' thing."[5] By discussing the immediate Semitic threat to society and the racial conflicts with the Chinese and Negro races, which still loomed ahead for the "European Aryans," Chamberlain intended to pose the alternatives of regeneration or decline, and thus conclude with the "Bayreuth *Weltanschauung*."

Only the first section, the two-volume *Foundations of the Nineteenth Century* [*Die Grundlagen des neunzehnten Jahrhunderts*], was ever completed, which is hardly surprising in view of the colossal proportions of the initial design. For the rest of his life, however, Chamberlain continued to gather research for the remaining two parts. "I have," he told his friend Lord Redesdale in 1908, "a huge lot of material for the *Neunzehntes Jahrhundert* [the second part] but have not yet commenced writing it." The *Kant* and *Goethe* books, to which he devoted the decade after finishing the *Foundations*, were, he added "an indispensable preparation."[6]

From February 1896 until September 1898 Chamberlain worked with great intensity. For the first year he read voraciously, taking notes and elaborating upon his first sketch (the only significant addition was the separate chapter on the *Völkerchaos*); then he began writing. The 1,200-page study was written and revised within the space of nineteen months—a truly remarkable feat, especially considering the fact that he contined to produce occasional articles for Bayreuth. The writing went smoothly, scarcely interrupted by the stormy political scenes in Vienna during Badeni's administration. Indeed, it is interesting that during the autumn of 1897, when German nationalist anger reached its height, Chamberlain was pouring out his feelings in the two chapters on "The Entry of the Jews into Western History" and the "*Völkerchaos*."[7]

Each morning, he told Eva Wagner years later, he knelt and prayed for God's guidance in his work and then immersed himself in his writing for eight hours. He shut himself off from Anna, setting up a bed in his study and spending his nights there. Nobody was allowed to interfere with his work, and even his walks were taken alone in the neighboring Esterhazy Park, pencil and notebook in hand. The evenings were spent either reading aloud with his wife and a few select friends or studying alone in preparation for the next day's labors; rarely did he consult the opinions of other scholars, except in their published writings. Even his correspondence with Cosima records the progress of the book rather than discussing its substance, although Chamberlain did acknowledge that his view of race differed from the theories of Gobineau, which until then had enjoyed such favor at Wahnfried. In his autobiography, the philosopher and mystic Hermann Keyserling, described Chamberlain's method of working. Mounted on a ladder in his library he would leaf quickly through numerous books, picking out quotations and using them deftly to fit the ideas and arguments with which he intended to concern himself during the day. An undisciplined reader in many respects, he seldom stopped to consider the contradictions of his thought or to ask himself whether these carefully selected quotations were typical, or his construction of their meaning valid. They were simply useful bricks in the edifice he was building. His thought and writing reveals a process of intellectual plundering; thus, while he claimed to use all pro-Roman and philosemitic sources to support his arguments attacking the Jews and the Papacy, his diaries show him—at the same time—pouring over writers like Drumont and Wahrmund, with the predictable result that his mind was never open to nonracial viewpoints.[8]

Chamberlain was one of the most successful exemplars of a new literary type: the popular synthesizer, the *terrible simplificateur* of Burckhardt's fears. His success in Imperial Germany—like that of cultural critics such as Julius Langbehn, Ernst Moeller van den Bruck, and the Monist, Ernst Haeckel—was symptomatic of a general dissatisfaction with traditional scholarship. The first salvoes in this critique of academic culture were fired by Nietzsche in the first of his "untimely meditations," attacking the rationalist critic of religion David Strauss in 1873. Afterward an increasing number of writers joined the fray, inveighing against the lowering of educational standards and the spiritual cost of recent technological progress. "We find ourselves," wrote the popular philosopher Rudolf Eucken, "in a serious intellectual and spiritual crisis, which we are unable to master."[9] Many contemporaries felt that the vitality of the German intellectual tradition had declined. The modern specialized academic was a mere caricature of the cultivated man, while the universities neglected their duty of educating the nation and providing a *Weltanschauung* which could unify and give direction to its experiences and strivings. A new breed of dilettante like Chamberlain sought to fill this gap between scholarship and life. "I believe," he wrote, "that the true dillettante is today a cultural necessity, as much for the scholar—enlivening his learning—as for the layman, by enriching his life through living, organized knowledge."[10]

Only a man of considerable conceit could have undertaken so enormous a task as the *Foundations* with so little preparation. "I know nothing of history," he wrote to Cosima Wagner, "nothing at all." But then his goal was "not scholarship but life, not theory but action: his avowed aim was not antiquarian interest in the disclosure of new facts but "to give shape to those that are well known, and to fashion them so that they might form a living whole in our consciousness," "to make knowledge a living, defining force for the present."[11] His conception of history, although intensely subjective, deserves some attention, for his ideas reflect on a superficial level a more profound debate among scholars about the nature and methods of historical scholarship.

The German historical tradition, like so many other aspects of German intellectual life, traced its origins to the Idealist philosophy of the Napoleonic wars and the period of national revival after 1800. These common philosophical antecedents gave to German historiography, as George Iggers has persuasively argued, a unity and continuity rare in other countries.[12] Ranke, Dahlmann, Droysen, Rotteck, and Welcker, to name only the most famous scholars of the "Prussian School," viewed history as a reflection of God's will, an expression of the divine in all its infinite subtlety and variety. Their painstaking scholarship was sustained by fervent Protestant conviction and a belief that historical truth both existed and was discoverable. Striving to overcome what they regarded as the rationalist simplifications of Enlightenment historiography, they tried, without subjecting the past to crude deterministic laws of development or falling into complete relativism, to lift the veil of the divine and to grasp the values inherent within each historical situation. In their focus upon politics, institutional studies, and foreign diplomacy, these historians endowed the state with a spiritual and ethical mission; they emphasized its uniqueness and historical individuality, and reduced to a minimum conflicts between the individual and society, and tensions between ethics and the pursuit of national power. In contrast to this their successors, in the exhilarating period of national unification, fell increasingly under the sway of the scientific method, absorbing the basically unphilosophical and confident empiricism of the scientific positivists. The ordered, religious plan of history contemplated by Ranke gave way before an ordered, rational system arranged according to scientific laws. History had been appreciably secularized.

From the 1880s, the positivist world view came under severe attack from several quarters. Philosophers, poets, novelists, psychologists, and social theorists had begun to challenge the prevailing assumptions of nineteenth-century rationalism, to focus attention upon the irrational in man, to raise questions about the nature and validity of scientific facts, and to question the applicability of the natural scientific method to other fields of knowledge. Coinciding with this general methodological and epistemological debate, which deeply affected the language and direction of all social and humanistic studies, historians and philosophers began to reexamine the very foundations of history as a discipline. In 1883 Wilhelm Dilthey demonstrated the range and originality of this reassessment with his *Einleitung in die Geisteswissen-*

schaften, while in the following years a spate of publications by the neo-Kantians Windelband, Rickert, and Cohen examined the subject further.[13]

It is difficult to summarize the results of this reevaluation, for the arguments advanced were extremely complex and when condensed lose their sophistication and true content. There were also marked differences of view between Dilthey, Windelband, and Rickert, although these are not important for the present discussion. All these writers sought to deepen the relation of the historical observer and the subject of his investigations, to refine the meaning of words like "understanding" and "knowledge," chart more carefully the limits of historical understanding, and formulate concepts of causation applicable to the study of human behavior and social evolution. Dilthey, for example, referred to all the products of man's spiritual and mental capacity as "objective *Geist*" and argued that the problem facing the historian was that of grasping the complex patterns and structures of these forms of "objective spirit." Clearly, if the defining element of the cultural sciences was their spiritual character, then a methodology derived from the natural sciences was untenable. Instead, Dilthey described historical consciousness in terms of "experience" (*Erleben*) and "intuitive understanding" (*das Verstehen*). He used these words to refer to a reexperiencing of the past through a supreme effort of intellect, emotions, and intuitive faculties. Historical understanding was viewed as an internal process, a highly personal penetration of the past, and an imaginative and artistic "recreation." Understandably this also encouraged a movement away from political and institutional studies, toward cultural, social, and intellectual history. Windelband, Cohen, and Rickert had a rather different view of the epistemological status of historical knowledge than Dilthey, but they too focussed upon the creative understanding of the mind, regulating perceptions and the formation of ideas according to its own modes of cognition.

In history, as in philosophy, this neo-Idealist critique of knowledge was soon popularized and bowdlerized. For some it offered the prospect of a solidly based idealistic world view, a secure refuge in an insecure materialist world. Other popularizers joined concepts like Dilthey's "immediate experience" to all manner of *völkisch* and racist theories, or borrowed them for some other kind of naïve appeal to irrationalism or attack on rational and conceptual thinking. Chamberlain's *Foundations* was one such attempt to clothe in philosophical jargon efforts to subdue the past to the author's subjective experience and intuition. Since, he argued, the past formed an organic unity and the historian himself was encased in the process of time, real understanding resulted from a certain creative intuition of the force of life. Rejecting prescriptions of objectivity as *"wissenschaftliche Bildungsbarbarei,"* Chamberlain embraced the Byronic formula of history as a "poem imitating truth."[14] He conceived of the *Foundations* as a unified *Gestalt*, of which each part should be judged in the perspective of the whole, and which—just as a painting can be weighed up at a glance—could be read easily in four or five days and judged in its entirety. In the first preface he put his view succinctly:

> What is written here, is experienced [erlebt]. Though many factual statements may be old mistakes, though many judgments may arise from prejudice and many conclusions from false reasoning, yet nothing is totally false. . . . A single thought can be without content, the error of an isolated individual, but a deep conviction is rooted in something outside and above the individual, and . . . it must contain at its core a living truth.[15]

The main problem for philosophers like Dilthey was how, given the limits of historical knowledge, it was possible to decipher in the flux of history the eternal values and truths they were convinced were inherent in the process. For Chamberlain this problem did not exist. Race was his yardstick of value. Bestowing a vague racial connotation to such words as *Einfühlung*, *Anschauung*, and *Lebensanschauung*, he represented the past as a continuous growth and disintegration of distinct human races, each cultural epoch being the work of a dominant human type. The historian—so far as his own racial *Gestalt* allowed—had to grasp this vital force of change. In this way his conception of historical knowledge merged with the vague subjective approach employed in his studies of Wagnerian aesthetics; both evinced the same vague, irrational *Anschauung*.

Racial history was already a well-established genre before Chamberlain wrote the *Foundations*. In France historians had actively propagated the Frankish and Gallic myths since the Revolution, while in England a host of writers, both professional historians and enthusiastic amateurs, sang the praises of the Anglo-Saxons, and traced the struggle between the Teutonic and non-Teutonic forces through such events as the Norman invasion and the Civil War and "Glorious Revolution" of the seventeenth century. In Germany, too, the racial tradition was firmly rooted in eighteenth century writers and rapidly won popularity during the early decades of the nineteenth century. Not only were the works of university scholars full of racial assumptions, but more popular accounts appeared which also attempted to use race as the key to all historical understanding. The works of Wolfgang Menzel, especially his *Geist der Geschichte* (1835) enjoyed a fairly large readership, while Gustav Klemm's ten volume *Allgemeine Kulturgeschichte der Menschheit* (1843–52) which explained the movement towards a unitary and egalitarian society in terms of interbreeding between "active" and "passive" races, was highly regarded by cultivated Germans; and, whether they read it or not, many of its arguments entered the racial rhetoric of the times. Gobineau's pessimistic *Essai sur l'inégalité des races humaines* (1853–55), the finest example of this type of writing, was too fatalistic for German taste and achieved little success until at least the 1880s, when it was taken up by Wagnerites and various aristocratic circles as a prognosis of decline which mirrored their own innermost anxieties about cultural degeneration. In the 1850s only the brilliant prophetic mind of de Tocqueville could predict to Gobineau that "alone in Europe, the Germans . . . could provide you with a really favourable audience."[16]

The decade of the 1890s, one in which Germany was torn by deep social and political divisions, saw the emergence of a chorus of cultural prophets and popularizers of history.

Admittedly academic historians still exerted great social influence—one has only to think of the works of Heinrich von
Treitschke and Heinrich von Sybel—but it seems as if a larger
middle class public than earlier was searching for bolder diagnosticians dealing in easy solutions. It was not (as has been
argued for example in the case of France[17]) that professional
historians after Treitschke retraced their steps to the ivory
tower and eschewed involvement in national affairs; rather,
their heavy scholarship, professional caution, and continuing
bias in favor of political and diplomatic history failed to suit
the mood of contemporaries and left to popularizers like
Chamberlain a large, enthusiastic readership in the area of
cultural history. (Spengler's success was the clearest indication
of this trend, and perhaps the last, for in the 1920s the popular
reader seems to have moved on from these vast historical can-
vases to that more easily read, shortcut to culture, the popular
biography.)

Chamberlain's superficial, eclectic style and glorification
of the German cultural tradition sustained the vanity and
deepest prejudices of his readers. Though full of contradictions
and at times very obscure, his thoughts were clothed in the
right philosophical garments and had sufficient contact with
broader debates going on in philosophy, anthropology, and history to impress readers as being both profound and informed.
He was not given to the vicious outbursts of a Duehring, nor
did he flirt with neo-paganism or the occult like Ludwig
Klages, Alfred Schüler and Lanz von Liebenfels. Chamberlain
was always respectable, and he sought to persuade rather than
antagonize. Endowing his work with a prophetic ring, he offered readers the impression of great erudition without tedious-
ness, sought to unearth the foundations of German *Kultur*
without becoming obscure and generally whetted the appetite
of his audience with a pleasing combination of detailed
analysis and bold, synthetic sweeps of judgment. In many
ways, as we shall argue later, he was for the troubled *Weltpolitik* era what Oswald Spengler later became for the period
of defeat after 1918—both sensed accurately the pulse of their
times.

Chamberlain's aim in the *Foundations* was to substantiate two fundamental convictions—that humanity was divided into distinct races which differed in their physical structure and mental and moral capacities, and that the struggle and interaction of these races was the main propelling force of history and the key to understanding cultural, political, and social development. Rejecting "the notion of humanity as nothing more than a linguistic makeshift," Chamberlain saw the past as a succession of cultural epochs, each characterized by the handiwork of a dominant racial type. "The whole of nature," he later informed his friend Kaiser Wilhelm, "shows us the fact of race as the foundation of all exceptional achievements . . . the origin of all the noblest cultural attainments."[18] His book was designed to show the Germanic or Teutonic race as the main architect of modern European civilization.

The *Foundations* discerned six major influences which had contributed to the development of nineteenth-century culture: Hellenic art and philosophy; Roman law and organization; the revelation of Christ; the racial chaos resulting from the fall of the Roman Empire; the negative and destructive power of the Jews; and finally, the creative and regenerative mission of the Teutonic—or, as he sometimes called it, the Aryan—race.

In the first part Chamberlain discussed the legacy of the old world. He began with ancient Greece, "an exuberantly rich blossoming of the human intellect," and the culture in which man first revealed his spontaneous creativity and achieved a synthesis of art and life. Chamberlain's vision of Greece owed much to the German Romantics. Echoing the laments of Wagner and Schiller's *Aesthetic Letters*, he depicted Hellenism as a tantalizing "lost ideal, which we must strive to recover," a marked contrast to the atomism and materialism of modern existence. "Among us," he reflected sadly, "every artist is a born slave. . . . art is for us a luxury, a realm of caprice; it is not a state of necessity and it does not lay down for public life the law that the feeling for beauty should pervade everything." Nonetheless, he predicted that the Teutons would eventually construct a new cultural unity, without the cruelty and slavery that marred Greek life. Bayreuth was clearly in his mind the modern torch-bearer of the Grecian aesthetic and philosophical legacy. Creative art was the unifying force of Greek civilization but, Chamberlain lamented, nineteenth-century educators still insisted on teaching the false legends of Greek history and politics, which merely revealed the tyrannical public life of a deeply divided people who lived by slavery and were deficient in statecraft.[19]

In contrast to Greece, the genius of Rome was unartistic and unpoetic. Patriotism, civic courage, respect for law and institutions, and a solid family structure—these were the moral virtues that characterized Roman civilization. Chamberlain's anxiety about contemporary attacks on the bourgeois family, his disapproval of feminism, and his insistence on strict obedience to the law were all evident in his nostalgic regard for Rome. "When discussing the burning question of the emancipation of women," he wrote, "or when forming an opinion with regard to those socialistic theories which, in contrast to Rome, culminate in the formula 'No family, all State,' the contemplation of this lofty height will be of invaluable service." It was Rome, he argued (making repeated references to Mommsen, von Savigny, and other standard authorities), that first rescued Europe from the cultural spell of the Semitic-Asiatic East, and created circumstances in which the Indo-Germanic races could develop independently, finally becoming "the beating heart and thinking brain of all mankind." "Greece always gravitated towards Asia, till Rome tore it away." Unlike Constantin Frantz and many other prophets of German superiority, Chamberlain did not contrast Roman and German law, claiming one was the emanation of the domineering statecraft of Rome and the other the creation of free men. He was criticized for this by the advocates of German law and was eventually persuaded by their view, but the text of the *Foundations* remained substantially unchanged in later editions.[20]

The heritage of Greece and Rome was not unblemished, and both succumbed to racial degeneration. In Greece, art eventually lost its vitality; religion became divorced from artistic relevation and fell prey to "priestly superstition and hypersubtle hunting after causality"; even philosophy turned away from the heights of Plato to the shallow rationalism of Aristotle and the narrow minded scholastics who succeeded him. This negative legacy, claimed Chamberlain, was still evident in the dogmatism of Thomas Aquinas and the sterile logic of men like David Strauss and J. S. Mill. Rome too "was great only as long as it remained physically and morally Roman." Whereas the early Romans had been ruthless in suppressing Semitic influences (as was evident in the total destruction of Carthaginian civilization), in later times "African half breeds, soldier emperors" like Caracalla, devalued the privilege of Roman citizenship by granting it indiscriminately to all subjects of the Empire. Like Gobineau and many other racist authors, Chamberlain believed that the protracted infiltration of the blood of slaves and freedmen, mostly of Semitic and African extraction, had transformed the Romans into an amorphous mass without definite racial character. "Like a cataract the alien blood poured down into the nearly depopulated city of Rome, and soon the Romans had ceased to exist." [21]

The third legacy of the ancient world was the revelation of Christ, whose birth Chamberlain regarded as the single most important event in world history. Christ epitomized a new dawn, the emergence of a new Germanic culture on the ruins of the old world. As "the God of the young, vigorous Indo-Europeans" Jesus had nothing in common—as some enthusiasts of comparative religion suggested—with Buddhistic pessimism and negation of the will. Nor, manifesting all the character traits typically Aryan or Teutonic, could Christ possibly have been Jewish—a notion as profoundly distasteful to Chamberlain as it had been earlier to Wagner. Though several thinkers had approached the problem before, it was in the *Foundations* that the theory of the Aryan Jesus gained its widest publicity. Since Christ was God and man unified, Chamberlain felt quite justified in investigating the probable racial heritage of the mortal half. Even a brief sketch of the history of Galilee, he argued, was sufficient to discredit the inherited delusion of the Savior's Jewishness, for the region was mostly populated by non-Jews—among them Greeks,

Phoenicians, and even some Indo-Europeans. In looks and speech (they had difficulty in pronouncing the Aramaic or Hebrew gutturals which every Jew and Semite accomplished with ease) these Galileans were, he concluded, racially distinct.[22]

This long and involved chapter demonstrates vividly the style of Chamberlain's racial dialectics. He was aware that although his readers might at heart prefer an Aryan to a Jewish Jesus, they would nonetheless require ingenious and careful coaxing to be convinced of the idea. Coating his prejudices with a veneer of biblical scholarship, Chamberlain cited numerous authorities like Robertson Smith, Wellhausen, Harnack, and Renan. Cautious in tone, he protested his objectivity, conceded his doubts and ignorance on several points, and even ascribed to the Savior a few Jewish traits for good measure. On one point only was he categorical: that Christ was not a Jew. The rest of his analysis was a *tour de force* of slippery and evasive reasoning, enticing his readers on to the conclusion that Christ was Aryan but without ever directly stating it. Scholars like Ernest Renan, who stubbornly refused to heed their own evidence, were suspected of ulterior motives and secret ties with the *Alliance Isráelite*.[23]

In contrast to the Berlin philosopher Eugen Duehring, who concluded that Christianity was a life-denying creed indissolubly bound to its Jewish origins, Chamberlain asserted that the teachings of Jesus were linked to the idealist religion of the Aryans, and not the legalistic and materialist faith of the Jews. This in turn led to reflection on why Christ had appeared in hostile surroundings. Among the Aryans, Chamberlain concluded, the religion of Jesus would have been stifled by luxuriant mythologies. Palestine provided the strongest possible antithesis, so that the faith evolved out of the tension between Christ and his surroundings. In Chamberlain's view there was no connection between Jewish-Hellenistic literature, the prophets and the Essenes, and the original message of Christianity. Yet, he felt compelled, as we have said, to concede a few Jewish traits to the Savior, so as to disarm criticism and avoid allegations that he was blinded by anti-Semitic intolerance. Though these were mere tactical expedients, Chamberlain received a critical response from Cosima

Wagner:

> Pages 247–249 ["*Christ a Jew*" where Chamberlain analyzes
> Christ's Jewish traits] I found deplorable. Also I cannot find
> adequate proof for your contention. Of course I know that you
> included this to strengthen your excellent assertion of the very
> opposite point and to reveal yourself an absolutely impartial re-
> searcher. . . . You began your chapter masterfully, I would have
> wished for an ending of the same quality. [24]

His answer was still more revealing, demonstrating the careful
calculation behind his statements. "When you search for my
motives," he told Cosima, "you are naturally on the right
track," and added:

> You would not believe how much—yes, *how much* renunciation
> a man in my position must suffer. Were I vain and full of self-
> pride, then I would write for all eternity. If I wanted more than
> to have an effect on people and then be floated away in the
> ocean of forgotten atoms—then I would not do much that I do,
> and would do many things that I leave undone. You may object
> that the right principle is to be "uncompromising." . . . But I
> ask you not to judge too quickly. For if you view my work as a
> whole you will observe it is an extremely "uncompromising"
> work. . . . But a concession here and there in small details
> works wonders and secures admission where one would other-
> wise be banned—so may the good seed of ideas flourish little by
> little and the husk (namely the book of the noble HSC with all
> its imperfections) be left behind. [25]

This in a nutshell was Chamberlain's aim. His manner of
expression was highly personal and ingratiating, first humble,
then superbly arrogant, sometimes openly dilettantish, then
making a great show of learning and expertise. For all its
contradictions, ambiguities, and errors of reasoning, the Christ
chapter is a carefully wrought example of the publicist's art.

The revelation of Christ completed the triple legacy of the
ancient world. Since then European history had arisen out of a
conflict of three major racial forces: a chaos of mixed races,
and two "pure" races: the Teutons and the Jews. [26]

The *Völkerchaos* or "Chaos of Peoples" was a central concept in Chamberlain's racial theory. Mostly in his work it

denotes the confusion of races left by the Roman Empire, although sometimes he used the term to refer to any "mongrelized" people. Rome had declined because of miscegenation, giving way to an "inextricable confusion of the most different races and peoples," a "chaos of unindividualised, species-less human agglomerates." Modern inhabitants of much of Europe manifested these mongrel origins, although it was only in the south and east that "real bastardizing, that is the crossing of unrelated or of noble and ignoble races," occurred. Moreover, it was through this decadent "nationless" mixture that the illustrious heritage of antiquity had been transmitted to the modern world. "Our whole intellectual development," Chamberlain lamented at one point, "is still under the curse of this unfortunate intermediate stage: it is this that supplies weapons to the anti-national, anti-racial powers even in the nineteenth century." In the fascist era, Nazism might be able to find guidance in Chamberlain's doctrines of Nordic superiority, but—after reading the *Völkerchaos* chapter—Mussolini understandably declared: "No such doctrine will ever find wide acceptance here in Italy." [27]

To illustrate the racial consequences of the *Chaos*, readers were provided with two major examples. First the Greek author, Lucian, who was clever, vainglorious, superficial, and unstable. "Utterly incapable of knowing what religion and philosophy are," this "gifted Syrian" nevertheless enjoyed great worldly success for he suited exactly the "totally bastardized, depraved and degenerate world around him." Equally typical was St. Augustine, whom Chamberlain portrayed as a hopelessly confused and self-alienated man: "In the world of his imagination we find the Jewish belief in Jehovah, the mythology of Greece, Alexandrine Neoplatonism, Romish priestcraft, the Pauline conception of God and the contemplation of the crucified Lord, all jumbled together in heterogenous confusion." A tragically schizophrenic mind, split between Aryan idealism and Semitic intolerance and superstition, Augustine, like Lucian, reflected the physical deterioration of the empire once halfbreeds like Caracalla and Heliogabalus had seized power. Rome perfectly exemplified Darwin's dictum: "crossing obliterates character." [28]

The heir to this "soulless congeries of humanity," Chamberlain maintained, was the Roman Catholic Church, which, in catering to the needs of a degenerate population, lost all contact with the pristine teachings of Christianity. The result was a faith distorted and corrupted by Semitic influences and a Papacy, devoid of spiritual depth, striving only to extend its political power. The Teutonic mission was to wrest Christianity from this alien grasp, expunge Semitic elements from their religion, and "sift" the revelation of Christ "from the threateningly perilous Jewish element." [29]

Clearly Chamberlain's description of the Roman *Chaos*, with its emphasis on Semitic influences, is closely related to his anti-Semitism. But for the moment at least, he kept *Chaos* and Jew separate. Arising out of the Roman chaos, the Teutons and the Jews dominated modern history. History advanced dialectically out of their combat; their battle for the heritage of the ancients and the legacy of Christ would determine the future of all mankind.

The second longest chapter of the *Foundations* is devoted to the Jews and their entry into European history. Chamberlain began cautiously, asserting that "the Jew is no enemy of Teutonic civilization and culture," and attacking "the revolting tendency to make the Jew the general scapegoat for all the vices of our time." He repeatedly denied any "personal animus against individuals belonging to the Jewish nation," and, as if to show his magnanimity, dedicated the book to a Jew, Julius Wiesner, his old professor in Vienna and Rector of the University. Reassuring readers that a certain distaste for Jews was both respectable and intellectually creditable, Chamberlain endowed his book with a valuable air of academic expertise, disassociating himself from vulgar anti-Semitism, and offering an apparently balanced and informed judgment. "Almost all pre-eminent and free men from Tiberius to Bismarck," it was argued, "have looked upon the presence of the Jew in our midst as a social and political danger." Before Germans could be immunized against foreign Semitic influences they had to know and recognize their enemy: Chamberlain's self-allotted task was to define the spiritual and physical charcteristics of the Jews. [30]

Researching the *Foundations*, Chamberlain for the first time began to read about the history of the Jews, although he merely used the information to bolster his existing prejudice. "I am reading here Renan's 'Histoire du peuple d'Israël'" he wrote Aunt Harriet in June 1896 "and have just finished the first volume. . . . I need hardly say that it is of absorbing interest. As Renan is an enthusiastic admirer of Hebrew religion, one gets the whole story of this people unfolded to one by a man who is full of real sympathy for it, which to my mind is essential." He added, however, "And yet in spite of Renan's efforts, I cannot help whilst I study the history, bible in hand, shuddering at the portentous, irremediable mistake the world made in accepting the traditions of this wretched little nation . . . as the basis of its belief."[31] Using Renan, Wellhausen, Stade, Robertson Smith, C. Steuernagel, and other authorities, whom he often seriously distorted, Chamberlain sketched the racial history of the Israelites, among whom the "real Jews," the descendants of the tribes of Judah and Benjamin, eventually developed as a distinct group.

The Israelite was claimed to be the product of crossbreeding between three different racial types. The "basic human material," argued Chamberlain, borrowing the terminology of the French racial anthropologist Vacher de Lapouge, was the Semitic Bedouin (*Homo arabicus*) of the desert, whose dominant personality trait was an excessively developed will power. Conditioned by the simple desert life, he was narrow-minded, unimaginative, and materialist in outlook. His influence was evident in the shallow, fanatical religious fervor of the Jews, which debased the relationship of man and God to a vulgar, legalistic contract. The second element was the broad-headed Syrian Hittite, physically strong but intellectually and morally inferior. His influence, claimed Chamberlain, could be detected in both the business acumen and the spiritual poverty of modern Jews. The intermixture of these two very different types produced the mongrel Hebrew.

There was also a third racial type, which, when crossed with the Hebrew, produced the Israelite: the Amorite (*Homo europaeus*) or Canaanite—a tall, fair skinned, blue-eyed Aryan from the north. The addition of this Amorite blood came too late to regenerate the corrupted Hebrew strain and was soon absorbed and disappeared. Such noble blood, however, enabled Chamberlain to explain away some of the more formidable qualities of the Jewish adversary and account for the "short period of splendour" enjoyed by the Israelites under David and Solomon—a brief glorious interlude before Syrian-Semitic elements triumphed completely.[32]

From the mongrelized Israelites the Jewish race developed through a unique interaction of racial will and historical circumstance. The conquest and enslavement of the more powerful northern kingdom of Israel by the Babylonians in 721 B.C. left the hitherto subordinate kingdom of Judea isolated. Chamberlain ascribed the emergence of a distinctive Jewish type largely to this historical natural selection. Later, the destruction of Judea by Nebuchadnezzar and the period of Babylonian captivity merely reinforced the separation of Judeans from other Israelites and helped to destroy almost all traces of their earlier common tradition. During and after the captivity a priestly caste manipulated Judean society, expurgating the books of the Old Testament, creating a new dogmatic religion and a fabricated historical tradition which deliberately concealed the mongrel origins of the people and laid down strict rules of endogamy. Chamberlain was especially fascinated by this prospect. "A handful of men," he wrote, "forced a definite national idea upon a people not at all inclined to accept it." The old traditions of Amos and Hosea were refashioned and distorted to represent the Jews as a chosen people—a notion which hardened into an unshakable dogma after the miraculous raising of the siege of Jerusalem by Sennacherib in 702 B.C. At that moment, argued Chamberlain, "the Jew was born and with him the Jehovah whom we know from the Bible."[33]

Often there was a distinct note of awe in Chamberlain's description. The race consciousness of the Jews, their strict adherence to social codes, and ceaseless enmity toward other races were characteristics which in a German would have been admirable. "Never for a moment," he reflected bitterly, "have they allowed themselves to forget the sacredness of physical laws because of humanitarian day-dreams. . . . We were the criminal abettors of the Jews . . . [and] we were false to that which every lowest inhabitant of the ghetto considered sacred, the purity of inherited blood."[34]

At times, as he warmed to his argument, Chamberlain's rhetoric evinced the same brutal, sadistic tones as were later found in the writings of Alfred Rosenberg. The goal of the Jew, the cornerstone of his religion, was "to put his foot upon the neck of all the nations of the world and be Lord and possessor of the whole earth." "Consider," Chamberlain warned, "with what mastery they use the law of blood to extend their power." Daughters of Jewish families were encouraged to marry outside the race, so that while the principal male line remained "spotless . . . thousands of side branches are cut off and employed to infect Indo-Europeans with Jewish blood." If no preventive measures were taken "there would be in Europe only a single people of pure race, the Jews, all the rest would be a herd of pseudo-Hebraic mestizos, a people beyond all doubt degenerate physically, mentally and morally."[35]

What role did the Jews play in Chamberlain's "Hymn to Teutonism"? His thought displays a vagueness and inconsistency common among anti-Semites. He wavered between calling the Jews a pure race, a negative *Gegenrasse*, and a mongrelized people whose whole history, arising out of the miscegenation of unrelated breeds, broke all the laws of racial breeding. Though he claimed to distinguish between Jews and Semites, Chamberlain used the terms almost interchangeably. Indeed, all racial enemies tended to coalesce in his mind into one anti-Teutonic monolith struggling to destroy the new world built by the superior peoples of northern Europe. In a vitriolic letter to his aunt explaining his "position with regard to the Jews," he warned against their cleverness, "that special poisoned talent of these mongrel half-semites . . . which acts on us northerners as a disastrous blight corroding all that is noblest in our nature, waking up, enticing on all that is low in our instincts, blinding us to our natural and therefore best qualities, teaching us to mock at all that is the holiest treasure of our heart of hearts."[36]

In the *Foundations* Chamberlain offered an orchestration of ideas, articulating the most cherished myths in which anti-

Semites sought refuge from the reality of mass politics, class division, and industrialization. The social and political concerns underlying his cultural idealism are at once apparent in the stereotypes he ascribed to the Jew. The Jew was identified with predatory capitalism, monopoly enterprise, and mobile, unearned wealth;his influence at the courts of princes, bishops and emperors was easily traced from the earliest Gothic times to the nineteenth century when "all the wars" were "so peculiarly connected with Jewish financial operations."[37] Responsible for the malfunctions of the economy and the class antagonisms they provoked, this urbanized, rootless race had reaped the benefits of modernization and accelerated social mobility—and at grave consequences to the health and unity of every Teutonic nation. The spread of international business syndicates and the expansion of international socialism were illustrations of Jewish power; so was liberal democracy. "With their gift for planning impossible socialist and messianic kingdoms," argued Chamberlain, "Jews threatened to destroy our whole laboriously won civilization and culture."[38]

In addition to these social and political stereotypes, Chamberlain also set out to repudiate any idea that Jews were possessed of special aptitude for religious thought and had brought monotheism to the rest of the world. Monotheism, he asserted, was a late addition to Judaism; the irate, vengeful tribal God, Jahweh, could not be compared to the God of the Hellenic Christians and the Indo-Europeans. Unlike some anti-Semites, Chamberlain did not reject the Old Testament altogether, but argued that recent advances by Protestant scholars made it possible to sift out the Indo-Aryan and Canaanite myths before they were engulfed or petrified by Semitic concepts[39]. By the 1880s, as Uriel Tal has shown, much of Protestant research was committed to the belief that pre-Christian Judaism had become barren and legalistic, and that Christianity, not modern Judaism, was the authentic heir to biblical monotheism. While claiming to rely on the studies of Wellhausen, Harnack and others, Chamberlain connected their ideas to an explicitly racial vision, radicalizing and distorting their conclusions.[40]

If the Jew was the destroyer of civilization, an ideogram for materialism, intolerance and social dissolution, the Teuton was his historical antithesis. Idealistic, mystical, loyal, free, and uncorrupted he fought to recapture the heritage of antiquity from the alien grasp of the Jew and the semitized *Völkerchaos*. Since the thirteenth century this race of Parsifals had been awakening to full consciousness of its historical mission to be the ennobler of mankind. Chamberlain rhapsodized about this virile, blond, long-skulled race which sprang from the northern woods and marshes; in some ecstatic passages, he echoed the most absurd enthusiasms of the contemporary *Blondheitskult*.[41] The geographical distribution of the race was left vague, and Chamberlain frequently used the terms "Indo-Germanic," "Indo-European," and "Aryan" as alternatives for Teuton. In general his description of the Teuton coincided with the category *Homo europaeus* used by Vacher de Lapouge, and included German, Celtic and Slavic peoples as branches of the race, although it was always implied that the German-speaking lands of Central Europe possessed the highest concentration and the purest strain of Teutonic blood. Elsewhere, especially in France and Russia, long periods of miscegenation had seriously undermined the race.

Though he had read the most important studies of contemporary ethnologists and racial anthropologists, Chamberlain avoided taking a side in the debate over the European or Asiatic origin of the Aryan race.[42] He was less interested in establishing the location of the cradle of civilization than in revealing the physical and spiritual characteristics of the superior race. He contemptuously dismissed scientists "who still did not know that the shape of the head and the brain structure have a decisive influence on the shape and structure of the thoughts," but avoided dogmatic statements about Teutonic physiology.[43] Hair color, skin texture, and skull shape were indicators of Teutonic blood, but had to be complemented by other moral and spiritual characteristics. Inner depth (*Innerlichkeit*), a firm sense of loyalty to a master they had freely chosen, and an inner spiritual and intellectual freedom—having nothing to do with the freedom preached by contemporary liberals or constitutionalists—were the salient qualities of Teutonic character. But, Chamberlain acknowledged, for all their innate superiority the Teutons still had their weaknesses. Too easily prey to the trickery and scheming of their enemies, some, like Charlemagne, had served the cause of Rome, others revealed a mystifying readiness to assimilate with other races. But gradually, in the face of unremitting Semitic enmity, they had struggled to form independent nation-states, to purify Christianity and rediscover Christ, and to build a new world based on racial foundations.

From the sixth century onward the Teutonic race had engaged in a continuous battle with the linked forces of Rome and *Judentum*. For the first six centuries this racial conflict was directed largely against the political and religious power of the Papacy, and for this reason Chamberlain sometimes argued that the *Foundations* was more anti-Roman than anti-Semitic.[44] In practice, however, this distinction made little sense, for both enemies were represented as co-conspirators sharing the same anti-Teutonic characteristics, and they tended to coalesce into one. "Rome," argued Chamberlain, "possesses born allies in all enemies of Teutonism" and "there cannot be a shadow of a doubt that the Roman ideal was the establishment of a universal state with Jewish priestly rule as a foundation." Roman Catholicism was "judaized" Christianity: its quest for universal power was mysteriously associated with the international aspirations of the Jews, and its intolerance and fanaticism reflected the unscrupulous and willful nature of the Semites. At times, Chamberlain linked Jesuits and socialists as protagonists of the "ideas of unlimited Absolutism," and lumped together Jews, liberals, the Roman Church, and the German Center Party under the rubric of Semitism. Hence his fears, frequently voiced in the *Foundations*, of a resurgent Roman campaign against Teutonism, evidenced in the decree of Papal Infallibility and the Syllabus of Errors, boil down to one aspect of a more generalized fear of Jewish or Semitic conspiracy. "Materialism in philosophy . . . the limitation of imagination, the forbidding of freedom of thought, deep-rooted intolerance toward other religions, red hot fanaticism—these are the things we must expect to meet everywhere to a greater or lesser extent where Semitic blood or Semitic ideas have gained a footing."[45]

The Semite was, to use Wagner's term, "a plastic demon," a hydra-headed monster whose activity was visible in all aspects of modern society which Chamberlain loathed or feared. He did not hate Jews, then in separate categories detest Jesuits, socialists, liberals, and parasitic capitalists. Whenever he looked hard, he discovered the same deadly foe:

His [the Jew's] physiognomy and form changes. He conceals himself, he slips through the fingers like an eel. Today he wears Court livery and tomorrow drapes himself in a red flag; servant of princes and apostle of feedom, banker, parliamentary spokesman, professor, journalist—anything you like; like the priest in his cowl, one doesn't recognize him; unnoticed he invades all circles.[46]

Behind the celebrated optimism of Chamberlain's writing lay a profound uneasiness which revealed itself in a markedly paranoid style of thought. This style—common to so many *völkisch* and racist thinkers—showed strong syncretic tendencies, reducing everything to the same racial dogma. Even in his occasional remarks on the Chinese, Chamberlain noted: "In many respects this human species bears a striking resemblance to the Jewish, especially in the total absence of all culture and the one-sided emphasizing of civilization." In brief, whether identified as Jew, Semite, or Rome the *Antigermanen* acted as a defining force: it was the anvil on which the image of the Teuton was hammered out. To mention the Teuton was to conjure up the image of his opposite.[47]

The two planes of this Manichaean struggle upon which Chamberlain focussed his attention were the religious and the political. His discussion of religion relied heavily upon the liberal Protestant tradition of the 1890s, which urged that Christianity must return to the original life and message of Jesus as the only way of emancipating Protestantism from the vestiges of pagan and Catholic ideas which had not been completely displaced by the Lutheran Reformation. To this Chamberlain added explicitly racial arguments culled from the writ-

ings of Lagarde and Wagner and his own interpretation of
Kantian religion. Christianity, he argued, had developed during the last centuries of imperial Rome into a hybrid faith
composed of two distinct and mutually opposed *Weltanschau-
ungen:* the religion of the Jews, historical and chronological,
and that of the Indo-Europeans, rich in symbolism and
mythology. As the Roman Church took over the political imperium of the decaying empire, so Christianity had succumbed
increasingly to Semitic materialism, to a preoccupation with
sin and punishment, and a literal interpretation of Aryan
myths and symbolism. Intolerance and rigidity stifled the living faith of Christ; a priesthood and a dogmatic Church replaced a religion of redemption, love, and divine Grace.

From the beginning, Chamberlain asserted, the Hellenic
and later the Teutonic spirit resisted this process. From the
Arian and Waldensian heresies, the efforts of Francis of Assissi
and Dante to change Catholicism from within, to the struggles of Wycliffe, Hus, and Luther, Chamberlain traced a
continuous tradition of Teutonic rebellion. But Rome had been
largely successful and, even after Luther had shattered the
unity of Catholic Christendom, the faith remained "imbued
with Roman superstition." Indeed, the Reformation had in
some ways strengthened Rome by removing its internal opposition and giving rise to the militant and "machiavellian" order
of Jesuits. "I see," Chamberlain wrote, "the greatest danger
for the future of the Teuton in the lack of a true religion
springing from and adequate to our own nature."[48] His hopes
lay in the Kantian religion of inner experience and the
emergence of "Germanic Christianity."

Rome's political battle against the emergence of independent nation-states had been less successful. Developing his
arguments around Goethe's dictum that individuals should be
"externally limited, internally limitless," Chamberlain represented the Teutons as a race which, by voluntary limitation of
the field of external action, had acquired infinite scope in their
inner spiritual world. In contrast to the universal strivings of
Rome, they had established racially based nations which
fostered freedom and individuality. Chamberlain intended to

dwell more fully upon political and social organization in the second part of his study and provided only a skeletal outline in the *Foundations*. He portrayed the Reformation as primarily a political revolution and Luther as a national hero; in contrast, he viewed the French Revolution as a last chaotic effort at rebellion by a population which had failed to achieve a Reformation in the sixteenth century and had become dominated by Jewish and Jesuit influences. Because France was racially debilitated, Chamberlain argued, its revolt was soon stifled by shallow rationalism and materialism and rapidly fell under the sway of Napoleon, a true representative of the *Völkerchaos*.

To each negative "Semitic" trait Chamberlain counterposed a Teutonic virtue. Kantian moral freedom took the place of political liberty and egalitarianism. Irresponsible Jewish capitalism was sharply distinguished from the vague ideal of Teutonic industrialism, a romantic vision of an advanced technological society which had somehow managed to retain the *Volksgemeinschaft*, cooperation, and hierarchy of the medieval guilds. The alternative to Marxism was "ethical" socialism, such as that described by Thomas More, "one of the most exquisite scholars ever produced by a Teutonic people, an absolutely aristocratic, refined nature." [49] In the rigidly elitist, disciplined society of Utopia with its strong aura of Christian humanism, Chamberlain found an approximation of his own nostalgic, communal ideal. "The gulf separating More from Marx," he wrote, "is not the progress of time, but the contrast between Teuton and Jew." There was even a Teutonic strain of Catholicism (Döllinger was an example in the nineteenth century), quite distinct from Rome and the universal church. Mindful that Catholics constituted one-third of the German population, Chamberlain could hardly exclude them all from his chosen race and he went out of his way to affirm their political loyalty in later prefaces to the *Foundations* (though continuing to view the Center Party as an agent of Rome). Even in 1900, he asserted, the *Antigermanisch* forces continued their attack both in the old form of Papal interference and in the new universalist guises of socialism, international finance, and liberalism. The "powers of darkness," he admonished readers, "are ever stretching out their polypus arms . . . and trying to drag us back into the Night out of which we Teutons are attempting to escape."[50]

The final and longest chapter of the *Foundations*, "The Rise of a New World," was devoted to a glorification of Teutonic achievements from 1200 until the dawn of the nineteenth century. Effortlessly, Chamberlain slipped into the assumption that all signs of greatness were *ipso facto* evidence of Teutonic blood—the Italian Renaissance and the genius of Giotto and Donatello as much as the Lutheran Reformation. Every thinker or intellectual trend of which he approved was accorded a place in the Teutonic pantheon. The result was, as G. P. Gooch wrote, "a glittering vision of mind and muscle, of large scale organization, of intoxicating self-confidence, of metallic brilliancy, such as Europe has never seen."[51] In Chamberlain's eyes a harmonious and well-integrated Teutonic *Weltanschauung* was taking shape whose configuration was visible in the evolution of science, religion, philosophy, and art.

Much of Chamberlain's discussion of a Teutonic world view was expanded later, particularly in his *Kant* and *Goethe*, while his convictions about the role of art in society had already been published in his books and articles on Wagner and Bayreuth. As a result only a brief summary of his survey in the *Foundations* is presented here. Hero worship was a salient feature of Chamberlain's intellect and personality, as is evident in his attitude toward cultural giants like Wagner, Kant, and Goethe, and later toward political figures like Tirpitz, Ludendorff, and Hitler. If Wagner was to be the central hero of the planned study of the nineteenth century, it was Kant, the cartographer of Teutonic thought, who dominated the *Foundations*. Kant towers over the last chapter, and much of Chamberlain's analysis reads like a preparatory effort for his next major work, a two-volume study of the philosopher.

Basing his analysis largely on the epistemology of Kant, the first Teuton to obliterate every trace of Roman dogmatism and Jewish materialism from his thought, Chamberlain plotted the limits of mechanical science and transcendental religion, and analyzed the stages in which, he believed, a critical

philosophy had developed—one which was cognizant of the
limits of human knowledge.

Behind Teutonic commercial drive and world-wide exploration, and in the onward march of science, Chamberlain discerned one basic quality: an unquenchable thirst for
knowledge of the physical universe. Parading his extensive
learning, he illustrated, with examples from botany, physics,
chemistry, and mathematics, the rise of a distinctive Teutonic
view of Nature which combined exact observation and intuitive perception (*Anschauung*). John Scotus Erigena, Francis
Bacon, Newton, Darwin, Hertz, Faraday, and many other
figures revealed the progressive victory of creative empiricism
over the obscurantism of Rome and scholastic narrowness. In
the modern era the main danger to science was not so much
priestly superstition as dogmatic scientism. The advance of
Teutonic science, Chamberlain insisted, required its strict
separation from all metaphysical and transcendental questions.
The scientific materialism of Büchner, which endeavored to
"explain" everything in the universe by force and matter, and
the efforts of Monists like Haeckel to transform Darwinian evolution into a cosmology repudiated all Kant's teachings on the
boundaries of human knowledge. Chamberlain reiterated
Liebig's call: "Back to Kant!" as the way to provide a sound
philosophical justification for empiricism, and the only means
of surmounting the positivist and materialist excesses of
modern scientific theorizing.

A mechanical science joined to a philosophical critique of
knowledge was complemented by ideal religion. Chamberlain
believed that in Teutonic philosophy and religion four groups
of thinkers had wrestled free of the intellectual straitjacket of
the Chaos. First, theologians like Duns Scotus, William of Oc-
cam, and later, Luther, had rebelled against Church orthodoxy
and paved the way for a religion based on individual freedom
and experience. Second, mystics like Meister Eckart, Jakob
Böhme and Giordano Bruno fostered a religion of love and
moral consciousness of the divine in place of historical religion.
Third was the sceptical humanism of Erasmus, Petrarch, and
Boccaccio, who forged fresh links with the cultures of ancient

Greece and Rome. Finally, there was the group of thinkers
Chamberlain called the "nature philosophers" (*Naturerfor-
scher*), exemplified by Locke and Descartes, who began to
chart the boundaries of reason and experience and who
recognized the active, formative operation of the mind in conceptualizing and ordering our experiences. Here again these
four groups were represented as achieving their fulfillment in
the philosophy of Kant and his nonhistorical religion of
experience.

To mechanical, empirical science and ideal religion
Chamberlain added a third facet of the Teutonic spirit: the
creation of artworks which elevated man, heightened his
awareness of life and of God, and continually renewed in his
soul the message of Christ. Echoing Wagner, Schiller, and
Kant, Chamberlain described art as a bridge between the inner realm of religion, inexpressible in words, and the world of
phenomena. Placing Homer, Dante, Dürer, Leonardo,
Rembrandt, Shakespeare, Beethoven, and many others within
one brilliant tradition, he began laying the foundations for his
treatment of Wagner as the chief legatee of this aesthetic heritage. Wagner would be revealed as the artist-redeemer who
had rescued and refashioned, in Teutonic form, the aesthetic
heritage of Greece. Actually, Chamberlain never wrote the
later sections of the study he had originally proposed to Bruckmann and there was no extended eulogy of Wagner or Bayreuth in the *Foundations*—something, as we shall see, which
caused considerable annoyance at Wahnfried.[52]

This long paean to Teutonic accomplishments brought
Chamberlain to the end of the *Foundations*. It was a remarkable work of synthesis, stamped indelibly with the mark of his
personality. Though he never wrote the final two parts his
plans are clear. Chamberlain intended to show the closing
nineteenth century as a critical age of transition, one in which
the forces of Teutonism met new dangers from an emancipated
Jewry, finance capitalism, the popular press, and the growth of
large-scale technology. It was also an era which witnessed the
rise to power of a unified Germany, led by the Hohenzollerns
and stablilized by the growth of a solid *Mittelstand* which offered a bulwark against both socialism and plutocracy.[53] Al-

ready in the *Foundations* the national mission of the Germans begins to prevail over other considerations; in the later parts the world mission of German culture was to have been the central theme, as the Reich, the last bastion of Teutonism, fought on against both the old racial enemies and the ominous threat, as yet on the distant horizon, of the yellow and black races.

There was little in the *Foundations* that was new. Chamberlain's visions of the Teutons as a chosen people, heirs of antiquity and torchbearers of Christianity can be found in the writings of others, while even in details his arguments rested heavily upon the large body of racist literature published since the mid-eighteenth century. In many respects it was the very familiarity of so much of what he had to say that made Chamberlain's book so acceptable to contemporaries and facilitated their approval of any new twists and turns he added. His book was steeped in the traditions of German idealism and romanticism, and was heavily indebted to the cultural speculations of Wagner and the vast historical canvas of Gobineau. A list of sources for the *Foundations* would be inordinately long and not very instructive, for Chamberlain ransacked scores of authorities to substantiate his own prior convictions. His writing exemplifies what George Mosse has called the "scavenger" quality of racist literature, pedantically piling up facts to demonstrate its contentions and annexing ideas from all the dominant trends of contemporary scholarship.[54]

As noted, racial history was a firmly established genre well before the *Foundations;* indeed, it is difficult to decide where in time to begin the history of racism. Every European country developed myths of origins, relating Christian and pre-Christian traditions to explain the heritage of man since Adam. The chief source for these speculations was, of course, the Bible, which traced the line from Adam to the patriarch Noah and to his sons, Japheth, Shem, and Ham. The main tradition attributed the paternity of Europeans to the children of Japheth, and that of Asians and Africans to Shem and Ham respectively. Other myths also flourished to account for differences between Europeans, to justify social inequalities within states, as well as to claim the supremacy of one people over another. In Spain, France, Italy, England, and the German states writers have from the earliest times invoked Gothic or Germanic superiority to explain the privileges of the nobility, the racial basis of the dynasty or governmental tradition, the inferiority of Celts, Gauls, or Iberians, and the physiological roots of military victories or popular insurrections. These ancient myths, described by one scholar as "compromises between pagan memories, dynastic ambitions and the teachings of the Church," may at first seem very remote from the theories of modern racism, but their preference for Germanic superiority prefigured and shaped the Aryan ideology; together they form the inherited wisdom about the identity of ancestors on which eighteenth-century race theory was built.[55]

From the Enlightenment onward, these racial myths of origin were strengthened by science. The eighteenth-century quest to define man's place in nature marks the beginning of racism as a coherent and systematic structure of thought. Widespread speculation about the concept of a Chain of Being; the path-breaking research of Cuvier, Linnaeus, Buffon, and Blumenbach; heated debates about the fixity of species and the role of climate and environment in causing differentiation between human beings: all attest to the enormous intellectual ferment, as traditional theories of supernatural order and metaphysical unity yielded ground to newer philosophies of secular reason, natural science, and romantic pantheism. Many theories, of course, were devised for distinct political ends: Edward Long's famous defense of slavery in Jamaica belongs to this category, so do the racially formulated denunciations of the French Revolution by Joseph de Maistre and the Comte de Montlosier.[56] But other theories, advanced more in the spirit of scientific objectivity, pieced together detailed investigations of physical characteristics and the observations of world travelers, as well as referring to contemporary philosophical speculation about the relationship of race and culture.

A second reservoir of racial ideas for the future was the anti-Enlightenment writings of Herder, Fichte, Chateaubriand, and Burke. Their focus on the collective personality of a people or *Volk*, springing from its common language, literature, and historical continuity was easily transmuted to suit the purposes of racial theorizing. This was particularly true of Herder, whose mystical concept of *Volksgeist* and emphasis upon the power of language in shaping a national culture, had a profound impact upon racial philology in the next generations, despite his own explicit rejection of racial classifications.

Later writers repeatedly harked back to this heritage of Enlightenment and Romantic thought. For example when, in the *Foundations*, Chamberlain touched upon pre-Adamite theories which distinguished the Jews as Adam's progeny from other groups of different ancestry, he recalled Goethe's conversations with Eckermann and sometimes the theories of Giordano Bruno.[57] Further, his assertions about language were often accompanied by references to Fichte, Herder, and Voltaire, while in Kant's racial speculations he could find a mixture of environmentalism and of an "inner life force" to account for human differences. Today it may seem a terrible distortion to focus upon the racial aspects of the thought of Kant, Hegel, Goethe, or Comte, but few thinkers from the mid-eighteenth century were free of racist notions, and later exponents of race understandably made the most of this illustrious pedigree. Chamberlain possessed a prodigious knowledge of early speculation about race; he also assumed that Germanic thinkers like Kant and Goethe must be intellectually compatible, their ideas fitting neatly together into a racial vision. Such assumptions not only led him to seize upon distorted interpretations of their work, but also to turn them into precursors of his own outlook; in this way, for example, he represented the prejudice of Kant against Judaism as a statutory and historical religion as akin to his own racial analysis.[58]

The Aryan or Teutonic myth was the central theme of European race thinking in the nineteenth century. "Today," remarked that dogged opponent of racism, Jean Finot, in 1906, "out of a thousand educated Europeans, 999 are persuaded of the authenticity of their Aryan origins."[59] Exaggerated though his remark was, it underscores the persistence of the Aryan idea more than a century after it was first "scientifically" formulated. The concept first achieved prominence in the late eighteenth century with a growing interest in the East and India, as philosophers and littérateurs attempted to free themselves from the constraints of Judaeo-Christian and Eurocentric thinking. Speculation about the original birthplace of man, together with romantic enthusiasm for Indian religion, encouraged study of the tribes that spread into northern India through the passes of the Hindu Kush around 1500 B.C. What really opened up the treasure trove of Eastern languages, texts, and cultures for the first time to Europeans were, however, the pioneering advances made in comparative linguistics and Sanskrit by a small group of philologists, most notably Sir William Jones, Franz Bopp, Jacob Grimm, and Friedrich Schlegel. Until then scholars had largely attempted to derive other languages from Hebrew, widely considered to be the original human tongue. But the new discoveries concerning grammatical structure postulated two distinct linguistic families—the Semitic and the Indo-Aryan or Indo-European—and pointed to the marked affinity between Sanskrit, Greek, Latin, Persian, the Germanic, and the Celtic languages. This quickly awakened a new sense of the significance of the Orient for Europe and rapidly established as the basic premise of scientific philology that European languages emerged from a common source akin to Sanskrit.

Not surprisingly, theories about language and speculation concerning the geographical origin of man were fused together, giving rise to the conviction that the Aryan-speaking peoples of northern India had migrated westward across the Eurasian land mass and were the distant ancestors of modern Europeans. In the 1840s and 1850s the voluminous scholarship of the German Indologist Christoph Lassen and the Oxford philologist Friedrich Max Müller did much to popularize and elaborate the hypothesis of a superior Aryan race (although Müller substantially altered his opinions later); Gobineau's

Essai transformed the Aryan drama into an ironic, tragic view of history, a pessimistic refutation of contemporary theories of progress; and in 1859 the Swiss philologist Adolphe Pictet published a massive eulogy of this conquering peasant race, depicting it as the chief architect of modern civilization:

> This was the race of the Aryas, who were endowed from the beginnings with the very qualities which the Hebrew lacked, to become the civilizers of the world; and nowhere does the evidence for a providential plan emerge more clearly than in the parallel courses of these two contrasting streams, one of which was destined to absorb the other. The difference between the two races could not be more marked. . . . The religion of Christ, destined to be the torch of humanity, was adopted by the genius of Greece and propagated by the power of Rome. Germanic energy gave it new strength, and the whole race of European Aryas under its beneficent influence, and by means of endless conflict, raised itself little by little to the level of modern civilization. . . . It is thus that the race of the Aryas, more favoured than any other, was to become the main instrument of God's plan for the destiny of mankind. [60]

Here, forty years before the publication of the *Foundations*, was a fairly close summary of its main themes. Probably the most important champion of Aryanism, however, was Ernest Renan. His vision of Aryan superiority and his analysis of Semitic languages as ossified, sterile, and incapable of self-regeneration—signifying the moral and biological decadence of the Semitic race—made a deep impression on contemporaries. It was he, above all, who analyzed Aryan and Semite in terms of language, history, race, and patterns of thought, and shaped the two myths to the intellectual climate of his time. Later writers, whether or not they agreed with his views, relied heavily on his writings. [61]

Around the middle of the century, voices of protest gradually began to challenge some of the sloppiness that had invaded linguistic-racial thinking. "A man's language," asserted E. B. Tylor, one of the English pioneers of cultural anthropology, "is no full and certain proof of his parentage." "Much bad anthropology," he added, "has been made by thus carelessly taking language and race as though they went al-

ways and exactly together."[62] By 1885, according to Isaac
Taylor, an Anglican clergyman and anthropologist, the
tyranny of Sanskrit over the study of race was ended, giving
way to a new era of exact science; but the change was more apparent than real, for the concepts of philology continued to
exercise a powerful impact on the new disciplines of ethnology,
anthropology, and the comparative study of social institutions.
Aryanism, as conceived by linguistic scholars, was challenged
and modified, but much of the older vocabulary, modes of
thought, and factual data was retained and played an important role in racial theory well into the twentieth century.

The main theoretical debate between the rival schools of
anthropology prior to the 1860s was the controversy over
monogenesis and polygenesis. Those who accepted Christian
orthodoxy and adhered to the biblical unity of mankind could
in practice assert the significance of race and the irreversible
inequality of human groups, but were compelled to explain
these qualitative differences as the outcome of powerful historical and environmental influences. Thus, Buffon and
Blumenbach were monogenists, but still believed that Negroes
were "degenerative" forms produced by such factors as climate, food, and modes of life, while James Cowles Prichard
(probably the most popular anthropologist in England in the
early nineteenth century) devised a complicated evolutionary
scheme whereby each higher specimen was bleached whiter
and the Negro transmuted into the European. Against these
views the polygenists denied vehemently that the action of the
environment was sufficient to cause human diversity (especially within the limited biblical timespans advanced in the
pre-Darwinian era). Their conclusion was that separate acts of
divine creation were responsible for the different human races.
Polygenism had important seventeenth- and eighteenth-century precursors, but it really began to win widespread favor in
the 1840s as more and more evidence of human diversity was
brought forward by biologists and anthropologists. According
to one recent writer, by the time Darwin's *Origin of Species*
appeared in 1859, polygenism was the predominant scientific
view and so fundamental did the debate seem that the
President of the Anthropological Society of London noted that

many people believed "ethnology merely attempts to solve the question of whether there was unity of origin for the different races of man." [63] It is often assumed that Darwinian evolution terminated the issue by offering a vastly expanded time-span for racial variations to occur and a more convincing mechanism to account for phylogenetic differences. But polygenism did not die out; rather, it survived in modifed forms, appropriating parts of evolution theory to suit its purposes. Chamberlain, for example, shied away from "metaphysical" questions about the origin of races, but he was adamant that they were quite distinct. Also, his professor at Geneva, Carl Vogt, insisted that the different races were descended from different anthropoid ancestors, as did Paul Topinard (one of the leading French anthropologists in the 1880s); thus the white European could at least be affiliated with a smarter ape than the rest. The external forces which nourished polygenist thinking—the gulf between the "civilized" white and the "savage" black, and the need to justify white imperalism—were strengthened after 1860, while specific racial problems such as miscegenation or the interfertility of mulattoes still produced strong backing for essentially polygenist viewpoints in scientific circles. [64]

The effect of the incorporation of Darwinian ideas of evolution and struggle into European race theory has often been described and requires no detailed restatement here. Darwin's theory was not inherently racist; indeed, one logical deduction was that by denying the separateness of varieties and species and by claiming that all life derived from a single primordial form, evolution repudiated the separateness and intrinsic inferiority or superiority of races. Yet Darwin's own statements about race were imprecise and often ambiguous; he did not reject the present reality of races and intimated that some were fitter than others and that certain kinds of racial crossings were biologically retrograde. [65] But whatever Darwin's opinions were, his theory was rapidly appropriated by racists as a powerful corroboration of the natural inequality of human groups and as proof of the possibility of racial upgrading and improvement. Whereas Gobineau's concept of race had been basically static, something "pure" created by God and

contaminated over the centuries by interbreeding, "natural selection" and the "survival of the fittest" injected into racial
thought a new dynamism and activism. Race was an entity in
constant flux: it could evolve to a higher or lower plane,
dissipate its energies, or adapt successfully to circumstances.
Fastened to earlier racial convictions and stereotypes and
translated into a tool of social and historical analysis,
Darwinism penetrated every aspect of racist theory, popularizing and legitimizing the vision of each society as an arena of
biological struggle and reinforcing nationalist sentiment by
proclaiming the nation the chief incubator and vehicle of racial
development.

In the decades after 1859, racial anthropology entered the
period of its efflorescence. Scholars no longer felt constrained
to make their research conform to scriptural texts and there
was a concerted effort to place the study of man upon firm
scientific foundations. For many investigators this meant sub-
merging it beneath a sea of quantitative data. In France, England, and Germany especially, scores of researchers, clutching
complicated calipers, craniometers, spirometers, and other
sundry gauges that measured scientific ingenuity more than
the human anatomy, scoured the countryside weighing skulls,
examining bones, classifying hair and eye color and skin pig-
mentation, and measuring noses, ears, heads, and every other
attribute of the physical frame. From the data accumulated,
large numbers of racial taxonomies were invented. From the
beginning there was general agreement that some measurements were more significant than others, notably the size and
shape of the skull which was said (until the experiments of
Boas on immigrants in the United States in the early twentieth
century) to be resistant to all environmental influences and
therefore an accurate indicator of racial type. The eighteenth-
century Dutch anatomist Pieter Camper had devised a "facial
angle" for comparing the skulls of Europeans, Kalmucks,
Negroes, and apes; later, in 1840, a Swedish anthropologist,
Anders Retzius, introduced the cephalic index, a figure
computed from the length and breadth of the head. From this
index two major types were classified: the dolichocephalic or
longhead (which included the Aryan in almost all the taxo-

nomies) and the brachycephalic or broadhead, together with a multiplicity of intermediary groupings. Debates about the qualities and merits of these types engaged the leading scholars of the age and racist assumptions, seldom seriously questioned, seeped into the most distinguished science of the time. The founder of the Anthropological Society of Paris, Paul Broca, who carried out pioneering research on the brain and dominated French anthropology until his death in 1880, managed to collect and classify over 2,000 skulls, while another researcher, A. von Török, took the quantitative mania to its absurd conclusion in 1900 by making over 5,000 measurements on a single skull.[66]

From this wealth of anthropometric evidence, racists hazarded a wide variety of social deductions. Anthroposociologists such as Georges Vacher de Lapouge and Otto Ammon carefully correlated skull shape, religious beliefs, urbanization, and statistics for wealth to show the effects of natural selection on social stratification. Drawing upon Broca, Darwin, and the Aryan theories of Gobineau and other scholars, they depicted history as a massive contest which produced a continual redistribution of racial elements within each nation according to the laws of racial and social selection. Ammon, for example, tried to demonstrate that the income distribution in Saxony in 1900 reflected the existence of a "natural" aristocracy; he also spent seven years measuring the skulls of army recruits in the Grand Duchy of Baden and arrived at sweeping conclusions about the differences between urban and rural populations and the deleterious effects of urbanization upon "superior" dolichocephalic types.[67]

From the ponderous treatises of anthroposociology, journalists and popularizers gathered valuable ammunition for use against their liberal and socialist enemies. Social welfare reform was decried for protecting the weaker, substandard elements of the population, democratic forms of government were judged contrary to the national interest in that they handed over power to those morally and intellectually least fit to wield it; criminals were said to be physiologically and racially distinct; and all kinds of schemes for "internal colonization" and land settlement were proposed to safeguard the health of the nation. Equally reflective of this growing desire to apply the results of racial analysis to contemporary situations was the vogue of eugenics or racial hygiene in the last two decades of the nineteenth century.[68]

The appearance of Francis Galton's *Hereditary Genius* in 1869 (he was a cousin of Darwin) is usually taken as the birth of eugenics, but such theorizing advanced rapidly around the turn of the century with the genetic research of de Vries and Weismann and the rediscovery of the Mendelian laws of heredity. Racial hygiene encompassed a variety of viewpoints: some writers focused upon differences among individuals, stressing the impact of modern civilization upon biological substance, others concentrated their attention on the differences between races and the evils of miscegenation. And while all agreed that natural selection had to be replaced by socially guided selection, there were sharp disputes over how this could be achieved, Many insisted that an educational crusade was needed to enlighten the public in its breeding choices; others urged the compilation of eugenic records by the state; and a few abandoned voluntarism altogether and favored varying schemes for government intervention. Eugenic fears of racial decay and speculations about the friction between individual liberty and collective responsibilities permeated contemporary controversy about the vitality of European culture, the expansion of bureaucratic structures and participatory politics, the threat posed by social levelling and socialism, the rapid march of European colonization, and the threat of war between the major powers.

Anthropological conferences in the last quarter of the century echoed with fierce debates between the rival proponents of different systems of racial classification and genetic theorizing. Contemporary chauvinism, as much as social and class biases, invaded the work of racists, and many forsook scholarship for the maelstrom of patriotic and xenophobic dispute. Most famous perhaps was the celebrated controversy between the prominent French anthropologist Armand de Quatrefages and Rudolf Virchow, the leading pathologist in Germany and a prominent figure in the Progressive Party in the *Reichstag*.[69] After the French defeat at Sedan in 1870 and the German bombardment of Paris, Quatrefages unleashed his anger at the Prussians by asserting that they were distinct from other Germanic groups and belonged not to the Aryans but to an earlier, indigenous population of northern Europe. The Prussians, he argued, were not blond dolichocephalics, but ruthless brachycephalic Finns or Slavo-Finns, the enemy of superior culture and civilization. Although later his anger subsided and he recanted to some extent, Quatrefages's attacks excited heated denials and abusive countercharges from the German press. Shortly thereafter, encouraged by Virchow and other leading figures, the German Anthropological Society established a commission to classify the racial composition of the German states and thereby also refute the French slurs. When the army refused requests to measure the skulls of its troops, the commission turned to that other passive resource for public experiments: school children. Using such criteria as hair and eye coloring, general countenance and complexion, some 6.76 million children were surveyed with the assistance of educational authorities in Germany, Austria, Switzerland, and Belgium. Jewish children were categorized separately, despite the recent achievement of Jewish emancipation in Germany—a procedure that must surely have reinforced consciousness of their distinctiveness and putatively separate origins. By 1885 this enormous experiment, involving over 15 million children, was concluded. The "Finnish theory" was demolished; Prussians were proven to be of Germanic stock, including large numbers of blond, blue-eyed dolichocephalics; fears were allayed that Germans in the extreme east of the Reich were being engulfed by Slavic types; and the honor of Prussia was redeemed. German racists interpreted this data in a variety of ways and used it selectively in later years to demonstrate a range of conclusions. It should be added that Virchow, a cautious and learned scholar who soon expressed serious doubts about the scientific validity of craniology, was a tireless opponent of these political uses of biology. Large numbers of other academics, however, proved less resistant to the temptation of inferring social and political doctrines from their racial research.

The French, Germans, and British all claimed to be the purest descendants of the original Aryans; in fact, as W. Ripley complained in 1899, "No other scientific question, with the exception perhaps of the doctrine of evolution, was ever so bitterly discussed or so infernally confounded at the hands of chauvinistic or otherwise biased writers."[70] Thus, at the time Chamberlain began the *Foundations* one of the hottest issues in academic debates concerned the exact location of the ancestral home of the Germanic or Aryan peoples. Whereas in the earlier part of the century most authorities settled for northern India, after 1850 a growing number of experts— including L. Geiger, T. Pösche, T. Benfrey, L. Wilser, K. Penka, I. Taylor, and G. Kossina—found a broad range of linguistic, cultural, archaeological, and anatomical reasons for situating civilization's cradle in their own backyard, especially in northern and central Germany, Scandinavia, and the Baltic plains. Disputes continued over whether the north Germans or Gauls were the closest to primitive Aryans, but the European theory of origins continued to gather support so that by the twentieth century the term "Nordic" began to displace Aryan, although for a time the two were used almost interchangeably (the Russian-born French anthropologist, Joseph Deniker, was among the first to refer to a *race nordique* in 1900). In the 1930s Hans F. K. Günther and his Nordic school developed even more elaborate proofs for a German seat of origin, from which superior blood flowed out into neighboring regions and invigorated their native populations with its transfusions.

In its various forms—Teutonic, Indo-European, Germanic, Frankish, Aryan—the doctrine of Aryan superiority dominated modern European race theory. Fundamentally Manichaean, it explained the world in terms of a relentless combat between the forces of Good and Evil. The existence of the Aryan, synonymous with everything Good, necessitated the presence of a destructive force of Evil—and increasingly this negative principle came to be identified with the Semite, and more narrowly, with the Jew. The tone of writers differed, so did the extent to which racial theories voiced the ideas of political anti-Semitism. But invariably when racists pondered the physique, style of mind, and moral qualities of Semites, they ended up drawing a neat antithesis to everything Germanic or Aryan. Thus, the linguistic studies of Friedrich Schlegel, Pichtet, Burnouf, Lassen, and Renan emphasized the disparity of Indo-European and Semitic languages and correlated this with different mental and cultural capacities. Gobineau equated "semitization" with degeneration and the contamination of the white race by black or negroid blood. Vacher de Lapouge injected a crude hatred for Jews into his work, so did Robert Knox, the Scottish anatomist and one of the key figures in English racism whose *Races of Man* (1850) achieved an important and often underrated impact. By 1860 the division of Aryan and Semite, according to Léon Poliakov, was "already part of the intellectual baggage of all cultivated Europeans."[71] It permeated theology, left an imprint on, for example, Matthew Arnold's distinction between Hellenism and Hebraism in *Culture and Anarchy* (1869), and found its way into popular novels, histories, and everyday language. The mass migration of Jews from the East in the 1880s, coupled with the emergence of new styles of anti-Semitic politics and more intellectualized forms of hatred which made the Jew the agent of decadent modernism and liberalism, further accentuated this trend. Race theory that aimed to be relevant to the concerns of the late nineteenth century had to confront the "Jewish question," whether writers strove to refute the crude political uses of science (Felix von Luschan's writings, for example) or endeavored to legitimize religious and social antipathy for Jews with pretentious pseudo-scientific terminology (Drumont, Wahrmund, Duehring, and Chamberlain).

One theme implicit throughout this brief analysis of racism deserves to be reemphasized. Many historians of anthropology have drawn a deep line of separation between university scholars and cruder race publicists such as Chamberlain. With some degree of justification, it has been suggested that these academics were far more objective in their research and focused more narrowly on questions posed by scientific data and previous traditions of scholarly inquiry. As racial science percolated through society, it became steadily more vulgarized and trivialized; the science of one generation, in other words, became the cultural prejudice of pseudoscience of the next. Appealing though this notion might be, it should not, however, be accepted without qualification, especially in the case of Germany, where considerable evidence points to cross fertilization of ideas and even personal contacts between the academics and race popularizers.

One example of this interaction was the essay competition sponsored in 1900 by the arms manufacturer and dilettante biologist, Friedrich Albert Krupp.[72] The subject of the contest was: "What can we learn from the principles of Darwinism for the application to inner political development and the laws of the state?" Judged by a committee of academics, chaired by the zoologist Ernst Haeckel, a leading Darwinian, the competition excited widespread interest and the major entries were subsequently published and extensively reviewed in all the leading newspapers and periodicals. All the essays of sufficient length and quality to merit consideration for prizes were by university graduates and most had doctorates. Among them were the Munich physician and eugenicist Wihelm Schallmeyer, who won first prize; the doctor and zoologist Ludwig Woltmann, who was outraged by the demeaning offer of third prize; and Ludwig Kuhlenbeck, a law professor who became well known for his Pan-German lectures and *völkisch* writings. Most of the entries were convinced that all true culture derived from superior races, most espoused Aryan superiority and some form of anti-Semitism, and several—including Schallmeyer—recommended some kind of government intervention, among other things the keeping of public records of family lineage to facilitate hygienic controls.[73]

The educational background of the entrants, their conscious effort to cite respectable academic sources in anthropology and genetics, their reliance in addition on ideas drawn from writers like Gobineau and Chamberlain, and the high praise these essays obtained from renowned scientists like Ammon, Haeckel, and Heinrich Ziegler (a professor of zoology and author of numerous works on genetics) illustrate the new ties between racial biology and social theorizing. Two journals founded shortly afterwards, Ludwig Woltmann's *Politisch-Anthropologische Revue* (1902) and the *Archiv für Rassen- und Gesellschaftsbiologie* (1904) edited by Alfred Ploetz, a leading exponent of race hygiene in Germany, also encouraged contributions from political publicists and popularizers as well as academics.

It cannot be denied that a wide gulf existed between professional scholars and popularizers in sophistication, depth of research, and theoretical complexity. But race research was not an ivory tower pursuit, cut off from contemporary politics and cultural criticism. Fritz Ringer has analyzed a "crisis of learning" among the academic mandarins of Germany beginning in the 1890s and has shown how the pressures of a mass society and the aspirations of German imperialism shaped the tone and direction of scholarship in the humanities and social sciences.[74] Although Ringer's study omits anthropologists and race scientists, their work was equally marked by the cultural anxieties and class attitudes of the *Bildungsbürgertum*. Their writings evinced in many cases the same disaffection with modernity, opposition toward democracy, and sense of themselves as the beleaguered guardians of culture in a hostile environment as can be found in Chamberlain. As a young *Privatdozent* at the start of his illustrious career, Eugen Fischer, warned contemporaries:

> Today in Italy, Spain, and Portugal, the Germanic blood, the Nordic race, has already disappeared. Decline, in part, insignificance is the result. France is the next nation that will feel the truth of this; and then it will be our turn without any doubt whatever, if things go on as they have and are going today.[75]

Chamberlain could easily have written this, and while Fischer was critical of the errors and inconsistencies in the *Foundations* he nonetheless affirmed that the basic gist of the argument was sound and could withstand attack. Even the most extreme visions of racial war voiced by contemporary publicists found occasional echo in the pages of learned journals, as when, for example, Vacher de Lapouge admonished readers of the *Revue d'anthropologie* in 1887:

> The conflict of races is now about to start openly within nations and between nations, and one can only ask oneself if the ideas of the fraternity and equality of man were against nature. . . . I am convinced that in the next century people will slaughter each other by the million because of a difference of a degree or two in the cephalic index. It is by this sign, which has replaced the biblical shibboleth and linguistic affinities, that men will be

identified . . . and the last sentimentalists will be able to witness the most massive exterminations of peoples.[76]

Finally, in terms of personal contacts, the links between publicists and academics were frequently closer than is often suggested. Chamberlain, for example, not only had a solid training in science, but was a close friend of the prominent biologist Jacob von Uexküll and of Ferdinand Hueppe of the University of Prague. Karl Penka, the Viennese Gymnasium professor and author of several important studies on the Aryans, was close to the circle of Lanz von Liebenfels, the leader of an Aryan mystical cult in the Austrian capital, while Ernst Haeckel had numerous contacts with the Pan-German movement.[77] The prestige of such academics and the frequency with which they moved from interpreting empirical phenomena to larger judgments about history and society did much to lend credibility to similar-sounding ideas expressed by journalists and publicists. The sympathy that Ploetz, Fischer and others later showed for the *völkisch* right and National Socialism was not merely a product of the First World War and the chaos of early Weimar, it also derived from the social and political assumptions that lay buried in their earlier scientific research.

In the climate of intensified national and imperial rivalry after 1890, race theorizing made rapid headway in most of Europe, but nowhere was the vogue of such ideas stronger than in Germany. In the Reich racism acquired immense prestige among wide segments of the population as a mental style that encompassed the vague but grandiose ambitions of *Weltpolitik*, explained the rising tension in international relations and class conflict at home, and reflected both the nagging fears of cultural decay and the brassy optimisim that simultaneously assailed contemporaries. The publication of the *Foundations* turned Chamberlain almost overnight into the prophet of race for educated laymen in Central Europe. Born in the same year that Gobineau's *Essai* appeared, he largely synthesized the different developments in racial ideology in the intervening period, drawing together the strands of science, nationalist mysticism and ethnocentric prejudice, and giving

Aryan supremacy a specifically German focus. Race, argued Chamberlain, was the key to understanding not only the past and the present, but also the future.

Although fond of quoting Disraeli's words in the novel *Tancred*, "All is race, there is no other truth,"[78] Chamberlain was particularly vague when it came to explaining what he meant by race and applied the term to a bewildering array of human groups: Jews, Teutons, Celts, Slavs, Chinese, Aryans, Semites, the ancient Greeks and Romans, Prussians, and occasionally even the British were all labelled races at some juncture in his writing. But the mixture of evasiveness, bold assertions, and contradictions that typify his racial references, while irritating to some professional scholars, elicited remarkably little objection from most readers. For one thing, race was widely used in a range of very different meanings and contexts in everyday speech. Anthropologists and ethnologists also employed the word to designate numerous human categories and subgroups, with little agreement as to criteria for classification or the composite characteristics of different "ideal" types. After 1880, writers increasingly doubted the reality of homogenous or "pure" races, yet older stereotypes like the Aryan and Semite proved curiously resistant to argument, and those same authors who insisted that no population was untouched by interbreeding nonetheless spent their time trying to re-create pure types out of the present heterogeneity. Enigmatic phrases like "unity in diversity" or "continuity in discontinuity" crept into the prose of even the most careful scholars as part of their quest for a fictive "pure" racial type lurking behind the mass of individual variations.[79] Similarly, simple associations between physical and mental traits, race, and national character abounded in all racial literature, both popular and academic, based not on logical analysis or convincing data, but on many different and conflicting emotions. Chamberlain may have been particularly remiss in using race as a catchall concept into which he poured his unsubstantiated feelings, but the difference was often one of degree rather than of kind.

By the end of the nineteenth century any race theory which hoped for success among intelligent readers had to appear scientific and incorporate the findings of anthropology

and biology. Wherever possible Chamberlain tried to buttress
his views with such scholarship, referring frequently to Virchow, von Luschan, Ratzel, Reinach, and others. Accompany-
ing the text were diagrams of skull shapes taken from the
French Aryanist Gabriel de Mortillet and illustrations of
Semitic and Germanic physiognomy. "There is perhaps not a
single anatomical fact," Chamberlain asserted, "upon which
race has not impressed its special distinguishing stamp," and
he furnished readers with a few remarks about hair coloring,
stature, and other anatomical indicators.[80] But he was also
quick to repudiate "rational anthropology" when it contradicted his own intuitive insights. By quoting out of context,
comparing contrary opinions, and poking fun at the jargon of
calipers and head indexes, he strove to discredit empirical research in favor of instinct and intuition: "Descartes pointed
out that all the wise men in the world could not define the
color 'white'; but I need only to open my eyes to see it and it is
the same with 'race.'" "The more we consult the experts," he
remarked with irritation, "the less able we are to find our bear-
ings."[81]

Chamberlain's polemics against the confusion of racial
science, while certainly reflecting his personal impatience at
scholarly caution and his intrepid defense of the dilettante,
also illustrated in some respects a real and growing crisis in
this whole field of study. By 1895, it has been estimated, over
25 million Europeans had been subjected to anthropometric
measurement and yet the more exact observation and quantifi-
cation became, the more artificial and purely statistical racial
classifications seemed. When, after years of research, Otto
Ammon was asked to supply a photograph of a "pure" Alpine
type from southern Germany, he had to admit that he had
never encountered one: "All his round-headed men were either
blond or tall, or narrow-nosed, or something else that they
ought not to be."[82] Virchow and Paul Topinard became
increasingly skeptical about interpreting the results of craniology; experts were deeply divided over heredity; and researchers found it impossible to show clearly the transmission
of combinations of racial traits from fathers to sons. Even
before 1900 Franz Boas, who was trained in the German tradi-

tion of Virchow, Ratzel, and Bastian, began using anthropometric data to develop a thorough-going critique of racial
thought. The metric torrent unleashed by scholarly investigations had, in other words, begun to weaken faith in the racial
concept itself, although few writers ventured to abandon the notion altogether. One general consequence, however, was an
increasing flight into subjectivity: skepticism about finding
exact physical criteria brought forth more extravagant claims
for racial psychology and more abstruse notions of racial
Gestalt or "race souls."

To some degree, then, Chamberlain's emphasis on direct
sensation and intuitive experience as the ultimate test of race
arose out of his desire to restate the themes of Aryan superiority and anti-Semitism without getting bogged down in the
unresolved issues which sharply divided the scholarly community. The goal of the *Foundations*, he explained, was "to
investigate and shape the race question for a person living in
the present." [83] Life did not wait for scientists. "If," he told
Kaiser Wilhelm, "we do not now resolve to investigate this
problem resolutely and to cultivate race on principle, it will
soon be too late and our Teutonic type will be lost forever." [84]
Racial *Gestalt* was an intricate unity of physical, mental and
spiritual attributes. Corresponding to its outward form or
physical characteristics were a range of moral and intellectual
qualities and even modes of life, institutions and forms of
government (variations and gradations occurred, as in the case
of physical type, but within definite limits). In general, Chamberlain preferred to rely on these "moral" criteria of race. He
continually reverted to what has been called the "systema-
tized anecdotal" method of classification, noting "the gloomy
passionateness of the Celt," the "idealism," "practicality,"
"loyalty," and "honor" of the Teuton, the "intolerance" and
"sterility" of the Semite, and so on. [85] His analysis of Christ's
racial ancestry was composed largely of this kind of reasoning,
inferring racial identity from the supposedly Aryan or Teutonic
nature of Christianity, complemented by a few broad generalizations about the ethnography of the Palestine region.

Sometimes he even seemed about to deny that race was
physical at all and came close to describing "Aryan" and

"Semite" as disembodied modes of thought and feeling detached from a specific physical structure:

> One does not need to have the authentic Hittite nose to be a Jew; the term Jew rather denotes a special way of thinking and feeling. A man can very soon become a Jew without being an Israelite; often it is necessary only to have frequent intercourse with Jews, to read Jewish newspapers, to accustom oneself to Jewish philosophy, literature and art. On the other hand, it is pointless to call the purest bred Israelite a Jew, if he has succeeded in throwing off the shackles of Ezra and Nehemiah and no longer acknowledges the law of Moses in his mind or despises others in his heart. [86]

Compounding the confusion, he added: "it is comparatively easy to become a Jew, difficult almost to the point of impossibility to become 'Teutonic.' "The richer the mind, the more closely and manifoldly it is connected with the substructure of a definitely formed blood." With such obscure comments, Chamberlain avoided a complete biological determinism: Jewish assimilation was impossible on a large scale, but not out of the question for exceptional individuals. And, more importantly, the excessive influence of "Jewish" ideas in Imperial Germany was not proof of irreversible miscegenation. Less candid than Karl Lueger, who bluntly remarked "I decide who is Jew," Chamberlain in practice followed the same intuitive impulse. [87]

"Life," he never tired of repeating, "is needed to understand life." Perhaps the height of his irrationality came in a passage where he asserted that children ("especially girls"), whose vision was unclouded by false egalitarian and humanitarian sentiments, possessed a particularly acute instinctual grasp of race. Similar convictions can be found in numerous racial novels, but Chamberlain used it deliberately to belittle the inconclusiveness of academic research:

> It frequently happens that children who have no conception of what "Jew" means, or that there is any such thing in the world, begin to cry as soon as a genuine Jew or Jewess comes near to them! The learned can frequently not tell a Jew from a non-Jew; the child that scarcely knows how to speak notices the difference. Is that not something? To me it seems worth as much as a whole anthropological congress or at least a speech of

Professor Kollmann. There is still something in the world
besides compass and yardmeasure. Where the expert fails with
his artificial constructions, one single unbiased glance can
illuminate the truth like a sunbeam. [88]

Science, Chamberlain argued, ought to refine and elaborate
that basic intuitive knowledge of which every member of a race
was conscious.

Chamberlain's attacks on scientific positivism and pe-
dantry, which absorbed more and more of his energies in the
years after he finished the *Foundations*, coincided with a
broader and more sophisticated debate throughout the world
concerning the philosophical foundations of science and the
limits of scientific explanation. Already in October 1896, when
he had scarcely begun the *Foundations*, he tried to pull
together his ideas in a brief sketch which he titled provi-
sionally "Toward a Doctrine of Life." [89] It comprised a series of
reflections on the scientific method, drawing upon the writings
of Ernst Mach, Heinrich Hertz, Hermann von Helmholtz, and
other leading scholars. Like them he also repeatedly went back
to Goethe, Lichtenberg, and especially Kant for a philosophical starting point for his speculations. Chamberlain condemned uncritical scientism and insisted that science must be
built upon a critique of knowledge; in particular, he rejected
the use of mechanical analogies in the life sciences and demanded a new methodology in these fields which would combine intuitive, mystical insights and empirical observation.
His radical subjectivism in the *Foundations* was, therefore,
justified by allusions to a range of respected authorities and
given a Kantian gloss. Chamberlain's highly idiosyncratic interpretation of Kant transformed the critique of reason into a
sweeping vindication of the mythic quality of all thought,
thereby allowing him to jettison science when it proved incon-
venient and to assert the validity of direct sensation and
unmediated experience. As Uriel Tal commented: "The intuitive experience of race thus becomes identical with the
existence of race itself and the principal criterion in judging
Judaism, Christianity, Germanism, religion, nationality and
culture in general." [90] At times Chamberlain seems to regard
race as a "category of the understanding," one of the *a priori*
principles through which the mind synthesizes and unifies

experience of the world. Human perception and the way reason operates are thus seen as a function of race. Elsewhere he comes close to identifying race as the underlying reality of things, the agent that shapes all feeling, morality, and religion as well as reasoning. In attempting to keep race immune from the onslaught of reason and empirical science, Chamberlain ran a grave risk of transforming it into a secular religion.

Given the irrationalist basis of Chamberlain's views, it may almost seem perverse to extract a racial theory from the *Foundations*. But the rudiments of a theory were nonetheless present. Chamberlain rejected Gobineau's view that originally pure races had undergone miscegenation so that the superior Aryan faced extinction. Gobineau's fatalistic lament, "We do not descend from the ape, but are headed in that direction," was unpalatable to more modern exponents of Teutonism, and Chamberlain offered a more optimistic and messianic vision. Gobineau's pessimism was "the grave of every attempt to deal practically with the race question" and left one honorable solution: "that we at once, put a bullet through our heads."[91] According to Chamberlain, race evolved historically; it was something dynamic and changing: "the result of a continuing effort to form itself, to arrive at and maintain a pure state."[92] Like most other racists, he grafted Darwinian struggle and plasticity of form onto older notions of a human hierarchy. "The early human race was a variable, comparatively colorless aggregate, from which individual types have developed with increasing divergence . . . the sound and normal evolution of man is therefore not from race to racelessness, but, on the contrary, to an ever clearer distinction of race." "You see," he told Edouard Dujardin, "I am a disciple of Darwin." He urged "wise cross-breeding of related races," and "wise defense against racial foreigners," using race not merely to explain the rise and fall of civilizations, but to hold out prospects for a future racial milennium. "Even if it were proved," he insisted, "that there had never been an Aryan race in the past, we will have one in the future; for men of action this is the decisive point of view."[93]

From animal breeding, botany, and history Chamberlain sketched out five laws or preconditions for the development of a noble race. (1) The presence of "excellent material," a statement he never attempted to clarify. For Chamberlain primordial man had a varied potential. (2) A continuous period of endogamy with little admixture of foreign blood. (3) A process of natural selection, toughening the racial material on the principle of the survival of the fittest. In discussing this process Chamberlain made the notorious statement, borrowed without acknowledgment from Vacher de Lapouge, praising "the exposure of sickly infants" as "one of the most beneficial laws of the Greeks, Romans and Teutons." (4) Controlled interbreeding depending on the capacity of the race to absorb new elements. (5) The mixtures of closely related types, where the infusion of new blood was swift and limited, followed by long periods of inbreeding, would produce the highest races. The island of Britain and the isolated valley communities of ancient Greece had offered especially propitious environments for this. In contrast, in the South American "mestizo" states the continued miscegenation of widely different types had "obliterated" race and produced a mongrelized chaos.[94]*

With humans, unlike animals, the results of interbreeding were not always immediately visible, but the large-scale experiments of history, Chamberlain asserted, sustained the validity of his five laws. His description of the racial evolution of the Jews was almost a parody of these rules for producing a noble race: the basic "material" was judged inferior, crossbreeding had occurred between widely dissimilar groups, but a rigid program of endogamy—ordained, Chamberlain argued,

---

* Fear of miscegenation runs throughout the *Foundations*, coupled with the conviction that inferior breeds possessed superior procreative power—or, to use Vacher de Lapouge's expression, that "bad blood drives out good." Thus in a letter to Kaiser Wilhelm in 1902, Chamberlain spoke of a professor of literature who had married "a pure German girl" and was horrified to find that their children showed marked Semitic traits. Upon investigation he added, it was found that the professor's grandmother had been a baptized Jew and that these characteristics had eventually predominated: "In one or two generations there is a fluctuation back and forth, but those that come after will be Syrian-Semitic, and will—with intellectual and moral dispositions corresponding to their race—act as "German" judges, professors, officers and deputies." Chamberlain also pondered the phenomenon of telegony or "remote impregnation." According to this notion, one "bad crossing" was sufficient to taint forever all subsequent offspring of the female. Explained in many textbooks, including the writings of Spencer and Darwin, this doctrine was largely applied to animal breeding, but racists soon appropriated the notion to apply to Aryans and Jews. During the First World War, Chamberlain's disciple, Artur Dinter, wrote a bestseller, *Die Sunde wider das Blut* [The Sin against the Blood] with a telegonic plot, and many Nazi publications centered on this theme. In 1935 the Nuremberg decrees turned the theory into law. *Briefe* 2: 153–54. For Dinter, see chapter 10.

by the Jewish religion—had saved this group from complete degeneration. Like other racial anti-Semites Chamberlain could never make up his mind whether Jews were a "pure" race, an "anti-race" or a mongrelized breed (a *Mischmaschvolk* was the expression of the Pan-German leader, Heinrich Class). A racial struggle for existence, Chamberlain admonished, was underway between Teuton and Jew: "where the struggle is not waged by cannon balls, it goes on silently in the heart of society by marriages." [95] Yet he offered few suggestions for state action to curb the influence of Jews, preferring instead to focus upon the spiritual and cultural regeneration of Germans. "If Chamberlain is right," concluded his French friend and translator, Robert Godet, "it is we who have created the Jewish peril by accepting in our organism a body which it could not assimilate. . . . We must therefore free ourselves from the Jewish yoke by spiritual means of our own." [96] Had Chamberlain completed his original plan, later volumes might have been more explicit. In the *Foundations* he preferred to describe the cultural situation as he saw it, and leave it to readers to draw their conclusions about social and political action.*

* On one occasion only did Chamberlain write in a more prescriptive tone. In 1900 the Bucharest journal *Nuova Revista Romana* sought contributions from several foreign writers as to whether political and civil equality should be accorded to Romanian Jews. Chamberlain saw himself as a middle-of-the-road observer, separate from the blind humanitarians and fanatical Jew-baiters ("on the one side genuine Zolas, Mommsens, Lombrosos and the like, on the other side rowdies à la Drumont"). His contribution appeared in 1900 and was subsequently reprinted in German newspapers. It was also used by the extreme right in 1918 to attack Foreign Minister von Kühlmann's treaty with Romania. Briefly, Chamberlain argued that the exclusion of Jews from England from 1290–1657 had enabled a strong, vigorous British race to grow and sustain itself. The glories of British history were a product of this, and only in the nineteenth century had the nation succumbed to Jewish influence in politics and cultural life. The lessons for Romania (a country with 25 times the proportion of Jews that were in England) were clear: a developing nation must curb the influence of this "destructive element." Assimilation was impossible and complete tolerance unwise. He argued for a restriction of Jewish civil and legal rights, their exclusion from politics, ownership of land, the press, publishing, and education. He also suggested monetary incentives to foster Jewish emigration. The Jew should become in other words an alien resident with much reduced rights. "We have the right and the duty," he wrote, "to take—without unfriendliness—strenuous protective measures against such a dangerous guest." His views coincided with those of much of the anti-Semitic movement in the period, and foreshadowed in many respects Nazi policy in the years 1933–38. "Ueber die Judenfrage in Rumänien," *Nuova Revista Romana* (1900) 10; reprinted in *Tägliche Rundschau* (Berlin) May 29, 1901, and again as "Rasse und Nation" in *Deutschlands Erneuerung* (July 1918) 2 (7).

All the major elements of German racism converge in Chamberlain's writing: Aryan supremacy, anti-Semitism, messianic and mystical notions of race, Social Darwinism, and recently developed doctrines of eugenics and anthroposociology. Above all he joined the Teutonic myth, German nationalism, and cultural idealism. For him—unlike Gobineau—race, nation, and *Volk* were almost identical. Admittedly, he was careful to include Slavs and Celts along with Germanic peoples in the Teutonic race, but his description made it clear that the purest and least corrupted specimens inhabited the German Reich. The vitality of Britain, Russia, and France had been exhausted by racial degeneration and their growing adherence to foreign, particularly Semitic, ideals. Only Germany, he reflected in 1906, could protect the "life-giving center of western Europe" from the "tartarized Russians," the "dreaming weakly mongrels of Oceania and South America," and the "millions of blacks, impoverished in intellect and bestially inclined, who even now are arming for the war of races in which there will be no quarter given." [97] As he repeatedly informed Kaiser Wilhelm in their early letters: the future of mankind was contingent upon the realization of Germany's national goals. German *Weltpolitik* was justified by a sacred mission—the preservation of Christianity and superior culture. As one American reviewer observed: "Imperialism, from gross aggression, becomes a moral duty and at last an article of faith." The deity of racial supremacy "not only justified the vast aggressions of Russia and England in the nineteenth century, but it also sanctions beforehand all that Germany may choose to appropriate in the twentieth." [98]

But the expansion of German power was predicated upon national and racial unity. It meant recovering German ideals, conformity to a whole conservative social and political order, and the eradication of those forces which threatened to enslave men—socialism, liberalism, materialism, and Catholic ultramontanism. Whereas Gobineau and many other racists used race primarily to explain social inequalities and class stratification within the state, Chamberlain employed race as a means of national integration. Rarely did he speculate about the relative racial worth of Germans; instead he urged them to recognize their deeper bonds of blood and to transcend class and ideological barriers. Race consciousness replaced liberal individualism and Marxist socialism—the two false creeds of the nineteenth century—as the basis for social organization. In practice this meant a rather vague affirmation of monarchy, authoritarian government, and conservative ideals, together with *völkisch* (and typically Wagnerian) appeals for a new politics that would translate the secret impulses of the nation into reality and fuse Germans into an organic and conflict-free society.

The *Foundations* became one of the principal texts of German racism, frequently cited in Pan-German and *völkisch* circles and later a model for many Nazi pseudo-philosophers. The Berlin professor Felix von Luschan might describe it as more poetry than science,[99] and historians may wince at its unsupported assertions and irrational claims, but large numbers of Germans were clearly enthralled by this kind of bold and opinionated "poetry." Many intellectuals delighted in Chamberlain's polemics against university scholarship, his irrational *Lebensphilosophie* coincided with a general growth of philosophic irrationalism, and his passion for culture and self-cultivation aroused widespread sympathy. Regardless of many errors, Chamberlain had shaped his knowledge into a personal creation; he had pieced together his own jigsaw puzzle of history, religion, philosophy, and science. Comparatively few readers were qualified to refute its wide-ranging erudition, and many more were highly vulnerable to this kind of racial and national doxology.

Chapter Six

Der Fall Chamberlain

CHAMBERLAIN'S *FOUNDATIONS*, admitted the *Frankfurter Zeitung* sadly, "has caused more of a ferment than any other appearance on the book market in recent years."[1] It was an immediate success despite its size and relatively high price and attracted widespread notice in the press. Three editions appeared in the first year of publication and a cheap "popular edition" in 1906 sold over 10,000 copies within ten days. By 1915 sales exceeded 100,000 and the book had become a much quoted classic in *völkisch* circles; translations soon appeared in English, Czech, and French, and by 1938 the German edition had gone through 24 large printings. Alfred Rosenberg, one of the leading ideologues of the Nazi movement, claimed in 1927: "Chamberlain's *Kampfbuch* is an indispensable accompaniment in the coming struggle for German freedom" and it is as a spiritual precursor of Nazi publications that the book has often been remembered by historians.[2] But it belonged, as its popular reception demonstrates, equally to the cultural milieu of Wilhelminian Germany. "Next to the national liberal historians like Heinrich von Treitschke and Heinrich von Sybel," Fritz Fischer has written, "Houston Stewart Chamberlain had the greatest influence upon the spiritual life of Wilhelminian Germany."[3]

Fischer's claim may well be an overstatement, but certainly the *Foundations* sparked a heated debate on cultural, religious, racial, and political grounds. Chamberlain had managed to capture the rhetoric of strength and heroism, the fretful appetite for power combined with fears of encirclement and incipient decline which pervaded so much of the thought and language of Imperial Germany; its mixture of popular idealism and national chauvinism was tempting to broad sections of the middle and upper classes. And yet it is very difficult to assess the impact of such a book upon readers. Memoirs are often sketchy, inaccurate, or distorted by later ideas and conclusions; published responses to a book at once raise the knotty issue of how representative a reviewer is of a broader public; and spontaneous comments, in private correspondences for example, are both difficult to find in substantial numbers and are frequently fleeting references, hastily written and very impressionistic. A broad sampling of all these sources, however, allows some basis for tentative statements about readership and the public impact of the *Foundations*, especially when joined to the results of related research upon German-Jewish relations and the emergence of what Fritz Stern and George Mosse have called "the Germanic ideology."

The *Foundations* was *the* literary fad of 1900 and maintained its tremendous appeal for several years. "The Chamberlain case," one contemporary recalled, "produced the same kind of response as the Spengler case after the World War."[4] It was extensively reviewed in the popular periodicals and provided an appropriate topic for discussion at literary and political meetings, historical societies, and philosophy lectures.[5] Yorck von Wartenburg, philosopher and son of a famous historical popularizer, informed Chamberlain in December 1899: "In Berlin . . . [your] book is the subject of daily conversation among all the cultivated people." Two years later Cosima Wagner wrote "I cannot tell you how often your name was mentioned in Berlin. For certain your *Foundations* is the book most read among all classes."[6] Another astute observer of the social scene, Baroness von Spitzemberg, recorded in her diary:

There is almost no page with which one might not disagree or at least question in astonishment: Is it so, can it be so? But there is not a page where one must not rejoice at the book's elegant style, its genial masculine, enthusiastic and spirited grasp of the subject! . . . wherever one goes the book is being read and has enthusiastic supporters, though there are others who call it superficial, unscholarly, and fantastic."

"The work," the Baroness admitted, "swarms with risky hypotheses, unproven assumptions, but it provides so much to think about, uplifts, strengthens and inspires the soul, destroys all monotonous theorizing and carping (*Nörgelei*)—Is that not sufficient praise in our feeble, cool, sceptical time?"[7]

The earliest reviews asked who this Chamberlain was, and some—much to Chamberlain's annoyance—spread a rumor that he was really Julius Langbehn who nine years before had surprised everyone with his enormously successful *Rembrandt als Erzieher*. Other newspapers asked whether he was related to Joseph Chamberlain, the British Colonial Minister and one of the most hated men in the Reich; indeed, several periodicals in the next years printed pictures of Austen Chamberlain, the statesman's son, by mistake.[8] Before long, however, Chamberlain's Wagnerite associations and his identity became quite widely known, especially after he was received by Kaiser Wilhelm. In Berlin salons like that of the fervent Wagnerite Countess Wolkenstein, where both Jews and Gentiles gathered, and at the more exclusive soirées of the old nobility, the book was discussed. As Dr. Samuel Sanger noted somewhat contemptuously in Harden's *Zukunft:* "In circles which are not exactly accustomed to participating in heated controversies over the philosophy of history and cultural criticism, and which are made uncomfortable by long-winded efforts to arrive dialectically at a *Weltanschauung* . . . the author of our *Foundations* has become a familiar name and an emphatically cited authority."[9] Hard pressed by declining land revenues and higher property taxes, resentful of the purchase of Berlin's sumptuous palaces by Jews, and eager to share the Kaiser's new fads, the aristocracy read the book, or at least made some efforts to appear knowledgeable about it.

The most vehement criticisms of the *Foundations* came from the socialist press and liberal newspapers like the *Frankfurter Zeitung* and *Berliner Tageblatt*. In the revisionist

Sozialistische Monatshefte Friedrich Hertz, who later wrote a book denouncing Chamberlain and other race theorists, ridiculed the subjective, irrational proofs adduced by Chamberlain to substantiate racial vanity. Yet, after showing the errors and inconsistencies of the book and its lack of clarity on the relative importance of biological race and ideas in history, Hertz warned that Chamberlain's "enthusiasm gathers up many readers, who become captives more of the ideals ... than his reasoning."[10] Hertz's articles were widely cited in the liberal and Jewish press, while *Vorwärts* also cautioned that the moderate tone at the start of the book soon gave way to intolerant anti-Semitism, and a misrepresentation of thinkers like Goethe that smacked of the worst sectarian excesses.[11] The sociologist Franz Oppenheimer, in an article that provoked an angry response from the Berlin *Post*, condemned the *Foundations* as "the characteristic product of a class which must break with true learning because it cannot bear honest scholarship, the product of a class which cannot possibly endure that its legal title to history and its ephemeral privileges be examined closely."[12] The *Vossische Zeitung* was equally careful to represent a fanatical *Judenhass* as the moving spirit behind the book, but this did not deter the *Berliner Tageblatt* from printing one laudatory article entitled "Chamberlain als Erzieher", and the reviewer, beguiled by Chamberlain's honest, modest temper, wrote:[13]

> Chamberlain's book is a "personality" from which we cannot pull ourselves away, with which we are continually fighting but must respect, which elevates and enriches us, makes us small and great, and educates us. The secret of his effectiveness lies above all in the fact that he does not lecture us with the supercilious attitude of one who is "accomplished." Rather he travels the same road as his readers and shares their searching, struggles, and hopes.

The Conservative and National Liberal press was not surprisingly more favorable—although not uncritical. In 1903 *Der Tag* used Chamberlain's denunciations of Rome to bolster its campaign against a proposed amendment of the anti-Jesuit law, but *Der Reichsbote* was somewhat troubled by the "materialistic" tone of the work and feared that its identification of the salvation of Indo-European culture with the power of the Germanic race gravitated away from Christian universalism toward a scientific naturalism. Friedrich Lange's *Deutsche Zeitung* and the radical right *Deutsch-Soziale Blätter* praised Chamberlain, so did the Munich *Allgemeine Zeitung* and the *Münchener Neueste Nachrichten*, whereas the *National Zeitung*, a staunch supporter of Germanism, took the opportunity to admonish readers: "one must not conceal the dangers which threaten Germanness, dangers mostly from inner enemies." "Since Chamberlain's epoch-making book," wrote the *Norddeutsche Allgemeine Zeitung*, "the race question stands in the foreground of scholarly and literary discussions"; but the business-minded *Hamburgischer Correspondent* complained: "the author devoted too much interest to the handling of the Jewish question and too little to economic problems." The *Preussische Jahrbücher* was consistently critical of Chamberlain, unlike the *Neue Deutsche Rundschau* and the *Deutsche Monatsschrift*, which even reprinted excerpts from the book. Most reviewers, whatever their detailed opinions, agreed with the writer in *Kunstwart*, a traditional battleground between conservatives and radicals, that it was "a book that everyone should read who needs to know the foundation on which the spiritual and material culture of the present day is built, that is to say every educated person."[14]

As was to be expected Chamberlain gained enthusiastic support for his views in *völkisch* circles. Local meetings of the *Deutsche Gesellschaft* and other groups discussed the merits of the work. In Austria, Pan-German newspapers like the Viennese *Ostdeutsche Rundschau* and *Deutsches Volksblatt*, and *Der Kyffhäuser* of Linz, invoked Chamberlain in their struggle, printing long, favorable analyses of the book.[15] We may surmise that few *völkisch* Germans lacked a copy after the success of the popular edition in 1906; and even those who had not read the book had ample opportunity to discover its contents, for newspapers and brochures associated with such organizations as the largest union of white collar employees, the *Deutschnationale Handlungsgehilfen-Verband*, eagerly popularized its contents. Its leader, Wilhelm Schack, commented happily on the success of Chamberlain and Gobineau in 1903 and looked forward to significant heightening of national and racial consciousness among the "broadest strata of society."[16] Among members of the *Alldeutscher Verband* Chamberlain's views also struck a sympathetic chord: Heinrich Class, the leader of the organization after 1908, "plunged" into Chamberlain, and some of the most extreme spokesmen of the *Verband* called themselves his disciples.[17] Among them was Josef Reimer, author of a remarkable book, *Ein Pangermanisches Deutschland*, published in 1905, which reiterated Chamberlain's racial and religious ideas as justification for the creation of a huge German empire stretching across the Continent and including much of Russia. Special commissions of anthropologists, "breeding experts," and doctors were to divide the subject population into "Germans," those capable of being "Germanized," and those incapable of racial improvement. Jews and Slavs were without exception consigned to the latter category, while all groups were to be subject to careful eugenic controls. Reimer's vision clearly went far beyond anything dreamed of by Chamberlain and anticipated Nazi practice in many horrifying aspects.[18]

Apart from the many letters addressed to Chamberlain by admirers, few readers give the impression of being convinced by his arguments. As the *Frankfurter Zeitung* argued: "The seed which [he] sows finds a soil ready prepared for it and that vastly heightens the danger of the book."[19] Intellectuals like Moeller van den Bruck, troubled by the secularism and philistinism of the age, discovered in Chamberlain a deep, contemplative spirit, striving courageously to come to grips with the problems of race, religion and cultural change. As one Viennese writer argued: "The book is not to be disputed if seen as a *whole*, because it is not a mechanical aggregate of assertions and opinions, but rather a living organism which already justifies itself by its mere existence. It is not to be read as a scholarly argument, but as a deep-moving, dramatic and lively monologue."[20]

Literary figures admired the overall accomplishment but were selective in their reading. Wilhelm Busch, the brilliant satirist of the German bourgeoisie, found "in the stimulating book, much that I did not know before"; Hugo von Hofmanns-

thal sent the *Foundations* to a friend, the historian Josef Redlich, describing Chamberlain as a "polyhistorian . . . who can
make the most relaxed head swim"; twelve years later he
lavished still higher praise upon Chamberlain's *Goethe*.
Hermann Bahr and other young Viennese writers were awed by
Chamberlain's powers of synthesis, while the German translator of Strindberg discovered a profound "inner relationship"
between Chamberlain's vision and the Scandinavian
dramatist, whom he called "the deepest living German
Dichter." Even the Förster-Nietzsche circle in Weimar,
generally cool toward devotees of Wahnfried, was apprecia-
tive.[21] One of the most satisfying reviews for Chamberlain was
written by the aristocratic novelist Ernst von Wolzogen for the
prestigious *Das Litterarische Echo* of Berlin. "Here a German
man," Wolzogen wrote, "has had the courage to trace the
Jewish question historically without being blinded by stupid
anti-Semitic passion." Wolzogen was what we might call a
genteel anti-Semite—one who would angrily deny any such
epithet, but whose very words belied his denials. After sniping
at Wagnerite vegetarianism and ridiculing the notion of an
Aryan Christ, he complimented Chamberlain on a remarkable
achievement:

> While not a few of those good Wagnerians inspired by the
> Master's essay on *Jewishness in Music* have produced in their
> minds only a stupid anti-Semitism which makes them smell
> ritual murder and Alliance Israelite everywhere, we find in
> Chamberlain's case such a fantastically impressive and serious
> scientific presentation of the subject that only the limited ho-
> rizon of the Jewish press coolies [*Presskulis*] could still see in it
> anti-Semitic animosity.[22]

Very different was the verdict of *Die Gesellschaft*, the influential champion of literary Naturalism. Heinrich Meyer-
Cohn, a Berlin lawyer and banker who was among the most active figures in Jewish defense organizations, wrote the review,
castigating the *Foundations* as "bad, unclear and illogical in
its train of thought and unpleasing in style, full of false
modesty and genuine superciliousness, full of real ignorance
and false affectation of learning."[23]

Chamberlain's popularity among academic youth appears to have been extraordinary. His name was invoked by nationalist organizations like the *Verein Deutscher Studenten* and university gymnastic clubs to justify the exclusion of Jews, while in military academies and among young guard officers the book was widely read and discussed. Both Hermann Keyserling and the Austrian mystic, Rudolf Kassner, were students when they first became infatuated with Chamberlain's ideas. Kassner later compared the excitement he felt at the nationalist idealism of the *Foundations* with "the kind of attraction that prevented me, like so many young people, from missing a single lecture of Heinrich von Treitschke at Berlin University." Somewhat later in 1909, seventeen-year-old Alfred Rosenberg discovered the book in Riga: "Another world rose up before me: Hellas, Judah, Rome. And to everything I assented inwardly—again and yet again." It was, Rosenberg claimed, the beginning of his education.[24]

The distribution of the book was helped when in 1903 August Ludowici, a wealthy south German manufacturer and amateur biologist, donated 15,000 marks to send it free to schools and public libraries. Believing Chamberlain the chief cultural prophet of the age, Ludowici generously augmented his finances in the next years, although with this first gift he unwittingly caused widespread speculation that none other than Kaiser Wilhelm, a fervent admirer of the *Foundations*, was the anonymous donor.[25] Wilhelm certainly did enhance the popularity of the book by his attentions but Chamberlain may well have mistaken strong words for actions when he reported happily to his aunt Anne Guthrie in 1903 "He [Wilhelm II] has now given orders that in all the 'Lehrerseminare' of Prussia, i.e. the schools in which schoolmasters are formed for their profession, the *Grundlagen* are to be studied, read and the new divisions of history introduced by me are to be used in the teaching of history in these Seminare."[26] But, whether the book had formal recommendation or not, it appealed to many high school teachers. One Protestant teacher later recalled:

> "I myself read the whole book in one go when as a young gymnasium teacher at Nürnberg it fell into my hands. And with a flushed face I put it aside full of excitement. I can picture the scene today [1927] and can reawaken the old feeling."[27]

Before long, like Lagarde and Langbehn, Chamberlain was raised to one of the culture heroes of the *Wandervogel*, and the memoirs of its early leaders attest his influence in the protracted debate over Jewish membership.

It is hardly surprising that many university scholars were vigorously opposed to the book. Baron von Taube, for example, remembered how his admiration for the *Foundations* caused a "vehement argument" with his history professor at Berlin, Theodor Schiemann, the political editor of the Conservative *Kreuzzeitung*. When Schiemann damned the book as "inexact and thoroughly misleading," Taube found himself arguing that although the factual evidence might be shaky or even false, Chamberlain's ideas "were great and penetrated deeply into the truth." [28] Another nationalist historian, Otto Hintze, was equally critical, rejecting all tendencies toward crude racial determinism and insisting that "nations"—a mixture of racial instinct, cultural evolution, and historical tradition—were the motor force of progress. Though he sympathized with Gobineau, "a fine, resigned aristocratic soul which . . . flees back from a democratic levelling age into the past," Hintze saw in Chamberlain "a more modern man . . . free from romantic whims, free from the fatalism of a declining social class, and free from the fetters of a Roman Catholic world view." In the same essay, Hintze himself felt the need to warn against "the massive influx of Slavic and other foreign racial elements from the east" and urged: "Let us take care then that a firm, compact, unified *Volkstum* results which is rooted not merely in the mind but also in the blood, the German [*deutsche*] race of the future." [29] Still more critical of Chamberlain's dilettantism was the reviewer in the *Historische Zeitschrift*, who deplored such superficial acquaintance with the sources and the endless repetition of a simplistic notion of racial causation. [30]

But other scholars found redeeming features in the sound instincts and patriotic judgments of Chamberlain and were prepared to overlook his unscholarly mode of reasoning. Hans Vaihinger, the editior of *Kant-Studien*, the Indologist Paul Deussen, and the theologian Otto Pfleiderer were among those impressed by the *Foundations*. Serious and for the most part favorable reviews also appeared in several of the more academic journals, while Werner Sombart, who a decade later was to reinforce many prejudices by his discussion of Jews in capitalism, urged Chamberlain to participate in the *Archiv für Sozialwissenschaft und Sozialpolitik*. Professor Arthur Drews, an evangelical pastor and later a leader in the German Faith Movement, probably expressed the feelings of many people when he praised the "originality," the "personal and artistic impulse" of the author "even where he is obviously at error." "A strong individuality," Drews added, "speaks from his words and we willingly pay heed because we have the impression that we will get to hear things from him which we would otherwise find in no learned work."[31]

One group of contemporary scholars and publicists might have been expected to welcome the book: those engaged in the study of race. In fact, Chamberlain gained a mixed reception. His cavalier methods of citing authorities out of context and his poking fun at the direction of research angered many anthropologists and ethnologists. Ludwig Wilser, Vacher de Lapouge, S. F. Steinmetz and Felix von Luschan all reprimanded the author, although they sometimes shared Chamberlain's basic feelings.[32] Quite a few racialists concurred with Friedrich Ratzel, professor at Leipzig and one of the founders of political geography, who wrote of Gobineau and Chamberlain:

> I sympathize completely with their goals of bringing to all an awareness of the importance of race in the life of peoples throughout history, but I cannot approve of the way they mistreat the facts of racial development and history. Both are good natured and unscholarly characters: Gobineau a kind of Victor Hugo in prose and like him seductive in rhetoric, Chamberlain more calm but no more level-headed—in him the Anglo-Celtic inclination is powerful, not caring about scholarly truth if it is a question of proving a pet theory.[33]

Among the younger generation of race popularizers—Heinrich Driesmans, Willibald Hentschel and, later, Alfred Rosenberg and Hans F. K. Günther—the *Foundations* did have a significant impact. Gobineau's followers however were incensed by Chamberlain's polemical statements: his denial of intellectual debts and disassociation of his theories from the "phantasmagorias" of the French aristocrat. Labelling Gobineau "a perverse anti-scientific spirit" was an action guaranteed to provoke an outcry from Ludwig Schemann and other leading Gobinists. One influential race thinker, Ludwig Woltmann, tried to mediate the subsequent dispute which flared up, saying: "In their deepest roots they are the same, like morning and evening stars." But notwithstanding this astral relationship, Schemann announced that he would not in future accept Chamberlain's subscription to the *Gobineau Vereinigung*.[34]

"The innocent reader," Jean Réal wrote about the *Foundations*, "was sometimes charmed into thinking that vexed points or insurmountable difficulties were resolved as if by magic with the intervention of Chamberlain's intuition and enthusiasm."[35] As the foregoing analysis reveals, few readers were innocent and many were all too vulnerable. Germans were accustomed to arguments stemming from racial and national pride, familiar with the prejudices articulated during and after the protracted struggle over the emancipation of German Jews, and very receptive to cultural interpretations of the German mission which suited the tone of the *Weltpolitik* era.

Chamberlain endowed the *Foundations* with a strongly Christian theme, demanding a new positive faith that would rediscover the pristine teachings of Christ and prepare the way for *völkisch* rebirth. Religious regeneration and the mission of Germany were inseparable. These arguments had been voiced before, notably by Lagarde and Wagner, but Chamberlain's elaborate restatement, alluding to recent scholaship on race and religion, sparked a heated debate especially among German Protestants.

Not surprisingly Catholic reviewers were deeply opposed to the book and distressed by its enthusiastic reception at Court. The *Foundations* seemed to coincide with a rising wave of anti-Catholicism around 1900, as evidenced by the agressive campaigns of the *Evangelischer Bund*, continued opposition to repeal of the Jesuit laws, and widespread protests against Catholic lobbying for new school legislation in Prussia. With Chamberlain, however, such sentiments seemed to have reached new heights verging on demands for a second *Kulturkampf*. Reviewers in Catholic journals meticulously refuted his historical distortions, especially his claim that the Roman faith reflected the needs of a mongrelized *Völkerchaos*, and attacked the notion of a Germanic religion as contrary to the very essence of Christiantity. On the subject of Jews Catholic reviews were largely silent. Replying to his Catholic critics in 1903, Chamberlain took pains to distinguish between "German Catholics" and ultramontane Romanists. In the same year he also strongly supported government plans for a Catholic theology faculty at the University of Strassburg believing that the scheme would help reintegrate Catholics into the German mainstream by reducing the power of the seminaries and the Vatican. To some degree Chamberlain's division between Catholicism and the Roman tradition pointed to the efforts of reformist Catholics like Albert Ehrhard and Hermann Schell who advocated greater assimilation of their coreligionists into German society (including the training of priests at universities). But, coming from so extreme an opponent, Chamberlain's clumsy efforts at compromise had no impact in Catholic circles.[36]

Protestants were much more divided over Chamberlain's book. Among Pietists and more orthodox Evangelicals his "positive Christianity" and his critique of organized religion were firmly rebuked.[37] Professor Baentsch of Jena rejected "Teutonic religiosity" as a vague, pantheistic surrogate for religion and wrote a long critique of Chamberlain's account of Semitic religion. The book of Job, the Psalms, the Prophets, the writings after the Exile, and the literature of Greco-Roman circles had all, he claimed, been ignored or misrepresented. No wonder Chamberlain found so little common ground between the Jewish and Christian traditions![38] The *Protestantenblatt* also deplored the "absurdities" of "Chamberlain's attempt to make Jesus probably of Aryan heritage"; so did the *Kirchliche*

Wochenschrift für Evangelische Christen. They were visibly disturbed at the way racial nationalism threatened to become a powerful religious substitute, promising salvation in a vague, secular form, yet masquerading behind conventional Christian terminology.[39]

Protestant reviewers usually had fewer objections when it came to Chamberlain's attacks on Rome. The *Strassburger Zeitung* agreed with his characterization of Rome as "the implacable enemy of Protestant and Germanic nations," and provincial Protestant presses, especially in Polish areas, were sympathetic to his attacks on "Jesuitism."[40] "Chamberlain's presentation," wrote Ernst von Wolzogen, "compels us to admire the extraordinary logic and inexorable consistency in the rule of the Roman hierarchy and, at the same time, opens our eyes to the most fearful enemy of German culture."[41] Similarly the Munich *Allgemeine Zeitung* announced in 1902: "It must be acknowledged unconditionally that [Chamberlain] has correctly recognized the significance of political Catholicism and the danger with which it threatens state and society, culture and *Bildung*."[42]

Extreme *völkisch* Protestant groups in Germany and Austria, of course, welcomed Chamberlain's racial and religious views. The *Gustav-Adolf Verein* and the *Evangelischer Bund* were both enthusiastic while J. F. Lehmann, the head of a flourishing publishing house and an important link between *völkisch* anti-Catholic organizations, discovered in Chamberlain a new spiritual guide. "My husband," Melanie Lehmann acknowledged, "believed he had found in Chamberlain a religious leader." The *Foundations* inaugurated, in Lehmann's eyes, a new era in the struggle aginst Rome: the twentieth century needed someone who could "unfold the banner of the true German spirit," as Luther had done. That man was Chamberlain.[43] They remained friends for many years and met on several occasions. Chamberlain's writings convinced Lehmann of conspiratorial links between Jewry and Roman Catholicism, a belief that he continued to hold and publicize till his death in 1935. Another influential figure in the racist Christian movement who looked to Chamberlain for advice and assistance was Wilhelm Schwaner, author of a *Germanen-*

bibel (1904). Schwaner, a village schoolmaster, was editor of *Der Volkserzieher*, a journal for anti-Semitic teachers, and played a prominent part in the German Youth Movement, urging them to exclude Jews and adopt a radically *völkisch* program.

But more important than Chamberlain's influence on *völkisch* extremists like Lehmann and Schwaner was his impact on German liberal Protestantism. This powerful school of thought, which began making great strides against conservative theology in the 1880s, reexamined the foundations of the Protestant faith, joining together the individualistic, emotional theology of Herder and Schleiermacher, the biblical criticism of the Tübingen school, and developments in neo-Kantian philosophy. The "modernists," as they were called, reassessed clericalism, dogma, and church history as a prelude to a freer, more rational religion, intellectually and emotionally more suited to the German middle classes and the spirit of the new Reich. But in their efforts to find a common ground between faith and knowledge, religion and science, Christianity and *Deutschtum*, the liberal Protestants—as Uriel Tal has shown—evolved a vision of a German *Kulturstaat* that was inherently antagonistic to the double aspiration of Jews for full integration into German society while preserving their Jewish singularity. While rejecting conservative theories of a Christian state, the liberal Protestants were equally determined to strengthen the exclusively Christian character of society and to permeate every facet of life with the spirit of the Gospels. Their counterattack against secularism and clerical dogma contained a vision of national unity and an implicit hope for Jewish conversion.[44]

By the end of the century this friction between Judaism and Protestantism, sustained and complicated by the wider tensions of Jewish-Gentile relations in the Reich, had seeped through a whole corpus of philological and historical research. In investigating the inter-testamental period and in discussing the relationship of Christ to Judaism, Protestant scholarship was deeply concerned to emphasize the distinctiveness of the two faiths and to depict Judaism as a mere precursor to Christianity, a religion that had deteriorated and become sterile.

Tal has persuasively argued that the common intellectual stance of liberal Protestants and Jews (their rationalist, historical, ethical and anthropocentric emphases) heightened this compulsion to restate and accentuate their differences. Whatever the case, by 1900 Protestant critiques of Rabbinic Judaism, with their obvious implications for contemporary Jews, had provoked a storm of controversy.

The highpoint of this religious debate coincided with the publication of a series of lectures entitled *Das Wesen des Christentums* (1900) by Adolf von Harnack, the leading spokesman of liberal Protestantism. Harnack's analysis, which received extravagant praise in many quarters, summarized the trends of recent research; he was pragmatic, determined to rescue the figure of Christ from the accretions of history and superstition, antipathetic to mysticism, and disparaging in his comments about Rabbinic Judaism. The book quickly provoked a furious response from Jewish scholars, including Leo Baeck, Martin Schreiner, and Moritz Güdemann. Two years later, the renowned Assyriologist Friedrich Delitzsch (of whom more will be said later) further enlarged and intensified the dispute by his campaign to prove the superiority of Babylonian culture and religion over those of the Jews. The dialogue between liberal Protestants and liberal Jews, Leo Baeck was forced to admit, had largely broken down and was no longer what it had been forty years before.

The religious polemic occasioned by the Harnack lectures was on a much higher plane than the discussion spurred by the *Foundations*, but to some degree Chamberlain's book benefited from the general atmosphere of the debate. Citing the leading Protestant authorities as his sources, Chamberlain had radicalized and vulgarized their views, grafting onto them a pronounced racist interpretation. Not only did Chamberlain's combination of racism and theology illustrate for Jews the hostile uses to which Protestant research could be put, but it also appealed emotionally to some Christians angered by Jewish criticism of Harnack and other scholars. Thus, *Christliche Welt*, the literary focus of liberal Protestantism, praised the work highly. "I believe," wrote one reviewer, "that this book can achieve for us today the service which Herder's *Ideen zur Philosophie der Geschichte der Menschheit* fulfilled for our forefathers . . . it carries in it an apologetic strength for which our 'Christian world' will have much to thank."[45] A second review by Pastor Max Christlieb even defended the racial perspective of the book:

> We theologians have even now failed to take up a real position but for the present continue to operate calmly with the notion of equality for all men before God, as if this also includes equality with each other. However, the emphasis on race expresses a new important knowledge for our time. Today even the Jews . . . no longer hide [this fact] as more and more they give vent in public to the racial consciousness which they have always had.[46]

A considerable number of pastors in Germany and Switzerland wrote letters congratulating Chamberlain on his accomplishment, while theology students in Württemberg, training for missions overseas, were also enamoured of the book.[47] Of course, it is impossible to ascertain what such people read into the argument, or to what extent they abstracted a "soft" or less dogmatic and racially conscious Chamberlain from it. Moreover, in the absence of a detailed sociological study of the Protestant clergy in the period, we can say relatively little about the relationship between the content of church periodicals, the viewpoints disseminated from local pulpits, and those held by the congregation. As Harnack himself once pointed out: as a compensation for their virtual exclusion from church government, the most divergent and heretical opinions were tolerated among the laity by the Protestant authorities. Certainly, many Protestants would have had little difficulty in accepting Chamberlain's racial, heroic Luther, for a whole intellectual tradition from Fichte, Jahn and Arndt to Treitschke had already depicted the reformer as a national hero, the archetypical German who "did not flee from the world but sought to rule it through the power of his moral will."[48]

Harnack's response to Chamberlain's book was undoubtedly complicated by Kaiser Wilhelm's outspoken praise for it. An admirer of both men, Wilhelm eagerly arranged a meeting in November 1901. As they walked around the grounds of Liebenberg, Prince Eulenburg's country estate, he exclaimed:

> Now come Professor Harnack, now you repeat to me what you
> said to me when we last met in May. Didn't you say that no
> other man in the world was capable of writing Chamberlain's
> chapter on Christ?—Yes, your Majesty I did.—And didn't you
> say that if all the theologians of the globe were to put their
> heads together, they couldn't succeed in doing it as he has done
> it?—Yes, I did, for it is my deliberate opinion.—And didn't you
> say that if you had written that one and only chapter of Cham-
> berlain's book you would be proud of yourself?—Your Majesty
> has an excellent memory.—Well Mr. Chamberlain, now you
> know what Harnack thinks of your work; he wouldn't have told
> you so in your face, and I think it's right you should know. [49]

Only Chamberlain's record of the encounter exists, and certainly the theologian was critical of the views advanced by the
book. Possibly, Harnack's comments were designed to humor
the sovereign (his answers seem to hint at this by their evasiveness); but it does appear that he did admire the vigor and
analytic boldness of Chamberlain's writing and their relationship remained congenial for many years.

More instructive is the exchange between the two men
more than a decade later when Harnack, after reading Chamberlain's _Goethe_ wrote five detailed letters to the author in
quick succession. He praised the work very highly in all the
letters, but then finally turned to his criticisms. Foremost
among these was the treatment of Jews:

> You really are possessed by an anti-Jewish demon, which dulls
> your vision and disfigures your excellent book with a stain.
> Where should I begin my polemic? I do not believe that Provi-
> dence created an infamous people [_Schandvolk_]. In general, I
> believe only very conditionally in sharp racial lines of character
> within the individual branches of the Aryans and Semites.

Harnack placed more importance on cultural and historic evolution in shaping the nature and qualities of a people; his next
words, however, expressed the hope for Jewish improvement
that had echoed through the writings of Christian proponents for Emancipation since the beginning of the nineteenth

century:

> [The Jews] have too long been oppressed, and through history it
> has been made very difficult for them to raise themselves up to
> the level of nobler mankind. But already I know of several Jews
> who in various ways compel my respect. Do we wish to help
> these people to progress? Certainly, there are great dangers in
> this. The bad Jew is today a terrible calamity for us, but all the
> greater must be our love and wisdom toward them. Your words,
> however, are only injurious, for then the Jew can say to himself:
> since we are racially as we must be, then we should consciously
> strive to remain so. [50]

Harnack found much to commend in Chamberlain's *Goethe*,
but rejected the racist theme that repeatedly surfaced in the
work. While both men advocated purging Christianity of Old
Testament elements, Harnack refused the racial argument
that assimilation was impossible and nourished an implicit
hope of Jewish conversion. Suggestive, but characteristically
enigmatic, is the conclusion to his final letter about the book:
"Still enough—the Jew shall not have the last word. Rather,
may he disappear completely [through conversion?] and may
there remain between us only the conviction of a broad and
deep unity and agreement [*Gemeinsamen*]."

Chamberlain's reply focused clearly on the ambiguity of
Harnack's response to his book. The so-called "errors" of
which Harnack had complained were "an integral part which
one cannot change, for they belong to the organic unity of the
whole." "You write me," he added, "'The worse the Jew, all
the greater must our love be'; and I will not deny that I find
the words beautiful from a proclaimer of the gospel." But,
insisted Chamberlain, the commandment to love thy neighbor
was directed toward forgiveness of individuals who had done
wrong, not a race which was collectively guilty:

> I do not view the commandment as meaning to love that which
> every day in all spheres defiles, poisons and drags down
> everything that is exalted and holy to me. . . . With all the
> strength in my soul, I hate it and hate it and hate it. [51]

For Chamberlain the very concept of love was impossible
without its antithesis, hate; the strength of his love for the

Germanic race was, as he admitted, enhanced and nourished by hate for the Jews. "Were I one time to stop hating, I would be impoverished in love."

The case of Harnack illustrates the complexity and selectivity of Protestant responses to Chamberlain. In unmodified form Chamberlain's religious viewpoint was too extreme for most, and his intuitive and heterodox faith was too sweeping in its departure from church doctrine. But in significant aspects the *Foundations* paralleled trends among several sections of the Protestant community. For example, his denunciation of Jesuits and Roman Catholicism coincided with a resurgence of such prejudice in the 1890s, while his attacks on scientific materialism found an echo in church campaigns against the League of Freethinkers and Haeckel's Monism. The fact that much of Protestant theology contained a marked anti-Jewish bias may well have desensitized readers to this more extreme version. Similarly, the intensification of nationalist feeling in the *Weltpolitik* era, which was reflected in the sermons and writings of the protestant clergy (it served, in part, to divert attention from the deep doctrinal and political disunity within their ranks) also helped make Chamberlain more "respectable."

Most significantly Chamberlain's *Foundations*, in the eyes of many readers, had not sacrificed Christian faith on the altar of "scientific" racism. He had incorporated Christ in a Germanic world view without dogmatizing or slipping into a crude biological determinism; he had preserved the duality of spirit and matter, assuring contemporaries of the importance of race without depriving them of the solace of religion. Since the 1870s political and racial anti-Semitism frequently involved not only attacks upon Jews and Judaism but also a wide-ranging critique of existing Christianity, which sometimes came close to a total rejection of the faith. While demanding reform of the church and the eradication of Semitic remnants in its doctrine, Chamberlain differed in style and tone from extreme critics like Fritsch, Wahrmund, and Duehring: his aim was to criticize and admonish rather than to alienate; to effect a compromise rather than to draw the line of battle. As a result, he was much more successful than previous writers in gaining a broad and sympathetic hearing for *völkisch* Christianity. For many, it would seem, the *Foundations* provided a convenient bridge between their growing national and racial prejudices and their basic Christian beliefs.

The failure of Christians to reject without reservation the claims of such books as the *Foundations* was deeply disturbing to German Jews and raised serious concern about the limits of their assimilation. Chamberlain's success was one of several blows dealt to the very principle of equality of rights and status at the end of the century. The Conservative Party's Tivoli Program of 1892 explicitly condemned "the multifarious and obtrusive Jewish influence that decomposes our people's life" and urged "Christian authorities and Christian teachers for our Christian people." Exclusion of Jews from government and academic posts, the judiciary, the military, and certain sectors of private industry was conspicuous. The old issue of ritual murder periodically resurfaced, as in the death of a Gymnasium student in Konitz, West Prussia, in 1900. Anti-Semitic political parties, though small, had gained a foothold in the *Reichstag*, and when Ludwig Bamberger, the liberal leader, left politics in 1893 he cited his disgust at the widespread tolerance of anti-Semitism as one of his chief reasons.[52] Liberal parties nominated fewer Jews as candidates than in the 1880s, and Jews frequently complained of growing social exclusion from youth groups, resorts, and hotels.* Assimilation had gone a long way, as Peter Gay has recently

---

* A growing number of Jews, Jacob Toury has argued, failed to vote. In 1907, for example, the inclusion of the National Liberals and Progressives in the Bülow bloc (which included anti-Semitic parties) left Jewish voters with an unpleasant choice between Social Democracy and the Center. The right-wing Prussian National Liberals found little sympathy among Jews, while relations with the two Progressive parties deteriorated in the 1890s. It was pointed out angrily by the *Centralverein* that the Progressives put up only baptised Jewish candidates at elections. There were no unbaptised Jews among Progressives in the *Reichstag* from 1893 to 1912. Also, more than once, Progressives threw their weight behind anti-Semites in runoff contests to avoid electing a socialist. After 1909 the liberal parties began putting up Jewish candidates again. In general, the decline of liberalism as a political force after 1890 encouraged Jewish organization to protect their civil rights. Jacob Toury, *Die politischen Orientierungen der Juden in Deutschland* (Tübingen, 1966); Ernest Hamburger, "One Hundred Years of Emancipation," *LBI* (1969) 14: 20–21.

reminded us, but for many Jews a feeling of disappointment
had begun to set in.[53]

There were of course deep religious, social, political, and
even national contrasts within German Jewry itself. Indeed,
this very fragmentation was an obstacle to the effective development of organizations to combat anti-Semitism and it enabled
the Prussian government to justify its refusal of demands for
reform that would strengthen Jewish communal organization.[54]
German Jews adopted a wide range of positions upon such
issues as assimilation, the danger of contemporary anti-Semitism, and the wisdom of forming organizations to pressure
governmental bureaucracies and the judiciary to live up to the
promises of emancipation. Although they were never able to
attract the majority of German Jews, the defense organizations
(the *Verein zur Abwehr des Antisemitismus* and the more important *Centralverein deutscher Staatsburger jüdischen Glaubens*) grew rapidly in the last decade of the nineteenth
century, a testimony to the continuing pressures of anti-Semitism as well as to the general increase of interest group organizations after 1890. As the most vocal segment of the Jewish
population, it is their response to the *Foundations*, rather than
that of the average Jewish *Bürger*, that can be accurately
described.

Both the *Centralverein* and the *Abwehr Verein* were
alarmed at the popularity of Chamberlain's book, for it confirmed their deepest suspicions about the pervasiveness of
anti-Semitic attitudes among the educated bourgeoisie and the
aristocracy. Chamberlain could not be lumped together with
rabble rousers like Graf Pückler, Ernst Henrici, or August
Böckel. In the *Foundations* anti-Semitism emerged as a
coherent ideology which traced its roots to the works of Lagarde, Fichte, Duehring, Ammon, Lapouge and even Kant and
Goethe. Commentators acknowledged Chamberlain's extensive
learning and ability to argue his views. "One must possess,"
wrote one critic, "a fundamental knowledge of the historical
facts and their interrelation to be able to catch the author, so
to speak, *in flagranti* and to uncover the arbitrariness of his
conclusions and replace them with the right interpretations."
"The book," he noted "has been taken up in the highest and

most exalted social circles," a reference to the Kaiser and his Court.[55] Chamberlain's elaborate and highly intellectualized form of anti-Semitism threatened, claimed *Im deutschen Reich*, the newsletter of the *Centralverein*, to erode traditional Christian restraints to prejudice, especially in the nation's elite.[56] It acted, warned the spokesman of liberal Judaism, Martin Schreiner, as "a moral narcotic to lighten the conscience of certain classes in the nation with regard to the injustices daily committed against Jews."[57] Moreover, the very fact that Chamberlain had been entertained at Court seemed to nullify the pride that Jews felt when exceptional figures like Bleichroeder or Ballin were admitted to the royal entourage; it was not as "protected citizens," warned the spokesmen of the defense organizations, but as equal citizens that Jews must gain their place in German society.[58]

There was little difference between the response of the *Centralverein* and that of the *Abwehr Verein*, originally formed by liberal and progressive Christian politicians to protest anti-Semitism. Both labored to refute and correct Chamberlain's errors, to challenge his misuse of sources and reverse his efforts to recast the German Enlightenment tradition in an illiberal and markedly anti-Jewish fashion. The *Abwehr Verein* gave more attention to reproducing criticisms of Chamberlain that had appeared in the Christian press and occasionally indicated that his book was more representative of English jingoism than of German qualities.[59] The *Centralverein* focused more upon the broader implications of the *Foundations* for attitudes in Central Europe. Neither group was taken in by the occasional note of magnanimity or moderation which crept into the book; both recognized a fanatical *Judenhass* as its underlying spirit—unlike many Christian reviewers. In addition, they were quick to use other essays and comments by Chamberlain to disprove his feigned scholarly impartiality and his artful disclaimers of any special hatred for Jews. *Im deutschen Reich*, seizing upon the results of a poll conducted by the *Staatsburger Zeitung* on the question of ritual murder, announced that Chamberlain had acknowledged that such a crime was possible.[60] Similarly, when Chamberlain advocated legal restraints upon Jews in an essay on Romania, reviewers were quick to note that he was reiterating the demands of the anti-

Semitic petition of 1880.[61] As far as the *Centralverein* was concerned, the new "scholarly" anti-Semitism was fundamentally the same as the *Radau-Antisemitismus* of political agitators like Liebermann von Sonnenberg, and they anticipated that the planned continuation of the *Foundations* would take a much more prescriptive tone, encouraging immediate state intervention in the problem. Chamberlain's rough plans for the later volumes vindicate their forecast.[62]

At the height of public debate over the *Foundations*, Berthold Feiwel wrote that "the maturing generation [of Germans] is flatly saturated with *Judenhass*."[63] His view was echoed in a growing number of articles in Jewish periodicals. Analyzing the growing exclusion of Jews from social groups, the newsletter of the *Abwehr Verein* concluded sadly, "So the Jews become more and more displaced from society and therefore compelled to found their own associations and to seek closer company with each other."[64] Still more pessimistic was Schreiner, who in his last book in 1903 mounted a vehement attack upon Chamberlain's portrayal of Jews and Judaism. "On several sides," he warned, "forces are working, consciously and unconsciously, for the destruction of Jewry," and went on to list the whole catalogue of racial theories, blood libels, and institutional obstacles to equality.[65] As more observers came to accept these gloomy conclusions, the rhetoric of the Zionists became more forceful and persuasive; in the years before 1914 the German-Jewish community became engulfed in the debate between assimilation and Zionism.

Chamberlain's name occurred in these internal disputes as well, especially in the celebrated case of Moritz Goldstein who had sent a highly controversial essay, entitled *"Deutsch-jüdischer Parnass,"* to the literary magazine *Kunstwart* in the Spring of 1912. Goldstein, who as a student at the University of Berlin experienced anti-Semitism and had been won over to Zionism, gave expression to the terrible dilemma of many contemporaries. Becoming a Zionist had settled nothing; rather, it had heightened the discrepancy he felt between his life as a German and a Jew. Unable to assimilate fully as a German, he could not accept the idea of exiling himself to Palestine. Similarly for the present generation of Jews there was no hope of creating a national literature in Hebrew; they were

indelibly German. His essay was a provocative exposition of this
inner schism, acknowledging the leading role played by Jews in
the cultural life of Germany, but concluding: "we are admini-
stering the spiritual property of a nation which denies our right
and our ability to do so." On the one side stood "the German-
Christian-Teutonic envy-ridden fools," on the other those
leaders of the Jewish community who closed their eyes to the
fact that assimilation was not working. Anti-Semitism, Goldstein argued, could not be explained away as the creed of
fanatical groups on the periphery of society: as the case of
Chamberlain showed, it pervaded the views of "the best
spirits, clever, truth-loving men who, however, as soon as they
speak of Jews, fall into a blind, almost rabid hatred." "Chamberlain," he added, "believes what he says and for that very
reason his distortions shock me. And thousands believe as he
does for the book goes through one edition after another and I
would still like to know how many Germanic types, whose self
image is pleasantly indulged by this theory, are able to remain
critical enough to question its countless injustices and errors?"[66]

Goldstein's essay occasioned an exceptionally heated debate among both Jews and Christians. But it was the assimilationist advocates of organizations like the *Centralverein* who
reacted most strongly to its conclusions, deploring the "excessive nationalism" and "racial Semitism" of the Zionists and
accusing them of reinforcing anti-Semitic propaganda. Yet *Im
deutschen Reich* never seriously replied to Goldstein's assertion that truth-loving Germans were embracing anti-Semitism
after having carefully weighed the arguments of both sides.
Instead it chose to berate Goldstein for his mild and forgiving
attitude toward Chamberlain, an outlook, it alleged, which
could only give weight to the forces of prejudice.[67]

The most famous enthusiast of the *Foundations* was Kaiser
Wilhelm II, of whom Walther Rathenau wrote: "never before

has a symbolic individual so perfectly represented an age." [68]
And in a country where parliamentary institutions were weak
and major decisions were taken behind the scenes by the
Kaiser and his ministers, rumor played an inordinate role. Rumors of Chamberlain's influence at Court certainly enhanced
the sales and popularity of his book, for it was considered
a means of understanding Kaiser Wilhelm and his global
political vision.

Wilhelm read the book in the early part of 1901 and his
quick but unsubtle mind was captivated by its footnotes and
feigned scholarship. Ulrich von Bülow, brother of the Imperial
Chancellor and a frequent visitor at Chamberlain's apartment
in Vienna, reported that the Emperor was "studying the book
a second time page for page" and reading selected parts to the
Empress in the evenings. "Bülow's opinion," Chamberlain
added, "is that the book will have considerable and salutary influence on the Emperor's opinions. May it be so!" After reading
the *Foundations*, wrote Prince Eulenburg, Wilhelm "became
more fascinated than ever by the 'mission of Germandom,'"
and more convinced in his belief in "a spiritual mission of the
German Kaiser based on his personal power." [69]

It was Eulenburg who, while ambassador in Vienna, wrote
to Chamberlain how much his work was appreciated at Court
and invited him to the embassy. They became friends and correspondents and Eulenburg, a Wagnerian and an anti-Semite
who had written Gobineau's obituary for the *Bayreuther
Blätter*, decided to arrange a meeting with the Kaiser. Chamberlain, he knew, "was very interested in the person of the
Kaiser and the furtherance of the German national cause, and
. . . welcomed with enthusiasm the suggestion of a personal
meeting." [70]

When Eulenburg's invitation arrived, Chamberlain was
spending a few days with his wife, Countess Maria Waller-
stein, and Adolphe Appia at the Countess Zichy's hunting
lodge near Berchtesgaden. He returned to Vienna and prepared for the long journey to Berlin and then eastward to Eulenburg's estate of Liebenberg. Chancellor Bülow, who had
taken the same train from Berlin, met him on the platform
and they discussed the *Foundations* and French literature en

route. Their arrival at Liebenberg typified the strange pseudo-medieval and theatrical world that Wilhelm liked to create for himself. "Our carriage," wrote Chamberlain, "whisked around a corner and there we suddenly were at the principal entrance—a sort of semi-circular garden arrangement. . . . And here at the foot of the steps congregated the whole party—men, ladies, servants with torches—grouped in a sort of half-moon,—and in the center the Emperor,"[71] As Holstein once remarked, Wilhelm had "dramatic rather than political instincts."

Before dinner Wilhelm, who had changed his hunting costume for an even more resplendent dress uniform, met alone with Chamberlain. "I thank you," he said, "for what you have done for Germany." "It was a big moment for both men," Eulenburg recalled, "and the Kaiser was moving in his gratitude to me for having arranged the encounter." After dinner, "standing smoking apart from other guests," Wilhelm "heard and saw nothing but Chamberlain all evening." The following day Adolf von Harnack was summoned from Berlin to join in their discussions on the Christian "mission of Germandom." Chamberlain, remarked Eulenburg, "was the most profound of the circle, the one whose remarks always touched on the inner and essential meaning of things, he was also the most taciturn." Wilhelm, he continued, "stood completely under the spell of this man, whom he understood better than any of the other guests because of his thorough study of the *Foundations*."[72]

The next day the group returned to Berlin, where Chamberlain was received by the Empress at a smaller, more intimate gathering. After this very successful meeting, Chamberlain and the Emperor corresponded over the next 26 years, until Chamberlain's death. They saw each other again in Vienna in 1903, and one biographer claimed they met during the Moroccan crisis of 1906—"not often, but in particularly favourable circumstances not provided by Court etiquette for secret and informal exchanges of views."[73] If the latter meetings occurred, Chamberlain left no record of them.

German and foreign newspapers were quickly aware of the Kaiser's infatuation with Chamberlain's *Foundations*. Guests at Potsdam were frequently treated to lengthy descriptions of the book, army officers like Anton von Mackensen suffered silently the endless evening readings from it at Court, and copies were presented to foreign visitors and members of Wilhelm's entourage. It was commonly said that the Kaiser, whose impatience seldom allowed him to finish any book, let alone one of over a thousand pages, could recite whole pages from Chamberlain by heart.[74] Such rumors led to considerable disquiet in some circles. The conservative *Reichsbote*, for example, was deeply worried at the prospect of Chamberlain's unorthodox religious opinions gaining sway at Court, while the liberal press lamented Wilhelm's open identification with a thoroughly racist book. Ullstein's *Berliner Zeitung*, for example, observed:

> Already for some considerable time there have been rumors both inside and outside the country about Herr Chamberlain's great influence on the Kaiser. . . . It cannot be a matter of indifference to the Kaiser and government that people overseas consider a man like Houston Stewart Chamberlain to be a most influential informal advisor of Wilhelm II. All serious judgments of Herr Chamberlain's book . . . have found it a terrible confused concoction. Apart from this the political opinions in the work are of a nature that compromises a German Emperor.[75]

To some extent these anxieties were justified, for Wilhelm did borrow Chamberlain's ideas and rhetoric freely to elaborate his own mystical-romantic visions of German *Kulturpolitik*. The impetuous, almost torrential rhetoric of the Aix la Chapelle, Posen, and Görlitz speeches in 1901 and 1902 was drawn directly from Chamberlain.[76]

The meetings at Liebenberg, Potsdam, and Vienna created a warm, personal bond between Wilhelm and Chamberlain. Their elaborate, wordy letters, full of mutual admiration and half-baked ideas, were transmitted by special messenger rather than through the postal service—often by Count Brockdorff-Rantzau, then attached to the embassy staff in Vienna. Reading them we enter the perplexing thought world of mystical and racist conservatism. They ranged far and wide in subject matter: the ennobling mission of the Germanic race;

the corroding forces of Ultramontanism; materialism and the "destructive poison" of *Judentum* were favorite themes. At times they focused upon the symptoms of decay in Germany, deploring the growing power of the "Jewish" press and the *Reichstag* and the insinuation of "Semitic values" into the very fiber of German education. At others, they dwelt on the place of Germany in the world, surrounded by hostile cultures, threatened by the Yellow Peril, "tartarized Slavdom," and the future danger of the black hordes. Chamberlain took the opportunity to advance many opinions which later found their way—almost verbatim—into his political writings after 1914; but he appears mostly to have reinforced the royal biases rather than to have converted Wilhelm to new ones. The correspondence reveals a striking coincidence of views on race, politics, and religion.

Occasionally Wilhelm became autobiographical. As a youth, he recalled: "I felt instinctively that we boys needed another course of preparation so as to continue the work of the new Reich. Our stifled youth had need of a liberator like yourself!" As a result, "all the mighty Germanic Aryanism that slumbered within me had to assert itself gradually in a difficult contest." After years of mental struggle the *Foundations* had appeared, synthesizing and bringing order to these racial and cultural ideals. "Then you come along and with one magic stroke bring order into the confusion, light into the darkness. You show the goals for which we strive and work, explain those things we had sensed only dimly, and reveal the paths which must be followed for the salvation of the Germans and thus the salvation of mankind! You sing a hymn in praise of everything German and above all of our magnificent language and you call out impressively to the Teutons: "Lay aside your quarrels and trifles; your duty on earth is to be God's instrument for the spreading of His culture, His teaching! To that end deepen, exalt, cultivate your language and through it science, enlightenment and faith!" What a salvation! So! Now you know, my dear Mr. Chamberlain, what was going on in my mind when I felt your hand in mine." [77]

Later in the same letter, amid further extravagant praise of Chamberlain, Wilhelm launched into his favorite theme of

Ultramontanism, or rather the need to win back German Catholics to a truly national stance. The following quotation captures the dream world the monarch at times inhabited as well as the emotional rhetoric and belligerant tone of his utterances:

> Truly, let us thank Him up there, that he still views us Germans with such favor; for God sent your book to the German people and you personally to me. You were chosen by Him to be my ally and I shall thank Him eternally that He did so. For your powerful language grips people and impels them to think and also naturally to fight, to attack! The German Michael is waking up and that is good for him, then he will be on the alert and will achieve something; and once he has begun to work he will accomplish more than anyone else. His science [*Wissenschaft*] in his own language is a colossal weapon and he must be continually reminded of this! For "reason," i.e. common sense, and "science" are our most dangerous weapons, especially in the struggle against "ubiquitous" Rome. Once the Teutonic Catholics have been brought by you into the open conflict between Teutons and Catholics, that is "Romans," then they will be "awakened" and will "know" that which the father confessors have been trying to hide from them—that they are being kept in humiliating subjection to "Rome" as an instrument against "Germany." Therefore, *Eritis sicut deus, scientes bonum et malum.*" In this regard we can now see some movement, and sales of your book have been frantic in these circles, praise God. . . .
>
> And now, for the New Year 1902, I wish God's blessing and Christ's strength to you my comrade-in-arms and ally in the struggle for the Teutons against Rome, Jerusalem etc. The feeling of fighting for a cause that is absolutely good and holy carries the guarantee of victory.[78]

With good reason did one close aide of Wilhelm regret that "religion and mysticism are now playing an increasingly large part in the Emperor's speeches." Even the Pope was not spared such theorizing. On a visit to Rome in 1903, Wilhelm informed Chamberlain, he "quoted whole pages" from the *Foundations* to Leo XIII until (whether out of politeness or sheer weariness we do not know) "the old man had to admit I was right."[79]

In spite of all these obvious signs of Wilhelm's enthusiasm, it remains difficult to gauge the exact impact of
Chamberlain's ideas upon him. The Kaiser was a kaleido-
scopic personality whose moods changed swiftly. Because he
entertained Jewish notables like Albert Ballin, Carl Fürsten-
berg and Max Warburg at Court, some contemporaries and
historians have failed to take seriously his anti-Semitism on
other occasions. But rhetoric and action were frequently at
odds in Wilhelm's life, as much when it came to Catholics as
Jews. In fact, from his student days at Bonn, his outlook was
decidedly anti-Catholic and anti-Jewish, although he might
make special exceptions of individuals. His closest advisers—
Herbert Bismarck, Alfred Waldensee and Philip Eulenburg—
were staunch anti-Semites, and he was greatly attracted by
Stoecker's mixture of racism, mild social reformism, and Christianity.[80] We must, conceded Wilhelm to his son, the Crown
Prince, in 1913, "firmly exclude Jewish influence from the army
and the administration, and restrict its power in all artistic and
literary activity"; but he never urged the revival of legislative
restrictions upon Jews and warned against those who advocated
their forcible expulsion from the Reich. The Jews, he argued,
"would take their enormous riches with them and we would
strike a blow against our national welfare and economy which
would put us back 100 years, and at the same time leave the
ranks of the cultured nations."[81] The *Foundations* seemingly
did not lead him to espouse a new outlook, but rather provided
him with new and more "scholarly" arguments to defend his
existing convictions. Chamberlain helped place Wilhelm's tangled and vaguely formulated fears of Pan Slavism, the black
and yellow "hordes," Jews, Ultramontanes, Social Democrats,
and free-thinkers into a global and historical framework
copiously footnoted and sustained by a vast array of erudite information. He elevated the Emperor's dream of a German
mission into an elaborate vision of divinely ordained, racial
destiny. The lack of precision, the muddle, and the logical flaws
that are so apparent to modern readers of the *Foundations* did
not bother Wilhelm: he eagerly submitted to its subjective, irrational style of reasoning.

Deeply interested in the history of Christianity and the
comparative study of religion, Wilhelm was especially at-

tracted by Chamberlain's demonstration that Christianity was completely separate from Judaism in its roots. Indeed, it was probably as a religious thinker, as the exponent of an undogmatic, 'positive,' German faith that Chamberlain achieved his greatest influence upon his royal friend. Their letters are crowded with pious declarations of faith and philosophical ramblings on such topics as the origin of evil. Both men sought to combine liberal Protestant ideas and *völkisch* nationalist traditions into a Germanic religion. But there was a tension within their thoughts between a racial vision of the Jew as the incarnation of an ineradicable evil and the Christian doctrine of universal salvation which allowed full assimilation. In the years before 1914, unlike many contemporary anti-Semites, neither of them wished to opt completely for racialism and neither advocated for example, dispensing with the Old Testament altogether.

This issue arose in January 1902 when the Assyriologist, Friedrich Delitzsch, gave to the German Oriental Society a highly controversial address entitled "Babylon and the Bible" (*"Babel und Bibel."*). In this and in subsequent lectures Delitzsch claimed the cultural superiority of Babylonia over Israel, arguing from the evidence of recent excavations at Nineveh and Babylon that the civilization of Israel showed strong Babylonian influences. Further, while acknowledging that Semites were the first monotheists, he attempted to prove from an analysis of cuneiform inscriptions that the monotheistic religion of the Old Testament was largely borrowed from Babylonian sources. Such assertions angered Jews and orthodox Christians alike, but elicited enthusiastic applause in certain anti-Semitic circles. Kaiser Wilhelm, who was present at the first lecture in January 1902, invited Delitzsch to a private audience a month later, at which time he was appalled to discover that the professor believed neither in the divinity of Christ nor the sacredness of the Old Testament. The *Babel-Bibel-Streit*, as it was known, aroused widespread public interest and provides an interesting commentary upon the relationship of Kaiser Wilhelm and Chamberlain.[82]

Chamberlain's contribution to the theological and historical debate appeared in the long preface to the fourth edition of the *Foundations*, completed in October 1902. In his book Chamberlain had repudiated the claim that the Jews were a "chosen people," endowed with a special aptitude for religious thought and experience. He had, of course, denied that the Israelites were ever true monotheists, interpreted the "splendid interludes" of Israel's history as a consequence of Indo-European influences, and proclaimed that Jesus was racially not a Jew. Rejecting Delitzsch's claims for Babylon, he offered his own interpretation of recently discovered cuneiform inscriptions and contended that Assyria was an area of nobler blood gradually overcome by Semitic influences. The monotheism of both Israel and Babylon was counterfeit—a crude and imperfectly grasped borrowing from ancient Persian and Aryan traditions. For him the continuing value of the Old Testament lay in its rich mythology, in what Israel had gleaned from a higher culture. The cumulative results of archaeology and biblical criticism would enable men to sift out these Semitic elements and to comprehend more fully the nature of the Aryan religion and thus the life of Christ. Like Wilhelm, Chamberlain was deeply troubled by the tendency of Delitzsch to minimize the uniqueness and divinity of Jesus, and angered by his reduction of Christianity to a series of Babylonian and Israelite cultural influences. Such "scholarly" studies, Chamberlain maintained, threatened to undermine the faith of Christians; indeed, much to the surprise of Jews engaged in attacking Delitzsch, he even hinted that the Berlin Assyriologist had spun a web of Semitic errors for this very purpose. Praising Babylon, he speculated, might be an adroit Semitic ploy to disguise the true import of present discoveries—namely, that Semites were not the pioneers of monotheism at all.[83] When the preface was published at the end of 1902, Chamberlain dispatched the first copy, with a long covering letter, to the Kaiser.

As head of the Evangelical Church and emperor of a predominantly Protestant nation, Wilhelm was somewhat embarrassed by the Babel-Bibel affair, all the more so because his own religious views were undergoing some change as a result of reading Chamberlain's Foundations. In early January 1903 Delitzsch again explained his theories before the Oriental Society, adding his dismay that churches and schools were completely

impermeable to the light of science when it came to the Old
Testament. With mounting criticism being voiced by orthodox
Christians, Admiral Hollman, president of the Oriental Society, hesitated before publishing the views of Delitzsch in the
society's bulletin; instead, he requested permission formally
from Wilhelm, thereby placing the monarch in a difficult position.

On February 15, by his own account, Wilhelm was finding
it very hard to answer Hollmann, mostly because he could not
clarify his own views. Then he opened a new letter from Chamberlain and discovered twenty or more densely packed pages
on the very same subject. His writing block disappeared and
within four hours he had drafted a satisfactory reply, which
brought together some of his own ideas together with others
taken word for word from Chamberlain. The letter constituted
Wilhelm's first major break with Protestant orthodoxy.[84]

The gist of Chamberlain's letter (cleverly phrased with
just the right blend of instruction and admiration for Wilhelm's taste) was that God's revelation in history was
continuous and not limited to Israel. In the modern era of secularism and materialism, Germany had a special mission: to
rediscover and safeguard the vital essence of Christianity.
Testimony to this was the sheer number of geniuses vouch-
safed the *Volk*—Kant, Goethe, Beethoven, Wagner, the
Hohenzollerns—all of them revelations of the divine more
brilliant than anything that had occurred on Sinai so many
centuries ago. As for Delitzsch, while his speculations might
stimulate the minds of scholars, they were pernicious when
spread so widely among an uninformed public and threatened
to unsettle the basic structure of their faith. In place of such
iconoclasm what was required was to teach Germans that the
faith of inner experience contained in Luther and Kant was the
highest expression of religion—and totally distinct from
Semitic and Judaic traditions.

Wilhelm's letter to Hollmann endeavored to harmonize
these ideas with a somewhat more orthodox position; the result
was confusing, but illustrative of the intellectual transition he
was making.[85] He reproached Delitzsch for his polemical style
and for disturbing the faith of many contemporaries, and went

on to discuss two distinct forms of revelation—"historical" and "purely religious, preparing the way for the future Messiah." The first was almost pure Chamberlain: there was a continuous revelation in history in figures like Hammurabi (the hero of Delitzsch), Homer, Charlemagne, Luther, Shakespeare, Goethe, Kant, and Kaiser Wilhelm I. For the sake of orthodoxy he added Abraham and Moses to the list. God, Wilhelm claimed, guided mankind's advance by "donating" to nations the great intellects of the world; he also "revealed himself differently to the different races according to their position and rank in the scale of civilization." With his description of the second, "more religious," form of revelation, Wilhelm attempted to draw closer to orthodox Protestants and fulfill his obligations as head of the church. Here he declared that a single thread of revelation ran from Abraham and Moses, through the Prophets and the Psalmists to Christ himself. Abraham's race was portrayed as "ever trying to hold fast to their monotheism" under repeated and heavy pressures, and protected by God until the heralded Messiah appeared. In the last parts of the letter, however, Wilhelm returned to Chamberlain, borrowing ideas and extracting whole phrases to argue that sections of the Old Testament were historical and "did not reveal God's word." Their value was symbolic only. From his constant repetition of the word "perhaps," it seems that Wilhelm both sensed his own underlying confusion and wished somehow to soften the contrast between himself and Protestant orthodoxy. Nonetheless he pressed on with a Chamberlain-style conclusion reaffirming his faith in the "one and only God," recognizing that modern research would alter perceptions of the Old Testament and predicting (in words drawn from Chamberlain) "that much of the nimbus of the chosen people [the Jews] will thereby disappear." [86]

Published on February 19, 1903, the Kaiser's letter caused an uproar. Some conservative circles saw it as marking a breach with Harnack and liberal Protestant theology, although they disapproved of the new direction Wilhelm had taken. Very few contemporaries suspected the influence of Chamberlain, although the *Leipziger Neuesten Nachrichten* noted quite correctly that the letter bore a striking resemblance to the tenor of Wilhelm's arguments in his recent Görlitz and Aix la Chapelle speeches—also heavily plagiarized from Chamberlain.[87] Actually Chamberlain was quite dissatisfied with the Hollmann letter and spent some twenty pages patiently enumerating his objections to the notion that Abraham was a herald of Christ or that Jews had developed a true monotheism. He denied that Abraham was a historical figure at all, calling him "a distant memory of the moon-worship of Harar." It was necessary, Chamberlain argued, to choose between the idea that the Old Testament was of historical and symbolic importance and the "Catholic" doctrine that every word of the Bible was "dictated by the Holy Spirit." He recognized Wilhelm's difficulties—a monarch could not say whatever he chose. Yet only if Germans embraced a purified Germanic Christianity could they carry out their divine racial mission. Chamberlain ended his letter with the assurance: "Were I not convinced that Your Majesty thinks the same as I on the fundamentals, I would never have ventured to write these pages."[88]

Under Chamberlain's guidance Wilhelm's opinions gradually shifted from Lutheranism to a racist Germanic Christianity; the Hollmann letter marks a stage in this journey. Moreover, the unrelenting hostility toward Catholicism and Judaism that fills this correspondence offers a vivid illustration of how closely the German state was identified with Protestantism and how deeply ingrained was repugnance to genuine religious pluralism in the highest circles of the land.

The humiliation of defeat in war and the social disintegration of the Reich in 1918 reinforced the worst racial fears of Wilhelm and Chamberlain. In its last decade their correspondence moved in that strange paranoid world of collapsed empires, Bolshevik terror, Jewish and Freemason conspiracies, and secret hopes for a new crusade against the forces of racial decay and materialism that is so characteristic of the writings and letters of the extreme right in the postwar era. Wilhelm blamed the Jews for Germany's defeat, his own exile, and the Weimar Republic, and accepted the notorious *Protocols of the Elders of Zion* as an accurate description of their unwavering conspiratorial resolve. His letters, very disjointed in thought, violent in rhetoric, and punctuated by scores of exclamation marks, reveal a mind derailed, a fertile intelligence brought— on the subjects of race and religion at least—to the borders of insanity.[89] He continued to read Chamberlain and was enthralled by *Mensch und Gott* in 1921.[90] By this time he had abandoned Abraham and the Old Testament altogether—his world, like that of Chamberlain, was one massive struggle, a vast theodicy of German and Jew.

It was not, of course, merely what Chamberlain wrote that won him Wilhelm's high regard, it was equally his style and manner. Prince Eulenburg once wrote to his protegé, Chancellor Bülow, "Never forget that His Majesty needs praise every now and then." This was crucial, if understated advice; Chamberlain grasped the fact instinctively. His letters brimmed with praise and illustrate clearly the dangerous Byzantine atmosphere that pervaded the Court. With constant flattery Chamberlain nourished Wilhelm's taut, restless ego, entering wholeheartedly into his escapist fantasies. The House of Hohenzollern was the "only trump card held by the German people" in "this extremely difficult world" and Wilhelm was "an Aryan soldier King," a glorious descendant of those martial rulers who acted consciously as "the true representatives of a moral world order." "Whenever nature creates states," he asserted, "she creates monarchy and unequal classes."[91]

Chamberlain encouraged Wilhelm's most stubborn and anti-democratic traits; he never lost faith in the "helmsman" despite the repeated failures and disputes over Morocco and the *Daily Telegraph* affair, or the Eulenburg scandal which Max Harden used to bring down Wilhelm's closest friend and adviser. "My powers," he wrote, "stand at your Majesty's command."[92] But their relationship was not one-sided and Wilhelm was not an aloof recipient of praise. If Chamberlain helped prop up the imperial ego, the Kaiser did no less a service for his English admirer. The attentions of Wilhelm convinced Chamberlain—as nothing else could—of his own "divine" mission as a German prophet; they bolstered his pretensions of being a *Weltschauer*, an intellectual guardian of the race and herald of a regenerated Christianity. Both of them were capable of extraordinary feats of self-delusion and hypocrisy. These two, troubled *poseurs* attracted each other like magnets.

In addition, both men were the product of two cultures, England and Germany, and both oscillated uneasily between the two. "My mother and I," the Kaiser exclaimed, "have the same character . . . that good stubborn English blood which will not give way." His bitterness at English arrogance and English imperialism always barely concealed a certain spirit of awe and emulation. As late as 1911, he admitted to Theodore Roosevelt: "I adore England." In 1907, on a state visit to England, Wilhelm stayed at the estate of Colonel Stuart Wortley, a relative of Chamberlain's. He reflected on the Eulenburg scandal and the actions of Harden and other publicists: "A trusted circle of friends was suddenly broken up by Jewish insolence, calumny, and lies." Powerless to stop "the names of one's friends being dragged through all the gutters of Europe," Wilhelm contrasted life at Wortley's Highcliffe Castle in Hampshire:

> Comfortable affluence, excellent people in all walks of life, with all classes giving clear evidence of culture in their elegance and cleanliness. . . . I could stay in a pure atmosphere among healthy people of character, while at home the mud was splashed as high as the roof-tops, and the *Reichstag* even took pleasure in soiling itself like a pig in the mire![93]

And if the Kaiser was a Prussian with an ingrained respect for English values and habits, Chamberlain was just as much an Englishman who was deeply ambivalent about his own birthplace and who revered German qualities and Prussian society. Almost unconsciously, as his vast correspondences show, he adopted an obsequious, scraping tone when addressing the lowliest of Prussian army officers. If Wilhelm was drawn to the very Englishness of Chamberlain, the author of the *Foundations* saw in the Hohenzollern prince—at least until the World War—the symbol of his idealized *Deutschtum*.

It is always hazardous for a historian to speculate about what readers saw in a large, sprawling book like Chamberlain's *Foundations*, to assess what they learned from it, how they received its dogmatic utterances, or even to guess whether most purchasers of the two stout volumes actually read them or merely arranged them on their bookshelves. There are, after all, always books that are proclaimed a must for any educated mind; books that are purchased enthusiastically, much quoted, but scarcely ever read. George Bernard Shaw and several other reviewers warned their public that those who failed to read Chamberlain's cultural synthesis would thereby exclude themselves from historical and sociological discussions for some time.[94] In fact, from a wide variety of private and published sources, it seems that the *Foundations* was read; certainly, it was widely discussed and received unusually large coverage in the press. Responses, as we have seen, varied enormously. Even among those favorable to the book, there was little unanimity. Some praised the author's candid profile of the Jew as eternal enemy of the Germans; others, like the Heidelberg student, Ernst von Meyenburg, attributed the book's effectiveness to its disdain "for the combative style of anti-Semitic demagogues"; still others liked it but were genuinely troubled by the hatred that simmered just below the surface of Chamberlain's rhetoric.[95] People read Chamberlain selectively; his rich prose yielded to their various interpretations. Yet a great many Germans regarded it as a book of the hour, an accurate portrayal of the mood of a new era. In view of this, although the evidence is sometimes brittle and unyielding, it is important to set the book within the broader framework of German anti-Semitism before 1914.

"I have not met a German," Nietzsche once wrote, "who was well-disposed toward the Jews." Even those who disavowed extremism and deplored the excesses of popular rabble-rousers reacted not "against the species of feeling itself but only against its dangerous immoderation."[96] Without accepting so total a condemnation we may acknowledge that

Nietzsche's grasp of the pervasiveness of anti-Semitic prejudice was closer to the truth than the predictions of so many optimistic contemporaries who viewed such hatred as a withering remnant of medieval obscurantism. The more honest self-questioners among Germans were frequently shocked and worried by their own brutal psychic response. Theodor Fontane, for example, admitted:

> I have been philosemitic since my childhood and have never experienced anything but kindness from Jews. Nevertheless, I have the feeling of their guilt, their unlimited arrogance, to such an extent that I not only wish them a serious defeat but desire it. And of this I am convinced, if they do not suffer it now and do not change now, a terrible visitation will come upon them, albeit in times that we will not live to see.

He added ominously: "I love Jews . . . but I do not wish to be ruled by them." [97]

Anti-Semitism in Germany was never monolithic. It varied widely in tone and intensity, in motivation and emphasis from one class or social group to another, between town and countryside, and from one region and confessional group to another. Without forgetting this diversity and complexity, however, it is convenient for the purposes of this brief analysis to divide political anti-Semitism during the years between 1870 and 1914 into two broad periods, with 1893–96 as a transitional divide between them. This roughly coincides with the periodization favored by many historians of the political and economic development of the *Kaiserreich*, distinguishing the severe downswings of the "Great Depression" and the political system of Bismarck from the prosperous, expansionist *Weltpolitik* era with its curious hybrid of monarchical authority, parliamentary, and extraparliamentary government. In response to the far-reaching economic, political, and social changes that occurred in the last two decades of the nineteenth century German anti-Semitism underwent a transformation. This is not to deny continuity between the prejudice of the 1880s and that of 1900; but it is important to clarify the differences of tone, the changes in the social groups that were affected, and the organizations that were most successful in disseminating anti-Jewish sentiment from one period to the next.

Some time ago Hans Rosenberg analyzed in detail the relationship between changes in collective attitudes, the resurgence of anti-Semitism, and the sharp economic contractions of the 1870s and 1880s.[98] Little needs to be added to his penetrating and persuasive analysis. Admittedly, German anti-Semitism crossed the threshold of the new Reich carrying a heavy intellectual baggage, accumulated over centuries of Protestant and Catholic prejudice, and added to more recently during the protracted debate over Jewish emancipation. But, in general, the main configurations of political anti-Semitism in the first two decades of the empire were shaped and fostered by the simultaneous and devastating impact of the pressures of nation building and the unsettled economic climate following the *Gründerkrach* of 1873. Ushered in by an atmosphere of heightened prosperity and raised expectations, Jewish emancipation coincided with a short-lived liberal era and soon encountered checks and opposition. Political and economic conditions for a consistent policy of liberalization did not exist in Germany, and the wealthy Jewish bourgeoisie—whose ascent in politics, commerce, and cultural life had indeed been meteoric—found itself the detested scapegoat of those who felt threatened, pushed aside, or culturally estranged by the heightened pace of social and industrial change.[99]

The collapse of the speculative boom of the *Gründerjahre* in 1873, together with a serious depression in agriculture, fostered a mood of crisis, unleashing a flood of books, pamphlets and newspaper articles against liberalism and Jews. Aggravated by sharp economic fluctuations, the social and psychological costs of the transition to industrial capitalism became the focus of a wide debate, intertwined with the issue of Jewish prominence in national life. Amid this climate of resentment and social aggression the first sustained attempts were made to forge anti-Semitism into a modern political weapon. The protests and grievances of craftsmen, shopkeepers, small businessmen, and peasants were the basis of a wave of anti-Semitic organizing: small parties and associations sprang up in many areas and popular leaders like l bermann von Sonnenberg, Otto Boeckel, and Alexander Pinkert (the dominant figure in Dresden when Chamberlain moved there) played upon this rebellion against the modernizing world, forging an ideology of racism and social conservatism and a new demagogic style of politics. At the same time, more educated and socially respected figures like Stoecker, Treitschke, Lagarde, and Richard Wagner refashioned older forms of Jew hatred into a comprehensive critique of modern society and its values. Between these two groups there was little or no interaction; both were spontaneous products of the same atmostphere of cultural dislocation and discontent with the life and values of the new Germany. Each group had its own goals, techniques of agitation, and clientèle; and each had a powerful impact in spreading suspicion and hatred for Jews among Germans.[100]

As late as 1890, however, the anti-Semitic movement (if we may call it such) had enjoyed few political successes; it was divided and weakened by ideological and class cleavages and split by personal feuds and disagreements over tactics. Isolated victories like Otto Boeckel's electoral success in Hessenland and the short-lived Berlin coalition organized by Adolf Stoecker in 1881 to contest the capital's *Reichstag* seats, provided ephemeral boosts of prestige. But, as a whole, anti-Semitic organizations lacked money and members and had little immediate hope of revoking Jewish emancipation or attracting the major power groups in Germany for their legislative priorities. Apart from confirming the susceptibility of certain occupational and social groups to anti-Jewish appeals, perhaps the most tangible result of this first wave of anti-Semitism in the 1870s and 1880s was the greater aura of respectability it achieved through association with such figures as Stoecker and Treitschke (and Bismarck, in whose circle were several outspoken anti-Semites, including his press secretary Moritz Busch). The image of the Jew as the incarnation of liberalism and liberal economics, as synonymous with the corrosive impact of modernity, was in these years first incorporated into a conservative critique of the bourgeois *ethos* of Imperial society.

Another significant development in the 1880s, related to the impact of Treitschke and other scholars, was a sudden generational shift in the attitudes of university youth and a deep tension between father and sons. There were many symptoms of the growing nationalism of academic youth in these years, of their anger and frustration at the "failures" of liberalism, their disaffection with contemporary society and spurning of bourgeois "reason". One significant consequence was the rapid spread of anti-Semitism through students societies, particularly the various branches of the *Verein deutscher Studenten*. So prevalent was such prejudice that one group of liberal students in Breslau issued a blanket condemnation of their contemporaries, warning:

> The undergraduates at the universities who ought to be the guardians of ideals, have absorbed anti-Semitic doctrines with the greatest enthusiasm and are eagerly at work to bring them to life. . . . The young people at the universities are looked upon as the future leaders of the nation who will influence the life of their country to a very great extent. The education of generations will be in their hands. . . . No end to this movement can be foreseen. Racial hatred will become a tradition and will increase from one generation to the next. The tension accumulated in this way may one day explode with elemental force over our heads. [101]

It was these middle class students who provided the chief contact between the cultural anti-Semitism of the *Bildungsbürgertum* and the grass-roots political agitation carried on by the various anti-Semitic parties and *Reformvereine*. As volunteers, they proved themselves capable canvassers and speakers in the campaigns fought by Boeckel and other leaders (Heinrich Class, for example, volunteered to help Boeckel while a student at Giessen). Their movement in the 1890s into responsible positions in government, medicine, teaching, private industry, and other spheres helped to secure the growing acceptance of racist and anti-Semitic styles of thought in society at large. [102]

"The Bismarckian system falls," announced the *Frankfurter Zeitung* in March 1890; "it withers before the fresh reality of a new age." [103] The Chancellor's resignation removed the single most powerful figure from the political scene, bequeathing a legacy of foreign policy successes and divisiveness at home, of repressive campaigns against internal "Reich enemies" and callous manipulation of the *Reichstag:* all of which left an indelible stamp on the nation's political culture. Clearly, the manifold changes in German society and politics over the next decade cannot be fastened to the fate of one individual, however extraordinary, or fixed chronologically to a single historical "turning point," but to contemporaries it did seem as if a new era had dawned. Within a brief period—as a result of forces which had long been developing—the world on which Bismarckian policies were predicated seemed remote. In the economic sphere the 1890s saw massive, if uneven, growth: the expansion of big business and banking, a shift in the nation's economic center of gravity from agriculture to industry, internal migration, and rapid urbanization. The class and occupational balance of this increasingly bureaucratized and commercialized society altered dramatically with the continued increase in the numbers of industrial workers and an even sharper rise in white-collar employees, executives, and service personnel. Simultaneously, the style and character of political life was transformed by the intensification of sociopolitical conflicts and the growth of the electorate. The extraordinary success of socialism, coupled with the bitter controversies over agricultural protection, and pressure from newly mobilized social groups, placed a heavy burden on the existing party structure and produced a dense network of new pressure groups and special-interest organizations. It is within this context of the emergence of a mass participatory politics and the cultural dislocations it wrought that the anti-Semitism of the post-Bismarckian era must be analyzed.

The years immediately after Bismarck's downfall brought a succession of triumphs for anti-Semitism. So alarming was this new proof of the tenacity of prejudice that it produced a basic shift in the mood and strategy of German Jews and spurred the foundation of defense organizations to protect their civic rights. The basis of the political victories gained by the anti-Semites was the belief of the Conservative Party leadership that anti-Semitism would be a valuable instrument for recruiting votes in small-town and rural constituencies in their efforts to galvanize opposition to Chancellor Caprivi's domestic policies and to offset the gains made by Social Democracy after the repeal of the anti-socialist legislation.* In its December 1892 Tivoli Program the Conservatives became the first major party to explicitly embrace anti-Semitism, despite fears within its ranks that the demagoguery and populism of the anti-Semites would be hard to keep within legitimate bounds. Some months later, the collaboration of Conservatives and anti-Semites in the national elections gave the latter their most impressive gains, enlarging their vote from 47,000 to 263,000 and increasing their seats from six to sixteen. Together with the Conservatives, this meant that the second largest bloc of seats in the *Reichstag* was openly anti-Semitic. As the earliest to focus upon peasant and *Mittelstand* grievances, the anti-Semitic parties were the first to benefit from the new post-Bismarckian political constellation. But, as Richard Levy has demonstrated in detail, their success was ephemeral; they soon entered a slow but continual decline, so that by 1912 they were reduced to 130,000 votes and six seats. In part their failure resulted from the unending tactical and personal disputes of the anti-Semitic leaders, their financial irresponsibility, penchant for scandal, and failure to build a tightly centralized movement. Equally significant, however,

---

* The bitter resistance that Chancellor Caprivi's (1890–94) trade and tariff policy aroused among the landed interests not only had a catalytic effect on the evolution of mass politics in Germany, but also significantly shaped conservative thought. As Kenneth Barkin has shown, the issue of agricultural protection became the focal point of a far-reaching debate over the social and political "costs" of industrialization, the relative importance of industry and agriculture, and the cultural and moral values of the nation. Akin in some ways to the struggle over the Corn Laws in England in the 1840s, this controversy established, broadly speaking, two conflicting visions of the Reich: as an organic, traditional *Agrarstaat* in which the disruptive forces of modernization were somehow held firmly in check, and as a technologically advanced, industrial society. The protection issue publicized widely the conservative, antimodernist critique; it also helped the wider diffusion of anti-Semitic ideas, the Jew being regularly identified in the literature of the Agrarian League as a supreme modernizer, synonymous with urban decadence and spiritual decline. Even after Johannes Miquel began re-creating the conservative *Sammlung* of landed and industrial interests in 1897 and after Bülow's tariff of 1902, the flexible imagery of anti-Semitism provided an outlet for anti-capitalist emotions without calling into question the socioeconomic system as a whole (thus Krupp, Stumm-Halberg, and Stinnes could be portrayed as models of German drive and ingenuity, quite separate from the *raffendes* capitalism of Jews); it mitigated those anti-modern sentiments that might otherwise have hampered a solid alliance of landowning and industrial groups. Kenneth D. Barkin, *The Controversy over German Industrialization 1890–1902* (Chicago: Chicago University Press, 1970); Dirk Stegmann, *Die Erben Bismarcks* (Cologne and Berlin, 1970).

was their lack of funds and heavy dependence on the Conservatives, which left them little political maneuverability. Anti-Semitic attitudes remained strong in Conservative circles, but the power of Adolf Stoecker in the party declined after Tivoli, and the success of the virulently anti-Semitic Agrarian League in consolidating the farm vote after 1895 greatly reduced the usefulness of the independent anti-Semites. Similarly, the emergence of local and eventually national protective associations among the *Mittelstand* further diminished their popular appeal. Thirty years of agitation produced no legislation reversing Jewish emancipation, nor had the realization of their goals ever seemed imminent; their lasting contribution was in keeping the "Jewish question" constantly and noisily in the public eye. During the First World War these independent parties disappeared altogether, melting into the "Victory Peace" coalition. [104]

Focusing too exclusively on the fortunes of these independent anti-Semitic parties, historians have often assumed that anti-Semitism was in general on the decline in the economically prosperous years after 1895. But examination of student and youth organizations, political rhetoric, newspapers, institutional discrimination, and the information meticulously compiled by the Jewish defense groups, points to the reverse conclusion. This varied—and to the present writer convincing—body of research suggests instead that the demise of parliamentary anti-Semitism was paralleled by its wider diffusion through society. [105] By 1900 anti-Semitism had become part of the mainstream of conservative ideas; it had permeated a wide range of social, cultural, occupational, as well as political groups, and in the writings of publicists like Chamberlain took on an increasingly elaborate intellectual apparatus. At times anti-Semitism has been portrayed as predominantly the reaction of *Mittelständler* whose lives were dislocated by the process of modernization. No one would dispute the fact that these strata supplied the grass-roots support of the innumerable anti-Semitic organizations that mushroomed from year to year. But equally striking, and often neglected, is the appeal of anti-Jewish styles of thought among the solid, prosperous bourgeoisie who were the beneficiaries of German capitalism and active "modernizers" in their daily lives. Admittedly, there were many contemporaries who deplored this constant recourse to a Jewish scapegoat to verbalize disaffection of various kinds, but broad segments of the middle classes, sometimes in subtle and elusive ways, were infected with such prejudice. And neither the fact that Jews constituted less than 1 percent of the total population, nor the painstaking, rational refutations of Jewish defense groups and their Christian sympathizers, made any appreciable difference.

Whereas in the period of Emancipation hostility was chiefly directed toward Jews as a distinct social and religious group, by the 1890s through a gradual process of abstraction, anti-Semitism had become one element (and not always the most important) in a broad conservative and nationalist cultural stance. In the words of Franz Oppenheimer, it had become "the inwardly turned face of aggressive chauvinistic nationalism."[106] Attacks were still launched against specific Jewish bankers, politicians, and immigrants, but increasingly anti-Jewish prejudice seeped into the thought and language of contemporaries in a vaguer symbolism which turned Jewry into a mythical entity, almost a metaphysical force, largely divorced from the concrete problem of relations between Gentiles and Jews. The Jew was a negative personification of the evils of capitalism, a symbol of modernity; he was responsible for the secularization of society, the decay of moral standards, the vulgarity and tastelessness of the age. Anti-Semitism permeated critiques of big-city life, warnings of the dangers of feminism,* and nostalgic longings for a remote, corporate past; it infiltrated the fashionable pessimism of the *Gebildete,* and

---

* Richard Evans, for example, illustrates the connection of anti-feminism and anti-Semitism in the campaigns of the commercial employees union (DHV). One of its publicists, Werner Heinemann, wrote in 1913: "We meet Jewry everywhere in the women's movement. The women's movement, the peace movement, Social Democracy and Jewry, these four are intimately related to one another, they are international and work in an international spirit." Claims that feminism resulted from the agitation of Jews were widespread on the right. Thus, the anti-Semitic *Deutsch-Soziale Blätter* commented: "This movement provides a possibility of subverting German ideals and destroying the heart and soul of the German woman—hence the remarkable zeal of the Jewesses in this connection." Evans, *The Feminist Movement in Germany 1894–1933* (London: Sage Publications, 1976), pp. 179–81. Chamberlain rejected women's suffrage with G. K. Chesterton's retort that women were too good for the vote. HSC to Sidonie Peter, Oct. 1, 1915 (CN).

attacks on the corruption and divisiveness of parliamentary politics. Anti-socialism and anti-liberalism found expression, simply and succinctly, in hostility toward Jews, while ambitious visions of *Weltpolitik* were made contingent upon a solid front against domestic *Reichsfeinde*. This was Chamberlain's principal theme in the *Foundations:* German culture and power depended on the capacity of Germans to resist alien influences and ideals. The rest of his ideas—his monarchism, anti-modernism, and opposition to democracy—were easily implanted into this general conception.

Anti-Semitism is a broad term; it encompasses a bewildering number of gradations of antipathy and many different chemistries of ideas. For extremists like Adolf Bartels, the literary critic and champion of *Heimatkunst*, the Jew was the foremost danger confronting the nation. "Who" he asked in 1906 "can today still dispute . . . that the fight against monarchism, the agitation against the officer corps, the struggle against so-called agrarianism (i.e. the toiling and striving landholders), the destruction of the *Mittelstand*, the adulteration of German art and scholarship, the depravity of the yellow press, the decadence of the metropolis are at bottom all traceable to Jewish influences?" [107] The Jew was responsible, in other words, for whatever was amiss. For Chamberlain also, the dialectic of German and Jew was the synthesizing principle of his world view, his means for understanding a rapidly changing reality. Other anti-Semites were less obsessed with this single issue and incorporated hostility toward Jews into a more differentiated context of ideas. The same variation existed between the dozens of anti-Semitic organizations: whereas some devoted their efforts exclusively to combating Jewry, others placed equal stress on a range of social and cultural goals (the regeneration of art and religion; improvement of education; imperialism; social protection for *Mittelständler*, etc.). The multifaceted stereotype of the Jew embraced a rich collection of attitudes and beliefs. But while many differences in tone and emphasis existed between anti-Semites, there were also numerous common themes that united them. Their cultural responses and style of thought overlapped; there was considerable interaction between the organizations to which they belonged; and their image of the tensions and conflicts that beset Imperial Germany bore striking resemblance beyond their shared hatred for Jews. Even those who would have refused the title of anti-Semite often disclosed patterns of thought similar to those of Chamberlain; so widespread and familiar was anti-Semitism as a form of discourse that whether readers accepted Chamberlain's arguments or not, they grasped immediately the range of cultural and political allusions they contained. As Shulamit Volkov explained recently in a trenchant analysis of this theme: "Professing anti-Semitism became a sign of cultural identity, of one's belonging to a specific cultural camp. It was a way of communicating an acceptance of a particular set of ideas, and a preference for specific social, political, and moral norms. Contemporaries, living and acting in Imperial Germany, learned to decode the message. It became part of their language, a familiar and convenient symbol."[108]

Indicative of this peculiarly cerebral and ideological nature of the *Judenfrage* in the last decade of the century was the very impracticality of most anti-Semites. Whereas the parliamentary anti-Semites devised a program of legislative priorities, the majority of those who railed against the Jews were remarkably vague about how the problem should be resolved. In spite of his cries of urgency, Chamberlain offered few concrete proposals and focused on exhortations for Germanic regeneration rather than detailed programs for defeating the Jewish menace. He rarely did more than hint at the need for controls on immigration and restrictions on the role of Jews in specific occupations and politics. As an integral part of a conservative nationalist vision, anti-Semitism was more a means of conceptualizing a complicated cultural stance and defining German values than a prescriptive creed. Only in the last years of peace, as doubts multiplied on the right about the capacity of the Imperial status quo to survive, did anti-Semitism develop a more prescriptive tone. Chamberlain's racism in the *Foundations* contained elements which could be fashioned into advocacy of more forceful, retaliatory action, but most of his comments were directed toward a spiritual transformation of

German society. Later, this cognitive distance between the symbolic Jew and actual Jews narrowed sharply.

In part the pervasiveness of anti-Semitic rhetoric and forms of argument in ever-widening middle-class circles reflects the continuing influence of Treitschke, Lagarde, Stoecker, and others who had done so much to cloak anti-Jewish prejudice in academic respectability. In part these patterns of thought were cultivated and reinforced by the reluctance of the state to fully implement Jewish emancipation, the discriminatory practices of the army and civil service, and the ingrained bias of other social institutions. But, additionally, the social and political forces at work in the 1890s greatly facilitated the spread of anti-Semitic ideology.

The political configuration of the period is familiar and requires no detailed analysis here.[109] Briefly, the staggering successes of Social Democracy and the sharp rise in the numbers of Germans participating in politics, posed a serious challenge to the traditional parties, forcing them to make large adjustments in ideology and organization. Extensive auxiliary organizations developed to strengthen the bonds of material interest and outlook between parties and their traditional sources of support. The Agrarian League, for example, was crucial in bringing the mass of rural voters into the national political scene—and, as Hans-Jurgen Puhle has shown, in disseminating a potent blend of romantic agrarianism and racist nationalism. Alongside the parties emerged new occupational groups and nationalist associations such as the Pan-Germans, the Naval League, the *Wehrverein*, and DHV which played an increasing role in opinion-making.[110] The result was a curious hybrid of parliamentary and extra-parliamentary politics and a growing polarization of German society after 1895 between the forces of social change, the liberals and socialists, and a broad conservative bloc of landowners, nationalist bourgeoisie, and *Mittlestand* groups. And whereas, to a great extent, the left worked for democratization through the *Reichstag*, the right—despairing of its chances at the polls—increasingly had recourse to anti-parliamentary means of pressure and attempted to deparliamentarize the system,

fostering a broad, "unpolitical" and anti-democratic nationalist consensus. There were significant differences in
interest and goals within this conservative alliance, but they
were united in their opposition to further liberalization. Within
this culture of the right anti-Semitism came to be accepted
"almost as a matter of course."[111]

In the years before 1914 failures in foreign policy (the
Moroccan crises and the *Daily Telegraph* fiasco especially) and
the intensification of class and political conflicts at home,
further radicalized the tone of the right. Government policy
proved unable to match the expectations of public opinion in
achieving greater security for the Reich or realizing its colonial objectives. Similarly, the Social Democratic electoral
landslide in 1912 confirmed the worst fears of the conservative
and bourgeois classes about the inability of the existing structure to restrain the march of socialism. Quickly dubbed "the
Jew elections" in the right-wing press, and blamed on "the incursion of Jewish capital," they provoked a new wave of racist
agitation and prophecies of national decline.[112] "Gobineau and
Chamberlain are gaining more attention," reported the voice
of big industry, the *Deutsche Arbeitgeberzeitung.* "With good
reason men strive to rescue the unique, physical and spiritual,
völkisch qualities of Germandom from the assault of foreign in-
truders."[113] "The race question," ran an article in the *Akade-
mische Blätter*, "is for us one of many, although among the
most important, which flow from our national ideology . . . But
as it proves impossible for us . . . to assimilate the Jewish race,
we are forced to conclude that we must expel it from the body
politic."[114] In this crisis atmosphere of parliamentary deadlock,
rumors of war and speculation about preventive strikes against
domestic and foreign enemies, the organizations of the far
right—the Agrarian League, the Pan-Germans and anti-Semites—achieved growing prominence and respectability in the
counsels of the conservative nationalists. Gradually the
German right was being reshaped and radicalized, although
the full extent of this was not apparent until the first World
War.[115]

There are numerous symptoms of a hardening of negative
attitudes toward Jews before the war. "Few outright anti-

Semitic attacks can be reported," observed the Jewish *Korrespondenz* in 1910," but only a few correspondents tell us about private contacts between Jewish and Christian Germans."[116] In the youth movement, holiday resorts, and in official circles, a tougher mood may be discerned; similarly, anti-Semitic literature continued to sell widely. Apart from Chamberlain's continuing success with the *Foundations*, Theodor Fritsch's *Handbuch der Judenfrage* sold over 4,000 copies within eight days of its publication in 1907, while Heinrich Class, the Pan-German leader, achieved a notable success with his pseudonymous tract, *Wenn ich der Kaiser wär* (1912). This rather crude compendium of racism, anti-Semitism, imperialism, and plans for a reconstructed authoritarian Reich, not only sold 25,000 copies by the spring of 1914, but was quite seriously attributed to such prominent personalities as Admiral Tirpitz, Count Posadowsky, and Baron von Stössel.[117] With its demands for a limitation to Jewish immigration and restrictions on the rights of Jews already in the Reich, Class's polemic epitomizes the shift to a more programmatic attitude on the far right. "A recovery of our *Volk* life in all its aspects: cultural, political and economic," he insisted, "is only possible if *Jewish influence is either completely excluded or restricted to tolerable, harmless proportions*."[118]

It was precisely these trends that prompted a man like Moritz Goldstein to challenge the Jewish strategy of assimilation; the position of the Jew, he concluded, was that of an unrequited lover—it promised unrelieved misery and no chance of ultimate acceptance. Yet Goldstein was in a minority. For all of the offensive treatment, the slights, rebuffs, and prejudiced language they had to cope with, German Jews were far from pessimistic. Much had been achieved; the authority of the state kept the most vicious rabble-rousers in check; there was no German equivalent of the Dreyfus affair and nothing remotely comparable to the pogroms in Eastern Europe. Sometimes historians have argued that the effect of the later tragedy of German Jewry has been to assign excessive importance to earlier examples of prejudice.[119] But a massive amount of documentation confirms the prevalence of anti-Semitic feeling; indeed, one scholar recently described

Wilhelminian society as "blanketed with overlapping critiques of Jews and Judaism," with each sector leveling its attack "from its own vantage point."[120] Few Jews who volunteered for combat in 1914 felt immediately threatened by anti-Semitism, but few also felt that Jews had attained their place in German society. The persistence of prejudice was deeply disappointing, but the danger it implied was masked to a considerable degree by the organizational disunity of the anti-Semites, and by the difficulty of accurately evaluating such feeling when it was so often voiced in vague ideological form and yoked to diverse other cultural and political grievances.[121]

From this analysis of the responses to the *Foundations* and of the broader trends in German anti-Semitism before the war, it is evident that Chamberlain owed his success to the way his book captured the mood of contemporaries. Sometimes moderate, at others extreme, full of lavish hopes for the supremacy of German culture and brooding fears of subterranean social and moral decay, it fitted anti-Semitism into a more or less coherent nationalist *Weltanschauung*. Chamberlain offered a "scholarly" evocation of the opinions and impulses current in conservative and bourgeois circles; he was a spiritual revolutionary and yet a conservative, cherished a pre-industrial social ideal and remained an adherent of economic and scientific progress, dreamed of world hegemony and still claimed to be defending mankind against the universal aims of an alien race.

His readers, of course, were chiefly from the middle classes; teachers, lawyers, businessmen, students, and pastors were prominent among his enthusiasts.[122] Exactly how far his influence reached into the *Mittelstand* (clerks, shopkeepers, craftsmen, peasants etc.) can scarcely be conjectured; the evidence is sketchy and more research is needed about the literacy and reading habits of these social groups. In general, while *völkisch* organizers certainly knew his work, the lower middle class probably encountered the themes of his book primarily in the form of reviews, newspaper excerpts, political speeches, and *völkisch* novels, rather than at first hand. Very important as well was the local press of Germany, where writers like Chamberlain and Bartels were often given space for articles and where their books obtained extensive comments. Thus, in one part of Austria, the *Foundations* became the focal point of a bitter dispute between two rival papers—the *Vorarlberger Volksblatt* of Bregenz and the *Vorarlberger Volksfreund* of neighboring Donbirn—which lasted from March until September 1904, with long weekly articles occupying the front pages of each journal. The crux of the debate was over Rome and clericalism; but what was said was less important than where—for such papers attracted a wide readership from across the local community and were the basic reading diet of shopkeepers, peasants, and workers in the area.[123] Lastly, the propagandist activities of the DHV probably helped publicize his ideas in circles not accustomed to reading fairly heavy two-volume works.

Chamberlain was himself sceptical about the possibility of publicizing his opinions to a mass audience. When August Ludowici, his friend and financial patron, offered to advance a substantial sum for printing a brief summary of the *Foundations*, Chamberlain flatly refused. Only after the educated classes had grasped his ideas, he told Kaiser Wilhelm, would they filter further down; the educated elite, he was convinced, was the source of all catalytic ideas that occasion major shifts in attitudes; their spirit, taste, and morality, their religious and political principles, determined the course of the nation[124] Without a unanimous sense of mission, shaped by its elite, a society drifted or disintegrated into warring factions; this, he admonished, was the danger confronting the Reich.

The crisis of the First World War caused him to modify his views somewhat. In his polemical wartime essays he put forth in simplified and more trenchant form the ideas contained in his previous books. His technique of weaving together fact and fiction, truth and assertion; his facile style and pseudo-scholarly air, made him highly successful in this genre as well. Until 1914, however, he viewed his task as that of formulating a Germanic ideology for the educated classes which others might publicize and convert into a political program.[125]

Chapter Seven

Kant and Goethe: Toward a Teutonic World View

THE *FOUNDATIONS* ESTABLISHED Chamberlain as a race popularizer and cultural prophet. Over the next fifteen years he kept up a prodigious pace, his life full of projects "in the service of *Deutschtum*." His major themes were familiar to readers of the earlier book: the superiority of German culture, the omnipresent threat of materialism, the relentless struggle with Rome and Jewry, and a German world mission that could only be fulfilled if the nation dedicated itself unstintingly to the historic task. To Chamberlain the new century brought terrible but surmountable dangers, while also holding out the prospect of German ascendancy. He did not despair of the future, nor did pessimism pervade his thoughts. His writings both flattered and criticized, admonished and exhorted Germans, always culminating in the same message: that a nation's power and prestige was a function of its ideals and cultural vitality. The future of the Reich depended on the success of Germans in rediscovering their racial character, in expunging foreign ideas and returning to German modes of thought: "inner superiority," argued Chamberlain, was the prelude to global dominance. "The issue now is," he told Kaiser Wilhelm, "to make or to mar!"[1]

At first it may seem that his central literary concerns in these years, two lengthy studies of Kant and Goethe, were far removed from the arena of power politics; but both books were inspired by the conviction that these thinkers were essential to the elaboration of a Teutonic world view and must therefore be made accessible to the mass of educated Germans. His aim, he wrote, was "to stimulate not speculation but deeds." "The hour has struck," he announced in his *Kant*, "when in our direst need we want this force not merely in the laboratories of a dozen learned men but outside for battle—for the battle of redemption."[2] Having little faith that university mandarins—overspecialized and hopelessly aloof from the public at large—would elevate the spirits and shape the minds of the nation, he assumed the task himself. He was not alone of course: the age inspired a vast output of nationalist prophecy; nor was his idealism original but drew from many sources and harked back to earlier moralists like Lagarde especially in his call for a Germanic religion. But works like Chamberlain's *Goethe* or Friedrich Lienhard's six volume *Wege nach Weimar* do, by virtue of their scope and sheer length, mark a new departure in *völkisch* cultural criticism.[3] They were more pretentious and scholarly in tone than their predecessors, heavily armed with erudite references, calculated to appeal to the educated amateur, yet betraying a secret wish for recognition from those same academics they so bitterly attacked. After 1918 these volumes became the gospels of a new generation of critics, source books for their denunciations of Weimar.

At the end of August 1898, apart from minor corrections, the *Foundations* was finished. For over two years Chamberlain had driven himself at a feverish pace; now, exhausted and apprehensive about the reception his bold ideas would get, he felt depressed, drained, and badly in need of a holiday. But even a few days in Salzburg did not lighten his cares for he was tormented by the thought of the unfinished second and third parts of the original design submitted to Bruckmann. Incapable of embarking on them right away, he decided to wire the publisher to use the title *Foundations of the Nineteenth Century* so that the book might appear more of a finished entity.[4] His doubts about completing the mammoth project were well founded, for over the next two decades, though he made extensive sketches and collected boxes of notes, Chamberlain repeatedly postponed the task and his interests shifted to other things. Possibly, he would have resumed it in 1914 had not the rapid deterioration of relations between the European powers and the outbreak of war absorbed his attention and deflected his energies to producing war propaganda. After the conflict, his health was too frail for anything that required such extensive research or so much writing. Yet it is clear that much of what he intended to say—about science, art, philosophy and politics—had already been anticipated in his other writings and in his extensive correspondence.

As we have seen, the *Foundations* was in some respects a hasty improvisation; it was not Chamberlain's own idea but grew out of Bruckmann's request. Yet even before completing the introduction Chamberlain, always full of new projects, began to sketch out another book altogether—one which developed slowly in his mind and was grounded in his earlier botanical studies with Wiesner. After a brief holiday in Italy in October 1896 he was so absorbed by the new idea that he interrupted his return journey and spent a few days at the Swiss resort Gardone to put some order into his jumbled thoughts. To Aunt Harriet, he admitted: "I have become such a prey to the *idée fixe* of the work I contemplate writing . . . that I decided to stay a week here and work out a sketch . . . not of the book but of my own idea. . . . Once a thing of that sort is clearly established, it becomes more easy to put it on one side than when it haunts one ghostlike."[5] His plan was vast: "nothing less than a theory intended to overthrow Darwinism," thus establishing a new philosophical basis for science—less analytic and mechanical, more intuitive and designed to grasp the forms and interconnectedness of life without slotting them into artificial theoretical schemata.[6] "Darwinism," he informed Cosima Wagner, "rules everywhere, it ruins our history and religion. It leads to social stupidities, it degrades our judgment of men and things."[7]

It was this grandiose idea that preoccupied Chamberlain after 1896. The modern age was one of science whose prevailing conceptions had penetrated every aspect of thought. Not only did mechanical, analytic science have its social counterpart in the atomistic theories of liberalism, but Darwinian Evolution, the chief paradigm of the age, had dispensed with God, reduced *Homo sapiens* to one animal among many, and endowed popular doctrines of progress, economic competition, and human perfectability with the sanction of scientific truth. To Chamberlain's mind, therefore, the central pillar of a Germanic world view had to be a new concept of life and an appreciation of race: a science, in other words, which was compatible with German religion and philosophy, freeing men of the illusion of self-evident and automatic human progress, awakening them to the threat of degeneration and harmonious with an elitist, hierarchical vision of social relations. Chamberlain's general attack on false ideologies began then with scientific materialism or its recrudescence in the works of popular Darwinians like Ludwig Büchner and Ernst Haeckel: for him they revealed in concentrated form the larger misconceptions of the age, while their widespread popularity made them especially dangerous. With its discussion of racial form and brief excursus on the German conception of Nature, the *Foundations* did contain some echoes of the Gardone sketch, but the latter was not really a blueprint for the book —as yet Chamberlain's ideas were far too hazy.

Shortly after the *Foundations* Chamberlain again returned to the "Life Doctrine" (or *Lebenslehre*, as he called it) but rapidly became aware that it required a great deal of preparatory work and a more systematic procedure. The sequence of his writings between 1900 and 1914 was largely dictated by this ulterior purpose. Since Goethe was the chief inspiration for his ideas, Chamberlain began a close study of the poet's scientific researches, using the definitive Weimar edition which had just become available. This in turn suggested another task—that of drawing up an index or register which would offer a convenient guide to Goethe's vast corpus of writings. Chamberlain quite correctly recognized that their sheer volume intimidated most readers, forcing them to rely on biographies or commentaries or to limit themselves to the best known literary compositions. A clear index, arranged by subjects and concepts, would enable the average man to approach all of Goethe, including his philosophy of Nature so necessary as an antidote to popular scientism.[8] "Without question," he wrote to Viktor Kommetter, a young law student, "Goethe is the greatest of all teachers about life. Every German should make it a rule to read Goethe every day—even if it is only a single page." [9]

After some months devising a general index, however, he abandoned the plan. He was still restlessly searching for an appropriate entry point into his larger project for a Nature philosophy and had convinced himself that Goethe must be the end rather than the beginning for his speculations. The first step, he decided, should be to examine the nature of knowledge itself, to show the limits of reason and its natural disposition to overstep the bounds of possible experience; this meant returning to the critical philosophy of Kant and his clear separation of metaphysical and scientific understanding.

Chamberlain had long cherished the idea of writing about Kant, but he was finally persuaded to begin after a series of conversations with two friends, Countess Marie Zichy and Baroness Marie Wallerstein-Oettingen. The plan of his *Damenbuch*, as he called it, was highly original. [10] It came to him suddenly in its entirety in April 1900, although the first weeks of rapid progress proved deceptive and the book took five years of intensive labor and many discarded drafts before the two volumes were ready for publication. As so often happens, what began as a short detour turned ineluctably into a major expedition. The book attempted, by drawing upon the vast secondary scholarship as well as the texts of Kant, to publicize the philosopher's "Copernican" insights in a series of comparisons and contrasts with other thinkers: Goethe, Leonardo da Vinci, Descartes, Giordano Bruno, and Plato. His object was not to supply a précis of Kant's philosophy nor to engage in technical analysis or what Chamberlain judged to be the hairsplitting exercises of academics (Vaihinger's exhaustive commentaries, for example, irritated him by their pedantic attention to detail); rather his aim was to show by numerous examples and instructive comparisons the underlying spirit and central focus of Kant's work, making it accessible to a broad educated public. The dualism of Kant, Chamberlain insisted, offered the perfect counterweight to monistic systems, whether those of scientists like Haeckel and Büchner or philosophers like Bruno and Hegel. It reestablished the moral autonomy of man, reconciled empirical science and idealism, and thereby provided a secure ground from which to evaluate both the claims of religious doctrines and of science. Kant had erected the scaffolding of the Teutonic world view.

Chamberlain's book, like himself, was a curious amalgam of contradictory qualities: intelligent and imaginative, crude and prejudiced, learned and yet astonishingly one-sided. A strong revival of interest in Kantian philosophy had been underway since the 1870s and by 1900 neo-Kantianism was the dominant *Schulphilosophie* in Germany, with its representatives occupying most of the university chairs.[11] Chamberlain peppered his text and notes with the names of these scholars, drawing upon them in selective manner and praising some of them highly—including Hermann Cohen and Paul Natorp—but the thrust of his arguments differed sharply from theirs. In general, in the process of denouncing the exalted claims made by others for reason—especially Roman Catholic writers and materialist scientists—he expressed his own deep distrust of rationalism and his reliance upon instinct and intuition as a source of knowledge. This may not always have been apparent to readers, since the greater part of the book was critical—aimed at exposing the false claims of others—while its range of subjects probably disguised his purpose to some extent. Interesting sections on plant physiology, optics, vitalism, evolution, analytic geometry, and hermetic philosophy were thoughtfully woven into the overall plan of illuminating Kant's central vision. The result was a highly sophisticated book, more subtle than the *Foundations*. It traced the limits that past thinkers had placed—or had failed to place—upon human comprehension and then moved quietly into an extended defense of religion and a kind of "voluntaristic" rebellion against reason, stressing intuition, will, or "life" as the ultimate test of truth. Earlier, Chamberlain had written: "Nothing is so convincing as the consciousness of race" and asserted: "Descartes pointed out that all the wise men in the world could not define the color 'white,' but I need only open my eyes to see it and it is the same with race." Now, in 1906, he argued that if Teutons realized their own inner strength and jettisoned false ideologies "no danger from outside would be invincible"; the Teutonic "empire of intellect" was under deadly assault "at the beginning of our much vaunted twentieth century" and its survival required a return to Kant.[12] For Chamberlain this meant a radical dualism, separating the realms of pure and practical reason, and thereby justifying an intuitive, irrational realm of racial values and racial religion beyond the reach of scientific or rational criticism.

In attempting to fashion a popular version of Kantian philosophy as a spiritual answer to the crisis of his times Chamberlain echoed a larger debate among German intellectuals about the relevance of Kant; his interpretation, with its emphasis upon the subjective and irrational and its effort to link Kant with a vague, mystical notion of a Teutonic spirit, also reflected contemporary disillusionment with the heritage of rationalism and liberalism. The cry that Germanic culture was in peril aroused murmurs of sympathy among readers; so did Chamberlain's analysis of the culprits: materialism, science, and technical progress; Roman Catholicism and dogmatic Protestantism; the proletarianization of culture and the growing might of socialism, which denied individuality and "undermined the dignity of man." The urban worker lived in an "artificial culture," his intellect dulled by "the monotony of his craft"; "the extreme specialization of every activity" and the diminution of leisure time made even the educated rely almost exclusively upon a mass distribution press to do their thinking and judging for them. "Everything," concluded Chamberlain, "tends to make us less able to see and less able to think." He devoted less space to berating Jewry, but clearly his exhortation that Germans acquire a deeper understanding of themselves also meant confronting the Jewish question: "In order to understand Kant [on religion] we must . . . begin by once and for all getting rid of the heavy burden of inherited and indoctrinated Jewish conceptions."[13]

Chamberlain's indictment of the modern age had a broad appeal among conservative groups in Imperial Germany, but he himself was bitterly disappointed with the reception that *Kant* gained and accused the liberal press and racial enemies of conspiring to defame and stifle his ideas. His discontent is at first difficult to fathom: after all, expensive, two-volume studies of Kant are not the most popular reading and the 30,000 copies eventually sold was very respectable. His dissatisfaction derived from the magnitude of his hopes and his conviction that this was a far superior and more carefully wrought study than the *Foundations*. The staggering earlier success nourished his hopes that he could publicize Kant and foster a religious revival; the care and years of study devoted to the task had awakened a belief that this time he would find praise even among the ranks of professional scholars. None of these things happened—at least to a degree that satisfied him.[14]

In fact, the book was reviewed widely and quite favorably. The critic F. J. Schmidt of the *Preussische Jahrbücher* praised it highly, commenting that Chamberlain was "a dilettante in the noblest sense of the word" who "reveals the purely-human worth of Kantian idealism in a clearer manner than learned experts." A. Wernicke, a Wagnerite, wrote a particularly glowing appraisal for the *Pädagogisches Archiv*, a journal influential among teachers. The Catholic press was understandably hostile, while scientists especially responded to his strictures with angry reviews. Most reviewers found aspects of the book with which they disagreed, and some noted that it was more for those who wished to worship Kant than to study him systematically; but in general responses were decidedly favorable. Even a man like Hermann Broch, the Austrian novelist, who converted from Judaism to Catholicism, described it as "very good" while admitting that he opposed its basic assumptions "however spirited and well-thought-out they may be." The Marburg philosopher Paul Natorp also found much to admire in it and—while admitting that he differed in his judgment of the state of German culture—predicted that it would familiarize broad circles with the task of philosophy. Much more extravagant in their appreciation were Chamberlain's close friends: Rudolf Kassner, Hermann Keyserling, and, of course, the Wahnfried circle, while Leopold von Schroeder dispatched a letter to Stockholm nominating Chamberlain for a Nobel prize.[15]

While Chamberlain's energies until 1906 were largely devoted to Kant, he also published a remarkable quantity of other essays on a variety of subjects. Scarcely a year went by without some new offering from his pen. His *Parsifal Märchen*, originally written for Cosima Wagner, appeared in 1900, followed by *Worte Christi*, a short religious manual for Christians estranged from existing churches. In 1902 a selection of his plays appeared with illustrations by Adolphe Appia, while in the following year he wrote the long fourth preface to the *Foundations*, defending himself against critics and attacking the arguments of Friedrich Delitzsch in the *Babel und Bibel* controversy. All the while he managed to keep up a steady flow of articles and book reviews, and in 1905, while laboring to finish the *Kant* manuscript, still found time to collect his essays on Indian literature and philosophy into a small introductory volume, *Arische Weltanschauung*.

Even before finishing *Kant* he was already busy making sketches for an even larger book on Goethe. Occupying him constantly for six years, it was to be the fullest exposition Chamberlain ever made of his own ideas and the most elaborate example of his style of popularization: a perplexing amalgam of wide-ranging scholarship, defiant subjectivism, original and valid insights, and glaring distortions. The book coincided with the peak of a Goethe renaissance that had been underway since the 1880s. "Everybody who was anybody among the new elite," Wolfgang Leppmann has written, "either belonged to the Goethe Society or otherwise made his bow toward Weimar."[16] Ernst Haeckel portrayed the poet as a forerunner of Darwin; Rudolf Steiner discovered in his writings the embryo of Theosophy; Bayreuth turned him into a dramatic poet in the tradition of Wagner; and the upper middle class *Bürger*, proudly displaying the finely bound collected works in his villa, looked to Goethe as the embodiment of the greatest qualities of the German spirit. Eight major biographies appeared in German alone between 1895 and 1909, followed in the next years by the huge studies of Chamberlain (1912), the sociologist Georg Simmel (1913) and of Friedrich Gundolf (1916), a prominent member of the Stefan George *Kreis*.

Chamberlain had written *Kant* during a period of personal unhappiness and uncertainty when, as we shall see, his marriage to Anna deteriorated rapidly, ending in their separation in 1906. At the same time his relations with Wahnfried had grown cooler because Cosima and Henry Thode, at least, were irritated by the paucity of direct references to Wagner in the *Foundations*. Ever watchful for possible heresy or treachery, they were suspicious of Chamberlain's reticence and Thode castigated him publicly for it.[17] The ill feeling that this squabble occasioned is reflected perhaps in the absence of any mention of Wagner in the Kant manuscript, although—seen in retrospect—it constitutes an important part of Chamberlain's larger achievement of linking Bayreuth with the broader currents of intellectual life and racist thought in Imperial Germany. In contrast, the composition of *Goethe* spans perhaps the happiest period in Chamberlain's life. Most of it was written after he had divorced Anna, moved from Vienna to Bayreuth, and married Eva Wagner, Cosima's youngest daughter. Welcomed back to Wahnfried as a son and celebrated *littérateur*, he experienced a new feeling of contentment and harmony. Not only did his *Goethe* resume the task of describing a truly Germanic view of life and nature, but it was also consciously a labor of love for Bayreuth—so much so that one reviewer wrote indignantly: "The spirit of Goethe has nothing to do with that of Bayreuth, which Chamberlain continually cites to buttress his gospel. They are two worlds as distinct as day and night. In one rules the sunshine of clarity and a passionate understanding of every creature, in the other the fog of mysticism governs."[18]

Chamberlain's *Goethe* is the most carefully crafted book he ever wrote; it contains the fruits of some twenty years of study and reflection. In the "Gardone sketch" of October 1896, he had first tentatively advanced the "new vision [*Anschauung*] of the form of living Being"; a brief section entitled "Afterthoughts" also suggested that this novel perception of life would trigger a wider revolution in thought. Philosophy, for example, would benefit from a new emphasis upon Being instead of evolution and Becoming; metaphysical speculation could achieve a sounder basis; the replacement of stifling materialism by an idealist outlook would allow art to flourish, while politics would be deflected from a liberal-democratic focus upon change to one that stressed continuity. It was through Goethe above all that Chamberlain hoped to clarify these assertions—a Goethe, one should add, whom he interpreted in the light of his knowledge of Wagner, Kant, and Plato. With some justice did he describe this in 1916 as "the most esoteric of my books."[19]

Divided into six long chapters, *Goethe* opens with a discussion of the poet's life which is largely straightforward and emphasizes the enormous significance of his Italian journey of 1786–88. Unlike most earlier biographies, which concentrated upon Goethe's youth, Chamberlain was fascinated by the latter stages of his life. His goal was to disclose the private side of Goethe, the interior of his personality, without confusing readers with excessive detail. The second chapter was more original and sought to uncover the basic elements, the "timeless *Gestalt*," of Goethe's character. His famous "God given harmony"—the figure of the Olympian Goethe—was only slowly and painstakingly achieved, Chamberlain argued, after years of inner strife. Many "diametrically opposed instincts, interests and abilities" coexisted in him which had to be repeatedly mastered and deflected into fruitful rather than destructive channels: it was this relentless struggle that endowed the poet's life with both its heroic and tragic elements. Briefly put, one side of Goethe was passionate, spontaneous, and thirsting for immediate sensual experience; the other was more thoughtful and contemplative, given to evolving complex abstract ideas. He was simultaneously a man of action and of reflection, statesman and artist, mystic and scientist, *Augenmensch* and theoretician. And because of this fundamental duality and his need to bridge the two halves of his nature, Goethe was deeply conscious of his own creative process: of the dialectical relationship between cognizing subject and object, the distinction between "experience" and "idea" and between observation and conceptualization. Goethe, in other words, was in Chamberlain's eyes instinctively a Kantian who was able to shape his powerful sense impressions into startlingly original scientific and philosophical insights and into poetry with a universal appeal. His personal triumph lay in recognizing the "antinomies" that cut across all his endeavors and in harnessing the creative power they released. As one of the first to question the earlier positivistic image of the Appolonian or Olympian Goethe, Chamberlain's achievement was considerable—the book, in Leppmann's judgment, contained "a great deal that is right, and much that was unquestionably new." [20]

The remainder of the book traced the consequences that these polarities in Goethe's personality had for different elements of his work. With the Weimar edition (the standard edition eventually numbered 143 volumes) it became possible for the first time to appreciate the incredible versatility of Goethe's achievement and, in particular, to reevaluate his non-poetic writings. Not surprisingly, the heated debates about Darwinian Evolution, and the widespread reaction against narrow scientism which figured so large in German intellectual life around 1900, stimulated new interest in Goethe's biological studies and his critique of Newtonian mechanics. Earlier writers such as the eminent physiologist and exponent of a mechanical world view, Emil DuBois-Reymond, had dismissed these speculations as a "stillborn pastime"; but by 1906 Rudolf Magnus found it possible to give a course of lectures at Heidelberg solely on Goethe's scientific researches. [21] Chamberlain's book—albeit in extreme fashion—exemplified the broader shift of opinion. It was more important, he argued, for the spiritual culture of the age to retrace Goethe's speculations about Nature than to ponder endlessly *Faust* or *Tasso*. [22] Goethe's writings on botany, anatomy, and optics offered a radically new approach to science, one which grasped the complexity of living forms and the all embracing unity of Nature. Chamberlain's sympathy for Goethe's viewpoint, coupled with his own expertise in botany, made him a clear and skillful commentator; his errors or exaggerations, where they occurred, originated in his uncontrollable desire to read his own convictions into the texts he was analyzing.

The sections dealing with Goethe's science were the most successful of the book and won high praise from a great many reviewers. His analysis of Goethe's poetic achievements, however, was seriously flawed by a determination to Wagnerize his subject and show him as a kind of poet-musician whose art had anticipated the Word-Tone dramas of Bayreuth. This involved, among other things, attributing great significance even to Goethe's minor dramas, while his sporadic efforts to reform the theater at Weimar were transformed into an early incarnation of the *Festspiele* idea.[23] In fact, this interpretation of Goethe was not Chamberlain's brainchild; it was anticipated in both Wagner's essays, *Beethoven* and *Actors and Singers*, and in his correspondence. Always seeking confirmation for his own beliefs, Wagner had also done his best to associate Goethe with notions of racial decline and regeneration.

In the final and longest chapter, "Goethe the *Savant*," Chamberlain went still further in the direction of turning Goethe into an exponent of his own views. Denouncing the myth of the "unphilosophical Goethe," he strove to represent him as one of the most original and incisive minds of all time. Denying that the poet had ever been a pantheist or disciple of the Jew Spinoza, even in his youth, Chamberlain averred instead that he was a consistent and faultless Kantian.[24] As for his social and political views: Goethe is portrayed as a bitter opponent of Herder's doctrine of humanity; a tireless foe of liberalism, the popular press, and narrow-minded academicians; and, finally, as a devout believer in "Germanic Christianity" and a courageous enemy of Jews. Selectively quoting from Goethe's writings, Chamberlain praised him as an adherent of legislation against German-Jewish intermarriage and a prescient seer who would not have "suffered among us" Jewish artists, professors, journalists, politicians, officers, and judges.[25] As we read on, so the versatile, rational and cosmopolitan Goethe, acclaimed by generations of writers, steadily recedes and is replaced by another: more mystical, intuitive, racist, and hate-filled. Bayreuth's Goethe had received his most comprehensive treatment. With some reason the *Centralverein's* journal *Im deutschen Reich* protested that the poet's name had been ruthlessly appropriated to enhance "a polemic about race politics, racial hygiene, and racial worth from the standpoint of a monomaniacal Judeophobia."[26]

Chamberlain's *Kant* and *Goethe* grew out of this same inspiration, and both books adopted the same crisis tone in decrying the lack of shared values and ideals in German society. Some differences are, of course, detectable—few writers go twelve years without some minor changes of emphasis. The principal development in this case was Chamberlain's increasing—and by 1912 almost total—identification with Goethe. Whereas in 1906 he was occasionally critical of the poet's philosophical confusion (as for example in the famous *Urpflanze* conversation with Schiller), six years later all reservations had disappeared. Beginning with Goethe's mistaken assertion to Eckermann, "Although independently, I was following a course similar to Kant's," Chamberlain turned him into a flawless Kantian.[27] Behind this shift of emphasis lay Chamberlain's increasing surrender to a purely intuitive *Lebensphilosophie* and his mounting disgust at the failure of society to counteract the deleterious influence of materialist scientists and dogmatic clerics. Goethe, a man radically at odds with both groups in his own day, impressed Chamberlain more and more as a kindred spirit estranged by the temper of his age.

The three pillars of a Teutonic outlook as discerned by Chamberlain were science, religion, and art. His artistic ideal, embodied in the dramas of Wagner and the *Festspiele* at Bayreuth, requires no further elaboration. Science and religion were the chief focus of his writing after 1900, and his efforts to achieve a balance between them both mirror a larger debate in Germany and demonstrate how *völkisch* publicists advanced race or the unity of the German spirit as the only means of resolving disputed issues and achieving an integral world view.

Science versus Religion: the dispute raged across Europe in the nineteenth century but nowhere was the struggle more intense or the arguments more exaggeratedly expressed than in Germany, a nation which was both deeply religious and pioneering in the development of modern science. Much has been written about the broad movement of criticism directed against Christian dogma in Germany. It arose from many directions: from the Young Hegelians; the startling findings of biblical criticism, comparative religion and church history; from the powerful challenges of individuals as different as Marx, Nietzsche, Schopenhauer, and Lagarde; and, of course, from natural science. In the 1850s, for example, a small group of bold popularizers including Ludwig Büchner, Karl Vogt, and Jacob Moleschott—an "unholy trinity" one of them quipped—campaigned for extreme materialism, insisting that all aspects of organic life and mental activity were reducible to laws of nature and the categories of physics and chemistry. Their defiant sayings ("no thought without phosphorus," "thoughts are secreted from the brain like bile from the liver and urine from the kidneys") were coined for shock effect and succeeded in creating fierce controversy. They depicted religion as superstition or a gross deception and soon welcomed Darwinian evolution as an alternative to Christian cosmology. Yet, for all the turmoil they caused, their influence both on scientists and laymen was relatively small.[28]

The extreme materialism of the mid-century exemplified by Büchner would have faded into oblivion but for the resurgence of scientism after 1880 in the writings of popular Darwinians like Ernst Haeckel. When the *Origin of Species* reached Germany in 1860 most of the older generation of scholars, still under the influence of romantic *Naturphilosophie*, rejected Darwin's theory. Over the next three decades, however, Darwinian evolution made rapid advances both in academic circles and among the public at large. Its most prominent and most extreme advocate was the Jena zoologist, Ernst Haeckel, whose popular statements of the social, political and religious implications of evolution reached a vast audience while also moving far away from the scientific precepts and underlying moral and philosophical views of its English originator. Haeckel's *Die Welträtsel* (1899) sold over 100,000 copies in the first twelve months and had exhausted ten large editions by 1919. It transformed evolution into a cosmology where life was generated spontaneously and the ascent of man was seen as a phase of cosmic development explicable solely in terms of energy and matter: in a single lecture in 1898, for example, Haeckel evolved humanity in 26 stages from chunks of carbon to *Pithecanthropus erectus*. From the beginning *Darwinismus*, as propagated by Haeckel, was a total system with far reaching consequences for the future of philosophy, science, religion, and social organization. The *Monistenbund*, founded in 1911, which soon boasted branches across Central Europe, campaigned vigorously for a "unified world view and vision of life on the basis of Nature." It derided Christian "mythology," both the Catholic and Protestant varieties, published pious confessions by individuals recently freed from the shackles of theology, and attracted to its ranks a diverse group of freethinkers and atheists. Darwinian theory was rapidly enthroned as a secular religion—a pantheistic celebration of the world spirit or cosmic force (in Haeckel's terminology *All-Natur*).[29]

Recently, several excellent analyses of the Monist movement have appeared and no purpose would be served in adding lengthy comments here.[30] Several points, however, are relevant to the present discussion. First, most scientists got on quietly with their experiments; they made no earth-shaking claims for their findings and saw no necessary contradiction between science and Christianity. For all the sound and fury, among the intellectual elite as a whole philosophical materialism (including the extremes of Darwinism) never possessed the continuity or pervasiveness in Germany of either idealism or critical positivism. Thus, in a famous attack, Rudolf Virchow, the distinguished pathologist, condemned Monism as a mere collection of poetic and religious fantasies, while the neo-Kantian philosopher Friedrich Paulsen was equally negative: "I have read this book," he wrote of *Die Welträtsel*, "with burning shame, with shame for the condition of the general and philosophical education of our people." He added: "That such a book was possible, that it could have been written, printed, read, produced, and believed among a people who possess a Kant, a Goethe and a Schopenhauer is painful."[31]

The intellectual elite may have for the most part rejected Monism, but Haeckel's careless and irreverent evangelism did excite the reading public with new questions and a vastly different explanation of the world than the one they had inherited. So much so that conservative and church groups especially became disturbed about the alleged diffusion of these ideas in schools and their spread among workers as a kind of scientific complement to atheism and socialism—although Haeckel was an outspoken opponent of Marxism. Two organizations, the Protestant *Kepler Bund* and the Catholic *Society for Science and Psychology*, were founded to meet the challenge by popularizing the compatibility of science and Christianity, while religiously oriented newspapers kept up a steady flow of abuse for the *"Affenprofessor* from Jena."[32] Among the most publicized attacks came one from a friend and correspondent of Chamberlain, the Kiel Ordinarius for Botany, Johannes Reinke. On January 11, 1906, speaking before the Prussian *Herrenhaus*, Reinke compared the development of Monism in the spiritual sphere to the growth of Social Democracy in the social and economic realm; it was, he argued, a revolutionary and atheistic style of thought, "a reversion to barbarism," propagated by fanatics like Haeckel even though distinguished scholars had proven them wrong. Reinke's plea was for a forceful campaign by the state against these theories, publicizing Monist errors and influencing educational curricula to ensure that schoolchildren were not infected. The correspondence between him and Chamberlain was full of similar warnings of "moral ruin"—on the subject of "Haeckelei" they were equally adamant and believed that more attention to science in schools would help to combat the excesses of scientific materialism.[33] "To make classical studies the foundation instead of the crown of education," wrote Chamberlain in 1914, "produces hollow and illusory knowledge, vain boasting, deeply rooted wrong-headedness, a false grasp of history, empty politics." Nature was "the true educator of man, especially of youth."[34]

It was in this general context that Chamberlain developed his bitter opposition to Darwinian thought. Around the turn of the century, as many historians have pointed out, a broad debate over the goals and direction of German culture took place. For men like Chamberlain and Reinke, Darwinism was as much a political and cultural issue as a scientific one: they viewed Haeckel's influence as synonymous with the destruc-

tion of religion and spiritually analogous to Social Democracy
and liberalism. The fact that many Monists were active in
radical and "irreligious" causes merely strengthened the conviction. Chamberlain's basic credo was not at all exceptional:
he wanted to keep science within bounds, so that religion could
once more reassert its influence and supply moral values and
spiritual ideals to a class-torn and ideologically divided nation.
His critique of exact science and his demand for a new biology
were inextricably linked to racial and social fears and his condemnation of Monist theorizing often spilled over into a wider
denunciation of scientists in general for failing to heed the
overwhelming significance of race.

The essence of Chamberlain's objections to contemporary
science is easily summarized. He voiced them as early as 1895
in an essay entitled "Büchner's Ruin"—a petulant answer to
Büchner's own "Ruin of Metaphysics," recently published in
Harden's *Zukunft*.[35] By reducing everything that had or would
happen to unchanging laws of matter found within the canon
of Newtonian mechanics, Chamberlain argued, Büchner had
transformed science into metaphysics. And while his notorious
Kraft und Stoff (1855) was an extreme example, it illuminated
a wider deficiency. The problem originated with the philosophical poverty of German science—its almost militantly
antiphilosophical stance—and its failure to grasp the distinction between experience and idea or to recognize that
knowledge is circumscribed by the limits of sensibility and by
the way the mind organizes what is presented to it. Scientific
"fact" was knowledge of reality as observed, not objective
knowledge of the "real essence" of things; it had therefore only
relative validity. Kant had solved such problems once and for
all, argued Chamberlain, but practicing scientists had failed to
apply his epistemology systematically. In fact, for some time
German philosophers and scientists had been engaged in a
heated debate about the status and validity of scientific information and Chamberlain both read and borrowed—often
carelessly—from these authorities. Ernst Mach and Wilhelm
Ostwald, for example, had vigorously attacked the inclination
of scientists to hypostatize their own concepts and characterized supporters of the atomic theory of matter as "thoroughly

naïve and crude."[36] Chamberlain, too, insisted that such terms as "atom," "aether," "cell," "species," "evolution" must be seen as convenient fictions—devices that depicted a fragment of the truth or tools for organizing the flux of impressions; they did not correspond to real entities.

Chamberlain's later criticisms take the same point of departure as the 1895 essay. What is noticeable, however, is an increasing tendency to regard all thinking as mythical and to obliterate any real distinction between scientific and other forms of thought. Myth, argued Chamberlain, bridged the gulf between perception and idea; a scientist was like an artist constructing symbolic representations of reality. In many instances Chamberlain sounds very modern (almost like a popular version of Mach, James, Bergson or Poincaré) but in fact he had little in common with such thinkers, and if he read them it was merely for confirmation of his own ideas. His thought was an untidy melange of romantic *Naturphilosophie* and pan-psychism, ideas drawn from vitalism and from Schopenhauer, Kant, and Goethe. So strong was his insistence upon the mythical nature of scientific theory that he removed any real possibility of choosing between one concept and another, thus opening the door wide to subjective arbitrariness. His distortion of Kantian dualism ended in casting doubt on reason and elevating instinctual knowledge or *Anschauung* as the source of the only reliable information about the world. As I have suggested earlier, Chamberlain recognized that it was becoming increasingly difficult, in the light of new research, to sustain the arguments of the old positive school of racism. By his radical dualism he avoided altogether the problem of verifying his race theory; it was a stratagem that the Nazis also used decades later, though some rejected dualism and switched to a monistic racial idealism.

It was not Chamberlain's intention, of course, to deny the vast progress of nineteenth-century science. What he did argue was that, given present assumptions and methods, it had come close to reaching its limits. This was particularly true of the life sciences and it was here, Chamberlain predicted, that the twentieth century would witness startling advances. The uncritical application of mechanical analogies in biology had deflected research into a hopeless "metaphysical" quest for first causes. Evolution, the most ambitious synthetic design of life's development, provided the most flagrant example of this quest, for it encouraged scholars to peer ever further back into the past, thus leading inevitably to the absurd claim that life was spontaneously generated out of inorganic matter.

Chamberlain's arguments against the Darwinians are easily summarized.[37] First, the philosophical point elaborated earlier in his essay against Büchner: "Only that observation of Nature," he wrote, "which begins with a critique of the observing subject is truly objective." "The understanding does not take its rules from Nature but dictates them to Nature."[38] Darwin, he asserted, had been a brilliant observer but an inferior thinker. "Species" was a concept devised by Linnaeus as a convenient way of organizing living forms and for referring to distinct and immutable categories of creatures. Not only had the Darwinians forgotten this and treated "species" as an objective reality, but they had even set out to disprove their very existence—at least as Linnaeus first conceived them. Chamberlain contended that the relationships between the various genera and species, as set forth in the ever more elaborate genealogical trees of the evolution theorists, had no basis in actuality, but existed only in the scientists' minds. His second objection focused more directly upon the evidence advanced for the theory. The enormous accumulation of facts, ostensibly in support of evolution, had not shown convincingly that one life form ever evolved into a completely different one, or that life began with the simplest structures and developed increasingly complex types. On the contrary, careful observation seemed to reveal a multiplicity of life forms, each with a remarkable stability and constancy, but also with a limited range of variability. Thus when vast geological and climatic change occurred, trilobites and dinosaurs had not been transformed but had simply died out, as they were incapable of adapting beyond a very limited scale. What the doctrine of natural selection boiled down to, Chamberlain argued, was a vulgar anthropomorphism: Darwinians assumed that nature followed the same utilitarian rules, the same principles of competition and success that the contemporary commercial age applauded—in short, it was the dogma of progress and perfectibility adapted to biology.[39]

Further advance in the biological sciences, Chamberlain averred, hinged upon the formulation of a new anti-Darwinian doctrine. The spiritual forbears (*Schutzgeiste*) he acknowledged were primarily Plato, Kant, Indo-Aryan thinkers, and, above all, Goethe. Goethe's approach, as exemplified in his *Theory of Colors* and *Metamorphosis of Plants*, was a mixture of careful, exact observation with an artistic and architectonic imagination. The methods more than the results reached in these two treatises excited Chamberlain: here was a science that recognized the limits of enquiry and preserved the poetry and mystery of life. Goethe neither imprisoned nature within the walls of abstract mathematics nor shackled science to the principle of causality. Instead he attempted by observation and intuition to grope toward the secrets of life, his goal being to see rather than explain, to obtain a synthetic vision of nature's complex unity, not dissect it into its most minute parts. When Goethe advanced the concept of an *Urpflanze*, or archetypal leaf, from which all others could be traced, he had been inspired by this goal: his biological focus had been upon Being rather than the mechanics of Becoming, on the nature of organic forms and the inner principle (*Bildungsgesetz*) which governed their organization.[40] Erich Heller, with characteristic skill, has described Goethe's purpose in biology: "To recognize living forms as such, to see in context their visible and tangible parts, to perceive them as manifestations of something within, and thus to master them, to a certain extent, in their wholeness through a concrete vision (*Anschauung*)." While not denying the modifying effects of external environmental forces, Goethe was captivated by "the self-revealed mystery" which preserves the basic unity of organic form through all its manifestations and modifications. His was a poet's attempt to restore a balance between analytic reason and the creative imagination: it fascinated Chamberlain and gave a stimulus to all his theorizing. Even Heller could not resist a parting shot at analytic science: "There may come a day when this Cinderella story will find a conclusion proper to such tales—but perhaps not before the new ecclesia of technology has had its consummate triumph by bringing to their explosive fusion the iciest mathematical abstractions and the hot appetite for power."[41]

The "Life Doctrine" which Chamberlain sketched at Gardone in 1896, returned to again four years later, and outlined in his *Kant* and *Goethe*, was never completed.[42] It remains a series of fragments. While confirming the legitimacy of mechanism in inorganic science, Chamberlain insisted that biology must start with a notion of *Gestalt* or organic form. This was what characterized life and made it quite different from, say, the identical forms of crystals or the forms of the planetary system. Here Chamberlain was rejecting the morphology of Haeckel, which aimed to find causal explanations for the structures organisms possess that were monistic—that is, which were true for all nature both organic and inorganic. *Gestalt* for Chamberlain was a multiplicity of different but mutually conditioning parts unified by an inner formative or organizing principle. While many Darwinians, including Haeckel, enlisted Goethe as an illustrious forerunner of Darwin, Chamberlain insisted—with a lot of evidence to support his contention—that Goethe had been concerned first with the stability of living forms and only secondarily with their variation.[43]

Chamberlain concluded that the Darwinian analogy between life and a piece of wax, shaped by exterior circumstances, had no basis in observation and ignored the complex balance or correlation between an organism's many parts and its whole (*Gestalt*). In its place he advanced the analogy between life and a pendulum. Each creature was endowed with an immutable sum of developmental potentials; variation was strictly limited in scope, and if one aspect of an organism experienced change there would be a corresponding economy of growth elsewhere. Just as conservation of energy was the basis of physics so the conservation of *Gestalt* was the key to understanding life. Environment and inner impulses together produced minor variations but a strong internal life principle worked to retain organic cogency. Other fragments of his speculations were even vaguer: he suggested, for example, that if the delicate balance within a *Gestalt* were upset (either

through changes in environment or the crossing of widely different types) a "formless chaos" would result—extinction, not
mutation, would ultimately occur. Similarly obscure is his notion of symbiosis. Advocating research upon the interdependent
links between specific groups of creatures, Chamberlain went on
to recommend that all life be viewed as a unity, governed by one
principle, thus making it impossible for one "species" to
"evolve" (that is, to be transformed into another) without disturbing the natural harmony of the rest. By an idiosyncratic
route Chamberlain appears to have moved very close to
Haeckel's notion of "cosmic force" and the idea of the "World
Soul," found in the Indian mystics and German romantics. [44]

Such were the elements of Chamberlain's life doctrine, out
of which he hoped to construct a new science of race; but he
never really expanded them to bring them in harmony with the
racism of the *Foundations*. To his mind what distinguished
groups of human beings was racial form or *Gestalt*, a combination of outward physical attributes and inner spiritual
qualities. Racial form, like any other, had limited potential for
variation: it could be improved—as history had shown—by
propitious interbreeding; it could be weakened or destroyed by
the crossing of unrelated physical types or even by the acceptance of alien intellectual and spiritual values. His mind
recoiled from the Darwinian vision of an atomistic, competi-
tive world whose outcome was uncertain: instead he conceived
a world that was governed by the laws of race, and where life
was a complex chain of being, arranged hierarchically, in
which the distinction between the highest and lowest men was
even greater than that between the lowest of *Homo sapiens*
and the apes. [45]

It is often forgotten that Darwinian ideas in Germany became so exaggerated and modified at the hands of Haeckel and
other Monists that they took on all the trappings of a secular
religion, and thereby provoked a vigorous opposition. Chamberlain's rejection of the mutation of species reflects a much
wider swell of opinion around 1900 and his borrowings from
Goethe and romantic *Naturphilosophie* (like those of Haeckel,
who also joined the same romantic ideas to his brand of evolution) attest to the residual strength of these traditions in

German biology. Moreover, while several historians have pointed to links between Darwinian theories, Social Darwinism, and Nazi racism, very little has been said about anti-Darwinian strands of racism, which were also quite common in Central Europe.[46] Chamberlain's *Lebenslehre*, for example, not only excited interest among such *völkisch* biologists as Jakob von Uexküll and the Nobel prizewinning physicist Philipp Lenard, but also prompted later a number of Nazi doctoral dissertations and articles.[47] If anything the Nazi regime found ideas of human evolution disquieting and its ideology tended to discourage or downplay belief in man's descent from animals. Although Haeckel and the Monists certainly contributed to Nazi race theory, Nazi racism was not a well-defined set of doctrines but a confusion of often conflicting ideas: apart from agreement on the general significance of race and the racial enmity of Nordics and Jews, all kinds of permutations of theory were tolerated. Nazi racism was not the political application of an aberrant strand of natural science; it was politics intruded into science. Theoretical precision and the academic quest for compatibility of ideas were not its concern.

At the beginning of the *Foundations* Chamberlain announced: "I see the greatest danger for the future of the Teuton in the lack of a true religion springing from and appropriate to our nature."[48] He returned to this theme repeatedly in later years, deeply troubled by the inability of the Protestant churches to combat effectively the secularizing trends of the age or to weaken the grip of Roman Catholicism over large sections of the population. In the electoral successes of socialism and the general prevalence of liberal and materialist values, Chamberlain saw the dismal failure of organized religion. Like many other conservative contemporaries he regarded the Reich as a Christian state whose social order, cultural vitality, and historic mission in the world were inherently religious. As the source of German ideas of freedom and duty, Christianity was an indispensable cohesive force in a class-torn nation; religious rebirth alone, he argued, could renew the spiritual basis of society, reaffirming the principles of monarchy, social hierarchy, loyalty, discipline, and race. For Chamberlain religion, not politics, was the basis of a new Germany.

Chamberlain's religious beliefs grew out of years of studying the Bible and theology, as well as church history, comparative religion, and anthropology. He was a deeply religious man who was undeniably well informed, although his interpretations were always fitted within a basically racialist framework. His letters and diaries are crammed with references to the works of Pfleiderer, Wellhausen, Schürer, Gunkel, Bousset, and Harnack, as well as to a host of English writers like Burkitt and Lightfoot. He also knew Indian religious texts well and numbered Leopold von Schroeder and Paul Deussen among his friends. From this wealth of sources Chamberlain fashioned a formless, undogmatic Christocentric faith which denied the validity of ecclesiastical doctrine and demanded a second reformation that would carry further the process of uncovering the gospel of Christ beneath the layers of theological dogma. And while his conclusions were extreme, aspects of his thought unquestionably had a wide appeal and paralleled the desire of many educated Germans for a revived Christianity outside the existing churches—one that would explicitly integrate religion and the mystique of a German racial mission. In the pre-1914 era Chamberlain found a sizable audience because he overlapped recent Protestant writing at many points, but it was especially after 1918 that *völkisch* Christian organizations looked to him, along with Paul Lagarde, as one of their chief prophets.

Fundamental to everything Chamberlain wrote about the Christian faith was his sharp distinction between Teutonic and Semitic religion. For him Christianity was not universally valid in the sense of being accessible to all: "It is hopeless," he wrote in 1904, "to want to say something coherent and true about religion in general and yet disregard the diversity of human types." Religion was a relationship between man and God, signifying an outward striving of the individual soul in an

attempt to draw closer to an unknowable god. Since "the
physical foundation of all expressions of the soul is race" did it
not follow that religious capacity mirrored the vast differences
between men?[49] Selectively raiding Protestant biblical scholarship concerning post-exilic Judaism and the early centuries of
Christianity, he portrayed Semitic religion as an arbitrary
legal code, a crude materialistic contract with God, which
pledged strict obedience and faithful worship in return for protection and territorial advantage over other nations.
Characterized by intolerance, obsession with sin, and shallow
rationalism, it formed an arid environment for Christianity
and one that profoundly scarred its evolution. The antithesis
to Semitic religion was the Teutonic one, which had assumed
several forms but demonstrated always the same aspiration to
achieve personal transcendence by drawing upon an inex-
haustibly rich fund of mythology and symbolism: it was emotional, ideal, and unencumbered by rationalist concepts which
so easily turned into dogma. One of the great ironies of history,
Chamberlain asserted, was that Jews had been represented as
the religious people when neither their self-serving monotheism nor their political concept of a Messiah had the remotest
relationship to Christianity.[50]

Rejuvenation of Christianity meant for Chamberlain lib-
erating the faith from the burdensome legacy of Semitic materialism and reasserting its Teutonic essence. "That is the fet-
ter," he wrote, "which hinders our every step": it was the
source of ecclesiasticism and of the narrow mentality that
prevented individuals from grasping the central paradox of religion—total devotion to a God whom one does not know and
cannot know. Several paths led toward liberation, the one
Chamberlain especially favored being via the transcendental
philosophy of Kant. Kant had cut through the layers of dogma
to reveal the kernel of religion—a "state of sensitivity" in
which man tries to give form and meaning to the unknowable
by use of myths and symbols, thus grounding morality in a
consciousness of the divinity. By consigning morality and religion to a sphere beyond time and place, Kantian epistemology
had at one blow repudiated the elaborate cosmologies that
centuries of reason had devised and nullified historical reli-

gions, the most prominent being Judaism. In brief, Chamberlain took the philosopher's interpretation of Judaism as a basically statutory and historical faith and his refutation of the theoretical claims of rational theology and radicalized them.[51] To Kant's critique of theology and his thesis of the autonomy of the will Chamberlain added a doctrine of racial subjectivism. For him Kant was the philosopher of "un-Jewish and anti-Roman *Deutschtum*," "the first totally free German" who had begun to rediscover "the living core of Christ's teachings."[52]

Another way of grasping the idealistic approach of Teutonic religion was through ancient Indian texts. Because of his ties to Bayreuth, Chamberlain had begun studying Schopenhauer as a young man in Dresden and then learned Sanskrit and delved into the fast expanding German scholarship on Aryan religion, his interest growing and overlapping his researches in racial history. Encouraged by Leopold von Schroeder and Paul Deussen, he wrote several essays and reviews pointing to the significance of the Vedas and Upanishads for the industrial civilization of Europe, and later collected them in a brief introductory book.[53] In Indo-Aryan writings Chamberlain found an enticing world and a much needed antidote to the lopsided materialism of modernity: here was a thoroughly aristocratic society, segregated by caste and devoid of the illusions of social leveling, a culture which dismissed the world of matter and concentrated upon the inner life. These texts, Chamberlain asserted, offered Germans the starkest contrast possible to the literalistic biblicism and dogmatics of organized Christianity and to Judaism. He admitted that Indo-Aryan absorption in the ideal had become total, stifling their development in other respects (in science, industry, and exploration for example) but this extremism made them all the more valuable as spiritual guides: "in the night of the inner life . . . the Indian . . . finds his way in the dark more surely than anyone."[54] Here was a body of Aryan thought, more easily tackled by the average reader than Kant, but leading directly to a sense of the harmony of man and nature and of the moral significance of the world which anticipated in many ways the teachings of Jesus. Making religion the very center of life, whose influence permeated art, law, technology, and philosophy, the Aryans had achieved an integral or unified world view; it was this that endowed everything they did with unity, purpose, and direction. This, most of all, was lacking in modern civilization—with its specialization and intellectual chaos, fragmented personalities, spiritual poverty, and almost desperate faith in the power of human reason. Chamberlain's vision of Hinduism was, as always, highly eclectic; primarily he saw it as a way of training the mind to think in idealistic terms—he never really made clear its relationship to Christian redemption.[55]

Kant led his readers back to the life and words of Jesus. What Indian religion lacked was such a mediator between man and God who could provide a focus for belief, a gathering point for all self-declarations of God. Chamberlain's religion was a worship of Jesus and he ridiculed the nineteenth century "madness" of that line of thinkers from D. F. Strauss to Arthur Drews who reduced Christ to a mythical figure.[56] For him there was no doubt about Jesus' historical existence and to help laymen concentrate more fully upon the Savior's life he published a small volume, *Worte Christi*, that attempted to report the actual words of Christ by comparing the variant texts of the gospels. It was very successful, especially during the War, when thousands of copies were sold to troops in special "trench" editions.[57] Jesus had spoken, Chamberlain wrote, in simple but profound parables or verbal pictures (examples of Teutonic symbolism) depicting an immanent God; his message was inner conversion and his emphasis was on grace freely given and redeeming love rather than law, penitence, sin, and punishment as was the case with the Old Testament deity. The Resurrection, Virgin Birth, and Last Supper, Chamberlain refused either to explain away or to accept literally—they were inpenetrable mysteries. Was Christ God? For Chamberlain the question was unanswerable: all that could be said was that God was knowable through Christ. Any other speculation meandered back into the stream of Semitic causal and materialist thinking.

Chamberlain never wrote about Christian ethics or their application in the world. His energies were devoted instead to sifting out the precepts of Jesus, divesting the gospels of their heavy encrustations of Jewish lore and Hellenic philosophy. Obviously, he was influenced by modern Protestant scholarship, especially Harnack's monumental *Lehrbuch der Dogmengeschichte* and his equally controversial lectures, *Wesen des Christentums*, although he often misused these authorities. From Jewish apocalyptic writings, Chamberlain wrote, had come the whole rigmarole of angels, devils, thorns of Heaven, and elaborate visions of the Last Judgment. Trying hard to accommodate the new faith to its Semitic environment, the Evangelists had falsely incorporated elements from the Jewish prophets, as in Matthew's account of Christ's birth and early life, while their emphasis upon miracles was a symptom of that society's moral and intellectual sickness.[58] Whereas the *Foundations* had given grudging praise to the Prophets, Chamberlain became harsher in his judgments later and never accepted the corollary of liberal Protestant criticism of postexilic Judaism—that Christianity was heir to the Prophetic and Psalmist traditions of early Judaism. For him the two were diametrically opposed. On balance it was the gospel of John that most appealed to him; its Hellenic perspective, he argued, was farthest from Semitic conceptions and provided a suitable starting point for analyzing the accounts set forth in the synoptic gospels. While he believed that significant aspects of Christianity had been distorted by efforts to make them comprehensible to the Greek world (as for example with the doctrine of the Trinity) Chamberlain found that culture less alien than the Semitic. As for the Old Testament, he did not advocate dispensing with it altogether since a critical knowledge of it was necessary for a proper analysis of the New. But, like Harnack—only on racial grounds—Chamberlain demanded that Christians stop treating it as a book of canonical authority: its continued use in this way by Protestants as well as Catholics was symptomatic of the paralysis of the faith.[59]

Echoing the polemics of Lagarde and exploiting the research of Harnack, Chamberlain denounced the existing Christian churches that had, he alleged, transformed the undogmatic and ideal faith of Jesus into a literal-minded and authoritarian religion. In apportioning blame for the moribund state of Christianity, Lagarde had singled out Paul for special

calumny, calling him "a Pharisee from head to toe" and denying that anything he said of Jesus "carried the stamp of relia-
bility."[60] Fichte and Renan had indulged in similarly bitter
polemics while liberal Protestant scholarship remained ambivalent—torn between the recognition that "Paul . . . delivered the Christian religion from Judaism" and that he was
the architect of church law and ecclesiasticism.[61] For Chamberlain, too, Paul was a perplexing figure. Unlike most other
exponents of a racial Germanic Christianity he was convinced
by his reading of Harnack and others that but for Paul Christianity would have disappeared altogether, absorbed into and
nullified by Judaism. And yet Paul had only preserved Jesus'
message of redeeming love by founding a universal church with
a theology that emphasized the Semitic notion of sin, enforced
by a dogmatic priesthood. For Chamberlain the only possible
explanation was racial: this dual heritage resulted from Paul's
being half Greek and half Jewish. It was a conclusion that enabled him to thread his way through Paul's Epistles, with their
varied tone and emphasis plucking out whatever suited his
own ideas and discarding the rest.[62]

Chamberlain's bitterest attacks were reserved for Roman
Catholicism, which the *Foundations* had depicted as a tyrannical power bent upon universal dominion. Rome, Chamberlain argued, had institutionalized Semitic elements within
Christianity and spread them throughout Europe, but since
the Fourth Lateran Council of 1215 Papal influence had been
slowly pushed back as the Germanic peoples struggled to build
their own independent nation-states. Toward the end of the
nineteenth century, however, he saw signs of a new Catholic
counteroffensive everywhere—from the promulgation of Papal
Infallibility to the excessive weight of the Center Party in
Reich politics, in the church's identification with Czech and
Polish nationalist movements, and most recently the Eu-
ropean-wide Catholic intellectual resurgence. Even the Chamberlain family itself was not immune; Houston's favorite
brother, Basil, had embraced Rome in 1899 although it turned
out to be a short-lived conversion.[63] Chamberlain also
repeatedly voiced the conviction that a Christian revival in
Germany would attract to its ranks not only Protestants but

German-spirited Catholics as well; for there was, he reflected, a strong dissident tradition among the Catholic population, whom foolish policies such as the *Kulturkampf* had driven *en masse* into the hands of the Roman hierarchy. He shared the proselytizing ambitions of organizations like the *Evangelischer Bund* but in the context of his own heterodox brand of faith.[64]

His desire for the conciliation of Catholics to the Reich was evident in two essays on education written for Karl Kraus's *Die Fackel* in 1901–2. The first, which included a sneering and astonishingly insulting attack on Theodor Mommsen, supported the Prussian government's decision to establish a chair of history to be restricted to Catholics at the new Alsatian university of Strassburg. The proposed chair, part of a wider plan to set up a whole Catholic theology faculty, brought a rash of objections from liberal academics, led by Mommsen and Lujo Brentano, on grounds of academic freedom and autonomy, although these protests also reflected a deeper liberal and Protestant prejudice that Catholics were generally incapable of the disinterested service to learning required of academics. Faculty anger reached new heights when it was announced that Martin Spahn, the son of the Center Party leader (and still a very young man) would be the first to occupy the disputed chair; not without reason his rapid preferment was explained as a direct result of the power wielded by the Center. Chamberlain's defense of the government was explicitly argued on the grounds that everything should be done to avoid the segregation of Protestants and Catholics.[65] Not only did a confessionally restricted professorship make sense on numerical grounds (Alsatians were overwhelmingly Catholic) but it was to be applauded as part of a wider plan to wean the upcoming generation of Catholics and priests in the region from narrow diocesan and Jesuit control. The opponents of Spahn, he alleged, were a ruling coalition of Protestant liberals and Jews ("a coterie of professors who threaten the state") who strove to retain control of university appointments. Exclusion of Catholics constituted "a far-reaching national danger; it sharpens religious antagonisms; supports ultramontane strivings . . . [and] embitters the serious minded, nationalist, independent Catholic scholars."[66] This self-perpetuating *Gelehr-*

tenmandarinat Chamberlain continued, had earlier tried unsuccessfully to block the appointments of Treitschke and Harnack and had thwarted the careers of such promising men as Eugen Duehring and Heinrich von Stein. He even claimed that the system worked to give disproportionate numbers of Jews representation on university faculties—something which the *Jüdische Volksblatt* of Vienna and a number of liberal newspapers quickly and heatedly disputed.[67]

Chamberlain's second article concerned the related issue of separate Catholic universities. Here again he demanded that proposals for such an institution at Salzburg be firmly resisted, because it would merely strengthen Rome and augment its political power: "Whoever speaks of Catholic universities means not Catholic in the sense of the great Catholic laiety . . . but Roman, totally subordinated to the clerisy and left defenseless to the Jesuits."[68] It was essential, he argued, that existing faculties mitigate their discrimination against Catholic scholars and prepare the way for true integration. In general, he advocated stronger state supervision of higher education. "The German professor," he informed Kaiser Wilhelm," is a colossal power 'for weal and for woe.' " Too often at university a student learned "to despise his Germanic nature and tread underfoot everything upon which the greatness of his ancestors rested." Under the guise of "objective scholarship," he added, liberal academics preached: "*Los von Gott, los von Königtum, los von Germanentum.*"[69]

Like other champions of Germanic Christianity Chamberlain also nurtured a strong distaste for the Protestant churches, believing that they had crushed the free spirit of Luther's rebellion and merely replaced Rome with their own authoritarian churchmanship. It was to Protestant laymen that Chamberlain addressed his appeals: from their midst alone, he believed, could a purer form of Christianity arise. They alone possessed the independence of mind to fuse the religion of Jesus with German idealism and the vision of national and racial redemption. After the First World War in *Mensch und Gott* (1921), the fullest statement of Chamberlain's religious views, he sketched proposals for nondenominational congregations that might facilitate such a Christian rebirth. Existing alongside established churches they would be open to all who believed in Christ the redeemer; their communal devotions of prayers and religious art would foster a timeless, inner religion designed to eliminate the distance that churches had interposed between man and God. These congregations would do without dogmas and official doctrines and would dispense with the sacraments altogether—for, as Goethe had said, in a truly Christian life every thought and action is a sacrament.[70] Designed to bring Christians of differing views together and to couple religion with faith in the Germanic race, Chamberlain's proposal left a deep impression on the numerous *völkisch* Christian sects that grew up during Weimar and culminated in the *Deutsche Christen* movement.[71]

One other aspect of Chamberlain's religious views deserves reiteration since it ran through everything he wrote—the unity of German art and German religion. From his earliest associations with the Wahnfried *Kreis* he had regarded great art as inherently religious, ennobling man and opening his heart to God. Art, he asserted, breathed fresh life into moribund religious mythology, preventing it from hardening into mere superstition; it heightened human sensitivity and continually enriched and renewed the message of Christ with its symbolism. "Only one human power," Chamberlain wrote, "is capable of rescuing religion from the double danger of idolatry and deism—that power is art." The works of the great German artists, which embodied the deepest emotions of the *Volk*, were, in Goethe's words, a "living momentary revelation of the inscrutable." And the culmination of religious art was to be found in Wagner's dramas—the fullest expression yet achieved in poetry, music, and drama of the Christian hope of regeneration. In his works (above all *Parsifal*), Wagner had drawn upon the purest Aryan symbols and myths to illuminate the teachings of Jesus. Thus Chamberlain's "positive Christianity" led predictably back to Bayreuth—where the Aryan Christian mysteries were celebrated in their pristine form, fusing race, culture, and religion into a powerful redemptive force. The Holy Grail was both the promise of Christian grace and of racial fulfillment.[72]

Chamberlain's thoughts on religion were a confusing combination of elements. His restless mind never stopped to consider the deep discordance between, say, Goethe's pantheistic doctrines of Nature and Kant's moralistic religion, or between Hinduism and Christianity. Out of them all he shaped a nationalistic *Kulturreligion* centered upon an Aryan Christ. He believed, like many contemporaries, that power was spiritual and that nations revealed their moral worth in confrontations and conflicts with other states; Christianity informed the German mission. But it was not clear whether he equated the expansion of German culture with the conversion of others to Christianity. Indeed, one rather doubts it, considering his emphasis upon the Germanness of the faith and his exclusivist attitudes toward Jews. Within Germany, Chamberlain's outlook clearly involved restrictions upon non-Christians. "The enemies of God," he informed Kaiser Wilhelm, "are my enemies. I will not permit my children to be educated, my youths to be raised, or my state to be ruled in cooperation with those who undermine Christian culture." Such, he insisted, should be the creed of every German.[73]

But his was not a revival of the old conservative Lutheran doctrine of the Christian state; his religion was merely a broad, formless, and intuitive set of beliefs centered around Jesus. He was seemingly tolerant and offered the widest scope possible to Christians—but, none at all to Jews, not even the option of conversion. When he urged a broad coalition of Christians it was as a prelude to determined exclusion of Jews. Unfair though the comparison may be, Chamberlain's misuse of liberal Protestantism nonetheless reinforces the argument of Uriel Tal that there were serious consequences for Jews inherent in the direction and influence of the theological modernism of scholars like Harnack, Schürer and Gunkel. Liberal Protestantism's disparagement of the later traditions of Judaism, its call for German national and cultural unity based on Christian principles, and its ingrained bias against Jewish efforts to preserve a separate existence were all easily adaptable by a thoroughgoing anti-Semite like Chamberlain. Also, though much has been written about the process of secu-

larization, it should not be forgotten that most middle class
Germans remained at bottom religious in their outlook: racism
and anti-Semitism appealed to them but only if it preserved a
Christian tone. Chamberlain's writings met this requirement:
they criticized existing churches but without slipping into a
denunciation of the faith itself.

Some years ago Karl Höfele analyzed the self-image and
cultural outlook of German *Bürgertum* before the First World
War as seen through yearly reports and speeches given in
educational establishments across the nation, adding information from some of the collections of essays by eminent scholars
about the state of German society.[74] The results are instructive
for understanding the position occupied by Chamberlain and
the degree to which his views paralleled those of the middle
classes as a whole.* Hermann Keyserling described the mood

* It is always dangerous to generalize about the "middle classes" and I do not wish to
suggest that the German bourgeoisie was uniformly antimodern, illiberal or equally
susceptible to the misgivings about German society and culture depicted in the next
pages. Obviously there were contemporaries who voiced great pride in the Reich's
achievements, who celebrated the record of urban growth and municipal activity,
expressed largely unqualified optimism about the future. More detailed study might
well reveal regional variations between, say Prussia, Hamburg, Baden, and Württemberg. But a large and varied body of research shows a widespread mood of
pessimism and ambivalence toward modern society after 1890, associated with nationalism, opposition to democracy, and a nostalgic passion for a mythical past.
Powerful social and institutional forces were at work after 1890 helping to forge a more
homogeneous conservative and nationalist ideological consensus—that cluster of ideas,
emotions and values often referred to as the "German ideology." Certainly, there were
important differences in tone and emphasis, over religion and specific political issues,
between the various elements of the German bourgeoisie. But they also had much in
common: by 1900—as many contemporary comments show—the beliefs, style of
thought and values of a Württemberg entrepreneur, academic, or civil servant often
sounded as "Prussian" as their counterparts further north. Höfele's data, though
limited in scope, is drawn from both north and south Germany. For further details
about bourgeois attitudes see the summary in Roy Pascal, *From Naturalism to
Expressionism, German Literature and Society 1880–1914* (New York: Basic Books,
1973) chaps. 1–5. Also, Dietrich Rüschemeyer, "Modernisierung und die Gebildeten im
kaiserlichen Deutschland," in P. C. Ludz ed., *Soziologie und Sozialgeschichte*
(Opladen, 1972) pp. 515–29.

of Germans around the turn of the century as restless and confused, tired of relativistic pronouncements and longing for a "sense of personal relation to the world."[75] Höfele's researches broaden and deepen this image. The temper of the age was critical but not predominantly pessimistic: most observers regarded the development of the nation since 1870 with pride and generally looked forward to a future that included increased prosperity and a further expansion of German power throughout the globe. Yet discontent and anxiety also fill these academic reports and speeches, together with an obsessive sense that the present formed an era of critical choices, a period of spiritual ferment and transition that would determine the whole future course of the nation. Their tone resembles that which echoes through Chamberlain's correspondence with Kaiser Wilhelm.[76]

Plenty of occasions arose for taking the pulse of the nation and diagnosing its complaints. Few brief spans of years have offered as many important centennials as 1900–14, each calling forth reflection upon the present in light of the past. There were celebrations for the deaths of Kant, Schiller, Kleist, and Fichte; for the birth of Wagner, the founding of Berlin University, and the battle of Leipzig. What emerges from this national self-analysis is a complex and many-sided representation of German society, but one that is remarkably consistent in its main themes. There was, for example, overriding emphasis upon the moral and cultural life of the nation, its politics being reduced to a symptom of its underlying spirit. Recurring frequently were complaints that modern society was devoid of firm and shared ideals, that its intellectual life was chaotic, spinning off in all directions at once and lacking a common ideological focus. Academic specialization was regretted deeply and seen as one instance of a wider curse which brought rapid advance but at the high cost of individual psychic and cultural impoverishment. Related to this, and much discussed, was the ironic reflection that a century of science had produced urban man, uprooted and out of touch with nature and history—a deeper penetration of nature's secrets having somehow worked to isolate men from her, so that few now knew anything of rural life or could distinguish one tree from another. It was this keen sense of loss, joined to critiques of utilitarian ethics and a strong element of aesthetic revulsion against the ugliness and drab uniformity of industrial civilization, that found expression in the *Wandervogel* movement that flourished in those years, and in the proliferation of schemes for land reform, "internal colonization," and garden cities. Both the haste of big-city life, and the crime, prostitution, and pornography commonly associated with it, encouraged a growing nostalgia for calmer epochs, a romanticization of peasant life and values, and a thriving *Heimatkunst* movement which catered to these moods while declaring it impossible for true art to arise from the poisoned soil of urban values.[77]

Such a collection of antimodernist sentiments might seem to belie the statement that the middle class temper was chiefly optimistic, were they not coupled with equally firm endorsements of the German character and its accomplishments. Friedrich Paulsen, for example, discerned a growing interest in philosophy among students that augured well for the future, while many observers took pleasure in what they believed was a marked revival of religious feeling, not registered so much in the numbers of churchgoers as in a more individualized quest for a faith without rigid forms and abstract dogmas. Anxieties about the mechanization of life and the threat of materialist science were answered—often in the same speech or essay—by enthusiastic praise of German technology and scientific prowess or self-congratulatory statements about the *Innerlichkeit* of the Volk. "We are," ran one school report of 1910, "the most broadly cultured Volk of the earth, the best sailors, the most intelligent soldiers. . . . in every aspect of scholarship, technology and art we stand pre-eminent."[78] The overwhelming emphasis of these analyses of society is, however, their nationalism and patriotism. This included fulsome praise of Prussian virtues, the Hohenzollerns, and the German army, disdain for the idea of popular sovereignty, and bitter denunciations of Social Democracy. And running through almost all of them was the conviction that God had prepared great tasks for Germans to perform, that His will underlay and sanctified a German national mission and the expansive thrust of German imperialism.

Even this brief catalogue of attitudes suggests the extent to which Chamberlain's writings articulated the self-image and cultural anxieties of the nationalist middle class. His *Kant* and *Goethe* raise every issue that Höfele discovered in his research, while elaborating an idealistic cultural stance that claimed to fuse the heritage of Wagner, Kant, and Goethe. Keyserling called Chamberlain the John the Baptist of the era, whose determination to shape a personal vision struck deep chords of sympathy even among those who objected to his specific biases and opinions. His warnings against overrating rationalism and exaggerating the benefits of material progress; his worries about the spiritually deadening impact of technology; his conviction that science—if unchecked—tended to overstep its legitimate bounds and stifle religious life: all these echoed the feelings of contemporaries. He was a man who claimed to be out of step with his time, but who—even in this assertion—was very much in tune with it. Whether he was condemning the *Reichstag* or exalting German *Kultur*, exhorting religious rebirth or warning about domestic and foreign dangers (Jews, Social Democrats, Anglo-Saxons, and even the "soulless" Yellow Peril) he found murmurs of understanding among conservative Germans.[79] Social, political, and, above all, racial fears constantly break through the sequence of Chamberlain's philosophical arguments to reveal his preoccupation with Germany's power and mission. Unlike Langbehn, he was not a crank ranting at the periphery of society: even a cursory look at his correspondence demonstrates the many threads linking him socially and intellectually to German conservatives of all shades. And where today we find a peculiar vacuity in his ideas and react negatively to the nebulosity of his language, contemporaries—well schooled in idealist and antimodern thought—found hidden meanings and allusions.

It is the natural response of many to turn to the past for guidance in uncertain times. In Germany, in the troubled years before 1914, this tendency often found expression in a cult of German classicism, a fascination with the era of Kant, Goethe, Schiller, and Humboldt as a kind of "golden age" or cultural *Urzeit*. Kant and Goethe especially provided a vast quarry from which ideas about aesthetics, science, religion,

and politics could be hewn. Here, it was argued, were the noblest exemplars of the German spirit; they could assist men in
constructing a philosophy appropriate to the twentieth century. And, as was so common with discussions of Germanness,
this often had implications for the issue of the role of Jews in
society. This was particularly true because Jewish publishers
and writers played a conspicuous part in the rapid increase of
studies about Kant and Goethe. Recently, an historian
described this as part of the continuing effort of Jews to
achieve a fusion of their two heritages—the goal of assimilation
required a clear image of the Germanness to which Jews should
conform.[80] Yet, if German Jews were eager to show themselves
equally "the children of the Torah and Goethe," *völkisch*
publicists were just as firmly resolved to deny that claim.
Thus, Chamberlain viewed his books as a task of literary pur-
gation, of rescuing Kant and Goethe from misinterpretation.
Those like Adolf von Harnack and Albert Schweitzer (he
described *Goethe* as his "sustenance" during the First World
War) who either ignored the racism of these books or praised
them in spite of it, failed to see that anti-Semitism was not in-
cidental to Chamberlain's outlook; it was the prism through
which everything else was refracted.

Part III

Prophet of Bayreuth

The war is a struggle between two Weltanschau-
ungen: *the Germanic which stands for morality, justice, loyalty and faith, real humanity, truth, and noble freedom against . . . worship of Mammon, the
power of gold, luxury, territorial acquisitiveness, lies,
treason, deceit, and not least assassination.*

—Kaiser Wilhelm II (1917)

What we need is a leader in völkisch, *practical statecraft. . . . I no longer believe we can transform public
life from the stage outwards. Where a fiery spirit like
Richard Wagner's did not prevail, lesser spirits strive
in vain.*

—Chamberlain (1916)

*I learned to recognize in Bayreuth the first symptoms
of that attitude which later became a scourge not
only of Bayreuth, but of the whole German nation.*

—Felix Weingartner (1937)

Chapter Eight

Private Life

CHAMBERLAIN, WHO SPENT years secluded in his library and shunned all publicity about his private life, was almost unknown to contemporaries apart from his published writings. Many aspects of his personality have already emerged in this study: he was shy and sensitive, many-layered, contradictory and difficult to know. While some of his friends like Edouard Dujardin portrayed his character as transparent and straightforward, the more astute among them found him something of a mystery and left strangely inconclusive and puzzled accounts, as if unable to say even years after his death what moved him. The historian has access to papers and comments closed to contemporaries; he can survey the range of Chamberlain's personal relationships and the staggering correspondence he kept up with family, friends, and casual acquaintances. But still the man behind the books and the mountains of letters remains very elusive, and large areas of his life and thoughts are in shadow. What follows is an attempt to sketch some of the salient traits of his personality and to describe the main events of his personal life during the period when he conceived and carried through his most important literary projects.

Weak and sickly as a child, Chamberlain was referred to by his two brothers as P.L.O., or "poor little one." From his photographs of the 1890s, however, he appears as a thick-set man, more than six feet tall with a tendency to overweight; his face was long and narrow with a high brow and deepset eyes;

his hair, once down to his shoulders, was now short and bald-
ing in places. Always well dressed, he looked somewhat different from the average middle class Viennese, preferring to
order his clothes from fashionable London tailors. Those who
visited the Blumelgasse apartment usually discovered a man
very different from their expectations. Rudolf Kassner, as a
Catholic, was surprised to find that the formidable opponent of
Rome that he expected was actually an agreeable, modest man
with no surface trace of racial or denominational hostility. A
witty and brilliant conversationalist, Chamberlain presented
to the world a kind of aristocratic ease and polished affability,
communicating to listeners an aura of learning and reasonableness. For Kassner he had "an ethical kind of fascination,"
Prince Eulenberg remembered his "fiery spirit and those eyes
and looks which speak volumes," while to Keyserling he
seemed foreign, an English "individualist" who "never saw
Germany as it really is" and "a cultivated man to the extent
that few in his time were equal."[1]

The one occasion when Chamberlain tried to analyze his
own personality in any detail occurred in 1895 in a letter to his
close Wagnerite friend (and at times financial benefactor) Alfred Bovet. A French graphologist had shortly before made a
study of Chamberlain's handwriting, and the letter was
intended to amplify the findings with his own reflections. He
depicted struggle as the key to his inner life, viewing himself as
locked in a continuous battle to overcome his weakness, indecision, and nervousness. Assertive and opinionated, he conceded
that in real life he was "extraordinarily timid" and highly
sensitive to the views and actions of others. There were sides to
this timidity, he admitted, that were humorous, but it cost
him much anxiety. "Nobody knows," he wrote, "how much
one suffers from this; very often this feeling ruins a life. I will
pass ten times in front of a café, really having a need to eat,
and then depart without having dared to enter. . . . If a smart
Swiss regards my tie with disdain, immediately I feel limp, I
am no longer a man, I am not even of the order of vertebrates.
I return by an anti-Darwinian progression to a piece of name-
less jelly, without form and barely endowed with the rudi-
mentary organs of sight and hearing, which permit me to beat

a retreat before the apocalyptic monster has devoured me completely."[2]

Coupled with this shyness was what he described as a "fear of discussion" (especially with those he revered) that at times amounted to obsequious and submissive conduct. He preferred not to argue or contradict, and when others uttered opinions contrary to his own he either agreed with them or quietly turned the conversation into less controversial channels. Chamberlain acknowledged that his personality was fluid and mobile, that he presented many different faces to acquaintances. Several of his closest friends sensed this; but among younger men his fear of open discussion expressed itself in a dogmatic narrowness. He championed causes and thinkers with all the fervor of a medieval scholastic: "He was haughty," Keyserling wrote, "as a Church father, viewing himself the guardian of the truth he possessed."[3]

Fame had brought Chamberlain a group of devoted admirers in Vienna. The Chamberlain *Kreis*, one might almost call it, usually met at the flat on the Blumelgasse. Starting in 1901 they held "reading evenings," discussing a variety of modern and classical authors and those working on books or essays also read selections from their writing. It was in this gathering, for example, that Chamberlain first developed the conception of his Kant book. Among the most frequent visitors on these occasions were the Indologist Leopold von Schroeder, Count Ulrich von Bülow (brother of the German Chancellor), Count Brockdorff-Rantzau (later Weimar's first Foreign Secretary and negotiator at Versailles), and several Wagnerites such as the music critic, Gustav Schonaich. Among the women usually present were Baroness Ehrenfels, Countess Marie Zichy, and Countess Marietta Coudenhove. The most vocal and impressive newcomers to Chamberlain's circle were, however, the two young writers, Hermann Keyserling and Rudolf Kassner.[4]

A capacity for friendship was one of the salient features of Chamberlain's personality, although there were few friends with whom he was really close. They fell, broadly speaking, into two categories: those like Agénor Boissier and Alfred Bovet who were considerably older than himself and helped guide his career, and much younger men who became his followers and intellectual disciples. The most important of the second group were Appia, Keyserling, Kassner, and later Felix Gross. Appia was the closest friend Chamberlain ever had; a constant visitor at the Chamberlain household in Dresden and Vienna, Appia owed, as we have seen, much of his education to Chamberlain and the rupture of their relationship in 1905 was a heavy blow to both of them.

In many ways Keyserling took the place of Appia, who had settled in Switzerland and saw less of the Chamberlains after 1895. A Baltic German of aristocratic family, Keyserling had studied geology at Dorpat and Heidelberg, but his intellectual interests changed radically after reading the *Foundations* in 1901. The book attracted him deeply with its "universality"—its demonstration of the way knowledge could be transformed into "a purely personal possession," offering "an unsuspected possibility of shaping my life." Seeing Chamberlain as "a type who could be the symbol and lodestar for my own journey," he traveled to Vienna and through Leopold von Schroeder soon came into contact with his literary hero.[5]

Having finished his doctorate in geology in 1902, Keyserling moved from natural science to philosophy, and his first book, *The Structure of the World*, was deeply indebted to Chamberlain's Kantian outlook. After 1903 their ideas began to diverge: Keyserling's call for spiritual rebirth, his vague nostalgic vision of a revived aristocratic leadership of society, and his obsession with social levelling remained close in many respects to Chamberlain's cultural and political views, but his reverence for Nietzsche, Bergson, and Schopenhauer displeased his former mentor. They continued to see each other frequently and vacationed together in the Swiss Alps, but personal as well as intellectual differences began to widen the rift between them.

Although he did not reach the height of his fame as a popular philosopher until the 1920s, Keyserling had an enormously inflated sense of his own genius; it was always hard for Chamberlain to accept intellectual independence in his disciples, but when they compared themselves (as Keyserling did) to Socrates, Jesus, St. Francis, Luther, Confucius, or similar figures, it became particularly difficult to tolerate. Chamberlain's opinion, expressed in a letter to his brother Basil, who was much taken with Keyserling's books, was characteristically put:

> We, the old intimate friends of K since he was a mere student, are becoming quite alarmed at the bent his mind has lately taken. . . . In a word: K is beginning to think he is the greatest man of his time, if not perhaps of all time—come to regenerate mankind and all that sort of thing. . . . He has got into the hands of millionaire Jews, especially a "Countess Fitz-James." . . . To Bruckmann . . . he said last summer, interrupting a discussion: "Before you judge of my works you must have studied my *personality*. I am in a way a blending of Immanuel Kant and Napoleon into one man; I possess the depth of the philosopher and the will of the conqueror." This was not fun but quite serious.[6]

Keyserling, who later—somewhat implausibly—denied that he had ever shared Chamberlain's racist views, remained a friend for several years, and after 1918 unsuccessfully sought the help of Bayreuth for his proposed School of Wisdom at Darmstadt.

The second disciple who came regularly to the "reading evenings" was Rudolf Kassner, the Austrian mystic and exponent of reformed Catholicism, who admitted he was infatuated by the "spirit of illiberalism" which enveloped the *Foundations* and felt impelled to seek out its author in 1900. Chamberlain was greatly impressed with Kassner, who reminded him of his earlier friend, Jules Laforgue; he took the younger man under his wing, introducing him to Indian religion and philosophy, broadening his reading of theology, and encouraging his study of English literature. It was, for example, at Chamberlain's suggestion that Kassner wrote his *Indian Idealism*, while his Platonist views bore strong traces of Chamberlain's influence. After 1906 the two began to drift apart as Kassner's intellectual tastes evolved in a direction different from Chamberlain's.[7]

Less important to Chamberlain was his association with the young philosophy student Felix Gross. When they met is unclear, but it was probably around 1907. Gross, whose father was a Jew, was then working on his doctorate. Consumed by self-doubt and guilt at being the offspring of a "mixed marriage," he drifted toward Chamberlain's circle, much as Arthur Trebitsch and Otto Weininger did.[8] Chamberlain seems to have fostered those feelings of self-abnegation in Gross while praising his religious and philosophical essays and assisting him financially. By 1910 Gross was acting almost as a secretary to Chamberlain, putting a new edition of his Wagner biography through the press and correcting galleys and proofs. He also wrote for the *Bayreuther Blätter* and contemplated settling in Bayreuth. Gross never escaped the tutelage of Chamberlain's ideas: as late as 1932, on the eve of a Nazi victory, he was still writing tracts about the Germanic ideology and urging Jews to forsake Zionism and assimilate to the heroic Teutonic ideal.[9]

These friendships were important to Chamberlain emotionally and intellectually. They provided him with an audience on whom to try out new ideas and helped to inflate his sense of worth as a writer and moralist; they also filled an emotional gap in his life during the slow disintegration of his marriage. Alternating between the roles of mentor and kind father, he encouraged the development of these younger writers, reading and commenting upon their manuscripts and recommending them to publishers and editors like Max Harden of *Zukunft*.[10] When they drifted away or rejected his views, he felt resentful or betrayed, for he had invested a great deal of energy in each of these relationships and they were highly charged with emotion and informed with a tinge of repressed sexuality. "He was," Keyserling reflected in his memoirs, "mimosaceous, sensitive, womanlike, as I was, and for that reason I found myself physiologically very close to Chamberlain."[11] Years later Kassner remembered this period as one of critical significance for his later career, while Keyserling, who saw clearly Chamberlain's many failings, nonetheless reflected: "If today I look back after forty years, I must recognize that among the minds I have known since then in Europe, there was no greater personality. He was a complete human being [*Vollmensch*], alive in a renaissance way, not wasted away leaving only the intellect."[12]

Probably the most pronounced side of Chamberlain's character after the enormous success of the *Foundations* was his conviction that he had a literary mission to fulfill. Cut off from the world apart from a few friends, he was driven to immense efforts by a feeling of sacred duty and threw himself into one work after another. And while at first acquaintance he might seem modest and unassuming, there could be little doubt about the significance he ascribed to his writings. Elated by the taste of success, he came to see himself after 1900 in the role of *praeceptor Germaniae*—a national prophet and moralist whose task it was to elaborate a Germanic world view in keeping with his vision of a world dominated by German culture. "Today," he told Wilhelm II, "God relies only on the Germans. That is the knowledge, the sure truth, which has filled my soul for years; I have sacrificed my peace in serving it; for it I shall live and die." Written in hypomanic periods of concentrated effort when the very act of writing seemed to release his inner tension, his books appeared at times to be the product of a will beyond his own. "Some supraindividual power," he informed an English admirer, Lord Redesdale, "invades the brain and illuminates it with a lucidity which is not normal in my rather hazy intellect." He attributed to himself a demon, or man within his breast, whose choices insinuated a common thread and gave a larger coherence and direction to his existence. In this way Chamberlain endowed his most intolerant and brutal utterances with a kind of religious aura; he saw himself—as did his friend Kaiser Wilhelm—as a willing tool of God. [13]

This fanatical and obsessive aspect of Chamberlain, although never far below the surface of his writing, was nevertheless disguised to many readers. They often praised his considerate tone, his air of learning, and his likable turns of phrase; cloaked in the familiar language of idealism, even his anti-Semitism seemed much less virulent and irrational than the crude polemics of many other *völkisch* thinkers. The recent judgment of a British anthropologist on the *Foundations* offers a reminder of this. After noting that it contained "much of interest and value," the writer adds, "it is obviously the work of an earnest and serious-minded person, the possessor of much detailed historical knowledge," although giving "too lit-

tle credit" to the Jews.[14] But close scrutiny of Chamberlain's
books, together with his correspondence and notebooks,
contradicts this image of moderation and uncovers a profoundly irrational mind, fearful, at times sadistic, and haunted
by notions of racial conspiracy. He reflected with a mixture of
pride and unease that he was the most dangerous foe of
"Rome" and "Jerusalem." "My lawyer friend in Munich," he
informed one acquaintance, "tells me there is no living being
whom the Jews hate more than me."[15] Even his dreams, which
he sometimes recorded in a small notebook after waking, disclosed the same preoccupation with racial enemies. Though
some of the entries are confused and disjointed, others only
partially remembered or unintelligible to the present writer,
they do seem to be a fairly accurate and honest record. Two
vivid entries from 1903—at the height of his literary success
and during a crisis period in his marriage—are particularly
graphic.[16]

His dream for the night of January 27 was described as
follows:

> I had been kidnapped by the Jews and so secretly that I had
> simply disappeared without anyone suspecting what had hap-
> pened to me. A kind of *Feme* court was to pass judgment over
> me. That I was to be killed was certain—only the means of
> execution was still to be decided. Meantime I was locked up in
> the room of a private house in a small town in Germany, com-
> pletely alone. Very calmly I walk up and down; there is no use
> thinking of help. Suddenly I notice in the corner of the room
> a new kind of telephone apparatus; it looks like a long plain
> book. As I turn the thing round and inspect it, I notice that I
> hear a faint, confused voice—as is normally the case with the
> telephone; and suddenly I can recognize it as Anna's voice!
> "Hello, hello" I call. She hears me but at first does not recog-
> nize my voice. Then, deeply stirred, she almost faints. "Where
> are you? Where are you calling from?" she asks. I tell her I am
> the prisoner of the Jews who wish to murder me in order to be
> rid of their most dangerous enemy. "Yes but *where* are you?" "I
> am in [illegible in MS.] near . . . (the name of the town escapes
> me)." Anna found it difficult to understand the name and asked
> me again and again. I became very excited because my one hope
> of rescue would disappear if she did not understand. Finally she

repeats the right name. "But now" I tell her "you must inform
the regime at once but in all secrecy; and they must quietly send
the police and the military so that nobody notices and reports the
fact here; and the troops must suddenly take control of this area
in the night. For if the Jews are warned fifteen minutes earlier
about me, they will kill me at once." To my despair Anna went
on talking: "Ah I see your eyes!" (It was actually a new invention
whereby next to the telephone was a kind of television
[*Fernseher*]). I implored her to fetch help at once; told her that
all would be lost if, by chance, someone came into my room. . . .
Finally she went. I then walked up and down; noticed that I
could also, if necessary, jump out of the window—felt, however,
that men were probably posted outside to kill me immediately.
And so I determined to wait for help which was now certain to
come.

Another entry, similar in many respects to the above, was
made for the night of June 7. Here his sense of martyrdom
results in a direct comparison between himself and Christ:

I had probably been drugged for I awoke in a large cellar after
being unconscious for a long time. It was poorly lit by flickering
torches. I had been abducted there by the Jews in order to be
crucified. The cross lay on the floor, pointing upwards in the air
a little at its top end. I was already bound fast to it with ropes.
At first I was terrified. But then a deep feeling of bliss came
over me: to die for one's convictions! To die as the Savior died!
Actually there would be no witnesses to the death in the cellar;
yet God's eyes were turned on me. Immeasurable consequences
would—I felt—result from this martyr's death. Happy and
proud I threw my head back (as far as the wood allowed) and
directed my eyes upwards and felt myself capable of suffering
every torment so as to will the truth. . . . Then I heard a noise
at the foot of the cross like old iron. I glanced down and saw a
man, who in the torchlight was choosing from a pile of huge
nails, the largest and the thickest. They were to be driven
through my hands and feet. At once all the pride and bliss
vanished from my heart. I felt only indescribable fear at the terrible pain which awaited me. My whole being trembled. I
looked around for help. Then I saw Anna. She had looked
everywhere for me and had, I don't know how, arrived there.
Now she stood next to me, ringing her hands. "Be quick!" I said
"the people have all gone away for the moment. Only the young

girl remains and she is good to me (this referred to a beautiful girl, roughly fifteen years old who earlier had stood next to my cross and regarded me with pitying eyes). Untie me!" This was accomplished clumsily in a frantic rush. And then all three of us fled out of the cellar window and into the street—as I reached daylight so I awoke.

These two dreams disclose the inner face of Chamberlain's racism, the profoundly irrational core of his thought which once led Adolf von Harnack to exclaim: "You are really possessed by an anti-Jewish demon!" The Jewish spectre invaded his ideas on every subject. His "struggle against the corrosive poison of Judaism," he informed Kaiser Wilhelm, was motivated "not by hatred of the Semites but by love of the Teutons"; but for the modern reader fear and hatred seem the motor force of his racial dynamic.[17]

Much has been written about the psychodynamics of anti-Semitic prejudice and what Theodor W. Adorno and his fellow researchers first described as the "authoritarian personality."[18] To Freud's own theorizing has been added the results of a large number of case studies of German prisoners of war, family structure in Central Europe, groups of soldiers and workers in several countries, and, more recently, detailed psychohistorical studies of prominent Nazis. These investigations have produced a fairly widely accepted picture of a closed-minded, prejudiced personality, consumed by feelings of weakness, worshipping power and strength, and resorting to racial and anti-Semitic hostility as a means of releasing inner tension and displacing unsettling aggressive urges. The formulation of such a model type does not account for anti-Semitism or minimize the complex matrix of cultural, social, political and historical factors which has shaped anti-Jewish feeling in modern Europe. But it does shed light on the problem of why a particular individual proved so vulnerable to racist interpretations of reality as well as helping to explain some of the contradictions and inconsistencies that typify racist thought. So far Chamberlain's ideas have been set against the backcloth of contemporary race theory, the aesthetic racial ideology of Bayreuth, and the political racism prevalent in Dresden and Vienna: these were the social and intellectual environments that shaped his development. But the intensity of his hostility and his imperviousness to pleas of reason (manifested in his letters and private papers more than his published writings) cannot be understood solely in terms of conformity to the ideas of his time or the circles in which he moved. Thomas Mann may have described the German character as "essentially anti-Semitic"; but there were many gradations, and Chamberlain belongs at the extreme end of the spectrum: his vision of the Jews as a collective embodiment of evil is symptomatic of a deeper distortion of the personality.[19]

The typical traits of the extreme anti-Semite, as described in the many case studies that have been compiled, may be summarized briefly. The Jew hater is represented as a deeply insecure, lonely, and perpetually vigilant person; someone who is plagued by self-doubt and whose vague and unstable identity is defined by detailed delineation of a negative non-self or out group. In his studies of Nazi prisoners in Britain, H. V. Dicks found a recurrence of certain personality characteristics: sexual ambivalence or anxieties about homosexuality; hypochondria or a morbid preoccupation with minor complaints; difficulty in establishing a satisfactory sex life; paranoid alternation between feelings of superiority and fears of weakness and dependence; and correspondingly marked variations of behavior from extreme aggressiveness to obsequious, ingratiating, and submissive conduct.[20] The resultant picture is of an anxious, confused and self-doubting personality, compensating for a submerged feeling of inferiority by fantasies of grandeur and strength; a "crippled self" for whom anti-Semitism has the well defined function of projecting onto the Jew all the unresolved conflicts, impermissible urges, and anarchic tendencies that threaten to overwhelm and destroy it. The diversity of stereotypes associated with the Jew, the enormous plasticity of his racial form in the anti-Semite's eyes, makes him a perfect projective screen for all these contradictory, ambivalent, and confused impulses. In discussing the etiology of such racial hostility most writers have focused on unresolved Oedipal conflicts: Norman Cohn, for example, in his analysis of the *Protocols of the Elders of Zion*, has argued that the image of the Jew in the document is essentially that of the

"bad father," a cruel, menacing f
hostility and ambivalence and arc
nerability originally inspired in
father.[21] Fear of a domineering p
complete identification with eithe
sivenss over sexual identity, and s
ing to a sharp differentiation of lo
out-groups; all of these, claim N.
hoda in their important study, are _____ .... .u..u.us of an authoritarian emotional syndrome in which anti-Semitism may
play a crucial defensive role.[22]

Certainly, many facets of Chamberlain's character do
seem to coincide with the personality structure developed in
clinical studies. He was nervous, shy, and insecure—excited at
one moment by grandiose ambitions and troubled at the next
by a nagging sense of inadequacy. Keyserling emphasized his
"almost sick sensibility" while Chamberlain himself, in the
letter to Bovet, pointed to timidity, hero worship, and a fear of
open discussion as among his salient characteristics. In person
he seemed modest, reasonable and tolerant, donnish in manner
and lifestyle, and far removed from the fanatical race hatred
his opponents accused him of. He even denied repeatedly that
he was an anti-Semite. Yet, as we have seen, his books and letters reveal a different self—aggressive in rhetoric, intoxicated
by his self-image as a militant, crusading *littérateur*, and convinced of the existence of racial plots. Possibly symptomatic of
his sense of vulnerability, of being menaced by unseen forces,
was the marked hypochondria that many of his friends noted.
Visiting the Blumelgasse flat one day, Kassner found his friend
totally distraught. Enquiring as to the cause he was told that
the doctor had been there all morning but had found nothing
amiss. Chamberlain's immediate conclusion was that he must
have something particularly rare and pernicious to confound
medical opinion in this way. Whether it was a matter of race,
the give and take of liberal politics, differences in intellectual
preferences or even medical diagnosis, Chamberlain seemed to
require clear cut, definite answers and abhorred uncertainity
and "formlessness."[23]

The genesis of Chamberlain's anti-Semitism could also be fit within the typical life histories developed by psychological studies. His difficult, peripatetic youth and feelings of uprootedness; the guilt feelings associated with the death of his mother so shortly after his birth; his sense of estrangement from a father he barely knew but who intervened suddenly and powerfully in his life; his weak health and acute sense of failure both at school and subsequently with the collapse of his speculations on the Paris *Bourse:* all were crucial shaping factors in Chamberlain's development. Already as a youth we find in his impassioned search for a spiritual home in Bayreuth and his eagerness to assimilate to German culture a determined attempt to overcome his sense of foreigness, his "marginality." He was in many ways the epitome of the uprooted intellectual of the late nineteenth century, a permanent outsider, striving to define himself into an in-group by carefully delineating what was un-German and "Jewish." Chamberlain's insistence on German superiority always reflected the exaggerated ardor of a convert; sensitive to his own paradoxical position as an English-born prophet of Germanism, he even ransacked his family past to discover a north German forebear from Lübeck so as to vindicate his own racial authenticity in an era of growing Anglophobia. [24]

Nevertheless, so much about Chamberlain's life that might be relevant to a psychological profile is unknown. Inadequate information survives, for example, about his early relationship to his father and relatives, his sexual life, marriage and friendships. His long and involved medical history presents a major problem. And even when the biographer has a source like the *Dream Book*, he knows nothing of the immediate circumstances surrounding a particular dream or those at the time it was recorded. Perhaps the clearest instance of a deficiency of evidence is the possibility that Chamberlain's first wife, Anna, was the daughter of a converted Jew. What added meanings could then be read into such statements as: "We were the criminal abettors of the Jews . . . and we were false to that which every lowest inhabitant of the ghetto considered sacred, the purity of inherited blood." [25]

Personal and cultural factors thus converge in Chamberlain's racism. His mental style may be termed paranoid, using the term not in a strict clinical sense, but to describe his persistent preoccupation with conspiratorial enemies and the air of fixed expectancy with which he looked at events and ideas, searching for the most part merely to confirm his own prior convictions. Chamberlain never discarded his theories in the face of troublesome facts; he forced information into a procrustean framework of predetermined racial categories. In his sleep he dreamed of plots directed specifically against himself; in his public utterances he identified his passion with the fate of German culture as a whole. What is most significant, however, is that his personal psychology made him particularly sensitive to the cultural and political mood of a large segment of German society.

Chamberlain was a reserved and private person; he confided in few people, and his correspondence, vast though it is, contains only superficial glimpses of his married life. For this reason it is difficult to unravel in any detail the long and emotionally exhausting marital crisis that coincided with his growing success as a writer. But it is clear that from the mid 1890s at least he was deeply unhappy, longed to be free of his wife, Anna, and yet could not bring himself to force a separation.

The first signs of later troubles were perhaps visible as early as his years in Dresden. As we have seen, Anna nursed him through long bouts of sickness and nervous exhaustion; she shared his interests in music, photography, and botany, encouraged his earliest literary efforts, and helped him by copying and editing manuscripts. To outward appearances they were generally well suited and happy, but a closer examination of those years seems to indicate that, as Houston immersed himself in the activities of the Wagner societies, Anna found herself pushed more and more to the periphery of his

existence. She never really entered the social world of Wagnerism, and after they moved to Vienna she felt herself
increasingly neglected and isolated. Ten years older than her
husband, she had aged prematurely and after 1890 suffered
from a variety of nervous ailments. Chamberlain, in contrast,
was healthier and more active than ever before. Completely
absorbed in his newly discovered vocation as a publicist, he
resented the smother of her good intentions and preferred to
spend his moments of leisure in the company of more stimulating and talented Wagnerite friends and a number of cosmopolitan upper class women like Baroness Emma von Ehrenfels
and Countess Marie Zichy. Neither socially nor intellectually
did Anna fit into this society, and Keyserling's rather snobbish
disdain for her "second rate governess nature" was probably
shared by a number of these acquaintances. [26]

"From 1893" Chamberlain later confessed to a friend,
"things were very bad." [27] Indeed, he reflected that Bruckmann's offer of a contract for the *Foundations* came as a welcome release from domestic pressures, enabling him to further
isolate himself and spend less time with his wife. Incapable of
leaving her and eager to minimize the friction between them,
he effected what amounted to a separation under one roof.
Within the large apartment they rented he created his own
quarters, shut himself in his library, and plunged into his work
on the book. He saw Anna mostly at their evening meal, and
these occasions, he told Countess Zichy, usually ended in rows,
recriminations, and bitterness. [28]

As Chamberlain grew increasingly self-absorbed and remote, Anna's health deteriorated; she complained of constant
headaches, dizziness, and frayed nerves. The success of the
Foundations further exacerbated matters, for it confirmed
Chamberlain's sense of his literary importance and made him
all the more determined to carry through the plans for books
that were flooding his brain. [29] Sorrow and guilt about Anna
prevented any escape from this personal *cul de sac*, but he was
resolved to work out a tolerable solution, and above all wanted
to minimize the strain these domestic troubles placed on his
work. "I can't sacrifice my life's work, begun so late, which it
is my God-appointed duty to labor at henceforth," he ex-

plained to Aunt Harriet "[and] I cannot make Anna ten years younger and myself ten years older which are in reality at the root of A's ailment."[30] Soothing his wife's rattled nerves became an increasingly irksome task:

> With such a load of work on hand and with great projects filling my head, I feel the strain of this extra duty painfully; in reality I would require someone to amuse *me* and to talk over my work and all sorts of things in a lively and cheery manner. . . . And instead of that I have to listen to endless complaints and to argue and soothe, and rack my head for entertaining nothings".[31]

At times he seemed resigned to the situation, fearful that Anna would collapse under the strain of a separation; at others, when his work seemed to grind to a halt—in 1903 especially he had difficulty in progressing with the Kant manuscript—he became desperate. Anna was to his mind the chief obstacle to his career and the continued tension unsettled him and made work almost impossible. He asked:

> Have I a mission to fulfill on earth? Or is that overestimation and should I give up everything, the work which makes me happy and exalts me and also the last hope of personal, intimate happiness, so as to perform modestly and obediently my simple middle class duty as a lawfully wedded husband according to my best understanding and conscience?[32]

For distraction and sympathy he looked to friends and, in particular, to two women. The first, Countess Marie Zichy, was the wife of the Austrian ambassador in Munich, but seems to have spent much of her time in Vienna. Her letters were removed from the Chamberlain *Nachlass* in 1930 and probably destroyed, but at Wahnfried she was regarded as the closest person to Chamberlain and he described her to Appia as "the admirable woman who entered my life like a guardian angel at a moment when everything was collapsing." He added that he considered her "the most exquisite, the most interesting, the most noble and proud creature that God ever created."[33] The sudden rupture of their relationship in the autumn of 1900 hurt him deeply. The other woman who became his constant companion after December 1903 was a widow, Lili Petri, a 34-

year-old actress of some repute. They met when she sought
permission to stage one of Chamberlain's plays published
earlier in the year. They were invited out together, traveled to
resorts and spas, and for a time Chamberlain found new zest for
life in the theatrical circles in which she moved. Since all Lili
Petri's correspondence was destroyed at her death in 1916 and
the relevant diaries of Chamberlain for the period are also
missing, the details of their relationship are sparse. Siegfried
Trebitsch, George Bernard Shaw's German translator, remembered Chamberlain working at the Petri house during the
day while she was out at rehearsals and recalled that once
Chamberlain confessed to him that she was "the woman he
most loved."[34] Trebitsch expected them to marry and Keyserling also predicted they would remain together, adding that
Chamberlain always tended to overrate the women he met.[35]
By 1905 this relationship seems to have reached a highpoint,
judging from the deluge of letters and telegrams dispatched by
Chamberlain, and it was probably the final impetus needed for
him to arrange a complete break with Anna.

By 1904 Anna's health was critical.[36] Her travels in previous years to Merano, an Italian mountain spa, and to relatives in Silesia had failed to improve her condition, but in
January 1905 she again left Vienna, traveling south to the
Mediterranean, accompanied by Adolphe Appia. Soon after
her departure Chamberlain reached a decision and declared it
was imperative that in future they live apart. "In my solitari-
ness," he wrote to Anna, "another self has awakened and I live
as in a state of continued delirium. I know what I am only
when I am alone. . . . It is like discovering oneself. I grow and
develop in every way." A second letter repeated this: "I want
and I must have myself. I must do this or I will perish." "You
embody the past," he wrote, "and often I have not the power
to prevail against it and that paralyses and tortures me."[37]

In March he visited Lili Petri near Cannes to discuss their
future and then saw Anna briefly near San Remo. Her doctors
had recommended that Anna enter a Paris clinic for nervous
disorders, but after treatment by injections and hypnosis she
grew worse and pleaded to be allowed to leave. It was Dujardin
who finally intervened, warning Chamberlain that her phy-

sician was "the most criminal of charlatans." Once more Chamberlain prevailed upon Appia to collect Anna and escort her to a sanatorium in Switzerland. Terrified that if he saw her he would go back on his decision to remain separated, Chamberlain flew into a rage when Appia reproached him for "deserting" his wife "in the most extraordinarily severe crisis." As a result their correspondence stopped abruptly and only eight years later was the feud partially patched up. Complaining to his brother Basil, Chamberlain wrote "[Appia] behaved foolishly last summer and was one of the causes that things took such a bad and stupidly disagreeable turn." [38]

For Chamberlain Anna's absence meant freedom and across a page in his diary he scrawled "New Life" in large letters.* The main issue still to be settled was financial. Chamberlain was greatly embarrassed by Anna's repeated complaints to their friends that his treatment of her was niggardly, and yet he was also troubled by the large expenses she was piling up. After she left the sanatorium and moved to Munich these did not decrease and, accusing her of a "squandermania" that would ruin him, he sought ways to limit his legal responsibilities for her actions. But although doctors agreed she was not normal they refused to certify her as irresponsible, so his lawyers pressed for a formal separation agreement and financial contract. [39]

It is difficult to assess Chamberlain's wealth with any accuracy. His expectations of family inheritances received several harsh blows, beginning in 1895, when his Aunt Catherine died at Versailles, leaving all her money to his brother Harry. Deeply worried about the future, Chamberlain contemplated moving to Munich and taking a job with the publisher

---

* He passed most of his days with Lili Petri and early in July they took a brief vacation at Marienbad. How long his relationship with Petri lasted is unclear, although they remained friends and correspondents until her death. That there were other women in Chamberlain's life is perhaps demonstrated by the assertions of a Viennese manicurist, Josephine Schinner, that Chamberlain was the father of her oldest child. In return for dropping the claim she received regular payments through his lawyers from at least 1909 until the end of 1921, but no other evidence on this matter survives. See the correspondence between the lawyer Otto Schwalb and HSC, eg. Schwalb to HSC 1 Dec. 1909; 22 Feb. 1911. In 1915 Schwalb attempted to find her employment (Schwalb to HSC 14 Oct. 1915); Schinner later changed her name to Schuster (J. Schuster to HSC 4 Dec. 1919 and 16 Dec. 1921).

Bruckmann, but the offer of a contract for the *Foundations* ended such thoughts. When Aunt Harriet died in 1899 he was the chief beneficiary of her modest estate, but his main hopes centered on Sir Neville Chamberlain, a childless widower. Houston was undeniably the favorite nephew and would quite probably have received the bulk of the inheritance but for a strange quirk of fate. Sir Neville died suddenly in 1902 before making a will and his fortune—worth over £ 90,000—passed to his brother Sir Crawford Chamberlain. Houston was given a life interest in £ 5,000 of securities, but two years later when Sir Crawford died the rest of the money went to his wife and out of the Chamberlain family. Houston's last hope was Aunt Anne Guthrie, the widow of a very wealthy financier. She assisted him with a regular and fairly liberal allowance and at her death bequeathed him a life interest from the revenues of £ 5,000 worth of stock. Houston's brother Basil also provided money for a secretary to help with his work and other small sums. In terms of legacies from his English relatives, Chamberlain was secure financially in 1906 but by no means as affluent as he had once hoped. Sometimes to friends he explained his disappointments saying: "I have had to pay dearly for the career I have chosen; all have disinherited me—and simply and solely because I have become a German writer! That was viewed by them as a kind of betrayal of the flag." But there seems to be no truth in this assertion. [40]

After 1900, with his growing fame as a writer, Chamberlain began to earn a sizable income from his books and articles, although there are signs of periodic irritation with Bruckmann about their relative shares of the proceeds. Nonetheless his accounts seem to indicate that his income from writing had climbed to about 12,000 marks a year and during the best years reached almost 30,000. Also, unknown to his family, Chamberlain did have other benefactors. The Swiss millionaire Agénor Boissier, who had been a close friend since his university days in Geneva, gave Chamberlain a regular stipend from the early 1890s, while August Ludowici, a wealthy south German manufacturer, who had subsidized the distribution of the *Foundations* to schools and public libraries, began giving him money in 1903. It was Ludowici, a complete convert to

Chamberlain's ideas, who came forward in the crisis with Anna, helping substantially with legal costs and medical bills in 1906 and giving Houston 100,000 marks worth of securities whose yield would pay most of Anna's living requirements; shortly afterward he presented Chamberlain with another 100,000 marks of stock for the purchase of a house. The money accumulated interest until 1908 when part of it was used to purchase a large villa opposite Wahnfried. Thus, adding the different revenues together, it would appear that Chamberlain's income in 1906–8 was well over 30,000 marks a year (and sometimes over 40,000), not including Ludowici's gift for the house. This made him an affluent man in a society where skilled workers and elementary teachers earned about 1,500 marks a year and full professors about 12,000; indeed, his income compares favorably with the salaries of the highest paid professors and with highly successful doctors and lawyers.[41]

Throughout 1906 and 1907, while Chamberlain busied himself with his writing, his lawyers negotiated for Anna's agreement to a divorce on grounds of "irreparable antipathy," the best means of avoiding a court case and scandal. The two parties were in sharp disagreement about a financial settlement and in the end it was Chamberlain's rapid courtship of Eva Wagner and his impatience to remarry that was to end the deadlock. In consequence, he was forced to raise his offer considerably but claimed later to be well pleased with the final agreement: "What with the large increase of income from my books and the simplicity of my life," he informed Basil, "I am now very well off and find that the £ 300 [6,000 marks] which go to Anna are after all an economy; with her one never knew what sums one might be called upon to pay next day."[42]

Apart from a brief meeting to win her consent to a speedy divorce in 1908, Chamberlain dealt with Anna only through lawyers and never saw her after March 1905. Anna lived in Munich until her death in 1924 and visited Vienna only once (in 1913, after Chamberlain had moved to Bayreuth) to attend an international conference on women's rights, a cause to which she devoted much of her time after the divorce. Her health improved considerably; she continued to idolize Chamberlain—sometimes arousing his anger as when she tried to ar-

range, without consulting him, for an English translation of
the *Foundations* in 1908—and her memoirs, which are brief
and uncritical, were designed merely as a kind of supplement
to his autobiography, which had omitted her name altogether.[43]

Siegfried Trebitsch fully expected Chamberlain to marry
Lili Petri, but in the summer of 1908 events took a different
course. Ever ready to discern the operation of fate behind his
life's twists and turns, Chamberlain later recalled: "It was as if
an invisible hand with strength of iron guided me. And it
turned me towards Bayreuth."[44]

In the first decade of the new century Bayreuth had
reached the zenith of its prestige and influence in the European musical world. Cosima's task of building the *Festspiele*
and publicizing Wagner's thought was largely completed. The
festivals were well attended by music lovers and socialites; her
son Siegfried was maturing as a conductor and composer and
would soon be old enough to assume full command; the
Wagner *Vereine* were still expanding and the composer's social
and political ideas enjoyed a new lease of life in the writings of
Thode, Chamberlain, Golther, and other literary luminaries of
the cult. Yet even in these "golden years" of Wagnerism storm
clouds hovered overhead, threatening the achievements of the
previous two decades. In 1913, thirty years after Wagner's
death, his music dramas would pass out of Bayreuth's control
and the substantial royalties they provided would suddenly
dry up; repeated efforts to secure a legal monopoly over *Parsifal* and an extension of the family's rights over the other
dramas failed. As early as 1903, the new Metropolitan Opera
House in New York, which was not a party to the thirty-year
rule, had staged *Parsifal*, obtaining the collaboration of an old
Bayreuth favorite, Felix Mottl. Cosima was powerless to
prevent this "desecration," and the loud outcry from Bayreuth

publicists against America's "rape of the Grail" was to no avail. Within Central Europe, at least, Bayreuth's influence was still sufficient to dissuade performances of Wagner's last drama, but the future looked uncertain and neither Kaiser Wilhelm nor other powerful friends of Wahnfried were able or seemed willing to set themselves up as active champions of the *Festspiele*.

Chamberlain's intensive work schedule, his bouts of ill health and the long marital crisis with Anna had kept him away from the festival after 1901. He was still active in fund-raising for the Bayreuth music school and wrote articles, though fewer in number than earlier, for the *Blätter*, but Wagnerism was no longer his all-absorbing cause. In part this was the result of a troubled private life and in part due to his conviction that with the *Foundations* he had reached a new stage in his literary career. But the change in his relations with Wahnfried was also to a considerable degree a consequence of the reception of his book among the "inner circle" of Wagnerites. Paradoxically, the *Foundations*, the most important work of the Bayreuth cult in these pre-War years, was the occasion of a rift between its author and Wahnfried, even though it was widely admired by Bayreuthians and was considered by some a composite of all the ideas of the cult expressed in the twenty years of issues of the *Blätter*. Wahnfried's reception of the book was mixed: admiration was coupled with the feeling that Chamberlain had been harsh in his judgment of Gobineau and, more importantly, had minimized his debts to Wagner and the cult. Enjoyment at the success of her disciple was soured for Cosima by a new air of independence and lack of due reverence he seemed to display.

While Chamberlain worked on the *Foundations* he corresponded frequently with Cosima and both envisaged the book as "*Ein Stück Bayreuther Arbeit*." On certain issues Chamberlain expected his views to be controversial among Bayreuthians. "With regard to race," he wrote to Cosima, "my main conception differs quite considerably from yours, but we will I believe understand each other excellently and agree in general aside from theoretical matters." He continued by explaining that inquiry into the origin of races was in his view a false path for speculation and that he could not accept the concept of originally pure races advanced in Gobineau's *Essai.*[45] As it happened, Cosima was highly impressed by Chamberlain's chapters on race and Hans von Wolzogen admitted he had long felt that race was not something given but rather had to be nourished and cultivated by distinct kinds of interbreeding and historical circumstances.[46] It was not so much what Chamberlain said but the way he said it which caused offense, for even staunch Gobinists like Schemann recognized that the *Essai* required updating and revision in accordance with the discoveries of contemporary racial science.

In fact Cosima had been troubled by an assertive and petulant tone in Chamberlain's writing even before the *Foundations* appeared. In December 1898, much to her delight, he was invited to address the prestigious Philosophical Society of Vienna University on the subject of "Richard Wagner's Philosophy." Given the disparagement with which Wagner's thought had long been regarded in many academic circles this was a symptom of the growing success of Wagnerism. But Chamberlain's lecture was not the paean to Wagner's greatness expected from so renowned a supporter of Bayreuth, for he had never really believed it possible to reconcile the several conflicting strands of Wagner's philosophy. Whereas Chamberlain's *Richard Wagner* in 1895 largely avoided the problems of the Master's thought, his lecture admitted that the ideas of Feuerbach, which influenced Wagner's early writings, were incompatible with the Schopenhauerean thoughts that dominated the later essays—and both fitted poorly with the basic Bayreuthian doctrine of aesthetic regeneration. Thus, instead of trying to represent these ideas as one unified and consistent philosophical doctrine, Chamberlain decided to depict the Master as a brilliant dilettante who lacked formal philosophical training but borrowed freely to illuminate his own insights. Feuerbach, Kant, Schopenhauer—Wagner, in Chamberlain's view, had never really understood any of them. He was the consummate artist, a man of deep intuitive genius, but *not* a philosopher![47]

In earlier years Cosima had enjoyed Chamberlain's occasional lack of conformism; she encouraged his jokes and criticism at the expense of other Wagnerites—even honored

but slow-witted friends like Glasenapp and Wolzogen.[48] But
there were limits to nonconformity, and with his lecture to the
Philosophical Society Chamberlain had just about reached
them. When the lecture was reprinted in the Munich press she
retorted stiffly: "You are in error regarding the facts. The relationship [of Wagner] to philosophy and his study of philosophers was quite different from what you have described.
. . . The noble spirits in your lecture hall will—so I fear—have
been sadly disturbed; the others, arrogant and superficial, will
have returned home regarding the *Gesammelte Schriften*
condescendingly as philosophical bungling."[49] But Chamberlain was not in the mood to accept criticism. He was still
smarting from his experience at Wahnfried during the festival
of 1896, when he had read to the "inner *Kreis*" the first draft of
his introduction to the *Foundations*. For all his affected
modesty he swallowed criticism with great difficulty and was
greatly irritated by the desire of his listeners that Wagner be
allotted a more explicitly central position. It was the first salvo
in a growing battle as Chamberlain tried to assume an independent position *vis à vis* Wahnfried.

Writing was the most important thing in Chamberlain's
life. It was through his books that he gained a sense of himself
and an assured feeling of his own importance. Anything that
challenged this provoked his fierce resistance and every
criticism of his work was taken as a personal attack. Similarly,
Wahnfried was feeling the need to place Wagner continually
before the nation so as to gain acceptance for Bayreuth as a
national shrine, to consolidate past achievements and marshal
support for some kind of legislative protection of the *Festspiele*. The situation was ripe for a clash between Chamberlain's ambitions and Cosima's single-minded pursuit of the
interests of Bayreuth.

Shortly after the publication of the *Foundations*, Cosima
imparted her first rapidly formulated impressions to Chamberlain. They were very favorable although she sensibly
criticized his handling of the Greeks and his iconoclastic efforts to deflate the achievements of Greek society. The Christ
chapter, the conceptualization of the *Völkerchaos* and the depiction of the role of the Jews in history all earned her praise.

"You are," she wrote, "the first who has had the courage to speak the truth that the Jew is a crucial factor in our present culture and that one must therefore investigate who he is." Her pleasure at the first volume was followed soon after by her unequivocal praise for the second with its masterful description of the rise of a new Teutonic world.[50]

Some months later, however, in October 1899, when Cosima was vacationing with her son-in-law, Henry Thode, she re-read and reflected upon the *Foundations* at greater length. Thode, the husband of Cosima's oldest daughter, Daniela von Bülow, was a distinguished art historian and a professor at Heidelberg. He and Chamberlain had disliked each other for years with a passion that bordered on sibling rivalry. Both had long been active supporters of Bayreuth, and Cosima had shown favor first to one then the other in a way which exacerbated their mutual ill feeling. The more she thought about it, the more critical Cosima became of the *Foundations;* she was irritated and disappointed because its intellectual debts to Wagner were inadequately acknowledged. Thode, her co-reader, was not the man to soothe her ruffled feelings, and he nursed his own grievances, believing that Chamberlain had tried to pass off as his own some of Thode's ideas about the Renaissance and Francis of Assisi.[51]

The first Bayreuth review appeared in April 1900. Written by Wolzogen, whose intellect Chamberlain did not regard highly, it was very laudatory but made little sense. "Hans von Wolzogen," Chamberlain reported to his Aunt Guthrie, "also gave a short notice last week in which he says that I have built a third flat onto the house which Herder began and Gobineau continued, etc.,—which seems to me rather absurd considering that my whole book is in fundamental opposition to Herder's central idea of 'humanity' and that I mention Gobineau only to refute him." Two other reviews followed in the *Bayreuther Blätter* by admirers of Chamberlain. Then, in March 1900, Henry Thode published a long review in the important journal *Literarisches Centralblatt für Deutschland*. While praising the book, Thode insisted that it was largely constructed out of the thoughts of Wagner and Gobineau, mentors who had received little thanks in what was generally so outspoken and heavily footnoted a volume. Possibly, he added angrily, Chamberlain felt he would "prejudice the effect of these thoughts if he quoted the source." The *Foundations*, it was asserted, borrowed Wagner's theories about the corruption of Christianity by Jewish and Semitic influences, the confusion of the Christian God with the warlike God of the Old Testament, and the raceless chaos that resulted from miscegenation in ancient Rome. As for the insight that modern culture was primarily the work of the Teutons, Gobineau had revealed this some forty years before. Chamberlain's celebrated synthesis was nothing more than an intelligent and appealing adaptation of the Bayreuth world view as expressed in Wagner's *Religion und Kunst* and in Gobineau's *Essai*.[52]

Nothing could provoke Chamberlain's anger more than this kind of attack upon his integrity as a thinker and he knew that Thode would never have written the review without the agreement of Cosima. Earlier he had often acted as defender of the faith at Cosima's request: now he was experiencing the same kind of attack himself. Chamberlain was correct: Cosima had not only read the review before publication but had actually suggested a few modifications of her own. Though he was furious Wahnfried's response could not have been a complete shock to Chamberlain in view of his first experience with the introduction in 1896. Meeting Thode in Munich early in 1899, he had remarked that the infrequent mention of one name in the book would undoubtedly evoke surprise at Bayreuth but, he added, he had his reasons. Thode clearly took this to mean that Chamberlain was afraid his book would be injured by association with Wagner.[53]

Cosima and Thode were convinced that had Chamberlain associated the *Foundations* more clearly with Wagner's name some of the purblind prejudice against the Master in scholarly circles might have been dispelled. Chamberlain had reached groups normally deaf to the beckonings of Bayreuth, but his reticence minimized the advantages Wagnerism could have gained from such a national success. What Cosima probably intended as a sharp rap on the knuckles became a more drawn out and acrimonious dispute because of Chamberlain's angry and unyielding response. He continued to write Cosima respectful and, on occasions, even affectionate letters, but gradually their tone with each other became more distant and cool. Cosima tried unsuccessfully to get Countess Zichy to intercede and smoothe out relations with Thode, but while Chamberlain assured Wahnfried that the whole thing was an unfortunate misunderstanding and that he recognized Thode never meant to impugn his intellectual honesty, he remained hurt and embittered. Obviously at Cosima's request, Thode wrote a brief apology denying any malicious intent, but did not retract any of his statements. In a fury, Chamberlain replied, dispensing with all polite fictions: "I feel toward my book as a mother towards her child. . . . I do not demand that people find my child beautiful, and even less that it should be heralded as a wonder child, but *my child* it is, 'free and well-born' and I will not permit it to be branded as a wretched bastard." If, he added, Thode's wish was a clear statement of debts to Wagner, his wish would be granted in a forthcoming preface. As for the implication that his earlier silence had been occasioned by fear of public disfavor, Chamberlain now announced that it resulted from an unwillingness to appear publicly as a critic of Wagner's errors.[54]

The preface to the third edition of the *Foundations* was published in September 1901, and Chamberlain allowed the press to reprint it for the benefit of those who owned earlier editions of the book. Without mentioning Thode by name it asserted emphatically that the ideas allegedly stolen from Wagner were either not originally his, or were notions the Master had misunderstood, or were quite contrary to Wagner's position. Misguided disciples in an almost hypnotic state, complained Chamberlain, were in danger of appropriating the whole European cultural tradition as the personal achievement of Wagner when, in fact, he often displayed a serious lack of understanding and critical acumen in his analysis of complex ideas. On the subject of race Chamberlain denied the influence of both Wagner and Gobineau, calling them "unscientific" in contrast to his book, which was built on the careful researches of men like Blumenbach and Darwin. Wagner's influence upon his own development was primarily aesthetic and in science and philosophy his patrons were Goethe and Kant. This preface represented an attempt by Chamberlain to map out the limits of his Wagnerism. Thode never replied to the counterattack. Cosima found it deeply distressing and disliking the publicity, probably restrained him. Even in 1912, after the rift with Wahnfried was fully repaired, Chamberlain reprinted the preface unchanged—it marked for him the independent position he had staked out within the "inner *Kreis*" of Bayreuth. [55]

The rapid success of the *Foundations* altered Chamberlain's self-awareness and magnified his ambitions. The book fed his ravening desire to be a presence in the world and convinced him of his own personal mission, related but nonetheless distinct from that of Bayreuth. Wahnfried declined to accept this at first and during 1902 relations between Cosima and Chamberlain remained rather cool. When Keyserling visited the festival in 1902 and 1904 he found his friend and mentor spoken of as a renegade by some of the most prominent Wagnerites. Even in 1905 Cosima admitted sadly to her friend Countess Wolkenstein that she still sensed a certain politeness, a lack of intimacy in her correspondence with Chamberlain which stood in the way of renewed affection. She invited him to the festival of 1904 but he did not attend. Not until early 1907 did they meet again, when Cosima, who had suffered a serious illness in the previous summer, journeyed south to recuperate, visiting Vienna en route. [56]

It was Siegfried Wagner with his insistent invitations who persuaded Chamberlain to return to Bayreuth for the *Festspiele* of 1908. Siegfried, a talented and genial man, had been friends with Chamberlain for years. It was not easy to be the son of Richard and Cosima Wagner, and he grew up in Wahnfried surrounded by admirers of his father and subject to the intense pressures of his mother, who pushed him forward as a composer and conductor. Only thirteen when his father died, Siegfried never managed to free himself from the intellectual and personal grip of his mother and sisters, while his wife, Winifred, whom he married in 1915, was the same dominating type of woman. Anti-Semitic, ardently nationalist, and conservative in his politics, he was raised to believe in the redemptive mission of Bayreuth and by 1896 was taking a considerable role backstage at the festival and helping with the conducting. After the

1906 *Festspiele*, which was marred by angry disputes between Siegfried and his brother-in-law, Franz Beidler, Cosima suddenly fell ill and suffered several heart attacks while visiting her friend Ernst zu Hohenlohe-Langenberg. Though she slowly recovered the time was clearly at hand for her son, now in his late thirties, to assume command.[57]

Thus Chamberlain returned to Bayreuth in the summer of 1908 to attend Siegfried's first *Festspiele*. He was accompanied by his brother Basil, who had returned to Europe in an effort to improve his declining health. Basil had remained close to Houston, despite the infrequency of their meetings, and was a steady supporter and confidant during the long crisis with Anna. After studies at the Sorbonne and Oxford he had tried for a brief period to undertake the banking career Admiral Chamberlain had advised for him. Ill health, however, made him, like his younger brother, a traveler and, after cruising to Australia, South Africa, and Shanghai, he had settled finally in Japan, living there for over forty years. As a professor of literature at Tokyo University he achieved considerable fame for his studies of Japanese culture, and his letters to Houston reveal the breadth of his knowledge and his continuing interest in European intellectual developments.[58]

Wahnfried was especially festive in 1908. Siegfried's performances were well received and Chamberlain was welcomed back into the fold. Cosima and Wolzogen, once so severe, had mellowed with age and were overjoyed to have Wahnfried's leading publicist return, "an intellectual wonder man, an excellent and prescient interpreter of the world" as Wolzogen once called him.[59] In these weeks at Wahnfried Chamberlain also rediscovered a peace and happiness which had eluded him for many years and he renewed his old friendship with Eva, Cosima's youngest daughter, who had for some years acted as her mother's nurse and secretary. By the end of August 1908 Chamberlain was convinced that he wanted to marry again. Eva was then 41 years old (twelve years younger than Chamberlain) and like the rest of the Wagner children suffered from a dominating mother and an exaggerated sense of her birthright. "Stately and imposing," wrote one contemporary, she had the reputation of being "clever but not very communicative." [60] In Eva, a rather repressed and prosy woman, Chamberlain found the "safe harbor" for which he had been searching. Lili Petri was forgotten and an incredible spate of letters passed between Bayreuth and Vienna in the last four months of the year. Eva, who presumably was in a position to know all the past gossip about him, wanted to know all about Emma Ehrenfels and Countess Zichy, and when the delicate question of Lili Petri was raised, Chamberlain had to resort to suitable Wagnerian analogies. "The Venusberg," he declared, referring to Miss Petri, "was the last stage in my education before arriving at you." In Eva he found "my holy Elizabeth." [61]

They decided to marry as soon as Chamberlain could complete divorce proceedings with Anna. The legal issues proved complicated. Anna at first refused to cooperate, but eventually consented and, after providing Adolf von Gross, Wahnfried's financial adviser, with a complete accounting of his income and sources of wealth, Chamberlain was married to Eva on December 26, 1908. It was a civil ceremony, since the Protestant church authorities refused to perform the service for a divorcé; a few days later a church wedding was carried out by a more obliging clergyman in Zurich. [62]

The Protestant clergy in Bayreuth were not alone in raising questions about his remarriage. Anne Guthrie, Chamberlain's last tie to the older generation of his family in England, was firmly opposed. "Though poor Anna never made herself acceptable to your family," she wrote, "I am sorry for her now—cast off because she is useless and has the misfortune of bad health." She even accused him of adopting German ways:

> I think you have imbibed *German* ideas, living so long among Germans, and it may be natural, but you do not see things *evidently* as the son of a respectable Englishman and I regret it my dear, and all the more as I know the bad impression that will be felt at home. . . . How a girl *accepts* a *married* man before he is even divorced is a disagreeable surprise to me, and it proves very *lax* views on matrimony,—but of course her *bringing up* accounts for that.

Chamberlain and his wife Eva

"She," continued Anne Guthrie, referring to Eva, "has been brought up by a mother who *left one husband to take another* and most naturally considers such a step correct." She died unappeased in 1912; Chamberlain never saw his aunt again and with her death lost his last real personal bond to England.[63]

Marriage to Eva was the culmination of Chamberlain's lifelong search; he saw it as the realization of his personal destiny. Thirty-eight years after first hearing the name Wagner as he sailed on Lake Lucerne, he now entered "the home of his soul," "the immortal 'Wahn-Fried.'" "After difficult years," he confessed to Kaiser Wilhelm, "first an intolerable married life, then a rewarding inner cultivation of the soul, often marked by aching loneliness, my life ship now glides in friendlier waters." Cosima too was delighted with her daughter's choice. To Countess Wolkenstein she admitted: "Had I reflected upon his character earlier I would have depicted him as uneven and excitable. He is even-tempered and friendliness itself. There is never a difficulty and, in a manner which inspires love, he accommodates himself to all the conditions of our existence." She looked back contentedly on the year that had passed: Siegfried had taken over the festival and her last daughter was married to someone worthy.[64]

Since Cosima was dependent upon Eva as a secretary, Chamberlain agreed to move to Bayreuth and a house opposite Wahnfried was purchased with the money given him by Ludowici. He slipped effortlessly into the daily regime of Wahnfried, working on his *Goethe* during the day and joining the family for readings and musical entertainment in the evenings. There were occasional trips to the Riviera with Cosima where he met Gerhart Hauptmann and other celebrities, and he soon began to take an important part in family decisions. To Keyserling, who hated the Wagners, this whole period of Chamberlain's life was a pitiable act of submission. Recalling a visit to Wahnfried, he wrote:

> [Chamberlain] who was once so anxious and careful about his outer independence so that he attached to his door on the sixth floor of Vienna's Blumeglasse a sort of short text so as to scare away possible visitors with its words, was now kept at Wahnfried like a harem woman and was soon quite subdued and domesticated. It made a devastating impression on me, how in the evening of my visit to Wahnfried in 1909 he read aloud almost humbly from Plutarch to Siegfried Wagner who paraded himself in a dressing gown on a kind of throne, and he acted enthusiastic about being awarded such a service. But he was undoubtedly so happy, much happier than he had ever been as a free man. And when he acknowledged his existence as a captive, the family naturally let him free and advanced his separate aspirations.[65]

In his own eyes, of course, Chamberlain returned to Bayreuth not so much as a disciple but as an independent figure of international reputation. Gradually, alongside Adolf von Gross, he assumed a leading role as a spokesman for Wahnfried. Cosima soon relied heavily on his judgment about a range of business dealings and in 1912 entrusted him with the delicate task of preparing Wagner's autobiography for publication. Still more indicative of his central position in family councils was his active part in the bitter feud that erupted between Siegfried and his sister Isolde over the Wagner inheritance. Earlier Isolde had received part of Hans von Bülow's estate, but in 1911, after the birth of her son, she began to campaign to get recognition as a legal heir of Wagner. Chamberlain and Eva were furious and orchestrated efforts first to get her to drop the claim and then to leave her husband, the conductor Franz Beidler, whom they suspected of being the real instigator of the dispute. A sensational court case of 1913–14 resulted in Isolde's defeat, but not before Cosima was forced to testify publicly against her daughter. Daniela von Bülow, who resented and disliked Chamberlain, blamed him for the disastrous course of events: "Our misery," she argued, "began in 1908 with Eva's marriage." [66]

As the most famous writer associated with the Wagner cult, Chamberlain became something of a model for the new generation of publicists contributing to the *Bayreuther Blätter* immediately before 1914. He enjoyed being an elder statesman at the center of an admiring throng, and accomplished a good deal of writing in this period, completing *Goethe* and making plans for successor volumes to the *Foundations*. But these years were also overshadowed by the depressing uncertainty of international politics and the slow movement of England and Germany toward war. Although he retained his English citizenship until 1916, Chamberlain felt increasingly hostile toward Britain and British politics. As for Germany, his correspondence records a deepening pessimism. "Has one ever seen a people so impoverished in political instinct?" he asked Kaiser Wilhelm in 1903. [67] The sensational disclosures of the Eulenburg scandal, failures in foreign policy, and Social Democratic electoral successes added to his disquiet in the next decade. Looking out at the world from Wahnfried he became convinced that time was short and that only drastic action from above could check the process of decay. He had faith in the values of Bayreuth, but no longer imagined that public life could be transformed from the stage outward. Mob and money, the forces unleashed by liberalism and modernity, could only be tamed by a thorough restructuring of the state. Slowly in the last years of peace, Chamberlain's racial and cultural idealism was transmuted into political activism.

Chapter Nine

Wartime Propagandist

DURING THE FIRST World War, because of his propagandist activities on the German side, Chamberlain was denounced as a "renegade" and turncoat by the British press. What literary reputation he had won outside the Reich was completely overshadowed by this new public image. In fact, Chamberlain's impassioned criticism of England was not sudden, born of the infectious emotionalism of August 1914. It was not the outbreak of hostilities which forced him to choose a side: the clash of armies merely confirmed a choice already made and hardened a conviction that Britain and her allies were pledged to annihilate Germany. At the outset of the war—despondent and embittered—he scolded his brother Basil: "No war has ever been simpler than this; England has not for a moment reduced her efforts to do everything humanly possible to bring it about and to destroy every peaceful impulse." "Germany's victory," he added, "will not be England's ruin; quite the contrary, it is the only hope for England's rescue from the total ruin in which she now stands. England's victory would be terrible for the whole world, a catastrophe."[1]

For Chamberlain politics were secondary, an outward symptom of deeper cultural and historical evolution. Although he admitted that a book such as the *Foundations* was "in a certain sense a political confession," he restricted his public comments upon contemporary issues and party debates to occasional asides or hit-and-run attacks on his enemies in the liberal camp.[2] His political vision, though not difficult to elicit in broad outline, was veiled in the jargon of philosophic idealism and spiritual regeneration. His letters to friends and family provide a better record of his reaction to everyday political events, although here too we find periodic bursts of interest rather than a continuous commentary.

As a student living in Geneva, Chamberlain first began to voice his strong disaffection with British politics, charging Disraeli with a large measure of the blame for the lowered tone of English public life. He regretted the collapse of the Liberal Party over Home Rule and opposed the aggressive colonial ventures of the Conservatives under Salisbury and their abandonment of the traditional British role of supporting Turkey against the Czar. The Franco-Russian alliance of 1894, Britain's unwillingness to become hitched to Austrian policy in the eastern Mediterranean, and widespread agitation in England against Turkish massacres of Christian Armenians were all critically appraised by Chamberlain. "The Armenian insurrection [of 1894]" he retorted to his Aunt Harriet's moral outrage against the Turks, "with the inevitable retaliation of massacres and persecution (of course *enormously exaggerated* by those greatest liars in creation, backed by their worthy friends the English journalists) was all got up at the precise moment when English politics required a 'diversion.'" Already Chamberlain had become accustomed to viewing the affairs of eastern and southern Europe from the perspective of Vienna or Berlin.[3]

But it was in the years after 1895, with Germany's commitment to a course of *Weltpolitik* and friction over British expansion in southern Africa, that Chamberlain's attitude toward England finally crystallized. Germany came late and unwelcome to the imperial feast, but from the mid 1890s the vision of an imperial destiny, of the nation's breakthrough to the stature of a world power, permeated political life and captured the imagination of wide sections of the bourgeoisie and intelligentsia. "We all felt," Friedrich Meinecke later reflected upon the national euphoria of the time, "that we were irresistibly outgrowing the saturated life of a continental great power."[4]

In a way *Weltpolitik* became the supreme goal and obsessive aspiration of that generation, the equivalent of national unification for the previous one. "Old empires are fading away and new ones are about to be formed," Kaiser Wilhelm told an audience in Hamburg in 1899, echoing the crude Social Darwinism that had become part of common parlance.[5] But since the world was largely divided up already, any readjustment of shares could only be acquired at the cost of international tension and heightened insecurity. Two consequences followed from this. First, Britain was regarded as both the leading example of imperial expansion and the chief obstacle to Germany's rise to world power status. The Prussian historian and publicist Hans Delbrück voiced the mood of many contemporaries when he wrote in 1899: "We want to be a world power and pursue colonial politics in the grand style . . . The entire future of our people among the great nations depends on it. But we can pursue this policy with England or without England. With England means peace; against England means war."[6] Second, since the German imperial design was shaped by the realities of power in Europe and the goal of enhancing the prestige of the Kaiser and the political system, it was fitful and erratic, not focused upon any one part of the world. The result was a widening gulf between vague, grandiose ambitions and fulfillment, which gave the nationalist movement an especially strident and irrational tone. Anglophobia, intensified by the accelerating naval race, merged with undefined schemes of Teutonic expansion and vague claims of German cultural superiority; the end result was a cultural critique of British power as a prelude to justifying German goals.

It was in this political and intellectual climate that Chamberlain formulated his judgment of England. At first he had cherished the hope that these two "consanguineous" powers might work together, that English strength and pragmatism could be joined to German *Geist* and efficiency.[7] As the march of events destroyed this dream, so he turned his mind increasingly to the question which puzzled many German racists; namely, if race determined character and both nations were of similar Nordic or Teutonic stock, why were their policies and interests so opposed? Chamberlain's answer was racial deterioration. Oliver Wendell Holmes once remarked: "The mind of a bigot may be compared to the pupil of an eye; the more light you pour on it, the more it contracts."[8] In this case the description is apt: Chamberlain never discarded his theories— he searched for clues to substantiate them, forcing events into a predetermined framework of ideas about racial and cultural evolution. Since he could never totally reject England or rid himself of a certain pride in its past, he rationalized his feelings by carefully distinguishing between the grand traditions of Burke and Gladstone, and the coarse, philistine late Victorian era. England, not Houston Stewart Chamberlain, had changed: England, not he, had become foreign.

Chamberlain's condemnation of British policy in southern Africa offers the most striking example of his growing estrangement from his birthplace. His comments on this subject for the first time anticipate the bitter polemics of his wartime pamphlets. As early as 1878 he had strongly opposed Disraeli's annexation of the Transvaal republic and irritated his relatives with his outspoken admiration for the pluck and determination of the Boers. Far from being "a few farmers incapable of governing the large country they hold," he argued, their victory at Majuba Hill proved them "as fine men as the English soldiers sent against them."[9] He also applauded Gladstone's decision to brave nationalist anger and concede independence to the Afrikaner republics under the British suzerainty. With the Jameson raid in December 1895, followed by a more or less continuous crisis until the outbreak of war four years later, Chamberlain's anger at British policies and his frustration with the patriotic sentiments of his relatives reached fever pitch. He fully endorsed the deliberately provocative telegram sent by Kaiser Wilhelm to President Krüger congratulating him on defeating the raiders, and when Aunt Harriet and Uncle Neville criticized the Anglophobic rhetoric of the German press, he answered:

> The English press is the most insufferably arrogant, generally ignorant, the most passionately one-sided and narrow minded in its judgments that I know; it is the universal *bully*, always laying down the law for everybody, always speaking as if it were umpire of the universe, always abusing everybody all round and

putting party spirit in all its judgments, envenoming thus the
most peaceful discussions. It is this and this only which has
made England hated all the world over. During the whole year
1895 I never opened an English newspaper without finding *War*
predicted or threatened. . . . No other nation in the whole world
has wanted war or done anything but pray for peace—England
alone, the world's bully, has been stirring it up on all sides.

The worst press after the English, he added in a more conciliatory tone, was the German: "only it seems on the whole better
informed, it is not as narrowly insular as ours."[10] Shortly afterward, in reply to a letter from Sir Neville defending British
policy in terms of a national struggle for existence, Chamberlain was still more condemnatory:

We are *the* heathen nation and race *par excellence*. War, conquest, commerce, money, and above all an eternal readiness to
knock every man down who stands in our way. And the only
thing thoroughly distasteful to me in England and Englishmen
generally, and English politics in particular, is this eternal co-
quetting with a religion to which every one of their feelings and
opinions and acts is in direct contradiction.[11]

Ironically, his own style of thought, as outlined in the *Foundations*, contained precisely this kind of national power politics
charged with religious purpose and sanction.

   In October 1899 Chamberlain's worst fears were realized
when the long-smoldering situation in south Africa erupted
into open warfare, setting off a wave of patriotism in England
and unleashing a storm of recrimination and fellow-feeling for
the Boers in Germany. For Chamberlain the circumstances
were further complicated by the fact that Uncle Neville, his
boyhood hero, had been recalled to active service, becoming
one of Lord Roberts's advisors in the campaign. By September
1901, however, Sir Neville regained the admiration of his
nephew when, after returning home and being promoted to
Field Marshal, he openly proclaimed his opposition to the
scorched earth policy, the barbed wire, the blockhouses and
concentration camps, which characterized the conduct of the
guerrilla war in its last two years. In the years after 1914
Chamberlain repeatedly cited Neville's actions as a family
precedent for his own repudiation of British policy.[12]

Chamberlain's celebrity as the author of the *Foundations* coincided with the highpoint of German agitation against Britain, and he was deluged with invitations to express his views on the conflict. He refused them all, restricting himself to a brief and melancholy poem in Harden's *Zukunft* on the theme of racial fratricide. "I prefer," he explained to Anne Guthrie, "holding my tongue. When questioned since my return from England, I always ward off the topic by saying: my countrymen are suffering from a fit of moral insanity, but they will recover; one must not make noise around a sick man's bed."[13] A few months earlier, in July 1900, he had described the war as sheer madness at a time when the Teutonic peoples were embattled on all sides:

> One thing I can clearly see, that is that it is criminal folly for Englishmen and Dutchmen to go on murdering each other for all sorts of sophisticated reasons, while the great Yellow Danger overshadows us white men and threatens destruction . . . The fact that a tiny nation of peasants absolutely untrained in the conduct of war, has been able to keep the whole united empire at bay for months and has only been overcome—and *has* it been overcome?—by sending out an army superior in number to the whole population including women and children, has lowered respect for England beyond anything you can imagine on your side of the water, and will certainly not remain lost on the minds of those countless millions who have hitherto been subdued by our prestige only.[14]

Cosima Wagner voiced the same opinion in her letters to Chamberlain: "This extermination of one of the most excellent Germanic races is so horrible that I know of nothing I have experienced which is comparable to it."[15]

The period between the Jameson Raid and the end of the Boer War in 1902 forms a watershed in Anglo-German relations. Not only did these years see the inauguration of German *Weltpolitik* and the initiation of a massive program of naval construction, but they also marked a more general transformation in the public consciousness of each society toward the other. British fears of a German impulse toward world power, coupled with a new awarness of the nation's diplomatic isolation, soon produced a sharp reorientation of British foreign policy, accompanied by a flood of propaganda against the "German menace." In the Reich as well, the reevaluation of Britain ranged from the loud chorus of Anglophobic jingoism in the Pan-German and nationalist press to more sober academic assessments. Chamberlain's family correspondence offers a vivid record of this polarization: his relatives seized upon the warlike objectives of Germany, and Houston insisted that England's policies were self destructive and had tarnished forever the notion of a civilizing mission.

In addition to public events, several intellectual influences played a role in the crystallization of Chamberlain's ideas. Most important perhaps was Treitschke, who in the 1880s had emerged as the first historian of stature to challenge the basically positive image of England in academic circles and to mount a comprehensive attack on English ideals and policies. Treitschke's prolific writings contained just about all the themes of anti-British propaganda before and during the First World War, and like other German nationalists, Chamberlain owed much to his scathing attacks on "the sly and violent policy of commercial self-interest passed off as a heroic fight for the good of humanity."[16] Also influential were a later generation of historians (Max Lenz, Erich Marcks, Otto Hintze, and Hans Delbrück, to name only a few) who engaged in a thorough and critical reassessment of British power in history. Finally, there was the day-to-day reportage of the nationalist and anti-Semitic press whose depiction of the Boer War as instigated by Jewish financial interests was echoed repeatedly in the correspondence of Chamberlain and Cosima Wagner.[17]

Essentially Chamberlain argued that there were two Englands: one aristocratic, courageous, industrious and mid-Victorian; the other modern, materialist, and atomized, a society whose virtues had been rotted away by trade. Yet even when he contemplated the generation of his father and Sir Neville, Chamberlain was ambivalent. He admired their individual strength and capacity, but regretted that these qualities were linked to an insularity of mind and an indifference to culture and learning. Capable of living for fifty years in Africa or India, they tolerated isolation, returned home, and reentered their London clubs without exhibiting any change of outlook resulting from their experiences. "This Englishman," Chamberlain wrote, "does not trouble a farthing about the whole culture of mankind. I believe that soap is the only achievement of civilization that [he] holds indispensable." [18]

Since the 1880s Britain had increasingly "chosen the service of Mammon." As always for Chamberlain, the agent of corrosion was the Jew. "This is the result," he told Cosima Wagner, "when one has studied politics with a Jew for a quarter century." [19] By this he meant Disraeli, whose flamboyance and consummate political artistry had, he alleged, veiled shallow selfish ideals; as for Lord Salisbury and Arthur Balfour, who dominated the Tories in the following years, they were typical of an emasculated aristocracy captivated by Jews. A brief visit to "the land of the Boer-eaters [*Burenfresser*]" in 1900 confirmed Chamberlain's despair. "My old England," he wrote "was nowhere recognizable." Local shops and businesses had been pushed out by unfair competition and fraudulent practices had undermined honest industry; the middle classes were philistine and self-satisfied; the monarchy was "irretrievably weakened and . . . scarcely more than a headdress [*Kopfputz*]," "a focus for social snobbery." [20] The nation's elite had been inundated by parvenus. "In fifty years," he predicted to Kaiser Wilhelm, "the English nobility will be a pure 'gold oligarchy' without racial solidarity or any relationship to the throne. . . . I inquired about and was told of a large number of 'new fledged' Lords. They were brewers, ink manufacturers, and shipowners." As for the general public, it had become "a herd which has no will and which a few newspapers and a handful of politicians manipulate as they wish." [21]

This image of England as a warning of the perils of indiscriminate commercialism, of parliamentarism and unfettered individualism, was identical to that painted in Chamberlain's wartime writings. English power, he concluded, could not last much longer, for it rested on no defensible moral basis; the nation had entered a period of slow, but inexorable decline. [22]

The world needed leadership. "There are periods," Chamberlain told Kaiser Wilhelm, "when history is, as it were, woven on a loom . . . in such a way that the warp and woof are established and are essentially unalterable; but then come times when the threads are introduced for a new fabric, when the type of material and the design must first be determined. . . . We find ourselves in such a time today." [23] France was in an advanced state of decline; Russia was degenerate and, but for its German dynasty, "nothing would remain but a decaying *matière brute*;" England offered no hope for the future, while the United States was a mere "Dollar dynasty":

> From dollars only dollars can come, nothing else; spiritually America will live only so long as the stream of European spiritual power flows there, not a moment longer. That part of the world, it may be proven, creates sterility; it has as little of a future as it has a past. [24]

Already employed as a synonym for modernity and materialism in the 1880s, "Americanization" entered the vocabulary of a wide range of cultural critics in the 1890s. Chamberlain, who turned down invitations to lecture at Yale and Johns Hopkins, had no grasp of American industrial power or military potential; for him "Anglo-Americanism" was more of a symbolic, moral entity—an antithesis to German *Kultur*.

"The future progress of mankind," Chamberlain insisted, "depends on a powerful Germany extending far across the earth." [25] This involved expansion in Europe and overseas; it required a battle fleet capable of shattering British control of the high seas; but, most importantly, it meant a restructuring of German politics and society. The twentieth century would demand a more systematic organization of society and state planning, for which Germans were well equipped, as their achievements in industry and science had proven; but this could only come about if the existing apparatus of parties and parliament were dismantled and if bourgeois liberalism gave way to greater state power and centralized authority:

> Germany—of this I am quite convinced—can within two centuries succeed in dominating the whole globe (partly through direct political methods and in part indirectly through language, culture, techniques etc.) if only it enters upon the "New Course" and that means bringing the nation to a final break with Anglo-American governmental (*Regierungs-*) ideals. [26]

This theme increasingly preoccupied Chamberlain after 1902,

as he grew more and more pessimistic about the possibility of containing the forces of social and political change within the existing Wilhelminian system. Germans, he complained, lacked a natural instinct for politics. He was deeply troubled by the rising strength of socialism, the reliance of successive Chancellors on the support of the Catholic Center, the virtual deadlock between the political parties produced by the 1912 elections, and the damage done to the Emperor's authority by the *Daily Telegraph* affair and the Eulenburg scandal. Never very specific or systematic in his political theorizing, Chamberlain convinced himself that only radical change could attain the hierarchical and fundamentally conservative society he envisioned; in this regard, as in others, he echoed the mood and conclusions of the Pan-Germans and other elements of the far right. In perpetual motion between an heroic Parsifal world and an advanced, scientific civilization, he groped for a framework which could encompass both. The result was a strange blend of romantic conservatism and a more programmatic vision of a disciplined, cohesive society on corporatist lines.

After two decades of national confrontations, crises, and talk of impending hostilities, the outbreak of war in 1914 did not come as a surprise to Chamberlain. Nor did it cause him any dilemma of allegiance, for his ties to England had already worn very thin. Admittedly, to Kaiser Wilhelm, Rudolf Kassner, and other friends, he seemed quintessentially English in style and manner. Hermann Keyserling, for example, regarded him as "an extremely charming English individualist," a kind of Rudyard Kipling in German idealist vestments.[27] But despite these general impressions, Chamberlain's knowledge and experience of Britain was very slight. His visits were seldom and brief: four in the forty years between 1874 and the war, a total of twenty weeks. Also, his closest personal links were severed by the death of his favorite relatives (Aunt Harriet in 1899, Uncle Neville in 1902, and Aunt Anne Guthrie in 1912). He largely gave up reading British papers, and his last occasions there were unhappy ones, overshadowed by the deep distaste he felt for the Edwardian ethos and by the rather demeaning task of keeping in the good graces of his Aunt Anne, a vigorous and sometimes cantankerous nonagenarian with a great deal of

money to dispose of. As for his brothers, Basil lived only intermittently in England even after his return from the Far East,
while Chamberlain was never close to Harry. Though Lord
Redesdale expressed the view early in 1914 that Englishmen
"may well be proud of a fellow countryman" who was
recognized as "one of the most brilliant writers and profound
thinkers of the day," Chamberlain was scarcely English, except
in name, and his image of his birthplace owed more to the
German nationalist press than first-hand experience.[28]

On July 22, 1914, less than a month after the assassination
of the Archduke Francis Ferdinand at Sarajevo, the Bayreuth
festival opened; it was to be the last international gathering of
Wagnerites for more than a decade. Tension mounted with
every performance and conversation rapidly turned from art
and music to politics as the European crisis deepened. As *Got-
terdämmerung* was being performed on July 29, the Austrian
army mobilized against Serbia; two days later, when the
performers began their new production of *Fliegende Holländer*,

Bayreuth in War: troops bound for the western front. Castle tower in the
background.

a bugler and military escort went through the streets of Bayreuth publicizing Germany's ultimatum to Russia. By now many seats in the *Festspielhaus* were empty as foreign visitors made haste to leave. For the last performance of the summer, *Parsifal* on August 1, only a few devotees remained: on that evening Germany declared war.

"My one wish," Chamberlain told his friend General von Roon, "was to hide myself like a sick animal in a dark corner; I was like a sailor who had lost his compass."[29] As recruits flocked to the colors and patriotic hysteria gripped the Reich, he retreated to the quiet of his study. After years of anticipation, the reality of war left him stunned. An improvement in Anglo-German relations in the previous year had, for one thing, encouraged a hope that England might remain neutral; now that hope had proved false he felt a deep sense of betrayal, directed especially against the Foreign Secretary, Lord Grey, and Edward VII. Friends plied him with advice: the literary historian and Wagnerite Max Koch urged him to emulate Carlyle's action in 1870 and address a manifesto to *The Times* denouncing Germany's enemies; others recommended that he renounce his British citizenship; and still others suggested that he retain it while proclaiming his condemnation of England. In fact, Chamberlain remained British until 1916 when he became a Bavarian subject. The war also revived the sense of rootlessness and isolation that he had experienced in youth: "I don't know," he wrote, "whether you can imagine what it means not to have lost a home, but never to have possessed a home, never to have moved in any community where everyone says: 'He is one of us.'"[30] Unable to endure inaction for long, after first unsuccessfully volunteering his services as an interpreter, he hurled himself into the task of writing war pamphlets and rapidly became one of the most prolific and extreme advocates of the German cause. To his brother Basil and some of his Wagnerite friends in France and England these polemics seemed to be the "rantings" of a man unhinged by the tragedy of his times, an "abyssmal aberration of a once intelligent man," but in fact they were remarkably consistent with his earlier opinions.[31] The European conflict had not suddenly politicized Chamberlain—it had exposed more fully the political vision he had earlier cloaked in the phrases of national idealism and spiritual regeneration.

The war demanded a complete mobilization of national resources, both material and intellectual. Academics, publicists, novelists, and poets succumbed no less enthusiastically than other strata of the population to the feverish spirit of August 1914. Chamberlain was one of dozens of writers who turned his talents to justifying German policies and attacking the assertions of enemy propagandists. Ensconced in his study and surrounded by large maps of the battlefronts, he devoured books on politics and history, searching out facts and ideas for his essays, and engaged in a vast

Bayreuth Station: embarcation of 6th Landwehr battalion for the front, 1914.

correspondence with soldiers and civilians. His trenchant, dogmatic style—well-honed in the service of Bayreuth—suited admirably the needs of the hour, and before long Chamberlain was one of the best known wartime publicists, receiving an Iron Cross in April 1915 in recognition of his services.

Like other writers Chamberlain's goal in the earliest weeks of the war was to demonstrate German innocence in the train of events which had led up to the conflict. His most detailed analysis of the forces at work behind the diplomatic crises before 1914 appeared in an essay titled "Whose fault is the War?" which was rapidly translated into English, French, Italian, and Spanish. [32] It was a fairly typical tract expounding arguments that were almost universally held in Germany during the early stages of the war. "Germany," Chamberlain asserted, "was the only country that sincerely wanted to preserve peace." Her enemies had carefully plotted to strip the Reich of markets and territory and to destroy her natural impulse to achieve the status of a world power. France had simmered with feelings of *révanche* since 1870 and would have precipitated a conflict at any point when the recovery of Alsace-Lorraine looked possible. Russia, on the other hand, "a vast amorphous body blindly bursting its bounds in every direction," had designs on the Hapsburg territories in eastern Europe and hoped to reduce Germany's ally to the ignominious status of "an eastern Switzerland." But the driving force of the coalition was England, whose controlling clique of politicians and businessmen had long planned to annihilate German commerce and industry, as well as to prevent the growth of a German fleet. While the French had been conciliatory in the last years of peace, recognizing their nation's weakness, the English had pushed ahead, bringing Europe to the brink of war over Morocco in 1905, sending agents to provoke trouble for Austria in the Balkans, encouraging Pan-Slav ambitions, and making preparations to use Belgium as a base for an invasion of the Rhineland. The British fleet, Chamberlain pointed out, had already been put on a war alert in July 1914, while Sir Edward Grey's much publicized last-minute peace moves were a clever subterfuge to avoid an unpopular conflict over Serbia. A "noose" had been pulled tight around Germany, and the

German invasion of Belgium on August 4, far from being an unprovoked thrust against a defenseless neighbor, as enemy propagandists claimed, was in fact an "iron-bound necessity," a legitimate last-minute act of self-preservation.[33]

That Chamberlain had launched his strongest attacks on England was not merely a function of private indignation at his birthplace; it also reflected a wider conviction in the Reich that England was the most dangerous threat culturally as well as militarily. German propagandists fulminated against English commercialism and materialism; they scorned English conceptions of freedom and the state, carped at British eccentricities and national habits, and depicted the central objective of the war as being to smash British power once and for all and to release the world from its despotism. Werner Sombart, for example, contrasted German heroism and the English trading mentality (*Händlervolk*), Ernst Haeckel charged that Sir Edward Grey was "a murderer of millions," while Ernst Troeltsch in more subtle fashion attacked the hypocrisy of English publicists, and defended German attitudes toward the state as a natural expression of German culture. Countless others voiced the same refrains, castigating perfidious Albion as the arch-enemy and spiritual antithesis of the Reich.[34] In a way Chamberlain benefited from the dominant prejudice, for England was a subject about which he could claim some measure of expertise. As an outspoken "renegade," he was seen by German patriots as one whose comments verified their assertions about British values and conspiratorial designs. Equally, Chamberlain's special position led the English press to single him out for particularly angry rebuttals. "The most ignorant of Germans," announced the *Times Literary Supplement*, "has not written greater nonsense," while the English translation of Chamberlain's early war essays (titled "Ravings of a Renegade") warned that his "exaggerated assertions and absolutely idiotic statements" were accepted by broad sections of the educated classes "in the unhappy country which has adopted him."[35]

Almost everything that Chamberlain said about England in his propaganda was anticipated in the letters he had written before 1914, although his tone had become more strident and unrestrained. In response to enemy publicists who distinguished between German culture and militarism, arguing that the latter had grown all-powerful and corrupted cultural life, Chamberlain replied that Britain was a ruthless, unintellectual "robber *Volk*," concerned only with money and self-aggrandizement. The English character, he alleged, had been molded by the Norman conquest and the transformation of the nation from an agricultural to a trading and commercial power in the sixteenth century. The first had established a foreign aristocracy with its own cultural traditions, thus creating a permanent division within the society so that even in the present war the British army visibly lacked the unity and camaraderie which sustained the forces of its German opponent. The second development—the rise of British commerce—had produced a mechanical and materialist civilization: opportunistic, destructive, and pledged to "further the interests of money making all over the globe." As always Chamberlain scattered many quotations from reputable sources throughout his tracts, misquoting historians like J. R. Green, W. E. H. Lecky, and J. R. Seeley, and appropriating the names of British cultural critics such as Ruskin and Carlyle to underscore his claims. He also occasionally resorted to anecdotes and personal reminiscences, dredging up memories of his unhappiness as a schoolboy and his later impressions of Edwardian society. The general image presented was of an acquisitive people, lacking in religion and art, misled by politicians and newspaper magnates, and distracted by *Sportsidiotismus*.[36]

Alongside these often absurd and petty strictures against England, Chamberlain indulged in the most extravagant praise of everything German. Repetitive, simplistic, more creations of style than of substance, his articles ranged from discussions of Luther, Wagner, and Bismarck as exemplars of German genius to tracts glorifying German humanism and freedom. Underlying everything he wrote, however, was the same simple polarity between German and western ideals (between *Kultur* and materialism, *Gemeinschaft* and *Gesellschaft*, conservatism and democracy). Chamberlain believed that the call to arms had rescued the heroic German spirit which had been almost extinguished in the pre-war years. The debilitating disunity created by party differences, class antagonisms, and sectional interests had suddenly evaporated; even the working classes, despite decades of socialist agitation, had rallied spontaneously to the nation's defense. What was necessary was to transform this national consensus into institutional reality, to repudiate western parliamentarism and liberal ideas so as to build a political system appropriate to the "spirit of 1914." But his early optimism did not last. By the second year of the war, as an increasingly tense domestic situation began to create splits in the *Burgfrieden*, or party truce, Chamberlain's tone grew more extreme and embittered. He redoubled his attacks on the so-called *"Englanderpartei,"* or political left at home, fusing the fight against foreign and domestic enemies into a single struggle for the survival of the Reich. In these essays, fabricated from many different strands of conservative thought, Chamberlain attempted to define the basic features of a political order appropriate to the German character; they represent the fullest expression he ever gave of his political philosophy.

His central theme was the distinction between German and western concepts of liberty. Contrary to English and French contractual theories of politics, men were not born free, their freedom originated in the state, which restrained selfish passions and incorporated the individual into the larger community. Confusing liberty with license, freedom with arbitrary impulse, the modern apostles of democracy had defined freedom as a sacred area of rights beyond the jurisdiction of the state. In contrast, the essence of German freedom was willing submission as a matter of conscience to legitimately constituted authorities; it implied duty more than rights and was something spiritual and internal for which each moral being had to strive. Consigning "liberty" to an inner, "nonpolitical," moral realm, Chamberlain closed off any discussion of the specific conditions for a free society and simply asserted that freedom was perfectly compatible with an authoritarian system of government. Similarly, he rejected the equation of freedom and equality. Except as a moral postulate of equality before God, egalitarian doctrines contradicted the abundant and unassailable evidence that human beings in fact varied enormously in talents, aspirations, and qualities. Translated into politics, "equality" invariably meant the triumph of mediocrity: "Whoever wants freedom cannot want equality, for it is the tyranny of the leveling will of the unintelligent majority." Indeed, the French revolutionary creed of "liberty, fraternity, equality," when transposed from the moral sphere into political organization, inevitably resulted in oppression, social division, and misgovernment.[37]

Not only were the basic principles of democracy false or destructive, but also the institutional forms of liberal parliamentary states appeared to Chamberlain to achieve the very reverse of what was avowed. Devised for small city-states in Greece, the system was ill-suited to large, populous nations and inevitably gave way to the rule of a small oligarchy. Democratic practice rested on the assumption that most voters understood issues, were capable of choosing delegates, and exercised sound judgment. In reality, none of these was true. The average voter was ill-informed in an era that demanded scientific government, and the whole system of electioneering, conducted by party machines, militated against sober decisions. Relying heavily on the work of Gustave Le Bon, Chamberlain concluded that in an age of mass politics the irrational "mass psychosis" of the crowd replaced the conscious, deliberate decisions of individuals.[38]

As a result, parliamentary regimes quickly fell under the thrall of narrow interest groups, party organizations eliminated free choice of eligible candidates, and the more talented of men retreated from public life, yielding to what the French writer Emile Faquet termed "the cult of incompetence."[39] In 1915 Chamberlain was terrified by the thought of the crowd's being hypnotized by liberal and socialist agitators; only in the 1920s did he acknowledge the rest of Le Bon's conclusions—that mass man was instinctually conservative and Caesarist—and contemplate the rise of charismatic leaders on the right.

The western enemies of Germany, Chamberlain contended, amply vindicated his claims in their everyday political life. Thus England was in the grip of a small plutocratic elite that wielded power behind the scenes: the Prime Minister and his colleagues in the cabinet controlled Parliament through the whips and House rules, thus nullifying the doctrine of the separation of powers, while popular newspapers ensured a compliant public opinion. The French representative system was also a sham. Here Chamberlain relied on two authors: Paul Bourget, the prominent novelist and *Action Française* member, and Francis Delaisi, a socialist critic whose *La Democratie et les financiers* caused a considerable stir on its appearance in 1910. Using Delaisi especially, Chamberlain attempted to show that a financial oligarchy manipulated the Third Republic, spending heavily on elections, backing radicals and even socialists where tactically convenient, and exploiting the state for their own selfish ends. Particularly noteworthy argued Chamberlain was Delaisi's suggestion that 55 men controlled France, only two or three of whom were political figures in the public eye—the rest were economic managers linked to Rome, freemasonry and Jewry. Only the continued operation of old monarchical institutions such as the *Conseil d'état*, he concluded, had saved France from total disaster. In both nations the expansion of the electorate had been accompanied by more rigid party discipline and political management; political freedom declined as a result.[40]

Still more glaring, in Chamberlain's eyes, was the gulf between rhetoric and reality in the United States. Supporting his arguments with copious references (to writings by Woodrow Wilson, James Bryce, John W. Burgess, and H. G. Wells among others) he described Congress as weak and ineffectual, firmly controlled by a President who over time had assumed all the authority of a king. Responsible only to this uncrowned monarch, ministers knew "nothing of the torments of a Reichstag as do German chancellors and state secretaries."[41] Here also a highly professionalized politics and a politically appointed judiciary catered to the interests of wealth, while the labor movement found itself more limited and constrained than anywhere in Europe. H. G. Wells, Chamberlain asserted, had gone to America anticipating a modern utopia; after coming face to face with the extreme exploitation of workers, the press corruption, and open venality of electoral contests, he returned totally disillusioned. This land, wrote Chamberlain, allegedly quoting an American visitor to Bayreuth, "is a hellish whirlpool in which all the contradictions of the world, all the greed, envy and lust brew and simmer; a wild struggle of millions of ignorant egotists, men without ideas, ideals, or traditions, without shared values, without any capacity for sacrifice, an atomic chaos endowed with no true power of nature [*Naturkraft*]."[42] It seems hardly surprising that before America's entry into the war, officials in the German Foreign Office worked to block the export of Chamberlain's pamphlets.

But what was the alternative to democracy in the modern age? Chamberlain's answer was summarized in an essay of more than a hundred pages entitled *Politische Ideale* (1915). It was a mixture of romantic conservatism, modern technocracy, nostalgia for the landed interest, and a vague corporatism designed to give it a populist flavor while in fact demanding fairly minimal rearrangements in the basic structure of contemporary society. Chamberlain began with the German idea of freedom, calling himself a Kantian in politics and arguing that the efflorescence of human technology and scientific skills in the modern world had been paralleled by the atrophy of man's moral and spiritual self. The emergence of liberal and socialist ideologies was one manifestation of this impoverishment, although he also somewhat paradoxically asserted that a need for guiding ideals had prompted so many Germans to take the false path of Social Democracy. He viewed the state as a natural, organic entity, a reflection of the "individuality" or genius of the nation. It shaped the individual, gave his existence a function and value, and provided a framework within which he could develop and realize his potential. By insisting on the logical priority of the whole and assuming that the individual parts attain meaning only within the whole, Chamberlain identified state power and freedom; he concluded that the task of political theorizing was to elucidate the conditions for a strong and durable state, rooted in the past, open to evolutionary change, reflective of the "personality" of the nation, but also capable of guiding and modeling its further development.

The pillars of a strong state were monarchy, the family, and private property. Monarchy, Chamberlain argued in the style of Justus Möser, Julius Stahl, and other conservative theorists, embodied the sacred principles of family, law and the common duty of all citizens to strive for the national good. Although he had by this time serious doubts about the caliber of Kaiser Wilhelm's leadership, he never wavered in his public support for a powerful monarchy, which superintended affairs largely free from constitutional and parliamentary restraints. Republican government led to anarchy and social atomization. "Whoever speaks of a republic in Germany," he wrote, "belongs on the gallows; the monarchical idea is here a holy law of life." [43] Monarchy was the natural order of things: his almost mystical belief in Kingship and the Hohenzollern dynasty was coupled with a dread that the downfall of the crown or even its transformation on the British or Scandinivian model would ensure the total and irreversible decline of the racially superior Germans and their culture.

Private property was the other touchstone of a healthy state. In using the term Chamberlain was vague, but then so were most völkisch theorists, desiring to condemn specific kinds of property while safeguarding others. Like many other social conservative theorists he sought a "third way" between unfettered laissez-faire capitalism with its worship of profit as an end in itself and the socialists' repudiation of ownership and control. The perilous instability, exploitation, and alienation that pervaded the modern social order resulted not from property itself, but from its parasitic and impersonal forms. While extolling the benefits of productive industry and emphasizing the significance of a strong landed interest, Chamberlain polemicized against the disruptive impact of mobile wealth associated with financiers and Jews:

> A man who possesses only a writing desk and a strong box can today be richer than the greatest landlord in the world. . . . Nobody can doubt that this threatens the continuance of the state. This kind of property has . . . no fatherland. War is as agreeable to it as peace; its increase is fostered not by sun and labor, but by heightened instability . . . so it loves unrest, change, and catastrophes of every kind. [44]

Coupled with romantic notions of the peasantry as a vital

source of national strength and synonymous with the virtues of sacrifice and duty, such ideas had long been the stock-in-trade of anti-Semitic publicists and demagogic leaders of the *Mittelstand*. The only remarkable thing in Chamberlain's case was that he had lived all his life largely by dividends and had even tried his hand—disastrously—as a broker on the Paris *Bourse*. His remedy, influenced by Lagarde's *Deutsche Schriften*, was simple: confiscation and nationalization of all financial and banking institutions, followed by government regulation of credit and the use of profits to ameliorate taxation and to pay for social reform. He never investigated how this could be achieved amid the complexities of a modern economic system or explained how far nationalization would extend. Chamberlain merely contented himself with the belief that planning and authority from above would be fairer, more predictable, and socially more cohesive than liberal capitalism. He was one of the many to voice such ideas, but Alfred Rosenberg later asserted that Gottfried Feder had specifically incorporated his proposal into the Nazi Party program of January 1920.[45]

In the context of war, Chamberlain refrained from all criticism of existing elites in German society. Unlike Lagarde he did not propose schemes for a new nobility or examine the structure of power in Wilhelminian society. He even included a few words of praise for the Prussian *Landtag*, long the sheet anchor of German Conservatism, and also for the German princes. Questions about the proper relationship between agriculture and industry, their ties to the state, and the role of intellectuals and officials in running society were largely ignored or left nebulous. The dominant impression given of the ruling elite in Chamberlain's ideal polity is of a vague coalition of aristocratic families and industrial, technical, and intellectual leaders creating together a new, harmonious order, run by experts and not liberal dilettantes, committed to the general good without the impious suggestion of subservience to popular will, and liberated from the diverse consequences of party politics. This, indeed, was the chief emphasis of the whole tract—the urgent need to dispense with parliamentary forms altogether. "Whoever wishes frankly to work for the emancipation of man," admonished Chamberlain, "should subscribe to no political party; politics is the enemy of freedom." [46]

In place of politics there was to be planning, scientific organization, and skilled administration by a small cadre of professional bureaucrats. Quoting extensively from his pre-war letters to Kaiser Wilhelm, Chamberlain pointed to the technological achievements and economic efficiency shown by German industry. The war had further illustrated the large reserves of skill and talent that the nation possessed. Now, he argued, the time had come to replace the *Reichstag* with a structure that employed these same principles of planning and expert administration to the tasks of government and legislation. The Wilhelminian political order was unsuited to the requirements posed by Germany's world mission. "It is not a question," Chamberlain wrote, "of carrying on the politics of others—namely that of the diplomats externally and the bankers internally—but of pursuing resolutely and openly a 'nonpolitics'; this alone will lead to the fulfillment of our goals." [47] The future called for a corporatist society, "a cohesive unity, disciplined and methodised," characterized by "true organic subordination." The German people were to be fashioned into a "national weapon of precision," a "nation acting according to a plan, a scientifically drilled nation." [48]

As a skilled publicist Chamberlain knew that it is often more effective to suggest than to detail ideas. Certainly his vision of scientific management remained highly impressionistic. The keynote of his new corporatist Reich was planned coordination, the achievement of a balance between an authoritarian central power and the mass of competing social and economic groups in society through the rule of impartial managers. No politics, only administration; no disagreement, only shared trust in the decisions of the nation's technical physicians. The disputes which had rent the Wilhelminian political order would be legislated away, and German workers, at present seduced by the promises of Social Democracy, would be reintegrated into society, regaining a consciousness of their function as laborers in a natural hierarchy. "By scientific organization," Chamberlain wrote:

> I mean the same consideration for scientific principles that has already produced unprecedented results in Germany in the areas of technology, research and even government in many cases. I include the most scrupulous exactitude in directing the available means toward the desired ends; also the application of forces in such a way as to achieve the maximum results from the minimum expenditure thus multiplying the resources at our disposal a hundredfold. In addition, I mean a division of labor which ensures that each individual does the work he understands and is fitted for according to his talents—this presumes practical systematization, that is to say, the carefully planned intermeshing of all the parts of every productive unit. [49]

Exactly what all this would look like when translated into concrete terms remained buried in the ambiguities of Chamberlain's prose; his mode of expression was that of a moralist rather than a political theorist. Like Augustus and the Romans, the new Germany would transform the world:

> Equipped with offensive and defensive weapons, organized as firmly and flawlessly as the army, superior to all in art, science, technology, industry, commerce, finance, in every field in short: teacher, helmsman, and pioneer of the world, every man at his post, every man giving his utmost for the sacred cause—thus Germany emanating efficiency will conquer the world by inner superiority. [50]

This passing reference to the army is instructive. Here, Chamberlain asserted, was "the first great component of the new state," a perfect blend of ancient traditions and modern technical efficiency and organization. The army with its "comradely unity" and hierarchical structure integrated all classes and confessions; it was the embryo of a new order growing within the old. As the war lengthened and his confidence in Kaiser Wilhelm and the civil leadership reached a new low, he increasingly pinned his hopes on Hindenburg, Ludendorff, and the military: "The present constitution of the state is not worthy of this army; state and military are in contradiction to one another." [51]

The nature of popular participation in Chamberlain's new state was never made clear. Like other *völkisch* critics of parliamentarism and professional politics, he was quick to invoke the name of the people as a source of legitimacy for his ideas, but his general viewpoint was decidedly more authoritarian than populist. He failed, for example, to make it clear whether local assemblies, provincial estates, or the *Bundesrat* would continue; he also never seriously dealt with the problem of competing social and economic interests, or the ways in which popular concerns could be recognized and addressed. The functions of government were to be handled by amateurs and professional bureaucrats in cooperation. "A completely factual picture of requirements" on a given issue would be made by sampling public opinion; then a specially appointed committee, selected from the public because of their knowledge of the subject at hand, would deliberate in secret and arrive at specific proposals. While he seems to have envisioned these committees as being composed of individuals from different occupational organizations, Chamberlain nowhere specified in detail a system of autonomous, but interlocking occupational estates such as existed in other corporatist theories. In any case, the proposals of these *ad hoc* committees (arrived at after consultation with appropriate government departments) were then to be forwarded to permanent state functionaries for drafting into law and execution as policy. Another central facet of the plan was a mobilization of the mass of the citizenry for public tasks, thus excluding the need for professional parliamentarians. Whereas democratic societies laid heaviest stress on individual rights, the new German order would emphasize social duty. Just as young men were eligible for military training, so older citizens would be subject to other kinds of service according to their education and ability. By using these reservoirs of talent—just as society had been forced to do during the present war—government could be cheapened, improved, and the population would receive an invaluable education in public affairs. "Whoever is unable to render service to the state," Chamberlain added, "be he rich or poor, noble or not, should not have the right to share in the dealings of the state nor obtain a voice in any other way." [52]

Such was Chamberlain's political creed; *Politische Ideale* was intended as a kind of political counterpart to the war-aims controversy. A German revolution or political rebirth, as Chamberlain called it, was the internal corollary of an annexationist peace and German dominance in the world. To the modern reader both his critique of democracy and his *völkisch* alternative remain exasperatingly vague, full of uncompleted ideas and obscure allusions. He never properly confronted the views of the liberal theorists he opposed; he showed no grasp at all of the ideological underpinnings of Social Democracy, preferring to lump socialism and democracy together as divergent strands of the "ideas of 1789"; and, finally, he failed to reconcile his vision of a system of estates with the complex requirements of a modern economy, even though his vision called for a technologically advanced and scientific nation. Chamberlain's aim seems to have been to suggest, rather than to specify; he was more concerned to convince readers of the failings of liberalism and parliamentarism than to prescribe a new order in intricate detail. Furthermore, *Politische Ideale* represents in many ways a transitional stage in his thinking and part of its sketchiness may derive from that. Before the war his hopes had centered upon a strong monarchy, but Wilhelm's inability to provide vigorous leadership, coupled with Chamberlain's growing contact with radical nationalist leaders, led him to contemplate a unified, mass based movement of the right which would bring about a general restructuring of German society. In this sense the essay is located ideologically midway between Chamberlain's viewpoints before 1914 and his conversion to the postwar populism of the Nazis.

One other aspect of his lack of clarity in these wartime writings deserves mention: the way in which he wove anti-Semitism into his tracts without too many explicit references to Jews, which might have brought the intervention of the government censors. At times he explicitly attacked Jews, but more often he employed innuendo and suggestive phrases without making direct assertions. There could be little doubt about the anti-Jewish connotations of his rhetoric against Mammonism and materialism, his obsessive concern with internal enemies and inflammatory language against the *Berliner Tageblatt* and other liberal press organs. By 1914, as we have said, the Jew symbolized a whole range of negative ideas among large sections of the German public. So close was the cognitive link that it also worked in reverse: certain catch phrases and styles of expression triggered a series of anti-Semitic associations whether the Jew was explicitly mentioned or not. Thus in a letter to a friend, Chamberlain admitted that he had excluded direct references to Jews from *Politische Ideale*, but added that the deeply anti-Jewish spirit of the tract would be easily grasped by Germans.[53] In the last days of the war, when censorship of the right was almost nonexistent, he was able to drop all such pretenses and subterfuges.

German Jews shared in the patriotic exultation that swept through the German nation in August 1914. Proud of their cause, confident of victory, and eager to demonstrate their willingness to sacrifice themselves for the Reich, they flocked to recruiting stations and volunteered their services for posts in government administration. Jewish organizations and the Jewish press continually urged that blood spilled in defense of the fatherland would wash away remaining anti-Semitic prejudice in society. The Kaiser's proclamation of a *Burgfrieden* on August 4 seemed to inaugurate an era of unity ("I recognize no more parties and no more confessions; today we are all German brothers and only German brothers") and the fact that Jews were invited to serve in responsible governmental positions in the new *Kriegsgesellschaften* and even breached that last bastion of exclusiveness, the Prussian officer corps, seemed tangible proof of a new climate of trust and acceptance. "The nation," wrote the dramatist Ernst Toller, an early army volunteer, "recognizes no races anymore, all speak one language, all defend one mother, *Deutschland.*"[54]

But this atmosphere of solidarity did not last very long before anti-Semitism, which had seemed to evaporate before the larger tasks of the war, quickly reasserted itself. Within two months Jews found it necessary to complain about the steady flow of anti-Semitic insults that appeared in the *völkisch* press. Anti-Semitic politicians and publicists deplored the presence of Jews in the economic administration of the war and actively propagated the old indictments of Jewish profiteering, shirking of duty, attachment to socialist ideas and cowardice, and added a few new flourishes specific to wartime conditions. Since these attacks violated the *Burgfrieden,* writers and publishers had at times to be careful to avoid intervention by the censors, and many resorted to various transparent stratagems, including attributing to England and the West ideas and qualities previously fastened upon Jews. As the publisher J. F. Lehmann wrote candidly: "The *Burgfrieden* compels us at all times to be very careful and the Jewish question . . . can often only be spoken of by way of intimation."[55] By and large, however, the military censors were erratic in their activities and generally lax on this issue. "We must never forget," wrote one Pan-German publicist, "that the English are not a *Volk* like others . . . the national type which it most closely approximates is the Jewish *Volk.*"[56] Another typical comment ran: "In the east the Slavs, in the west the Romance peoples, pervaded by Jewishness, then the cool, calculating shopkeeper mentality of the English, produced by the same Oriental spirit—thus is the encircling ring around the Teutons completed."[57] Chamberlain was particularly adept at linking English and Jewish ideals, depicting the conflict as a mighty struggle against Semitic commercialism and Mammon, and by the beginning of 1915 the Jewish press was regularly complaining of his slanders. Thus, irked by the success of Ernst Lissauer's (a Jew living in Vienna) patriotic poem entitled "A Hymn of Hate against the English," Chamberlain reminded readers that "he stems from a *Volk* that—in contrast to Germans—at all times has fostered hatred as its main charac-

teristic." The chief purveyors of enemy lies, he added, came
from the same people.[58]

During 1915, as the western front became stabilized and
the prospects of a swift victory disappeared, the deep social
and political rifts in German society reopened and the extreme
right, including powerful organizations like the Pan-German
League and the Agrarian League, gave up all pretense of
observing the domestic truce. Their propaganda against Jews
intensified and soon anti-Semitism became interwoven with
the issues of war aims, provisioning, manpower, and the prospect of postwar reconstruction. Nor was it only the tradi-
tionally anti-Semitic organizations that channelled their fears
and frustrations into the campaign against Jews. The war had
a general effect of drawing the different elements of the
German right more closely together and of further enhancing
the influence of the Pan-Germans and *völkisch* groups. As the
conflict lengthened and conditions in Germany deteriorated, so
large sections of the right, including powerful industrial and
landed groups that had previously avoided the cruder forms of
anti-Semitism, now began to see the benefits of using Jewry as
a kind of lightning rod for deflecting popular resentment and
as a way of forging a broad movement in opposition to a negotiated peace and its domestic complement of social and
political reforms. It is difficult to assess the relative quotients
of sincere anti-Semitic conviction and cynical manipulation in
some of this propaganda, but the result was the same: a rising
tide of allegations against Jews which achieved a considerable
impact among a population subjected to the hardships and
privations of war.

Chamberlain's correspondence in these years captures the
mood and intensity of this internal war against the Jews waged
by the far right; in addition, his success as a propagandist
illustrates the growing significance of racist groups within the
broad "national opposition" to any peace talks or constitutional concessions. He was not a political organizer, nor did his
health permit him to travel across the country giving lectures
and holding meetings like Dietrich Schäfer and other writers
and teachers, but his influence was such that most of the lead-

ing figures in Pan-German and anti-Semitic circles made
contact with him during the conflict.

In the early months of fighting, as the German armies advanced into France and Hindenburg and Ludendorff dealt
crushing blows to the Russian forces at Tannenberg and
the Masurian Lakes, Chamberlain rejoiced at the prospect of a
swift and victorious war. "I thank God," he wrote to his friend
Prince Max von Baden in September, "that I have been allowed
to experience these two exaltations—1870 and 1914—and that I
was both times in Germany and saw the truth with my own
eyes." [59] Viewing the army as an agent of cultural renewal, he
asserted that Germany was still the strongest nation in the
world despite its *Reichstag*, and predicted that the conflict
would usher in an era of German peace and supremacy. At
Christmas, although the Germans had sustained heavy
casualties in Flanders, he was still optimistic. Daily, he
reported, there arrived in Bayreuth "a mass of greetings from
the field and the military hospitals, even from the front line
trenches—sometimes on scraps of paper, dirtied by mud or
tallow." "One finds in them," he added, "a wonderful
Germany: so modest, so trusting in God, so simple and heroic,
so rich in healthy humor." [60]

His mood became darker over the next months. Although
momentous successes had been achieved and German troops
everywhere occupied enemy soil, a decisive triumph eluded
their grasp and Chamberlain slowly became aware that the
war would be a long and severe test of the nation's will, ideals,
and political endurance. Like his Pan-German friends, he was
deeply distrustful of Bethmann-Hollweg, regarding the chancellor as weak-willed, anglophile, and far too conciliatory
toward Social Democracy. Fearful that Germany's political
leaders would accept for a negotiated settlement, Chamberlain
welcomed the ultra-annexationist campaign mobilized by the
Pan-Germans and the agrarian Conservatives in the early
months of 1915 and signed the so-called Address of the Intellectuals presented to the chancellor in July by some 1347
professional men, theologians, teachers, artists, writers and
academics; he also joined the Independent Commission for a

German Peace (*Unabhängiger Ausschuss für einen deutschen Frieden*), founded by the Berlin theologian Reinhold Seeberg and the historian Dietrich Schäfer, which began a nationwide effort to build support for extensive territorial acquisitions.[61] Only a decisive victory, Chamberlain was convinced, would achieve German world dominance and permanent security; anything short of it would mean the decline of Germany and a substantial shift toward democracy at home. The external enemy could be safely left to the skillful professionalism of Hindenburg, Falkenhaym, and Scheer (Admiral of the High Seas Fleet), but internally the Reich stood "leaderless" against the dangers of defeatism, profiteering and pressures for constitutional reforms.[62]

Not surprisingly the savage *fronde* against the Bethmann system rapidly assumed the characteristically anti-Semitic tone of Pan-German rhetoric. Both explicitly and by insinuation, it was bruited that the chancellor was a puppet of Jewish interests. Typical of the mood in these circles was a letter of Chamberlain to Prince Max von Baden:

> I learned today from a man who is especially well-placed to observe these things—even when they go on secretly—that the Jews are completely intoxicated by their success in Germany—first from the millions they have gained through the war, then because of the praise showered on them in all official quarters, and thirdly from the protection they and their machinations enjoy from the censor. Thus, already they are beginning to lose their heads and to reach a degree of insolence which may allow us to hope for a flood-tide of reaction. May God grant it![63]

Deploring, in another angry letter, Kaiser Wilhelm's "well known absolute incapability of judging character," Chamberlain added: "If times were not so tragic, one could laugh that a sovereign who twenty-six years ago 'dismissed' Bismarck should now be forced to obey a Frankfurt pimp." The last reference was to Bethmann, whose ancestors were merchants and bankers from Frankfurt. "Is it really necessary that a Dernberg, a Ballin, a Bethmann, a miserable Jagow, a washed finance rat *à la* Helfferich, and in the background another dozen Jews and mixed breeds should control the destiny of this great *Volk*?"[64] It is significant that Prince Max registered no surprise or misgivings about such opinions: they were fairly commonplace. "It's not the Kaiser and Bethmann who rule in Berlin," as Theodor Fritsch wrote, "but Ballin, Rathenau and Co."[65]

As indicated by these outbursts, the Kaiser's apparent support for the "weak" policies of the chancellor was a source of great consternation among the annexationists, and they frequently explained it as a consequence of his seclusion, purposely cultivated by the supporters of moderation. "Valentini, Müller, Bethmann, and to some extent also Falkenhaym," complained the publisher Lehmann to Chamberlain, "seek to close the Kaiser off from the world and make it impossible for the voices of upright men to get to him."[66] Being one of the privileged few to have direct access to the Crown, Chamberlain was potentially at least a valuable ally. He dispatched copies of his pamphlets to Wilhelm along with letters full of patriotic fervor. These tracts aroused not a little indignation among more liberal members of the royal entourage; thus, the Chief of the Naval Cabinet, Alexander von Müller, recorded in his diary: "This evening at scat the Kaiser read us a presumptuous article by the writer Chamberlain on the lack of will to victory of the German people and the mediocrity of our statesmen. There was general unexpressed indignation on the part of his audience."[67] Several plots were hatched in 1916 to breach the Kaiser's seclusion and oust Bethmann, especially after the resignation of Tirpitz over unrestricted submarine warfare. Chamberlain's role in these intrigues is obscure, although he evidently took an active part in one attempt—along with Prince Ernst Hohenlohe-Langenburg, Prince Max von Baden, Count Zeppelin, and several leading Pan-Germans. Their aim was to persuade King Ludwig of Bavaria to head a deputation to Wilhelm voicing deep dissatisfaction with the handling of the war and suggesting that Tirpitz replace Bethmann. Ludwig, who was more preoccupied with his own territorial ambitions, dallied with the scheme for a while, then counselled delay and it collapsed.[68]

Tirpitz was Chamberlain's choice as the man likely to offer the kind of vigorous and ruthless leadership that would bring victory. Along with the mass of the German public

Chamberlain urged unrestricted submarine warfare as the only way to force England into submission; his expectations of this "miracle weapon" were fantastic, and as late as 1922 he insisted that "the success of this weapon would still have brought about peace negotiations already in the summer of 1917, but for the unfortunate Peace resolution of the *Reichstag* which opened to all eyes the inner weakness of Germany." [69] In addition to an all-out submarine campaign, he also publicly advocated a simultaneous assault on England from the air. In 1915, after a long meeting with Count Zeppelin, who complained of endless restrictions upon the use of Germany's air power, Chamberlain demanded massive attacks on London to bring the war home to the "upper ten thousand" and their "*Bourse* king." [70] He showed little concern that America might enter the conflict as a result of a total blockade. Indeed viewing the war primarily as one of contending moral values and ideals, he had always considered Germany locked in struggle with the materialist and democratic spirit of America. From 1917 the connection between "Jew" and "American" became increasingly common in *völkisch* and annexationist circles; in the Weimar republic it was incorporated into an anti-Semitic interpretation of reparations.*

Chamberlain's growing prominence in the war aims movement and his relentless campaign against "internal saboteurs" from time to time brought intervention from the censors. Throughout 1915 he complained of delays in the publication of

---

* Typical of his views was a letter to Kaiser Wilhelm in January 1917 (two months before the United States declared war). After a tirade of abuse against Britain, Chamberlain announced: "England has fallen totally into the hands of the Jews and the Americans. A person does not understand this war unless he realizes that it is in the deepest sense the war of *Judentum* and its near relative Americanism for the control of the world—a war against Christianity, against *Bildung*, moral strength, uncommercial art, against every idealist perspective on life, and for the benefit of a world that would include only industry, finance, and trade—in short, unrestricted plutocracy. All the other additional factors—Russian greed, French vanity, Italian bombast, the envious and cowardly spirit of the neutrals—are whipped up, induced, made crazy; the Jew and the Yankee are the driving forces that operate consciously and that in a certain sense have hitherto been victorious or at all events successful. . . . It is the war of modern mechanized "civilization" against the ancient, holy and continually reborn culture of chosen races. Machines will crush both spirit and soul in their clutches." HSC to Kaiser Wilhelm January 20, 1917 (*Briefe* 2: 252). Wilhelm had used almost the same expressions in his previous letter to Chamberlain (*Briefe* 2: 250) and repeated them in a speech marking the occasion of the thirtieth jubilee in June 1918.

his essays, blaming the Foreign Office under Jagow for hindering their circulation overseas and hinting that official circles were cutting short paper supplies to his publisher Bruckmann. "As regards the direction of the censorship against me personally by the Chancellor," he wrote to his friend in the Kaiser's suite, Oscar von Chelius, "I have the testimony of a German prince, and as for the other business [the enmity of the Foreign Office] we possess two original letters from the office concerned."[71] In February 1916 he announced to another friend that an essay entitled "Germany's War Aims," which was scheduled for publication "in more than two hundred newspapers with a total circulation of over one million copies" was withdrawn at the last minute after pressure was exerted "from a quarter close to the government."[72] But while the censors acted against particularly flagrant violations of their guidelines, Chamberlain's popularity, not least with the Kaiser (who awarded him an Iron Cross for these "spiritual grenades"), left most of his writings untouched.[73]

The attacks on Jews that accompanied the Pan-German campaign to get rid of Bethmann-Hollweg was only one sign of the intensification of anti-Semitism as the war entered its second year. With the allied blockade and the ever growing demand for supplies for the war fronts, serious shortages and rising prices at home provided a fertile soil for malice. Artisans, craftsmen, and small businessmen, hard hit by the rationalization of war production and the allocation of government contracts and raw materials to large-scale producers, were particularly susceptible to anti-Semitic appeals; so, too, were white collar employees whose incomes and living standards declined sharply relative to the wages of industrial workers negotiated by the unions. Denunciations of the role of Jews in retail, provisioning, and government agencies, claims that Jews were avoiding military service, and less focused accusations that the struggle was against "Jewish commerce and finance" were common in both rural and urban areas across the Reich.[74] Nor was it only rich Jews who provided a target for German anger: an equally bitter mood developed against the impoverished *Ostjuden*, whose lands the German armies had overrun in eastern Europe. For the first time, German soldiers came into contact with more than two million Jews in the Pale of Settlement, and the image of the foreign, unassimilable, ghettoized Jew increasingly became a favorite stereotype of the anti-Semitic press. Even liberal journalists admitted they were deluged with racist letters and articles from troops on the eastern front, and when the military authorities began transporting Jewish labor to relieve the pressing manpower shortages in the Reich, protests burst forth with new intensity. The Reich, it was alleged, was being swamped with Jews. (Finally, in April 1918 the Prussian government yielded to pressure and published an order specifically prohibiting the entry of Jews from Poland.) [75]

But perhaps the most glaring illustration of this general resurgence of prejudice was the so-called *Judenzählung* of November 1, 1916. German casualties in that year reached staggering numbers (the battles of Verdun and the Somme added over 800,000) and as the shortage of men fit for combat grew acute, public resentment against cowards and slackers mounted. Anti-Semitic publicists made every effort to channel these protests against Jews, whom they accused of inveigling cushy office jobs behind the lines. In this agitation they were greatly assisted by the decision of the Prussian War Ministry in October to conduct a statistical enquiry into the role of Jews in the different units of the army. The genesis of the "Jew count" is complicated, as Werner Angress has shown. [76] It appears to have resulted from a combination of the anti-Semitic predisposition of high-ranking army officers, the flood of denunciations against Jews that flowed into the War Office from civilians, and a number of bureaucratic considerations, including a fear of seeming to ignore the mass of complaints at a time when manpower was very scarce. The replacement in August of Falkenhaym by Hindenburg as Chief of the General Staff and the growing authority of General Ludendorff, a fanatical anti-Semite, also probably encouraged more forceful expression of prejudice against Jews. Public awareness of the survey spread rapidly when the *Reichstag* budget committee also entertained for a while a proposal for investigating the religious affiliation of persons serving in the government war agencies as well. Though German Jews vigorously protested being singled out by the army in this way, the War Office replied that its enquiry would dispel once and for all the ignorance and misrepresentations surrounding the issue of combat service.

Subsequent events belied this claim. The prevalence of anti-Semitism among the officer corps was no secret and the collection of data was left up to local commanders who (as Franz Oppenheimer later showed) frequently juggled the figures.[77] Thus, Jews who were hospitalized with battle wounds as well as those on leave from the front or in transit to new units were often wrongly designated as serving behind the lines. Commenting upon the change of mood in the trenches, Julius Marx reflected sadly: "For some time it has been evident that I am regarded suspiciously as a Jew. At the outbreak of war . . . there were only Germans. Now once again one hears the odious old ways of talking. And suddenly one is alone among comrades of whom one has grown fond, with whom one shares hardships and marches in a common cause."[78]

Once the enquiry was completed, the War Office refused to release its findings despite strong pressure from Jewish organizations; no official pronouncements were made and only in 1919 were selected fragments published—made available to the anti-Semite Alfred Roth for his accusations against the Weimar "*Judenrepublik.*" It was left to Jewish groups, particularly the *Reichsbund jüdischer Frontsoldaten*, to retrieve Jewish honor by publishing their own figures of participants and casualties. But the lie proved more potent than the truth, and charges of malingering and ineptitude on the battlefront continued, seemingly given sanction by the official silence. (Anti-Semites claimed that the War Office was once more trying to shield Jews from the full fury of public indignation.) Even more disillusioning, admitted the writer Ernst Simon, was the irrefutable fact that the "Jew count" was a "thoroughly popular cause, an authentic expression of the [people's] true will."[79]

In 1917 the German military situation further deteriorated with the collapse of the Verdun offensive, the failure of unrestricted submarine warfare to defeat England, and the decision of the United States to enter the conflict. At the same time the rifts in German society widened, as the left demanded a clear commitment to constitutional reforms and opinion began to mount in favor of early peace negotiations. Since the very first days of the conflict the right had warned that only a victorious and profitable conclusion to the war would safeguard the political and social order from pressure from below. A "peace of renunciation," in the words of Wolfgang Kapp, a rising figure among the Conservative politicians, would mean "an irremediable weakening of the government . . . which would immensely strengthen parliament and . . . endanger the future of the German empire." [80] The outbreak of the revolution in Russia, coupled with Bethmann's renewed efforts for peace and assurances that political reforms would be forthcoming, and finally the passage of a Peace Resolution through the *Reichstag* (July 1917) inflamed the paranoia and desperation of the right. The annexationists prepared for a war to the knife against the chancellor and domestic "traitors."

This mood of desperation is well illustrated by the essays and correspondence of Chamberlain in the last two years of the conflict. There is little in either to suggest that he had an accurate grasp of how the war was going. Though a number of military officers, including Count von Roon, supplied him with details of the battlefronts, and though he understood the weakness of the Hapsburg Monarchy, Chamberlain still clung to the hope that a knockout blow would produce a peace commensurate with Germany's future strategic needs and with the nation's enormous sacrifices. His essays, which became increasingly irrational and choleric, returned obsessively to two themes: that Germany could still triumph if only the population willed victory and that the war was a struggle between two world philosophies (Idealism and Materialism; German and Anglo-American; Teuton and Jew) which made any reconciliation impossible. It was a struggle for existence that must result in the destruction of one or the other. [81] It might take thirty years or even longer before a secure and lasting peace could be attained. [82] Letters to his friends echoed with the same sentiments, interspersed with more gloomy reflections about the breakdown of domestic discipline and morale and the possibility of revolution. The time had come—indeed it was long overdue—"to make revolution from above so that it should not come from below." [83]

Like other Pan-Germans, Chamberlain rejoiced at the resignation of Bethmann-Hollweg in July 1917 and the establishment of a virtual military dictatorship under Hindenburg and Ludendorff. Hero worship had always been a salient feature of Chamberlain's intellect and personality, and the war gave him ample opportunity to indulge his passion to the full; he placed almost boundless faith in the genius of these two leaders, foreshadowing in some ways his later faith in Adolf Hitler. "Had Hindenburg and Ludendorff stood on the first day in their rightful place," he later wrote, "the peace would in all probability have been dictated in Paris before the end of 1914." [84] Now, he believed, the circumstances were ripe for a final showdown with the *Reichstag* majority that had joined together in favor of the Peace Resolution. Indeed, as German society continued to polarize in the last year of the war, he became almost completely preoccupied with the internal struggle. Victory over the "inner enemy" was indispensable—the destruction of the so-called *"Englanderpartei"* was the first step toward achieving German world supremacy. There were, he asserted, anticipating the rhetoric and tone of *völkisch* polemics during Weimar, two nations, mutually antagonistic, living side by side in Germany. One included such figures as Hindenburg, Tirpitz, Ludendorff and Pan-Germans like J. F. Lehmann, Wolfgang Kapp, and Count Reventlow; the other, totally different in physiognomy and values, a different breed, comprised men like Bethmann, members of the *Reichstag* majority such as Scheidemann, David, and Erzberger, and the mass of liberal and socialist journalists. [85] No coexistence between them was possible. Chamberlain even admitted that he preferred to see Germany divided, whatever the short-term consequences, for this alone could provide a sound basis for postwar reconstruction and the eventual resumption of Germany's struggle.

Given the fanaticism of Chamberlain's wartime writing it is scarcely surprising that public responses were either very positive or totally negative. Alfred Roth, an anti-Semitic activist who was to play an important role in Weimar, com-

mented in 1915: "Whoever has observed, as I have, the profound results that Chamberlain's essays have wrought on the
battlefields and in the trenches among thousands of our
soldiers may be hopeful and joyful."[86] Another writer, and
onetime admirer of the *Foundations*, recalled: "I can personally testify that young officers in the field to whom I sent
these tracts found them repulsive."[87] Whatever their actual
impact, however, the number and wide circulation of these
essays placed their author among the best selling propagandists of the day. His first series of war essays, for example,
sold 160,000 copies in six months, the second more than 75,000
copies in six weeks, and a tract such as *Politische Ideale* sold
out 34,000 copies in just over a month. It is probable that
somewhere between 750,000 and one million copies of his
essays were bought during the course of the war—and this does
not include the countless excerpts and reprints, quotations, reviews, and analysis that appeared in the press, constantly
placing his name and ideas before the German public.[88] As
early as December 1915 the *Abwehr Verein* estimated with
alarm that his pamphlets had been read by over three million
people—by the end of the war the figure was much higher.[89]*

Success of this magnitude brought Chamberlain considerable favor within ultra-nationalist circles. Leaders of the annexationist campaign wrote to him; some visited Bayreuth or
met him on his infrequent trips to Munich and Bad Gastein.
New right wing publications solicited his support and
requested articles, including Wilhelm Kiefer's *Bühne und Welt*
and *Unser Vaterland*, a journal published by Count Karl von
Bothmer and the young playwright, and later Nazi ideologue,
Dietrich Eckart. More importantly, when the Pan-German
League bought the *Deutsche Zeitung* in April 1917, Chamberlain was proposed for its editorial board and provided a
front page article for the first new issue.[90] At the same time he
also collaborated with J. F. Lehmann, Dr. Erich Kühn, Hein-

---

* Chamberlain refused to accept payment for his wartime essays, regarding his efforts
as a patriotic duty and not a profitable enterprise. The revenues were, in fact, quite
considerable and caused some friction with the publisher Bruckmann who it was
alleged did profit handsomely from them. Royalties were distributed to army commanders for buying extra supplies for their troops and other sums were sent to Lili
Petri who until her death in 1916 ran a field hospital for the wounded.

rich Class, Dietrich Schäfer, and other leaders of the "national opposition" in founding *Deutschlands Erneuerung*, which rapidly became one of the most important journals of the extreme anti-Semitic and anti-democratic right. Although by this time Chamberlain was too sick to shoulder much in the way of editorial duties, it is noteworthy that the first number began with a long essay by him on "The German *Weltanschauung*." [91] Another cause which he championed in the final year of the war was the *Vaterlandspartei*, organized by a coalition of nationalists headed by Wolfgang Kapp and Admiral Tirpitz. Created in response to the *Reichstag* Peace Resolution in September 1917, within a year this "party" numbered over 800,000 members in 2500 local branches. It was by far the most successful attempt to build a unitary mass movement of the right pledged to resist a "Jewish peace" of renunciation and to strengthen opposition to internal political reform. [92] *

Right wing slanders seldom led to legal proceedings, especially in the last two years of the war when the overwhelming power and jurisdiction of the military afforded extra protection to annexationist and anti-Semitic publicists. Jewish organizations and the liberal press published rebuttals of charges against them, and occasionally individuals replied publicly or privately to allegations made against them. Astonishing for its patience and stubborn belief in the reasonableness of men is a letter to Chamberlain from Walther Rathenau in July 1916. As a Jew and organizer of the Raw Materials Department of the

---

* Just how close in rhetoric and interpretation of the war the founders of the new organization were to Chamberlain is demonstrated by the comments of Tirpitz at its first meeting: "The war has developed into a life and death struggle between two world philosophies: the German and the Anglo-American. The question today is whether we must sink down and become manure for others. . . . The colossal struggle which Germany is now waging is therefore not one for Germany alone; what is really at issue is the liberty of the continent of Europe and its peoples against the all-devouring tyranny of Anglo-Americanism." The same vision can be found repeated time and again in Chamberlain's essays and letters. Welcoming the *Vaterlandspartei* with a brief essay, he lashed out against Bethmann and his accomplices, the *Frankfurter Zeitung* and *Berliner Tageblatt*, who had systematically worked to undermine the Reich. This new party, he proclaimed, would triumph over all others so that finally no parties would exist at all. Fritz Fischer has observed that the *Vaterlandspartei* constituted "a step towards the anti-parliamentary, dictatorial, one party state." In terms of Chamberlain's hopes, at least, the description is apt. Fritz Fischer, *Germany's Aims in the First World War* (New York: Norton, 1967), pp. 432–33; Chamberlain, "Die Deutsche Vaterlandspartei," *Deutsche Zeitung*, Nov. 9, 1917, pp. 1–2.

War Ministry, Rathenau became one of the principal targets of
the growing wave of accusations against "Semitic domination"
and "profiteering." Responding to a thinly disguised attack by
Chamberlain, he enclosed with his letter a balance sheet of his
finances and three personal affidavits from the War Minister,
the Deputy War Minister, and the Chancellor as proof of innocence. Ever patient and restrained he seems to have hoped
that, after furnishing such evidence, the accusations would be
publicly retracted. Chamberlain—as far as can be told—
ignored the implied request.[93]

But Chamberlain's bitter attacks on the liberal press
finally provoked more determined action against him. Most of
his essays contained a harangue against the *Frankfurter
Zeitung* and *Berliner Tageblatt*, accusing them of fabricating
the lie of German militarism, of working to weaken and de-
moralize the Reich, and of sharing the same commercial and
liberal philosophy as Germany's western enemies.[94] Finally in
an essay on the *Vaterlandspartei* he abandoned all caution: "No
knowledgeable person," he wrote, "can doubt that the enemy is
at work among us," adding that years before Bismarck had
noted that, "whenever England has something up her sleeve
against the interests of Germany, she uses the *Frankfurter
Zeitung*." This influential newspaper, Chamberlain insisted,
was the mouthpiece of Anglo-American financial interests: its
ideals and interests were profoundly unpatriotic, promoting always "England's supremacy and Germany's humiliation."[95] It
was a clear case of libel, and Bernhard Guttmann, the dynamic
leader of the *Frankfurter*, seized the chance to press charges,
even though his legal advisers warned that the action
would be unwise given the inflamed mood of national opinion.[96]

It was not until August 1918 that the case finally came to
trial, but it quickly attracted widespread notice. Most of the
prominent figures associated with the newspaper were present
in the courtroom; so were many leading lawyers and judges
from the Frankfurt area. The newspaper was represented by a
Dr. Hertz and by Conrad Haussmann, a prominent member of
the Progressive Party and a leading opponent of the annexationists. Chamberlain—permitted to remain in Bayreuth on

account of his poor health—was defended by two well known figures of the far right, Heinrich Class, the head of the Pan-German League, and Adolf Jacobsen, a Hamburg lawyer who became active in counterrevolutionary politics after 1918.

The presiding judge opened the proceedings with a plea to both sides to refrain from using the courts as a forum for political propaganda. Then Hertz presented the case against Chamberlain, carefully recounting the charges Bismarck had once made against the newspaper and the subsequent verdict of the Berlin courts that they were totally unfounded. He also pointed to prior accusations by the right wing press, in particular the *Deutsche Zeitung*, which had been retracted once legal action was threatened. As for Chamberlain's claim that the paper had direct connections with Anglo-American finance, Hertz demonstrated that the whole of its one million marks capital was in the hands of German citizens. Heinrich Class met these arguments with a harangue deploring the consistent stand of the *Frankfurter* for anti-German causes: it was common knowledge, he announced, that the newspaper had hindered the work of Bismarck, that it had opposed the acquisition of Alsace-Lorraine, fought against military expenditures, undermined the home front, and slandered the German army with cries of militarism. Even its ties with high finance, he remarked allusively—referring to its Jewishness—were simple fact. But this political polemic failed to sway the court: Class, as Chamberlain angrily noted, was ill-prepared and made no systematic attempt to substantiate his claims. After a trial of only seven days a verdict was returned against Chamberlain on August 16.[97]

"In normal times," the judge admitted in his summation, "the penalty, in view of the seriousness and unscrupulousness of the libel, would have been imprisonment." But the times were not normal and, in view of the age (now 63) and sickness of the defendant, he preferred to impose a fine of 1500 marks plus all costs. In addition, he charged that every newspaper which had published the libel must print a retraction. The decision provoked nonetheless an uproar in right wing circles: the *Deutsche Zeitung*, among other papers, devoted column after column to restating the case against the *Frankfurter*, going all the way back to its founder Leopold Sonnemann and labeling him an "internationalist" opponent of order and a "declared republican and enemy of monarchy." Chamberlain's admirers quickly donated money to pay for the trial expenses and Class was instructed to appeal the decision. But before this could happen, the war ended and in 1919 an Appeal Court in Frankfurt dismissed the case on the grounds that it came within the general political amnesty. Chamberlain and his friends regarded the outcome as yet another blatant illustration of Jewish power in the German press and judiciary.[98]

The atmosphere surrounding the trial and the howls of rage from nationalist ranks at its outcome are one small indication of the broadening campaign against Jews as the Wilhelminian empire tottered and collapsed. Despite the surrender of Russia, which had raised high expectations among the annexationists, the battered and weakened German armies were unable to produce a decisive victory in the west. Ludendorff's last offensive brought a sudden advance and momentarily shattered the Allied front, but was then repulsed at the cost of heavy German casualties. All at once the military situation seemed hopeless; German dreams of vast conquests now yielded to the spectre of defeat and internal disintegration. Anti-Semitism thrives on despair, frustration, deprivation, and chaos; in the late summer and early fall of 1918 all were present in abundance. Across eastern Europe and Russia Jews were the victims of violent outbreaks; and in Germany itself Jewish organizations expressed deep anxiety about possible mob action. "When," asked the Social Democrat, Georg Davidsohn, "will the first real Jew pogrom begin in Berlin or elsewhere in Germany, if things continue as they are."[99] "Our Kaiser has failed," wrote J. F. Lehmann in October, "also our *Volk* has sinned against its blood . . . We must teach our *Volk* to think racially, so that all foreign born and alien elements may be expunged from it. Is that not a great and wonderful duty?"[100] The horrors of war, as George Mosse has observed, nurtured everywhere "the adversary habit of mind" which craved an enemy and was "ready for the politics of confrontation in postwar Germany."[101] For men like Class, Lehmann, and Chamberlain the war was not over in November 1918; it had merely entered a new stage, and they prepared to wage a new battle against the liberal and socialist elements that had gained the initiative as a result of the defeat.

Chapter Ten

Bayreuth and Nazism

BY AUGUST 1918 the final German offensive in the West had ground to a halt and the Kaiser's armies, exhausted and outnumbered, were forced to retreat, sustaining heavy casualties. Germany's allies, Austria-Hungary and Bulgaria, were on the brink of collapse, while the Turkish front buckled and gave way under the pressure of new assaults. This caving in of the German war fronts triggered a rapid sequence of changes within the Reich. The military, fearful of a complete rout, insisted upon an immediate armistice; liberal demands for broadening the basis of the government could be deferred no longer; and, in a matter of weeks, naval mutinies and widespread urban disorders undermined the monarchy altogether. On November 9, a republic was proclaimed and Kaiser Wilhelm departed for Holland; Prince Max von Baden, who had reluctantly assumed the role of Chancellor one month before, now transferred power to the Social Democrat, Friedrich Ebert. The Weimar Republic had come into being: born of the humiliation of defeat, led by indecisive men intimidated by their sudden attainment of power, grudgingly accepted by some Germans, and vilified by many others.

The armistice took Chamberlain, like so many Germans, by surprise. The German armies still occupied foreign soil and hopes of total victory had been heightened by the withdrawal of Russia from the war and the annexationist treaty of Brest-Litovsk in the spring. In his propaganda Chamberlain had sometimes conjured up the prospect of defeat, but largely for the purpose of exhorting compatriots to greater sacrifice and exertion in the cause of eventual victory. He had never seriously contemplated the collapse of the Hohenzollern empire: it was almost incomprehensible, running contrary to every conviction he held about the superiority of German ideals and the ordained cultural mission of the Germanic race. Now, quite suddenly, everything was in flux: his friend and correspondent throughout the war, Prince Max von Baden, had helped depose Wilhelm, the Bavarian monarchy was overthrown, and in Bayreuth, as in other towns, a Workers and Soldiers Council worked alongside the local administration. "It could well be," he wrote sadly to the painter Paul Croeber, "that the Germans have already accomplished their highest achievements and that Providence is now breaking a vessel which is incapable of producing something higher."[1]

Since 1916 Chamberlain's health had deteriorated rapidly: he was largely confined to bed, his limbs were partially paralyzed, and he was barely capable of speech. Struggling against extreme pain and discomfort, he tried to go on with his literary plans, aided by Eva (and local friends like Paul Pretzsch who later helped publish Chamberlain's correspondence) to whom he dictated his letters and essays in an almost unintelligible stammer. The exact nature of his illness remains uncertain—possibly it was multiple sclerosis, or as Chamberlain once guessed, a rare form of Parkinson's disease. Some of his admirers discerned darker forces at work. Thus, Ludwig Roselius, a prominent Bremen businessman and co-founder of the *Vaterlandspartei*, was sure that the English had got at Chamberlain's tea!—a very un-British action but an occupational anxiety perhaps coming from one of the chiefs of Kaffee HAG.[2] Equally certain of foul play was Arthur Trebitsch, a Viennese Jew and tragic example of *Selbsthass*, who even travelled to Bayreuth to warn Chamberlain—a curious journey reminiscent in some ways of Langbehn's celebrated trip to the Jena asylum to cure Nietzsche.[3]

Though physically worn out, Chamberlain remained mentally alert, keeping up a vast correspondence and continuing to publish, albeit at a slower rate than before.* His first task was to revise a series of autobiographical reflections, upon which he had been working intermittently since 1916. Organized as a collection of long letters to friends describing his family, education, scientific studies, and early experience of Bayreuth, these recollections carefully excluded personal and marital matters—Anna, for example, was omitted altogether. The book, *Lebenswege meines Denkens* (*Life Journey of My Thinking*), as indeed its title indicated, was a biography of his mind: a justification of his journey toward Bayreuth and *Deutschtum*, and a means of providing readers with a glimpse of the man behind the published works. Partly because he chose not to discuss politics or religion, these reflections contain remarkably little rancor against racial enemies and very little that was explicitly anti-Semitic. He emerges as a cultivated Englishman, steeped in German and European culture, passionately engaged in his writing and led by his fervent idealism to Bayreuth, the "home of his soul." It is a picture of Chamberlain as he saw himself—and, admittedly, as many of his friends saw him—a striking contrast to the hatred and racial anger which filled the letters and political tracts he wrote in those same last years of the war.

Next he returned to an older project, a major study of Christianity, for which he had been collecting notes for several years. The idea, which had originated with Julius Lehmann and the theologian Otto Pfleiderer, had over time changed from a historical survey to a more personal exposition of Chamberlain's beliefs. In 1919 he found it a pleasant escape from the turmoil of Weimar politics to bury himself in the early Christian centuries and to puzzle over biblical criticism

---

* Chamberlain also found himself in considerable financial difficulty after the war. He had donated his revenues from wartime propaganda to charitable causes, while his investments in Austrian and Hungarian state bonds became worthless paper. His stock and dividends in England were confiscated, then appropriated as part of reparations. Chamberlain made efforts to recover the confiscated wealth, but without success. The liberal press took some delight in his dilemma, accusing him of trying to avoid the consequences of his change of nationality (e.g., *Berliner Tageblatt* Aug. 5, 1921, *Frankfurter Zeitung* Aug. 4, 1921). In the postwar years he was aided financially by his patron, August Ludowici, and by his brothers with whom something of a reconciliation had been made. After Chamberlain's death, his wife's needs were met by a life annuity established by Basil Hall Chamberlain.

and comparative religion. Finished in 1921, *Mensch und Gott*, was a continuation and elaboration of the religious reflections in Chamberlain's earlier writings. Drawing upon Kant, Goethe, Wagner, the German Romantics and Indian religion, he constructed an eclectic, somewhat formless and highly intuitive Christianity. His focus upon Jesus, the intercessor between God and man, and his vision of religion as a manifestation of racial soul place him squarely in the tradition of Germanic Christianity. What is slightly different, say, from the work of Lagarde, is the delight Chamberlain took in Paul's Epistles and his conviction that Paul was the chief preserver of Christ's doctrines, rather than the main corrupter and Semitizing influence. Further, as a prophet of Bayreuth, he placed special emphasis upon the connection of art and religion. The final chapter of the book returned to the familiar themes of aesthetic, religious, and social regeneration. Art, Chamberlain argued, gave shape and form to religious feeling, allowing the Christian truth to be continually re-expressed without degenerating into idolatry or rationalist dogmatism. Quoting his lifetime mentors, Schiller and Wagner, he concluded that man's salvation could be grasped through religious art—the Aryan art of Bayreuth; and the book closes suggesting the significance of Bayreuth and the Wagnerian drama in the task of spiritual rebirth. Not surprisingly, Chamberlain's last religious testament won widespread praise both among supporters of Wahnfried and the numerous adherents of Germanic Christianity.[4]

Apart from these two books, Chamberlain published a very successful collection of essays (mostly completed before the war) and wrote several short political articles for newspapers.[5] His literary output during Weimar, though remarkable under the circumstances, was small and of no special significance; his career as a writer was largely over. Yet, in the 1920s the impact of his ideas both on Bayreuth and the German right was arguably greater than ever before, and hundreds of letters attest to the devoted following he had collected among Germans of all walks of life. To these admirers he was a prophet who had warned of the dangers threatening German culture, and whose prescience had gone unheeded. Labeled a "renegade" in England and sharply criticized in the liberal press, Chamberlain found himself a hero in nationalist circles: Bayreuth made him a freeman of the city; the anti-republican press celebrated his seventieth birthday in 1925 with columns of praise; he became the most cited authority of a new generation of Wagnerites; and many political and cultural groups solicited his name and interest for their organizations. The image of Chamberlain as court philosopher of Kaiser Wilhelm and cultural prophet of the Wilhelminian bourgeoisie gradually receded before a new *persona*—the "sage of Bayreuth," or the "apostle and founder of the German future" as Alfred Rosenberg once called him.[6] Almost inevitably his story in these years becomes that of an onlooker rather than an active participant; for though he received abundant news of events from visitors and correspondents, his own thoughts too often remain obscure and the written evidence for his responses to situations all too fragmentary.

The experience of Weimar found in Chamberlain's correspondence is that of a lived nightmare. His worst fears had materialized; the foundations of his world had crumbled, and a new Reich had risen on its rubble epitomizing everything that he abhorred. He brooded over the lost chances, moral surrenders, and mistakes of the past, and apportioned blame liberally. Although the army had remained superior in battle, the nation had rotted from within, subverted by its press and politicians, who detested the very structure on which it rested. Bethmann-Hollweg had betrayed the Reich while Kaiser Wilhelm had ignominiously failed it. "In 1890," he wrote, "Bismarck wanted to have strikers committing acts of terror shot; it is reasonable to nip the cancer in the bud and thereby implement the teachings of our gentle Saviour. But, moved by misguided humanitarianism, Kaiser Wilhelm preferred to separate himself from the greatest statesman of all time rather than punish a few hundred murderous knaves for their crimes." "Today," he added, "the noble lord is harvesting his reward." [7] "How was it," he puzzled, that the German workers "who at the outbreak of war behaved so marvellously and so consciously German, soon after allowed themselves to be captured by their Jewish leaders and seducers?" [8] He deplored the *Halbbildung* and political immaturity of Germans in letters to Prince Eulenburg, a sick and despairing recluse at Liebenberg, and to Admiral Tirpitz, now busy writing his memoirs. As a result of the war, he told Alfred Jacobsen, the Balkan chaos extended to Hamburg and Dresden. No Wilsonian Peace, he predicted, would for long contain the anarchic forces unleashed by the collapse of the Hapsburg, Hohenzollern, and Romanov dynasties. [9]

Contemplating the situation in 1919, Chamberlain found everywhere the conspiratorial design of Jews: as "the vultures of revolution," the beneficiaries of democracy, the agents of socialism, and the principal architects of the reparations agreements. "One can say," he wrote to the biologist Jacob von Uexküll, "without exaggeration that what we are experiencing today is the supremacy of the Jews. When newspapers today speak of eighty to a hundred Jews in the so-called government, this is inaccurate for among the remaining twenty there are many half breeds." [10] His friends expressed similar opinions. The vast scope and pace of political change seemed to exhaust more conventional and familiar categories of explanation, and they yielded to various kinds of secret society myths and tales of Semitic plots. Tirpitz, for example, railed against "the influx of un-German elements from the east" who had "broken the inner strength of the *Volk;*" Dr. Wildgrube, a prominent Conservative, reflected bitterly on "the dictatorship of a handful of Jews;" and Baron Uexküll, whose Baltic estates had been expropriated, voiced his enthusiasm for the *Protocols of the Elders of Zion*, which were being reprinted in vast numbers by the right. "We stand close to the time," he wrote, "when the power in all states will fall into Jewish hands." He speculated, however, that their own cleverness might yet thwart the Jews, resulting not in their hegemony, but their eradication

[*Ausrottung*].[11] Lastly, another friend, the opera singer H. Bennet Challis, advocated "planned scientific breeding" as the only way to national recovery, while another friend confessed to Chamberlain: "I grow more and more convinced that the whole world can only be relieved of its misery with the elimination [*Ausmerzung*] of Jewry."[12]

Early Weimar offers numerous examples of this sudden escalation in the violence of racial language,[13] and no purpose is served here in examining every detail of these outbursts of frustration and fear from Chamberlain's circle of friends. Yet one series of letters does deserve closer attention, not because they are typical (far from it), but because of the light they throw on the extraordinary career and personality of Artur Dinter, a particularly successful author of racist novels and subsequently a prominent figure in the early history of the Nazi party. The story of Dinter—told here for the first time—reminds us again that merely to reduce racism and anti-Semitism to notions of their social function is to neglect the fact that such prejudice can be a total experience, encapsulating all thought within the same interpretive scheme and enveloping every aspect of a person's existence.

Born in 1876 in Alsace, Dinter was the son of a senior customs official; he studied philosophy and science at the universities of Strasbourg and Munich and then became a teacher, occupying for a time the post of *Oberlehrer* at the German school in Constantinople. But, after a promising start, he threw up this career, returned to Germany and followed his long-cherished ambition to work in the theater. Before the war he wrote a number of plays, directed others in several provincial centers, and helped found the *Verband deutscher Bühnenschriftsteller*. His first contact with Chamberlain's ideas apparently came sometime between 1907 and 1910, during a long nervous crisis brought on by an unhappy love affair: the *Foundations*, Dinter claimed, struck him with the force of a revelation. The book acted like a "giant magnet" giving direction to his efforts, "a natural center point around which all my feeling and thinking, writing and striving, activity and suffering crystallized."[14]

It was in July 1916 that Dinter, then a young infantry captain on the western front, first wrote to Chamberlain. After
volunteering in 1914, he had received multiple wounds and was
awaiting his medical discharge. If anything the war had hardened his anti-Semitism into an obsession: it was the center of
his personal and political life. It had been his goal for some
time, he told Chamberlain, to write a fictional extension of
Chamberlain's world view which would reach those who were
intimidated by a bulky two-volume study like the *Foundations*.[15] Finished in the next year and dedicated to Chamberlain, his immensely popular *Die Sünde wider das Blut* (*The
Sin Against the Blood*) came with notes on sources, suggestions
for further study, and a short, didactic Afterword on the need
for racial and Christian rebirth. Later editions contained
lengthy comments on the political upheavals of Weimar. It
would merit little notice had it not become *the* best seller in
Germany at the end of the war. By 1922 some 200,000 copies
had been sold, and some estimates have placed Dinter's
readership as high as 1.5 million.[16] Some *Gymnasium* teachers,
it was claimed, had read it aloud or recommended it to their
students. A sequel, published in 1921, also sold more than
100,000 copies in the first year.[17]

The contents of *Die Sünde* may be briefly summarized.
Hermann, the hero, is a young Aryan scientist, born of honest
peasant stock. He is married twice, first to the daughter of a
wealthy Jewish financier, then to a Gentile, and the story
depicts his gradual enlightenment about race and the "dia-
bolical" role of the Jews in modern culture. The plot twists
and turns, and there are lengthy debates between the main
characters, which enable Dinter to include just about every
Jewish stereotype and voice every possible accusation against
them. When his second wife gives birth to a child with
pronounced Semitic features, Hermann learns that, in her
youth, she had been seduced by a Jewish army officer and—in
accord with the "laws" of race—that this one "crossing" had
been sufficient to drive out good German blood. Further, he
learns that this was no chance occurrence but part of a
concerted racial policy. Private papers come into Hermann's

hands disclosing the full horror of the Jewish conspiracy and their subjugation of the working masses:

> Hundreds of thousands, even millions of working people with sweat on their faces, in all parts of the globe, jumped (like marionettes) on his [the Jewish financier's] wires. Like a spider he sat in his Berlin office. . . . He was the great pitiless heart which sucked out men's blood to exchange it for ready cash, whether it sprang from the veins of white or black, yellow or red peoples, Christians or heathens. He laughed off the corpses of men and families, even of whole peoples, if he could make money from them.

Gradually, Hermann begins to understand the manipulative role of the Jews in parliamentary politics, their systematic campaign to ruin the industrious *Mittelstand*, their control of advertising, and incitement of the masses against the established order. And so it goes on, as the story moves slowly to its climax (not without discussions of Darwin, Kant, Goethe, the need for a second Reformation, and the issue of Jesus' Jewishness).

Finally, Hermann kills the Jewish officer who had dishonored his wife (in the meantime, she has killed herself and the child). Then, conducting his own defense, he warns listeners at the trial: "If the German Volk does not succeed in shaking off and rendering harmless . . . the Jewish vampire, which it has unsuspectingly nourished with its heartblood, then it will be destroyed in the foreseeable future." Acquitted, Hermann volunteers at the beginning of the war and is shot through the heart on Christmas day 1914: "So now," runs the last sentence, "his wish was fulfilled—to die for the holy Fatherland." [18]

It would be difficult to imagine a more contrived, cheaply sentimental, and distasteful story. It was not explicitly pornographic like the writings of Dinter's friend, Julius Streicher, but seems to have excited a complicated mixture of fear, disgust, prurience, and moral outrage. Insisting that the plot was based on accurate theoretical foundations, Dinter called for immediate legal action amounting to a virtual apartheid system: the restriction of Jewish immigration, exclusion of Jews from the law, teaching, and politics, and the nullification of their equal civil rights. (In short, the extreme anti-Semitic program drawn up as early as the 1880s.)

The case of Dinter illustrates how racism can invade every aspect of a person's life. Indeed, his long and autobiographical letters to Chamberlain not only reveal in wearisome detail the creation of this novel, but also provide a lurid commentary upon the relationship between his writing and his personal life. "All my books," he once wrote, "go back to personal experiences."[19] Dinter's chief preoccupation seems to have been to find a suitable wife, and his letters (one suspects that they must have tried Chamberlain's patience to the limits) describe one ill-fated liaison after another. Thus, in 1918, his affections were directed toward a young noblewoman from Württemberg whose parents objected to his bourgeois origins and anti-Papal prejudices. A lapsed Catholic, Dinter in turn suspected them of dangerous Jesuitical leanings and decided to search instead for a peasant girl. Within three months he had found a suitable candidate (some 24 years his junior) and marriage was seriously discussed. A further series of difficulties intervened, however: the Württemberg fiancée returned to the scene, a third woman threatened Dinter with a paternity suit, and he finally admitted, he was already married and had been seeking a divorce since 1917! He had abandoned his wife, he confessed, upon discovering that she had been the mistress of a Jew, by whom she had had a child. The overlapping strands of Dinter's fiction and life become very tangled indeed.[20]

Even the passion for his peasant girl, one Gertrud Dreyse, soon turned sour. Racial anxieties plagued Dinter. By July 1919 he was sending pictures of her grandfather, parents, and brothers to Chamberlain for his expert opinion on their racial physiognomy. Hard-pressed, Chamberlain finally decided that Gertrud might stem from "Indian gypsies," but by this time the prospective bride, considering herself of solid Alpine stock and sick of Dinter's persistent researches, had the sense to end the relationship. As for Dinter, he found a bride in 1921—a friend of the Ludendorff family, above reproach, a "sublimely blond and blue-eyed" woman from "a racially pure Thuringian family of teachers and pastors." She was "an excellent *Hausfrau*." "Now," he wrote, "I am finally at rest."[21]

Dinter's fanatical mind regarded the whole world—not without a certain crazy, inner logic—with a fixed and preoccupying expectancy, looking behind everything for hidden motives and special meanings. His private miseries converged with wider collective anxieties in the early postwar era, transforming personal fear into successful racist propaganda and political action. Not only was his novel a stunning success, but Dinter also toured the country on behalf of *völkisch* organizations, treating crowds to harangues against Weimar and the indignities of Versailles. When he spoke in Bayreuth in October 1919, at the end of a tour of thirty towns, the audience overflowed the hall and spilled out into the streets. "We will not rest," he raged, "until northern Schleswig is restored and an undivided part of the Reich. . . . 'til Posen, Danzig, Schleswig-Holstein, Alsace-Lorraine, and the Saar are again German. We will not rest till the last black rogue* has disappeared from the Rhineland and till the whole Rhine is once more free and German." To his *"verehrter Meister"* Chamberlain he confessed that Germany's defeat was not an unmitigated disaster. A victory would merely have sanctified the corrupt old order and condemned the nation to a slow, but inexorable decline. "I do not weep tears," Dinter confessed. "Hitherto I had no idea of the ungodly dilettantism of our leadership." Wilhelm's flight "like a thief" had cleared the path for a new order that would throw off the shackles imposed by domestic and overseas enemies.[22] Dinter's rise within the radical right was meteoric: by 1926 he had become Nazi *Gauleiter* in the critically important state of Thuringia and received the high honorary party number of 5. His career is one further indication of the continuing intellectual influence of

* This refers to the Moroccan and Senegalese troops used by the French in occupying the Rhineland 1919–1920. For the public outcry that this provoked see: Keith L. Nelson, "The Black Horror on the Rhine" *Journal of Modern History* (1970), 42:606–27. In *Mein Kampf* (Boston: Houghton Mifflin, 1943), p. 325, Hitler commented: "Just as [the Jew] systematically ruins women and girls, he does not shrink back from pulling down the blood barriers for others, even on a large scale. It was and it is Jews who bring the Negroes into the Rhineland, always with the same secret thought and clear aim of ruining the hated white race . . . and himself rising to be its master."

Chamberlain on this younger generation of anti-Semitic activists.*

Dinter could never be described as typical, not even of the extreme right. But the hardships of a protracted war, followed by national humiliation and the convulsion of revolution produced a dramatic upsurge in anti-Semitism and widened the appeal of anti-Semitic politics. The efforts of Pan-German and *völkisch* circles in the previous decades to harness the different layers of German antipathy toward Jews for a more focused political campaign achieved sudden success. In several areas officials and spokesmen for Jewish organizations reported with mounting anxiety that a "pogrom mentality" was sweeping the land; rabbis in some localities issued warn-

* Dinter's fall from favor with Hitler was equally rapid. As a Chamberlain disciple, Dinter spent much of his time advocating the need for a religious reformation and an all-out campaign against Rome as well as the Jews. As early as 1924 Hitler began to crack down on multiple allegiances among Nazi party members and he particularly wished to avoid religious disputes that might divide Protestant and Catholic adherents of the party. There were complaints against Dinter's leadership in Thuringia and, after some hesitation, Hitler began to look for a new leader—in 1927 he chose Fritz Sauckel (the labor boss of the Third Reich). But Dinter was not pushed aside so easily. He had earlier published a series of criticisms in *Der Nationalsozialist* (of which he was the editor); and now he sought to air the matter before the next general meeting of the party. He even demanded that a party Senate be elected to advise Hitler, hoping in this way to check the excessive concentration of power in the *Führer's* hands. When these efforts failed, Dinter continued a campaign against the party in his journal *Geisteschristentum* ("only the blind, uncritical admirer of Hitler or those people . . . who do not want to admit the truth, can still doubt that the Hitler party is a Jew party, which under the *völkisch* banner carries on the business of Rome"). He was expelled from the party in 1928, but later made his peace with Nazism and worked actively for the Nazi Christian movement. After 1945 he was summoned before the courts in Baden to answer charges that he was continuing to agitate for a racist *Volkskirche*. Dinter died in 1948 at the age of 72. A. Dinter, "Der Kampf um die Vollendung der Reformation: Mein Ausschluss aus der Nationalsozialistischen Deutschen Arbeiterpartei," *Geisteschristentum* (Sept–Oct., 1928), 1; *Der Nationalsozialist* (Weimar) September 12, 1925; Dietrich Bronder, *Bevor Hitler kam* (Hannover, 1964), p. 262; also, Albrecht Tyrell, *Führer befiehl . . . Selbsterzeugnisse aus der Kampfzeit der NSDAP: Dokumentation und Analyse* (Düsseldorf: Droste, 1969).

ings to their congregations not to linger around synagogues
before and after services; there were a few cases of physical
violence and (in Bamberg, for example) of Jewish homes being
daubed with swastikas. Compared to eastern Europe actual
violence was minimal, but brutal rhetoric became almost commonplace. "A sleepy meeting," the Conservative leader, Count
Westarp, remembered, "would wake up and the house applaud
as soon as I started on the subject of the Jews."[23] Golo Mann
has argued that these immediate postwar years evinced a more
widespread and ferocious popular anti-Semitism than any period of recent German history, including the Depression and
the Third Reich. As the recent research of Werner Jochmann
has demonstrated, there is considerable evidence to support
the claim. With appalling readiness an embittered, alienated
and fearful population resorted to the same scapegoat. From
the pulpits of the clergy, in police barracks and army messes,
at student gatherings and in workshops, a polyphony of voices
intoned variations upon the same anti-Semitic theme.[24]

The line of continuity between pre-war and Weimar anti-
Semitism is clear. One would have to look hard in the anti-
Semitic literature of the 1920s, as Peter Pulzer has observed, to
find a novel argument or point which had not already been
used before 1914.[25] Nonetheless, there were some changes of
emphasis or accentuations of ideological trends present in the
Wilhelminian period, in addition to the general increase in
threatening language and the more vicious tone of the attacks.
First, there was a far wider acceptance of racial theories of
anti-Semitism than in previous decades. Building on the writings of Chamberlain, Duehring, Gobineau, and Schemann, as
well as the research of ethnologists and anthropologists, a new
generation of race publicists largely tailored the already well-
established Aryan myth to the circumstances of post-1918
Europe. Among the most successful were Hans F. K. Günther
and the Nordic School, whose ideology was strongly anti-
Semitic and whose writings achieved much acclaim in *völkisch*
and right wing circles.[26] The increasing popularity of such intellectualized and racialist anti-Semitism since the 1880s implied a larger shift of opinion away from older religious and
economic forms of prejudice to a belief that the Jew was

unassimilable and did not belong to the German *Volk*. The logic of unalterable biological facts precluded the hope of a German-Jewish fusion through conversion to Christianity.

Strangely enough, alongside the vogue of racial theorizing, with its pretentious apparatus of scientific terms, there was also an increase in the use of images and language drawn from medieval demonology and reminiscent of such religious fanatics as August Röhling in Austria in the 1880s. In a skillful piece of literary detective work, Norman Cohn has analyzed the origin and dissemination of the *Protocols of the Elders of Zion* in terms of a revival, in secularized form, of Christian apocalyptic beliefs. Fastened to this image of the Jew as Satan's accomplice were also a variety of secret society or masonic myths, which had been steadily cultivated since the eighteenth century.[27] Before 1918 such notions had limited currency in Germany, but in the aftermath of the November revolution they became the subject of numerous pamphlets and speeches. A tract by Artur Dinter on the Talmud, for example, sold over 60,000 copies in one year, while the Lehmann press had considerable success with a study of freemasonry, world war, and world revolution by Dr. Friedrich Wichtl, which focused on a Jewish plot centered in England. Henry Ford's *The International Jew* was also a huge publishing success and was eagerly devoured by Chamberlain in the last months of 1923.[28] Lastly, in addition to these features, the language of postwar anti-Semitism contained many more expressions derived from parasitology, identifying the Jew as a poison, a pestilence, a deadly bacillus, parasite, or beast of prey: all of these suggesting his complete separation from the rest of society and implying that his removal or elimination was vital to the health of the nation.

Jewish stereotypes remained much the same in Weimar as before, although the depiction of Jews as socialist insurrectionaries—now Bolshevik conspirators—understandably gained special prominence in the wake of the revolutionary outbreaks across Europe between 1917 and 1920. Similarly, the alleged international ramifications of Jewry excited more attention in the light of the Comintern and the international financial controls imposed upon the Reich.

There was also considerable continuity in the sociology of anti-Semitism before and after the war. Its main political strength was concentrated in the diverse groups of the *Mittelstand*. Teachers, tradesmen, small businessmen, officials, salaried employees, parsons, lawyers, artisans, and peasants were all well represented in the multiplicity of anti-Jewish organizations that sprang up in eariy Weimar. The economic grievances against big business and big labor, the anxieties over status, the ideological identification of themselves with the true values of German culture, which had prompted many in these strata to embrace nationalist and anti-Semitic politics before 1918, were much intensified by political and economic trends in the new republic.[29] In contrast, the organized industrial working class proved largely impervious to racist propaganda, although scholars are somewhat divided as to the incidence of anti-Semitism among workers outside the SPD and its auxiliary associations.[30] Higher up the social scale, among aristocrats, industrialists, academics, and the *Bildungsbürgertum*, anti-Semitism had made considerable and continual progress since the 1890s; but particularly after 1914, the inhibitions of these social groups about engaging in demagogic anti-Jewish movements were whittled away by the pressures of war and revolution. The campaign for annexationist war aims and the *Vaterlandspartei*, launched by the Pan-German League, had played a significant part in this process.

Among the young, both those who shared the *Fronterlebnis* and those who spent the war in high school or entered university shortly afterward, antipathy toward Jews was also conspicuous. Ex-officers and demobilized soldiers, confronted with the problems of reintegrating into civilian society, were easily recruited into many *völkisch* associations and militant nationalist *Bünde*. University students, hard-pressed by inflation and worsening prospects for employment, were also highly receptive to anti-Semitic appeals, and demonstrations against Jewish professors (unheard of before 1914) and the adoption of exclusionary "Aryan paragraphs" by student *Burschenschaften* were not uncommon. In the Berlin student elections of 1921, almost two-thirds of the total vote was cast for anti-

Semitic candidates. The same radicalizing trends were also present in the Youth Movement (even before the war 92 percent of the *Wandervogel* had no Jewish members and Jewish participation had been a hotly debated issue), where a number of new right wing militant *Bünde* emerged. Racialist, nationalist, anti-communist, and more conscious of politics than their predecessors, these groups called for a "German Revolution" that would destroy the Weimar system and establish a new society on *völkisch* principles.[31] "The German," Hans Blüher, the first historian of the Youth Movement, predicted in 1922, "will soon know that the core of all political issues is the Jewish question."[32]

Finally, the general intensification of anti-Semitism was also registered in the attitudes of the Protestant clergy. Politically conservative, patriotic, ardently monarchist and anti-republican, the pastorate became rapidly embroiled in bitter disputes with the political left over education, the corporate status, property, and privileges of the churches. The Stoecker tradition remained strong among the clergy, while the search for a new politically relevant theology, attuned to the circumstances of the postwar era, brought many churchmen closer to the *völkisch* nationalist standpoint.[33] Anti-Jewish pronouncements by prominent pastors and theologians were commonplace, as Richard Gutteridge has recently shown. For example, Paul Althaus, who became professor of theology at Erlangen in 1925, demanded that the significance of the Jewish question be fully recognized: "Evangelization" he insisted "is today opposed on all sides by a mentality under Jewish influence in business, the press, art, and literature." He especially upbraided Weimar's left intelligentsia and inveighed against "the demoralized and demoralizing urban intellectual class which is represented primarily by the Jewish race."[34] Similar blanket association of liberal, socialist, and atheistic ideas with Jewry filled the pages of the evangelical periodicals which were widely read and influential in middle-class homes. Week after week, as Ino Arndt has shown, they repeated the standard stereotypes and included reviews of current anti-Semitic publications.[35] Moreover, in the wake of the German defeat, a number of racist Christian sects were founded. As early as

1917, on the occasion of the Luther anniversary celebrations, a small group of racist Christians led by Pastor Friedrich Andersen, Professor Adolf Bartels, and Hans von Wolzogen issued a manifesto demanding that all Semitic doctrines be expunged from Protestantism and stressing Luther's anti-Semitic statements and his abhorrence of democracy. Four years later, together with Chamberlain, Karl Grunsky, Arthur Bonus, and other prominent Wagnerites and anti-Semites, they established a *Bund für eine deutsche Kirche* which achieved considerable publicity in the Reich. Similar groups arose elsewhere: for example, the Leipzig *Deutsche Christenbund*, the Prussian *Christlich Deutsche Bewegung*, and the *Thüringer Deutsche Christen* (in which Dinter was a leading figure), the last of which soon openly identified the goal of a Christian renaissance with the aims of the embryonic Nazi movement and cooperated eagerly with local *Ortsgruppen* of the party.* Although these right wing fringe groups aroused some concern and embarrassment among national leaders of the church, almost nothing was done to check the general radicalizing of the clergy and the laity, and no forthright de-

---

* As we have seen, Chamberlain played a major role in formulating and popularizing the doctrines of Aryan or Germanic Christianity. To many Germans he had successfully incorporated Christ into a Germanic world view, providing a convenient ideological bridge between their growing racial and nationalist sentiments and their basic Christian beliefs. Chamberlain and the Wahnfried circle remained important ideological influences. Friedrich Anderson, for example, admitted that his break with Lutheran orthodoxy was decisively influenced by reading Chamberlain; similarly, Dinter and Max Maurenbrecher did much to publicize his ideas among the Thuringian German Christians. After these extremist sects were unified in 1932 into a pro-Nazi coalition (the *Glaubensbewegung Deutsche Christen*) Chamberlain's works were frequently quoted as examples of a successful synthesis of religion, politics, and race. Also, after 1935 when Christianity came under attack from various sections of the Nazi party, a number of pamphlets used Chamberlain to argue that a Christian rebirth had to be an element of a successful Nazi revolution. But Chamberlain was also invoked for quite different purposes. Thus, *Junge Kirche* (the mouthpiece of the *Bekennende Kirche*, which voiced its opposition to Nazi policies) rejected angrily in 1936 the appropriation of Chamberlain's name for assaults on the church. It insisted that he was "outstanding among the confessors of Jesus Christ at the turn of the century." As late as 1940, Pastor Georg Schott founded a *H. S. Chamberlain Vereinigung* in Dresden with a religious program, but it attracted little support and was dissolved within two years. (*Junge Kirche*, quoted in R. Gutteridge, *The German Evangelical Church and the Jews 1889–1950*, New York, 1976, p. 35). For anti-Jewish sentiments among Catholics and their reformulation in racist terms, see: Hermann Greive, *Theologie und Ideologie: Katholizismus und Judentum in Deutschland und Österreich 1918–1933* (Heidelberg, 1969).

nunciation of anti-Semitic agitation was officially sanctioned during Weimar.[36]

In the Wilhelminian period, despite the openly anti-Jewish stance of a range of small parties, occupational groups and nationalist *Verbände*, political anti-Semitism remained deeply fragmented. This disunity continued in early Weimar, although immediately after the November revolution strenuous efforts were made by the Pan-Germans, Agrarians, and racists to make their influence felt in a broad "national opposition" to the republic. The result was the *Deutschnationale Volkspartei* (DNVP), an amalgam of Conservatives, Christian Socialists, and anti-Semites which was in many ways the successor to the *Vaterlandspartei* coalition. Its basic program, proclaimed in April 1920, explicitly condemned "the predominance of Jewry in government and public life," and its electoral speeches, slogans and placards attempted to harness the anti-Semitic mood so widespread in the Reich. "What has Berlin become?" asked one handbill circulated in 1920. "A playground for Jews!" In 1924 another election poster proclaimed a "Struggle against Jewish influence on all fronts," while much of the party's everyday propaganda employed crude racial stereotypes and caricatures of "Jewish types" to condemn the republican leadership.[37] Admittedly *völkisch* elements never managed to secure complete control of the party, but their pressure on the leadership for a more forceful expression of racism won considerable success especially in the years before 1922. As the largest party of the right, the DNVP played a crucial role in transmitting *völkisch* ideology to the mass of German electors and in endowing anti-Semitic accusations with a patina of respectability. As George Mosse has observed: "While respectable DNVP personalities in top hats and frock coats moved in the best social circles, their aides were on the street corners disseminating racist propaganda."[38] But this effort to incorporate all the anti-Weimar forces into a single political coalition, fusing traditional conservative and more radical populist elements, ran into difficulties once the various factions switched from a common defense against the threat of left-wing revolution to more specific aims and issues. Early hopes that the party might absorb Stresemann's *Deutsche*

Volkspartei proved false, the extreme racist wing finally se-
ceded after considerable friction in 1922, and, most important,
the DNVP largely failed to build a lasting base of support
among the *Mittelstand*. After a brief alignment with the party
many of the Protestant middle strata turned to a range of
small regional religious or special interest groups.[39] Not until
the Nazi electoral victories of 1930 were these fragmented elements of the *Mittelstand* integrated into a broad populist
movement of the right.

Apart from the DNVP and older pressure groups such as
the Pan-Germans, the right waged its war on the republic
through a staggering number of veterans organizations,
cultural associations, occupational groups, rifle and gymnastic
clubs, religious sects, and paramilitary formations. At one end
of the spectrum was the *Deutschnationale Handlungsgehilfen-
Verband* (DHV) or commercial employees union founded in
1893 with a large membership and considerable funds for all
manner of political and publishing ventures, whose leaders
were prominent in many radical right organizations. At the
other pole were numerous small occultist sects and "blood and
soil" breeding communities for upgrading the Nordic race. Although there were many differences in ideology, rhetoric, and
goals between them, these groups together formed a vast and
complex network with overlapping memberships, personal ties
between their leaders, and certain basic similarities in outlook—among the most important of which was anti-Semitism.[40]

One organization, founded in February 1919 by the Pan-
Germans and other anti-Semitic groups, deserves additional
comment both because of its swift and extraordinary success
in capturing a mass following and because it acted as a way
station for many right-wing personalities (including several
disciples of Chamberlain) on their journey toward Nazism.
This was the *Deutschvölkischer Schutz-und Trutzbund*
(DVSTB), perhaps the first organization to achieve a mass mobilization of the *völkisch* movement by combining anti-Semitic
ideology largely fashioned before 1918 with mass political techniques and methods of organization that anticipated the
Nazis. Led by Alfred Roth (who was also Secretary of the

DHV) the *Bund* launched a remarkable recruitment drive designed to publicize, in the words of its charter, "the pernicious and destructive influence of Jewry" and to make anti-Semitism the pivotal issue of Weimar politics. Membership rose rapidly, numbering 25,000 in 1919, 100,000 a year later, and shortly before its dissolution by the Weimar authorities in 1922, it had over 280,000 members (veterans, artisans, teachers, students and apprentices were heavily represented). It held hundreds of demonstrations, arranged lecture tours by Dinter and Bartels, and unleashed propaganda blitzes of unprecedented magnitude. (In just one year, 1920, it distributed 7.6 million pamphlets, 4.7 million handbills and 7.8 million stickers). Organized into some 600 local branches, the *Bund* engaged in wide-ranging activities, including efforts to infiltrate schools, universities, and cultural institutions, campaigns to influence church elections to achieve the appointment of anti-Semitic church officials and clerics, and the holding of patriotic German Day celebrations around the country. It also had a clandestine arm, set up by Alfred Jacobsen (Chamberlain's lawyer in the *Frankfurter Zeitung* trial) and maintained contacts with various *Freikorps* and with Organisation Consul, an assassination group responsible for the murders of Erzberger and Rathenau. Chamberlain's friends and correspondents were prominent in the *Bund* and sent him news of their activities; among his acquaintances on its advisory board were, for example, Lehmann, Dinter, Bartels and Fritsch, while Carl Cesar Eiffe was among those who contributed money.[41]

This, then, was the confusing political environment of Chamberlain's last years. After the initial shock of the November revolution and a stunned reaction to the establishment of a democratic state, his spirits began to improve somewhat. The wave of left wing reforms that swept spontaneously over the

Reich in the first year of peace soon ebbed as traditional political patterns and power structures began to reassert themselves. Weimar politics and culture were anathema to Chamberlain—the triumph of everything he had opposed—but the continuing economic dislocations and deep political discord that prevented the consolidation of the republic in its first four years gave him grounds for hope that the system could be overthrown. Out of the ashes of the *Kaiserreich*, he predicted, would arise the phoenix of a new Germany, hardened by its trials and ready once more to assume a dominant position in the world. He compared the anti-republican cause to that of the early Christians whose "times were without ideals," and who through their unbroken faith and moral power had eventually transformed a hostile world. "It is magnificent, indeed overwhelming," he wrote to Prince Eulenburg, "to realize the power of a pure idea, to see it grow from small beginnings and not only survive the collapse of a giant empire, but go on to conquer the conquerors. . . . One comes to the conviction that far greater things might be in the offing than those now in power could possibly suspect." [42]

From newspapers, conversations with visitors to Bayreuth, and through a large correspondence, Chamberlain pieced together his own assessment of conditions in the Reich; a prisoner in his house at Bayreuth, he lived in an encapsulated *völkisch* world without any point of contact with the liberal and progressive spirit of Weimar. Like so many others, Chamberlain longed for a right wing coup that would take advantage of the growing crisis in the nation to topple the "*Judenrepublik*". Though on principle opposed to any involvement in the morass of party politics, he nonetheless valued the DNVP as a temporary counterweight to the left, but was soon troubled by its internal divisions and by reports of "sad experiences behind the scenes" from friends active in the party (i.e. the efforts of moderate and traditional Conservatives to resist a *völkisch* takeover). [43] Pondering the alternatives, Chamberlain pinned his hopes chiefly on the army and the *Freikorps:* perhaps, he speculated, new leadership would emerge from the officer corps or among the troops fighting the Poles on the eastern borders, or from the ranks of the Youth

Movement.[44] In these early postwar years he embarked on a political journey, a vicarious one for the most part, largely conducted through letters; he followed his friends and informants through the maze of nationalist organizations, and like many of them eventually arrived at the Nazi party.

The first major attempt to destroy the republic came in March 1920 with the Kapp-Ehrhardt *putsch*, which was defeated in five days by the concerted action of German workers in calling a general strike and also by the refusal of the *Reichswehr* leadership to give it their support. Hitherto, Chamberlain had been an admirer of Wolfgang Kapp, one of the most active wartime opponents of Bethmann-Hollweg and a founder of the *Vaterlandspartei*, but in the wave of criticism and recrimination that followed the dismal collapse of the coup his opinions changed radically (unlike Ludwig Schemann, who later wrote a passionate defense of Kapp).[45] One of Chamberlain's young disciples, Josef Stolzing-Cerny, a minor anti-Semitic poet and journalist of Czech origin, had been a press organizer during the *putsch*. Reporting angrily on his experiences, he declared: "Unfortunately [Kapp] was not at all 'the man with the lion heart,' much rather the man with the beer heart, for he continually used all his energies befuddling his brain with alcohol. . . . In the same situation a Bismarck or a Napoleon would have hunted the whole Jewish-socialist republic to the devil." Stolzing-Cerny (the name Stolzing came from *Die Meistersinger*) was furious at Kapp's refusal to turn the Ehrhardt brigade loose for a full-scale attack on Berlin Jewry.[46]

Meantime, Artur Dinter had spent the brief period of the Kapp regime in the Ruhr, the heart of the strike movement, where he watched the Red Army mobilize and drive out the *Reichswehr* forces and police units stationed in the area. His impressions illustrate the kind of information on which Chamberlain based his opinions and also point to a broader shift of views in *völkisch* circles in the wake of the Kapp débâcle.

> The miserable Kapp attempt, which one must call childish if not criminal, caught me in the middle of my lecture tour through the Ruhr region. I witnessed terrible fighting, fought my way through various adventures on a freight train to

Neudietendorf, then walked for seven hours to my house in the woods, only to find the same conditions there. Here too were dead and wounded. A proclamation was posted that every man of 18–45 years capable of bearing arms was at once to enlist in the Red Army, and that all weapons were to be handed over at once. I, of course, did neither one nor the other. I hid part of my collection of firearms and kept my Browning pistol in my pocket, determined to sell my life as dearly as possible if things took a turn for the worse. But nothing happened. Although a sentry was placed in front of the house, nobody came in. I am increasingly convinced that we are heading for long years of civil war. We are unquestionably entering a new era of Bolshevism—a wholly natural reaction to the one-sided materialism of the last fifty years directed solely at enjoyment, profit and greed. Bolshevism undoubtedly has a healthy core even if the path which the blind, uncritical masses take is indistinguishable from chaos. The propertied and the leaders of society are themselves to blame because they regard acquisition and possession as goals in themselves viewing them as the only things which give life meaning. In consequence they fail to appreciate the spiritual and psychic nature of human beings and their eternal destiny. Now comes the inevitable backlash. I have spoken a great deal with these fanatical workers and I was deeply moved by the powerful impression of their well-disciplined workers' battalions. Each fellow in them was a born and trained soldier, willingly subordinating himself to a freely chosen leader. And then the enormous impression made by the General Strike! The terrible power it reveals of bringing all the wheels to a standstill by a command! No army and no authority is effective against it! The world and the organization of the state must be placed on wholly new foundations! The next decades will see the death of one order and the evolution of another—may God grant us a leader who properly understands the signs of the times. Men like Kapp and the right wing of our party are living corpses from whose bodily organs the rhythm of life has been extinguished.[47]

Here, as in other letters to Chamberlain at the time, Dinter concluded that nothing further could be expected from moribund conservatives like Kapp. A new dynamic and populist politics of the right was required, adapted to the crisis conditions of postwar Germany and capable of crystallizing the energies of the "front generation" into a powerful movement. "We want," Dinter wrote, "to pull together the whole German people into a great sacred work community, which knows one goal, that of service, the *Volk* and the fatherland." [48]

Though the details of Chamberlain's thoughts remain a mystery, his friends were becoming increasingly disenchanted with the elitist style and bourgeois composition of groups such as the Pan-Germans and the DNVP; they dismissed these organizations as anachronistic and incapable of building the mass following which (as the Kapp failure illustrated) was necessary to challenge the power of the left. Their answer was "German socialism," an amorphous term signifying a radical nationalist alternative to liberal individualism and Marxism. It conjured up nebulous images of corporatism, class solidarity and social cooperation, a spiritual revolution against materialism, and the subservience of the individual to the needs of an authoritarian state. There were many variants: Spengler closely associated this "authentic" socialism with the traditional Prussian virtues of duty and self-sacrifice; Moeller van den Bruck described it in terms of the spiritual unity of the *Volk* and claimed that class enmity and party divisions would miraculously evaporate with the reassertion of German values. For Chamberlain, German or "ethical" socialism was equally vague—an amalgam of idealism, corporatism, technocratic planning, and Wagnerian nostalgia for an idyllic past. [49] Like later fascist ideologues he saw no contradiction between such socialism and the defense of property rights; his ideal of class reconciliation was synonymous with racial and national solidarity, and any gaps or problems in his logic were overcome by heavy doses of unifying rhetoric.

There were many rival political groups in the early years of Weimar that proclaimed themselves the true bearers of German socialism, promising a dynamic blend of racial nationalism and populist politics. But it was the National Socialist movement that especially began to attract members of Chamberlain's circle by its success in drawing large numbers of recruits from the petty bourgeoisie and the working classes. By the summer of 1923, chiefly through Hitler's talents as a party organizer and tactician and through his spellbinding oratory, the Nazis had been transformed from one of many small discussion groups of mostly skilled workers and veterans meeting in the smoke-filled beer halls of Munich into a party of some 50,000 members (and about 150,000 sympathizers in Bavaria alone). Those disgruntled at the inaction and unimaginative *Kampfstil* of more traditional *völkisch* groups found in Nazism a more radical and determined alternative; its barrage of rallies and processions, its ruthlessness toward opponents, military discipline, and careful attention to the symbolism of politics proved irresistible to many of the most activist elements of the nationalists. "The new movement," Hitler announced, "aims to provide what the others have not: a nationalist movement with a firm social base, a hold over the broad masses, welded together in an iron-hard organization, filled with blind obedience and inspired by a brutal will, a party of struggle and action."[50] By the beginning of 1923 Hitler occupied a leading position in the Bavarian radical right and, encouraged by the example of Mussolini's successful "march on Rome," was seeking for a chance to consolidate his position in the south and take action against the republic.

Conditions in Munich were especially favorable for the growth of the extreme right. Bavaria had suffered heavily from the war and the revolution had been bloodier there than elsewhere, culminating in a short-lived Soviet Republic that was brutally suppressed by *Freikorps* forces. Dread of communism among the propertied classes, together with deep conservative and particularist suspicions of Berlin, made the city a base for the enemies of Weimar. In addition, whereas the Kapp *putsch* had failed in Berlin, a simultaneous coup in the south under Gustav von Kahr had succeeded, turning the state even more into a right wing stronghold, a "cell of order" which attracted like a magnet all the anti-republican elements dislodged from other parts of the Reich (especially when the republican authorities began to take firmer action after the Rathenau murder in 1922). The idea began to spread among the proliferating nationalist and racist groups that Bavaria might act as a staging ground for a triumphant "march on Berlin."

By early 1923 the circle of Chamberlain's friends and disssciples intersected with that of Hitler at numerous points. As

an up-and-coming young politician with an ability to lure
workers into the nationalist camp, Hitler was soon cultivated
by a number of wealthy Munich families, among them the
Bechsteins and Chamberlain's publisher, Bruckmann. As early
as 1920, Elsa Bruckmann, who had been devastated by the
death of her nephew (the poet Norbert von Hellingrath) at
Verdun, invited Hitler to her salon. She soon became one of his
ardent admirers and, according to Karl Alexander von Müller,
discovered in her activities for the party a new reason for living
and hope for the future.[51] J. F. Lehmann, who had continued
to play an active role in racist politics after the war and was
briefly jailed for planning a coup against the revolutionary
Eisner regime, also made early contact with the Nazis. Indeed,
he may well have acted as an intermediary for right wing
funds, since his financial support for Hitler in the summer of
1920 coincided with the first efforts of the Pan-Germans to
draw the Nazi party into their orbit. As the publisher of
Deutschlands Erneuerung and much other bestselling racist
literature, he also became acquainted with Dietrich Eckart
and several other Nazi writers, and it was Lehmann who first
gave the young Baltic Russian, Alfred Rosenberg, a job when
he came to Munich in 1919.[52] Dr. Erich Kühn, the chief editor
of *Deutschlands Erneuerung* (and a correspondent of Chamberlain) was also involved with Nazism from its earliest days
under Anton Drexler.[53]

Furthermore, in the wake of the Kapp fiasco, Stolzing-
Cerny appeared in Munich and after a brief spell working for
Lehmann became an editor for the Nazi *Völkischer Beobachter*; a letter from him to Chamberlain in January 1921
sang the praises of "Adolf Hitler, an Austrian worker, a man
of extraordinary oratorical talents and an astonishingly rich
political knowledge who knows marvellously how to thrill
the masses."[54] Lastly, there was Dinter, whose path toward
Nazism is more obscure: his first contacts seem to date from
1922 and he was probably influenced by his friend Julius
Streicher, who in that year allied his followers in Nuremberg
with Hitler.[55]

As early as 1915 Chamberlain had called for an "iron
broom" to sweep Germany clean (an expression the Nazis
quoted repeatedly); even so, it is doubtful that he envisioned a

sweeper as radical as Hitler.[56] But the subsequent failures of traditional conservatism and the chaos of early Weimar convinced him of the need for a completely new style of politics, while several members of the Wahnfried household were quick to voice their enthusiasm for D'Annunzio and Mussolini in Italy.[57] Along with many adherents of the *völkisch* right, Chamberlain put his faith in a broad coalition marching behind a national hero—Ludendorff being the most likely choice. The role assigned to Hitler in this scheme was that of a "drummer" who could mobilize broad public support against the republic. It was probably the widely reported pitched battle that Hitler and his followers fought against the communists in the neighboring town of Coburg that confirmed Chamberlain's ideas about the potential political value of Nazism, while the French incursion into the Ruhr, and the political and economic crisis it created, convinced him that the time was ripe for action. He still nourished some apprehension about the Nazi leader, however, and it was not until they met in October 1923 that all his doubts were assuaged. Then it was Hitler's personal charisma and deference to the cause of Wagnerism that completely won the old man over. Since the war Bayreuth had become more and more identified with *völkisch* politics; now in Hitler Wahnfried found a man dedicated to the destruction of the republic who openly connected his own mission to that of Wagnerism. During his last years the two central preoccupations of Chamberlain's existence—the future of Germany and of Bayreuth—became centered upon the fortunes of the Nazi *Führer*.

After marrying Eva and settling in Bayreuth, Chamberlain had assumed a range of family responsibilities. The prestige and cultural influence of the festival was at its peak when Cosima handed over the reins of power to her son in 1907. All Wagner's dramas had been performed on the festival stage; the family income was sufficient to meet its immediate needs; and the Wahnfried interpretation of the Master's ideas and artistic intent had triumphantly driven all others from the field. Yet, just beneath the surface, treacherous rocks and shoals threatened this outwardly buoyant vessel. The New York *Parsifal* performance of 1903, staged despite Cosima's bitter opposition, was a reminder of the tenuous hold Wahnfried had over the dramas—especially since all copyright controls were due to expire in 1913. Then, the inheritance struggle between Isolde and Cosima, culminating in a savage court battle, raised the ominous prospect of a division of the Wagner legacy should the matriarch—76 on the eve of the war—die or her son Siegfried remain unmarried or childless. And, since Siegfried was totally preoccupied with running the festival and lacked experience in what might be called the "politics of art," it was upon Chamberlain's shoulders that the larger problems of family business devolved.[58]

Thus, before the war, he and Eva—who remained Cosima's secretary—took charge of such matters as the publication of Wagner's autobiography, the seemingly endless task of building the Wagner archive, and the recruitment of new writers for the *Bayreuther Blätter*. Over Hans von Wolzogen Chamberlain exerted an especially strong influence and the *Blätter* became noticeably more *völkisch* and more in tune with the *Foundations* and his other major works. With the loss of Wahnfried's copyright controls imminent, the "inner circle" of Wagnerites was particularly anxious to demonstrate the importance of the *Festspiele* in the cultural and racial mission of the Reich: essays by such devotees as Friedrich Gross, Arthur Seidl, and Leopold von Schroeder were more devoutly phrased than ever, describing Bayreuth as an Aryan temple, a sacred place of pilgrimage for the race.[59] More practical were efforts, again choreographed by Chamberlain, Wolzogen, and Friedrich von Schoen, to obtain a special dispensation from the *Reichstag* for *Parsifal*; yet in 1912, just as in 1901, the request met with a refusal, despite a petition with over 18,000 signatures. Controversial since its inception the "Bayreuth Idea" had many enemies.

The other major issue which destroyed the peace of Wahnfried in these years was Isolde's claim for a share of the family inheritance. It was Chamberlain and Eva who were most incensed at the demand and led the opposition. Their vehemence in part reflected Eva's jealous pride in being Wagner's only recognized daughter; but it was also inspired by a bitter hatred for Franz Beidler—Isolde's husband—and a fear that their control over the festival would be seriously weakened if Isolde were successful, for she alone had produced a son. Indeed, while the courts were deciding the issue, Siegfried and the Chamberlains proposed a complete revision in the financial and administrative structure of the festival by establishing a *Richard Wagner Stiftung für das deutsche Volk*—a foundation that would control all the family possessions, including the festival house, its funds, Wahnfried, and the Wagner archives. While Michael Karbaum has suggested that this was a device for further increasing the Chamberlains' power, their motives appear to me to be less selfish. Not only did a foundation guarantee the transference of the Wagner inheritance and control of the festivals in the future, rather than leaving this to the vagaries of inheritance by birth (especially since Siegfried at 45 was still a bachelor) but it also nullified the arguments of those who opposed special state protection for Bayreuth on the ground that it would merely enrich the Wagner family. But the closing of the festival during the war, Cosima's victory over Isolde in 1915, and Siegfried's marriage led to a postponement and then a permanent shelving of the plan.[60]

The war years brought many changes in Bayreuth. The festival theater was closed; large numbers of ticket returns in the summer of 1914 due to the worsening international situation, burdened it with heavy losses; and inflation, which reached disastrous proportions after 1918, seriously reduced the festival funds carefully gathered in the last decade of peace. The *Blätter* continued its strongly racist and political emphasis with essays affirming the righteousness of Germany's struggle and demands from Wolzogen and Professor Paul Förster of Berlin that special attention be paid to the molding of a new postwar generation. Since there were no festival gatherings it was left to the *Blätter* to continue the links between Wagnerites in Central Europe and to argue the spiritual and intellectual relevance of "the Bayreuth Idea" for the victory and redemption of the Reich. But the audience for the journal was very small, and Bayreuth would have been almost forgotten in those years but for the staggering success of Chamberlain as a propagandist. He alone had a wide national and international reputation; he alone was constantly in the news. And as the chief link between Wagnerism and the political strivings of the right during the war, he not only helped weld Bayreuth and the *völkisch* movement more closely together, but also became the undisputed prophet of the Wahnfried circle, the figure around whom the new generation of Wagnerites congregated. In this respect the war acted as a catalyst continuing and strengthening the politicization of the Wagner cult—a trend which reached a culmination in its postwar identification with the Hitler movement.

Haus Wahnfried itself was much altered. Rising costs for fuel forced the family to close off most of its drafty rooms while outside the lawns were dug up and potatoes and cabbages replaced beds of flowers. The daily life and atmosphere of the mansion were also changed by the arrival in rapid succession of a new brood of Wagners—thus relieving the worries of all the older generation. For in 1914 one of the principal anxieties of Cosima and the Chamberlains was that Siegfried appeared much too content as a bachelor. Eva gave him explicit instructions as he prepared for a visit to Berlin: "*All* who love and admire you look anxiously into the future and cherish with us the deep wish that you will find the right woman. . . . so find your little kitten [*Katerlieschen*] and bring young life into our dear Wahnfried! . . . It is time!"[61] Ever obliging and dutiful, Siegfried began searching in earnest and in September 1915 married Winifred Williams, the adopted daughter of the pianist Karl Klindworth, a pupil of Liszt, and a longtime friend of Wahnfried. A lively young woman, only eighteen years old, Winifred must have found her new household awesome and oppressive. The family's insistence that Siegfried find a wife had never dispelled their doubts about there being anyone good enough for the honor. Thus his older sisters Eva and Daniela regarded the newcomer with a mixture of jealousy and suspicion: to them she was young and needed guidance and train-

ing. Cosima was much the same "requiring her to write daily
French exercises and dust the library for half an hour every
morning"—tasks she afterward carefully inspected.[62] All fears
about the succession, however, vanished as Winifred quickly
bore four children—Wieland, Friedelind, Wolfgang, and
Verena. Wahnfried became a house of two generations:
downstairs all was noise and youth; upstairs sat Cosima, a
skeletal figure, dressed in black, attended by her two
daughters, Eva and Daniela. On rare occasions she could be
seen, leaning heavily on Siegfried's arm as they walked in the
Hofgarten; sometimes she visited Chamberlain after he had
moved into the house across the road; but mostly she sat in her
room, surrounded by mementoes of her life and cut off from
the turbulence of the world outside.

Bayreuth experienced revolution more or less at second
hand in 1918-19—from newspaper reports, rumors, and eyewit-
nesses of events in Munich, Berlin, and the other centers of
major unrest. With only 30,000 inhabitants evenly divided
between factory workers, public officials, and white collar employees, there was no hard nucleus around which the extreme
left could organize. Food shortages, high prices, and unemployment caused by scarcities of raw materials resulted in minor
demonstrations, but that was all. The Workers, Peasants,
and Soldiers Council set up in November pursued a moderate,
conciliatory policy, cooperating closely with existing local authorities, and the town remained surprisingly uninfluenced by
radical developments in Munich.[63] Not that the local elite was
free from fear: Cosima, for example, was briefly very alarmed
that Wahnfried or the festival house might be targets of
wanton destruction; but no violence actually occurred. The
very peacefulness of Wahnfried and Bayreuth seemed, as if by
contrast, to magnify the horror that Chamberlain, Wolzogen,
and other members of the "inner circle" of Wagnerites felt at
the chaos engulfing the Reich. It was as if there were "two Ger-
manies," dramatically different but existing side by side: that
of the small towns, shaped by the German past, and that of
the large cities, violent, ruthless and nihilistic. The Wahnfried
habitués shared the mixture of disgust and alarm, of racial
hatred and religiosity that characterized Chamberlain's re-

sponse to early Weimar. Even Siegfried, often portrayed in later years as a moderate on the Jewish question, was prone to outbursts about the racial degeneracy of revolutionaries and the identicality of Bolshevism and Semitism.

Siegfried's energies were divided between his own compositions and the imposing task of resuming the *Festspiele*. Scarcities of necessary materials and of available rooms for guests in Bayreuth, coupled with higher wage rates and a rapid depletion of the festival funds through inflation, made the question of timing especially hazardous. Plagued by the belief that a premature and unsuccessful reopening would pile up such immense debts that the festival would be destroyed forever, he made extensive concert tours to raise money and went abroad to Scandinavia and, in 1924, to America (there, among others, he met Henry Ford whose public vendetta against Jewry aroused false expectations of a handsome donation). These tours brought in some revenue, but overall the results were disappointing, and the continuing spiral of inflation—at least until the end of 1923—made the task appear almost impossible. It was only in the summer of 1924, after some semblance of monetary stability had returned to the Reich, that the first post war festival took place, but even then its financial footing remained precarious and within five years it was again hard hit by economic collapse and nationwide depression.

When Chamberlain first heard Hermann Levi conduct the *Ring* at Munich in 1878, the very words Wagner and Bayreuth connoted artistic modernism, "the artwork of the future." Wagnerites overlapped the avant garde in all the arts, and a young devotee like Chamberlain—a founder of *Revue Wagnérienne*, admirer and friend of the Symbolists—considered himself emphatically "modern." Yet over the next three decades, as Wagnerian music gradually became more widely accepted, a conservative atmosphere descended over Bayreuth. And while Chamberlain might appreciate Adolphe Appia's startlingly new ideas for staging Wagner's music, or the psychological dramas of Ibsen and Strindberg, Cosima firmly resisted all new artistic experimentation; in fact there was little that she appreciated in any of the arts after 1885. After the war such resistance to the new in art became a central part of

Bayreuth's national mission; indeed, its outright rejection of the incredible wave of aesthetic experimentation that marked Weimar was the reverse side of its boast to be the shrine and mecca of the *völkisch* movement. Like everything else in these years, art was thoroughly politicized. In the eyes of the political right the abstractions of Klee and Kandinsky, the atonal "Jewish music" of Schoenberg and his disciples, as much as the irreverent antics of Dada or the proletarian theater of Piscator, were symptoms of the chaos and decadence that had overtaken Germany. Bayreuth—as Chamberlain, the composer Hans Pfitzner, and others never tired of explaining—was the antithesis of this *"blutleere Afterkunst"* of Weimar;[64] it was the home of German religious art, a link to the sacred heritage of Goethe, Schiller, and Beethoven, and the epitome of those national and racial values which alone could regenerate the Reich.

Most supporters of Bayreuth agreed in thinking that the future of the festival could only be assured if the mission of Wagnerism and the task of reviving the beleaguered spirit of nationalist Germany were widely recognized to be identical. In their efforts to achieve lasting financial stability for their cultural bailiwick the Wagners had always cultivated the rich and the powerful. Thus, aside from his patron Ludwig II of Bavaria, Richard Wagner requested help from Bismarck and wrote the tasteless *Kaisermarsch* of 1870 in the hope of procuring public funds or protection from the Hohenzollerns. Later Cosima endeavored to win over Wilhelm II and attempted to secure special concessions from the *Reichstag*. In fact, Bayreuth always used two strategies: that of winning direct protection from the Crown or the law-making body, and the more populist course of building a constituency among the wealthy German middle classes. After 1918 the situation was transformed. Protection from the Wittelsbachs was abruptly removed by revolution while the creation of a liberal republican Germany dashed any hopes of government subventions. Everything depended upon the sympathies of German *Bürgertum*, many of whose finances were badly diminished by more than a decade of high inflation. The rescue of Bayreuth, or so it seemed to Chamberlain, was linked to the material and spiritual recovery of the German bourgeoisie, and ultimately to the replacement of Weimar by a *völkisch* nationalist state that would protect its sacred cultural inheritance. The nearest it came to achieving this goal was in the years after 1933 when Wahnfried received funds directly from Hitler and the festivals became almost state occasions, part of the elaborate ritual of the Nazi regime.[65]

Thus, with its characteristic blend of pragmatism and passion, the Bayreuth *Kreis* in the 1920s set about the task of forging closer links with the broad movement of *völkisch* politics. As we have seen, strong ideological and personal ties already existed: Hans von Wolzogen, for example, had long-standing contacts in anti-Semitic circles and Ludwig Schemann, as founder of the *Gobineau Vereinigung*, was in touch with a broad range of prominent politicians and thinkers of the German right. But it was Chamberlain above all who in his writings had joined the Bayreuth cult to the mainstream of the Germanic ideology, and his wartime success as a propagandist had strengthened and expanded both his fame and his personal contacts. His correspondents spanned the whole of the Weimar opposition from Tirpitz to demagogues like Dinter and Theodor Fritsch; his endorsement was eagerly sought after for cultural associations like the Fichte Society and for new racial and political publications; and postwar racial Christian sects, nationalist youth organizations, and counterrevolutionary groups usually numbered him among their spiritual and intellectual forebears. No longer capable of writing large numbers of essays himself, Chamberlain encouraged a new generation of Bayreuthians to do so: among the most prolific were Wolfgang Golther, Paul Bülow, Karl Ganzer, Karl Grunsky, Erich Schwebsch, Richard Du Moulin Eckart, Otto Daube, Georg Schott, and Paul Pretzsch. Together they launched a cultural offensive designed to convince Germans of the truth of Siegfried Wagner's national appeal in 1921: "Whoever loves Germany and wants to do something for its health and its future as a *Kulturvolk* must come to Bayreuth's assistance."[66] "Here," declared a typical article, "lie the roots of a new *Weltanschauung*, free of Jewish spiritual domination, which can guide the Volk—through a religious concept that cor-

responds to its very being—to economic and political autonomy."[67] Bayreuth, they argued, was "the flagship of the
German spirit."[68]

For the most part, the new generation of publicists were
mere epigoni, adapting the well-honed themes of Wagnerism to
the mood and circumstances of post 1918 Europe, and their
essays were largely undistinguished and derivative of earlier
writers like Chamberlain, Wolzogen, Thode, and Leopold von
Schroeder. In one area, however, a distinctly new beginning was
made with the founding of the *Bayreuther Bund für deutsche
Jugend* in August 1925 for those of 15 years and over. A special
women's division of the Wagner Association had long existed,
but this was the first effort to engage youth for the cause—an
outgrowth of proposals made in the *Blätter* during the war and
symptomatic of *völkisch* claims to represent the German future.[69] Under the leadership of Otto Daube, a young and energetic music teacher from Leipzig, the *Bund* expanded rapidly
and by the summer of 1927 boasted 50 local branches, a
monthly journal, and a long calendar of meetings, lectures, and
other activities.[70] With the inner Wahnfried *Kreis* very sympathetic to the *Bund*, it quickly became a major part of the cult,
and one which soon developed links with various elements of the
Bündische Jugend. Thus, in July 1926, together with the *Adolf
Bartels Bund*, another cultural youth group with a pronounced
anti-Semitic outlook, Daube organized a German Festival in
Weimar. Works by Wolzogen, Friedrich Lienhard, Siegfried
Wagner, and Wilhelm Kotzde, the leader of the *Adler und
Falken* youth group, were read or performed. Such authors,
argued Daube, epitomized German art, in contrast to the mass-
produced radio culture of the moderns; "a powerful
counterforce to the aesthetic demoralization of our day," as
Albert von Puttkamer called them. A second festival followed in
1929, and there were additional gatherings at the *Festspiele* in
Bayreuth.[71] It was all part of a drive to awaken Germans to
another Weimar (that of Goethe, Schiller, and Nietzsche as
seen by the *völkisch* right) antithetical to the values and taste of
the Republic which had appropriated the name. From its outset
the *Bayreuther Bund* was welcomed by the Nazis as a friendly
organization and later on it became a corporate member of the

party's youth movement. Chamberlain, like other members of the Wagner family, was an honorary member of its governing board.

The growing ties between Bayreuth and *völkisch* politics also opened up the complicated issue of whether Jews should participate as artists and visitors in the *Festspiele*. August Püringer, a vehement anti-Semite, suggested that they be excluded altogether. The language of Siegfried Wagner's reply in 1921, as quoted by his daughter Friedelind, was strongly critical.[72] "Among the Jews," he wrote, "we count a great many loyal, honest, and unselfish adherents who have given us numerous proofs of their devotion." To exclude such people would not be humane, Christian, or German; nobody should be banned "just because he is a Jew," he added, recalling the names of Davidsohn, Tausig, Porges, Rubinstein, and Levi. Foreigners, too, had played an important role in the Bayreuth story, at times when the German bourgeoisie were largely indifferent to Wagner. "On our Bayreuth hill we want to do positive work not negative. Whether a man is a Chinese, a Negro, an American, an Indian, or a Jew, that is a matter of complete indifference to us." "It is we," Siegfried concluded, "who must bear the blame for the hopeless state of affairs in our Fatherland because we have no national pride, because we leave our men in the lurch." Indeed, Germans might well "learn from the Jews how to stick together and how to give help. . . . I see how the Jews assist their artists. . . . If I were a Jew my operas would be performed in every theater. As things are, however, we must wait till we are dead."

Interpreting this letter is not easy: the sentiments are clear but in view of the rest of Wahnfried's activities the message rings false. Questions of color and ethnicity were not a matter of indifference at Bayreuth; and although Jews and foreigners had always participated in the cult, their special position and their inferior status to Germans was seldom allowed to be forgotten. Also, on other occasions, Siegfried had protested loudly against Jewish influence in the Reich and had courted the leading anti-Semites of the day. The emotional center of the letter would appear to be his angry reminder that Germans were responsible for the neglect of their culture, coupled with a conviction that any assistance should be accepted in this year of Bayreuth's national appeal for funds. Any ban, such as that suggested by Püringer, would undoubtedly seriously injure the fund drive, and one can imagine the problems of defining who was a Jew and implementing an exclusionary policy. Cosima's policy, it will be recalled, had also been to accept help wherever it came from, and Chamberlain too made special exceptions for Jews like Hermann Levi or Friedrich Gross. Siegfried, like many contemporaries, detested "Jewishness" in the abstract, but often responded sympathetically to individual Jews. Yet this did not make him any the less an admirer of Hitler after 1923 nor, after the ravages of inflation in that year, any the less bitter about Jewry. His Christmas greetings to Nora Eidam, an old friend of the family, show quite another side of his personality: "The times of the Spanish Inquisition," he wrote, "have returned. Perjury and treachery are spoken of highly and Jew and Jesuit proceed arm in arm to eradicate *Deutschtum*. But perhaps Satan has miscalculated this time!"[73] Siegfried's views, we may conclude, were changeable: he preferred to stress the positive aspects of Germanness rather than negative hatred of the Jew, but such hatred was an inescapable, integral part of the Bayreuth Idea. The views of Chamberlain and other members of the "inner circle" on the issue of Jewish participation in 1921 have not survived, but it would seem that they too were not ready for any Aryan paragraph—both because they cherished exceptions and because the festival would almost certainly suffer as a result.

Just as Bayreuth solicited closer ties with the right, so *völkisch* political leaders welcomed these contacts, for association with Wagnerism enhanced their social and intellectual respectability and coupled their strivings with the legacy of German music. And for all his revolutionary rhetoric and abrasive anti-bourgeois style, no one wanted acceptance at Bayreuth more than Hitler. Since his adolescence in Vienna he had been a Wagner enthusiast; he talked incessantly about the composer and regarded the dramas as the highest expression of the German soul.[74] Entry into Wahnfried was for him like walking on holy ground; it also meant a special kind of social acceptance that relieved his painful sense of being an outsider in bourgeiois society. On his frequent visits both before and after 1933, he even seemed to find amid the Wagner children a semblance of family life otherwise lacking in his exclusively political existence. As for Wahnfried, its members soon nourished extravagant hopes for their tribune-of-the-people and predicted a better future for Bayreuth as a consequence. Their relationship was always a two way street.

The Nazi movement made steady progress in the region of Franconia, and Bayreuth had an active *Ortsgruppe* from November 1922. Among its most energetic members were Hans Schemm, an elementary school teacher who later became Bavarian Kultusminister, and Christian Ebersberger, a businessman well known to the Wagner and Chamberlain families. Wahnfried, however, played little part in these local party activities during the first year, although—as Winifred Wagner remembered—news of Hitler's remarkable skill as a speaker and organizer reached the Wagner household as early as 1920 through visitors from Munich like Josef Stolzing-Cerny and Michael Georg Conrad (the German champion of Naturalism and an old acquaintance of the Bayreuth "inner circle"). In addition, as we have seen, Chamberlain had several of his own sources of information.[75] But it was not until October 1923 that Hitler entered Wahnfried and the relationship between him and the Wagners began.

The succession of crises that convulsed Germany in 1923 is familiar and requires no detailed recounting. The French invasion of the Ruhr in January to compel reparations payments produced passive resistance against the aggressors and this in turn triggered a sequence of events that brought the republic to the verge of political and economic disintegration. The Reich's currency and financial structure collapsed, resulting in a catastrophic inflation that wiped out the savings of millions of Germans; large-scale strike movements broke out in several areas; separatist agitation intensified in Bavaria; and plans for anti-republican coups were hastily drawn up by the *Freikorps* and the extreme right. By July 1923 the central government had no effective control over the country. In Bavaria, as prices and unemployment rose sharply, pressure upon the Kahr

Hitler in Bayreuth, September 30, 1923. Hitler is without his hat. Julius Streicher is diagonally in front of him.
Courtesy of Mr. Bernd Mayer, Bayreuth.

government increased and the numerous racist and para-military groups openly called for a march through the neigh-boring left-wing-controlled states of Thuringia and Saxony and on to Berlin. Impatient and anxious lest the opportunity slip from his grasp, Hitler directed all his energies toward uniting the Bavarian right and forcing the Kahr government to give the signal for decisive action.[76]

As part of the Nazi party's feverish propaganda activity in these months, Hitler came to Bayreuth on September 30 to ad-dress a German Day rally. After reviewing the local sections of the S.A. and its *Freikorps* allies, *Oberland* and *Wiking*, he gave a speech at the Reithalle. Some hours later he sent a message via Christian Ebersberger asking to see Chamberlain; they met briefly the same evening and, on the following morn-ing, Hitler was invited to visit Wahnfried. He came, Winifred Wagner commented, "as a respectful admirer of the German genius Richard Wagner, not as a political agitator." He was shown over the house, stood in silence before the Master's

Deutscher Tag in Bayreuth.

Programm:

Samstag, 29. September 1923.

Ab 1 Uhr nachmittags: Empfang der auswärtigen Gäste am Bahnhof.
Ausgabe der Festabzeichen, Zuteilung der Unterkünfte etc.

Ab 8 Uhr abends: Begrüßungsabend unter Mitwirkung verschiedener Musikkapellen.
Ansprachen von Führern der nationalen Bewegung und zwar
für die National-Sozialistische Deutsche Arbeiter-Partei,
Oberland, Reichsflagge im Sonnensaal;
„ Bund Bayern und Reich: . . . Bürgerressource, Reichsadler;
„ Bund Blücher, Wicking, Jungdeutscher
Orden, Sturmtrupp Frankenland: Frohsinn;
„ alle übrigen Verbände: . . . . Harmonie und Schloßdiele.

Sonntag, 30. September 1923.

6³⁰ Uhr: Wecken.

9⁴⁵ Uhr: Abholen der Fahnen.

11 Uhr: Feldgottesdienst auf dem Exerzierplatz (Leopoldshöhe)
1. Fanfarenruf
2. Militärgebet
3. Ansprache des Pfarrers
4. Weihe der Fahne
5. Niederländisches Dankgebet.
Hierauf geschlossener Abmarsch der Verbände in ihre Standquartiere.

1³⁰ Uhr: Sammeln zum Festzug (Ort wird den Führern noch bekannt gegeben).

2³⁰ Uhr: Festzug durch die Stadt

Straßenfolge: Aufmarsch in der Lisztstraße, durch Wahnfriedstraße, Richard Wagnerstraße,
Opernstraße, Bahnhofstraße, Bürgerreutherstraße, Wilhelmstraße, Wilhelms-
platz, Schulstraße, Maxstraße (hier Gegenzug); kurz vor der Spitalkirche:
Stehen des Zuges und kurzer Gedenkakt für die Gefallenen
des Weltkrieges unter dem Geläute der Glocken. (Teilnehmer in
Zivil nehmen Hut ab, Führer Hand an der Mütze) / / / Zug geht dann weiter durch:
Sophienstraße, Friedrichstraße, Dammallee, Leopoldstraße, Kasernstraße,
Heldstraße, Jean Paulplatz, Ludwigstraße.
Der Vorbeimarsch erfolgt am neuen Schloßplatz vor unseren Führern und Ehrengästen.
Auflösen des Zuges und geschlossener Abmarsch der Verbände in ihre Standquartiere (Säle)
vom Kutscherplatz.

Ab 4 Uhr: Vorträge in sämtlichen Sälen, sowie in der Markgrafenreithalle von
den bedeutendsten Führern der nationalen Bewegung.

Ab 8 Uhr: Zusammenkunft in den bekannten Sälen.

Von den Rednern haben ihr Erscheinen fest zugesagt: Herr Adolf Hitler, Herr Weber, Herr Esser,
Herr Dr. Kloß, Herr Gesselmann, Herr Dr. Herold, Herr Jonson, Herr Streicher u. a.

A German Day Program, 1923.
Courtesy of Bernd Mayer, Bayreuth.

grave, and held further discussions with Chamberlain, but did not, it seems, meet Cosima.[77]

The visit was a huge success. Hitler's genuine reverence for Wagner and regard for Chamberlain, his emotional promise to restore to Bayreuth full rights over *Parsifal*, and his burning conviction that the National Socialist movement would eventually rule Germany, all made a strong impression on the Wagner family. So enthusiastic was Chamberlain that a week later he made a public declaration of faith in the Nazi leader. It is remarkable not only for its contents, but also because Chamberlain had never before aligned himself so wholeheartedly with any political figure:

> Most respected and dear Herr Hitler:
>
> You have every right to be surprised at this intrusion having seen with your own eyes how difficult it is for me to speak. But I cannot resist the urge to address a few words to you. I view this, however, as an entirely one-sided act, i.e. I do not expect an answer from you.
>
> I have been wondering why it was you of all people—you who are so extraordinary in awakening people from sleep and humdrum routines—who recently gave me a longer and more refreshing sleep than I have experienced since that fateful day in August 1914 when I was first struck down by this insidious sickness. Now I believe I understand that it is precisely this that characterizes and defines your being: the true awakener is at the same time the bestower of peace.
>
> You are not at all, as you have been described to me, a fanatic; in fact, I would call you the complete opposite of a fanatic. The fanatic inflames the mind, you warm the heart. The fanatic wants to overwhelm people with words, you wish to convince, only to convince them—and that is why you are successful. Indeed, I would also describe you as the opposite of a politician—in the commonly accepted sense of the word that is—for the essence of all politics is membership of a party, whereas with you all parties disappear, consumed by the heat of your love for the fatherland. It was, I think, the misfortune of our great Bismarck that he became, as fate would have it (by no means through innate predisposition), a little too involved in politics. May you be spared this fate.
>
> You have immense achievements ahead of you, but for all your strength of will I do not regard you as a violent man. You

know Goethe's distinction between force and force. There is the force that stems from and in turn leads to chaos, and there is the force which shapes the universe. . . . It is this creative sense that I mean when I number you among the constructive men rather than those who are violent.

I constantly ask myself whether the poverty of political instinct for which Germans are so often blamed may not be symptomatic of a much deeper talent for state-building. In any case the German's organizational skills are unsurpassed (viz. Kiaochow!) and his scientific capacity is unequalled—in the essay *Politische Ideale* I pinned my hopes on this. The ideal kind of politics is to have *none*. But this non-politics must be frankly acknowledged and forced upon the world through the exercise of power. Nothing will be achieved so long as the parliamentary system dominates; for this the Germans have, God knows, not a spark of talent! I consider its prevalence to be the greatest misfortune; it can only drag us continually into the mire and ruin every plan for a healthy and revitalized fatherland.

But I am digressing, for I wanted only to speak of you. That you brought me peace is related very much to your eyes and hand gestures. Your eye works almost as a hand: it grips and holds a person; and you have the singular quality of being able to focus your words on one particular listener at any given moment. As for your hands, they are so expressive in their movement that they rival your eyes. Such a man brings rest to a poor suffering spirit!

Especially when he is dedicated to the service of the fatherland.

My faith in Germandom has never wavered for a moment, though my hopes had, I confess, reached a low ebb. At one blow you have transformed the state of my soul. That Germany in its hour of greatest need has given birth to a Hitler is proof of vitality; your actions offer further evidence, for a man's personality and actions belong together. That the magnificent Ludendorff openly supports you and embraces your movement: what a wonderful combination!

I was able to sleep without a care; nothing caused me to awaken again. May God protect you![78]

In January 1923, when the French army marched into the Ruhr, Chamberlain had predicted that if Germans worked for a "conscious shaping statecraft, organized on scientific principles" the Reich would "in a few years succeed in ruling the whole world morally, intellectually and thereby in every other decisive aspect."[79] Now in Hitler he saw the savior of Germany in her "hour of greatest need." Ludendorff is clearly relegated to the role of a supporter of the movement. When the Munich *putsch* occurred a month later, there was no doubt in Wahnfried about who was its true leader. Always a hero-worshipper, in his last years Chamberlain had discovered a new idol. Nazi ideology seemed in many respects close to his own *Politische Ideale*, while in Hitler himself he saw the prospect of strong, race-conscious leadership which would firmly control the popular masses and forge a new national order.

With this letter Chamberlain became the first person of national and even international reputation as a writer to align himself with the Nazi movement; it brought elation at party headquarters in Munich. In Stolzing-Cerny's words, Hitler rejoiced "like a child;" "Herr Hitler," he added in a letter to Eva Chamberlain, "continually enthuses about Bayreuth and not least about the Wagner family and its charming children. We hope that our movement gains its objectives quickly, for then also Bayreuth will become what your great father wished."[80] At that moment Hitler was facing one of the most difficult decisions of his career: Chamberlain's faith in his historic destiny came, in the words of Joachim Fest, "as the answer to his doubts, as a benediction from the Bayreuth Master himself."[81]

Hitler and his inner circle of advisers had been planning a coup ever since May of 1923; how well their plans were formulated in early October and whether any mention had been made of them to Chamberlain will never be known. Whatever the case, the unsuccessful Beer Hall Putsch of November 9, far from dampening Wahnfried's enthusiasm for Nazism, confirmed and strengthened it. As it happened, Siegfried and Winifred Wagner were in Munich for a Wagner concert at the Odeon Theater and after witnessing the police fusillade outside the Feldherrnhalle and the rout of Hitler's followers, they brought the news back to Bayreuth. In name at least Chamberlain was also present, for the front page of the *Völkischer Beobachter* on that day carried a brief article of his along with news of the events of the Beer Hall the previous night. Entitled "God Wills It!" Chamberlain's essay is an appeal for action:

> Breathless we stand and await the coming events; for everyone feels with a greater or lesser degree of certainty that we have reached a turning-point in world history. . . . we conclude that not merely human but divine forces are at work. The existence of *Deutschtum* and of Germanic thought is at stake in this action.

It ended with another obvious reference to Hitler:

> Admittedly we now painfully miss three million of the best Germans in our struggle against "the other Germany"; yet in between a new generation is growing up that promises to be worthy of its fathers. If they find a man whose heart beats in harmony with theirs—a born leader—then I shall not be anxious about Germany's future. And is it not whispered everywhere that the man has appeared and waits among us for this hour?

The failure of the *putsch*, followed by Hitler's capture and imprisonment on November 11 was viewed at Wahnfried as a tragedy; but nobody in the house believed it to be the end of the *Führer's* career. "We are deeply affected by this tragic fate," Chamberlain told his friend, August Ludowici, "Jew and Jesuit can now triumph again!"[83] Siegfried Wagner used almost identical words in a Christmas letter to Rosa Eidam, adding: "Should the German cause really succumb, then I will believe in Jehovah the God of revenge and of hate. My wife struggles like a lioness for Hitler!"[84] What had seemed to some observers bad comic-opera, took on epic qualities in the eyes of the Wagners. Winifred, in particular, once very much in the background, now emerged as a political activist. After speaking before the local Nazi group she published a particularly effusive declaration of support for Hitler, "this German man . . . who has taken upon himself the dangerous task of getting the working class to open their eyes to the inner enemy and to Marxism and its consequences." "I frankly admit," she wrote, referring to the whole Wahnfried household, "that *we* too stand under the spell of this personality, and that we too, who stood with him in days of fortune, now hold true to him in his days of need."[85] Over the next months, together with Eva and Daniela Thode, she helped collect food, money, and clothing for the families of convicted Nazis and helped gather some 10,000 signatures on a petition to the state government for Hitler's release.

Chamberlain was also eager to reaffirm publicly his faith in the Nazis. He followed developments in the party closely and carefully studied a small volume of Hitler's speeches that appeared at the end of 1923.[86] On Christmas Eve, he published a brief essay, "The Touchstone," in the Pan–German *Deutsche Zeitung* which proclaimed that the litmus test of a true *völkisch* movement was "its choice of a leader." Rarely were true leaders drawn from the ranks of professional parliamentarians—"mostly it is some complete outsider, about whom nobody knows a thing; a man who arises out of the movement he calls forth." What Germany needed, he insisted, was not party resolutions and ministerial ordinances but a "roaring hurricane."[87] Then, on New Years Day 1924, he wrote his most adulatory letter yet, recording for a friend his impressions of Hitler; it was published some three months later to celebrate the *Führer's* birthday.[88] Forgotten in later years, it neatly illustrates the growing cult of Hitler, his transformation into a figure of mythic stature and even an instrument of the Divine. The *Führer*, he claimed, was one of those "rare beautiful beings [*Lichtgestalten*] . . . a true *Volksmensch*," a man of genuine simplicity, with a "fascinating gaze," whose words "always come directly from the heart":

> One can distinguish two classes of significant men, according to whether their head or heart dominates. I would definitely categorize Hitler as a man of the heart not because I rate his intellectual capacities low—on the contrary—but because the central organ, the source that kindles his passion and forges his thoughts is the heart. This distinguishes him from most politicians; he loves the Volk, he loves his German people with a burning passion. Here we have the core of his politics, his economic theories, his enmity toward the Jews, his battle against the corruption of values and so on.

Hitler, argued Chamberlain, had nothing in common with the

run of opportunist politicians—the word "opportunist," he
noted, was introduced by the "Jew Gambetta." Whereas
others built self-serving *Reichstag* coalitions he had embarked
on a "war of destruction" (*Vernichtungskrieg*) against Germany's enemies. The prime characteristic of Weimar politics
was obfuscation, intentional vagueness designed to bamboozle
the nation; but the essence of Hitler's personality and politics
was candor and directness; he was "a great simplifier" (*Verein-
facher*) who cut through the web of disingenuous phrases spun
by others, said what he meant, and said it with a power, logic,
consistency, and seriousness that won people "by storm." He
could be understood by the simplest of men, and that was the
secret of his "unprecedented effectiveness" among the "alienated workers." He alone was able "to convert them in bands to
healthier views," destroying the power of Marxism and building
another force in its stead.

Nor did Chamberlain recoil at the viciousness of Hitler's
anti-Semitism. In a startling passage he announced his
agreement with the Nazis and confessed that what drew him to
Hitler was the faith that his angry speeches were blueprints for
future action:

> Because . . . [Hitler] is no mere phrasemonger but consistently
> pursues his thoughts to an end and draws his conclusions from
> it, he recognizes and proclaims that one cannot simultaneously
> embrace Jesus and those that crucified him. That is the
> splendid thing about Hitler—his courage! . . . In this respect he
> reminds one of Luther. And whence comes the courage of these
> two men? It derives from the holy seriousness each has for his
> cause. Hitler utters no word he does not mean in earnest; his
> speeches contain no padding or vague, provisional statements .
> . . but the result of this is that he is decried as a visionary
> dreamer [*Phantast*]. People consider Hitler a dreamer whose
> head is full of impossible schemes and yet a renowned and
> original historian called him "the most creative mind since Bis-
> marck in the area of statecraft." I believe . . . we are all in-
> clined to view those things as impracticable that we do not al-
> ready see accomplished before us. He, for example, finds it im-
> possible to share our conviction about the pernicious, even mur-
> derous influence of Jewry on the German Volk and not to take
> action; if one sees the danger, then steps must be taken against

it with the utmost dispatch. I daresay everyone recognizes this, but nobody risks speaking out; nobody ventures to extract the consequences of his thoughts for his actions; nobody except Hitler. . . . This man has worked like a divine blessing cheering hearts, opening men's eyes to clearly seen goals, enlivening their spirits, kindling their capacity for love and for indignation, hardening their courage and resoluteness. Yet we still need him badly: May God who sent him to us preserve him for many years as a "blessing for the German fatherland." [89]

The tenor of Chamberlain's description, his air of religious exaltation, and his determination to see in Hitler a messianic figure, closely resembles the responses of others who hurled themselves into the Nazi movement around this time. For Chamberlain Nazism was a crusade, a redemptive force such as he had yearned for in his wartime propaganda and even earlier; it was Wagnerism in politics with Ludendorff as a "Siegfried personality" "of childlike guilelessness" and Hitler a Parsifal who alone could recover the Holy Grail and heal the nation's wounds. [90]

The remainder of Chamberlain's life is uneventful. He had made his political choice and never wavered from it. Indeed Hitler's defiance of the Munich court, transforming ignominious defeat into a national propaganda victory, strengthened Chamberlain's faith in the Nazi leader. "Today more than ever," he congratulated Hitler, "we feel and cherish a love for you, trust in the purity of your being and have faith in the conquering power of your cause." [91] Ludendorff, who was acquitted of all charges, visited Chamberlain shortly afterward in Bayreuth while trying to gather votes for the völkisch block formed to fight the Reichstag elections of 1924. Hitler also wrote to him from the Landsberg jail, but these letters disappeared shortly after the end of World War II. [92]

From several friends and correspondents Chamberlain received reports of the tensions and cleavages within the party during Hitler's imprisonment—some complained of Streicher and Esser, others of Rosenberg or of the growing contempt within Nazi ranks for older leaders of the right like Ehrhardt and Ludendorff. Chamberlain was dismayed by the factional squabbling, but offered no substantive opinions about it. "When a man stands," he told his architect friend, Ludwig von Hofmann, "with one foot in the next world, he sees many things in a new light. . . . I wish I could put several of the leaders of the *völkisch* movement in my place for a day. Their eyes would be opened. On the central issue—the sacred issue—we are all united; why haggle over lesser things? The old, petty failing of the Germans could bring a man to despair in this hour when unity is more necessary than ever." [93] Dinter, who rose rapidly in the party, becoming *Gauleiter* of the key state of Thuringia, soon began to make enemies by his personal crusade for a "positive" or racial Christianity and his bitter denunciations of Catholicism. Thus, on Chamberlain's seventieth birthday in 1925, while the Nazis and the nationalist press published long eulogies, Dinter gave his encomiums a special twist by warning that the *völkisch* movement was in danger of coming adrift from its spiritual moorings. Eager to avoid the potentially divisive issue of religion, Hitler moved cautiously to oust Dinter from his position of leadership in the Gau, and in 1927 replaced him with Fritz Sauckel. [94] Chamberlain left no comment on these tensions; probably he was too sick to pay much attention. But it is very possible that had he lived he too would have been disappointed by the growing organizational emphasis of party efforts and the downplaying of religious issues which might hamper its electoral ambitions.

Bayreuth's close identification with the far right was made especially clear when the *Festspiele* finally reopened in the summer of 1924. Nationalist colors flew on the *Festspielhügel*, nationalist *Verbände* held parades, and Ludendorff and Dr. Rudolf Buttmann, one of the leaders of the *völkisch* wing of the German Nationalists, made political speeches. At the end of *Meistersinger* the audience sang "Deutschland, Deutschland über alles" and petitions circulated urging the Bavarian government to order Hitler's release (10,000 signatures were collected in Bayreuth alone). Not long before the festival, Hitler had written to Siegfried Wagner expressing his deep regrets at not being able to attend; his hope, he admitted, had been to come to Bayreuth in triumph (it lay "on a direct line of march to Berlin") as "the first witness and herald" of the coming German rebirth. This, he added, would have been the best medicine possible for Chamberlain's rapidly declining health.[95] But Hitler's ambition to visit the festival was realized the following year, and after 1933 he came regularly and provided funds for the performances at critical movements. Gradually the festival changed: Siegfried and Cosima died in 1930, Winifred took over its direction, and a new era began.[96] The pre-war cosmopolitan atmosphere was not reestablished: audiences remained almost exclusively German and Nazi dignitaries were everywhere in evidence. This "nationalization" of Bayreuth went even further after the outbreak of war in 1939: in addition to party officials, convalescent soldiers, invalids, munitions workers, and nurses filled performances, brought there through the beneficence of the state. *Parsifal* was dropped from the Bayreuth repertoire, a casualty of the growing Nazi campaign against the churches and religion; ironically on his first visit in 1923, after seeing the Master's grave, Hitler had told the Wagners in an emotional outburst: "Out of *Parsifal* I will make a religion."[97] The last wartime festivals were little more than state rites—the final two, in 1943 and 1944, featured one work only, *Die Meistersinger*, now universally regarded as a Nazi hymn. The *Führer* himself was too busy to attend after 1941.

Chamberlain never saw any of this. After a long and painful illness he died on January 9, 1927 in his seventy-second year. The funeral service was attended by members of the Wagner family (with the exception of Cosima), friends like Dinter, civic leaders of Bayreuth, local Nazis, and representatives of the Pan-German League and *Bund Wiking*. Hitler attended in person for the National Socialists and Prince August Wilhelm came on behalf of the Hohenzollerns.[98] Chamberlain was eulogized as a prophet who had devoted his life to Wagnerism and Germany, and whose writings contained the vision of a new "glorious and light-filled future" for the German Reich. Just a few months before his death, he had been visited by Hitler for the last time. The staccato prose of

Goebbels' diary recorded the meeting:

> Shattering scene: Chamberlain on a couch. Broken, mumbling
> with tears in his eyes. He holds my hand and will not let it go.
> His big eyes burn like fire. Greetings to you spiritual father.
> Trail-blazer, pioneer! I am deeply upset. Leave-taking, he
> mumbles, wants to speak, can't—and then weeps like a child!
> Farewell! You stand by us when we are near despair. Outside
> the rain drums on the pavement! I want to cry out, to weep. [99]

These sentences indicate why Chamberlain occupied such a
special place in the Nazi pantheon in later years. In 1926 the
party's fortunes were at their lowest point; it had made a poor
showing in state elections; Hitler was banned from speaking in
much of the Reich and future prospects for the radical right
seemed unencouraging. After the chaos of 1923, the Republic
had achieved a degree of stability and public support in the
era of Stresemann and Locarno. Hitler's genuine and lasting
affection for Chamberlain and Wahnfried was due in no small
measure to their continued faith and confidence in this difficult period. The obituary in the *Völkischer Beobachter* called
Chamberlain "one of the blacksmiths whose weapons have not
yet found in our day their fullest use," and later in the year Alfred Rosenberg published a brief study praising him as "the
pioneer and founder of a German future." [100] Well before its attainment of power National Socialism had begun to make
Chamberlain its own special prophet and herald.

Chamberlain and Eva shortly before his death

Epilogue

CHAMBERLAIN NEVER LIVED to see the Third Reich, but his name is forever associated with it. Few "precursors" acknowledged by the Nazis attained an equal status in the annals of the regime. This self-appointed prophet of Germanism became the subject of a vast array of speeches, articles, radio programs and school lessons. Many of his writings were reissued or anthologized, the dates of his birth and death were marked by solemn tributes in the party press, and a steady flow of doctoral dissertations proclaimed his significance for the creation of a new order in Germany.[1] "Chamberlain's world view," wrote one observer in 1936, "has become today the cornerstone of a new era. What he thought about the great epochal questions of human history . . . has today become the basic property of a great stream of culture."[2] After the defeat of the Third Reich he continued to be regarded as one of the leading Nazi doctrinaires and in the ever-expanding literature on Hitler routinely gains a mention as one of the tribe of pseudo-intellectuals and crackpots from whose works the *Führer* pieced together his own Germanic vision. Probably the most common image of Chamberlain today is that of a sick and broken man, clutching at Hitler's hand in October 1923, magnetized by the young politician's personal charisma.

But for all this it is exceedingly difficult with Chamberlain, as with other so-called ideological mentors of Nazism, to define his influence with any precision. The evidence is ambiguous and it is rarely possible to separate his impact from that of other cultural critics, journalists, and popularizers of similar views who together played a major role in molding the consciousness and self-image of Germans. An examination of Nazi writings about him reveals that they fall into two broad categories. The first and by far the largest comprises the straightforward hagiographic literature designed to give Chamberlain a prominent niche in the Nazi gallery of ancestors, to place him alongside Fichte, Jahn, Lagarde, Nietzsche, and many others in one Germanic tradition of which National Socialism was said to be the legitimate spiritual descendant.[3] Repetitive, platitudinous, and unanalytical, these writings invariably have the same format—a brief summary of his life, large doses of praise for his campaign against racial decadence, a few comparisons with Nietzsche and other heroes, and a conclusion describing how Chamberlain had in the earliest years hailed Hitler as the Savior of the Reich. Another variant of this genre were articles devoted more specifically to his connections with Bayreuth and the importance of Wagnerism for the new Germany.[4] The second category of writings consists of somewhat more detailed and analytical accounts of aspects of Chamberlain's thought. Dissertations appeared about his "life doctrine" and the need for a Nazi methodology in science; there were attempts to ferret out a theory of history underlying the *Foundations*, and discussions of his interpretation of Indo-Aryan texts, Kant, and Goethe.[5] Most numerous of all were commentaries upon his religious ideas, primarily concerned to show the compatability of race and Christian doctrine, and to argue that Germanic Christianity was a necessary and integral part of a Nazi Revolution.[6] Taken together Chamberlain's works constituted the most sustained and ambitious attempt before 1933 to formulate a Germanic world view. His sweeping intellect moved easily across the fields of science, religion, philosophy, history, and the arts; and his writings contained an arsenal of facts and arguments to bolster racial opinions as well as being crafted with a clarity and style that few of his putative disciples could match. Though sometimes treated critically, in scope and method Chamberlain's works were generally well suited to become models for those charged with providing a more systematic exposition of Nazi ideology after 1933 and with rewriting school texts in conformity with the basic tenets of the regime.

There is little question that Chamberlain's thought was permeated with many of the attitudes, values, and doctrines that formed the central themes of Nazi writing. Unlike many alleged forebears, his books required no skillful editing, abridgement, or drastic reinterpretation to square with the party line. In a negative sense especially, there was a striking family resemblance. Chamberlain's loathing for liberalism and Marxism, his attacks on finance capital and bourgeois materialism, and his obsessive focus on the sinister power of Jewry all foreshadowed the accusations of Nazism. Other affinities were equally evident: the theory of Teutonic or Aryan superiority, Germanized Christianity, agrarian romanticism and vague corporatist notions of social organization, to name only a few. But there were equally significant differences. Thus, until the last years of his life, Chamberlain was a staunch defender of monarchy; reverence for aristocracy and traditional German institutions pervaded much of his work. His preoccupation with spiritual and aesthetic regeneration, while echoed in some Nazi literature, was very different from the party's rhetoric of social and political revolution; indeed, Chamberlain all his life dreaded the kind of total political mobilization of every aspect of life that Nazi propaganda proclaimed as a goal. The parallels between Chamberlain's racism and the pseudo-scientific race doctrines of the Third Reich are considerable, and the general outline of history put forward in the *Foundations* was repeated by scores of writers in the 1930s. But while the outward similarities were great, it must also be noted that in style and tone Chamberlain was more genteel and refined, his language generally less violent, and his arguments less crudely deterministic than many later race thinkers. Lastly, his writings were based on a firm sense of the role of a cultivated and educated elite in society. They had little in common with the class rhetoric and aggressive populism of much of Nazi propaganda, despite the superficial resemblances of romantic *völkisch* phraseology. In sum, although many of Chamberlain's

views pointed forward to the doctrines of Nazism, there
remained conspicuous differences of style, values, and social
perspective between them.

Among the chief problems with attempting to establish
clear lines of continuity between Wilhelminian thinkers and
Nazi ideology is the heterogeneous character of the latter. The
Third Reich's propaganda proclaimed that a specific Nazi
Weltanschauung existed, a coherent and unified set of attitudes and ideas appropriate to the new "fascist man." But,
as historians have often pointed out, the reality was an extraordinarily confusing assortment of precepts and doctrines,
some of which were conveniently ignored once the party
assumed power. The Nazis' cynicism about ideas, their exploitation of party principles and the frequent divergence
between the pronouncements of the regime and its practice
have caused some scholars to largely ignore ideology in their
work or to accept some variation of Hermann Rauschning's
thesis that it was a mere intellectual coating, a collection of
slogans and ill-conceived arguments, useful for manipulating
the masses.[7] The thread of consistency in Nazi actions, it is
often argued, was not ideological so much as a radical drive for
power and conquest. Some historians have even gone a long
way toward a functional explanation of Nazi racism, viewing it
as a tool to which the elite had recourse to legitimize and
bolster their power and to mobilize the nation for territorial ag-
grandizement.[8] The Nazi elite, it has been pointed out, were
quite capable of contradicting the precepts of their alleged
ideological forebears in domestic and foreign policy while continuing to praise them as heralds of the new order.

But it is a mistake to doubt the power of Nazi ideology,
however crude and makeshift it may sometimes seem. Political
and ideological factors were inextricably intertwined in Nazi
policy: short term improvisations were often at odds with long
term objectives and tactical and military requirements made it
impossible to adhere to the avowed principles of the regime at
every step. But the driving force of a crude and unsophisti-
cated Social Darwinism, the geopolitics of *Lebensraum*, anti-
Bolshevism, *völkisch* nationalism, and above all racial anti-
Semitism in the history of the regime is undeniable. What the

class struggle is to Marxism, racial conflict was to Nazism: the reality underlying historical events, the central concept upon which the theory and practice of National Socialism was predicated. It was, Leonard Krieger has written, at once a "tenet of faith and operational ideal that threads pervasively through Nazi thought and action" from the beginning of the movement until its end.[9]

Yet, although it was the cornerstone of the official ideology, Nazi racism was confused and vague; it cannot be reduced to a well-defined, systematically argued, and theoretically precise set of doctrines. Here as in other areas, there was a good deal of diversity. Thus Hitler's outlook derived mostly from Wilhelminian *völkisch* traditions; he focused on hatred of Slavs and Jews and harnessed this to an intense national chauvinism, placing no importance upon technical questions like the exact criteria and characteristics of a race, and frequently muddling the concepts "race," "nation," and *Volk.* Himmler, in contrast, cherished a somewhat different supranational Nordic ideal, while further variations can be found in the work of Rosenberg and of race scholars like Hans F. K. Günther, whose writings were highly regarded by the party. No single theory prevailed, although all theories shared certain basic ingredients. What emerged, in other words, was a series of fundamental assumptions, which acted as the lowest common denominators of all Nazi racism—an obsession with racial "purity," the conviction that the modern era was characterized by a world struggle between Aryan and Jew, and the belief that other nations had become miscegenated and decadent, leaving Germany as the standard-bearer of Aryanism. Though elaborated and reformulated by an army of race experts in the twelve years of the regime, these ideas ultimately derived from nineteenth-century traditions and from the *völkisch* ideology disseminated in the period before 1914.[10]

In view of what has been said, it is hardly surprising that evidence for Chamberlain's direct influence on individual Nazis is both contradictory and inconclusive. Abundant documentation exists to show that the leaders of the party had at least a passing acquaintance with his writings. Even the most cursory glance at early recruits repeatedly turns up his name as

one of the most respected authorities on race, and he was obviously much cited in the early ideological debates of the movement. His well-publicized adherence to Hitler also probably
brought it some new followers: W. S. Allen's analysis of the evolution of the party in Northeim in Lower Saxony, for example,
refers to the town's first Nazi, a bookstore owner, as an admirer
of Chamberlain.[11] At a more exalted level in the movement
Hitler, Hess, Goebbels, Eckart, Himmler, von Schirach, and
above all Rosenberg had read Chamberlain and professed to
have been influenced by him. Hans Kerrl, the Minister for
Church Affairs, and Hans Schemm, the Bayreuth schoolmaster
who became Bavarian *Kultusminister*, were also firm admirers,
while Nazi intellectuals such as Hans F. K. Günther, Alfred
Baeumler, Walter Frank, Ernst Krieck, and the Nobel physicist
Philipp Lenard showered him with filial respect.[12] Beyond
these superficial traces of ideological linkage, however, it is difficult to proceed. In the case of Hitler, while he read the *Foundations*, Chamberlain's biography of Wagner, and some of the
war pamphlets, it is fruitless to try to define the impression
they made on him. The *Führer* was a fitful, erratic, and
voracious reader who imbibed the contents of dozens of books,
pulling out ideas and arguments that coincided with his basic
outlook or could be adapted to it. His anti-Semitism, for
example, reveals traces of Austrian Pan-Germanism, Gobineau, Lapouge, Chamberlain, Eckart, Rosenberg, Lanz von
Liebenfels, and several others; and while portions of *Mein
Kampf* (especially his discussions of the characteristics of the
Aryan) seem to echo the *Foundations*, the sources for the book
were numerous and all were transmuted and remolded by
Hitler. The mental world of the other Nazi leaders was equally
eclectic and loosely defined. They were administrators and
politicians concerned with the exercise of power; theoretical
precision and the academic quest for compatibility of ideas
were not their concern. Thus, Himmler praised Chamberlain's
essays on race and clearly shared many of his ideas, but he also
found portions of Chamberlain's writings "hard to read" and
"hard to understand" and his astrological and occultist leanings would have appeared sheer nonsense to Chamberlain.[13]

Of the chief personalities of the Third Reich only Alfred
Rosenberg can properly be called a Chamberlain disciple.
When as a youth in Riga he first encountered the *Foundations*,
it struck him with the force of a revelation. "Another world
rose up before me: Hellas, Judah, Rome. And to everything I
assented inwardly—again and yet again. And then I ordered
Wellhausen's *History of Israel and Judah* and Bernhard
Stade's *Bible Research* and other books of that kind. . . . The
political events that happened later therefore seemed to me a
necessary commentary." Eight years later, in 1917, he occupied himself studying Chamberlain's *Goethe* and *Kant*, and
read aloud most of the latter to his wife while spending a few
weeks in the Crimea.[14] Nor did he tire of these books, but continually returned to them for inspiration, citing Chamberlain
not only as an authority on race, but also on politics.[15] Rosenberg's chief work, *Der Mythus des zwanzigsten Jahrhunderts*
[*The Myth of the Twentieth Century*, 1930], which became one
of the central texts of Nazi ideology, reflects the extent of his
debts throughout its 700 pages. Its general historical outline,
discussion of Christ's racial heritage, anti-Romanism, and attacks on church doctrine—even its phraseology and use of a concept like *Völkerchaos*— all hark back to the ideas of his English
mentor. And while many historians have downgraded the importance of Rosenberg, viewing him as a somewhat pitiful figure
on the periphery of power, it should not be forgotten that as the
Führer's plenipotentiary for ideological training and education,
he exercised a considerable authority over cultural and church
affairs. Furthermore, through its inclusion in school and training college syllabi and its adoption for SS courses, *Der Mythus*
achieved a large audience. As Robert Cecil has observed,
Hitler's comments on the work were by no means all critical,
and there is some reason for believing that Rosenberg's early influence on him has been underrated in the light of later events.[16]

In the final analysis it is less rewarding to speculate about
the influence of Chamberlain on specific individuals or groups
within the Nazi movement than to consider the general legacy
of pre-war *völkisch* thought. Spanning the period from the
1880s until the 1920s, Chamberlain's career as a publicist

is well suited for that purpose. His writings illuminate in
particular the character and appeal of Teutonic or Aryan
racism in the years before the First World War and show how
widespread anti-Semitism had become as an integral part of a
broad "Germanic ideology." Most of the basic ingredients of
Chamberlain's thought were already present in the works of
Treitschke, Lagarde, Duehring, Wagner, and others; his own
contribution was to elaborate and update their vision, incor-
porating more systematically the findings of racial "science"
and adapting it to the complicated mood and changed circumstances of the *Weltpolitik* era. Although sometimes regarded as
a peripheral figure, isolated from the mainstream of German
and European culture, Chamberlain was in fact very much a
product of his times, shaped by the dominant intellectual
currents of the nineteenth century. Whether it was neo-
Kantianism, modern biblical criticism, Darwinian ideas, neo-
idealism in history, or the critical reevaluation of positivist
science, Chamberlain faced on some level the major intellectual issues confronting contemporaries. His formulations
may appear totally unsatisfactory today, but to many readers
at the time they had a distinct appeal providing a pseudo-
scientific justification for German aspirations to world power
and disclosing a mixture of racial pride, cultural ambivalence,
and political uneasiness prevalent among middle- and upper-
class Germans. His influence on Rosenberg and Hitler has
often been the subject of speculation, but equally it should be
remembered that he won the friendship and esteem of such
diverse personalities as, for example, Kaiser Wilhelm, Ernst
von Wolzogen, Heinrich Class, Hermann Keyserling, Paul
Deussen, and Otto Pfleiderer. Intellectually and emotionally,
Chamberlain was very much a Wilhelminian.

There is considerable disagreement among historians
about the extent and significance of German anti-Semitism in
the two decades before 1914. In part the controversy arises
from different definitions of the subject: some scholars limit
their focus to parliamentary parties and other explicitly
political or governmental forms of prejudice; others adopt a
broader approach examining many areas of national life outside the political arena. Another related problem is the

increasingly abstract quality of anti-Semitism in the 1890s and
the way that antipathy toward Jews or Jewishness was integrated into a broad structure of beliefs and values, a conservative and nationalist cultural stance. A book such as
Chamberlain's *Kant*, for example, may well be viewed as only
minimally anti-Semitic: comments on Jews occupy very little
space in its pages. And yet in the context of Chamberlain's
overall philosophy, our judgment would be quite different. The
point is that for liberal and Jewish contemporaries in the years
before 1914, and for us today, it is often extremely difficult to
assess the importance of anti-Jewish turns of phrase or racial
stereotypes when they form just one constituent element in a
much larger and more complicated structure of ideas and attitudes. In the opinion of this writer, anti-Semitism of varying
forms and intensity permeated the political and cultural views
and the vocabulary of large numbers of Germans before 1914.
Cultural reform movements like Wagnerism, books such as the
Foundations, campaigns by pressure groups and political
parties, and a host of other religious, literary, occupational,
and social associations helped promote this prejudice and
fostered an atmosphere of tolerance for anti-Semitic viewpoints. Though not at the forefront of national politics, anti-
Semitism was very much a part of the ethos and mental style
of the German right.

The hardships and national humiliation of the first World
War further radicalized *völkisch* ideology and broadened the
appeal of anti-Semitic politics. Racist elements, in particular
the Pan-Germans, achieved a more prominent place in the
counsels of the right, and publicists like Chamberlain by their
association with the annexationist cause gained an even wider
and socially more diverse readership than earlier. Since the
1890s the distinction between "popular" and "intellectual"
anti-Semitism had been considerably eroding; the war continued and extended this process, further dismantling the barriers of tone and style that had separated "scholarly" or "middle brow" anti-Semitism from more populistic strains. Not only
did the letters of Chamberlain's cultured correspondents in the
first years of Weimar at times sound like the rantings of anti-
Semitic political agitators, but figures like Artur Dinter, whose

demagoguery was cloaked in pretentious pseudo-scholarship, took over and vulgarized pre-war "Germanic ideology" for the widest possible consumption.[17] After 1923 the tide of anti-Semitism receded and the republic enjoyed a brief period of economic recovery and relative political stability, but the legacy of the previous crisis years was all too evident in the ideology of Nazism and other racist movements founded in the wake of the November revolution.

National Socialism was the inheritor, although not the only one, of *völkisch* ideology. This does not imply that earlier thinkers envisioned Nazi policies of terror and violence, culminating in racial genocide. The anti-Semitism of Chamberlain and other Wilhelminian figures discussed in this study was not exterminatory: their most extreme utterances called vaguely for legislative restrictions which would have reduced Jews to the status of resident aliens with specific positions in society closed to them and no voice in political affairs.[18] Most of the time these anti-Semites offered no solutions at all—their anti-Semitism was more of a "defensive" creed, a language for defining German values and exhorting cultural rebirth, than an offensive prescriptive doctrine demanding specific action against Jews. But, as we have seen, the racism of Chamberlain and others contained marked dynamic and messianic elements that could easily be fashioned into advocacy of more forceful retaliatory measures. Nazism did this: it acted like a reflector, catching the rays of *völkisch* ideology and retransmitting them in a much intensified form. Nazi racial policies grew out of a nexus of ideology, the though patterns and psychology of the leading Nazis, the process and methods by which the party obtained and consolidated power, and finally the circumstances of a total war. It is a mix that defies precise analysis, but significantly, these policies were phrased in the same terms—the same language, stereotypes, symbolism, and patterns of argument—as those employed by pre-war *völkisch* thinkers. Though a revolutionary departure in German political life in so many ways, National Socialism inhabited the same "semantic field" as racist nationalism during the *Kaiserreich;* it drew upon the latter, but radicalized and transformed its meaning.[19]

This is a part of the reason why so many conservative Germans, faced with economic depression and the political failures of Weimar, placed their hopes in Nazism. When Chamberlain met Hitler in October 1923 he looked on him as one who shared his own attitudes and beliefs; he viewed Hitler as an exponent of pre-war ideas who had allied them with a new dynamic political practice more suited to the republican era. Many others made the same error; many simply ignored the aspects of Nazism they found deplorable. Recently a number of regional analyses of the Nazi party have appeared which trace in detail its evolution from a small fringe group to a mass movement. They have focused primarily upon the novel structure and propaganda techniques of the party, and have in several cases cast strong doubts upon the significance of anti-Semitism in drawing recruits to the party and in attracting votes after 1929. In the case of Northeim, for example. W. S. Allen has argued that many who flocked to National Socialism just "ignored or rationalized" its hatred of Jews; similarly, in a fine monograph on Bavaria, Geoffrey Pridham concluded that "although they had warnings in the racialist hatred of Nazi speakers who made threats about the position of Jews in the future Nazi state, the majority of voters did not seem to realize how seriously the Nazis meant to put their ideas into practice."[20] Leaving aside the complex issue of voter motivation, what is more relevant in the present context is the simple fact that virulent rhetoric and threats against Jews did not deter voters. Anti-Semitic agitation over a long period not only created a large pool of racist activists in Germany, it also helped to de-sensitize large numbers of others to the dangers of racial hatred, and to the possibility that brutal rhetoric might one day be translated into murderous action. Discussing the crisis of early Weimar, Werner Jochmann concluded that in 1923 "while one large part of the population hated and despised Jews, the other, just barely the majority, had either inwardly given them up or showed no inclination to get involved on their behalf."[21] Ten years later, when another period of national crisis brought Hitler to the helm of Germany, a similar combination of prejudice, insensitivity, and indifference prevailed. The legacy of Chamberlain and others like him is then twofold: it lies both in the influence they had on the evolution of an anti-Semitic right wing politics in Germany and in the slow process by which so many became anaesthetized to the deadly possibilities inherent in ideological Jew hatred and racial argumentation.[22]

Appendix

The Foundations in Britain and the United States

Chamberlain grew increasingly critical of Britain and the United States in the years before 1914. He dismissed their parliamentary institutions and liberal ideals as a sham, depicted their artistic and cultural life as frivolous and commercialized, and claimed that even the English language was debased and no longer an appropriate medium for the advancement of knowledge. Some of these opinions were published, but they were mostly confined to private correspondences until Chamberlain launched his wartime polemics. Considering the German nationalist flavor of his writing, his early reputation in England and the United States was surprisingly favorable. Admittedly, some reviewers were passionately critical but many were positive: in sharp contrast to the bitter denunciations of "the renegade" or "turncoat" Englishman that appeared after the outbreak of war.

In Britain and the United States, as in Central Europe, it was the *Foundations* which brought Chamberlain renown. His biography of Wagner, translated into English by Ainslie Hight in 1897, received widespread attention in musical circles, so did his passionate defense together with William Ashton Ellis of the "orthodox" Wagner against Ferdinand Praeger.[1] But these were limited successes. Even the *Foundations* drew only brief comment in the Anglo-American press (except for German-language newspapers in the United States), until it was published in English by John Lane in 1910.[2]

The story behind the English translation is long and tangled. As early as 1902, Chamberlain informed Kaiser Wilhelm that a Dr. Strong, who was librarian for the House of Lords, wanted to undertake the translation. He was prevented, or so it was alleged, by

Sir Rowland Blennerhasset, an "Irish ultramontane" and Germanophobe who "ran from publisher to publisher to incite them all against my work."[3] Whatever the truth of the matter, during the next few years the project lay dormant, and was not revived until 1908—and then from an unexpected quarter. Unknown to Chamberlain, Anna had secretly contacted W. H. Dawson, a lecturer in history at Edinburgh University. He in turn passed the matter on to John Lees, a friend and lecturer in German at Aberdeen, who agreed to provide an English translation for a fee of £100 and a percentage of the royalties.[4] It was probably an attempt by Anna to regain Houston's affection; they had been separated for some time and she was eager to reopen contact between them. It backfired from the beginning: not only was Chamberlain deeply distressed by this meddling in his affairs but he was also outraged by the efforts of John Lane, the proposed English publishers, to scale down his fees and royalties.

Eventually an agreement was made; Lees started the translation and Chamberlain switched his efforts from obstructing the book to trying to assure that it would gain a favorable response. To this end, in November 1908, through his brother Basil, he contacted Lord Redesdale, a diplomat, scholar, and close friend of Edward VII. Redesdale, whose admiration for this book was known, was asked if he would write a brief introduction to the English edition, since "the work of a totally unknown writer may fall flat, whereas if duly introduced, it might succeed."[5] His Lordship agreed, although he did not know Chamberlain, and in this fashion unwittingly embarked on a course which made him Chamberlain's chief spokesman and helper in England before 1914—something that proved to be a considerable embarrassment to him in subsequent years.

Redesdale's involvement with the work became progressively larger as he entered into a friendly correspondence with Chamberlain and when it became clear that Lees's translation was completely unsatisfactory to the author. After reading proofs of the translation in December, Chamberlain once more thought of scuttling the whole enterprise, or of disclaiming any responsibility for it. Appalled by Lees's work he wrote: "It is a mere verbatim rendering of German words into English words, often also into Scottish dialect." He added: "No wonder that fool man got through the whole in three or four months." Lees was understandably irritated by Chamberlain's verdict on his work: "You will readily understand," he informed the publisher, "that I cannot step aside at this juncture. My professional reputation is at stake and it is my firm determination to protect it by every means in my power."[6] Lees ascribed Chamberlain's atti-

tude to Anna's involvement in the project. In fact, all the cor-
respondence—and there is a great deal of it—points simply to both
Houston and Basil's dissatisfaction with the style and tone of the
English version.

The result, in any case, was that Lees continued his work while
Redesdale, at Chamberlain's entreaty, took a larger role correcting
and revising the translation. (Lees, who was deeply hurt by the whole
episode, could—had he known—have taken some satisfaction from
the fact that Chamberlain was equally appalled by the French version—"an atrocious, bad translation").[7] The young lecturer succumbed quietly to the awesome Redesdale and soon accepted all his
suggested changes without a murmur: from the exchange of letters it
is evident that his Lordship's responsibility for the book reached far
beyond the introduction with which he was credited. As for Chamberlain, he was deeply flattered by Redesdale's devoted and patient
efforts, recognizing that his close association with the book guaranteed a sympathetic hearing in the British press.

Well before the translation was finished, Redesdale began to
prepare the way for the forthcoming book. In January 1909 he wrote
and had privately printed "An Appreciation" of the *Foundations*,
which he dispatched to a wide circle of influential friends. (The same
essay was later printed as an introduction to the book.) The "Appreciation" was a long paean to Chamberlain's genius: it described the
book, gave a brief account of its author, and offered a mild and sympathetic interpretation of its main themes. Redesdale saw in Chamberlain an honest, kind-hearted, and cultivated inquirer after truth:

> To me the book has been a simple delight—the companion of
> months—fulfilling the highest function of which a teacher is capable,
> that of awakening thought and driving it into new channels. That is
> the charm of the book. The charm of the man is his obviously
> transparent truthfulness. Anything fringing on fraud is abhorrent to
> him, something to be scourged with scorpions. And in one passage he
> himself says the enviable gift of lying has been denied to him.[8]

It is astonishing how eager Redesdale was to embrace the vision of
Chamberlain. He was enthralled by the sections on Greece and
Rome, on Christ, "the mephistic vapours of Roman dogma and
Roman imperialism," and the significance of race; he noted enthusiastically that the Teutons were north Europeans and included
the Celts and the races that inhabited Britain. Of one aspect alone
was he critical: Chamberlain's anti-Semitism. He accepted the account of the origin of the Jewish race, acknowledged "the stubborn

singleness of purpose and dogged consistency which have made the
Jew what he is," but insisted that Jews had rendered great social,
economic and political services.[9] In January 1914, in the *Edinburgh
Review*, he added: "It would almost appear as if the low Polish Jew,
whom we see in the sweated tailor of the East End, had sat as model
for his [Chamberlain's] picture. but even he . . . is what persecution
and evil surroundings have made him."[10]

Among the recipients of Redesdale's "Appreciation" was
Edmund Gosse: poet, essayist, and cultivator of literary connections;
he enjoyed an inflated reputation on the Continent as a literary critic
and was a natural target for Redesdale's efforts to publicize Chamberlain. Gosse, at that time librarian to the House of Lords, was also
a terrible snob, eager to please his coroneted friends: he responded
warmly, praising Redesdale's essay and welcoming the idea of an
English edition of the *Foundations*. The Conservative leader A. J.
Balfour also expressed his thanks and described Redesdale's essay as
"exactly what I wanted"; among the Liberals, Viscount Morley, Secretary of State for India, and R. B. Haldane, Secretary for
War, were both encouraging in their remarks, although Haldane
clearly had some reservations about Chamberlain's views. Another
correspondent, Lucien Wolf, the editor of *Jewish World* and a
prominent spokesman for British Jewry, replied politely—doubtless
relieved that Redesdale had carefully disassociated himself from
anti-Semitic prejudice but also troubled by the imminent appearance of Chamberlain's work in English: he foresaw, he told
Redesdale, that he would find much to quarrel with in the forthcoming book.[11] Little should be inferred from these letters: the replies
were very brief and people are rarely quite candid in assessing the
literary enthusiasms of friends, even less when the author is a peer
and a friend of the King—politeness and propriety easily stifled more
exacting evaluation of Redesdale's essay or its subject.

While Redesdale sought to awaken interest in the forthcoming
translation, publisher John Lane began to line up prospective reviewers. "I am now," he wrote, "considering the best men in this
country to write special articles on the book." Chamberlain was
asked to suggest names "of well-known men in this country who
would be in sympathy with your work."[12] How significant these special efforts were is difficult to gauge. Certainly, after its appearance
in December 1910, the translation was widely reviewed. In the same
month *The Times Literary Supplement* announced: "this is unquestionably one of the rare books that really matter," and described

Chamberlain as, "a remarkable literary force [who] has in recent years made [his] appearance in German literature." There followed a well-crafted review that expounded the basic themes of the book, praised its style, and acknowledged calmly that the author's "judgments of men and things are deeply and indisputably sincere and are based on immense reading." The reviewer did not proclaim his wholehearted agreement; rather his tone is a mixture of enthusiasm and determined noncommittal. Here was an excellent, imaginative and weighty book that deserved to be read seriously. In general, the aggressive, brutal side of Chamberlain was downplayed: "It would be unfair to confuse Mr. Chamberlain's attitude toward the Jew with the crudities of anti-Semitism; yet he unquestionably regards the Jew—partly because he, like the Teuton, has the mysterious strength of pure race—as a most dangerous force in modern life." The reviewer was clearly troubled by the handling of "the Jewish question" but also unwilling to dispense with racial categories altogether: "While we admit," he wrote, "as we probably must, the broad truth of his account of Judaism and the Jews, it is certainly not true that every Jew reflects in every particular the character of his race. . . . nor is it true that race character itself is a dead unchangeable thing, cast once for all in an iron mould." [13]

Redesdale was overjoyed at public reactions: "The book," he informed Chamberlain jubilantly in December 1911, "has been much read and by the best people. Wherever I go I am asked all manner of questions about 'the wonderful Mr. Chamberlain.'" During Redesdale's visit to the First Lord of the Admiralty, Winston Churchill, the latter "at once launched into unmeasured praise of the *Grundlagen*, the English version of which was lying on his table." [14] The "fortuitous" presence of the book before Churchill when the Baron arrived serves once again to remind us that the desire to please him undoubtedly colored response among the political and social elite and was a major factor in the work's success. Reviews multiplied: *The Athenaeum* and the *Bookman* were mixed in their response; so was the *Quarterly Review*. Each recognized that this was an important book but were troubled by its vision of history as "an Iliad of conflict between German and Semite." Provincial newspapers like the *Birmingham Daily Post* and the *Glasgow Herald* were, as Colin Holmes has pointed out, more enthusiastic, while the *Spectator* called the book "a monument of erudition." Specific assertions and arguments came in for sharp criticism but most commentators were disposed to dwell on the positive qualities of the *Foundations*. "It is," concluded the *Review of Reviews*, "impossible to withhold admiration for the vast learning, the splendid critical acumen, and the deductive manner in which facts are marshalled in support of the thesis."[15]

Two responses to the English edition of the *Foundations* further illustrate the strange appeal it could exert, at least among literary-minded Germanophiles. In June 1911 *Fabian News* printed an astonishing panegyric by G. B. Shaw. Its extravagance reveals what we might call "the other side" of Shaw—his elitist scorn for democracy, the autodidactic quality of his learning, and the deep confusions and contradictions in his ideas—all overlaid by the Shavian love of paradox and assertion. "This very notable book," he began, "should be read by all good Fabians"; "it is a masterpiece of really scientific history," and, "It will show many Fabians what side they are really on, lifting them out of mere newspaper and propaganda categories into their right camp." Shaw delighted in Chamberlain's unconcealed bias, his bold generalizations "as distinguished from the crowd of mere specialists . . . and accumulators of hard dead data"; he applauded Chamberlain's firm protest "against the lumping together under the general name of 'Humanity' of people who have different souls." Nonetheless, Shaw disagreed that the battle between Teuton and Chaos still raged, concluding that the Chaos had triumphed and with it superstition, national conceit, militarism and mediocrity: the "short round skull" of a British greengrocer, more than that of the Jew, turns out to be the deadly adversary of G. B. S.[16]

No less enthusiastic, according to the researches of Emile Delavenay, was D. H. Lawrence, who read the book in 1911 and discovered that it synthesized many of his own thoughts about art, the mystique of blood, and the mechanical, disintegrated amorphous character of modern mass society. Among the several intellectual influences swaying Lawrence in the direction of a profoundly irrational and elitist vitalism, Chamberlain, in Delavenay's view, was the most effective—the essay on Hardy, *Twilight in Italy*, *The Rainbow*, and especially his *Movements in European History*, published in 1919, are said to have been shaped by the dialogue between Lawrence and the *Foundations*.[17] No adequate evidence exists for testing Delavenay's assertions and, in any case, Lawrence used and transformed what he read so drastically that it bore little resemblance to the original—yet it is quite plausible that this English Germanophile and Wagner enthusiast found the message of Chamberlain enticing.

English readers were, not surprisingly, far better disposed toward Chamberlain before than after 1914. They read the book because its entry onto the book market was well-prepared and because it was known to have created an immense impact in Germany. For all the chauvinist antagonism between the two nations each was deeply intrigued by the other: Germans were deeply ambivalent about England; Englishmen, critical of their own land, often found the answer to these deficiencies in their illusions about the Reich. Reviewers in both countries were highly receptive to this new brand of dilettantism, with its extravagant flattery of "the northern races." But while anti-Semitism in Britain had recently been fanned by an influx of Jews from Russia and an acrimonious public debate over immigration restrictions, there is no evidence that this enhanced sales of the book. What occasionally surfaces in contemporary comments is an older, snobbish disdain for Jews rather than the more political anti-Semitism so common in Germany. Jewish writers were sometimes greatly troubled by Redesdale's efforts on behalf of so notorious an anti-Semitic work but most were like Lucien Wolf who informed Claude Montefiore, President of the Anglo-Jewish Association, that a public refutation of Chamberlain would merely serve to draw attention to the book.[18] In general, then, until World War I Chamberlain received guarded praise in the land of his birth: even as late as 1915, in his Creighton lecture, James Bryce described him as "an able and very learned Anglo-German writer." But the war soon brought a sudden change of opinion. Chamberlain was depicted as the "Turn-coat son of Britain," a "renegade," and his literary success was deemed "one of the measures of the demoralization of the German intelligence by the religion of *Macht*."[19]

In the United States too the war marked a similar turning-point in Chamberlain's reputation, although his *Foundations* never aroused there the degree of interest it had on the other side of the Atlantic. The original German version achieved a number of reviews, mostly reserved or critical in tone, but again it was the English edition which first spurred any wider public interest. Certain pro-German figures such as Professor John W. Burgess of Columbia University and Senator Albert T. Beveridge professed to be strongly influenced by the book; so did the Immigration Restriction League, at the time engaged in a campaign to curb the free entry of "non-Aryan elements" into the country. Madison Grant, for a quarter century the Vice President of the League, was especially impressed by Chamberlain, and his own racial treatise, *The Passing of the Great Race* (1916) was to bear traces of its European counterpart. Henry Cabot Lodge, Prescott F. Hall, and Alfred P. Schultz were among the chief adversaries of the new immigration into America who found sympathetic ideas in Chamberlain.[20] Another was Ellery

Sedgwick, the dynamic editor of the conservative and genteel *Atlantic Monthly*. "Not, I think, since my boyhood days, when I first surrendered to the fascination of Buckle," wrote Sedgwick to Chamberlain, "have I been so stimulated by a product of contemporary thought." He also requested an essay which "will apply to the U.S. those principles which you deduce from your consideration of the hybridization of races," noting that "if the results which you describe are inevitable, they must show themselves in sharper outline in this country than elsewhere in the civilized world." [21]

The most famous reviewer of the *Foundations* was Theodore Roosevelt, who found the book brilliant and suggestive, if also full of "startling inaccuracies and lack of judgment." Yet, despite its defects, the ex-President was obviously attracted by its illiberal and inegalitarian doctrine: he especially sympathized with Chamberlain's denunciation of "the prevalent loose and sloppy talk about the general progress of humanity, the equality and identity of races, and the like." Chamberlain was at the least a beneficial antidote to "well-meaning and feebleminded sentimentalists." Quite different was the response of Lyman Abbott, chief editor of the same magazine (*The Outlook*): "We do not know where one would find anti-Semitic prejudice more intense or the grounds for it more skillfully marshalled, or misrepresentation of a people more artistically presented than in this work." [22]

Most surprising for the exaggerated nature of his response was the distinguished historian Carl Becker, who wrote a long and eulogistic review for the New York magazine *Dial*. "On every page," he asserted, "wide and accurate knowledge, masterly grasp of an immense subject, the profound reflection of a powerful mind, and courage" were displayed. Though at first hesitant about Chamberlain's use of the race concept, Becker brushed aside these doubts in his eagerness to enter the mood of the book, to experience its intuitive judgment of history from within: "among historical works," he argued, it was, "likely to rank with the most significant of the nineteenth century." "One despairs," he added, "of conveying any adequate idea" of its "intellectual mastery," "keen analysis," "brilliant originality," and "trenchant humor." [23]

For all Becker's enthusiasm few Americans turned to the book: it was very Eurocentric in design and doctrine and did not address, in most contemporaries' eyes, the problems confronting the United States. Apart from a brief flicker of interest during the first two years of the war, when the German-American Literary Defense Committee and other Germanophile groups distributed his propaganda, Chamberlain caused barely a ripple on the American intellectual scene. As John Higham has argued, Americans by and large were not reading European racists in these years; they generated their own racial literature, tailored to specific conflicts in North America, without transatlantic inspiration. [24]

After 1918 Chamberlain was forgotten for a while in Britain and the United States. At his death the English press contained several bitter obituaries, focussing especially upon his chauvinistic propaganda for Germany during the First World War, but it was not really until after the Nazis came to power that interest in his career and writings revived. From then on it was Chamberlain's role as a forerunner of National Socialist ideology that preoccupied writers and the *Foundations* was interpreted not as an expression of Wilhelminian *Weltpolitik* but as a book that shaped the views of Hitler and Rosenberg and anticipated Nazi racialism.

Notes

Abbreviations

BB	*Bayreuther Blätter*, (1878–1938)
Briefe I, II	*Briefe 1882–1924 und Briefwechsel mit Kaiser Wilhelm II*, ed. Paul Pretzsch (Munich: Bruckmann, 1928).
Briefwechsel	*Cosima Wagner und Houston Stewart Chamberlain im Briefwechsel 1888–1908*, ed. Paul Pretzsch (Leipzig, 1934).
(CN)	Chamberlain *Nachlass*, Richard Wagner Gedenkstätte, Bayreuth.
CW	Cosima Wagner.
Dilettantismus	*Dilettantismus, Rasse, Monotheismus, Rom. Vorwort zur 4. Auflage der Grundlagen des Neunzehnten Jahrhunderts* (Munich: Bruckmann, 1903).
Foundations I, II	*Foundations of the Nineteenth Century* trans. John Lees, with the assistance of Lord Redesdale (London: John Lane, 1910).
Goethe	*Goethe* (Volksausgabe) (Munich: Bruckmann, 1931).
Grundlagen	*Die Grundlagen des XIX. Jahrhunderts* (Volksausgabe; Munich: Bruckmann, 1932).
HSC	Houston Stewart Chamberlain.
Kant I, II	*Immanuel Kant*, trans. Lord Redesdale, (London and New York, 1914).
LBI	*Leo Baeck Institute Yearbook*, various years.
Lebenswege	*Lebenswege meines Denkens* (Munich; Bruckmann, 1922).
Mitteilungen	*Mitteilungen aus dem Verein zur Abwehr des Antisemitismus* (Berlin).
Richard Wagner	*Richard Wagner*, 11th ed. (Munich: Bruckmann, 1942).
Richard Wagner (Hight trans.)	*Richard Wagner*, trans. Ainslie Hight (London, 1897).

All other references to Chamberlain's works are first editions except where otherwise stated.

Introduction

1. Konrad Heiden, *Der Fuehrer, Hitler's Rise to Power*, trans. Ralph Manheim (New York: Fertig 1969), p. 232.

2. A. B. Paine, *Mark Twain: A Biography* (New York, 1912), 2:922.

3. Max Nordau, *Entartung* (Berlin, 1893), 1:380.

4. A. B. F. Mitford (Lord Redesdale) *Bayreuth in 1912* (London: privately printed, 1912).

5. Fritz Stern, *Gold and Iron. Bismarck, Bleichröder and the Building of the German Empire* (New York: Knopf, 1977), p. xx.

6. Martin Duberman, *The Uncompleted Past*. (New York, Random House, 1969).

7. P. Loewenberg, "Psychohistorical Perspectives on Modern German History," *Journal of Modern History* (June 1975), 47(2).

8. For references see chapter 8 footnotes 18, 20-22.

9. "Shrinking History," *The New York Review of Books*, Feb. 22 and March 8, 1973.

10. F. Weinstein and G. M. Platt, "The Coming Crisis in Psychohistory," *Journal of Modern History* (June 1975), 47(2).

11. M. D. Biddiss, *Father of Racist Ideology. The Social and Political Thought of Count Gobineau* (London, 1970). See also Janine Buenzod, *La formation de la pensée de Gobineau* (Paris, 1967).

12. Stern, *Gold and Iron*, p. xxiii.

13. I. Schorsch, "German Antisemitism in the Light of Post-War Historiography," *LBI* (1974), 19:270.

14. R. Rürup, "Emancipation and Crisis—the 'Jewish Question' in Germany 1850-1890," *ibid.* (1975), 20:25.

15. J. Réal, "H. S. Chamberlain: The Religious Conception of Race," In E. Vermeil, ed., *The Third Reich* (New York, 1955), p. 285.

Chapter One: An Englishman Uprooted

1. Albert Schweitzer to Eva Chamberlain Feb. 19, 1927 (CN).

2. *Lebenswege* chap. 1.

3. Henry Orlando Chamberlain (1773-1828); his second wife was Anne Eugenia Morgan (1785-1867). Admiral William Charles Chamberlain (1812-78). When Houston was born, William was Captain of the Port at Chatham, England's largest naval dockyard; later he became Commander of the Harbour at Devonport. Colonel Charles Chamberlain (?-1871); Lieut.-General Thomas Hardy Chamberlain (1826-79), Indian Army Bombay. Sir Crawford Trotter Chamberlain (1821-1902), General, took part in many campaigns in India, including the Afghan and Sikh Wars, cited for courage in the Mutiny, commands of various cavalry regiments, many honors. Field Marshal Sir Neville Chamberlain (1820-1902), prominence in Munity etc., command of Madras Army, final service with Roberts in South Africa.

4. Captain Basil Hall (1788-1844) entered the navy in 1802, served in the Napoleonic Wars, travels on the Continent 1817-19, Fellow of the Royal Society. Published several books of travel. Married to Margaret, daughter of Sir John Hunter, British Consul-General in Spain. Sir James Hall (1761-1832), eldest son of Sir John Hall, 3rd

Baronet of Dunglass, educ. Christs College, Cambridge, friend of the geologist Hutton, married to daughter of the Earl of Selkirk, MP 1807–12.

5. Basil Hall Chamberlain (1850–1935) originally intended for a banking career but gave it up because of poor health; educated at Oxford and the Sorbonne, eventually Professor at Tokyo University and author of many books on Japanese literature. See, for example, K. Koizumi, ed., *Letters from B. H. Chamberlain to Lafcadio Hearn* (London, 1936). Henry Chamberlain (1853–1923), referred to as "Harry," went into business.

6. W. L. Burn, *The Age of Equipoise. A Study of the Mid-Victorian Generation* (London), 1964).

7. *Lebenswege*, p. 15.

8. Harriet Mary Chamberlain to Baroness Amelie Ropp Feb. 7, 1857; Nov. 14, 1859 (CN).

9. *Lebenswege* p. 24.

10. *Ibid.*, pp. 37 ff. Most of Chamberlain's early letters and schoolbooks have been lost. He referred to these schoolboy experiences several times in his essays published during World War I.

11. *Ibid.*, p. 73.

12. Fragment written in Dresden, probably in the spring or winter of 1888 (CN).

13. C. M. Bowra, *Memories 1898–1939* (Cambridge: Harvard University Press, 1967), p. 32.

14. For the André family see David S. Landes, *Bankers and Pashas. International Finance and Economic Imperialism in Egypt* (Cambridge: Harvard University Press, 1958).

15. *Lebenswege*, pp. 34–35, 30.

16. "Erinnerungen aus dem Jahre 1870," *Deutsches Wesen*. The essay first appeared in *Der Merker* (Vienna) April 15, 1915.

17. *Lebenswege*, p. 54.

18. "Chamberlain und sein deutscher Lehrer. Brief an Prof. Otto Kuntze in Stralsund," *Deutsche Bücher. Almanach der Münchener Verleger* (1916); also, Erich Gülzow, "Otto Kuntze, der deutsche Lehrer H. S. Chamberlains," *Baltische Studien*, n.s., 42. Most of the Kuntze correspondence has been lost, though some letters are in the Chamberlain *Nachlass*.

19. "Chamberlain und sein deutscher Lehrer," p. 15.

20. *Ibid.*, pp. 22–23.

21. HSC to Admiral William Chamberlain Nov. 8, 1874; also Dec. 2, 1874 (CN).

22. *Lebenswege*, p. 59.

23. "Chamberlain und sein deutscher Lehrer," p. 23; Leopold von Schroeder, *H. S. Chamberlain. Ein Abriss seines Lebens* (Munich, 1918); *idem* in *Ostdeutsche Rundschau. Weihnachtsbeilage*, no. 294, Dec. 24, 1916; Anna Chamberlain, *Meine Erinnerungen an H. S. Chamberlain* (Munich, 1923) contains some details of Chamberlain's early life.

24. Anna Chamberlain, *Meine Erinnerungen*, chap. 1.

25. *Ibid.*, p. 27.

26. *Ibid.*, pp. 28–30. The letter was reprinted several times during the First World War—e.g. *Süddeutsche Monatschefte* (Munich) April–Sept. 1917, p. 36.

27. Chamberlain wrote several plays and poems in these years. See: HSC to Macmillan Co., London, Sept. 20, 1875; Murray's Press to HSC Dec. 7, 1875. He sought advice, among others, from the German liberal nationalist poet Gottfried Kinkel (e.g. HSC to Kinkel April 15, 1876; Kinkel to HSC Sept. 13, 1876). Kinkel was

critical but encouraging about these literary efforts; he may also have influenced the language and tone of Chamberlain's Seville letter. Anne Guthrie to HSC Oct. 14, 1908 refers to the family's frosty attitude toward Anna. (CN).

28. B. H. Chamberlain to HSC April 30, 1878 (CN). "Fan" was Chamberlain's mother's sister, Fan Hall, who married a banker, Alfred Christian, and lived in Malta for many years. She died in London in 1905.

29. Anna Chamberlain, *Meine Erinnerungen*, p. 32.

30. Anna's correspondence has not survived and most of Chamberlain's letters to her were destroyed after her death in 1924. Otto Graf zu Stolberg-Wernigerode in *Neue Deutsche Biographie* (1956), 3:187 writes that Anna's father was a converted Jew. He gives no source and I have found nothing to corroborate this in the Chamberlain papers, although Dr. Wilhelm Einsle, who organized the *Nachlass*, wrote in his diary: "Anna soll ein Judin sein."

31. On the way from Breslau to Florence they stopped in Munich and attended the première there of the *Ring*. Soon after Chamberlain joined the Bayreuth *Patronatsverein. Lebenswege* p. 85.

32. *Lebenswege*, p. 86.

33. Notebooks (CN); Dean of Geneva Univ. to HSC Oct. 28, 1881; HSC to Harriet Chamberlain Oct. 30, 1881 (CN).

34. *Lebenswege* pp. 102-3.

35. *Ibid.*, pp. 103-4.

36. *Ibid.*, p. 107.

37. Chamberlain gave the impression in his autobiography that overzealous application to his scientific researches caused the nervous breakdown.

38. Adolphe Appia was one of those who frequently visited the Chamberlains at Vert Pré. On Appia see chap. 3. HSC to CW Aug. 11, 1900 (CN); HSC to Harriet Chamberlain June 15, 1881 (CN).

39. HSC to Harriet Chamberlain Feb. and March 1883 (CN).

40. *Ibid.*, Nov. 26, 1883 (CN).

41. *Ibid.*, March 25, 1884 (CN).

42. *Ibid.*, March 27, April 2, 1884 (CN).

43. *Ibid.*, April 6, 1884 (CN).

44. *Ibid.*, June 6 1884; also, June 18 (CN).

45. *Ibid.*, Sept. 7, Oct. 23, Nov. 12, 1884 (CN).

46. Anna Chamberlain to Harriet Chamberlain Dec. 25, Dec. 13, 1884 (CN).

47. Anna Chamberlain to Harriet Chamberlain Dec. 29, 1884; Dr. Battersby to Harriet Chamberlain Dec. 13, 1884; Anna Chamberlain, *Meine Erinnerungen*, p. 49.

48. HSC to Harriet Chamberlain Aug. 22, Sept. 18, 1885 (CN).

49. E.g. E. V. Stonequist, *The Marginal Man. A Study in Personality and Culture Conflict* (New York: Russell, 1961; report of 1937 ed.).

50. E. Dujardin, *Rencontres avec Houston Stewart Chamberlain* (Paris, 1943), p. 31.

Chapter Two: The Education of a Wagnerite

1. *Lebenswege*, p. 180; "Erinnerungen aus dem Jahre 1870," in *Deutsches Wesen*.

2. *Lebenswege*, pp. 167 ff, quote from pp. 181-82.

3. *Ibid.*, p. 192.

4. For the Pernerstorfer circle see W. J. McGrath, *Dionysian Art and Populist Politics in Austria* (New Haven: Yale University Press, 1974).

5. *Lebenswege*, p. 206 (the original letter is missing from the *Nachlass*).

6. Compare his comments in *Revue Wagnérienne* (Jan. 1886) no. 12 and *Richard Wagner* (1895). The first Bayreuth production of Lohengrin in 1894 altered Chamberlain's views on the work.

7. Anna Chamberlain, *Meine Erinnerungen* p. 35; *Lebenswege*, p. 211.

8. For the conservative tradition of cultural criticism in Germany see Fritz Stern, *The Politics of Cultural Despair* (Berkeley: University of California Press, 1961). Also, G. Kratzsch, *Kunstwart und Dürerbund* (Göttingen, 1969); George L. Mosse, *Crisis of German Ideology; Intellectual Origins of the Third Reich* (New York: Grosset and Dunlop, 1964); Roy Pascal, *From Naturalism to Expressionism, German Literature and Society 1880–1918* (London: Weidenfeld, 1973).

9. Hans von Wolzogen, *Lebensbilder* (Regensburg, 1923); also HSC to CW Aug. 1, 1890 (CN). Some additional information can be found in Erik Böhm, "Hans von Wolzogen," Diss., Munich 1943.

10. R. W. Gutman, *Richard Wagner. The Man, His Mind and His Music* (New York: Harcourt, 1968), p. 393.

11. MS in Chamberlain *Nachlass*; a portion of the essay is reprinted in *Lebenswege*, pp. 219–20.

12. *Ibid.*

13. *Ibid.*

14. *Lebenswege*, p. 218.

15. *Ibid.*; BB (1878), pp. 29–42; 85–92; 171–77; (1879) 121–35; (1880) "Religion und Kunst," pp. 269–300; (1881) "Erkenne dich Selbst," pp. 33–41; "Heldentum und Christentum," pp. 249–58.

16. HSC to Harriet Chamberlain July 31, 1882 (CN); *Lebenswege*, pp. 236–41.

17. See the excellent study by Winfried Schüler, *Der Bayreuther Kreis von seiner Entstehung bis zum Ausgang der wilhelminischen Ära* (Münster, 1971). On Stein see HSC and Friedrich Poske, *Heinrich von Stein und seine Weltanschauung* (Munich, 1903).

18. HSC to Harriet Chamberlain July 13, July 25, 1883; soon after, he was introduced to Liszt. See HSC to Harriet Chamberlain Aug. 2, Aug. 28, 1883 (CN).

19. HSC to Antonin Lascoux Oct. 31, 1885 in André Coeuroy, *Wagner et l'esprit romantique* (Paris, 1965) pp. 148–50. Edouard Dujardin, *Rencontres avec Houston Stewart Chamberlain* (Paris, 1943), chaps. 1–2. HSC to H. Vauplane Feb. 1884 (CN).

20. HSC to Harriet Chamberlain March 22, 1886; also, March 1, 21, Nov. 27, 1887 (CN).

21. His sickness may have been psychological or physiological, the evidence is unclear. It may even have been the first stages of multiple sclerosis, which some have argued was the eventual cause of his death.

22. HSC to CW June 2, 1889; CW to HSC June 6, 1889; HSC to Harriet Chamberlain Sept. 11, 1889 (CN).

23. Isabelle Wyzewska, *La Revue Wagnérienne. Essai sur l'interpretation esthetique de Wagner en France* (Paris, 1934). Also, E. L. Duval, *Theodor de Wyzewa. A Critic without a Country* (Paris, 1961). Edouard Dujardin in *Revue musicale* (Paris) Oct. 1, 1923. Léon Guichard, *La musique et les lettres en France au temps du Wagnerisme* (Paris, 1963).

24. Romain Rolland, *Musicians of Today* (New York, 1915), p. 277.

25. Dujardin, *Rencontres*, p. 12.

26. HSC to Harriet Chamberlain Nov. 7, 1885 (CN).

27. Rolland, *Musicians of Today*, p. 67.

28. C. Mauclair, *Servitude et grandeur littéraires* (Ollendorf, 1922) quoted in Guichard *La musique et les lettres*. p. 242–43.

29. Among the contributors were: Léon Leroy, Edouard Schuré, Edouard Rod, Catulle Mendès, Stephane Mallarmé, Villiers de l'Isle-Adam, Huysmans, Maurice Barrès, Verlaine, Fantin Latour.

30. Edouard Dujardin, *Revue musicale* (Paris) Oct. 1, 1923; A. Coeuroy, *Wagner et l'esprit romantique*, chap. 9.

31. HSC to Dujardin Aug. 2, 1887 (CN); *Revue Wagnérienne* 1886–87 contains a description of the growing dispute. "L'Or du Rhein," *La Revue Wagnérienne* (Oct. 1885), no. 8. Also HSC to Dujardin May 20, 1885, in Dujardin, *Rencontres* pp. 25–29.

32. Jacques Barzun, *Darwin, Marx, Wagner* (New York: Doubleday, 1958) p. 289.

33. "Notes sur Tristan und Isolde," "Notes sur Parsifal," in *La Revue wagnérienne*, Feb. 1887; Aug. 1886.

34. Edouard Dujardin, in *Revue musicale* Oct. 1, 1923.

35. Hans von Wolzogen to Ludwig Schemann, July 1, 1887 in Schüler, *Der Bayreuther Kreis*, p. 59.

36. "Die Sprache in Tristan und Isolde und ihr Verhältnis zur Musik," *Allgemeine Musik-Zeitung* (1888), 15(29–30)(31–32); HSC to Harriet Chamberlain Oct. 29, 1888; Hans von Wolzogen to HSC March 5, 1887 (CN). It is not clear why Chamberlain had "long been on bad terms" with Levi.

37. "Kunstlerisches Dankbarkeit," in *Sächsische Landeszeitung* May 16, 1888. *Briefwechsel*, p. 7.

38. On Heinrich von Stein see Schüler, *Der Bayreuther Kreis* and Günter Ralfs, ed., *Heinrich von Stein. Idee und Welt* (Stuttgart, 1940). On Schemann see his autobiography, *Lebensfahrt eines Deutschen* (Leipzig, 1925).

39. Anna Chamberlain, *Meine Erinnerungen* chap. 3; Hans von Wolzogen to HSC June 19, 1888 (CN).

40. On Cosima Wagner see: Richard Du Moulin Eckart, *Cosima Wagner* (Berlin, 1931); Max Millenkovich-Morrold, *Cosima Wagner* (Leipzig, 1937). After a long legal dispute Cosima's diaries have finally been published. When she died they passed into the keeping of Chamberlain's second wife, Eva, and when she died in 1942, she left instructions that they were not to be opened until thirty years later. Subsequently, there was a dispute between the town of Bayreuth and those who had been in custody of the diaries over fees. They have been issued in a fine two-volume edition: Cosima Wagner, *Die Tagebücher 1869–1883* (Munich, 1976–77). An English-language edition of the first volume has been published (New York: Harcourt, 1978).

41. Quoted in Geoffrey Skelton, *Wagner at Bayreuth* (New York: Braziller, 1966), pp. 71–72.

42. Cited in Schüler, *Der Bayreuther Kreis*, p. 81–82.

43. HSC to CW June 24, 1888 (CN); HSC to Zahn March 6, 1891, in *Briefwechsel*, p. 8.

44. Skelton, *Wagner at Bayreuth*, p. 72. The quotation comes from Chamberlain's article: "Die ersten zwanzig Jahre der Bayreuther Bühnenfestspiele," *BB* (1896), *19*.

45. HSC to Hans von Wolzogen in *Briefwechsel* p. 7; HSC to Harriet Chamberlain Nov. 17, 1891 (CN).

46. Ilse Lötz, *Cosima Wagner. Die Hüterin des Grals* (Görlitz, 1936) p. 242. Baroness Wolkenstein, formerly Baroness von Schleinitz was a leading patron of Bayreuth

in Berlin and was instrumental in getting Kaiser Wilhelm to attend the festival in 1876. Richard Du Moulin Eckart relied heavily on the Wolkenstein-Cosima Wagner correspondence for his biography.

47. CW to HSC Oct. 12, 1888 (CN) etc.

48. Dujardin, *Rencontres*. Chap. 2 has some comments on Chamberlain's reading in these years, while Chamberlain's letters to Harriet Chamberlain also contain discussions of his views on contemporary French writers.

49. "Brief an Hans Sachs über die Bestimmung der Wagnervereine," *BB* (1910), *33*; "Richard Wagner in seinem Verhältnis zu den Klassikern der Dicht- und Tonkunst," *BB* (1897), *20*.

50. "Richard Wagners Regenerationslehre," written in 1893 and published two years later in *BB*, (1895), *18*.

51. *Lebenswege* p. 161; also, Chamberlain's letter in the *Dresdner Tageblatt* Dec. 29, 1885 "Offener Brief an Opernsänger Riese."

52. Thomas Mann, *Essays* (New York: Vintage Books, 1957) p. 249–50.

53. HSC to Harriet Chamberlain April 24, 1881 (CN).

54. *Ibid.*, Dec. 7, March (n.d.), 1881 (CN).

55. *Ibid.*, March (n.d.) 1881 (CN).

56. *Ibid.*, April 14, 1881, Jan. 29, 1881 (CN).

57. *Ibid.*, Feb. 17, 1883 (CN).

58. *Ibid.*, April 24, March 25, 1881 (CN).

59. *Richard Wagner* (Hight trans.) p. 140.

60. The research on the Bismarckian Reich is staggering and no attempt can be made here to include even the most important studies. For a general interpretation see: Hans-Ulrich Wehler, *Das Deutsche Kaiserreich 1871–1918* (Göttingen, 1973). Also, Helmut Boehme, *Probleme der Reichsgründungszeit, 1848–79* (Cologne and Berlin, 1968); another important monograph is Hans-Ulrich Wehler's *Bismarck und der Imperialismus* (Cologne and Berlin, 1969). James J. Sheehan, ed., *Imperial Germany* (New York: New Viewpoints, 1976) contains a good selection of essays. Sheehan's recent book, *German Liberalism in the Nineteenth Century* (Chicago: University of Chicago Press, 1978), especially chaps. 4–5, offers a very illuminating analysis of the political evolution of of liberalism. Also, very insightful on the whole subject of German political culture is Fritz Stern's collection of essays, *The Failure of Illiberalism* (New York: Knopf, 1972).

61. HSC to Harriet Chamberlain July 12, 1889 (CN).

62. HSC to Anne Guthrie Jan. 8, 1889 (CN).

63. See especially: Hans Rosenberg, *Grosse Depression und Bismarckzeit. Wirtschaftsablauf, Gesellschaft und Politik in Mitteleuropa* (Berlin, 1967); Fritz Stern, *Gold and Iron: Birsmarck, Bleichröder and the Building of the German Empire* (New York: Knopf, 1977) provides a fascinating analysis of the whole period, placing the career of Bleichröder in the context of Germany's social and political development. Also useful for the crash is James F. Harris, "Eduard Lasker: The Jew as National German Politician," *LBI* (1975), 20.

64. Reinhard Rürup, *Emanzipation und Antisemitismus* (Göttingen, 1975), especially the first essay: "Judenemanzipation und bürgerliche Gesellschaft in Deutschland."

65. See, for example, Ismar Schorsch, *Jewish Reactions to German Anti-Semitism 1870-1914* (New York, 1972), pp. 13–21; Monika Richarz, "Jewish Social Mobility in Germany during the Time of Emancipation (1790-1871)," *LBI* (1975), 20; Steven M. Lowenstein, "The Pace of Modernisation of German-Jewry in the Nineteenth

Century," *ibid.*, (1976), 21; Jacob Toury, "Der Eintritt der Juden ins deutsche Bürgertum," in Hans Liebeschütz and Arnold Paucker, eds., *Das Judentum in der Deutschen Umwelt* (Tübingen, 1977). An 1895 survey revealed 56% of Jews engaged in business and commerce, 19.3% in industry, 1.4% in agriculture as compared to 10%, 36% and 36% for the German labor force as a whole, "In 1871, 43% of the inhabitants of Hamburg earned less than 840 marks a year, but only 3.4% of the Jews belonged to this low income group." In education, Jews accounted for about 6% of all secondary school students by 1860 although only about 1% of the total population.

66. See especially Rürup, *Emanzipation und Antisemitismus*; *idem*, "Emanzipation und Krise—Zur Geschichte der 'Judenfrage' in Deutschland vor 1890," in W. E. Mosse and A. Paucker, eds., *Juden im wilhelminischen Deutschland 1890-1914* (Tübingen, 1976).

67. Stern, *Gold and Iron* chap. 18; *idem*, "Money, Morals and the Pillars of Society," in *Failure of Illiberalism*; Rürup, "Emanzipation und Krise." For the development of Jewish stereotypes in the first half of the century see Eleonore Sterling, *Er ist wie Du* (Munich, 1956) the second edition has a new title: *Judenhass* (Frankfurt, 1969).

68. P. J. Pulzer, *The Rise of Political Anti-Semitism in Germany and Austria* (New York, 1964); W. Boehlich, ed., *Der Berliner Antisemitismusstreit* (Frankfurt, 1965). For Lagarde, see Fritz Stern's *The Politics of Cultural Despair*. Among the helpful articles published on the subject in *LBI* are: Hans Liebeschütz, "Treitschke and Mommsen on Jewry and Judaism" (1962); M. A. Meyer, "The Great Debate on Antisemitism" (1966); and Henry Wassermann, "Jews and Judaism in the Gartenlaube" (1978).

69. The best analysis is Richard S. Levy, *The Downfall of the Anti-Semitic Parties in Imperial Germany* (New Haven: Yale University Press, 1975); for Hessen, see Dan S. White, *The Splintered Party* (Cambridge, Mass.: Harvard University Press, 1976) especially pp. 136-48. Some information on Bernhard Förster and his relationship to the Bayreuth circle can be gained from H. F. Peters, *Zarathrustra's Sister* (New York: Crown, 1977).

70. A. Levy, *Geschichte der Juden in Sachsen* (Berlin, 1900), p. 108 and fn. For Fritsch see: R. H. Phelps, "Theodor Fritsch und der Antisemitismus," *Deutsche Rundschau* (1961), 87; Levy, *The Downfall of the Anti-Semitic Parties* (chap. 4 has a good analysis of the 1893 election).

71. The letter is undated, probably from 1889 (CN).

72. Advertisements for these journals appeared in *BB* (on the covers). Others included: *Pionier, Unverfälschte Deutsche Worte*, and *Westphälische Reform*. The judgment on the membership of the Dresden Verein is made from its annual lists included in *BB* (its size was 23 in 1884, 40 in 1886, and 67 in 1887). As already indicated Bernhard Förster was an enthusiastic Wagnerite: he lectured to Wagner societies, including that in Berlin, and gained the enthusiastic support of Wolzogen for his Aryan colonization scheme, Nueva Germania, in Paraguay. Peters, in *Zarathrustra's Sister*, quotes a letter of Elizabeth Nietzsche from 1883: "He (Förster) is filled with a magnificent enthusiasm for Wagner's efforts to regenerate our country. We feast on compassion, heroic self-denial, Christianity, vegetarianism, Aryanism, southern colonies." Once in Paraguay they sent back reports and appeals, printed in *BB* and elsewhere: discussing drainage schemes etc.; Förster writes "How far all these activities seem from the sacred hill of Bayreuth. But we feel in our hearts that it is precisely this kind of work that makes us the spiritual heirs of Richard Wagner." (pp. 71, 102-3).

73. HSC to CW Feb. 17, 1889 (CN).

74. HSC to Harriet Chamberlain June 26, 1888 (CN).

75. Chamberlain's friendship with Laforgue meant a great deal to him though few details have survived. He visited Laforgue several times in Berlin and on Dec. 13, 1887, wrote to Aunt Harriet: "The death of Laforgue in August last robbed me of the only man I ever felt I could be really intimate with. He was in all senses of the word a 'genius'" (CN).

76. For lists of his reading see his *Tagebücher* (CN).

77. HSC to Harriet Chamberlain June 26, 1888 (CN).

78. *Ibid.*

Chapter Three: First Years in Vienna (1889–92)

1. HSC to Harriet Chamberlain Oct. 19, 1889 (CN); Edouard Dujardin, *Rencontres avec Houston Stewart Chamberlain* (Paris, 1943), p. 67–70.

2. *Lebenswege* p. 117; see also Wiesner's comments in a letter to Leopold von Schroeder, *H. S. Chamberlain* (Munich, 1918) p. 63–64.

3. *Lebenswege*, p. 122; *Natur und Leben*, pp. 117 ff.

4. *Recherches sur la sève ascendante* (Neuchatel, 1897).

5. HSC to Harriet Chamberlain July 18, 1890 (CN).

6. Dujardin, *Rencontres* p. 86.

7. HSC to Harriet Chamberlain Sept. 7, 1890 (CN); Anna Chamberlain, *Meine Erinnerungen* chap. 9; Anna Chamberlain to Harriet Chamberlain Dec. 29, 1892; HSC to Harriet Chamberlain Nov. 1, 1890 (CN). *The Illustrated London News* printed some of his photographs: see the letters between HSC, Anne Guthrie, and William Simpson in 1892 (CN).

8. L. von Schroeder, *H. S. Chamberlain*, p. 72; R. Kassner, *Buch der Erinnerung* (Leipzig, 1938) pp. 156–57; *Foundations*, 2:511.

9. HSC to Agénor Boissier Nov. 12, 1890 (CN).

10. HSC to Harriet Chamberlain March 22, 1886; also March 1, 21, and Nov. 27, 1887 (CN).

11. "La Bosnie sous le protectorat del'Autriche," *Bibliotheque universelle et Revue suisse* (1892), 54; "Bosnische Bilder," *Ostdeutsche Rundschau* (Vienna) Dec. 2, 1893; "Bosnia for a Holiday," *Manchester Guardian* April 13, 1895.

12. "Bosnische Reise," unpublished ms. Oct. 1890. HSC to Harriet Chamberlain Aug. 27, 1892 (CN); "La Bosnie sous le protectorat," pp. 5–6.

13. *Briefe* 1:33; *Briefwechsel* p. 208; HSC to Harriet Chamberlain Aug. 27, 1891 (CN); "La Bosnie sous le protectorat," pp. 356, 360–66.

14. "Bosnische Reise," ms.

15. "Bosnia for a Holiday."

16. HSC to Ali Cehic Nov. 5, 1895, *Briefe* 1:31–32.

17. *Briefwechsel*, p. 369. Note also his reflections on leaving Bosnia: "Of course, one thing strikes one most forcibly on reentering Europe and that is the preponderant role of women. I will not defend the paradox that this is a misfortune—but certainly it seems to me the chief reason for our want of dignity and pride," HSC to Harriet Chamberlain Sept. 28, 1890 (CN).

18. Dujardin, *Rencontres*, p. 74–75.

19. The chief sources for the following account are the extensive Appia-Cham-

berlain correspondence in the Chamberlain *Nachlass*; R. Vollbach, *Adolphe Appia. Prophet of the Modern Theater* (Middletown, Conn.: Wesleyan University Press, 1968); *idem*, "Adolphe Appia und H. S. Chamberlain," *Die Musik Forschung* (1966), 4. Vollbach does not seem to me to strike the right balance in his analysis of the relationship, partly because of a strong desire to separate Appia from the taint of Chamberlain's racial and political views. He also ignores Appia's repeated efforts to revive the friendship after the break over Anna and Chamberlain's divorce.

20. Vollbach, *Adolphe Appia* p. 40.

21. Geoffrey Skelton, *Wagner at Bayreuth, Experiment and Tradition* (London, 1965) p. 151. In addition to helping Appia in Dresden and Munich Chamberlain also, in 1900, provided him with introductions to prominent people in Paris and urged wealthy patrons to assist him.

22. Vollbach, *Adolphe Appia* p. 40.

23. Quoted in a letter from HSC to Appia Oct. 31, 1888 (CN).

24. *Richard Wagner* (Munich ed. 1942) p. 289 fn.

25. CW to HSC May 13, 1896 (CN); HSC to Appia Feb. 13, 1894 (CN).

26. *Die Musik und die Inszenierung* (Munich: Bruckmann, 1899). Though their friendship cooled after 1906 Appia still wrote warm letters to Chamberlain. See, for example, his four letters praising *Mensch und Gott* in 1923 (CN).

27. Rolland quoted in Jacques Barzun, *Darwin, Marx, Wagner* (New York: Anchor, 1958) p. 392. On Bahr see his own *Selbstbildnis* (Berlin, 1923).

28. For a fine study of early Wagnerism in Austria see W. J. McGrath, *Dionysian Art and Popular Politics in Austria* (New Haven, 1974). For the intellectual background there are, of course, the excellent essays by Carl Schorske: "The Transformation of the Garden: Ideal and Society in Austrian Literature," *American Historical Review* (1967), 72; "Politics and Psyche in *fin de siècle* Vienna: Schnitzler and Hofmannsthal," *American Historical Review* (1960–61), 66.

29. Almost nothing has been written about the Vienna Wagner Society. Some details can be pieced together from the *Bayreuther Blätter* and the annual reports of the Verein. See, for example, the *Achzehnter Jahresbericht des Wiener akademischen Wagner-Vereins 1890* (Vienna, 1891).

30. HSC–CW correspondence (CN) 1890–1892. The published version of the correspondence omitted these letters. HSC to Friedrich Glasenapp April 25, 1892 (CN).

31. *Briefwechsel*, pp. 243–44; HSC to CW Oct. 26, 1891 (CN). On the night that Chamberlain spoke, a prominent member of the *Neuer Verein*, Karl Haller, also addressed the club on "Deutsche Kunst und deutsche Politik." Also *Briefwechsel* pp. 260ff. HSC to Glasenapp April 25, 1892 (CN); HSC to Friedrich Schön May 27, 1896 (CN); Karl Haller–HSC correspondence for 1892–3—e.g., Jan 11 and 14, 1892 (CN). *Verein* meetings were reported in the Pan-German *Ostdeutsche Rundschau*. Some lectures were directly on the Jewish question—e.g. Theodor Antropp's talk entitled "Goethe und das Judentum" on April 6, 1893 (*Tagebücher*-CN). The *Verein* was restricted to Germans, and Chamberlain had to obtain special dispensation to become a member.

32. For the Graz lecture see *Briefwechsel*, p. 317. In a lecture to the *Deutscher Jugendbund* Chamberlain asked: "Whose fault is it if the Jewish press possesses so enormous an influence? Who compelled us to drink from the poisoned stream and . . . how could we relish such a draught." "Festvortrag" *Deutscher Jugendhort* (Vienna) (1897), 1. H. Ahorner, "H. S. Chamberlain" *Deutschlands Erneuerung* (Munich, 1933), 17.

33. There are many studies of Austria prior to 1914. Among the most helpful are: Carl Schorske, "Politics in a New Key: An Austrian Triptych," *Journal of Modern*

History (1967), 39; Andrew G. Whiteside, *The Socialism of Fools. Georg Ritter von Schoenerer and Austrian Pan-Germanism* (Berkeley: University of California Press, 1975); *idem, Austrian National Socialism before 1918* (The Hague, 1962); Peter G. J. Pulzer, *The Rise of Political Anti-Semitism in Germany and Austria* (New York: Wiley, 1964); W. J. McGrath, "Student Radicalism in Vienna," *Journal of Contemporary History* (1967) 2(3); W. M. Johnston *The Austrian Mind* (Berkeley: University of California Press, 1972) contains a good bibliography.

34. HSC to Harriet Chamberlain April 12, 1890 (CN).

35. *Briefwechsel*, pp. 523–24; HSC to Harriet Chamberlain May 30, 1897 (CN). See also Chamberlain's comments at the death of one of the *Jugendbund* leaders, written in a letter of 1896 and published in the *Völkischer Beobachter* (Munich) Oct. 19, 1926, p. 2.

36. Heinrich von Treitschke *Politics* (abridged by Hans Kohn, New York, 1963), p. 132. Chamberlain greatly admired Treitschke and sent copies of his earliest writings to him.

37. *Foundations*, 1:327. For the impact of the Habsburg Monarchy on Chamberlain see also: Gerd-Klaus Kaltenbrunner, "Houston Stewart Chamberlains Germanischer Mythos," *Politische Studien* (Munich) (1967), *18*. I found this article very insightful.

38. *Foundations* 1:301.

39. *Rasse und Persönlichkeit*, pp. 83, 86. It would also seem that the campaign which the Pan-Germans launched against Roman Catholicism also left a deep imprint on Chamberlain's writings. Schoenerer's slogan "Ohne Juda, ohne Rom wird erbaut Germanias Dom" could easily have served as a closing incantation to the *Foundations*. The success of Karl Lueger's Christian Social movement in mobilizing mass support in Vienna strengthened Chamberlain's fear of a Catholic resurgence, artfully disguised under the slogans of Christian socialism. For Chamberlain, as for Austrian Pan-Germans, Rome was not merely a historical foe of Germanism but a present danger.

40. Arthur Schnitzler, *My Youth in Vienna* (New York: Holt, 1970), pp. 5–6. See also his novel, *Der Weg ins Freie* (Berlin, 1908); also insightful is Adolf Gaisbauer, "Der historische Hintergrund von Arthur Schnitzlers 'Professor Bernhardi," *Bulletin of the Leo Baeck Institute* (1974). For Austrian Jews see J. Fraenkel, ed., *The Jews of Austria. Essays on Their Life, History, and Destruction* (London: Valentine, 1967). Also helpful for the general topic of anti-Semitism is Dirk van Arkel, *Antisemitism in Austria* ms, Leiden 1966.

41. HSC to Harriet Chamberlain Aug. 30, 1894 (CN).

42. HSC to Anne Guthrie Sept. 2, 1895 (CN).

43. Several kinds of anti-Semitism coexisted and overlapped in Austria. One form stressed socioeconomic issues and predominated among the many protest organizations formed by craftsmen and small businessmen; another was heavily religious and harked back to medieval demonology. The major propagators of this brand of fanaticism were wayward priests like Joseph Deckert and August Rohling, whose *Talmudjude* caused a sensation in 1871. Finally, there was also racial or biological anti-Semitism—note, for example, Schoenerer's comments: "We regard anti-Semitism as the cornerstone of our nationality. . . . Our anti-Semitism is not directed at their religion but at their peculiar racial qualities" (Whiteside, *Socialism of Fools*, p. 120).

44. *Briefwechsel*, pp. 356–58.

45. *Drei Bühnendichtungen* (Munich, 1902). There are several other unpublished plays (CN). Another work which occupied him in these years but was not published till much later was *Herr Hinkebeins Schädel* (Munich, 1921), a humorous sketch revolving around idealist philosophy.

46. *Lebenswege*, p. 125.

47. HSC to Wolzogen March 24, 1893; see also Schüler, *Der Bayreuther Kreis*, p. 161 fn. *Tagebücher* (CN); see also R. Louis, *Die deutsche Musik der Gegenwart* (Leipzig, 1912).

Chapter Four: The Bayreuth Publicist

1. On this theme see Fritz Stern, *Politics of Cultural Despair* (Berkeley: University of California Press, 1961).

2. W. Schüler, *Der Bayreuther Kreis* (Münster, 1971) is excellent for the personalities of the Wagner cult and its evolution to 1918. It is somewhat weaker on Chamberlain's role and the political significance of Bayreuth.

3. HSC to C. F. Glasenapp Dec. 30, 1896 (CN).

4. HSC to Wolzogen March 24, 1893 (RW Gedenkstätte); HSC to W. Golther March 22, 1896, *Briefe* 1:38.

5. Stern *Politics of Cultural Despair* (1974 reprint); p. 89–90; R. W. Lougee, *Paul de Lagarde* (Cambridge: Harvard University Press, 1962); Ludwig Schemann, *Paul de Lagarde. Ein Lebens—und Erinnerungsbild* (Leipzig, 1919).

6. Short reports on both organizations can be found in *BB's* annual reports. For the youth Bund see chapter 10.

7. Membership lists in *BB* give some hints about the social background in local *Vereine*.

8. Thus Ottomar Beta, a fiercely anti-Semitic advocate of land reform, wrote for both *BB* and journals like Fritsch's *Hammer*, so did Willibald Hentschel.

9. *Briefwechsel zwischen Cosima Wagner und Fürst Ernst zu Hohenlohe-Langenburg* (Stuttgart, 1937). Georg Meurer "Bayreuther Eindrücke" *Hammer* (1902), 1. See also B. Schemann, *Cosima Wagner. Briefe an Ludwig Schemann* (Regensburg, 1937).

10. *The Guardian* (London) July 20 1898.

11. Quoted in Schüler *Der Bayreuther Kreis*, p. 53.

12. HSC to Siegfried Wagner July 18, 1896, *Briefe* 1:43.

13. Du Moulin Eckart, *Cosima Wagner* 2:499.

14. C. F. Glasenapp's six-volume *Das Leben Richard Wagners* (Leipzig, 1905-1911) was the "offical biography." Bayreuthians put forward Glasenapp's name for a Nobel Prize in 1902. For Chamberlain's "intuitive" method see HSC to Harriet Chamberlain March 27, 1893 (CN); "The Personal Side of Richard Wagner" and "How Richard Wagner Wrote His Operas" in *Ladies Home Journal* (Philadelphia) Nov. 1898; "Richard Wagner: Schematische Lebensübersicht" *Weekblad voor Muziek* (Amsterdam) Sept. 14, 21; Oct. 5, 19; Nov. 2, 1895.

15. *Richard Wagner* (Hight trans), p. 35. HSC to A. Hight July 18, 1897 (CN).

16. *Richard Wagner*, especially pp. 88, 93–95. See also M. Wesendonck to HSC Jan. 13, 1896 and Chamberlain's reply Jan. 20, 1896, *Briefwechsel*, pp. 431–35.

17. "Richard Wagner und die Heimgarten" *Ostdeutsche Rundschau* (Vienna) May 22, 1894. *Richard Wagner* (High trans.) p. 358. See also HSC to Glasenapp July 12, 1897 (CN). Richard Wagner *Gesammmelte Schriften* 10:343. Also Chamberlain's "Offenen Brief an Herrn Fritzsch" *Musikalisches Wochenblatt* (Leipzig) Oct. 1899.

18. "Richard Wagner und die Heimgarten;" *Richard Wagner* (Hight trans.), p. 358. For Hanslick see his autobiography *Aus meinem Leben*, 2 vols. (Berlin, 1894). *Richard Wagner* (Hight trans.), p. 175.

19. H. Dinger, *Richard Wagners geistige Entwicklung* (Leipzig, 1892). HSC to CW Oct. 18, 1892, *Briefwechsel*, p. 302. Also Chamberlain's "La littérature Wagnérienne an Allemagne," *Revue des deux Mondes* (Paris) 1894, pp. 782–810. The essay appeared under the name of one of Chamberlain's acquaintances, Jean Thorel, but he actually wrote it. Also "Unter uns" *BB* (1894) pp. 73–78.

20. HSC to CW Feb. 16, 1893, CW to HSC Feb. 19, 1893; HSC to CW Feb. 22, 1893 (*Briefwechsel*, pp. 316–21). The lecture was published in *BB* later in 1893.

21. *Richard Wagner* (Hight trans.), pp. 55, 58; "Richard Wagner und die Politik," in *BB* (1893) "Über Richard Wagner" *Der Wartburgerbund* (Dresden 1896), 2 (13–16). See also HSC's introduction to *Richard Wagner's Letters to August Roeckel* (trans, London 1897); "Richard Wagner's politische Grundsätze," *Neue Musikalische Presse* (Vienna) (1900), 9. Chamberlain was very anxious that Wagnerites close to court circles in Berlin bring his reinterpretation of Wagner's politics before the Kaiser: HSC to Wolzogen March 18, 1893 (CN).

22. Dinger, *Richard Wagners geistige Entwicklung; F. Praeger, Wagner wie ich ihn kannte* (Leipzig 1892; a translation, *Wagner as I Knew Him*, appeared in the same year in London and New York). Also W. Blissett, "English Wagnerism before 1900," *The Wagner Society News Letter* (London, 1959), no. 39.

23. "Ferdinand Praegers 'Wagner wie ich ihn kannte" *BB* (1893), 16.

24. "Nachtrag zu Richard Wagners Briefe an Ferdinand Praeger," *BB* (1894), 17; *Briefwechsel*, pp. 316 ff, 357 ff.

25. Postcard to Harriet Chamberlain Aug. 14, 1893 (CN). Notices of the refutation appeared, for example, in *Der Kunstwart*, Sept. 1893, *Ostdeutsche Rundschau* (Vienna) Aug. 20, 1893; *Le Guide Musicale* (Paris) Feb. 25, 1894.

26. Breitkopf and Härtel, publishers, to HSC March 29, 1895; Breitkopf and Härtel to Lord Dysart Sept. 24, 1894 (CN). Also, *Neue Freie Presse* (Vienna) Oct. 29, 1898.

27. W. A. Ellis "Praeger and Wagner's Letters" *The Musical Standard* (London and New York) Feb. 24; March 10, 17, 24, 31; April 7, 1894. Mrs. Leonie Praeger *The Musical Standard*, April 14, 21, 28, 1894; Ellis rejoinder in the same magazine May 12, 26, 1894; editorial summing up of the dispute June 2, 1894. Wilfred Praeger to *The Musical Standard* Aug. 17, 1895; HSC's reply Aug. 31, 1895. Lord Dysart to HSC July 16, 1895. HSC-Rechtsanswalt Bernstein correspondence (CN).

28. Lord Dysart to Bernstein July 16, 17, 25, 1895 (CN). *Richard Wagner. Echte Briefe an Ferdinand Praeger* (Bayreuth, 1894, 2nd ed. 1908).

29. E. Newman, *Fact and Fiction about Wagner* (New York, 1931), p. 168. Ellis to HSC April 19, 1894; HSC to Wolzogen March 28, 1893; HSC to CW Oct. 30, 1893 (CN). See also "Nocheinmal Richard Wagner und P. Rosegger," *Ostdeutsche Rundschau* (Vienna) July 10, 1894, no. 187. The quotation is from "Nachtrag zu Richard Wagners Briefe," *BB* (1894).

30. *Ostdeutsche Rundschau* (Vienna) July 20, 1894, Aug. 20, 1893; *Allgemeine Musikzeitung* (Berlin) August 1894; *Deutsche Zeitung* (Berlin) April 4, 1895; *Deutsche Wacht* April 7, 1895; *Revue des deux mondes* (Paris) Nov. 15, 1893.

31. "Eine Entgegnung auf unser 'offenes Wort' über die Neu-Inszenierung des Lohengrin in München," *Ostdeutsche Rundschau* June 12, 1894. "Münchener Lohengrin Witze," *ibid.*

32. "Musikausstellung und Festspiele," *BB* (1892); "Richard Wagner als Schriftsteller," *Tägliche Rundschau; Beilage* (Berlin) May 22–23, 1902, nos. 116–17. "Richard Wagner als Erzieher," *Ostdeutsche Rundschau* Dec. 23, 1899. Wolzogen, *Bayreuth* (1904), p. 80. The final quote is from C. Schorske, "The Quest for the Grail: Wagner

and Morris," *The Critical Spirit. Essays in Honor of Herbert Marcuse* (Boston: Beacon, 1967), p. 229.

33. "Bayreuth und die Kritik," *Deutsche Revue* (Berlin) Aug. 1897.

34. L. Schroeder, *Die Vollendung des arischen Mysteriums Bayreuth* (Munich, 1911), p. 211, quoted in Schüler, *Der Bayreuther Kreis*, p. 219. On Chamberlain's work for the Stipendiumsstiftung see HSC-Friedrich von Schön correspondence (CN).

35. *Richard Wagner* (Hight trans), p. 273.

36. J. M. Stein, *Richard Wagner. The Synthesis of the Arts* (Detroit, 1960); R. W. Gutman, *Richard Wagner* (London, 1968).

37. "Versuch einer Inhaltsübersicht von 'Oper und Drama,'" *Die Musik* (Berlin) 1902; *Briefwechsel*, p. 304; "Zwei offene Briefe an Herrn Fritsch," *Musikalisches Wochenblatt* (1893) 24 (17, 22); "Bewusstsein und Unbewusstsein bei Wagner," *Neue Zeitschrift fur Musik*, March 2, 1893.

38. G. Skelton, *Wagner at Bayreuth. Experiment and Tradition* (London, 1965), p. 79.

39. "Tannhäuser Nachklänge: Aus dem Brief eines Englanders an einen Franzosen," *BB* (1892); "Une défense de Tannhäuser," *L'Artiste* (Paris) Dec. 1891. *Revue Wagnérienne* (Jan. 1886), 12; "Lohengrin in Bayreuth," *Ostdeutsche Rundschau* (Vienna) July 22, 28; Aug. 14; Sept. 13, 27; Oct. 9, 20, 1894.

40. A. Coeuroy *Wagner et l'esprit romantique* (Paris, 1965), p. 319.

41. "1876–1896. Die ersten zwanzig Jahre Bayreuther Bühnenfestspiele," *BB* (1896) 19. HSC to Wolzogen Nov. 11, 1895 (CN).

42. For the Bayreuth music school see *Du Moulin Eckart* 2:442 ff; *Briefwechsel*, pp. 303, 314, 321. Also "Zur Eröffnung der Stilbildungsschule in Bayreuth" *Freie Bühne* (1893), 4(11); "Wie man in Bayreuth studiert," *Ostdeutsche Rundschau* (Vienna) March 8, 1895; "Konzert Gulbranson" *Ostdeutsche Rundschau* Dec. 18, 1900; "Bayreuther Betrachtungen," *Deutsche Zeitung* (Beilage) nos. 114–15, Aug. 15–16, 1896; "Bayreuther Briefe," *Berliner Börsen Courier* Aug. 2–20, 1896.

43. L. Lehmann, *My Path Through Life* (New York, 1914), pp. 433, 422.

44. HSC to CW July 29, 1888, May 3, 1890; CW to HSC Feb. 28, 1895, May 13, 1896, and Sept. 17, 1902 (CN). HSC to Appia Jan. 26, 1889, Sept. 13, 1892, March 5, 1893, Oct. 21, 1888, Feb. 13, 1894 (CN).

45. "Wie man in Bayreuth studiert," *Ostdeutsche Rundschau* March 8, 1895. F. Weingartner, *Buffets and Rewards. A Musicians Reminiscences* (London: Hutchinson, 1937), pp. 147–8.

46. F. Weingartner, *Bayreuth 1876–96* (Berlin, 1896).

47. *Lebenswege meines Denkens*, p. 243.

48. "Richard Wagners Regenerationslehre" *Bayreuther Blätter* (1895). This brief essay provides a good summary of Chamberlain's view of Bayreuth's regenerative role in German culture. It compares Wagner's concept of regeneration (accessible to all, discoverable through intuition, not reason and knowledge) with ideas in Schopenhauer, Indian texts, Rousseau, and Christianity. Contrasting Wagner's regeneration with the individual salvation preached by the Christian churches and with Rousseau's state of nature, Chamberlain finds it significant that in Germany the artist-visionary should be the one to explain the meaning of such "rebirth" or "renewal." After discussing the interconnection of art and religion in typically Bayreuthian terms, Chamberlain points to the racial orgins of man's "fall," viewing the Jew, in particular, as the "apostle of progress" and enemy of true "rebirth." Racial miscegenation is also blamed for steady deterioration of the "higher races." The conclusion of the essay broaches the harmful effects of alcoholism and meat-eating, two other common Wagnerite themes.

49. *Rasse und Persönlichkeit*, pp. 134–35.

50. *Briefe* 2:229.

51. M. Boucher, *The Political Concepts of Richard Wagner* (New York: Exposition, 1950). A. S. Tirrell, *Richard Wagner's Ideas on Nationalism, Culture, and Religion* PhD Diss. Columbia Univ., New York, 1952.

52. *Richard Wagner* (Munich), p. 285.

53. Letter of 1896, printed in "Brief an Hans Sachs über die Bestimmung der Wagnervereine," *BB* (1910).

54. *Gesammelte Schriften* 5:94. See also Otto Dov Kulka "Richard Wagner und die Anfänge des modernen Antisemitismus," LBI, (1961) 4(16) (Bulletin). Rather misleading is R. E. Herzstein, "The Wagnerian Ethos in German History 1848–1933," PhD Diss. New York Univ. 1964.

55. See M. D. Biddiss, *Father of Racist Ideology. The Social and Political Thought of Count Gobineau* (London: Weidenfeld, 1970).

56. The Gobineau *Nachlass* at Strasbourg contains some 28 letters from Cosima to Gobineau and 2 from Wagner. L. Schemann, *Gobineau. Eine Biographie* (Strassburg, 1913–16) 2:560. Also L. Deffoux *Les origines du Gobinisme en Allemagne* (Paris, 1925).

57. "Heldentum und Christentum," *BB*. (1881), pp. 249–58.

58. L. Schemann, *Gobineau und die Deutsche Kultur* (Leipzig, 1910); *Die Rasse in den Geisteswissenchaften* (Munich, 1928–31), 3 vols.

59. HSC to Wolzogen Nov. 15, 1897, *Briefe* 1:56.

60. *Briefe* 1:77 (HSC to "Jugend").

61. CW to HSC Sept. 28, 1894; HSC to Harriet Chamberlain Jan. 16, 1896 (CN).

62. T. Adorno, *Versuch über Wagner* (Knaur, 1964), p. 15.

63. F. Weingartner, *Buffets and Rewards* (London, 1937), p. 146.

64. CW to HSC March 1, 1900, *Briefwechsel*, p. 589–90.

65. "Richard Wagners Briefe an Hermann Levi," *BB* (1901), 24. Reprinted in part in *Rasse und Persönlichkeit*.

66. Paul and Bernhard Förster, prominent in anti-Semitic circles, wrote for *BB*. Wahrmund wrote one article for it in 1895 (see also Wolzogen's prefatory remarks).

67. Cosima Wagner-Hohenlohe Langenburg *Briefwechsel*, p. 42. (from a letter of 1893).

68. Schüler, *Der Bayreuther Kreis*, p. 248.

69. *Ibid.* (Hans von Wolzogen to HSC Nov. 3, 1894—CN).

70. HSC to Karl Haller Jan. 6, 1899, *Briefe* 1:69.

71. "Festvortrag," *Deutscher Jugendhort* (Vienna) (1897), 1 (1–5).

72. W. Frank, *Hofprediger Adolf Stoecker und die Christlichsoziale Bewegung* (Hamburg, 1935), pp. 320 ff; Du Moulin Eckart *Cosima Wagner* 2:451; *Briefwechsel*, pp. 314, 316, 323–26. Uriel Tal, *Christians and Jews* (Ithaca, 1975) pp. 248–59. W. Kampmann, "Adolf Stoecker und die Berliner Bewegung," *Geschichte in Wissenschaft und Unterricht* (1962), 13(9). Du Moulin Eckart *Cosima Wagner* 2:663–64.

73. *Gesammelte Schriften* 10:297.

74. W. J. McGrath, *Dionysian Art and Populist Politics in Austria* (New Haven: Yale University Press, 1974) p. 93.

75. G. B. Shaw, "Bayreuth and Back," *The Hawk* Aug. 13, 1889; quoted in E. Zuckermann, *The First Hundred Years of Wagner's Tristan* (New York: Columbia University Press, 1964), p. 56.

76. *Briefwechsel* pp. 626–29.

77. *BB* carried many articles on *Parsifal*—e.g., Erich Schwebsch, "Klingsor und

die heilige Lanze," *BB* (1915). See also Kurt Overhoff, *The Germanic-Christian Myth of Richard Wagner* (Bayreuth, 1955).

78. Schorske, "The Quest for the Grail: Wagner and Morris," p. 231.

79. *Wagner's Prose* Works, ed. William A. Ellis 6:282.

80. F. Stern, *The Politics of Cultural Despair* (Berkeley: University of California, 1974 ed.) p. 90.

81. H. von Wolzogen "Unter uns: Ein brief uber Kunst und Kirche" *BB* (1895), pp 183 ff. Chamberlain's disciple Friedrich Gross developed an elaborate mystical-religious view of Wagner in a series of essays in *BB*—e.g., "Die Religion der Zukunft," *BB* (1909).

82. HSC to Hans von Wolzogen July 13, 1895 (CN). See also Tal, *Christians and Jews*.

83. See Chaps. 7 and 10. Also Tal, "Religious and Anti-Religious Roots of Modern Antisemitism, " *Leo Baeck Memorial Lecture* (1971).

84. Thomas Mann, *Essays* (New York: Vintage, 1957) pp. 240, 242.

85.Robert Musil, *The Man Without Qualities* (New York; Putnam, 1965), p. 74.

86. Robert W. Gutman, *Richard Wagner. The Man, His Mind and His Music* (London: Penguin, 1971) p. 360. Also on this theme Bryan Magee's excellent *Aspects of Wagner* (New York, 1969).

87. Max Nordau, *Entartung* (Berlin, 1893; English trans., 1905).

88. For public festivals and mass politics see George L. Mosse's provocative *The Nationalization of the Masses* (New York: New American Library, 1975).

Chapter Five: The Foundations of the Nineteenth Century

1. *Drei Vorworte*, pp. 22–24; *Briefe* 1:132. Chamberlain–Bruckmann correspondence (CN).

2. HSC to A. Boissier Dec. 28, 1895; A. Boissier to HSC Jan, 3, 1896 (CN).

3. First Outline, ms (CN); HSC to CW Feb. 18, 1896 (CN).

4. *Drei Vorworte* pp. 24 ff.

5. *Foundations* 1:xxiv.

6. HSC to Redesdale Nov. 25, 1908.

7. *Tagebücher* (CN).

8. HSC to Eva Wagner Sept. 25, 1908 (CN). Keyserling, *Reise durch die Zeit* (Switzerland, 1948), pp. 134–35.

9. R. Eucken, *Geistige Strömungen der Gegenwart* (Berlin, 1918), pp. 1–10, as quoted in Fritz Ringer, *The Decline of the German Mandarins. The German Academic Community 1890–1933* (Cambridge: Harvard University Press, 1969), p. 254.

10. *Dilettantismus* (Munich, 1903), p. 48.

11. *Briefwechsel*, p. 444; *Foundations* 2:563.

12. George G. Iggers, *The German Conception of History. The National Tradition of Historical Thought From Herder to the Present* (Middletown, Conn.: Wesleyan Univ Press, 1968).

13. On the neo-Kantians see: T. E. Willey "Back to Kant, The Revival of Kantian Idealism in Germany 1870–1914" PhD Diss., Yale Univ 1965. Also L. Krieger, *The German Conception of Freedom. History of a Political Tradition* (Boston, 1957).

14. *Lebenswege*, pp. 143–44.

15. *Grundlagen* (foreword to 1st ed.).

16. M. Degros, ed. *Correspondence d'Alexis de Tocqueville et d'Arthur de Gobineau* (Paris, 1959), p. 267. Biddiss, *Father of Racist Ideology*, pp. 148 ff.

17. See William R. Keylor, *Academy and Community: The Foundation of the French Historical Profession* (Cambridge: Harvard University Press, 1975).

18. *Briefe* 2:151.

19. *Foundations* 1:38, 40, 38.

20. *Ibid.*, pp. 166; 121; on Frantz see Vermeil, ed., *The Third Reich* (London, 1955); Louis Sauzin's essay, "The Political Thought of Constantin Frantz." On Chamberlain and Roman Law, see B. Matthias "Chamberlain und das römische Recht," *Deutsche Rundschau* (1901) 106:405–17.

21. *Foundations* 1:72, 70, 172, 124; F. Hertz, *Race and Civilization* (New York: Macmillan 1928) chap. 7.

22. *Foundations* 1:200; 187ff; 200ff; 221ff. Also "Christus eine Germane" *Zukunft* (Berlin, 1904), 46.

23. *Foundations* 1:212 ff, 211 fn.

24. *Briefwechsel*, p. 564.

25. *Ibid.*, pp. 567–58.

26. Also *Rasse und Persönlichkeit*, pp. 78–79.

27. *Foundations* 1:299; 284; 299–300. Emil Ludwig, *Talks with Mussolini* (Boston: Little, Brown, 1933). Ortega y Gasset, on the other hand, was deeply influenced for a time by the *Völkerchaos* concept as a cause of North European "superiority"—*Obras Completas* (Madrid, 1961–63) 1:345. After returning to Spain after study in Germany he proclaimed the superiority of northern Europe: "Mediterranean" culture cannot match Germanic science—philosophy, mechanics, biology—with its own products. As long as it was pure, that is, from Alexander to the Barbarian invasion, there is little doubt. Later, with what certainty can we speak of "Latins" or "Mediterraneans"? Italy, France, Spain are overwhelmed by Germanic blood. We are essentially impure races; through our veins flows a tragic psychological contradiction. Houston Stewart Chamberlain speaks of "chaotic races." Ortega also, like Chamberlain, included Rousseau and Michelangelo among the Germanic types.

28. *Foundations* 1:388, 311. Also "Lucian," *Zukunft* (Berlin) March 11, 1899.

29. *Foundations* 1:250.

30. *Ibid.*, p. xl; HSC to Joseph Jacobs June 4, 1914 (CN); *Br* 1:111, 77; *Wehr und Gegenwehr*, p. 44 *Foundations* 1:353.

31. HSC to Harriet Chamberlain June 7, 1896 (CN).

32. *Foundations* 1:385–86.

33. *Ibid.*, pp. 492, 451.

34. *Ibid.*, pp. 331, 350. "How," Chamberlain asked an audience in Vienna (referring to the liberal *Neue Freie Presse*) "could a paper have become a real power, which derides and defiles daily everything which since time immemorial is holy and peculiar to we Teutons? . . . How would that have been possible if every German knew his duty." "Festvortrag," *Deutscher Jugendhort* (Vienna) (1897), 1 (1–5).

35. *Ibid*, pp. 479–80, 331. For some details of the influence of Chamberlain on Alfred Rosenberg see A. R. Chandler, *Rosenberg's Nazi Myth* (Ithaca: Cornell University Press, 1945); R. Cecil, *The Myth of the Master Race. Alfred Rosenberg and Nazi Ideology* (New York: Dodd Mead, 1972). Rosenberg's own *H. S. Chamberlain als Verkünder und Begründer einer deutschen Zukunft* (Munich, 1927) is also very revealing.

36. HSC to Harriet Chamberlain July 30, 1899 (CN).

37. *Foundations* 1:344.

38. *Grundlagen* (2nd ed. Munich, 1900), p. 450.

39. In general for liberal Protestantism and Jews in Germany see Uriel Tal, *Christians and Jews* (Ithaca: Cornell University Press, 1975).

40. *Ibid.*, p. 285.

41. See also E. Bierhahn, "Blondheit und Blondheitskult in der deutschen Literatur," *Archiv für Kulturgeschichte 46* (1964).

42. *Foundations* 1:518.

43. *Ibid.*, p. 210.

44. HSC to Harriet Chamberlain Feb. 30, 1899 (CN).

45. *Foundations* 2:134, 9; also quoted in M. Biddiss, "Prophet of Teutonism," *History Today*, January 1969. A typical passage in which Chamberlain joins socialism and Catholicism as both being antinational and therefore anti-German is the following: "All consistently reasoned Socialism leads to the absolute state. . . . It honestly admits its internationalism; its character is revealed however, not in disintegration, but in a wonderfully developed organization, copied, as it were, from a machine. In both points it betrays its affinities to Rome. In fact it represents the same Catholic ideas as the Church, although it grasps it by the other end. For that reason too, there is no room in its system for individual freedom and diversity, for personal originality. . . . Socialism is imperialism in disguise; it will hardly be recognisable with hierarchy and Primacy; in the Catholic Church it finds a pattern of socialistic, anti-individualistic organization." *Foundations* 2:176–77.

46. *Rasse und Persönlichkeit*, p. 59.

47. *Foundations* 2:248; also, "Die Seele des Chinesen," *Neues Wiener Tageblatt* April 5–6, 1900. In general on the "Yellow Peril" see Heinz Gollwitzer, *Die gelbe Gefahr* (Gottingen, 1962).

48. *Foundations* 2:258–59.

49. *Foundations* 2:362 and fn.

50. Chamberlain later made this distinction between Rome and Catholicism clearer: See *Dilettantismus;* "Die Ultramotane Bedeutung der Klöster," *Allgemeine Zeitung* Nov. 20, 1902. *Foundations* 1:328.

51. G. P. Gooch, *Germany* (New York: Scribner, 1925), p. 118.

52. See chap. 8.

53. First outline ms. (CN).

54. George L. Mosse, *Toward the Final Solution. A History of European Racism* (London: Dent, 1978), p. 234.

55. Léon Poliakov, *The Aryan Myth. A History of Racist and Nationalist Ideas in Europe* (New York: Basic Books, 1974), p. 326.

56. Jacques Barzun, *The French Race* (New York: Columbia University Press, 1932) and *Race. A Study in Superstition* (New York: Harcourt, 1937).

57. *Foundations* 1:336.

58. For Kant and Judaism, see: Nathan Rotenstreich, *The Recurring Pattern* (London: Weidenfeld, 1963).

59. Jean Finot, *Le préjugé des races* (Paris, 1906), pp. 354–57.

60. Poliakov, *The Aryan Myth*, p. 260.

61. Edward Said, "Renan's Philological Laboratory," in *Art, Politics, and Will: Essays in Honor of Lionel Trilling*, eds. Quentin Anderson et al (New York: Basic Books, 1977); Théophile Simar, *Étude critique sur la formation de la doctrine des races au XVIIIe siècle et son expansion au XIXe siècle* (Brussels, 1922). J. Chaix-Ruy, *Ernest Renan* (Paris, 1956).

62. Poliakov, *The Aryan Myth*, p. 257; also G. W. Stocking, *Race, Culture and Evolution* (New York: The Free Press, 1968), chap. 4.

63. Marvin Harris, *The Rise of Anthropological Theory* (New York: Crowell, 1968), p. 93.

64. Stocking, *Race, Culture and Evolution*, chap. 3. Also Andrew Lyons, "The Question of Race in Anthropology," PhD Diss. Oxford University 1974.

65. Gertrude Himmelfarb, *Darwin and the Darwinian Revolution* (New York: Norton, 1968), pp. 412-31; Hannsjoachim W. Koch, *Der Sozialdarwinismus. Seine Genese und sein Einfluss auf das imperialistische Denken* (Munich: C. H. Beck, 1973); R. J. Halliday, "Social Darwinism: A Definition," *Victorian Studies* (1971), p. 14.

66. Barzun, *Race. A Study in Superstition*, p. 117.

67. There is no adequate study of Anthroposociology. For Ammon's research on Saxony see: *Die Gesellschaftsordnung und ihre natürlichen Grundlagen. Entwurf einer Sozialanthropologie* (Jena, 3rd ed., 1900). For Vacher de Lapouge's views see: *L'Aryen. Son rôle social. Cours libre des sciences politiques* (Paris, 1899). Also, E. J. Young, *Gobineau und der Rassismus* (Meisenheim an Glan, 1968).

68. Hedwig Conrad Martius, *Utopien der Menschenzüchtung. Der Sozialdarwinismus und seine Folgen* (Munich, 1955); H. G. Zmarzlik, "Social Darwinism in Germany seen as a Historical Problem," in H. Holborn ed., *Republic to Reich. The Making of the Nazi Revolution* (New York: Vintage, 1972); C. P. Blacker, *Eugenics: Galton and After* (Cambridge: Harvard University Press, 1952). Hans Querner, "Ideologisch-Weltanschauliche Konsequenzen der Lehre Darwins," *Studium Generale* (1971), p. 29.

69. R. Virchow's articles in *Zeitschrift für Ethnologie* (1872) 4; *Archiv für Anthropologie* (Jan. 1886) 16. H. E. Ackerknecht, *Rudolf Virchow* (Madison, 1953); A. de Quatrefages, *La race prussienne* (Paris, 1871); Poliakov, *The Aryan Myth*, pp. 261-66; Lyons, "The Question of Race," section 6.

70. Christine Bolt, *Victorian Attitudes to Race* (London: Routledge and Kegan Paul, 1971), pp. 13-14.

71. Poliakov, *The Aryan Myth*, p. 255.

72. H. E. Ziegler's introduction to the collected essays: *Natur und Staat. Beiträge zur naturwissenschaftlichen Gesellschaftslehre* (Jena, 1903). The best analysis of the essay contest is an unpublished essay by F. W. Frey of Yale University who kindly allowed me to see his work.

73. Conrad Martius, *Utopien der Menschenzüchtung* chap. 2; Wilhelm Schallmeyer, *Vererbung und Auslese im Lebenslauf der Völker* (Jena, 1903); Ludwig Woltmann, *Politische Anthropologie* (Leipzig, 1903). Among the reviews see: Otto Ammon in *Naturwissenschaftliche Wochenschrift* (1904) 14; A. Nordenholz in *Archiv für Rassen und Gessellschaftsbiologie* (1905), pp. 456-63, 619-22. For the criticisms by F. Toennies: *Schmollers Jahrbuch* (1905), pp. 1089-1106; (1907), pp. 487-552.

74. F. Ringer, *The Decline of the German Mandarins*. See also: Russell McCormach, "On Academic Scientists in Wilhelmine Germany," *Daedalus*, Summer 1974.

75. Eugen Fischer, *Sozialanthropologie* (1910), as quoted in Hans F. K. Günther, *The Racial Elements of European History* (New York, 1927; reprint: New York, Kennikat, 1970), p. 266. For Fischer's comments on Chamberlain: L. Snyder, *Race* (New York: Alliance Books, 1939), p. 135.

76. Poliakov, *The Aryan Myth*, p. 270; also, E. J. Young, *Gobineau und der Rassismus*, pp. 209-23.

77. Chamberlain-Uexküll letters (CN); *Briefe* 2:195-96; for Penka see: Hans-

Jurgen Lutzhöft, *Der Nordische Gedanke in Deutschland* (Stuttgart: Klett, 1971), p. 112. D. Gasman, *The Scientific Origins of National Socialism. Social Darwinism in Ernst Haeckel and the German Monist Movement* (London and New York: Mac-Donald, 1971).

78. *Rasse und Persönlichkeit*, p. 80; *Dilettantismus*, p. 19.

79. Stocking, *Race, Culture and Evolution* chap. 3.

80. *Foundations* 1:518.

81. *Dilettantismus*, p. 20; *Foundations* 1:267. Also, "Die Rassenfrage," in *Rasse und Persönlichkeit*.

82. Stocking, *Race, Culture and Evolution*, p. 58.

83. *Rasse und Persönlichkeit*, p. 69; also HSC to Ludwig Stein Sept. 19, 1904 in *Briefe* 1:150.

84. *Briefe* 2:153.

85. Julian Huxley and A. H. Haddon, *We Europeans: A Survey of "Racial" Problems* (London, 1935). *Foundations* 1:512, 542-78.

86. *Foundations* 1:491.

87. *Ibid.*, pp. 519-20.

88. *Ibid.*, p. 537.

89. The manuscript was published in *Natur und Leben* (Munich: Bruckmann, 1928); see also chap. 7 for more details.

90. Uriel Tal, *Christians and Jews in Germany*, p. 282.

91. *Dilettantismus*, pp. 16, 18. *Foundations* 1:263.

92. E. Dujardin, *Rencontres avec H. S. Chamberlain* (Paris, 1943), p. 115.

93. *Foundations* 1:296; Dujardin, *Rencontres avec H. S. Chamberlain*, p. 115. *Rasse und Persönlichkeit*, p. 84. *Foundations* 1:266 fn.

94. *Foundations* 1:275-89.

95. *Ibid.*, p. 578.

96. Godet quoted in Poliakov, *The Aryan Myth*, p. 318.

97. *Kant* 2:332.

98. "An Imperialistic Chosen Race," *New York Evening Post* Jan. 23, 1904.

99. Mosse, *Toward the Final Solution*, p. 127.

Chapter Six: *Der Fall* Chamberlain

1. *Frankfurter Zeitung* April 30, 1902.

2. Alfred Rosenberg, *H. S. Chamberlain als Verkünder und Begründer einer deutschen Zukunft* (Munich, 1927), p. 29.

3. Fritz Fischer, *Krieg der Illusionen* (Düsseldorf, 1969), p. 66.

4. Otto Taube *Wanderjahre. Erinnerungen aus meiner Jugendzeit* (Stuttgart, 1950), p. 158.

5. E. Diederichs, *Leben und Werk* (Jena, 1937), letter of December 4, 1901.

6. HSC to CW Nov. 27, 1899; CW to HSC Feb. 15, 1902 (*Briefwechsel* pp. 580, 627).

7. *Das Tagebuch der Baronin Spitzemberg* (Göttingen, 1960), p. 403.

8. *Staatsburger Zeitung* (Berlin) November 5, 1901; HSC to Anne Guthrie July 27, 1902 (CN); R. Dreyfus "H. S. Chamberlain," *La Revue de Paris*, May 1, 1935, pp. 33-35; *Oesterreichische Wochenschrift* (Vienna) Dec. 13, 1901.

9. "Chamberlain als Erzieher" *Die Zukunft* (Berlin) July 12, 19, 1902.

10. *Sozialistische Monatshefte* (Berlin) 1902, pp. 876 ff, 962 ff. Also Friedrich Hertz, *Moderne Rassentheorien* (Vienna, 1904). See also the comments of the socialist poet R. Dehmel, *Ausgewählte Briefe*, 1:421 and 2:160 (Berlin 1922). Hertz's views were reproduced in *Berliner Tageblatt* July 2, Nov. 11, 1901 and were widely commented upon in the press of the Jewish defense organizations.

11. *Vorwärts* quoted in *Mitteilugen* (1901), 11(46):381–82.

12. *Frankfurter Zeitung*, March 1, 1901; also April 3 and 30, 1902. *Post* (Berlin) June 6, 1903. See also *Neue Deutsche Rundschau* (1902), 13:123 ff.

13. *Vossische Zeitung* (Berlin) April 10, 17, 1904; March 9, 22, 1902. Theodor Kappstein "Chamberlain als Erzieher" *Berliner Tageblatt*, Nov. 11, 1901 (*Beiblatt*).

14. *Der Tag* (Berlin) Sept. 27, 1903; *Der Reichsbote* (Berlin) Nov. 3, 1901. *Deutsche Zeitung* Aug. 30, 1899, Dec. 20, 1902, Jan. 22, 1905. Also *Deutsches Welt* (*Deutsche Zeitung* supplement) Feb. 8, 1903. *Deutsch-Soziale Blätter* Nov. 2, 1904; *Allgemeine Zeitung* Dec. 21–22, 1899. *Münchener Neueste Nachrichten*, Sept. 22, 1899, Jan. 13, 1903, April 15, 1903. *National Zeitung*, April 16, 1902, March 4, 18, 1904. *Norddeutsche Allgemeine Zeitung*, March 24, 1901. *Hamburgische Correspondent*, March 24, 1901. *Preussische Jahrbücher* reviews of Chamberlain's books were written by J. F. Schmidt and were often critical. *Neue Deutsche Rundschau*, Oct. 1899; *Deutsche Monatsschrift*, Nov. 1902. *Kunstwart*, Sept. 1, 1899.

15. *Ostdeutsche Rundschau* April 19, 1899, March 22, 1900, etc. *Deutsches Volksblatt* (Vienna) July 30, 1903. *Der Kyffhäuser* Aug. 1, 1900.

16. Iris Hamel, *Völkischer Verband und nationale Gewerkschaft* (Frankfurt, 1967), pp. 89 ff.

17. H. Class, *Wider den Ström* (Leipzig, 1932), p. 87.

18. Josef Reimer, *Ein pangermanisches Deutschland. Versuch ueber die Konsequenzen der gegenwärtigen wissenschaftlichen Rassenbetrachtung fur unseren politischen und religiösen Probleme* (Berlin-Leipzig, 1905).

19. *Frankfurter Zeitung*, April 30, 1902.

20. Moeller van den Bruck, *Zeitgenossen* (Minden, 1906), pp. 120 ff. *Oesterreichische Rundschau* (Nov 1905–Jan 1906) 5:455.

21. Wilhelm Busch, *Sämtliche Briefe*, ed. Friedrich Bohne (Hannover, 1969) 2:211, 220–21. *Hugo von Hofmannsthal—Josef Redlich Briefwechsel* (Frankfurt, 1971), pp. 4, 164–65. H. Bahr, *Tagebuch* (Vienna, 1918) April 10, 1917; also the volume for 1919, pp. 74, 95, 292–98. E. Schering to HSC Nov. 15, 1901 (CN). *Gesellschaft der Freunde des Nietzsche Archivs* (E. Thierbach, 1937) (1901) 8(11):83, 95, 96.

22. *Das Litterarische Echo*, Feb. 1, 1900. Also HSC to Ernst von Wolzogen Feb. 5, 1900 (*Briefe* 1:83).

23. *Die Gesellschaft* (Munich), Dec. 1900.

24. *Briefe* 2:167. R. Kassner in *Europäische Revue* (1929), 5(1). Alfred Rosenberg cited by R. Cecil, *The Myth of the Master Race* (New York: Dodd Mead, 1972), pp. 12–13.

25. Chamberlain-Ludowici letters (CN).

26. HSC to Anne Guthrie Sept. 22, 1903 (CN).

27. P. Joachimsen in *Zeitwende* (Munich, 1927), p. 352.

28. Traube, *Wanderjahre*, p. 158.

29. Otto Hintze, "Rasse und Nationalität und ihre Bedeutung für die Geschichte" (1903), reprinted in *Soziologie und Geschichte* (Göttingen, 1964).

30. *Historische Zeitschrift* (1902), 88:479–82.

31. H. Vaihinger, *Kant-Studien* (1902), no 4. HSC-Deussen letters (CN). *Vierteljahrsschrift für wissenschaftliche Philosophie* (1901), 25:57–59. *Zeitschrift für Philoso-*

phie und Pädagogik (1901) 8:232–46. Werner Sombart to HSC June 17, 1904 (*Briefe* 1:147) A. Drews in *Die Gegenwart*, Aug. 12, 1899.

32. *Wehr und Gegenwehr* pp. 38 ff. *Archiv für Rassen- und Gesellschafts-biologie* 2:739 ff. Felix von Luschan, *Völker-Rassen-Sprachen* (Berlin, 1922), pp. 25, 93.

33. *Türmer Jahrbuch* (1904), p. 75.

34. L. Schemann *Gobineaus Rassenwerk* (Leipzig, 1910), p. 274; *Vierter Bericht über die Gobineau Vereinigung*, July 1900; *Allgemeine Zeitung* (Munich), *Beilage* (1900), nos. 130–32; L. Woltmann in *Politische Anthropologische Revue* 2:550; L. Schemann to Hans von Wolzogen Feb. 20, 1902 (R. Wagner Gedenkstätte).

35. E. J. Vermeil, ed., *The Thrid Reich* (UNESCO, 1955), p. 276.

36. *Germania*, Aug. 13, 1902; H. Grauert in *Historisch-Politische Blätter* (1904), 131–32; *Stimmen aus Maria Laach, Katholische Blatter* (1901), 60:409–24; *Briefwechsel*, pp. 581–82; *Dilettantismus;* and Chamberlain's letter in *Allgemeine Zeitung* (Munich) April 19, 1907. Albert Ehrhard in *Leo Gesellschaft: Vorträge und Abhandlungen*, 14; On Schell, see the account in *Badischer Beobachter* (Karlsruhe), March 29, 1903.

37. Even the conservative theologian Reinhold Seeberg showed some approval of Chamberlain's work along with that of Lagarde and Richard Wagner in the years before 1914; Arnold Horowitz, "Prussian State and Protestant Church in the Reign of Wilhelm II," Ph.D. Diss. Yale Univ. 1976, p. 338.

38. D. Baentsch in *Pädagogisches Magazin 246* (1905).

39. *Protestantenblatt* (Bremen) July 11, 1903; *Kirchliche Wochenschrift für Evangelische Christen*, Dec. 11, 1903. Also HSC to J. F. Lehmann Feb. 12, 1904 (CN).

40. *Strassburger Zeitung*, Nov. 11, 1903. There were numerous short reviews in local papers, e.g. *Magdeburgische Zeitung*, March 19, 1903.

41. *Das Litterarische Echo*, Feb. 1, 1900.

42. *Allgemeine Zeitung* (Munich) Nov. 20, 1902.

43. M. Lehmann, *J. F. Lehmann. Ein Leben im Kampf für Deutschland* (Munich, 1935), pp. 25, 96, 102. The Lehmann publishing house in Munich would make an interesting study in itself, illustrating among other things the ties between academic race theorists and race popularizers. Beginning as the publisher of the *Münchener Medizinische Wochenschrift* in 1890, which rapidly became the leading medical journal in Germany, the firm moved on to become a leading distributor of Pan-German, *völkisch*, and extremist Protestant literature. Among its publications were the *Archiv für Rassen- und Gesellschaftsbiologie, Volk und Rasse, Heimdall*, and *Deutschlands Erneuerung*. Among the authors Lehmann signed up were Artur Dinter, Eugen Fischer, Alfred Rosenberg, L. F. Clauss, Ludwig Schemann, Paul Schultze-Naumburg, Fritz Lenz, and Alfred Ploetz. Lehmann also befriended Hans F. K. Günther in 1919, and encouraged him to write the best-selling *Rassenkunde des deustschen Volkes* (1922). After the Nazis came to power, the firm flourished more than ever; when the NSDAP issued a list of 23 works most highly recommended on race, 17 bore the imprint of Lehmann. In many ways Chamberlain was the decisive influence on Lehmann's racial thought. See also the obituary notices for Lehmann in *Deutschlands Erneuerung*, (1935), 19(5). In 1904, when he first came into contact with Chamberlain, Lehmann was very active for the *Evangelischer Bund*. This organization, founded in 1886. was strongly nationalist and militantly anti-Catholic. Its membership rose from 74,000 in 1890 to over 500,000 in 1914, and A. Horowitz ("Prussian State and Protestant Church") has estimated that about a third to a half of the Prussian pastorate was drawn into its ranks, indicating once again how closely nationalist and anti-Roman sentiments were bound together among Protestants.

44. Tal, *Christians and Jews in Germany* (Ithaca: Cornell University Press, 1975);

also, "Theologische Debatte um das 'Wesen des Christentums'" in W. E. Mosse and A. Paucker, eds. *Juden im Wilhelminischen Deutschland, 1890–1914* (Tübingen, 1976) pp. 599–632.

45. *Christliche Welt* (Oct. 18, 1900), 11(42).

46. *Ibid.*, Dec. 24, 1903. For a negative assessment see: "Die Babel- und Bibel-Literatur," *Ibid*, March 19, 1903.

47. Werner Hermann, "Erinnerungen aus Seminar und Stift," in *Blatter für württembergische Kirchengeschichte* (1953), pp. 158–62.

48. K. Kupisch, "Bürgerliche Frommigkeit im wilhelminischen Zeitalter," in H. J. Schoeps, ed., *Zeitgeist im Wandel, Das wilhelminische Zeitalter* (Stuttgart, 1967).

49. Report of the conversation by HSC to Anne Guthrie Nov. 11, 1901 (CN).

50. Adolf von Harnack to HSC Nov. 24, 1912 (CN). The other letters are dated November 3, 17, 19, 21.

51. HSC to Adolf von Harnack Dec. 9, 1912 (CN).

52. S. Zucker, "Ludwig Bamberger and the Rise of Anti-Semitism in Germany," *Central European History* (Dec. 1970), 3(4).

53. Peter Gay, "Begegnung mit der Moderne—Deutsche Juden in der deutschen Kultur," in *Juden im wilhelminischen Deutschland* (Tübingen, 1976).

54. For Jewish responses to German anti-Semitism see: I. Schorsch, *Jewish Reactions to German anti-Semitism 1870–1914* (New York, 1972); J. Reinharz, *Fatherland or Promised Land* (Ann Arbor: Univ. of Michigan Press, 1975). M. Lamberti, *Jewish Activism in Imperial Germany: The Struggle for Civil Equality* (New Haven: Yale University Press, 1978).

55. *Frankfurter Zeitung*, April 30, 1902 (written by the sociologist Franz Oppenheimer).

56. *Im deutschen Reich*, 7:610 ff; 9:580; 15:567.

57. M. Schreiner, *Die jüngsten Urteile über das Judentum* (Berlin 1902), p. 157.

58. *Im deutschen Reich* 9:580.

59. *Mitteilungen* 1902–4 contains numerous references to Chamberlain, e.g. 10(21):161–64; 11(32):268–70; (46):381; 17(11):82–83.

60. *Im deutschen Reich*, 7(8):406 ff and 7(11):610 ff.

61. *Die Welt* (Zionist in position), 5(34):5.

62. *Im deutschen Reich*, 7(4):198. *Die Welt*, 5(34):5.

63. Quoted in S. Ragins, "Jewish Responses to Antisemitism in Germany 1870–1914," PhD Diss. Brandeis Univ. 1972, p. 233.

64. *Mitteilungen*, 16(25):191.

65. M. Schreiner, *Die jüngste Urteile*, p. 164.

66. M. Goldstein, "Deutsch-jüdischer Parnass," *Kunstwart*, (March 1912), 25(11). Also M. Goldstein, "German Jewry's Dilemma. The Story of a Provocative Essay," *LBI*, 2 (London, 1957).

67. *Im deutschen Reich*, 18(10):439 ff. Goldstein's reply followed in 19(3):98–99.

68. Walther Rathenau, "Der Kaiser. Eine Betrachtung," *Gesammelte Schriften* (Berlin, 1925–29), 6:301.

69. HSC to Anne Guthrie March 17, 1901 (CN); Philipp Fürst zu Eulenburg-Hertefeld, *Erlebnisse an deutschen und fremden Höfen* (Leipzig, 1934), 2:321.

70. *Ibid.*

71. HSC to Anne Guthrie Nov. 11, 1901 (CN).

72. Eulenburg *Erlebnisse* (trans. in J. C. G. Röhl, *From Bismarck to Hitler* [London: Longmans, 1970 p. 41–2]). Also Anna Chamberlain, *Meine Erinnerungen* pp. 125 ff.

73. J. von Kurenberg, *The Kaiser* (New York, 1955), p. 249.

74. Lamar Cecil, "Wilhelm II und die Juden," in *Juden im wilhelminischen Deutschland*, p. 330. Among the foreign educators who received a copy from Kaiser Wilhelm was John W. Burgess of Columbia University.

75. *Reichsbote* Nov. 3, 1901. for comments see *Mitteilungen* (1901), pp. 381–82 and *Im deutschen Reich* (1901), pp. 612–13. Also Agnes Zahn-Harnack, *Adolf von Harnack* (Berlin, 1936), p. 341. *Berliner Zeitung*, Nov. 13, 1901.

76. *Briefe*, 2:156–57, 165. See also the comments in *The Times* (London) June 21, 1902. Most but not all of the Chamberlain-Kaiser Wilhelm correspondence was published in *Briefe*, 2.

77. Kaiser Wilhelm to HSC Dec. 31, 1901 (*Briefe*, 2:141–42).

78. *Ibid.*

79. The aide was Graf Robert Zedlitz-Trützschler. Wilhelm's audience with the Pope is related in HSC to Anne Guthrie Sept. 22, 1903 (CN).

80. Cecil, "Wilhelm II und die Juden."

81. Document reproduced in part in Röhl, *From Bismarck to Hitler.* Also E. Zechlin, *Die Deutsche Politik und die Juden im ersten Weltkrieg* (Gottingen 1969), pp. 48–49.

82. F. Delitzsch, *Babel und Bibel. Ein Vortrag* (Leipzig, 1902); *Zweiter Vortrag uber Babel und Bibel* (Stuttgart, 1904).

83. *Dilettantismus;* Also *Briefe* 2:155, 165, 167, 171, 188 ff, 199, 201–3.

84. Jean Réal, "La lettre a l'Amiral Hollmann, *Études germaniques* (Paris, 1951), 6:303–12. Kaiser Wilhelm to HSC Dec. 21, 1902, Feb. 16, 1903; HSC to Kaiser Wilhelm Feb. 4, 1903.

85. Wilhelm's letter was published in *Grenzboten* and received widespread comment.

86. Réal, "*La lettre.*" Also J. Finkelstein, "Bible and Babel," *Commentary* (1958) 26:431–44.

87. Réal, "*La Lettre.*"

88. *Briefe* 2:193–212 (letter of March 27, 1903).

89. These last letters of Kaiser Wilhelm 1925–31 (the last to Eva Chamberlain) were never published.

90. Sigurd von Ilsemann, *Der Kaiser in Holland: Amerongen und Doorn 1918–1923* (Munich, 1967), p. 191.

91. Bülow as quoted by M. Balfour, *The Kaiser and His Times* (New York: Norton, 1972), p. 149. *Briefe* 2:140, 134; *Politische Ideale*, p. 72.

92. *Briefe*, 2:140.

93. *Ibid.*, p. 226. The celebrated interview that led to the *Daily Telegraph* affair, which greatly embarrassed Wilhelm, took place at Highcliffe.

94. G. B. Shaw, *Fabian News* (June 1911) 22:53–54.

95. E. von Meyenburg to HSC May 30, 1899 (CN).

96. F. Nietzsche, *Beyond Good and Evil* (New York: Vintage Books, 1966), p. 187.

97. Theodor Fontane as quoted in G. Masur, *Imperial Berlin* (New York, 1970), p. 149.

98. Hans Rosenberg, *Grosse Depression und Bismarckzeit* (Berlin, 1967).

99. F. Stern, *The Failure of Illiberalism* (New York: Knopf, 1972), pp. 27–57. See also Stern's *Gold and Iron. Bismarck, Bleichroeder and the Building of the German Empire* (New York: Knopf 1977) chapter 18.

100. For the anti-Semitic parties: Richard S. Levy, *The Downfall of the Anti-Semitic Parties in Imperial Germany* (New Haven: Yale University Press, 1975); P. W. Massing, *Rehearsal for Destruction. A Study of Political Anti-Semitism in Germany* (New York: Harper, 1949). On craftsmen: Shulamit Volkov, *The Rise of Popular Anti-

modernism, *The Urban Master Artisans 1873–1896* (Princeton: Princeton University Press, 1978). On Treitschke: W. Boehlich, ed., *Der Berliner Antisemitismusstreit* (Frankfurt a. Main, 1965); Ernest Hamburger, *Juden im öffentlichen Leben Deutschlands* (Tübingen, 1958), pp. 99–100.

101. *LBI* (1957) 3:122.

102. For student participation in Boeckel's electoral campaigns: Levy, *The Downfall of the Anti-Semitic Parties*, pp. 22, 58–59, 195. Heinrich Class, *Wider den Strom* (Leipzig, 1932); P. J. Pulzer, *The Rise of Political Anti-Semitism in Germany and Austria* (New York: Wiley, 1964), pp. 247–57.

103. Quoted by J. A. Nichols, *Germany after Bismarck* (New York: Norton, 1968), p. 26.

104. Ismar Schorsch, *Jewish Reactions to German Anti-Semitism*, pp. 103–16; Levy, *The Downfall of the Anti-Semitic Parties*.

105. The best account of the period is Werner Jochmann, "Struktur und Funktion des deutschen Antisemitismus," in *Juden im Wilhelminischen Deutschland*, pp. 389–477.

106. Oppenheimer, quoted in E. Zechlin, *Die deutsche Politik und die Juden*, p. 53. On the transformation of anti-Semitism see also: Reinhard Rürup, "Emanzipation und Krise zur Geschichte der 'Judenfrage' in Deutschland vor 1890," in *Juden im Wilhelminischen Deutschland*, pp. 1–56.

107. Bartels, quoted by Klaus Bergmann, *Agrarromantik und Großstadtfeindschaft* (Meisenheim an Glan, 1970), p. 117.

108. Shulamit Volkov, "Antisemitism as a Cultural Code," *LBI* (1978) 23:34–35.

109. Dirk Stegmann, *Die Erben Bismarcks* (Cologne and Berlin, 1970); Michael Stürmer, ed., *Das kaiserliche Deutschland. Politik und Gesellschaft 1870–1918* (Düsseldorf, 1970); Hans-Ulrich Wehler, *Das deutsche Kaiserreich 1871–1918* (Göttingen, 1973). Between 1871 and 1912 the German electorate doubled, while the number of voters participating tripled.

110. H. J. Puhle, *Agrarische Interessenpolitik und preussischer Konservatismus im wilhelminischen Reich 1893–1914* (Hannover, 1966); Konrad Schilling, *Beiträge zu einer Geschichte des radikalen Nationalismus in der wilhelminischen Ära*, Phil. Diss. Cologne, 1968; Geoff Eley, "Reshaping the German Right: Radical Nationalism and the German Naval League, 1898–1908," *Historical Journal* (1978), 21:327–54. For the *Wehrverein:* Martin Kitchen, *The German Officer Corps 1890–1914* (Oxford: Clarendon Press, 1968), pp. 136–39. Also, H. Pogge von Strandmann, "Nationale Verbände zwischen Weltpolitik und Kontinentalpolitik," in *Marine und Marinepolitik im kaiserlichen Deutschland 1871–1914*, ed. H. Schottelius and W. Diest (Düsseldorf, 1972). The *Reichsverband gegen Sozialdemokratie*, founded in 1904, also played an increasingly important role in the struggle against the S.P.D. and in forging a conservative nationalist consensus (with anti-Semitic overtones, especially in the last years of peace). For the failure of the liberal parties and organizations to meet the challenge of mass politics in Imperial Germany, see: James J. Sheehan, *German Liberalism in the Nineteenth Century* (Chicago: University of Chicago Press, 1978), pp. 219–83.

111. Reinhard Rürup, "Emancipation and Crisis," *LBI* (1975), 20:25. On the different political milieux of Germany see: M. Rainer Lepsius, "Parteien und Sozialstruktur: Zum Problem der Demokratisierung der deutschen Gesellschaft," in G. A. Ritter, ed., *Deutsche Parteien vor 1918* (Cologne, 1973) pp. 56–80.

112. Jochmann, "Struktur und Funktion des deutschen Antisemitismus," p. 464; Stegmann, *Die Erben Bismarcks*, pp. 257–62.

113. Fritz Fischer, *War of Illusions. German Policies from 1911 to 1914* (New York: Norton, 1975), p. 256.

114. *Ibid.*

115. This whole subject will be treated at length in Geoff Eley's forthcoming study, *Reshaping the German Right* (New Haven: Yale University Press, 1980). See also: Uwe Lohalm, *Völkischer Radikalismus. Die Geschichte des Deutschvölkischen Schutz- und Trutz-Bundes 1919–1923* (Hamburg, 1970).

116. George Mosse, *The Crisis of German Ideology* (New York: Grosset and Dunlap, 1964), p. 134.

117. Stegmann, *Die Erben Bismarcks* pp. 293–304. Posadowsky was State Secretary of the Ministry of the Interior until 1907; von Stössel was a leading Pan-German.

118. Heinrich Class, *Wenn ich der Kaiser wär* (Leipzig, 1914 ed.), p. 76. Italics in the original.

119. For example, Peter Gay, "Begegnung mit der Moderne—Deutsche Juden in der deutsche Kultur," in *Juden im Wilhelminischen Deutschland*, especially pp. 300–11.

120. Ismar Schorsch, "German Anti-Semitism in the Light of Post-War Historiography," *LBI* (1974), 19:269.

121. Jochmann, "Struktur und Funktion des deutschen Antisemitismus," pp. 459–60, 468–89. The efforts of individuals like Class, Bartels, Fritsch and Wilhelm Schwaner to unify the different anti-Semitic groups met with little success; also, the attempts to forge a common strategy through such organizations as the *Germanen Orden, Reichshammerbund* and the *Verband gegen Ueberhebung des Judentums* made little headway before the war. More than twenty new anti-Semitic organizations were founded 1912–1914.

122. Letters to HSC (CN).

123. *Vorarlberger Volksfreund* (Donbirn) March 2, 19, 30; April 7, 23, 30; July 2 etc. 1904. *Vorarlberger Volksblatt* (Bregenz) March 10; April 2; June 12, 19, 26; July 3, 10, 17, 23, 31; Aug. 7, 14, 27; Sept. 17, 24, 1904.

124. *Briefe* 2:161.

125. Note the comment of the *Gothaische Tagblatt* Dec. 21, 1915: "If one asks which writer in the last decade before the war had the greatest impact on the national consciousness and world view of the educated classes, the almost unanimous answer would probably be Houston Stewart Chamberlain."

Chapter Seven: Toward a Teutonic World View

1. *Briefe*, 2:139.

2. *Kant* (Redesdale trans London, 1914), 2:338.

3. Lienhard (1865–1929) considered his work closely related to the cultural mission of Bayreuth and included letters from Chamberlain, Schemann, and Wolzogen in the diaries he published at the end of each volume of the *Wege*.

4. *Drei Vorworte*, pp. 24 ff.

5. HSC to Harriet Chamberlain Oct. 25, 1896 (CN); *Lebenswege meines Denkens*, pp. 125 ff; HSC to Gräfin Zichy Feb. 26, 1899 (CN). "Gardone Entwurf" ms (CN), published in *Natur und Leben*, pp. 103–36.

6. HSC to Anne Guthrie June 24, 1900 (CN).

7. *Briefwechsel*, p. 478.

8. *Lebenswege meines Denkens*, p. 141.

9. HSC to Viktor Kommetter Sept. 19, 1902 (*Briefe*, 1:98).

10. *Lebenswege meines Denkens*, pp. 141 ff; *Briefe*, 1:132–33, 292–94.

11. See T. E. Willey, "Back to Kant. The Revival of Kantian Idealism in Germany 1870–1914," PhD Diss. Yale University 1965. Also Fritz K. Ringer, *The Decline of the German Mandarins. The German Academic Community 1890–1933* (Cambridge: Harvard University Press, 1969).

12. *Foundations*, 1:269; *Dilettantismus*, p. 20; *Kant*, 2:331.

13. *Kant* 2:334–36, 390.

14. *Kritische Urteile* (3rd enlarged edition, Munich 1909).

15. *Preussische Jahrbücher* (1906), 3; *Pädagogisches Archiv* (1906), 2; *Hochland* (1906–7), 4:752; *Neue Freie Presse* (Vienna) Dec. 7, 1905; Paul Natorp to HSC Jan. 28, 1906 (CN); Hermann Broch to Ludwig von Ficker (publisher of *Der Brenner*) in *Gesammelte Werke* 10:255; Leopold von Schroeder to HSC Jan. 26, 1906. Earlier in 1902 the Bayreuth *Kreis* had unsuccessfully recommended Friedrich Glasenapp (Wagner's biographer) for a Nobel Prize. For Kassner and Keyserling's relationship to Chamberlain see chapter 8.

16. Wolfgang Leppmann, *The German Image of Goethe* (London: Oxford, University Press, 1961), p. 106.

17. See chapter 8.

18. Review by Dr. Ernst Traumann, *Frankfurter Zeitung*, Jan. 7, 1913.

19. "Gardone Entwurf," *Natur und Leben*, p. 136. On Chamberlain's *Goethe* see the essay by Jean Réal, "Houston Stewart Chamberlain et Goethe," *Études germaniques* (Paris) (1950), 5. *Briefe*, 2:25. Although Chamberlain was disappointed at the reception *Goethe* obtained, the book was widely reviewed and highly praised. For a sample of reviews see: *Reichsbote* (Berlin) March 11, 1913; *Kölnische Zeitung* March 18, 1913; *Berliner Tageblatt* May 7, 1913; *Deutsche Tagezeitung* (Berlin) Jan. 13, April 28, June 16, 1913; *The Times* (London) July 17, 1913; *Zeitschrift fur Philosophie und Pädagogik* (June 1914) 21(9).; *Die Grenzboten*, March 5, 1913; *Goethe-Jahrbuch*, (1913), 34; *Bühne und Welt*, Sept. 1913. A large number of reviews also appeared in the influential local press throughout Central Europe.

20. W. Leppmann, *The German Image of Goethe*, p. 176.

21. Emil Du Bois-Reymond, *Goethe und kein Ende* (1882); Rudolf Magnus, *Goethe als Naturforscher* (Leipzig, 1906).

22. *Kant*, 1:46.

23. *Goethe* chap. 5 (esp. pp. 564–78).

24. *Goethe*, pp. 324, 709, 730.

25. *Goethe*, pp. 715–24, 748.

26. *Im deutschen Reich* (Berlin) (1913), *11*.

27. For Goethe's interpretation of Kant see Ernst Cassirer, *Rousseau, Kant and Goethe* trans. Peter Gay (New York 1963).

28. A. Aliotta, *The Idealistic Reaction against Science* (London, 1914); Karl Löwith, *From Hegel to Nietzsche. The Revolution in Nineteenth Century Thought* (English version: New York, 1964); O. Chadwick, *The Secularization of the European Mind in the Nineteenth Century* (Cambridge, 1975).

29. For Haeckel see D. Gasman, *The Scientific Origins of National Socialism. Social Darwinism in Ernst Haeckel and the German Monist League* (London and New York: MacDonald, 1971).

30. In addition to Gasman see: N. R. Holt, "The Social and Political Ideas of

the German Monist Movement 1871-1914 PhD Diss. Yale Univ. 1967; F. Bolle "Darwinismus und Zeitgeist," in H. J. Schoeps, ed., *Zeitgeist im Wandel. Das wilhelminische Zeitalter* (Stuttgart, 1967).

31. Virchow had been Haeckel's teacher at Würzburg; Friedrich Paulsen, "Ernst Haeckel als Philosoph," *Preussische Jahrbücher*, (1900) 101.

32. Bolle in Schoeps, *Zeitgeist im Wandel*, p. 258.

33. *Ibid.*, pp. 258-63; Chamberlain-Reinke letters (e.g., J. Reinke to HSC June 30, 1907—CN).

34. "Antwort auf einer Rundfrage über die Wert und Bedeutung des realistischen Bildungswesens," *Bayerische Zeitung für Realschulwesen* (April 1914), 22(4) 156-57.

35. "Büchners Sturz," *Neue Deutsche Rundschau* (June 1895), 6:572-84.

36. S. F. Mason, *A History of the Sciences* (New York, 1962), pp. 500-501.

37. See, for example, Chamberlain's summary in the Plato chapter of *Kant* (1906).

38. *Natur und Leben*, pp. 115, 23.

39. *Ibid.*, pp. 140-49.

40. *Goethe* chap. 4. See also "Goethe, Linné und die exakte Wissenschaft," in *Rasse und Persönlichkeit*, pp. 112-125.

41. E. Heller, "Goethe and the Idea of Scientific Truth," in *The Disinherited Mind. Essays in Modern German Literature and Thought* (New York: Farrar Strauss, 1959), pp. 14, 8-9. The first is a quotation from Goethe.

42. His manuscripts were published after his death by his biologist friend Jacob von Uexküll in *Natur und Leben* (Munich: Bruckmann, 1928).

43. *Goethe*, pp. 628-63.

44. *Natur und Leben*, pp. 149-78; *Goethe*, pp. 610, 657-63.

45. *Mensch und Gott*, pp. 20, 13. Gasman *The Scientific Origins* p. 164 quotes a similar statement from Haeckel and speculates that some of Hitler's notions about the "distance" between human types were derived from the Monist leader. In fact such expressions were widespread in Imperial Germany.

46. Though several studies of Social Darwinism in Germany exist, none is entirely satisfactory and there is room for a new detailed analysis. See Hans-Günter Zmarzlik, "Der Sozialdarwinismus in Deutschland als geschichtliches Problem," trans. in H. Holborn, ed., *Republic to Reich. The Making of the Nazi Revolution* (New York: Pantheon, 1972). Also, Hedwig Conrad Martius, *Utopien der Menschenzüchtung* (Munich, 1955); Hannsjoachim W. Koch, *Der Sozialdarwinismus. Seine Genese und sein Einfluss auf das imperialistische Denken* (Munich, 1973). For an older account see Oskar Hertwig, *Zur Abwehr des ethischen, des sozialen, des politischen Darwinismus* (Jena, 1918).

47. Uexküll and Lenard letters (CN). Among the Nazi writings on Chamberlain's "Lebenslehre" and racial "science" are: Waldtraut Eckhard, *H. S. Chamberlains Naturanschauung* (Leipzig, 1941); Willi Nielsen, *Der Lebens—und Gestaltbegriff bei H. S. Chamberlain* (Kiel, 1938); Alfred Rosenberg *H. S. Chamberlain als Verkünder und Begründer einer deutschen Zukunft* (Munich, 1927).

48. *Foundations* 2:390.

49. HSC to J. F. Lehmann Feb. 12, 1904 (*Briefe* 1:110). Lehmann had requested that Chamberlain write a book on comparative religion for him.

50. The following analysis is based upon several of Chamberlain's works: *The Foundations, Kant, Goethe, Worte Christi,* and *Mensch und Gott.*

51. For Kant see-Nathan Rotenstreich, *The Recurring Pattern. Studies in Anti-Judaism in Modern Thought* (New York, 1964).

52. "Immanuel Kant," *Tägliche Rundschau* (Unterhaltungsbeilage), March 14, 1902; *Foundations* 2:490–95.

53. *Arische Weltanschauung* (Berlin, 1905). The essays had first appeared in articles in the *Tägliche Rundschau* and the Munich *Allgemeine Zeitung*.

54. *Ibid.*, p. 71.

55. No detailed analysis of German interest in eastern cultures (a revealing mirror of contemporary scepticism of the goals and direction of western society) exists as yet.

56. *Mensch und Gott*, p. 75.

57. For wartime reviews of *Worte Christi* see: *Die Post* (Berlin) July 13, 1915; *Kölnische Volks-Zeitung*, July 22, 1915; *Neue Preussische Kreuzzeitung*, Dec. 7, 1915; *Literarisches Centralblatt fur Deutschland* (1915), 11; *Berliner Morgenpost* March 14, 1915; *Heimat und Welt* (1915), 9.

58. *Mensch und Gott*, pp. 156 ff, 170–73.

59. *Dilettantismus*, pp. 43–95; *Mensch and Gott*, pp. 29, 109 ff.

60. Fritz Stern, *The Politics of Cultural Despair* (New York: Anchor, 1965), p. 68.

61. Adolf von Harnack, *What is Christianity?* (New York: Harper and Row, 1957), p. 176. On Harnack see G. Wayne Glick, *The Reality of Christianity. A Study of Adolf von Harnack as Historian and Theologian* (New York and London, 1967).

62. *Mensch und Gott*, pp. 178–79. Given their general views it is hardly surprising that Chamberlain and the Kaiser were fascinated by the figure of Marcion (the second-century leader of a heretical movement within Christianity) who had tried to eradicate all trace of the Old Testament from Christianity and demanded a "de-Judaized" Gospel. See Kaiser Wilhelm to HSC June 6, 1925, May 10, 1927. (CN).

63. *Foundations* 2:134–35; HSC to Basil Hall Chamberlain July 8, 1899, Dec. 31, 1901 (CN).

64. *Dilettantismus*, p. 75; *Briefe* 1:104.

65. "Der voraussetzungslose Mommsen," *Die Fackel* (Vienna) (1901), 3(87). Cosima Wagner was deeply troubled by this attack on so eminent a scholar as Mommsen and asked Chamberlain to withdraw the essay from publication (CW to HSC Dec. 29, 1901—CN).

66. *Ibid.*, p. 6.

67. *Jüdisches Volksblatt* (Vienna), Feb. 13, 1903.

68. "Katholische Universitäten," *Die Fackel*, Jan. 24, 1902; reprinted *Rasse und Persönlichkeit*, pp. 41–65.

69. *Briefe* 2:194–95, 186; "Der voraussetzungslose Mommsen." Chamberlain argued that the university should become "a second supplementary army . . . instead of being a second republican church."

70. *Mensch and Gott*, pp. 267–99.

71. See chapter 10.

72. *Kant*, 2:502; *Foundations*, 2:503; *Mensch und Gott*, pp. 280–87.

73. *Briefe*, 2:209–10.

74. "Selbstverständnis und Zeitkritik des deutschen Bürgertums vor dem ersten Weltkrieg," *Zeitschrift fur Religions-und Geistesgeschichte* (1956), 8.

75. Hermann Keyserling, *Reise durch die Zeit* (Switzerland, 1948), p. 133.

76. *Briefe*, 2:139.

77. Höfele, "Selbstverständnis etc." On the *Wandervogel* see W. Z. Laqueur, *Young Germany* New York: Basic Books, 1962); M. Domandi, "The German Youth Movement" PhD Diss. Columbia Univ., 1960. For the garden city movement and attitudes toward peasant culture: Klaus Bergmann, *Agrarromantik und Großstadtfeindschaft* (Meisenheim an Glan, 1970); Peter Zimmermann, *Der Bauernroman.*

Antifeudalismus-Konservatismus-Faschismus (Stuttgart, 1975). During the First World War Chamberlain expressed his support for the "internal colonization" ideas of Adolf Damaschke. See letter of February 9, 1916, quoted by G. L. Mosse *The Crisis of German Ideology* (New York: Grosset and Dunlap, 1964), p. 109.

78. Höfele, "Selbstverständnis etc."

79. For Chamberlain's fears of the "Yellow Peril," see his essay "Die Seele des Chinesen" *Neues Wiener Tageblatt* (Vienna) April 15–16, 1900.

80. S. M. Bolkovsky, *The Distorted Image. German-Jewish Perceptions of Germans and Germany* (The Hague, 1976).

Chapter Eight: Private Life

1. Anna Chamberlain, *Meine Erinnerungen*, p. 4; R. Kassner, "Erinnerung an Houston Stewart Chamberlain," *Europäische Revue* (Berlin) (April 1929); 5; *idem, Buch der Erinnerung* (Leipzig, 1938), p. 153; Philip Fürst zu Eulenburg-Hertefeld, *Erlebnisse an deutschen und fremden Höfen* (Leipzig, 1934), 2:330. Hermann Keyserling, *Reise durch die Zeit* (Leichtenstein Verlag, 1948), pp. 133, 125.

2. "Petite étude graphologique et réponse," *L'Écriture*, (Paris) 1896, pp. 71 ff. (quotation is from p. 76).

3. Keyserling, *Reise durch die Zeit*, p. 127.

4. Anna Chamberlain, *Meine Erinnerungen*, pp. 126, 149 ff. Also, Kassner, Keyserling correspondences with Chamberlain (CN); Leopold von Schroeder, *Lebenserinnerungen* (Leipzig, 1921), pp. 121 ff.; Chamberlain's letters to Baroness von Ehrenfels (CN).

5. Keyserling, *Reise durch die Zeit*, pp. 133, 120. On Keyserling see:W. Struve, *Elites against Democracy. Leadership Ideals in Bourgeois Political Thought in Germany, 1890–1933* (Princeton, 1973), chap. 9: H. Adolph, *Die Philosophie des Grafen Keyserling* (Stuttgart, 1927); M. Boucher, *La philosophie de Hermann Keyserling* (Paris, n.d.); M. G. Parkes, *Introduction to Keyserling* (London, 1934).

6. HSC to B. H. Chamberlain Feb. 20, 1908 (CN).

7. R. Kassner, "Erinnerung" and *Buch der Erinnerung*; also letters 1900–1906 (CN). Kassner's works are now being republished: *Sämtliche Werke*, 6 vols. (Pfullingen 1969–).

8. HSC—Felix Gross correspondence (CN), e.g., HSC to Gross May 16, 1907. Both Trebitsch and Weininger regarded themselves as Chamberlain's disciples; both exemplified what Theodor Lessing described as Jewish *Selbsthass*, attempting to absolve themselves of the burden of their Jewishness by actively denouncing their co-religionists and accepting the accusations of anti-Semites. Weininger's brief and tragic career (1880–1903) is well known. A convert to Protestantism, he achieved overnight success with *Geschlecht und Charakter* in 1903, which contrasted Jewish and Aryan traits and preached arduous self conquest as the only panacea for Jews. A few months later, still only 23, he committed suicide in the house where Beethoven died. Trebitsch (1879–1927), whose blond appearance made him the center of a sick cult in Vienna, was also drawn to anti-Semites; his writings publicized the menace of Jewry until he killed himself in 1927—the year of Chamberlain's death. Theodor Lessing, *Der jüdische Selbsthass* (Berlin, 1930); S. Liptzin, *Germany's Stepchildren* (Philadelphia, 1944); Chamberlain—Trebitsch letters (CN); Hans Kohn, *Karl Kraus, A. Schnitzler, Otto Weininger. Aus der jüdischen Wien der Jahrhundertwende* (Tübingen, 1962).

One of the early Nazis, Kurt Ludecke, recalled meeting Trebitsch in the mid-1920s: "Trebitsch was a peculiar and pathetic personality, a full-blooded Jew who was an apostate from his people and his religion. . . . Seriously believing that he looked very much like Houston Stewart Chamberlain . . . he produced as proof one of his pamphlets which showed their pictures facing each other. Looking at his eyes and fair hair, I had to admit that the photographs bore a striking resemblance. . . . Trebitsch sought to convince me that he could be a valuable ally in the Nazi struggle. . . . Needless to say, there was no place for him in the party." K. Ludecke, *I Knew Hitler* (New York: Scribner, 1937), pp. 188–89.

9. Chamberlain provided Gross with introductions to literary circles in Vienna and Paris; he also got Jacob Von Uexküll to work with Gross in Heidelberg. See Gross, "Kant und wir," *BB* (1913), pp. 16–31.

10. HSC to Max von Harden Feb. 26, 1901 and Oct. 11, 1905 (CN).

11. Keyserling, *Reise durch die Zeit*, p. 123. Eugen Diederichs, the highly eccentric *völkisch* publisher, who visited Chamberlain in an attempt to get him to join his stable of authors, was completely captivated. "They sat facing each other. Diederichs gazed at Chamberlain, became more and more effusive in his expressions of admiration, pushed his chair closer and finally cried out: 'Herr Chamberlain, I love you!'" Otto von Taube, *Stationen auf dem Wege. Erinnerungen an meine Werdezeit vor 1914* (Heidelberg, 1969), p. 13.

12. Keyserling, *Reise durch die Zeit*, p. 127.

13. *Briefe*, 2: 138; HSC to Lord Redesdale Aug. 6, 1910 (Redesdale Papers, Gloucester).

14. J. R. Baker, *Race* (Oxford: Oxford University Press, 1974), pp. 50, 59.

15. HSC to Major Kotze, April 3, 1915 (*Briefe*, 1:307–8).

16. *Traumbuch* (CN).

17. A. von Harnack to HSC Nov. 24, 1912 (CN); *Briefe*, 2:138.

18. Theodor W. Adorno et al., *The Authoritarian Personality* (New York: Harper, 1950); R. M. Lowenstein, *Christians and Jews, A Psychoanalytic Study* (New York; International Universities Press, 1951). The August 1962 issue of *Psyche* was devoted to anti-Semitism; see also the two articles by M. Wangh in the *International Journal of Psychoanalysis* 1965, pp. 386–95; 1968, pp. 210–22. For a list of recent works in psychohistory: P. Loewenberg, "Psychohistorical Perspectives on Modern German History," *Journal of Modern History* (June 1975), 47(2). Gordon W. Allport, *The Nature of Prejudice* (Cambridge: Harvard University Press, 1953); Peter Watson, ed., *Psychology and Race* (London: Penguin, 1973) are also good introductions to the subject of racist psychology.

19. Thomas Mann, *Doktor Faustus* (Stockholm, 1947), p. 620. English language edition: New York: Knopf, 1948; paperback, Vintage, 1973.

20. H. V. Dicks, "Personality Traits and National Socialist Ideology," *Human Relations*, June 1950.

21. Norman Cohn, *Warrant for Genocide* (New York: Harper, 1966), pp. 251–69. See also P. Loewenberg, "The Unsuccessful Adolescence of Heinrich Himmler," *American Historical Review* (Feb–June 1971), 76.

22. N. W. Ackermann and M. Jahoda, *Antisemitism and Emotional Disorder* (New York: Harper, 1950).

23. R. Kassner, *Buch der Erinnerung*, p. 154.

24. *Lebenswege*, p. 21; letters concerning Böckmann family (CN).

25. *Foundations*, 1:350. See chap. 1 fn. 30.

26. The sources for Chamberlain's private life are sketchy: two of his diaries are

missing and his correspondence with Baroness von Ehrenfels, Countess Marie Zichy, and others is incomplete. Anna Chamberlain's letters have not survived, while her memoirs offer only a blurred and uncritical picture of events. Hermann Keyserling's *Reise durch die Zeit* is informative, so are Chamberlain's letters to August Ludowici (CN).

27. HSC to Countess Zichy, June 22, 1900 (CN).

28. *Ibid.*

29. HSC to August Ludowici Aug. 4, 1902 (CN): "The duties of my life are so clearly marked out for me that probably I cannot do anything other than them—as long as Providence gives me the strength to complete them one after another, without veering off to the left or the right." Also, HSC to Harriet Chamberlain Aug. 28, 1899 (CN) describes how Anna hoped their life would be more social after the completion of the *Foundations*; her lonely existence in Vienna, Chamberlain admitted, "she has got[ten] to *dread* positively."

30. HSC to Harriet Chamberlain Aug. 28, 1899 (CN).

31. HSC to Anne Guthrie Sept. 3, 1899 (CN).

32. HSC to August Ludowici May 11, 1906 (CN). This and other letters referred back to the troubles in Chamberlain's private life since the early 1890s.

33. HSC to Adolphe Appia, Sept. 10, 1900 (CN).

34. Siegfried Trebitsch, *Chronicle of a Life* (London, 1953), pp. 68–69; HSC to Anne Guthrie, April 26, 1903; HSC to Adolphe Appia June 5, 14, 24, 1906 (CN). *Tagebücher*—Lili Petri appears as LP. Petri's letters were destroyed at her death—see Dr Otto Schwalb-HSC correspondence (CN).

35. H. Keyserling, *Reise durch die Zeit*, p. 130.

36. HSC to Anne Guthrie and B. H. Chamberlain Sept. 4, 1904; HSC to Appia Feb. 25, 1904; Anna Chamberlain, *Meine Erinnerungen* pp. 154 ff. Anna required a full-time nurse at this point.

37. The original letters are missing; they are published however, in Anna Chamberlain, *Meine Erinnerungen*, pp. 156, 160.

38. Anne Guthrie to HSC May 2, 1905; E. Dujardin to HSC June 26, 1905; B. H. Chamberlain to HSC June 2, 1905; HSC–Appia correspondence, especially July–Aug. 1905; HSC to B. H. Chamberlain Feb. 15, 1906 (CN). For Anna's account of her experiences in the Paris clinic see *Meine Erinnerungen*, pp. 188–97.

39. HSC–Professor and Greta Weese correspondence 1905-6 (CN); HSC to Adolphe Appia Sept. 6, 1905; HSC to B. H. Chamberlain Feb. 15, 1906 (CN).

40. HSC to A. Boissier Dec. 28, 1895; Harriet Chamberlain to HSC March 3, 1896; family correspondences 1902; HSC to Ludowici May 11, 1906. Arbuthnot Guthrie left approximately 50 million marks when he died in 1897, according to Chamberlain (HSC to Ludowici 11 May 1906). The last quotation is from HSC to Ludowici May 11, 1906. He greatly exaggerated when he said: "I have actually no capital—with the exception of my brain. By rights I should now have very handsome capital assets."

41. See the lengthy HSC-Bruckmann Verlag correspondence (CN); also Chamberlain's financial account books; Boissier seems to have given HSC about 5,000 Austrian florins a year (e.g., Boissier to HSC Jan. 31, 1895); Ludowici to HSC, April 27, May 14, July 12, 16, 21, 1906 (CN). HSC to Adolf von Gross Oct. 26, 1908 (CN).

42. HSC to B. H. Chamberlain June 30, 1908 (CN).

43. Anna Chamberlain, *Meine Erinnerungen*, p. 201.

44. S. Trebitsch, *Chronicle of a Life*, p. 69.; HSC to Eva Wagner Oct. 15, 1898 (CN).

45. *Briefwechsel*, pp. 442–44, 500, 528, 541, 544.

46. H. Wolzogen to HSC March 20, 1899; CW to HSC April 25, 1899 (CN).

47. The lecture was held on Dec. 16, 1898 and published in the *Münchener Allgemeine Zeitung*, Feb. 25–28, 1899.

48. HSC to CW July 29, Aug. 1, 1890 (CN).

49. CW to HSC March 26, 1899 (CN).

50. CW to HSC April 25, 1899; April 7, 1899; also Du Moulin Eckart, *Cosima Wagner*, 2:584–85.

51. *Briefwechsel*, pp. 574–78.

52. HSC to Harriet Chamberlain April 30, 1899; he is referring to Wolzogen's review in *Deutsche Welt. Wochenschrift der Deutsche Zeitung* July 2, 1899. Two reviews appeared in the *Bayreuther Blätter* by A. Wernicke and W. Golther. H. Thode in *Literarisches Centralblatt für Deutschland* (Berlin) March 10, 1900.

53. CW to Countess Zichy (undated, autumn 1901) (CN).

54. HSC to CW March 23, 1901; H. Thode to HSC April 25, 1901; HSC to H. Thode May 1, 1901 (CN).

55. Foreword to 3rd ed., reprinted in *Wehr und Gegenwehr* (Munich, 1912).

56. H. Keyserling, *Reise durch die Zeit*, p. 130; Du Moulin Eckart, *Cosima Wagner*, 2:783, 827.

57. On Siegfried Wagner: Zdenko von Kraft, *Der Sohn. Siegfried Wagner, Leben und Umwelt* (Graz/Stuttgart 1969). For Chamberlain on Siegfried see, for example, HSC to CW Jan. 22, 1896 (CN); also his articles: "Siegfried Wagner in Wien," *Wiener Rundschau*, April 15, 1899; "Jung Siegfried" *Jugend* (Munich), Aug. 12, 1899; "Siegfried Wagner und die Bärenhäuter," *Die Zukunft* (Berlin), April 22, 1899; "Brief über Siegfried Wagners Bärenhäuter," *BB* (1899), 22; "Siegfried Wagner," *Allgemeine Zeitung* (Munich) Sept. 5, 1908.

58. HSC-B. H. Chamberlain correspondence for 1908 (CN).

59. Hans von Wolzogen, *Lebensbilder* (Regensburg, 1923), p. 100.

60. Berta Geissmar, *Two Worlds of Music* (New York: McClelland, 1948), p. 48.

61. HSC to Eva Wagner Dec. 4, 1908; HSC to Eva Wagner Oct. 15, 1908 (CN). Eva sent about 240 letters and telegrams in about four months and Chamberlain was almost as prolific.

62. HSC to Adolf von Gross Oct. 26, 1908 etc. (CN). Du Moulin Eckart, *Cosima Wagner*, 2:833–38.

63. Anne Guthrie to HSC Oct. 14, Nov. 7, 1908 (CN).

64. *Lebenswege*, pp. 246–47; *Briefe*, 1:231; Z. von Kraft, *Der Sohn*, p. 154.

65. H. Keyserling, *Reise durch die Zeit*, p. 130.

66. Quoted by Geoffrey Skelton in his introduction to *Cosima Wagner's Diaries 1869–1877* (New York: Harcourt, 1978), p. 18. See also HSC-Adolf von Gross correspondence (CN).

67. *Briefe*, 2:174, 139.

Chapter Nine: Wartime Propagandist

1. HSC to Basil Hall Chamberlain Oct. 30, 1914 (CN).

2. *Lebenswege*, p. 6.

3. HSC to CW Sept. 16, 1900 (*Briefwechsel*, p. 605); HSC to Anne Guthrie Jan. 8, 1889; Ms of two articles on British colonial and foreign policies submitted unsuccessfully to the *Standard* and *Saturday Review* in 1897. The quotation is from HSC to

Harriet Chamberlain Jan. 4. 1896. See, also: his letters of Dec. 23, 1894 and May 9, 1897 to Aunt Harriet (CN). Also, HSC to Mr Johnstone March 10, 1897 (CN).

4. Meinecke as quoted by Konrad H. Jarausch, *The Enigmatic Chancellor. Bethmann Hollweg and the Hubris of Imperial Germany* (New Haven: Yale University Press, 1973), p. 185.

5. Quoted by V. R. Berghahn, *Germany and the Approach of War in 1914* (London: Macmillan, 1973), p. 35.

6. *Preussische Jahrbücher*, Nov. 26, 1899 (as quoted by J. Steinberg, "The Copenhagen Complex," *Journal of Contemporary History* 1 (3):27. See also: Ernst Köhler, *Bildungsbürgertum und nationale Politik* (Berlin, 1970).

7. Cosima Wagner had similar views, see *Briefwechsel*, p. 507 (letter of March 12, 1897).

8. As quoted in Ashley Montagu, *Man's Most Dangerous Myth. The Fallacy of Race* (New York: Meridian, 1964), p. 180.

9. HSC to Harriet Chamberlain Jan. 29, 1881 (CN).

10. HSC to Harriet and Neville Chamberlain Jan. 12, 1896 (CN).

11. HSC to Harriet and Neville Chamberlain Jan. 25, 1896 (CN).

12. Anne Guthrie-HSC letters, 1900 (CN); Neville Chamberlain to HSC Dec. 20, 1900 (CN); Neville Chamberlain to H. J. Ogden Sept. 20, 1901 (printed in the *Manchester Guardian*); Neville Chamberlain to HSC Aug. 7, 1901 (CN); also, *Lebenswege*, pp. 25–26. Neville's actions permanently estranged his former commander, Lord Roberts.

13. *Die Zukunft*, Feb. 25, 1900, p. 291 (reprinted in the *Ostdeutsche Rundschau* Feb. 18, 1900). The poem closed with the words: "When Teuton battles Teuton, whoever wins, God is defeated." HSC to Anne Guthrie Dec. 9, 1900; see also: HSC to *Die Woche* Jan. 24, 1900; HSC to Max Harden Feb. 19,1900 (CN).

14. HSC to Anne Guthrie July 15, 1900 (CN).

15. CW to HSC Sept. 20, 1900 (*Briefwechsel*, p. 605).

16. See the analysis of Treitschke's influence in Charles McClelland, *The German Historians and England* (Cambridge, 1971). Quotation from p. 181.

17. On the political responses to the Boer war in Germany: Pauline Anderson, *The Background of Anti-English Feeling in Germany 1890–1902* (Washington D.C., 1939). For the Anti-Semites: R. S. Levy, *The Downfall of the Anti-Semitic Parties in Germany*, pp. 210–17. *Briefwechsel*, pp. 586, 589, 581, 605. Chamberlain wrote that German journalism had "made immense progress since the creation of large and prosperous anti-Semitic papers, the *Tägliche Rundschau*, the *Deutsche Wacht*, etc., for the other papers can no longer lie with impunity." (HSC to Harriet and Neville Chamberlain Jan. 12, 1896).

18. HSC to Harriet Chamberlain Jan. 25, 1896 (CN).

19. HSC to CW Sept. 16, 1900 (*Briefwechsel*, p. 605).

20. "Ueber die Judenfrage in Rumänien," *Nuova Revista Romana* (Bucharest) 1900, p. 10. This essay was reprinted several times in Germany. *Briefe* 2:158, 168–69. Also, "Das heutige England," *Deutsche Monatsschrift* (Berlin), Nov. 1902.

21. *Briefe* 2:169.

22. *Ibid.*, p. 139. Also, "Kaiser Wilhelm II," *Jugend* (Munich) May 28, 1900 (reprinted in *Deutsches Wesen*). HSC to Anne Guthrie July 15, 1900 (CN).

23. *Briefe* 2:139 (letter dated Nov. 15, 1901).

24. *Ibid.*, pp. 138; 169 (Feb. 4, 1903).

25. *Ibid.*, p. 138.

26. *Ibid.*, p. 160 (letter of Feb. 20, 1902).

27. Hermann Keyserling, *Reise durch die Zeit*, p. 135.

28. Lord Redesdale, "Houston Stewart Chamberlain," *Edinburgh Review* (Jan. 1914), 219:79.

29. HSC to General von Roon April 28, 1915 (*Briefe* 1:310).

30. Quoted in "The Sage of Bayreuth," *Times Literary Supplement*, Aug. 28, 1953.

31. For example: Maurice Kufferath, a Wagner enthusiast in *Revue Bleue* 1915 (see Léon Poliakov, *The Aryan Myth*, New York: Basic Books, 1974, p. 320).

32. *Wer hat den Krieg verschuldet?* (Wiesbaden, 1915).

33. *Ibid.; England und Deutschland* (Bruckmann, 1915); "Deutsche Friedensliebe," *Internationale Monatsschrift für Wissenschaft, Kunst und Technik* (Oct. 1914), 1.

34. For the responses of German academics to the war: Klaus Schwabe, *Wissenschaft und Kriegsmoral. Die deutschen Hochschullehrer und die politischen Grundfragen des ersten Weltkrieges* (Göttingen, 1969). Ernst Haeckel, "Weltkrieg und Naturgeschichte," *Nord und Süd* (1914) 151:146. Ernst Troeltsch, "Die deutsche Idee von der Freiheit," *Deutsche Zukunft* (Berlin, 1916); Werner Sombart, *Händler und Helden* (Munich, 1915); Rudolf Kjellén, *Die Ideen von 1914: Eine weltgeschichtliche Perspektive* (Leipzig, 1915). For Max Scheler's wartime writings see: John R. Staude, *Max Scheler 1874–1928. An Intellectual Portrait* (New York, 1967). Thomas Mann, *Betrachtungen eines Unpolitischen* (Berlin, 1918). On Mann, see the interesting essay by W. H. Bruford, *The German Tradition of Self-Cultivation* (Cambridge: Cambridge University Press, 1975), chap. 11.

35. "The Sage of Bayreuth," *Times Literary Supplement*, Aug. 28, 1953 (The *TLS* made this statement in 1916). *The Ravings of a Renegade, being the War Essays of Houston Stewart Chamberlain*, translated by C. H. Clarke (London, 1916).

36. *England und Deutschland*; a translation of the first part appeared in *North American Review* (1915), 202:30–52. "Deutsche Friedensliebe" (1914); Grundstimmungen in England und Frankreich," *Tägliche Rundschau* Jan. 9, 11, 12, 1915. Typical of the personal recollections was the following ("England"): "Even today, although the suffrage has been extended to a large portion of the common people, the old outrages of the ruling class have not fallen into desuetude. Most of my readers will recollect Dickens's description of an election in Pickwick papers. . . . I had an opportunity of establishing how well the old account would fit modern instances. . . . The whole day was spent shouting and fighting. . . . In the evening I experienced it in my own person—for, at that time, I was a pupil at a college, and of the eighty inhabitants of my "house" the only one who wore the Liberal badge, thus confessing himself an adherent of Gladstone. Not even the prayers of the master prevailed upon me to lay aside the colors of my convictions and replace them by those of Disraeli, and so the whole pack fell upon me, knocked me down and beat me. . . . I learned more on that day—it is now forty-six years ago—about the English constitution and the English conception of liberty than later from the books of Hallam and Gneist."

37. The major themes of his thinking are contained in *Politische Ideale* (1915) and *Demokratie und Freiheit* (1917); quotation from "Deutsche Weltanschauung," reprinted in *Rasse und Persönlichkeit*, p. 18. See also: Leonard Krieger, *The German Idea of Freedom. History of a Political Tradition* (Boston: Beacon, 1957).

38. *Politische Ideale*, pp. 60–63; *Demokratie und Freiheit*, pp. 77–78.

39. *Demokratie und Freiheit*, pp. 60–65.

40. *Ibid.* ("Demokratie"), p. 35–38, 49–60.

41. *Ibid.*, p. 44.

42. *Ideal und Macht* (1916), pp. 23–24.

43. *Politische Ideale*, p. 76.

44. *Ibid.*, pp. 54–55. Bruckmann hoped that the *Bund der Landwirte* would subsidize the circulation of *Politische Ideale* because of its praise for the landed interest—Hugo Bruckmann to HSC Oct. 30, 1915 (CN).

45. Alfred Rosenberg, *H. S. Chamberlain als Verkünder und Begründer einer deutschen Zukunft* (Munich, 1927), p. 54.

46. *Demokratie und Freiheit*, p. 14.

47. *Rasse und Persönlichkeit*, p. 32 ("Deutsche Weltanchauung," 1917).

48. *Briefe* 2:159; *Politische Ideale*, pp. 68–69.

49. *Politische Ideale*, pp. 76–77; also *Die Zuversicht* (1915), pp. 20–21.

50. Quoted in Konrad Heiden, *Der Fuehrer, Hitler's Rise to Power* (Boston: Beacon, 1969) p. 241.

51. *Politische Ideale*, p. 116. (also pp. 72, 114–15).

52. *Ibid.*, pp. 92–116; quote from p. 113.

53. *Briefe* 1:324.

54. E. Zechlin, *Die Deutsche Politik und die Juden im Ersten Weltkrieg* (Göttingen, 1969), p. 92. For this whole subject see also the fine symposium: W. E. Mosse and A. Paucker eds., *Deutsches Judentum in Krieg und Revolution* (Tübingen 1971).

55. J. F. Lehmann to Dr. Karl Geiger, 1917 n.d. in Melanie Lehmann, *Verleger J. F. Lehmann. Ein Leben im Kampf für Deutschland* (Munich, 1935), p. 137.

56. Paul Ernst in *Der Tag* (Berlin) June 9, 1915. As early as Aug. 28, 1914, Alfred Roth and other associates of *Reichshammerbund* were planning their strategy against Jews: "We must today already be perfectly clear that the Jewish question will be a burning issue after the war." Quoted by Werner Jochmann in "Die Ausbreitung des Antisemitismus," in *Deutsches Judentum in Krieg und Revolution*, p. 411 fn.

57. Walter Otto of the DHV writing in *Hammer*, Sept. 1914 (quoted by Iris Hamel, *Völkischer Verband und nationale Gewerkschaft*, Frankfurt, 1967, p. 105).

58. *Die Zuversicht* (1915). At the very beginning of the war Chamberlain had made a few conciliatory comments about the patriotism of German Jews—e.g., *Kriegsaufsätze*, 1st series, p. 46. But his private comments were deeply antagonistic. By early 1915 the Jewish press was beginning to voice its outrage at his anti-Semitic crusade: e.g. "H. S. Chamberlain als Störer des inneren Friedens," in *Mitteilungen* (Jan. 27, 1915); 25: 5; also Aug. 11, pp. 61–66; and Dec. 29, p. 143.

59. HSC to Max von Baden Sept. 22, 1914 (*Briefe* 1:250–51).

60. HSC to Max von Baden Dec. 24, 1914 (CN).

61. Karl Ludwig Ay, *Die Entstehung einer Revolution. Die Volksstimmung in Bayern während des ersten Weltkrieges* (Berlin, 1968), p. 73. Also, the essay by K. H. Schädlich on the Independent Commission in Fritz Klein ed., *Politik im Kriege 1914–18* (Berlin, 1964).

62. *Ideal und Macht* (1916), p. 11.

63. HSC to Max von Baden March 19, 1915 (*Briefe* 1:299–300); see also HSC to Major von Kotze April 3, 1915 (*Briefe* 1:307–8). For the campaign against Bethmann-Hollweg: Wilhelm Deist ed., *Militär und Innenpolitik im Weltkrieg 1914–18* (Düsseldorf, 1970); Konrad H. Jarausch, *The Enigmatic Chancellor*; Dirk Stegmann, *Die Erben Bismarcks. Parteien und Verbände im Spätphase des Wilhelminischen Deutschlands* (Cologne and Berlin, 1970) pp. 458–519. On the Pan-German League: Alfred Kruck, *Geschichte des Alldeutschen Verbandes 1890–1939* (Wiesbaden, 1954).

64. HSC to Max von Baden Dec. 24, 1914 (CN); April, 27, 1915 (CN).

65. Theodor Fritsch to HSC March 17, 1916 (CN).

66. Letter of Sept. 11, 1915, in Melanie Lehmann, *Verleger J. F. Lehmann*, p. 133. Max von Baden was also deeply worried by the isolation of the Kaiser, see Baden to HSC Aug. 19, Sept. 4, Nov. 26, 1916 (CN).

67. Walter Görlitz, ed., *The Kaiser and His Court. The Diaries, Notebooks, and Letters of Admiral Georg Alexander von Müller 1914-1918* (New York, 1964) entry for Jan. 4, 1917.

68. Letters of Carl Cesar Eiffe (a prominent Pan-German) and HSC Aug.-Nov., 1916 (CN). Also, Ernst zu Hohenlohe-Langenburg to HSC July 27, 1916 and Dec. 21, 1916 (CN). Eiffe to HSC Nov. 6, 1916: "I agree absolutely with your statements about the danger of revolution. . . . Already last winter I said to Fürst Salm [Horstmar—President of the Navy League and very prominent in right wing circles] that we must make the revolution from above so that it does not come from below. You know that I don't mean that literally. And now that I am working on *how*, I am very pleased at your friendly renewed invitation to talk things over—perhaps on my next journey from Munich" (CN).

69. *Rasse und Persönlichkeit*, p. 195.

70. *Hammer oder Amboss*, pp. 43-48, 27.

71. HSC to Oscar von Chelius Oct. 12, 1915 (*Briefe* 1:325); also, Bruckmann-HSC correspondence (CN); HSC to Max von Baden March 19, 1915, Feb. 27, 1915; HSC to Alfred de Bary Feb. 25, 1915; HSC to Alfred Conn Feb. 25, 1915; HSC to Admiral von Thomson June 18, 1915, Friedrich von Schoen to HSC June 29, 1915 (CN).

72. HSC to Major General Pfeil July 26, 1916 (*Briefe* 2:26).

73. Wilhelm Deist, *Militär und Innenpolitik im Weltkrieg 1914-18*, 1:63-181; Werner Jochmann, "Die Ausbreitung des Antisemitismus," p. 420; Martin Kitchen, *The Silent Dictatorship. The Politics of the High Command under Hindenburg and Ludendorff* (London, 1976), pp. 56-58. HSC-J. F. Lehmann letters—e.g., Lehmann to HSC Aug. 25, 1915 (CN).

74. The best accounts of wartime anti-Semitism are: W. Jochmann, "Die Ausbreitung des Antisemitismus," and E. Zechlin, *Die Deutsche Politik und die Juden im Ersten Weltkrieg*. A brief sketch is also included in Jürgen Kocka, *Klassengesellschaft im Krieg 1914-1918* (Göttingen, 1973), pp. 103-5. Some details are also included in C. Ehlers, "Julius Streicher and the Bourgeois Transition to Nazism," PhD Diss. Univ. of Colorado, 1975, chaps. 3-5.

75. G. L. Mosse, *The Crisis of German Ideology* (New York: Grosset and Dunlap 1964), p. 136. Also, S. Adler-Rudel, *Ostjuden in Deutschland 1880-1940* (Tübingen, 1959) and *idem.*, "East European Jewish Workers in Germany," LBI (1957) 3.

76. Werner T. Angress, "Das deutsche Militär und die Juden im Ersten Weltkrieg," in *Militärgeschichtliche Mitteilungen* (1976), 19:77-146.

77. .W. Jochmann, "Die Ausbreitung des Antisemitismus," pp. 425-27.

78. Julius Marx, *Kriegstagebuch eines Juden* (Zurich, 1939), p. 32.

79. Quoted in E. Zechlin, *Die Deutsche Politik und die Juden im ersten Weltkrieg*, pp. 532-33. On the Jewish veterans see: Ruth Pierson, "Embattled Veterans," LBI (1974), 19:139-54. Note the comments of Hitler in *Mein Kampf* (Boston: Houghton Mifflin, 1943) p. 193: "to be a slacker passed almost as a sign of higher wisdom. . . . The offices were filled with Jews. . . . I was amazed at the plethora of warriors of the chosen people [i.e., behind the lines] and could not but compare them with their rare representatives at the front."

80. R. H. Lutz, ed., *The Fall of the German Empire*, 1:103 (letter of May 1916).

81. "Der Wille zum Sieg" (1917); "Das eine und das andere Deutschland" (1917);

"Hammer oder Amboss" (1916). Like all such extreme rhetoric, Chamberlain's phrases contained an element of anxiety, an anticipation of failure, for which he was already providing the explanation. Loss or betrayal of Will was the cause of defeat (the fault of the weak-willed and treacherous). Propaganda against internal enemies was an indispensable part of the ideology of Will. Much of Chamberlain's language anticipates the tone of fascist writers. Thus, at the outbreak of war in 1939, Hitler announced: "If our will is so strong that no affliction can subdue it, then shall our will and our German state overcome every affliction and triumph over it." J. P. Stern, *Hitler. The Fuehrer and the People* (New York: Collins, 1975) p. 63. Compare: *Hammer oder Amboss* 3rd series of war essays (1916), pp. 9, 27, 36. *Der Wille zum Krieg und andere Aufsätze* (1918), p. 45; *Ideal und Macht* (1916), pp. 32 ff.

82. HSC to Max von Baden May 16, 1916 (*Briefe* 2:16); also, "Der hundertjährige Krieg" (1915) in *Hammer oder Amboss*, 3rd series of war essays.

83. These were actually the words of Carl Cesar Eiffe to HSC (Nov. 6, 1916), but similar expressions can be found throughout Chamberlain's correspondence.

84. *Rasse und Persönlichkeit*, p. 193.

85. "Das eine und das andere Deutschland" first published in *Deutsche Zeitung* Oct. 11, 1917.

86. Alfred Roth in *Deutschvölkischer Blätter* (1915), quoted in *Mitteilungen* (*Abwehr Verein*) Dec. 1, 1915, p. 125. Note also the comment of Professor Rein of Jena in a review of *Politische Ideale*: "We see more clearly each day how necessary the war is for our progress. We welcome the great purification that it brings. It strengthens our resolve to energetically do away with all the un-German elements in our *Volk*." *Der Tag* April 24, 1915.

87. Paul Joachimsen, *Zeitwende* (1927), 3:437.

88. The Bruckmann Verlag-HSC correspondence (CN) contains all the details of Chamberlain's sales. The *Nachlass* also includes large numbers of reviews.

89. *Mitteilungen* (*Abwehr Verein*) Dec. 1, 1915, p. 125. Chamberlain's essays were heavily criticized by liberal writers. For examples see: F. W. Foerster, *England in H. S. Chamberlains Beleuchtung* (Munich, 1918) and "H. S. Chamberlain als Interpret der westlichen Zivilisation," in *Die Neue Rundschau* (1917), 28; H. Molenaar, *Anti-Chamberlain* (Leipzig, 1915); L. Spitzer, *Anti-Chamberlain. Betrachtungen eines Linguisten über H. S. Chamberlains Kriegsaufsätze* (Leipzig, 1918).

90. Chamberlain was in contact with the leaders of the *Verband gegen die Ueberhebung des Judentums*; he also corresponded with Wilhelm Stapel, the editor of *Deutsches Volkstum*. Lehmann was the publisher of *Unser Vaterland*. For more details see: R. M. Engelmann, "Dietrich Eckart and the Genesis of Nazism" (PhD Diss. Univ. of Washington, 1971), pp. 94–98. His essay for the *Deutsche Zeitung* April 2, 1917, after its purchase by the Pan-Germans was titled "Der Deutschgedanke."

91. "Deutsche Weltanschauung," *Deutschlands Erneuerung* (April, 1917).

92. For further details see: Dirk Stegmann, *Die Erben Bismarcks*, pp. 497–519; K. Wortmann, *Geschichte der Deutschen Vaterlandspartei 1917–1918* (Halle, 1926).

93. W. Rathenau to HSC July 17, 1916 (CN).

94. For example: *Demokratie und Freiheit*, pp. 32, 59; *Politische Ideale*, p. 102; "Das eine und das andere Deutschland."

95. "Die Deutsche Vaterlandspartei," *Deutsche Zeitung* Nov. 9, 1917. Also *Frankfurter Zeitung*, Oct. 14, 1917 (attack on the "renegade" Chamberlain).

96. B. Guttmann, *Schattenriss einer Generation 1888–1919* (Stuttgart, 1950), pp. 224–25.

97. Trial transcript (CN). Ludwig Müller von Hausen to HSC Aug. 18, 31, 1918 (CN).

98. *Deutsche Zeitung* Aug. 17, 18, 1918; Ernst Diederichs to HSC Aug. 18, 1918 (CN); W. Rust to HSC Oct. 5, 1918 (CN). *Süddeutsche Zeitung* (Stuttgart) Aug. 20, 1918. J. F. Lehmann to HSC Aug. 28, 1918 (CN).

99. Quoted in E. Zechlin, *Die Deutsche Politik und die Juden im Ersten Weltkrieg*, p. 550. The issues of *Im deutschen Reich* also reveal a growing apprehension.

100. Melanie Lehmann, *Verleger J. F. Lehmann*, p. 150.

101. George L. Mosse, "The Jews and the German War Experience 1914–1918," *LBI Memorial Lecture* (1977), p. 15.

Chapter Ten: Bayreuth and Nazism

1. *Briefe* 2:67.

2. Ludwig Roselius to HSC Aug. 1, 1917 (CN). A disciple of Chamberlain, Roselius was a patron of folk arts and crafts. In 1933 he became a member of the executive committee of the *Deutscher Werkbund*.

3. T. Lessing, *Der Jüdische Selbsthass* (Berlin 1930) pp. 125–29. See also the comments on Max Steiner, pp. 133–37.

4. *Mensch und Gott* was widely reviewed in the press. Cosima and Hohenlohe-Langenburg were deeply impressed by it. See their *Briefwechsel* (Stuttgart, 1937) p. 393. For a Catholic criticism see P. D. Feuling "Zur H. S. Chamberlains Betrachtungen über Religion und Christentum," *Historisch-politisch Blätter für das Katholische Deutschland* (Munich) (1922), 169:13–28, 65–79.

5. *Rasse und Persönlichkeit* (Munich 1925).

6. Alfred Rosenberg, *H. S. Chamberlain als Verkünder und Begründer der deutschen Zukunft* (Munich: Bruckmann, 1927).

7. HSC to Captain Crome Nov. 24, 1919 (CN).

8. *Rasse und Persönlichkeit*, p. 198.

9. See, for example: HSC to Admiral von Tirpitz Nov. 16, 28, 1919; Jan. 20, 1920 (CN). Eulenburg to HSC March 18, 1919 (CN). "Halbbildung," *Deutsche Zeitung* Aug. 14, 1921. HSC to Jacobsen Nov. 21, 1918 (*Briefe* 2:53–98).

10. HSC to Jacob von Uexküll Jan. 8, 1919 (*Briefe* 2:68–71).

11. Admiral von Tirpitz to HSC Jan. 9, 1920; Dr. Wildgrube to HSC Dec. 30, 1918; J. von Uexküll to HSC May 17, 1920. See also: HSC to Uexküll March 20, 1919; Uexküll to HSC Dec. 30, 1918 (CN).

12. H. Bennet Challis May 9, 1919 (CN); E. Diederichs (a member of *Volksbund rettet die Ehre*) to HSC May 11, 1921 (CN).

13. On the language of anti-Semitism: A. Bein, "Der jüdische Parasit. Bemerkung zur Semantik der Judenfrage," *Vierteljahrshefte für Zeitgeschichte* (April 1965), 13 (2). J. P. Faye, *Langages totalitaires* and *Théorie de récit* (Paris, 1972) constitute the most ambitious attempt so far to investigate the "language field" of Nazism from a structuralist and Marxist perspective. On the *Protocols of the Elders of Zion* and the whole climate of racism in post-war Central Europe: Normal Cohn, *Warrant for Genocide* (New York: Harper, 1966).

14. A Dinter to HSC Aug. 12, 1916; Aug. 10, 1916 (CN).

15. A. Dinter to HSC Aug. 10, 1916; Oct. 3, 1917, July 21, 1918, June 25, 1918 (CN).

16. *Deutsches Judentum in Krieg und Revolution*, p. 460 fn 177.

17. A. Dinter *Die Sünde wider das Blut* (Leipzig 1918), p. 276. See also Alex Bein, "Die Judenfrage in der Literatur des modernen Antisemitismus als Vorbereitung zur Endlösung" *Bulletin of Leo Baeck Institute 21* (1963). *Mitteilungen des Vereins zur Abwehr des Antisemitismus* (April 1920), 30:64, (March 1919), 29:39. *Im deutschen Reich* 1919-1921 also contains a number of comments about Dinter's impact. See also by Dinter: *"Lichtstrahlen aus dem Talmud": offene Brief an des Landes-Rabiner von Sachsen-Weimar-Eisenach Herrn Dr. Wiesen et al.* (Leipzig, 1920); also the vehemently anti-Catholic *197 Theses zur Vollendung der Reformation: die Wiederherstellung der reinen Heilandslehre* (Leipzig, 1926). The sequel to his first novel was *Die Sünde wider den Geist* (Leipzig, 1921). He completed the trilogy with *Die Sünde wider die Liebe* (Leipzig, 1922).

18. *Die Sünde wider das Blut* (Leipzig, 1919), pp. 240, 371.

19. *Die Sünde wider den Geist* (Leipzig, 1921) p. 235.

20. A. Dinter to HSC Dec. 11, 1918; May 5, 1919; May 8, 1919; July 26, 1919; Jan. 6, 1920 (CN).

21. A. Dinter to HSC July 7, 9, 12, 17, 1921; Dec. 11, 1921.

22. On Dinter in Bayreuth: *Briefwechsel zwischen Cosima Wagner und Fürst Ernst zu Hohenlohe-Langenburg* (Stuttgart, 1937), p. 383, letter from Cosima Oct. 14, 1919. Uwe Lohalm, *Völkischer Radikalismus. Die Geschichte der deutschvölkischer Schutz- und Trutzbundes 1919-23* (Hamburg, 1970), pp. 204-5. A Dinter to HSC Dec. 11, 1918 (CN).

23. Quoted by Lewis Hertzman, *DNVP. Right-Wing Opposition in the Weimar Republic 1918-1924* (Lincoln: University of Nebraska Press, 1963), p. 129.

24. Mann as quoted in Saul Friedländer, "Die politischen Veränderungen der Kriegszeit und ihre Auswirkungen auf die Judenfrage" in W. E. Mosse and A. Paucker, eds., *Deutsches Judentum in Krieg und Revolution* (Tübingen, 1971), p. 49. Werner Jochmann's fine essay: "Die Ausbreitung des Antisemitismus" in the same volume (pp. 409-510) is based on a wide range of published and archival sources.

25. Peter G. Pulzer, *The Rise of Political Anti-Semitism in Germany and Austria* (New York: Wiley, 1964), p. 300.

26. Hans-Jurgen Lutzhöft, *Der nordische Gedanke in Deutschland 1920-1940* (Stuttgart: Klett, 1971); Geoffrey G. Field, "Nordic Racism" *Journal of the History of Ideas* (July–Sept. 1977), 38(3):523-40. Hans F. K. Günther's major work, *Rassenkunde des deutschen Volkes* appeared in 1922 and had gone through six editions by 1926. See also Karl Saller, *Die Rassenlehre des Nationalsozialismus in Wissenschaft und Propaganda* (Darmstadt, 1961); Karl Thieme ed., *Judenfeindschaft Darstellung und Analysen* (Frankfurt, 1963).

27. Norman Cohn, *Warrant for Genocide*. For Röhling see: I. A. Hellwing, *Der konfessionelle Antisemitismus im 19. Jahrhundert in Oesterreich* (Vienna, 1967); J. S. Bloch, *Erinnerungen aus meinem Leben* (Vienna and Leipzig, 1922). Jacob Katz, *Jews and Freemasons in Europe 1723-1939* (Cambridge: Harvard University Press, 1970). For a very insightful analysis of secret society mythology in the French Revolution and Restoration see J. M. Roberts, *The Mythology of the Secret Societies* (London: Secker and Warburg, 1972).

28. A. Dinter, *"Lichtstrahlen aus dem Talmud"*; for Wichtl see: Norman Cohn, *Warrent for Genocide*, p. 132. For Chamberlain's reading: *Tagebücher* (CN) e.g. December 1923, January 1924. Chamberlain regarded Rudolf Steiner's Anthroposophy

as an offshoot of freemasonry and a danger to German values: HSC to Engineer V.O. April 1, 1919 (*Briefe* 2:91–92); HSC to General von Gleich May 28, 1921 (*Briefe* 2:116–17); Dr. Victor Scholz to HSC May 19, 1921 (CN), etc.

29. W. Jochmann, "Die Ausbreitung des Antisemitismus." For the political and economic position of the *Mittelstand* during the republic: H. A. Winkler, *Mittelstand, Demokratie und Nationalsozialismus* (Cologne, 1972).

30. Donald L. Niewyk, *Socialist, Anti-Semite and Jew. German Social Democracy Confronts the Problem of Anti-Semitism 1918–1933* (Baton Rouge: L.S.U. Press, 1971). More stress is placed upon antipathy toward Jews on the left by Hans Helmuth Knütter, *Die Juden und die deutsche Linke in der Weimarer Republik 1918–1933* (Dusseldorf, 1971) and George L. Mosse, "German Socialists and the Jewish Question in the Weimar Republic" LBI (1971) 16.

31. On students: W. Jochmann, "Die Ausbreitung des Antisemitismus," pp. 474–77; Michael H. Kater, *Studentenschaft und Rechtsradikalismus in Deutschland 1918–1933* (Hamburg, 1975), pp. 145–62 etc. The best general account of the Youth Movement is Walter Z. Laqueur, *Young Germany: A History of the German Youth Movement* (London, 1962).

32. Hans Blüher, *Secessio Judaica* (Berlin, 1922), p. 49.

33. Karl W. Dahm, *Pfarrer und Politik* (Cologne, 1965); Gottfried Mehnert, *Evangelische Kirche und Politik 1917–1919* (Düsseldorf, 1959).

34. J. R. C. Wright '*Above Parties.' The Political Attitudes of the German Protestant Church Leadership 1918–1933* (Oxford: Oxford University Press, 1974), p. 54. R. Gutteridge, *The German Evangelical Church and the Jews 1889–1950* (New York, 1976) reveals the prevalence of anti-Semitic views among the clergy.

35. Ino Arndt, "Die Judenfrage im Licht der evangelischen Sonntagsblätter 1918–1933," PhD Diss. Tübingen 1960; Wolfgang Altmann, "Die Judenfrage in evangelischen und katholischen Zeitschriften zwischen 1918 und 1933," Diss. Munich 1971.

36. Friedrich Andersen to HSC Dec. 28, 1921; Friedrich Andersen, *Der deutsche Heiland* (Munich, 1921); Rita Thalmann, "Protestantisme et National-Socialisme: les débuts des 'Chrétiens Allemands'" *Revue d'Histoire Moderne et Contemporaine* (1965), 12, pp. 287–308. For the *völkisch* tradition in German theology; Wolfgang Tilgner, *Volksnomos-theologie und Schöpfungsglaube* (Göttingen, 1966). Among the analyses of Chamberlain's religious ideas: Adolf Geprägs, *Germanentum und Christentum bei H. S. Chamberlain* (Göttingen, 1938); F. Beckmann, *H. S. Chamberlains Stellung zum Christentum* (Diss. Tübingen, 1943); H. W. Beyer, *H. S. Chamberlain und die innere Erneuerung des Christentums* (Berlin, 1939); W. Bülck, *Christentum und Deutschtum bei Arndt, Bismarck, H. S. Chamberlain und heutigen Dichtern* (Gütersloh, 1937); G. Frischmuth, *H. S. Chamberlain als Christ* (Gütersloh, 1937); R. Grabs, *Paul de Lagarde und H. S. Chamberlain* (Weimar, 1940); Herbert von Hintzenstern, *H. S. Chamberlains Darstellung Urchristentums* (Weimar, 1941); Anton Jirku, *H. S. Chamberlain und das Christentum* (Bonn, 1938); W. Vollrath, *H. S. Chamberlain und seine Theologie* (Erlangen, 1937). For the failure of the Protestant leadership to issue any denunciation of anti-Semitism among the clergy: J. R. C. Wright "*Above Parties.*"

37. G. L. Mosse, "Die deutsche Rechte und die Juden," in Mosse and Paucker, eds., *Entscheidungsjahr 1932. Zur Judenfrage in der Endphase der Weimarer Republik* (Tübingen, 1966), p. 229. Also, Annelise Thimme, *Flucht in den Mythos: die Deutschnationale Volkspartei und die Niederlage von 1918* (Göttingen, 1969).

38. G. L. Mosse, *The Crisis of German Ideology* (New York: Grosset and Dunlap, 1964), p. 243.

39. For this process of fragmentation: H. A. Winkler, *Mittelstand, Demokratie und Nationalsozialismus*; see also Robert Gellately, *The Politics of Economic Despair Shopkeepers and German Politics 1890–1914* (London, Beverly Hills: Sage, 1974), pp. 197–209 ("Epilogue 1914–1939").

40. The literature on these organizations is very large. For the Pan-Germans in early Weimar, in addition to works already cited, there is B. S. Chamberlin, "The Enemy on the Right. The Alldeutscher Verband in the Weimar Republic," PhD Diss., Univ. of Maryland, 1972. On the DHV: Iris Hamel, *Völkischer Verband und nationale Gewerkschaft. Der Deutschnationale Handlungsgehilfen-Verband 1893–1933* (Frankfurt, 1967); the best discussion of the various occultist sects and breeding schemes is G. L. Mosse, *The Crisis of German Ideology*, especially pp. 108–26. Also, Michael H. Kater, "Die Artamanen-Völkische Jugend in der Weimarer Republik," *Historische Zeitschrift* (1971), 213:577–638. H. J. Gordon, *Hitler and the Beer Hall Putsch* (Princeton: Princeton University Press, 1972) contains a detailed discussion of the various paramilitary and *völkisch* groups active in Bavaria in the first five years of the republic.

41. Uwe Lohalm, *Völkischer Radikalismus. Die Geschichte der Deutschvölkischer Schutz- und Trutzbundes 1919–1923*. This excellent study is indispensable for an understanding of the continuities in the radical right and anti-Semitism from the Kaiserreich to early Weimar.

42. Quoted in J. C. G. Röhl, *From Bismarck to Hitler. The Problem of Continuity in German History* (London: Longman, 1970), pp. 32–33.

43. Prof. Max Koch to HSC May 1, 1919 (Koch was Rektor of Breslau University).

44. HSC to von Riepenhausen Jan. 23, 1919 (*Briefe* 2:78–80).

45. Ludwig Schemann, *Wolfgang Kapp und die Märzunternehmung vom Jahre 1920: Ein Wort der Sühne* (Munich and Berlin, 1937).

46. J. Stolzing-Cerny to HSC Jan. 1, 1921 (CN). Also, the letters of Wilhelm Kiefer (editor of *Bühne und Welt*) to HSC, e.g., Oct. 19, 1921 (CN).

47. A. Dinter to HSC April 2, 1920 (CN).

48. *Ibid.* Also A. Dinter, *Ursprung, Ziel und Weg der deutschvölkischen Freiheitsbewegung* (Weimar, 1924), p. 17. Dinter's anger at the pre-war *völkisch* leaders had been growing since the November revolution, e.g. Dinter to HSC Dec. 11, 1918 speaks of "the high-handed autocracy and the supposition of personal infallibility [of Heinrich Class]," which is "characteristic of the "old system" that has its fossilized counterpart in the *Alldeutscher Verband*."

49. On "German" or "true" socialism see the very insightful analysis by Herman Lebovics, *Social Conservatism and the Middle Classes in Germany, 1914–1933* (Princeton: Princeton University Press, 1969). O. Spengler, "Prussianism and Socialism," in D. O. White, ed. *Selected Essays* (Chicago: University of Chicago Press, 1967); for Moeller van den Bruck: *Das Dritte Reich* (Berlin, 1923) and Fritz Stern, *The Politics of Cultural Despair* (New York: Doubleday Anchor, 1965), pp. 301–25. Hermann Keyserling also advocated a vague German socialism joining nostalgia for a romanticized past to dreams of a meritocratic and efficient future: *Deutschlands wahre politische Mission* (Darmstadt, 1919). He tried unsuccessfully to obtain financial help from Chamberlain and other Wagnerites for his School of Wisdom in Darmstadt, stressing its significance in the struggle against Marxism. Chamberlain who had by this time become estranged from Keyserling refused. Chamberlain first used the term "ethical socialism" in *Politische Ideale*; see also the fragment intended

as a continuation of this tract: "Der deutsche Staat" Ms (CN) and *Deutsche Zeitung* May 1, 1920.

50. Quoted by Geoffrey Pridham, *The Nazi Movement in Bavaria 1923-1933* (New York: Harper and Row, 1973), p. 9. For a detailed analysis of the Nazi Party in 1923 see H. J. Gordon, *Hitler and the Beer Hall Putsch.* On the growing dissatisfaction with the political style of older *völkisch* organizations: Jeremy Noakes, *The Nazi Party in Lower Saxony 1921-1933* (Oxford: Oxford University Press, 1971), pp. 1-86. Also on the early years of the party: A. Tyrrell, ed., *Führer befiehl . . . Selbsterzeugnisse aus der Kampfzeit der NSDAP* (Düsseldorf, 1969); *idem.*, *Vom 'Trommler' zum 'Führer'* (Munich, 1975).

51. Karl Alexander von Müller, *Im Wandel einer Welt. Erinnerungen* (Munich, 1966), 3:300.

52. M. Lehmann, *Verleger J. F. Lehmann. Ein Leben im Kampf fur Deutschland* (Munich, 1935); obituaries in *Deutschlands Erneuerung* (1935), 19(5). On Lehmann's financial ties to Nazism see B. S. Chamberlain, "Enemy on the Right" p. 216. On his aid to Alfred Rosenberg see the latter's *Memoirs* (New York, 1949), pp. 48-49. On Lehmann and the *putsch* see Gordon, *Hitler and the Beer Hall Putsch* p. 290. His son-in-law was Dr. Friedrich Weber, the leader of *Bund Oberland.*

53. When Hitler gave his first speech at the Hofbräukeller in October 1919, Kühn was billed as the main speaker. Kühn's party number was 587.

54. J. Stolzing-Cerny to HSC Jan. 1, 1921 (CN). Another acquaintance of Chamberlain, the Pan-German Ludwig Roselius, also met Hitler in 1922: Roselius, *Briefe und Schriften zu Deutschlands Erneuerung* (Oldenburg, 1933). Pastor Georg Schott, an admirer of Chamberlain who wrote several books and articles about him after 1927, joined the Nazi party in September 1920.

55. The Chamberlain-Dinter correspondence does not indicate when Dinter joined. A friend of Hermann Esser and Julius Streicher, he probably entered the party sometime in 1922, when Streicher linked the Nuremberg branch of the *Deutschsozialistische Partei* to the NSDAP. On Thuringia: D. R. Tracey, "The Development of the National Socialist Party in Thuringia 1924-1930" *Central European History* (March 1975), 8(1); *idem.*, "Thuringia under the Early Weimar Republic," PhD Diss. University of Maryland, 1966.

56. *Politische Ideale*, p. 101.

57. Manfred Gravina to HSC Sept. 30, 1919 (CN). Cosima at first hoped that Ludendorff would become dictator of Germany. By the end of 1920 this hope had faded, but she continued to believe that most Germans desired and needed a dictatorial leader. In 1923 she wrote: "At present the Italians appear to possess a statesmanly personality in Mussolini." *Briefwechsel zwischen Cosima Wagner und Fürst Ernst zu Hohenlohe-Langenburg*, pp. 387-88, 390, 393. In march 1924 Siegfried Wagner met Mussolini in Rome and was greatly impressed. Finding the situation of Germany "a depressing contrast" to that of Italy, he jotted a few comments about the Duce in his diary: "Everything is will, force, almost brutality. A fanatical eye, but none of the power of love that one finds in Hitler and Ludendorff. Romans and Germans! We spoke chiefly of ancient Rome. There is something of a Napoleon about him. A man of fine and true race! . . . It is devastating how low Germany has sunk." Zdenko von Kraft, *Der Sohn: Siegfried Wagners Leben und Umwelt* (Graz and Stuttgart, 1969), p. 247.

58. A brief, but excellent summary of the postwar period in Bayreuth is given by Michael Karbaum, *Studien zur Geschichte der Bayreuther Festspiele 1876-1976*

(Regensberg, 1976), pp. 61–80; especially valuable are the documents collected in the second half of the book. Also Chamberlain-Adolf von Gross correspondence (CN) for Chamberlain's part in the Wagner family affairs.

59. There are many examples: H. Kühnhold, "Die Regenerationslehre Richard Wagners und die Neugeburt des deutschen Volkes," *BB* (1913), pp. 276–89; Max Seiling, "Gegen den Monismus," *BB* (1908); Felix Gross, "Die Religion der Zukunft," *BB* (1909); Leopold von Schroeder, "Der arische Naturkult als Grundlage der Sage vom heiligen Gräl," *BB* (1911). Also the anti-Semitic attack on finance by Ottomar Beta, "Fass und Volk der Danaïden," *BB* (1909).

60. Karbaum, *Studïen zur Geschichte*, pp. 57–58.

61. Zdenko von Kraft, *Der Sohn*, p. 193.

62. Conversation of author and Frau Winifred Wagner in Bayreuth. Friedelind Wagner, *Heritage of Fire* (New York: Harper, 1945), p. 5.

63. The best account of Bayreuth in the revolution is Berndt Zinner, "Revolution in Bayreuth? Die Stadt in der Jahren 1918–1919," *Archiv für Geschichte von Oberfranken* (1973), 53:337–412.

64. The expression comes from Albert von Puttkamer's "Die Weimarer Festspiele 1926 des Bayreuther Bundes der deutschen Jugend," *Bayreuther Festspielführer* (1927), p. 75. See also the article by the attorney Jenne in the same issue, "Um den Ewigkeitswert Bayreuths." There were a number of reinterpretations of Wagner's works in the Weimar period, but not in Bayreuth (e.g. Otto Klemperer and Jürgen Fehlings *Fliegende Holländer* in Berlin which had expressionist aspects). Hans Mayer has recently described Siegfried as a particularly conservative and unoriginal mind, deeply opposed to all innovation. At the opening of the *Festspiel* in 1924 Siegfried announced: "Bayreuth is not there for any sort of hyper-modern vogues. This would contradict the style of works which after all were not written and composed as cubist, expressionist or dadaist." Hans Mayer, *Richard Wagner in Bayreuth* (New York: Rizzoli Publications, 1976), p. 103.

65. Karbaum, *Studien zur Geschichte*, pp. 81–93; Hans Mayer, *Richard Wagner in Bayreuth*, pp. 131–55; Kraft, *Der Sohn*, pp. 301–36; also the *Bayreuther Festspielführer* for these years.

66. Karbaum, *Studien zur Geschichte* part two p. 62.

67. Reinhard Vieweg, "Lohengrin und Christus" *BB* (1919) p. 211.

68. Karbaum, *Studien zur Geschichte* p. 58, the phrase was used by Du Moulin Eckart *Cosima Wagner*, 2:836.

69. Paul Förster, "Der deutsche Schule der Zukunft" *BB* (1916); Hans von Wolzogen "Wagnervereine nach dem Kriege" *BB* (1919).

70. Reports on the Bayreuther Bund can be found in *BB* and the *Bayreuther Festspielführer*, as well as the *Monatsblatt Bayreuther Bund der Deutschen Jugend*.

71. A von Puttkamer, "Die Weimarer Festspiele"; O. Daube, "Bayreuther Bund des deutschen Jugend," *Bayreuther Festspielführer* (1927); Z von Kraft, *Der Sohn*, pp. 263–66. On Bartels see Hans Severus Ziegler, *Adolf Hitler: aus dem Erleben dargestellt* (Göttingen, 1965).

72. Friedelind Wagner, *Heritage of Fire*, pp. 105–6. Püringer considered himself a Chamberlain disciple: see, for example, his eulogy on Chamberlain's seventieth birthday in *Deutsches Volkswart* (Sept. 1925), 7(12).

73. Christmas letter to Nora Eidam 1923, quoted by Karbaum, *Studien zur Geschichte*, part two, p. 65. Chamberlain used almost the same words in his letters to August Ludowici at this time.

74. "Whoever wants to understand National Socialist Germany," Hitler once

said, "must know Richard Wagner." His friend as a boy, August Kubizek, remembered their visits to the opera: "When he listened to Wagner's music, he was a
changed man; his violence left him, he became quiet, yielding and tractable. His gaze
lost its restlessness; his own destiny, however heavily it may have weighed upon him,
became unimportant. He no longer felt lonely and outlawed and misjudged by society.
He was intoxicated and bewitched. . . . From the stale, musty prison of his back room,
he was transported into the blissful regions of German antiquity, that ideal world
which was the lofty goal for all his endeavors." August Kubizek, *The Young Hitler I
Knew* (New York: Tower publications, n.d.), p. 175. Also, George G. Windell, "Hitler,
National Socialism, and Richard Wagner," *Journal of Central European Affairs*
(1963), 22(4):479–97.

75. The most detailed study of Nazism in Bayreuth is Benedikt Lochmüller's 2-
volume biography, *Hans Schemm* (Munich, 1935). There are a large number of
references to Chamberlain's intellectual influence on Schemm. Conversation of the
author with Winifred Wagner in Bayreuth. Winfried Schüler, *Der Bayreuther Kreis*, p.
85n.

76. H. J. Gordon, *Hitler and the Beer Hall Putsch*, pp. 140–269.

77. There are several accounts of the visit. Karbaum quotes Hans Konrad,
Studien zur Geschichte, part two p. 305. Also Christian Ebersberger, *Drei Generationen im Haus Wahnfried* (Ms. memoirs—Richard Wagner Gedenkstätte, Bayreuth),
and "An historische Stätte in Bayreuth," *Nordische Rundschau* (Kiel) Jan. 8, 1937.
Winifred Wagner as quoted in von Kraft, *Der Sohn* p. 305.

78. HSC to Adolf Hitler Oct. 7, 1923 *Briefe*, 2:124–26.

79. *Rasse und Persönlichkeit*, p. 36 (the essay "Kultur und Politik" was originally
published in *Deutschlands Erneuerung*, Jan. 1923 pp. 1–4).

80. J. Stolzing-Cerny to Eva Wagner Chamberlain Oct. 19, 1923 (CN). See also
Paul Bülow "Hitler und der Bayreuther Kulturkreis" *Aus Deutschlands Werden*
(Leipzig, 1933) 9.

81. Joachim Fest, *Hitler* (New York: Vintage, 1975), p. 181.

82. "Gott will es! Betrachtung über den gegenwärtigen Zustand Deutschlands"
Völkischer Beobachter Nov. 9, 1923, p. 1.

83. HSC to August Ludowici Nov. 26, 1923 (CN); see also Dr. Johannes Bierbach
to HSC Dec. 7, 1923 (CN).

84. Karbaum, *Studien zur Geschichte* p. 65, part two.

85. *Ibid*, part one p. 68.

86. *Tagebücher*, 1923–4 (CN).

87. "Der Prufstein" *Deutsche Zeitung* Dec. 24, 1923.

88. "Adolf Hitler" *Deutsche Presse* (Munich), April 20–21, 1924, p. 1. It is not
clear to whom this letter was originally written. Possibly there were several recipients.
He did inform August Ludowici, Jacob von Uexküll and a number of other friends
about his impressions of Hitler.

89. *Ibid*.

90. "Gedanken eines Invaliden," *Grossdeutsche Zeitung* (Munich) May 4–5,
1924, p. 2.

91. HSC and Eva Chamberlain to Adolf Hitler Dec. 1, 1923 (CN).

92. They were on Chamberlain's desk during the Second World War and were
probably stolen at its end (W. Einsle's *Tagebuch*, Bayreuth, Richard Wagner
Gedenkstätte).

93. J. Stolzing-Cerny to HSC May 8, 1924 (CN); Carl Cesar Eiffe to HSC June
1924 (CN); HSC to Ludwig von Hofmann *Briefe* 2:126–27; Stolzing-Cerny to HSC

Dec. 23, 1923, speaks of Hitler's release from the Landsberg jail. It was he who read the proofs of *Mein Kampf* and not Chamberlain as suggested by Karl Alexander von Müller, *Im Wandel einer Welt* p. 306.

94. A. Dinter in *Der Nationalsozialist*, Sept. 12, 1925: Chamberlain "is in truth the actual creator of the present *völkisch* movement. . . . The great danger for the present *völkisch* movement is that it threatens to bog down once more in the purely materialist aspects of the anti-Semitic struggle. The warning to pay attention to Chamberlain cannot be proclaimed forcefully enough."

95. Karbaum, *Studien zur Geschichte*, part two pp. 65–66.

96. Wolzogen was the last of the old guard to die, in 1937.

97. *Winifred Wagner* a 1975 film directed by Hans Jürgen Syberberg. Review by Robert Kraft in *The New York Review of Books* Nov. 11, 1976, p. 14.

98. *Monatsblatt: Bayreuther Bund der deutschen Jugend* (Feb. 1927) 2(2). Cosima was not told of Chamberlain's death.

99. H. Huber, ed., *The Early Goebbels Diaries* (New York, 1962), p. 83. The dates of Hitler's visits to Chamberlain after Oct. 1923 were: March 1925, Summer 1925 (for the festival), Nov. 1925, and May 1926.

100. *Völkischer Beobachter*, Jan. 11, 1927; Alfred Rosenberg, *H. S. Chamberlain als Verkünder und Begründer der deutschen Zukunft*.

Epilogue

1. The 24th edition of *The Foundations* was published in 1938. For typical anthologies: O. Döring, *Ein Deutscher namens H. S. Chamberlain: sein Lebensbild nach sein eigenen Worten* (Berlin, 1937); H. L. Schmidt, *H. S. Chamberlain: Auswahl aus seinem Werken* (Breslau, 1934). On the 10th anniversary of his death tributes were paid to him in all schools by order of the Education Ministry, and scores of articles appeared in the press on Jan. 10, 1937: *Berliner Tageblatt (Beiblatt); Völkischer Beobachter, Berliner Lokalanzeiger; Munchener Neueste Nachrichten; Frankfurter Zeitung; Kolnische Zeitung*, etc.

2. Desiderius Breitenstein, *H. S. Chamberlain. Ein Wegbereiter des rassischen Weltbildes* (Warendorf, Westphalia, 1936), p. 12. Written by a Catholic critic of Chamberlain.

3. For example: W. Essmann, "Chamberlains Weg zum Deutschtum," in *Der Weltkampf* (1936), 13:56–62; W. Gross, "Die Propheten Nietzsche, Lagarde, und Chamberlain und ihrer Bedeutung für uns," in *Nationalsozialistische Monatshefte* (April, 1930); F. Peuckert, "Chamberlain und Nietzsche" *Nationalsozialistische Monatshefte* (April 1934), 49:299–305. Pastor Georg Schott was one of the most prolific writers about Chamberlain, whose books and articles were particularly adulatory. See: *Auf des Lebens Höhe* (Munich, 1927), *Das Vermächtnis H. S. Chamberlain* (Stuttgart, 1940).

4. For example: R. Reinhardt, "H. S. Chamberlain" and "H. S. Chamberlain—Der Deutsche" in *Bayerische Kurier* Jan. 9, 1943 and July 23, 1943. Otto Trobes, "H. S. Chamberlain und der Bayreuther Gedanke" *Deutsche Allgemeine Zeitung*, Jan. 9, 1937.

5. Willi Nielsen, *Der Lebens- und Gestaltbegriff bei H. S. Chamberlain* (Kiel, 1938). Waldtraut Eckhard, *H. S. Chamberlains Naturanschauung* (Leipzig, 1941). Eckhard relies heavily on the work of Ernst Krieck, the Nazi educational theorist, and

is critical of Chamberlain's Kantianism. This is altogether a much more political tract than Nielsen. On Chamberlain's historical method: Josef Fahringer, *H. S. Chamberlain als Historiker* (Vienna, 1941); Karl Keudel, *Methode und Grundsätze der Geschichtschreibung H. S. Chamberlains* (Göttingen, 1939). By far the most competent study of Chamberlain is Hugo Meyer, *H. S. Chamberlain als völkischer Denker* (Munich: Bruckmann, 1939) which is based on a wide range of published sources. It goes as far as the publication of the *Foundations*.

6. Thus, Adolf Geprägs asserted: "Whoever today places in mutual opposition Christianity and the fruits of our race research, has fundamentally misunderstood the seer of our age." *Germanentum und Christentum bei H. S. Chamberlain* (Göttingen, 1938). For a list of other sources see the bibliography and chap. 10 n. 36.

7. H. Rauschning, *The Revolution of Nihilism* (New York, 1939); *The Voice of Destruction* (New York, 1940). The divergence between Nazi rhetoric and practice in domestic policies is analyzed by David Schoenbaum, *Hitler's Social Revolution. Class and Status in Nazi Germany 1933–1939* (New York, 1966). A call for a fresh enquiry into the ideology of the early party was sounded by Barbara Miller Lane, "Nazi Ideology: Some Unfinished Business" *Central European History* (March 1974), pp. 3–30.

8. See, for example, Walter Struve, *Elites against Democracy. Leadership Ideals in Bourgeois Political Thought 1890–1933* (Princeton, 1973), pp. 420–25.

9. L. Krieger, "Nazism: Highway or Byway?" *Central European History* (March 1978), p. 11.

10. There is no single study of Nazi racial ideology that surveys all aspects of the subject in detail. See, Karl Saller, *Die Rassenlehre des Nationalsozialismus in Wissenschaft und Propaganda* (Darmstadt, 1961); R. Breitling, *Die nationalsozialistische Rassenlehre* (Meisenheim an Glan, 1971) is very brief. Patrik von zur Mühlen, *Rassenideologien. Geschichte und Hintergründe* (Bonn, 1977), pp. 236–46. Hans-Jurgen Lutzhöft, *Der nordische Gedanke in Deutschland 1920–1940* (Stuttgart, 1971) provides an excellent analysis of the Nordic School and much else besides. On Himmler: J. Ackermann, *Heinrich Himmler als Ideologe* (Göttingen, 1970).

11. The bookstore owner, Walther Timmerlah, came from an old and respected family in the town. Returning to Germany in 1921 after nine years abroad he was overwhelmed by the changed circumstances of the Reich and estranged from the Republic. "Shortly before the Munich *Putsch* he heard, at a literary tea, that Chamberlain said of Hitler, 'There's a man I could follow with my eyes shut,' and consequently Timmerlah joined the NSDAP as the first member in Thalburg." Well liked in the town and active in its social life, he was a significant factor in getting others to join: "People said, 'If he's in it, it must be all right.'" W. S. Allen, *The Nazi Seizure of Power: The Experience of a Single German Town 1930–1935* (Chicago: Quadrangle, 1965), p. 26. One should also remember, of course, that there were many who admired Chamberlain's writings and claimed to have been influenced by him who never were attracted to the Hitler movement or repudiated it after a brief flirtation.

12. See, for example: W. Frank, *Geist und Macht* (Hamburg, 1938), p. 48 ff.; Alfred Baeumler, *Politik und Erziehung* (Berlin, 1939), pp. 29–32; Ernst Krieck, *Mythologie des bürgerlichen Zeitalters* (Leipzig, 1939), p. 82. Paul Lenard had been an admirer of Chamberlain since the war; they occasionally corresponded.

13. For Hitler's reading see: W. Maser, *Hitler. Legend, Myth and Reality* (New York, 1971), chap. 5; Ernst Hanfstaengl, *Hitler. The Missing Years* (London: McClelland, 1957); Hans Frank, *Im Angesicht des Galgens* (Munich, 1953). Also, E. Jäckel, *Hitlers Weltanschauung. Entwurf einer Herrschaft* (Tübingen, 1969); Hugh Trevor-

Roper, "The Mind of Adolf Hitler," preface to *Hitler's Table Talk 1941-1944* (London, 1953). For Hitler's criticism of Chamberlain's Christian spiritual values see p. 114. For Himmler: Bradley F. Smith, *Heinrich Himmler. A Nazi in the Making 1900-1926* (Stanford: Stanford University Press, 1971), pp. 122, 147.

14. Robert Cecil, *The Myth of the Master Race. Alfred Rosenberg and Nazi Ideology* (New York: Dodd Mead 1972), pp. 12-13, 18-19.

15. For example, Rosenberg quoted Chamberlain in a letter to Gregor Strasser explaining his opposition to the establishment of Nazi trade unions in 1927. *Ibid*, p. 57.

16. *Ibid*, p. 101-2. Also, Rosenberg's collection of writings and speeches contains several references to Chamberlain: *Blut und Ehre* (Munich, 1935). His brief study, *H. S. Chamberlain als Verkünder und Begründer einer deutschen Zukunft* (Munich, 1927) reveals an accurate and detailed knowledge of Chamberlain's writings, although the interpretation is radicalized and politicized. For a portrait of Rosenberg as a pathetic idealist with little influence: J. C. Fest, *The Face of the Third Reich* (New York: Ace Books, 1970), pp. 241-75. More recently his influence on Hitler has been thought more significant, e.g. Geoffrey Stoakes, "The Evolution of Hitler's Ideas on Foreign Policy 1919-1925," in P. D. Stachura ed., *The Shaping of the Nazi State* (New York: Barnes and Noble, 1978). On Rosenberg and the Nordic School of racists see: Lutzhöft, *Der nordische Gedanke in Deutschland*.

17. Norman Cohn, *Warrant for Genocide* (New York: Harper and Row, 1969), pp. 136-37 provides the example of a meeting in 1924 reported by one Jewish observer: "In Berlin I attended several meetings which were entirely devoted to the *Protocols*. The speaker was usually a professor, a teacher, an editor, a lawyer or someone of that kind. The audience consisted of members of the educated class, civil servants, tradesmen, former officers, ladies, above all students, students of all faculties and years of seniority. . . . Passions were whipped up to boiling point. There, in front of one, in the flesh, was the cause of all ills—those who had made the war, and brought about the defeat, and engineered the revolution, those who had conjured up all our suffering . . . . German scholarship allowed belief in the genuineness of the *Protocols* and in the existence of a Jewish world conspiracy to penetrate ever more deeply into all the educated sections of the German population."

18. It is arguable that the Nuremberg Laws and other anti-Jewish decrees in the first five years of the Third Reich were a fulfillment of the program outlined by the anti-Semitic parties of the Wilhelminian era. In the case of Chamberlain and many other anti-Semites, however, their goals are too vague to guess what they believed the role of Jews should be.

19. Shulamit Volkov, "Anti-Semitism as a Cultural Code" *LBI* (1978), 23:45-46; J. P. Faye, *Languages totalitaires* and *Théorie du récit* (Paris, 1972). For two very different interpretations of Nazi policy: Lucy S. Dawidowicz, *The War against the Jews 1933-1945* (New York: Holt, 1975) argues that the destruction of Jewry was the goal of Nazi policy throughout; Karl A. Schleunes, *The Twisted Road to Auschwitz. Nazi Policy Toward German Jews 1933-39* (London: Deutsch 1972) depicts the Nazis as "stumbling toward a policy" and argues that the Final Solution as it emerged in 1941-42 was not the product of a grand design. K. Pätzold, *Faschismus. Rassenwahn. Judenverfolgung. Eine Studie zur politischen Strategie und Taktik des faschistischen deutschen Imperialismus 1933-1935* (Berlin, 1975) analyzes anti-Semitism and persecution of the Jews as instruments of manipulation and mobilisation, denying the inevitability of the Final Solution.

20. W. S. Allen, *The Nazi Seizure of Power*, p. 76. "If Nazi anti-Semitism held any appeal for the townspeople, it was in a highly abstract form, as a remote theory unconnected with daily encounters with real Jews. . . . Many who voted Nazi simply ignored or rationalized the anti-Semitism of the party, just as they ignored other unpleasant aspects of the Nazi movement." Geoffrey Pridham, *Hitler's Rise to Power. The Nazi Movement in Bavaria, 1923–1933* (New York: Harper and Row, 1973), pp. 237–44 (quotation p. 244).

21. Quoted in Ismar Schorsch, "German Anti-Semitism in the Light of Post-War Historiography," *LBI* (1974), 19:267.

22. For additional comments on this theme during the Third Reich: Norman Cohn, *Warrant for Genocide*, pp. 209–15. Also, M. Müller-Claudius, *Der Antisemitismus und das deutsche Verhängnis* (Frankfurt, 1948).

Appendix

1. For English reviews of Chamberlain's *Richard Wagner* see: *The Musical Standard* (London) Dec. 1895; *The Meister*, 1896, 32; *The Evening Standard*, Feb. 5, 1896; *The Spectator*, March 26, 1898; *The Guardian* (London) July 20, 1898; *Times*, Sept. 24, 1897. For the United States see *Critic* (New York) (Jan. 1898), 32; *Nation*, Nov. 25, 1897.

2. *Quarterly Review* (Oct. 1903) 198:406–12; *New Yorker Staats-Zeitung* July 29; Aug. 5, 12, 16, 19, 26, 1899 and Sept. 2, 9, 1900; *The New York Times* March 14, 1903. *New York Evening Post*, Jan. 23, 1904.

3. HSC to Kaiser Wilhelm Feb. 20, 1902, *Briefe*, 2:162.

4. Professor Weese to HSC Feb. 23, 1909 (CN)—Weese was Anna's nephew. HSC to Anne Guthrie April 19, 1908 (CN). See also the detailed analysis by Colin Holmes, "Houston Stewart Chamberlain in Great Britain," *The Wiener Library Bulletin* (1970), 24(2): p. 31–6.

5. B. H. Chamberlain to Redesdale Nov. 12, 20, 1908 (Redesdale Papers located in the County Record Office, Gloucester). B. H. Chamberlain to HSC Jan. 13, 1909 (CN); John Lane publishers to HSC Dec. 18, 1909, Nov. 2, 1910 (CN). In fact, John Lane had suggested in 1907 that Basil Chamberlain might undertake the translation; he declined owing to poor health. John Lane to HSC Nov. 28, 1907 (CN).

6. HSC to Redesdale Jan. 17, 1909; Lees to John Lane Jan. 28, 1909 (Redesdale Papers). Also John Lane to HSC Nov. 2, 1910; B. H. Chamberlain to HSC Jan. 20, 1911 (CN).

7. HSC to Redesdale Aug. 6, 1910; also May 19, 1910 (Redesdale papers). Geness first contracted to do the French translation; he was replaced by Robert Godet in 1910. The translation appeared in 1913, but its sales were soon injured by the outbreak of war.

8. *Die Grundlagen des Neunzehnten Jahrhunderts. An Appreciation* (London 1910), p. 6. See also: *idem*, "Bayreuth in 1912" (Privately printed, London 1912).

9. *Ibid.*

10. *Edinburgh Review* (Jan. 1914), 219:82.

11. Edmund Gosse to Redesdale March 19, 1909; Arthur Balfour to Redesdale March 18, 1909; R. B. Haldane to Redesdale June 4, 1909; Morley to Redesdale Dec. 24, 1910; Lucien Wolf to Redesdale June 17, 1909 (Redesdale Papers). Redesdale also

sent copies to Lady Londonderry and Lord Rosebery (a brief letter of thanks with an illegible signature, sent from Mentmore, the Rosebery estate, is included in the Redesdale papers).

12. John Lane to HSC Nov. 2, 1910 (CN). Holmes, "Houston Stewart Chamberlain," p. 33.

13. *Times Literary Supplement*, Dec. 15, 1910.

14. Redesdale to HSC Dec. 28, 1911 (CN); Redesdale to HSC Jan. 25, 1912 (CN). Churchill was married to a niece of Redesdale.

15. *Athenaeum* April 1911, 8; *The Bookman* (1911), 39:277; *Quarterly Review* (1903), 198; Holmes, "H. S. Chamberlain in Great Britain," p. 32. *Review of Reviews*, Oct. 1911.

16. *Fabian News* (June 1911) 22:53–54.

17. Emile Delavenay, *D. H. Lawrence: L'Homme et la genèse de son oevre. Les années de formation 1885–1919* (Paris, 1969). The comments on Chamberlain are interspersed throughout the book. See especially pp. 406–12, 424–31.

18. L. Wolf to Claude Montefiore Jan. 12, 1911 (David Mowshowicz Collection File 32, Nos. 2899–2900, Yivo Institute, New York).

19. *Race Sentiment as a Factor in History* (Creighton Lecture, London 1915). For other wartime comments see: *Literary Digest* (1915) 51:666–67; J. M. Robertson, "Herr Chamberlain and the War," *Contemporary Review* (July–Dec. 1915), 108; *Westminster Gazette*, April 11, 1916; *Times* obituary Jan. 11, 1927.

20. The Kaiser sent a copy to Burgess; Beveridge visited Chamberlain in Bayreuth in 1915 (HSC to Hugo Bruckmann Feb. 11, 1915, *Briefe*, 1:279). Alfred Schultz to HSC Aug. 13, 1908 (CN). R. B. Aldcroft to HSC May 25, 1911 (CN). See also John Higham, *Strangers in the Land. Patterns of American Nativism 1860–1925* (New York: Atheneum, 1970), p. 362.

21. Ellery Sedgwick to HSC Aug. 7, 1912 (CN).

22. *The Outlook* (July 29, 1911) 98:728–34.

23. *The Dial* (May 16, 1911), 50:387–91.

24. Higham, *Strangers in the Land*.

Bibliography

To attempt to cite all the sources used in the preparation of this book would result in a very long bibliography of limited use to most readers. I have chosen instead to list here all the writings of Chamberlain, followed by the major books and articles about him. Following these is an annotated bibliography of major sources consulted on European racism, German anti-Semitism, Wagner and Bayreuth. A certain amount of overlap between these categories is inevitable, but titles have only been mentioned once.

Chamberlain's Works

Unpublished Sources

The chief source for this biography is the large Chamberlain *Nachlass*, classified and organized by Dr. W. Einsle, and housed in the Richard Wagner Gedenkstätte, Bayreuth. Also important were the papers of Cosima Wagner and various prominent Wagnerites located in the same archive. Other sources of lesser significance included the papers of Lord Redesdale in the County Record Office, Gloucester, England, and those of Ludwig Schemann at the university library in Freiburg.

The Writings of Houston Stewart Chamberlain:

The most nearly complete bibliography to date is Albert Vanselow, *Das Werk Houston Stewart Chamberlains. Eine Bibliographie* (Munich, 1927). It contains, however, a number of mistakes and omissions. I have not listed all the editions of Chamberlain's books and articles, only their first publication.

This bibliography does not include foreign translations: for a list of these see Vanselow.

Das Drama Richard Wagners. Leipzig: Breitkopf and Härtel, 1892.

Richard Wagner. Echte Briefe an Ferdinand Praeger. Leipzig, 1894.

Richard Wagner. Munich: Bruckmann, 1896.

Recherches sur la sève ascendante. Neuchâtel: Attinger, 1897.

Die Grundlagen des Neunzehnten Jahrhunderts. Munich: Bruckmann, 1899.

Parsifal-Märchen. Munich: Bruckmann, 1900.

Vorwort und Nachträge zur dritten Auflage der Grundlagen des XIX. Jahrhunderts. Munich: Bruckmann, 1901.

Worte Christi. Munich: Bruckmann, 1901.

Drei Bühnendichtungen. Munich: Bruckmann, 1902.

Dilettantismus. Rasse. Monotheismus. Rom. Vorwort zur 4. Auflage der Grundlagen des XIX. Jahrhunderts. Munich: Bruckmann, 1903.

Heinrich von Stein und seine Weltanschauung. Leipzig and Berlin, 1903. (With Friedrich Poske.)

Immanuel Kant. Die Persönlichkeit als Einführung in das Werk. Munich: Bruckmann, 1905.

Arische Weltanschauung. Berlin, 1905.

Briefwechsel zwischen Schiller und Goethe. Jena: Diederichs 1905 (Introduction only).

Wehr und Gegenwehr. Vorworte zur dritten und zur vierten Auflage der Grundlagen des Neunzehnten Jahrhunderts. Munich: Bruckmann, 1912.

Goethe. Munich: Bruckmann, 1912.

Kriegsaufsätze. Munich: Bruckmann, 1914.

Neue Kriegsaufsätze. Munich: Bruckmann, 1915.

Politische Ideale. Munich: Bruckmann, 1915.

Wer hat den Krieg verchuldet? Wiesbaden, 1915.

Die Zuversicht. Munich: Bruckmann, 1915.

Deutschlands Kriegziel. Oldenburg, 1916.

Deutsches Wesen. Munich: Bruckmann, 1916.

Ideal und Macht. Munich: Bruckmann, 1916.

Hammer oder Amboss. Munich: Bruckmann, 1916.

Demokratie und Freiheit. Munich: Bruckmann, 1917.

Der Wille zum Sieg und andere Aufsätze. Munich: Bruckmann, 1918.

Lebenswege meines Denkens. Munich: Bruckmann, 1919.

Mensch und Gott. Betrachtungen über Religion und Christentum. Munich: Bruckmann, 1921.

Herr Hinkebeins Schädel. Gedankenhumoreske. Munich: Bruckmann, 1921.

Drei Vorworte. Munich: Bruckmann, 1923.

Rasse und Persönlichkeit. Munich: Bruckmann, 1925.

Natur und Leben. Munich: Bruckmann, 1928. Ed. J. von Uexküll.

Briefe 1882–1924 und Briefwechsel mit Kaiser Wilhelm II. Ed. Paul Pretzsch 2 vols. Munich: Bruckmann, 1928.

Cosima Wagner und Houston Stewart Chamberlain im Briefwechsel 1888–1908. Ed. Paul Pretzsch. Leipzig, 1934.

Selections from Chamberlain's works appear in:
H. L. Schmidt, ed. *Houston Stewart Chamberlain. Auswahl aus seinem Werken.* Breslau, 1934.
Oskar Döring, ed. *Ein Deutscher namens Chamberlain. Sein Lebensbild nach seinen eigenen Worten.* (Langensalza, 1937).
Paul Pretzsch, ed. *Richard Wagner der Deutsche als Künstler. Denker und Politiker.* Leipzig, n.d.

Articles by Chamberlain:

1885
"La Revue de Bayreuth (Bayreuther Blätter). Analyses des numéro de fevrier 1885." *Revue Wagnérienne* (March 1885), no. 2.
"La Revue de Bayreuth (Bayreuther Blätter). Analyse du numéro de mars 1885." *Revue Wagnérienne.* (April 1885), no. 3.
"L'Or du Rhein: traduction française litterale de la première scene." *Revue Wagnérienne* (Oct. 1885), no. 8.
"La Revue de Bayreuth (Bayreuther Blätter). Analyses des numéros de juillet et d'août 1885." *Revue Wagnérienne,* (November 1885), no. 10.
"Correspondance sur la représentation de la Walkure a Dresde." *Revue Wagnérienne* (Dec. 1885), no. 11.
"Offener Brief an den Opernsänger Riese." *Dresdner Tageblatt* (Dec. 1885), 29.

1886
"Notes sur Lohengrin." *Revue Wagnérienne,* (January 1886), no. 12.
"La Revue de Bayreuth (Bayreuther Blätter). Analyse des numéros IX–XII." *Revue Wagnérienne,* (Feb. 1886), 2(1).
"La Revue de Bayreuth (Bayreuther Blätter). Analyse des numéros II–III." *Revue Wagnérienne,* (April 1886), 2(3).
"Notes sur la Goetterdaemmerung." *Revue Wagnérienne,* (June 1886), 2(5).
"Notes sur Parsifal." *Revue Wagnérienne,* (Aug. 1886), 2(7).
"La Revue de Bayreuth (Bayreuther Blätter). Analyse des numéros IV–VI." *Revue Wagnérienne,* (Dec. 1886), 2(11).
"Les Portraits de Wagner par Ernst Kietz." *Revue Wagnérienne,* (Dec. 1886), 2(11).

1887
"La Revue de Bayreuth (Bayreuther Blätter). Analyse des numéros VII–XII." *Revue Wagnérienne,* (Jan. 1887), 2(12).

"Notes sur Tristan et Isolde I." *Revue Wagnérienne*, (Feb. 1887), 3(1).
"La Walkure de Richard Wagner et la Valkyrie de M. Victor Wilder." *Revue Wagnérienne*, (September–Oct. 1887), 3(7).
"Notes sur Tristan et Isolde II." *Revue Wagnérienne*, (Nov.–Dec. 1887), 3(8).

1888
"Kunstlerische Dankbarkeit." *Sächsische Landeszeitung*, May 16, 1888.
"Notes chronologiques sur l'Anneau du Nibelung." *Revue Wagnérienne*, July 1888.
"Die Sprache in Tristan und Isolde und ihr Verhältnis zur Musik." *Allgemeine Musik-Zeitung XV Jahrg.*, nos. 29–30, 30–31, 1888.

1891
"Une défense de Tannhäuser." *L'Artiste*, Dec. 1891.

1892
"Tannhäuser-Nachklange: Aus dem Briefe eines Engländers an einen Franzosen." *Bayreuther Blätter* (1892), pp. 51–57.
"La Bosnie sous le protectorat de l'Autriche." *Bibliothèque universelle et Revue suisse* (1892), 54, pp. 5–21, 349–368.
"Parsifals Christbescheerung: Ein Weihnachtsmärchen." *Bayreuther Blätter*, (1892), pp. 28–34.
"Musikausstellung und Festspiele." *Bayreuther Blätter* (1892), pp. 382–407.
"The Wagner Museum." *Daily News* (London), Dec. 9, 1892.

1893
"Zur Eröffnung der Stilbildungsschule in Bayreuth." *Freie Bühne*, Feb. 11, 1893, pp. 188–96.
"Parsifals Gebet." *Bayreuther Blätter* (1893), pp. 97–105.
"Zwei offene Briefe an Herrn Fritzsch." *Musikalisches Wochenblatt* (1893), 24(17, 22).
"Richard Wagner und die Politik." *Bayreuther Blätter* (1893), pp. 137–58.
"Ferdinand Praegers: Wagner wie ich ihn kannte." *Bayreuther Blätter* (1893), pp. 201–40.
"Bosnische Bilder." *Ostdeutsche Rundschau* (Vienna) Dec. 2, 1893.
"Bewusstsein und Unbewusstsein bei Wagner." *Neue Zeitschrift für Musik*, March 2, 1893.

1894
"Ein Nachwort zum Gastspiele Mounet Sullys." *Ostdeutsche Rundschau* (Vienna), Jan. 23, 25, 1894.
"Nachtrag zu Richard Wagners Briefe an Ferdinand Praeger." *Bayreuther Blätter* (1894), pp. 19–29.
"Die Bedeutung des Todes bei Richard Wagner." *Bayreuther Blätter* (1894), pp. 30–40.

"Unter Uns." *Bayreuther Blätter* (1894), pp. 73–78.

"Parsifals Tod." *Bayreuther Blätter* (1894), pp. 152–60.

"Praeger and Wagner's Letters." *The Musical Standard* (London) May 5, 1894, pp. 381–2.

"Richard Wagner und der Heimgarten." *Ostdeutsche Rundschau* (Vienna), May 22, 1894.

"Eine Entgegnung auf unser "Offenes Wort" ueber die Neu-Inszenierung des 'Lohengrin' in München." *Ostdeutsche Rundschau* June 12, 1894.

"Münchener 'Lohengrin'-Witze." *Ostdeutsche Rundschau*, June 12, 1894.

"Wie man in Bayreuth Geschäfte macht." *Ostdeutsche Rundschau* June 17, 1894.

"Dr Paul Deussens Uebersetzung der Sûtras des Vedânta." *Bayreuther Blätter* (1894), pp. 249–64.

"Nocheinmal Richard Wagner und P. Rosegger." *Ostdeutsche Rundschau* July 10, 1894.

"Lohengrin in Bayreuth." *Ostdeutsche Rundschau* (1894), July 22, 28; Aug. 7, 14; Sept. 13, 27; Oct. 9, 20; Nov. 18.

"Briefe aus Bayreuth." *Berliner Börsen—Courier* (1894), Aug. 8, 13, 22.

"Jean Thorel: La littérature Wagnérienne en Allemagne." *Revue des Deux Mondes* May 15, 1894.

1895

"Wie man in Bayreuth studiert!" *Ostdeutsche Rundschau* March 8, 1895.

"Bosnia for a Holiday." *Manchester Guardian* April 13, 1895.

"Praeger-Wagner Controversy." *The Musical Courier* (London) Aug. 31, 1895.

"Mr. Chamberlain is Angry." *The Musical Courier* (New York) Oct. 19, 1895.

"Richard Wagners Regenerationslehre." *Bayreuther Blätter* (1895) pp. 169–82.

"La Doctrine Artistique de Richard Wagner." *Revue des Deux Mondes*, Sept.–Oct. 1895.

"Büchners Sturz." *Neue Deutsche Rundschau* June 1895.

"Die Kunstwerke Richard Wagners." *Neue Musikalische Presse* (Vienna) June 23, 30 1895.

"Richard Wagner. Schematische Lebensübersicht." *Weekblad voor Muziek* (Amsterdam, 1895), Sept. 14, 21; Oct. 5, 19; Nov. 2.

1896

"1876–1896. Die ersten zwanzig Jahre der Bayreuther Bühnenfestspiele." *Bayreuther Blätter* (1896), pp. 1–67.

"Petite étude graphologique." *L'Ecriture* (Paris) 1896.

"Tendenz oder Sentenz?" *Bayreuther Blätter* (1896), pp. 193–96.

"Ueber Richard Wagner." *Der Wartburgbund* (Dresden), 2(13–16).

"Vor den Coulissen." *Berliner Börsen—Courier* July 31, 1896.

"Bayreuther Briefe." *Berliner Börsen—Courier* (1896) July 30; Aug. 2, 30.

"Richard Wagner et le génie français." *Revue des Deux Mondes* (Paris) July 15, 1896.

"Die Bayreuther Festspiele." *Die Zukunft* (Berlin) July 18, 1896.

"Richard Wagner." *Die Redenden Künste* July 29, 1896.

"Bayreuther Betrachtungen." *Rundschau. Unterhaltungsbeilage der Deutschen Zeitung* (Berlin) Aug. 15, 16, 1896.

"Bayreuth 1896." *Ostdeutsche Rundschau*, Sept. 13, 16, 19, 1896.

"Bayreuth im Jahre 1896." *Die Zukunft* (Berlin) Sept. 26, 1896.

1897

"Allegorische Dramen." *Ostdeutsche Rundschau* Jan. 3, 1897.

"Offener Brief ueber Bayreuther Honorare." *Weekblad voor Muziek* (Amsterdam) March 6, 1897.

"Nach dem Ringe." *Bayreuther Blätter* (1897), pp. 100–105.

"Richard Wagner in seinem Verhältnis zu den Klassikern der Dicht- und Tonkunst." *Bayreuther Blätter* (1897), pp. 189–213.

"Die Upanishads deutsch." *Bayreuther Blätter* (1897), pp. 299–300.

"Recherches sur la sève ascendante." *Die Zukunft* (Berlin) June 12, 1897.

"Fest-Vortrag." *Deutscher Jugendhort* (Vienna) 1 (1–5).

"Bayreuth und die Kritik." *Deutsche Revue* (Berlin) Aug. 1897.

"Allgemeine Geschichte der Philosophie." *Bayreuther Blätter* (1897), pp. 348–71.

"Redevoering gehouden te Bayreuth den 18 August 1897, na afloop der 'Festspiele.'" *Weekblad voor Muziek* (Amsterdam) Nov. 20, 1897.

"De la Sainteté." *Le spectateur Catholique* (Paris) Nov. 1897.

"Eine neue Geschichte der deutschen Literatur." *Ostdeutsche Rundschau* Dec. 21, 22, 1897.

1898

"Ueber indisches Denken." *Beilage zur Allgemeinen Zeitung* (Munich), Aug. 18–19, 1898.

"The Personal Side of Richard Wagner." *The Ladies Home Journal* (Philadelphia) Oct. 1898.

"How Richard Wagner Wrote His Operas." *ibid.* Nov. 1898.

1899

"Briefe ueber Siegfried Wagners Bärenhäuter." *Bayreuther Blätter* (1898), pp. 13–18.

"Richard Wagners Philosophie." *Beilage zur Allgemeinen Zeitung* (Munich) Feb. 25, 27, 28, 1899.

"Lucian." *Die Zukunft* (Berlin) March 11, 1899.

"Siegfried Wagner in Wien." *Wiener Rundschau* April 15, 1899.

"Bülows Briefwechsel." *Die Zeit* (Vienna) April 22, 1899.

"Siegfried Wagner und der Bärenhäuter." *Die Zukunft* (Berlin) April 22, 1899.

"Jung Siegfried." *Jugend* (Munich) Aug. 12, 1899.

"Werther." *Ibid.*, Aug. 26, 1899.

"Offener Brief an Herrn Fritzsch." *Musikalisches Wochenblatt* (Leipzig) Oct. 1899.

"Der Kampf um der Staat." *Neue Deutsche Rundschau* (Berlin) (Oct. 1899), 10.

"Paul Deussen und die Bedeutung der Altindischen Weltanschauung für das Leben der Gegenwart." *Beilage zur Allgemeinen Zeitung* (Munich) Oct. 7, 9, 1899.

"Das gibt's nicht!" *Jugend* Oct. 28, 1899.

"Schiller als 'Lehrer im Ideal.'" *Ibid.*, Dec. 16, 1899.

"Gedichte von Albert Roffhack." *Ostdeutsche Rundschau* Dec. 20, 1899.

"Richard Wagner als Erzieher." *Ibid.*, Dec. 23, 1899.

1900

"Die Racenfrage." *Die Wage* (Vienna) Jan. 7; Feb. 25, 1900.

"Der Krieg." *Die Zukunft* (Berlin) Feb. 17, 1900.

"Welches Werk Richard Wagners halten sie für das beste?" *Ostdeutsche Rundschau* Feb. 18, 1900.

"Richard Wagners politische Grundsätze." *Neue Musikalische Presse* (Vienna) March 25, 1900.

"Classicität und Germanismus." *Wiener Rundschau* April 1, 1900.

"Die Seele des Chinesen." *Neues Wiener Tagblatt* April 5–6, 1900.

"Magyar Czigányzene." *Budapester Tageblatt* April 8, 1900.

"Kaiser Wilhelm II." *Jugend* (Munich) May 28, 1900.

"Ueber die Judenfrage in Rumänien." *Nuova Revista Romana* (Bucharest, 1900), 10.

"Un philosophe Wagnérien. Heinrich von Stein." *Revue des Deux Mondes* (Paris) June 15, 1900.

"Richard Wagners geschichtliche Stellung." *Jugend* (Munich) Sept. 23; October 1, 1900.

"Konzert Gulbransson." *Ostdeutsche Rundschau* Dec. 18, 1900.

"Werther réhabilité." *La Vogue* (Paris) March 15, 1900.

1901

"Die Preussische Rasse." *Beilage zur Täglichen Rundschau* January 18, 1901.

"Volkstum und Weltmacht in der Geschichte." *Unterhaltungs-beilage zur Täglichen Rundschau* (Berlin) February 1901.

"Richard Wagners Briefe an Hermann Levi. Zur Einführung." *Bayreuther Blätter* (1901) pp. 13–17.

"Das Wesen der Kunst." *Festschrift der Karlsruher Künstlerschaft*, March 1901.

"Gedanken aus Goethes Werken." *Ostdeutsche Rundschau* March 16, 1901.

"Richard Wagners Bayreuth." *Die Woche* (Berlin) June 1, 1901.

"Goethe und der Typus des germanischen Genius." *Beilage zur Allgemeinen Zeitung* (Munich) Oct. 12, 1901.

"Berichtigung." *Beilage zur Allgemeinen Zeitung* (Munich) Nov. 6, 1901.

"Rasse und Nation." *Unterhaltungsbeilage zur Täglichen Rundschau*, May 7–9, 1901.

"Der voraussetzungslose Mommsen." *Die Fackel* (Vienna) Nov. 1901.

1902

"Katholische Universitäten." *Die Fackel* (Vienna) Jan. 1902.

"Die Natur als Lehrmeisterin. Ein neues Bildungsideal." *Der Tag* (Berlin), Jan. 26, 29, 1902.

"Versuch einer Inhaltsübersicht von 'Oper und Drama.'" *Die Musik* (Berlin) Feb. 1902.

"Immanuel Kant." *Unterhaltungsbeilage zur Täglichen Rundschau* (Berlin) March 14, 1902.

"Richard Wagner als Schriftsteller." *Unterhaltungsbeilage zur Täglichen Rundschau* (Berlin) May 21–22, 1902.

"Paul Deussen: Elemente der Metaphysik." *Unterhaltungsbeilage zur Täglichen Rundschau*, July 24, 1902.

"Der Bayreuther Festspielgedanke." *Unterhaltungsbeilage zur Täglichen Rundschau*, July 26, 1902.

"Kantbiographien." *Deutsche Monatsschrift* (Berlin) Sept. 1902.

"Ueber Dilettantismus." *Deutsche Monatsschrift* (Berlin) Nov. 1902.

"Die Rassenfrage." *Unterhaltungsbeilage zur Täglichen Rundschau* (Berlin), Nov. 4–6, 1902.

"Das heutige England." *Deutsche Monatsschrift* (Berlin), Nov. 1902.

"Immanuel Kant." *Deutsche Gedenkhalle*, 1902.

"Heinrich von Stein." *Bayreuther Blätter* (1902), 25.

1903–1913

"Deutschland und England." *Strassburger Zeitung* Jan. 3, 1903.

"Christus eine Germane." *Die Zukunft* (Berlin) Jan. 23, 1904.

"Lettre à M. Edouard Dujardin." *Mercure de France* (Paris) Feb. 1904.

"Briefwechsel zwischen Schiller und Goethe." (Introduction to work of the same title) Jena, 1905.

"Grundlagen." (Letter of Chamberlain to Oskar Pöffel). *Entwicklung* (Vienna) June 15, 1907.

"Goethe, Linné und exakte Wissenschaft der Natur." *Wiesner-Festschrift* (Vienna, 1908), pp. 225–38.

"Siegfried Wagner." *Allgemeine Zeitung* (Munich) Sept. 5, 1908.

"Entgegnung an Dr. L. Sofer." *Die Umschau* (Frankfurt) Nov. 20, 1901.

"Immanuel Kant." *Bayreuther Blätter* (1909), 32.

"Brief an H. S. (Hans Sachs) über die Bestimmung der Wagnervereine." *Bayreuther Blätter* (1910), pp. 225–28.

"Richard Wagner. Auswahl seiner Schriften." *Ibid.*, pp. 289–96.

"Richard Wagner und Frankreich." *Ibid.*, (1911), pp. 91–111.

"Bericht ueber die Enthüllung der Büste Adolf von Gross." *Oberfrankische Zeitung* (Bayreuth) June 2, 1911.

"Richard Wagners 'Mein Leben.'" *Bruckmanns Almanach für das Jahr 1912*, pp. 19–26.

"Dante und Goethe." *Die Neue Rundschau* (Berlin) (1912), 23(11).

"Die Bhagavadgitâ". *Unterhaltungsbeilage zur Täglichen Rundschau* (Berlin) Jan. 3, 1913.

1914

"August Ludowici: Das genetische Prinzip." *Bayreuther Blätter* (1914), pp. 48–49.

"Antwort auf eine Rundfrage ueber Wert und Bedeutung des realistischen Bildungswesens." *Bayerische Zeitung für Realschulwesen* (Munich) (April 1914), 22(4).

"Deutschland als führender Weltstaat." *Der Volkserzieher* (Berlin) (Sept. 1914), 18(20).

"Die deutsche Sprache." *Unterhaltungsbeilage zur Deutschen Tagezeitung* (Berlin) Oct. 3, 1914.

"Deutsche Freiheit." *Der Volkserzieher* (Berlin Oct. 1914), 18(21).

"Deutsche Friedensliebe." *Internationale Monatsschrift für Wissenschaft, Kunst, und Technik* (Leipzig, Oct. 1, 1914), 9(1).

"England." *Unterhaltungsbeilage zur Täglichen Rundschau* (Berlin) Oct. 27–29, 1914.

"Englische Gelehrte." *Unterhaltungsbeilage zur Täglichen Rundschau* (Berlin) Nov. 21, 23, 24, 1914.

"Gipfel der Menschheit." *Deutsche Weihnacht, eine Liebesgabe deutscher Hochschüler* (Cassel) Dec. 1914.

1915

"Grundstimmungen in England und Frankreich." *Unterhaltungsbeilage zur Täglichen Rundschau*, Jan. 9, 11, 12, 1915.

"Bismarck der Deutsche." *Bismarck-Beilage zur Täglichen Rundschau* (Berlin) April 1, 1915.

"Brief an die Schriftleitung ueber die Aussichten der internationalen Zusammenarbeit auf dem Gebiete der Kultur." *Svenska Dagbladet* (Stockholm) May 12, 1915.

"An die Neutralen." *Neue Preussische (Kreuz-) Zeitung* (Berlin) May 21, 1915.

"Erinnerungen aus dem Jahre 1870." *Der Merker* (Vienna, April 15, 1915), 6(8).

"Freiheit." *Deutsche Zeitung*, July 5, 1915.

"Erinnerungen an den Buchhandel." *Börsenblatt für den Buchhandel* (Leipzig) Aug. 21, 1915.

"England und Deutschland." *München-Augsburger Abendzeitung* (Munich) Sept. 19, 1915.

"Martin Luther." *Bühne und Welt* (Hamburg) (Dec. 1915), 17.

"Der Weltkrieges letzte Phase." *Unterhaltungsbeilage zur Täglichen Rundschau* (Berlin) Dec. 8, 1915.

1916

"Brief an einen Bayerische Soldaten." *Der Champagne-Kamerad. Feldzeitung der 3. Armee.* March 26, 1916.

"Hammer und [sic] Amboss." *Unterhaltungsbeilage zur Täglichen Rundschau* (Berlin) March 30, 1916.

"Shakespeare." *Unterhaltungsbeilage zur Täglichen Rundschau* (Berlin) April 22, 1916.

"Kultur und Politik." *Deutsche Politik* (Weimar, July 1916), 1(1).

"Ideal und Macht." *München-Augsburger Abendzeitung* (Munich) July 15, 16, 1916.

"Chamberlain und sein deutscher Lehrer." *Deutsche Bücher 1916. Almanach der Münchener Verleger*, pp. 10–24.

"Die Englanderpartei." *Ostdeutsche Rundschau* July 23, 1916.

1917:

"Der Wille zum Sieg." *Das Grössere Deutschland* (Dresden, Jan. 13, 1917), 4(2).

"Ein Brief aus Sevilla vom 23. Mai 1876." *Süddeutsche Monatshefte* (Munich) (April 1917) 14(7).

"Deutsche Weltanschauung." *Deutschlands Erneuerung* (Munich) (April 1917) 1(1).

"Der Deutschgedanke." *Deutsche Zeitung* April 2, 1917.

"Zeichnet Kriegsanleihe!" *Unterhaltungsbeilage zur Täglichen Rundschau* (Berlin) April 10, 1917.

"Die Antwort an den Papst." *Deutsche Zeitung* (Berlin) Sept. 27, 1917.

"Aufruf zur Zeichnung der 7. Kriegsanleihe." *Flugblatt des Zeitspiegels* (Flensburg) Oct. 1917.

"Das eine und das andere Deutschland." *Deutsche Zeitung* (Berlin) Oct. 11, 1917.

"Werkzeuge oder Geld." *München-Augsburger Abendzeitung* (München) Oct. 15, 1917.

"Die deutsche Vaterlandspartei." *Deutsche Zeitung* (Berlin) Nov. 9, 1917.

"Ein Brief ueber Heinrich Heine." *Deutschlands Erneuerung* (Munich) (Dec. 1917), 1(9).

1918–1927.

"Rasse und Nation." *Deutschlands Erneuerung* (Munich) (July 1918), 2(7).

"Der Deutsche Staat." *Deutsche Zeitung* (Berlin) April 1, 1920.

"Richtigstellung einer Bemerkung im II. Morgenblatt der Frankfurter Zeitung vom 4 August." *Frankfurter Zeitung* Aug. 13, 1921.

"Halbbildung." *Deutsche Zeitung* (Berlin) Aug. 14, 1921.

"Dr. Hans Günther, Rassenkunde des deutschen Volkes." *Der Bücherwurm* (Dachau, 1922), 4.

"Dankschreiben an den Stadtrat für die Verleihung des Ehrenbürgerrechts der Stadt Bayreuth." *Oberfränkische Zeitung* (Bayreuth) June 15, 1922.

"An die 'Deutsche Zeitung.'" *Deutsche Zeitung* (Berlin) Jan. 30, 1923.

"Gott will es! Betrachtung über den gegenwärtigen Zustand Deutschlands." *Völkischer Beobachter* (Munich) Nov. 9, 1923.

"Brief ueber die Persönlichkeit." *Ibid.*, Oct. 19, 1923.

"Der Prüfstein" *Deutsche Zeitung* (Berlin) Dec. 24, 1923.

"Kultur und Politik." *Deutschlands Erneuerung* (Munich) Jan. 1923.

"Houston Stewart Chamberlain über Franz Liszt." *Bayreuther Blätter* (1923) pp. 18–19.

"Brief an Adolf Hitler." *Deutschlands Erneuerung* (Munich) (Jan. 1924), 8(1).

"Gedanken eines Invaliden." *Grossdeutsche Zeitung* (Munich), May 4–5, 1924.

"Adolf Hitler." *Deutsche Presse* (Munich) April 20–21, 1924.

"Ein Brief Chamberlains: über die Bayreuther Ringaufführungen von 1896." *Offizieller Bayreuther Festspielführer* 1924.

"Die Rassenfrage." *Beilage zum Völkischer Beobachter* (Munich), May 24–25; May 31–June 1, 1925.

"Die Wirkung der Mimen." *Bayreuther Blätter* (1927), 50.

Letters of Chamberlain, Otherwise Unpublished

Briefwechsel zwischen Cosima Wagner und Fürst Ernst zu Hohenlohe-Langenburg. (Stuttgart, 1937).

Friedrich Lienhard, *Wege nach Weimar*. 3rd. ed. Stuttgart, 1917.

"Houston Stewart Chamberlains Briefe an Schemann." *Deutschlands Erneuerung* (June 1938), 22(6).

A Selection of Books and Articles about Chamberlain

Ahorner, H. "Houston Stewart Chamberlain." *Deutschlands Erneurung* (Munich, 1933), 17.

Baentsch, D. "H.St. Chamberlains Vorstellungen über die Religion der Semiten spez. der Israeliten." *Pädagogisches Magazin* (Langensalza, 1905), 246.

Ballmann, Heinrich. *Houston Stewart Chamberlain und das Deutschtum.* Bonn: Nolte, 1939.

Beckmann, Fritz. *H.St. Chamberlains Stellung zum Christentum.* Diss. Tübingen, 1943.

Beyer, Hermann Wolfgang. *Houston Stewart Chamberlain und die innere Erneuerung des Christentums.* Berlin, 1939.

Biddiss, Michael D. "Houston Stewart Chamberlain: Prophet of Teutonism." *History Today* (London) Jan. 1969.

Breitenstein, Desiderius. *Houston Stewart Chamberlain: ein Wegbereiter des rassischen Weltbildes.* Westphalia: Warendorf, 1936.

Bülck, Walter. *Christentum und Deutschtum bei Arndt, Bismarck, H.St. Chamberlain und heutigen Dichtern.* Gütersloh, 1937.

Chamberlain, Anna Horst. *Meine Erinnerungen an Houston Stewart Chamberlain.* Munich, 1923.

Conrad, Herbert. "Mit Appia nichts zu schaffen." *Festspiel Nachrichten.* Bayreuth, 1966.

Crommelin, Armand. "Houston Stewart Chamberlain." *Offizieller Bayreuther Festspielführer 1924.*

Curtiner, Egon B. *Chamberlain gegen Schopenhauer, Eine Untersuchung der von H.St. Chamberlain in seinem 'Immanuel Kant' an Schopenhauer geübten Kritik.* Düsseldorf, 1910.

Dettelbach, Hans. "Der englische Verkünder des deutschen Kulturgedankens." *Deutschlands Erneuerung* (1932), 16.

Dippel, Martin. "Houston Stewart Chamberlain." *Deutscher Verlag* (Munich) 1938).

Dinter, Artur. "Houston Stewart Chamberlain." *Der Nationalsozialist* (Weimar) Sept. 12, 1925.

Dujardin, Edouard. "Erinnerungen an H.St. Chamberlain." *Münchener Neueste Nachrichten.* April 26, 1927.

——— *Rencontres avec Houston Stewart Chamberlain.* Paris, 1943.

Eckhard, Waldtraut. *Houston Stewart Chamberlains Naturanschauung.* Leipzig, 1941.

Eichler, F. *Einheit in der Mannigfaltigkeit. Eine Einführung in die Leitgedanken der H.St. Chamberlain-Vereinigung.* Dresden, 1941.

Einsle, Dr. W. "H.St. Chamberlain und der Bayreuther Gedanke." *Festspiel Nachrichten* (Bayreuth 1955).

Erdmann, Hugo. "Der 'Renegat' Chamberlain." *Neues Leben.* (1918), 12(10).

Essmann, Walter. "Chamberlains Weg zum Deutschtum." *Der Weltkampf* (Munich, 1936) 13:56–62.

——— "Chamberlain-der Diener am Deutschtum." *Der Weltkampf* (March 1935), 13(147):98–110.

Fahringer, Josef. *H.St. Chamberlain als Historiker. Methode seiner Geschichtsdarstellung.* Diss. Vienna, 1941.

Foerster, Friedrich W. *England in H.St. Chamberlains Beleuchtung.* Munich, 1918.

——— "H.St. Chamberlain als Interpret der westlichen Zivilisation." *Die Neue Rundschau* (1917), 28.

Frischmuth, Gertrud. *Houston Stewart Chamberlain als Christ.* Gütersloh: Verlag C. Bertelsmann, 1937.

Geprägs, Adolf. *Germanentum und Christentum bei Houston Stewart Chamberlain.* Göttingen, 1938.

Golther, Dr. Wolfgang. "Auf der Warte." *Der Türmer* (March 1927), 29(6).

Grabs, Rudolf. *Paul de Lagarde und Houston Stewart Chamberlain.* Weimar: Deutsche Christen, 1940.

Grauert, Hermann. *Dante und Houston Stewart Chamberlain.* Freiburg im Breisgau: Herdersche Verlagshandlung, 1904.

Gross, Dr. "Die Propheten Nietzsche, Lagarde und Chamberlain und ihrer Bedeutung für uns." *Nationalsozialistische Monatschefte* (April 1930), 1.

Gruenberg, L. and P. Habermann. *Houston Stewart Chamberlain: eine Auswahl aus seinem Briefen.* Bielefeld and Leipzig, 1941.

Grunsky, Karl. "Chamberlain." *Bayreuther Blätter*, 1923.

Grützmacher, R. H. *Kritiker und Neuschöpfer in zwanzigsten Jahrhundert.* Erlangen und Leipzig, 1921.

Gülzow, Erich. "Otto Kuntze, der deutsche Lehrer Houston Stewart Chamberlains. *Sonderdruck aus: Baltische Studien*, New series 47.

Hansen, A. "Die Lebenswege H.St. Chamberlain und die Naturwissenschaft." *Naturwissenschaftliche Wochenschrift* (Berlin) Nov. 23, 1919.

Hartmann, Ludwig. "Houston Stewart Chamberlain." *Bayreuther Land* (1934) nos. 6/7.

Hermann, Otto. *Chamberlains Bedeutung für die Prägung einer christlich Weltanschauung in den gebildeten Ständen.* Sonderdruck, n.d.

Hess, M. W. "H. S. Chamberlain: Prophet of Nazism." *The Commonweal* (New York) (May 1939), 30.

Hintzenstern, Herbert v. *H. St. Chamberlains Darstellung Urchristentums.* Weimar, 1941.

Hofmiller, Josef. "H. St. Chamberlain." *Süddeutsche Monatsheft.* (Dec. 1915), 13.

Hommel, Hildebrecht. *H. St. Chamberlain und die Griechen.* Verlag Moritz Diesterweg, Frankfurt 1939.

Horn, Walter. "Der Mensch Houston Stewart Chamberlain." *Deutsche Zeitung* March 19, 1928.

Hundt, Gerhard. "Houston Stewart Chamberlain der Deutsche." *Deutsche Festspiele in Weimar Offizieller Führer*, 1926.

Jirku, Anton. *Houston Stewart Chamberlain und das Christentum.* Bonn, 1938.

Joachimsen, P. "Houston Stewart Chamberlain." *Zeitwende* (1927), 3.

John, Johannes. "Houston Stewart Chamberlain und der Kunstwart." *Bühne und Welt* (Hamburg, 1915), 17.

Kaltenbrunner, Gerd-Klaus. "Houston Stewart Chamberlains Germanischer Mythos." *Polische Studien* (Munich, 1967).

Kassner, Rudolf. *Buch der Erinnerung.* Leipzig, 1938.

——— "Erinnerung an Houston Stewart Chamberlain." *Europäische Revue* (Berlin, April 1929), 5(1).

Keudel, Karl. *Methode und Grundsätze der Geschichtschreibung Houston Stewart Chamberlains: Ein Beitrag zur Historik der Gegenwart.* Würzburg, 1939.

Keyserling, Hermann. *Reise durch die Zeit* Leichtenstein, 1948.

Koch, Max. "Arndt, Chamberlain, Görres." *Breslauer Hochschul-Rundschau*, June–July 1923.

Kock, Karl. "Houston Stewart Chamberlain und Immanuel Kant." *Festschrift für Musik*, April 1924.

Kranz, C. *Chamberlains Grundlagen des 19. Jahrhunderts in ihrer Stellung zu Christus und zum Christentum.* Stuttgart, 1906.

Lehmann, Melanie. *Verleger J. F. Lehmann: Ein Leben im Kampf für Deutschland.* Munich, 1935.

Leistner, J. F. "Houston Stewart Chamberlains Staatsanschauung." *Deutschlands Erneuerung* (Munich, 1935), 19(4).

Literary Digest. (1915), 51:666–67. "Turncoat Son of Britain." (Author not given.)

Lubosch, Wilhelm. "H. St. Chamberlain, Natur und Leben." *Bayreuther Blätter* (1929), 51.

Maurenbrecher, Max. "Die Chamberlain Briefe." *Glaube und Deutschtum* June 24, 1928.

——— "Houston Stewart Chamberlain." *Deutsche Zeitung* Dec. 4, 1923.

——— "Kind und Profet: zum Gedächtnis H. St. Chamberlain." *Glaube und Deutschtum* (Dresden) Jan. 30, 1927.

Meyer, Hermann. "Die Nationalsozialistische Bewegung und ihre Führer von Lagarde, Treitschke, und Chamberlain ausgesehen." *Nationalsozialistische Monatshefte* (Feb. 1931) 1(11).

Meyer, Hugo. *Houston Stewart Chamberlain als völkischer Denker.* Munich: Bruckmann, 1939.

Meyer, Karl Alfons. "Houston Stewart Chamberlain." *Schweizer Monatshefte für Politik und Kultur.* (1926–27), 6(11).

Mitford, A. B. F. (Lord Redesdale). "'Die Grundlagen des Neunzehnten Jahrhunderts' by Houston Stewart Chamberlain. An appreciation." Privately printed for author by John Lane, London 1910.

——— "Houston Stewart Chamberlain." *The Edinburgh Review* (Jan. 1914), 219.

Molenaar, Heinrich. *Anti-Chamberlain.* Leipzig, 1915.

Netzle, Christof. "Chamberlains Stellung in der deutschen Literatur." *Literarisches Echo* (Stuttgart and Berlin). 1924.

Nielsen, Willi. *Der Lebens—und Gestaltbegriff bei Houston Stewart Chamberlain.* Kiel, 1938.

Peuckert, Fritz. "Houston Stewart Chamberlain." *Internationale Zeitschrift für Erziehung,* eds. A. Baeumler and P. Monroe (Berlin, 1937) 6(6).

Platz, H. "Houston Stewart Chamberlain und die Mystik." *Hochland,* (1940–41), 38(5).

Pretzsch, Paul. "H. St. Chamberlain der Deutsche." *Bayreuther Kurier* Jan. 9, 1927.

——— "Houston Stewart Chamberlain in Bayreuth." *Bayreuther Land* (1928).

—— "Ich schreibe nichts lieber als Briefe." (H. St. Chamberlain zum Gedenken). *Bayreuther Land* (1936), no. 1.

Püringer, August. "Der Gralsleiter ohne den 'deutschen König': zu H. St. Chamberlains 70 Geburtstag." *Deutscher Volkswart* (Sept. 1925), 7(12).

Réal, Jean. "The Religious Conception of Race: Houston Stewart Chamberlain and Germanic Christianity." E. Vermeil, *The Third Reich*. New York: UNESCO, 1955.

Réal, Jean. "Houston Stewart Chamberlain et Goethe," *Études germaniques* (Paris, 1950, 5.

Réal, Jean. "La lettre à Amiral Hollmann ou Guillaume II a l'école de H. S. Chamberlain," *Etudes germaniques* (Paris, 1951), 6.

Reinhardt, Richard. "Houston Stewart Chamberlain." *Bayerischer Kurier*, Jan. 9–10, 1943.

—— "Houston Stewart Chamberlain der Deutsche." *Bayreuther Kurier* July 23, 1943.

Robertson, J. M. "Herr Chamberlain and the War." *Contemporary Review* (July–December 1915), 108.

Roeder, Hans. *Worte für Menschen zur Entgegnung auf Chamberlains Worte Christi* Berlin, 1905.

Roosevelt, Theodore, and Lyman Abbott. "The Foundations of The Nineteenth Century." *The Outlook* (New York) 98:728–34.

Rosenberg, Alfred. *Houston Stewart Chamberlain als Verkünder und Begründer einer deutschen Zukunft*. Munich: Bruckmann, 1927.

Rouché, M. "Houston Stewart Chamberlain." *Études Germaniques* (Paris), Oct. 1962.

Schack, Herbert. *Denker und Deuter: Männer vor der deutschen Wende.* Stuttgart: Alfred Kroner, n.d.

Schmitz, Eugen. "Cosima Wagner und Chamberlain im Briefwechsel." *Dresdener Nachrichten* Oct. 10, 1934.

Schneider, E. "Houston Stewart Chamberlain." *Die Völkische Schule* (1925), 3(9).

Schott, Georg. "H. St. Chamberlain zum Gedächtnis." *Bayreuther Bund* (January–February 1937), 12.

—— "Auf des Lebens Höhe: zum Gedächtnis H. St. Chamberlain." Munich: Lehmann, 1927.

—— *Auf des Lebens Höhe.* Munich, 1927.

—— *Das Lebenswerk Chamberlains in Umrissen.* Munich, 1927.

—— *Das Vermächtnis Houston Stewart Chamberlains.* Stuttgart, 1940.

Schroeder, L. von. *Houston Stewart Chamberlain. Ein Abriss seines Lebens.* Munich: Lehmann, 1918.

—— "Chamberlains linker Arm." *Ostdeutsche Rundschau* Dec. 24, 1916.

Schwaner, Wilhelm. "Für Chamberlain." *Der Volkserzieher.* (Berlin, 1916), 20(10).

Schweinitzhaupt, Franz. "H. St. Chamberlain zum 70 Geburtstag." *Deutschlands Erneuerung* (Munich, Sept. 1925), 9, 9.

Silverman, Maurice. "Shattering Chamberlain's Foundations." *The Reflex* (Chicago, Jan. 1929), 9(1).

Spanier, Dr. M. "Zum Charakteristik Houston Stewart Chamberlains." *Abwehrblätter* (Berlin, Feb. 1929), 39.

Spitzer, Leo. *Anti-Chamberlain: Betrachtungen eines Linguisten über Houston Stewart Chamberlains 'Kriegaufsätze' und die Sprachbewertung im allgemein.* Leipzig, 1918.

Stodte, Hermann. "Houston Stewart Chamberlain." *Die Wegbereiter des Nationalsozialismus* (Lübeck) 1936.

Stutzinger, Gerhard. *Die politischen Anschauungen Houston Stewart Chamberlains.* Berlin, 1938.

The Times (London) Jan. 10, 1927.

Tirala, Lothar Gottlieb. "Cosima Wagner und Houston St. Chamberlain im Briefwechsel." *Deutschlands Erneuerung* (Munich, 1935), 19(1).

—— "Houston Stewart Chamberlain: Ein Gedenkblatt." *Deutschlands Erneuerung* (Munich, March 1927), 11, 3.

—— "Houston Stewart Chamberlain zum Gedenken." *Bayreuther Festspielführer* (1927), pp. 83–95.

Trobes, Otto. "Chamberlain und der Bayreuther Gedanke (zu Wiederkehr des Todestages Jan. 9, 1927) *Bayerische Ostmark*, Jan. 9, 1927.

—— "H. St. Chamberlain und seine Bedeutung." *Bayreuther Bund*, Jan.–Feb., 1937.

Uexküll, Jacob von. "Austen [*sic*] Stewart Chamberlain." *Deutsche Rundschau* May 1927.

—— "Houston Stewart Chamberlain: Die Persönlichkeit." *Bücher des Verlages F. Bruckmann A. G.* München 1928.

Unruh, Ernst von. *Herr Houston Stewart Chamberlain und die Weltgeschichte.* Leipzig, 1908.

Vollbach, Walther R. "Adolph Appia und Houston Stewart Chamberlain." *Die Musik Forschung* (1966), no. 4.

Vollrath, Wilhelm. "H. St. Chamberlain und sein britisches Erbgut." *Zeitschrift für Deutsche Geisteswissenschaft* (1939) Jena: Eugen Diederichs Verlag, 1939, 1(6).

—— *Houston Stewart Chamberlain und seine Theologie.* Erlangen, 1937.

—— *Th, Carlyle und H. St. Chamberlain, zwei freunde Deutschlands.* Munich: Lehmann, 1935.

Wachler, Ernst. "H. St. Chamberlain über Goethe." *Allgemeiner Beobachter* (Hamburg) Feb. 15, 1913.

Westernhagen, Curt von. "Houston Stewart Chamberlains Briefe." *Bayreuther Bund der deutschen Jugend.* (May 1928) 5, 3.

Wolff, Hans. "Houston Stewart Chamberlain." *Deutsches Volkstum* (Hamburg) March 1928.

Wolzogen, Hans von. "Houston Stewart Chamberlain." *Bayreuther Blätter*, 1927.

—— "Houston Stewart Chamberlain." *Beilage zum Deutschen Tageblatt* (Berlin) Sept. 9, 1925.

———— "Kunst und Kirche. Offener Brief an Houston Stewart Chamberlain." *Xenien Bücher* (Leipzig, 1913), no. 3.

Wüst, Fritz. *Eine Entgegnung auf 'Die Grundlagen des 19. Jahrhunderts' von Houston Stewart Chamberlain.* Stuttgart, 1905.

Annotated Bibliography

European Racism:

The literature on this subject is staggering. Among the general surveys available are: Jacques Barzun, *Race. A Study in Superstition* (New York, 1937); Louis L. Snyder, *Race. A History of Modern Ethnic Theories* (New York, 1939); Jean Finot, *Le préjugé des races* (Paris, 1905); Theophile Simar, *Étude critique sur le formation de la doctrine des races au XVIII siècle et son expansion au XIXe siècle* (Brussels, 1922). More recently there is: Léon Poliakov, *Le Mythe Aryen. Essai sur les sources du racisme et des nationalismes* (Paris, 1971; Eng. trans., New York 1974); George L. Mosse, *Toward the Final Solution. A History of European Racism* (London, 1978); and Patrik von zur Mühlen, *Rassenideologien Geschichte und Hintergründe* (Berlin, 1977). Also extremely useful is Andrew Lyons, "The Question of Race in Anthropology from J. F. Blumenbach to Franz Boas" (unpublished Oxford University D.Phil. Thesis, 1974). Michael D. Biddiss of Leicester University, England, is currently completing what will undoubtedly be a discerning and carefully researched general study of racism.

There are several books about individual race theorists, but particularly valuable for this study were those analyzing the career of Count Gobineau. For the best general account see the two books by Michael D. Biddiss, *Father of Racist Ideology. The Social and Political Thought of Count Gobineau* (London, 1970) and *Gobineau: Selected Political Writings* (New York, 1970). Janine Buenzod, *La Formation de la pensée de Gobineau* (Paris, 1967) is a mine of information for Gobineau's early development and has an exhaustive bibliography. Also useful are: Gerald Spring, *The Vitalism of Count Gobineau* (New York, 1932) and, for Gobineau's impact on later thinkers, E. J. Young, *Gobineau und der Rassismus* (Meisenheim an Glan, 1968). The most important follower and publicist of Gobineau's views in Germany was Ludwig Schemann, at one time closely linked to the Wahnfried circle. See his *Gobineau; eine Biographie* (Leipzig, 1913–16); and *Gobineaus Rassenwerk* (Leipzig, 1910).

There is no detailed study of Social Darwinism in Germany and Austria. Hannsjoachim W. Koch, *Der Sozialdarwinismus. Seine Genese und sein Einfluss auf das imperialistische Denken* (Munich, 1973) offers a brief but useful survey. Also noteworthy is Hans-Günter Zmarzlik, "Der Sozialdarwinismus in Deutschland als geschichtliches Problem," *Vierteljahrshefte für Zeitgeschichte* (July 1963), 11; now reprinted and translated in H. Holborn, ed. *Republic to Reich, The Making of the Nazi Revolution,* (New

York, 1972). Among older works on the subject, see: Oscar Hertwig, *Zur Abwehr des ethischen, des sozialen, des politischen Darwinismus* (Jena, 1918) and Hedwig Conrad Martius, *Utopien der Menschenzüchtung* (Munich, 1955). On Ernst Haeckel and the Monist movement there is the provocative study by Daniel Gasman, *The Scientific Origins of National Socialism* (London, 1971). In addition to reading the writings of racists such as Ludwig Woltmann, Heinrich Driesmans, Vacher de Lapouge, Wilhelm Schallmeyer, Otto Ammon, Alfred Ploetz, Hans F. K. Günther, and others mentioned in the text and notes, the best way of achieving a sense of the scope and direction of race research in the Wilhelmine and Weimar periods is through two journals: the *Archiv für Rassen- und Gesellschafts—biologie* and the *Politisch-anthropologische Revue*.

The history of German interest in eastern cultures—a revealing mirror of contemporary scepticism with the goals and direction of western society—remains to be written. Attitudes toward the "Yellow Peril" have, however, received close study in Heinz Gollwitzer's excellent *Die gelbe Gefahr*, (Göttingen, 1962). On Nordic racism there is the fine systematic study of its origins and development by Hans-Jürgen Lutzhöft, *Der nordische Gedanke in Deutschland 1920–1940*. See also my comments in "Nordic Racism," *Journal of the History of Ideas* (July–Sept., 1977), 38(3). Surprisingly enough, although there are many books and articles which touch on Nazi racism, few discuss the subject in detail. Karl Saller, *Die Rassenlehre des Nationalsozialismus in Wissenschaft und Propaganda* (Darmstadt, 1961) and Rupert Breitling, *Die Nationalsozialistische Rassenlehre* (Meisenheim an Glan, 1971) are both very brief. Also helpful is Léon Poliakov and Josef Wulf, eds., *Das Dritte Reich und seine Denker: Dockumente* (Berlin, 1959). On Alfred Rosenberg see the general account by Robert Cecil, *The Myth of the Master Race: Alfred Rosenberg and Nazi Ideology* (London, 1972), and R. Bollmus, *Das Amt Rosenberg und seine Gegner* (Stuttgart, 1970); on Himmler there is Joseph Ackermann, *Heinrich Himmler als Ideologe* (Göttingen 1970) and Bradley F. Smith, *Heinrich Himmler: A Nazi in the Making 1900–1926* (Stanford, Calif., 1971). A very detailed account which threads its way through the bureaucratic maze of the SS organizations is Michael S. Kater's excellent *Das "Ahnenerbe" der SS* (Stuttgart, 1974).

Finally, some of the general studies on race which shaped my ideas are: George W. Stocking, *Race, Culture and Evolution: Essays in the History of Anthropology* (New York, 1968); Pierre van den Berghe, *Race and Racism* (New York, 1967); Marvin Harris, *The Rise of Anthropological Theory* (New York, 1968); and Ashley Montagu, *Man's Most Dangerous Myth: The Fallacy of Race* (New York, 1964).

Anti-Semitism in Germany before 1933:

The historical scholarship on German Jewry and German anti-Semitism is vast and continually growing. I have focussed primarily on recent research and on those studies I have found particularly helpful. Those requiring a fuller list or titles on aspects of the subject not covered here should consult first the "Select Bibliography of Books and Articles" included in each issue of the *Leo Baeck Institute Year Book* (London, 1955–present); for older titles there is also Ilse R. Wolff, ed., The Wiener Library Catalogue Series: *From Weimar to Hitler—Germany 1918–33* (London, 1964) and *German Jewry. Its History, Life and Culture* (London, 1964). Many of the books listed below also have excellent bibliographies.

The best starting point for this whole subject is the various publications of the Leo Baeck Institute: *The Leo Baeck Institute Year Book*; the *Leo Baeck Institute Bulletin* (Tel Aviv, 1957–present); the *Leo Baeck Institute Memorial Lecture* (New York, 1956–present); and the *Schriftenreihe wissenschaftlicher Abhandlungen des Leo Baeck Instituts*, a series in which some thirty-five volumes have appeared thus far. Particularly important are the essays contained in four of these volumes: Werner E. Mosse and Arnold Paucker, eds., *Entscheidungsjahr 1932. Zur Judenfrage in der Endphase der Weimarer Republik* (Tübingen, 1965); *idem, Deutsches Judentum in Krieg und Revolution 1916–1923* (Tübingen, 1971); *idem, Juden im wilhelminischen Deutschland 1890–1914* (Tübingen, 1976); and Hans Liebeschütz and Arnold Paucker, eds., *Das Judentum in der deutschen Umwelt* (Tübingen, 1977). With a few exceptions I have not cited the essays in these collections separately.

The best studies of the independent anti-Semitic parties formed in the wake of the stock market crash of 1873 are: Paul Massing, *Rehearsal for Destruction* (New York, 1949); Peter G. J. Pulzer, *The Rise of Political Anti-Semitism in Germany and Austria* (New York, 1964); and Richard S. Levy, *The Downfall of the Anti-Semitic Political Parties in Imperial Germany* (New Haven, 1975). On Massing himself see the excellent analysis of the Frankfurt School by Martin Jay, *The Dialectical Imagination* (Boston, 1973). Levy's discussion of these parties is the most detailed. For my opinion of his book see the review essay in *The Journal of Social History* (1977) 11(1):99–109. An older study is still useful: Kurt Wawrzinek, *Die Entstehung der deutschen Antisemitenpartei 1873–1890* (Berlin, 1927). Walter Mohrmann, *Antisemitismus. Ideologie und Geschichte im Kaiserreich und in der Weimarer Republik* (Berlin, 1972) is a brief attempt at a Marxist analysis but adds nothing new. A good source for the regional activities of many of these small parties is *Im deutschen Reich* (1895–1914), the monthly organ of the Centralverein. On the Great Depression and its political and social consequences see the superb study by Hans Rosenberg, *Grosse Depression und Bismarckzeit* (Berlin, 1967). A great deal of research is now underway on various aspects of the *Mittelstand* in the Imperial period. Two recent works which are highly illuminating are: Shulamit Angel-Volkov, *The Rise of Popular Anti-Modernism in Germany. The Urban Master Artisans 1873–1896* (Princeton, 1978) and Robert Gellately, *The Politics of Economic Despair. Shopkeepers and German Politics 1890–1914* (London, 1974).

The long and complicated history of Jewish Emancipation in the German states has recently been the subject of intensive research. Of exceptional value is the collection of essays by Reinhard Rürup, *Emanzipation und Antisemitismus. Studien zur "Judenfrage" der bürgerliche Gesellschaft* (Göttingen, 1975); the volume also has an extensive bibliography. By the same author there is also: "Emanzipation und Krise—Zur Geschichte der 'Judenfrage' in Deutschland vor 1890," in W. E. Mosse and A. Paucker, *Juden im wilhelminischen Deutschland 1890–1914* (Tübingen, 1976). Another first-rate analysis of the emancipation process is Jacob Katz, *Out of the Ghetto. The Social Background of Jewish Emancipation 1770–1870* (Cambridge, Mass., 1973). The literature on German Jewry is growing rapidly. A fascinating collection of memoirs is currently being edited by Monika Richarz: *Jüdisches Leben in Deutschland. Selbstzeugnisse zur Sozialgeschichte* vol. 1 (1780–1871), vol. 2 (1871–1891) (Stuttgart, 1976–1979); a third and final volume covering the years of Weimar and the Third Reich is in preparation. A mine of information on the role of Jews in German society is Ernest Hamburger's *Juden im öffentlichen Leben Deutschlands* (Tübingen, 1968). On Jewish political affiliations see Jacob Toury, *Die politischen Orientierung der Juden in Deutschland* (Tübingen, 1966). Fritz Stern, *Gold and Iron. Bismarck, Bleichroeder and the Building of the German Empire* (New York, 1977) is a monumental study that puts the career of Gerson Bleichroeder in the cultural and political context of German Unification and the Imperial period. Another noteworthy study of German-Jewish business success is Lamar Cecil, *Albert Ballin. Business and Politics in Imperial Germany 1888–1918* (Princeton, 1967). Little has been written on the subject of the *Ostjuden*; for a brief introduction see: S. Adler-Rudel, *Ostjuden in Deutschland 1880–1940* (Tübingen, 1959). Jack L. Wertheimer is at present engaged in a major study; meantime, see his important doctoral thesis "German policy and Jewish Politics: The Absorption of East European Jews in Germany 1868–1914." Ph.D. Diss. Columbia Univ. 1978.

Other accounts of importance are: A. Ruppin, *Soziologie der Juden*, 2 vols. (Berlin, 1930–1931), and Jacob Toury, *Soziale und politische Geschichte der Juden in Deutschland 1847–71* (Düsseldorf, 1977). Peter Gay's essays, *Freud, Jews and Other Germans* (New York, 1978) are full of important and challenging insights.

My comments on the activities of the Jewish defense organizations are based on a reading of *Im deutschen Reich* and the *C.V.-Zeitung*, organs of the Centralverein deutscher Staatsbürger jüdischen Glaubens, and the *Mitteilungen aus dem Verein zur Abwehr des Antisemitismus*, published by the Abwehr-Verein. A number of excellent monographs have also appeared: Ismar Schorsch, *Jewish Reactions to German Anti-Semitism 1870–1914* (New York, 1972); Arnold Paucker, *Der jüdische Abwehrkampf gegen Antisemitismus und Nationalsozialismus in der letzten Jahren der Weimarer Republik* (Hamburg, 1967), and by the same author: "Zur Problematik einer jüdischen Abwehrstrategie in der deutschen Gesellschaft," in W. E. Mosse and A. Paucker, eds., *Juden im welhelminischen Deutschland*. Also illuminating are: S. Ragins, "Jewish Responses to Anti-Semitism in Germany 1870–1914," PhD Diss. Brandeis Univ., 1972 and Jehuda Reinharz, *Father-*

land or Promised Land. The Dilemma of the German Jew 1893–1914 (Ann Arbor, Mich. 1975). An excellent analysis of Jewish pressure group politics is provided by Marjorie Lamberti, *Jewish Activism in Imperial Germany and the Struggle for Civil Equality* (New Haven, 1978). S. M. Bolkovsky, *The Distorted Image. German–Jewish Perceptions of Germans and Germany* (The Hague, 1976) contains a good deal of useful information but its psycho-historical analysis seems to me frequently flawed and overdone.

There are several excellent studies of *völkisch* ideology. See especially: Fritz Stern, *The Politics of Cultural Despair* (Calif., 1961) and George L. Mosse, *The Crisis of German Ideology* (New York, 1964) and *Germans and Jews* (New York, 1970). Also insightful is Wolfgang Emmerich, *Zur Kritik der Volkstumsideologie* (Frankfurt, 1971). On the *völkisch* youth movement the best introduction is Walter Z. Laqueur, *Young Germany* (London, 1962).

For anti-Semitism in the first half of the nineteenth century, there is the classic study by Eleonore Sterling, *Er ist wie Du. Aus der Frühgeschichte des Antisemitismus in Deutschland 1815–1850* (Munich, 1956), based on a wide array of archival materials. A new edition of the book has recently appeared: *Judenhass. Die Anfänge des politischen Antisemitismus in Deutschland 1815–1850* (Frankfurt, 1969). Two controversial but theoretically significant books are Eva G. Reichmann, *Hostages of Civilisation* (London, 1950) and Hannah Arendt, *The Origins of Totalitarianism* (New York, 1951); the latter connects the fate of Jews in Europe to the demise of the nation-state. Léon Poliakov, *Histoire de l'antisémitisme*, 3 vols. (Paris 1955–68), contains a vast amount of information while among the many collections of essays on the subject the following are useful: Koppel S. Pinson, ed., *Essays on Antisemitism* (New York, 1942); Hermann Huss and Andreas Schroeder, eds., *Antisemitismus: Zur Pathologie der bürgerlichen Gesellschaft* (Frankfurt, 1965); and Karl Thieme, ed., *Judenfeindschaft. Darstellung und Analysen* (Frankfurt, 1963).

By far the most illuminating new additions to the literature on Anti-Semitism in the Imperial and early Weimar periods are the two long and meticulously researched articles by Werner Jochmann in the Leo Baeck symposia cited above: "Struktur und Funktion des deutschen Antisemitismus," in *Juden im wilhelminischen Deutschland* and "Die Ausbreitung des Antisemitismus," in *Deutsches Judentum in Krieg und Revolution*. Jochmann reveals clearly the pervasiveness of anti-Semitism in German society and institutions, and describes the development of an integral nationalist ideology in which anti-Semitism played a crucial role.

Little has yet been written about the language of anti-Semitism but for some introductory comments see Alexander Bein, "Der 'jüdische Parasit.' Bemerkung zur Semantik der Judenfrage," *Vierteljahrshefte für Zeitgeschichte* (April 1965), 13. Also, Christoph Cobet, *Der Wortschatz des Antisemitismus in der Bismarckzeit* (Munich, 1973). J. P. Fay, *Langages totalitaires* and *Théorie de récit* (Paris, 1972) attempt to investigate the "language field" of Nazism from a structuralist and Marxist perspective. K. Felden, "Die Uebernahme des antisemitischen Stereotyps als soziale Norm

durch die bürgerliche Gesellschaft Deutschlands 1875–1890," Diss. phil.
Heidelberg, 1963, summarizes a good deal of interesting material but is con-
ceptually weak.

On attitudes toward Jews in Christian theology and the Christian
churches see the superb analysis by Uriel Tal, *Christians and Jews in
Germany. Religion, Politics and Ideology in the Second Reich 1870–1914*,
trans. from Hebrew (Ithaca: Cornell Univ. Press, 1975). Tal carefully
unravels conservative, liberal, and racist attitudes toward Jews and places
them within the framework of a gradual secularizing process. Based on a variety of new archival sources and containing an extensive bibliography, his
book is indispensable for the whole subject of Christian attitudes. Also
noteworthy is Tal's "Religious and Anti-Religious Roots of Modern Anti-
Semitism," The Leo Baeck Memorial Lecture (New York, 1971), 14. Two
other useful studies are Stefan Lehr, *Antisemitismus—religiöse Motive im
sozialen Vorurteil 1870–1914* (Munich, 1974) and Wolfgang Tilgner, *Volks-
nomostheorie und Schöpfungsglaube* (Göttingen, 1966). The most important
analysis of Catholic attitudes toward Jews is Hermann Greive, *Theologie und
Ideologie. Katholizismus und Judentum in Deutschland und Österreich
1918–1935* (Heidelberg, 1969). The historical scholarship on Protestantism is
much larger. In addition to the essay by Hans-Joachim Kraus in the Leo
Baeck symposium, *Entscheidungsjahr 1932*, see Richard Gutteridge, *The
German Evangelical Church and the Jews 1879–1950* (New York, 1976). The
latter is much better for the period after 1933; the earlier sections are
somewhat superficial. Also helpful is Ino Arndt, "Die Judenfrage im Licht der
evangelischen Sonntagsblätter von 1918–1933," Diss., Tübingen, 1960. Other
significant accounts related to this general subject are: Arnold M. Horowitz,
"Prussian State and Protestant Church in the Reign of Wilhelm II," PhD
Diss. Yale Univ., 1976; K. W. Dahm, *Pfarrer und Politik. Soziale Position und
politische Mentalität des deutschen evangelischen Pfarrerstandes zwischen
1918 und 1933*; G. Mehnert, *Evangelische Kirche und Politik 1917–1919*
(Düsseldorf, 1959); J. R. C. Wright, *"Above Parties." The Political Attitudes
of the German Church Leadership 1918–1933* (Oxford, 1974). In preparation
for this study I read a number of church periodicals; particularly helpful was
Christliche Welt, the literary focus of liberal Protestantism.

The prevalence of anti-Semitism in the major German political parties
and pressure groups has attracted a good deal of scholarly attention. Only a
few titles can be mentioned here. On the *Bund der Landwirte* see: Hans-
Jürgen Puhle, *Agrarische Interessenpolitik und preussischer Konservatismus
im wilhelminischen Reich* (Hannover, 1966). For white collar organiza-
tions: Iris Hamel, *Völkischer Verband und Nationale Gewerkschaft. Der
Deutschnationale Handlungsgehilfenverband 1893–1933* (Frankfurt, 1967),
and Heinrich A. Winkler, *Mittelstand Demokratie und Nationalsozialismus*
(Cologne, 1972). There are several important works on the Pan-German
League. In addition to the autobiography of Heinrich Class, *Wider den
Ström* (Leipzig, 1932) see: Alfred Kruck, *Geschichte des Alldeutschen
Verbandes 1890–1929* (Wiesbaden, 1954) and Konrad Schilling, *Beiträge zu*

*einer Geschichte des radikalen Nationalismus in der wilhelminischen Ära
1890-1909* (Diss., Cologne, 1968). For liberal organizations see: Stanley
Zucker, *Ludwig Bamberger: German Liberal Politician and Social Critic*
(Pittsburgh, 1975); James F. Harris, "Eduard Lasker: The Jew as National
German Politician," *Leo Baeck Year Book* (1975), 20; Dan S. White, *The
Splintered Party* (Cambridge, Mass., 1976) which offers a fine analysis of
National Liberalism in Hessen; and John L. Snell, *The Democratic Move-
ment in Germany 1789-1914* (Chapel Hill, 1976). Useful for Weimar is
Robert A. Pois, *The Bourgeois Democrats of Weimar Germany*, Transactions
of the American Philosophical Society (Philadelphia, July 1976), 66 part 4. A
number of recent works should be consulted for the German left: Hans-
Helmuth Knütter, *Die Juden und die deutsche Linke in der Weimarer Republik 1918-1933* (Düsseldorf, 1971); Donald L. Niewyk, *Socialist, Anti-
Semite and Jew* (Baton Rouge, 1971); George L. Mosse, "German Socialists
and the Jewish Question in the Weimar Republic," *Leo Baeck Year Book*
(1971), 16; and most recently, Rosemarie Leuschen-Seppel, *Sozialdemokratie
und Antisemitismus im Kaiserreich* (Bonn, 1978).

Two other indispensable works for World War I and the early Weimar
period are: Egmont Zechlin, *Die Deutsche Politik und die Juden im ersten
Weltkrieg* (Göttingen, 1969) and Uwe Lohalm *Völkischer Radikalismus: die
Geschichte des deutschvölkischen Schutz—und Trutz—Bundes 1919-1923*
(Hamburg, 1970). More than a study of one organization, Lohalm's monograph examines the whole subject of the continuity between *völkisch*
ideology in Imperial Germany and Weimar. My ideas on the extreme right
were also shaped by reading contemporary periodicals, among them *Hammer*
(1902-1914) and *Deutschlands Erneuerung* (1917-1936). Finally, for the history of the Protocols of Zion there is the excellent piece of detective work by
Norman Cohn, *Warrant for Genocide. The Myth of the Jewish World
Conspiracy and the Protocols of Zion* (London, 1967).

Much less scholarly attention has been devoted to anti-Semitism in
Austria. In addition to P. G. J. Pulzer's book cited above, several studies deserve mention: Andrew G. Whiteside, *The Socialism of Fools. Georg Ritter
von Schoenerer and Austrian Pan-Germanism* (Berkeley, 1975); J. C. P.
Warren, "The Political Career and Influence of Georg Ritter von Schoenerer," PhD Diss. London Univ. 1963; Carl E. Schorske, "Politics in a New
Key: An Austrian Triptych," *Journal of Modern History* (1967), 39; and Dirk
van Arkel, *Antisemitism in Austria* (Diss. Leiden, 1966).

Wagner and Bayreuth

My major sources were the papers and correspondence of the various
prominent members of the Wagner movement, which are housed in the
Richard Wagner Gedenkstätte in Bayreuth. Winfried Schüler's excellent *Der
Bayreuther Kreis von seiner Entstehung bis zum Ausgang der wilhelminischen Ära* (Münster, 1971) is a thorough study of these same materials.

Bibliography

In places my interpretation differs from his and the emphasis of the present
study is more on politics and racial politics in the Wagner movement.
Schüler's book also contains an exhaustive bibliography and footnotes, very
helpful for futher research. In addition to Richard Wagner's *Sämtliche
Schriften und Dichtungen* (Leipzig, 1911) in twelve volumes and his *Mein
Leben* (Munich, 1963), readers will find Robert Gutman, *Richard Wagner,
The Man, His Mind and His Music* (London, 1968) insightful and entertain-
ing. Ernest Newman, *The Life of Richard Wagner* (New York, 1933–1947) in
four volumes, is indispensable, although I would agree with Gutman's
critical assessment of the final volume for failing among other things to treat
adequately Wagner's racialism and political vision. Important for understanding the Wagner *Kreis* and still useful in other respects is Carl Friedrich
Glasenapp, *Das Leben Richard Wagners* (Leipzig 1905–1911), 6 vols. The
bibliography of works on Wagner and the music dramas is vast. Readers may
find the following books helpful: Theodor Adorno, *Versuch über Wagner*
(Knaur Verlag, Munich 1964); Bryan Magee, *Aspects of Wagner* (London,
1968); Kurt Overhoff, *The Germanic-Christian Myth of Richard Wagner*
(Bayreuth, 1955); Jack Stein, *Richard Wagner. The Synthesis of the Arts*
(Detroit, 1960); Elliot Zuckerman, *The First Hundred Years of Wagner's
Tristan* (New York, 1964); Maurice Boucher, *The Political Concepts of
Richard Wagner* (English trans., New York, 1950); and Jacques Barzun,
Darwin, Marx, Wagner (Boston, 1941).

While there are many books about Cosima Wagner, none have adequately described her role in the Bayreuth cult and her special position as a
woman in the musical world of Central Europe. For her life with Wagner the
best source is the recently published diaries, *Die Tagebücher 1869–1883*
(Munich 1976–1977) in two volumes. Still the most informative biographies are Richard Du Moulin-Eckart, *Cosima Wagner* (Berlin, 1929–31), 2
volumes; and Max Millenkovich-Morold, *Cosima Wagner* (Leipzig, 1937),
but both are uncritical and adulatory. For some other details see the brief
study by Ilse Lötz, *Cosima Wagner, die Hüterin des Grals* (Görlitz, 1936).
Cosima's letters to Chamberlain have already been cited. In addition to the
unpublished correspondence located in the Richard Wagner Gedenkstätte,
Bayreuth, see: Bertha Schemann, ed., *Cosima Wagner, Briefe an Ludwig
Schemann* (Regensburg, 1937); Erhart Thierbach, ed., *Die Briefe Cosima
Wagners an Friedrich Nietzsche* (Weimar, 1938–40); Max von Waldberg, ed.,
Cosima Wagners Briefe an ihre Tochter Daniela von Bülow (Stuttgart, 1933);
*Briefwechsel zwischen Cosima Wagner und Fürst Ernst zu Hohenlohe-Lan-
genburg* (Stuttgart, 1937). There is a need for a new full-scale biography of
Cosima, placing her life more satisfactorily in the context of Wagnerism and
German cultural history.

Surprisingly, Cosima's diaries have added little new information about
the troubled relationship of Nietzsche and Richard Wagner. For good general
summaries see Robert Gutman's biography mentioned above and R. J. Hollingdale, *Nietzsche. The Man and His Philosophy* (Baton Rouge, 1965); also
informative is F. R. Love, *Young Nietzsche and the Wagnerian Experience,*

University of Carolina Studies in German Language and Literature (1963), no. 39. For their letters see: Elizabeth Förster-Nietzsche, *Wagner und Nietzsche zur Zeit ihrer Freundschaft* (Munich, 1915; Eng. trans., London 1922).

On Siegfried Wagner there is Zdenko von Kraft, *Der Sohn: Siegfried Wagners Leben und Umwelt* (Graz/Stuttgart, 1969). For Appia, see the detailed study by R. Vollbach, *Adolphe Appia. Prophet of the Modern Theater* (Middletown, Conn.: Wesleyan University Press, 1968).

In addition to Schüler's fine monograph already cited, I have found Michael Karbaum's *Studien zur Geschichte der Bayreuther Festspiele 1876-1976* (Regensburg, 1976) particularly helpful for the history of the festival and for the relationship between Bayreuth and Nazism. The choice of documents which make up the bulk of the book is excellent; the introduction is less successful and does little to relate the Wagner cult in detail to cultural and political developments in the Reich as a whole. Also informative, though brief, is Geoffrey Skelton, *Wagner at Bayreuth: Experiment and Tradition* (London, 1965) and Egon Voss, *Die Dirigenten der Bayreuther Festspiele* (Regensburg, 1976). Useful memoirs include: Ludwig Schemann, *Lebensfahrt eines Deutschen* (Leipzig, 1925); Hans von Wolzogen, *Lebensbilder* (Regensburg, 1923); F. Weingartner, *Buffets and Rewards. A Musician's Reminiscences* (London, 1937); Friedelind Wagner, *Heritage of Fire* (New York, 1945); Rosa Eidam, *Bayreuther Erinnerungen* (Ansbach, 1930); and Christian Ebersberger, *Drei Generationen im Hause Wahnfried* (privately bound typescript, Richard Wagner Gedenkstätte). By far the richest source for the Wagner cult is, however, the *Bayreuther Blätter* (1878-1938), edited by Hans von Wolzogen; some additional information for the later period can also be obtained from the *Bayreuther Festspielführer* (1924-1939), edited by K. Grunsky, O. Strobel, and P. Pretzsch. For the Bayreuth youth movement I consulted the *Monatsblatt Bayreuther Bund der deutschen Jugend*. On Hitler and Bayreuth, additional sources are: Paul Bülow, *Adolf Hitler und der Bayreuther Kulturkreis* (Leipzig, 1933) and by the same author, *Bayreuth, die Stadt der Wagner Festspiele 1876-1936* (Leipzig, 1936). Rather sketchy is George Windell, "Hitler, National Socialism and Richard Wagner," *Journal of Central European Affairs* (1962-63), 17.

On Wagnerism in Austria, there is the excellent monography by W. J. McGrath, *Dionysian Art and Populist Politics in Austria* (New Haven, 1974) which discusses the Pernerstorfer circle. No accounts exist for the period of the 1890s and beyond, nor has anyone looked closely at the Wagner societies in Austria. On France there is Léon Guichard, *La musique et les lettres en France au temps du Wagnérisme* (Paris, 1963); André Coeuroy, *Wagner et l'esprit romantique* (Paris, 1965); and, specifically on *Revue Wagnérienne*, Isabelle Wyzewska, *La Revue Wagnérienne: Essai sur l'interpretation esthetique de Wagner en France* (Paris, 1934). I know of no good study of Wagnerism in England, but see: William Blisset, "English Wagnerism before 1900," *The Wagner Society News Letter*, (1959), no. 39.

Index